OCEAN BRIDGE
THE HISTORY OF RAF FERRY COMMAND

CARL A. CHRISTIE WITH FRED HATCH

Ocean Bridge:
The History of RAF
Ferry Command

UNIVERSITY OF TORONTO PRESS
Toronto and Buffalo

© University of Toronto Press 1995
Toronto and Buffalo
Printed in Canada

ISBN 0-8020-0638-8

Printed on acid-free paper

Canadian Cataloguing in Publication Data

Christie, Carl A. (Carl Andrew), 1942–
  Ocean bridge : the history of R.A.F. Ferry Command

Includes bibliographical references and index.
ISBN 0-8020-0638-8

1. Great Britain. Royal Air Force. Ferry Command.
2. World War, 1939–1945 – Aerial operations,
British. 3. World War, 1939–1945 – Canada.
I. Hatch, F.J. II. Title.

D786.C57 1995   940.54'4941   C95-930206-9

University of Toronto Press acknowledges the financial assistance to its
publishing program of the Canada Council and the Ontario Arts Council.

This book has been published with the help of a grant from the Social
Science Federation of Canada, using funds provided by the Social Sciences
and Humanities Research Council of Canada.

This book is dedicated to
all those who gave their lives
ferrying aircraft

Contents

Preface

The late Fred Hatch began work on what eventually became this book many years ago. He undertook a study of various aspects of Canadian involvement in transatlantic operations as part of the preparatory work for the official history of the Royal Canadian Air Force. This followed quite naturally after his research into the British Commonwealth Air Training Plan made significant contributions to Canadian and aviation historiography. When Fred retired from the Directorate of History of the Department of National Defence in 1980, the then senior historian, Brereton Greenhous, gave me the daunting task of carrying on the work that Fred had been doing on Ferry Command.

My continuation of the historical research on Ferry Command resulted in a 182-page narrative, 'Trans-Atlantic Ferrying and Air Transport Operations, 1940–45,' now deposited with other unpublished narratives, research reports, and draft chapters in the public archives of the Directorate of History in Ottawa. All of us working on the history of the RCAF realized that the story of Ferry Command – interesting and important though it may be – did not belong in the official account of a Canadian institution. Despite the large number of Canadians involved, and despite having its headquarters in Montreal, Ferry Command was essentially part of the history of a foreign service, the British Royal Air Force. We did decide to compress the findings into a short appendix to volume 2 of that definitive work, *The Creation of a National Air Force*, in order to place on record a brief description of the remarkable achievements of the delivery service operating out of Canada. In the meantime, Dr W.A.B. Douglas, the director of history and principal author of volume 2, generously gave Fred Hatch and me permission to publish our own book on Ferry Command if we wished to continue the work in our own time.

Throughout this period I was privileged to develop a close friendship with Fred Hatch and I benefited greatly from his experience and counsel. Unfortunately, Fred succumbed to cancer in October 1987. Had we not already agreed to dedicate this book to the memory of those who gave their lives ferrying aircraft, I would have inscribed it to Frederick John Hatch, CD, PhD.

Of the history presented here, Fred prepared the rough drafts of the first chapter, the account of Flight Lieutenant H.A. Wills's brief experience with Ferry Command, the description of the trans-Africa airway, and the discussions of developments in the area of air traffic control. In addition, we worked together on an article for the *Canadian Defence Quarterly* on 168 Squadron, the RCAF's famous bomber mail service, a story tangential to that of Ferry Command. We discussed problems of research, organization, and approach on many occasions. In the end, the constant tinkering during the actual writing and editing process of the last few years has brought many changes to our original vision. Still, Fred can take much of the credit for any merit this book may possess; I must take the blame for its deficiencies. I am indebted to Fred's daughter, Virginia Hatch Stewart, for the privilege of helping to sort her father's papers and for permitting me to have anything I found on Ferry Command. She also agreed to the inclusion of Fred's name on the title page in recognition of his important contribution to this book.

Acknowledgments

Many people contributed in various ways to this book. Dr W.A.B. Douglas, director general history at National Defence Headquarters until his retirement in June 1994, has been unfailing in his support, as was Professor Norman Hillmer, for several years senior historian at the Directorate of History and now at Carleton University. Owen Cooke, chief historical archivist, and Liliane Grantham and her successor Suzanne Burgeois, my colleagues in the inquiries section, have given constant encouragement, as indeed have all the historians on staff. The now retired librarian, Réal Laurin, and his successor, Jean Durocher, were always a great help, particularly with my interminable interlibrary loan requests. The same can be said of Faye Nicholson, now with the Department of Transport but formerly archival assistant in the Directorate of History, and her successor, Warren Sinclair, who put up with my frequently unreasonable demands for files. Loretta Storey, Grace Scaini, and Diane Rhéaume, successively the Archival and Inquiries Section's secretary for the last fifteen years, have helped in innumerable ways.

Bill Constable drew the map of Ferry Command routes, originally published in *The Creation of a National Air Force*. I hereby acknowledge the generosity of the Department of National Defence in permitting its reuse, as well as the map of North Atlantic Ferry Routes (originally drawn in the old Army Historical Section for an unpublished study of Canadian defence policy), and the photographic reproductions of the maps of RCAF-controlled air traffic control areas from *R.C.A.F. Regulations for Control of Aircraft Movements* (CAP 365). I am also grateful that the department permitted the reproduction of official photographs. I acknowledge permission to use photographs from the collections of the Montreal *Star* and the Montreal *Gazette* held by the National Archives of Canada. Other illustrations came from veterans. I appreciate their ingenuity in taking snapshots – often where it was prohibited in wartime conditions – and in sharing them with a historian half a century later. Many more were viewed than could be used in this book; all helped build an understanding and appreciation for the breadth, scope, and variety of Ferry Command's reach and activities.

Many visiting researchers to the Directorate of History have helped. Three in particular, John Edwards, Bob Smith, and Hugh Halliday, have been ever willing to share their voluminous knowledge of Canadian air force history and its sources. Bob deserves a special mention for helping to identify the dozen or so women pilots recorded briefly in Ferry Command documents, for carefully reading the manuscript, and for painstakingly checking my appendix on losses against his own copious notes. He contributed to the accuracy and saved me some embarrassments.

Professor Michael Behiels, now of the University of Ottawa, served as a constructive critic of my paper on the establishment of Ferry Command in Bermuda to the Bermuda/Canada conference at Bermuda College in February 1984. As that presentation evolved in chapter 5 of this book, Michael's questions and comments helped me to put the whole story into context. Similarly, Professor David Beatty of Mount Allison University performed the same useful function for my paper on Canadian contributions to Ferry Command that I delivered to the annual meeting of the Canadian Historical Association in 1992.

People I have never met took an interest in the project and offered information. For example, in addition to Ferry Command veterans mentioned below, Matthew Rodina shared his own findings about Ferry Command acquired during his research into civilian-military transport operations during the war. My responsibility for the inquiries service of the Directorate of History has brought me more useful contacts than I can ever delineate.

I wish to give special thanks to Glenn Wright. Now with the RCMP historical section, he made significant suggestions when he was responsible for RCAF records at the National Archives of Canada, and he pushed me to finish the manuscript when we were, too briefly, colleagues at the Directorate of History. He even volunteered to read the manuscript.

Other archivists at the National Archives of Canada have provided assistance at various stages of the project. They include Barbara Wilson in Government Archives, on whose knowledge of military sources I have so often leaned; Bob McIntosh and Paul Marsden, admirably capable replacements for Glenn Wright in Military Records; Ann Martin, who put me onto some interesting Department of Transport files; George Lafleur and Dan German, who had the thankless task of reviewing them to ensure that I did not see some mysterious wartime secret; Tim Dubé in the Manuscript Division, whose familiarity with aviation sources is helpful to many researchers; and Peter Robertson, who (with the able assistance of Helen De Roia, Sarah Montgomery, and Irene Van Bavel) once again has ensured that a book on Canadian military history is adequately illustrated with appropriate photographs.

Ann Bilodeau from the National Research Council Archives and archivists from the Newfoundland Provincial Archives in St John's, the Harriet Irving Library at the University of New Brunswick in Fredericton, and the Provincial Archives of Manitoba have assisted by answering requests made through the mail and in person. With the exception of one visit to the Public Record Office in London, England, documents from other institutions were mostly read in copy form in Ottawa. Transcripts/translations of crown-copyright records in the Public Record Office appear by permission of the controller of Her Majesty's Stationery Office.

Ray Crone sent me photocopied material from his own collection. J.A. 'Red' Scanlan answered questions about aircraft maintenance and air force terminology. Paul Drover and Terry Strocel provided information about current Canadian Forces' search and rescue procedures.

My wife, Gail, has had to put up with my preoccupations about ferrying aeroplanes for far too long. I cannot say how much I appreciate her patience and understanding. Similarly I want to thank my parents, Helen and Andy Christie (the latter the best fabric worker, parachute rigger, safety equipment and then safety systems technician – not to mention athlete – that the RCAF ever had) not just for raising me as 'an air force brat,' but also for reading this manuscript with a critical eye.

I would also like to thank Professor A.M. Jack Hyatt (University of Western Ontario) for inspiring me to pursue a career in military history and Professors Frederick A. Dreyer (University of Western Ontario) and Christopher J. Bartlett (University of Dundee) for being extremely helpful and understanding thesis supervisors as I tried to develop my skills as a historian.

At the University of Toronto Press, there are probably more people to thank than I even know. Nonetheless, I should like to make special mention of four. Virgil Duff expressed interest in the project and invited me to make an early submission, and Gerald Hallowell has constantly offered encouragement and wise counsel. Rob Ferguson has been helpful, and Rosemary Shipton improved my style as she edited the manuscript.

Perhaps most importantly, I must express my appreciation to the veterans of Ferry Command, who have offered endless encouragement and, best of all, information – both orally and in writing. The list of veterans (as well as relatives and friends of same) who have assisted either Fred Hatch or me is long. However, risking the embarrassment of forgetting someone (for which I apologize in advance), I thank the following people: Don Bennett, Bill Baker, Mel Boles, Stevie Cameron (daughter of Squadron Leader H.C. 'Whitey' Dahl), A. Mowatt Christie (brother of Squadron Leader George Patterson Christie), Dolly Coulter (daughter of George Evans), Henry Flory, Gerry Forrette (nephew of Robert Byrne), John Griffin, Kenneth Harris, George Hindmarsh, Fred Hotson, Robert Jones, Jimmy and Betty Jubb, Mary Kellaway, Bill Kidd, Gerry Lagrave, Al Lilly, Don Macfie, Tom McGrath, Earl McIlroy, Don McVicar, Griffith 'Taffy' Powell, George Seward, Bob Short, Art Stark, J.U. Stephens, H.R. 'Red' Syrett, Arthur Teulon, and Gladys Wills and Gale Bauman (wife and daughter of Harold Wills).

Finally, I should make special note of the assistance and encouragement I received from the late Lloyd and Lillian (Hanson) Wheeler, who were, respectively, a radio operator with Ferry Command and secretary of the RAF Ferry Command Association. It is sad that Lillian did not live to read the book that she supported so enthusiastically right from the beginning. Many of the contacts and much of the source material came directly or indirectly through her.

I hope I have done justice to the story of Ferry Command's role during the Second World War. Should I have fallen short it is not for lack of admiration and appreciation for an important story too long untold.

Abbreviations

A/C (or a/c)	aircraft
AFC	Air Force Cross
AFHQ	Air Force (RCAF) Headquarters, Ottawa
AG	air gunner
AIR	Air Ministry records at the PRO
Am	American
AMS	air member for supply
ANS	Air Navigation School
AOC	air officer commanding
AOC-in-C	air officer commanding-in-chief
AOS	Air Observer School
ASR	air/sea rescue
ASRO	air/sea rescue officer
ASV	air-to-surface vessel radar
AT	Atlantic Transport
ATA	Air Transport Auxiliary
ATC	Air Transport Command (of the USAAF)
ATFERO	Atlantic Ferry Organization
Aus	Australia(n)
AWOL	absent without leave
BAC	British Air Commission
BAFO	British Air Forces of Occupation
BC	British Columbia
BCATP	British Commonwealth Air Training Plan
BE	Bluie East (as in BE-2 airfield)
BFC	British Ferry Command
BMAP	British Ministry of Aircraft Production

BOAC	British Overseas Airways Corporation
Br	British
BR	Bomber-Reconnaissance (anti-submarine)
BW	Bluie West (as in BW-1 and BW-8 airfields)
CAHS	Canadian Aviation Historical Society
CAP	Canadian Air Publication
CAS	chief of the air staff
CB	Companion of the Bath
CD	Canadian Forces Decoration
Cdn	Canadian
CFI	chief flying instructor
CFR	contact flight rules (ie, within sight of the ground)
CGS	chief of the general staff (of the Canadian militia [army])
C-in-C	commander-in-chief
civ	civilian
CMG	Companion of St Michael and St George
CNR	Canadian National Railways
CO	commanding officer
CPR	Canadian Pacific Railway
CWAC	Canadian Womens Army Corps
CWC	Cabinet War Committee (Canadian)
DC	District of Columbia
DCER	*Documents on Canadian External Relations*
DF	direction finding
DFC	Distinguished Flying Cross
DHist	Directorate of History, National Defence Headquarters, Ottawa
DM	deputy minister
DMS	director of medical services
DND	Department of National Defence (Canadian)
DOT	Department of Transport (Canadian)
DR	dead (or deduced) reckoning
DRO	daily routine order
DSO	Companion of the Distinguished Service Order
E	east
EAC	Eastern Air Command, RCAF
EATS	Empire Air Training Scheme
Eng	engineer
ETA	estimated time of arrival
FBI	Federal Bureau of Investigation (USA)

FE	flight engineer
GBE	Knight Grand Cross Order of the British Empire
GMT	Greenwich Mean Time
GRS	General Reconnaissance School
HMS	His Majesty's Ship
HQFC	Headquarters Ferry Command
hr	hour
hrs	hours
ic	in charge / in command
JAN-CAN	Joint Army, Navy-Canadian
JATP	Joint Air Training Plan
JATS	Joint Air Training Scheme
KC	kilocycles
KCB	Knight Commander of the Bath
LCol	Lieutenant Colonel
Lt	Lieutenant
Maj	Major
MAP	Ministry of Aircraft Production
MBE	Member of the Order of the British Empire
MC	Military Cross
MG	Manuscript Group
MO	medical officer
MP	member of parliament
N	north
NA	National Archives of Canada
Nav	navigator
NB	New Brunswick
NC	North Carolina
NCO	non-commissioned officer
ND	North Dakota
NDHQ	National Defence Headquarters, Ottawa
NE	northeast
Nfld	Newfoundland(er)
no.	number
np	no place of publication given, or no pagination
NPA	Newfoundland Provincial Archives
nr	near
NRC	National Research Council
NS	Nova Scotia
NW	northwest

NY	New York
NZ	New Zealand(er)
OBE	Officer Order of the British Empire
obs	observer
OC	officer commanding
oic	officer in charge / officer in command
OM	Order of Merit
Ont.	Ontario
ORB	operations record book
OTU	Operational Training Unit
PAAF	Pan American Air Ferries
PAF	Polish Air Force
Pass	passenger
PEI	Prince Edward Island
PHP	Post Hostilities Problems (Committee, in Canada)
PICAO	Provisional International Civil Aviation Organization
PM	Prime Minister
PRO	Public Record Office
QDM	course to steer
QM	Quartermaster
QTE	bearing
Que.	Province of Quebec
QUG	I am going to ditch
RAAF	Royal Australian Air Force
RAF	Royal Air Force
RAFFC	Royal Air Force Ferry Command
RAFTC	Royal Air Force Transport Command
RCAF	Royal Canadian Air Force
RCCS	Royal Canadian Corps of Signals
RCMP	Royal Canadian Mounted Police
REMU	Reserve Equipment Maintenance Unit
RFS	Return Ferry Service
RG	Record Group
RN	Royal Navy
RNAF	Royal Norwegian Air Force
RNZAF	Royal New Zealand Air Force
RO	radio officer / radio operator
S	south
SAL	Scottish Aviation Limited
SAR	Search and Rescue

SASO	senior air staff officer
SFTS	Service Flying Training School
SSgt	Staff Sergeant
Swed	Swedish
TCA	Trans-Canada Air Lines
TWA	Trans World Airlines
UK	United Kingdom
u/s	unserviceable
US	United States
USAAC	United States Army Air Corps
USAACS	United States Army Airways Communication System
USAAF	United States Army Air Forces
USATC	Air Transport Command (of the USAAF)
USN	United States Navy
USofS	undersecretary of state
USS	United States Ship
USSR	Union of Soviet Socialist Republics, or Soviet Union
VE	Victory in Europe
VIP	very important person / personage / passenger
VJ	Victory over Japan
W	west
WAC	Western Air Command, RCAF
WAG (or WO/AG)	wireless operator/air gunner
WASPs	Women Airforce Service Pilots
W/T	wireless telegraphy
'X' Depot	Explosives Depot
'Y' Depot	Embarkation Depot
YMCA	Young Men's Christian Association
Z	GMT or Greenwich Mean Time

RANKS: COMMONWEALTH AIR FORCES

A/C/M	Air Chief Marshal
A/M	Air Marshal
A/V/M	Air Vice-Marshal
A/C	Air Commodore
G/C	Group Captain
W/C	Wing Commander
S/L	Squadron Leader
F/L	Flight Lieutenant

F/O	Flying Officer
P/O	Pilot Officer
WO1	Warrant Officer First Class
WO2	Warrant Officer Second Class
FSgt	Flight Sergeant
Sgt	Sergeant
Cpl	Corporal
LAC	Leading Aircraftman
AC1	Aircraftman First Class
AC2	Aircraftman Second Class

OCEAN BRIDGE
THE HISTORY OF RAF FERRY COMMAND

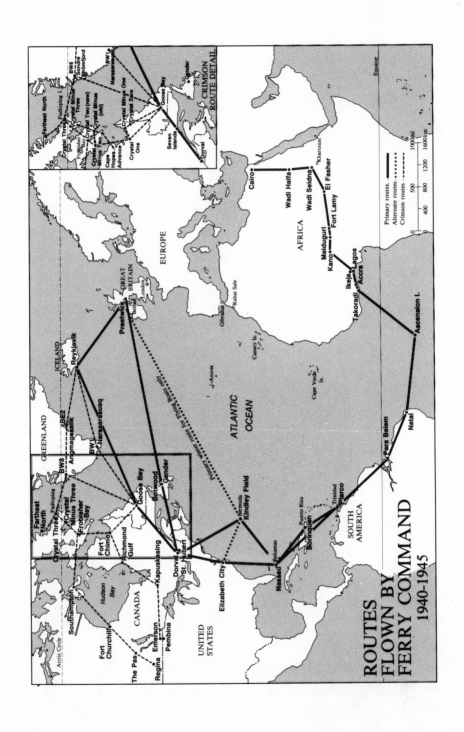

ROUTES FLOWN BY FERRY COMMAND
1940-1945

CRIMSON ROUTE DETAIL

Primary routes ....
Alternate routes ....
Crimson routes ....

0   400   500   800   1000 mi
0   400   800   1200   1600 km

1

Atlantic Pioneers

Descriptions of air battles of the Second World War, like accounts of battles fought on land and at sea, tend to ignore the vast infrastructures that supplied and supported the competing forces. Thus it is that histories of the Allied air offensive against Germany, of air operations in the Battle of the Atlantic, of the campaign in North Africa, or of the recapture of Burma, for example, seldom, if ever, make any reference to the transoceanic ferrying organization that delivered some ten thousand desperately needed military aircraft from the factories of the United States and Canada to airfields in the United Kingdom and other theatres of war. Yet this long-range aircraft supply line, based in Montreal but operated, for the most part, by the Royal Air Force, was essential to the development and projection of Allied air power, and was one of the most spectacular achievements of the war. Those responsible for the successful delivery of these aircraft not only helped to win the war, but also made remarkable advances in long-range flying. Anyone who has crossed an ocean in the comfort of a modern airliner is forever in their debt.

When the ferrying organization delivered its first aircraft, a flight of seven Lockheed Hudson reconnaissance bombers, in November 1940, transatlantic aviation was still in its infancy. Between 1919, the year of the first non-stop aeroplane crossing from North America to Europe, and the outbreak of war in September 1939, fewer than a hundred successful crossings had been made. Approximately fifty attempts had failed because of rough weather, engine problems, or overloading. Some of the crews were plucked from the sea by rescue vessels, but at least sixteen flights ended with the notation 'lost at sea' or 'aircraft and crew disappeared.'[1]

How frightening the North Atlantic weather could be, even in the summer, was graphically demonstrated in the first non-stop flight by John Alcock and Arthur Whitten Brown, which won them the £10,000 (the equivalent of about $50,000 at that day's rate of exchange) purse offered by Lord Northcliffe of the London *Daily Mail*. Taking off from St John's, Newfoundland, in the late afternoon of 14 June 1919 in a twin-engine Vickers Vimy biplane, a First World War bombing machine fitted with extra fuel tanks for the 1900-mile stretch over the open sea, the two British flyers soon found themselves sandwiched between heavy layers of fog and cloud. There were times when they could not see the wing tips of the Vimy, and now and then the nose disappeared from view. To hold the aircraft straight and level, Alcock kept his feet planted firmly against the rudder pedals throughout the flight, and his hands never relaxed their grip on the control column except to take snatches of food and drink offered by Brown. Even so, at one point they lost all sense of direction and went into a long spin, levelling out just above the wave tops and with the aircraft heading back towards North America.[2]

The only thing in their favour was a strong tail wind, but coming at an angle it blew them off course. For an hour and a half before they sighted land, with poor visibility preventing any astro-navigation, they had no idea where they were. Eventually, after almost sixteen hours of flying over nothing but ocean, landfall was made at the northern tip of Ireland about one hundred miles from Galway, the intended destination, where a reception party of reporters and dignitaries anxiously scanned the skies for the first glimpse of the Vimy.

Flying south along the coastline as far as Clifden, the weary flyers ran into more fog and, with hills looming ahead, Alcock decided to end the flight then and there. Spotting what looked like 'a lovely field,' he brought the flight to a sudden and jarring halt in an Irish bog, with the aircraft mired up to its axles in the wet, spongy ground. Both men were shaken up, but sustained no injuries. Speaking to a reporter from the *Daily Mail*, the exhausted Alcock gave a brief but vividly honest account of the adventure:

We have had a terrible journey. The wonder is we are here at all. We scarcely saw the sun or the moon or the stars. For hours we saw none of them. The fog was very dense, and at times we had to descend to within 300 feet of the sea.

For four hours the machine was covered in a sheet of ice caused by frozen sleet; at another time the sleet was so dense that my speed indicator did not work, and for a few seconds it was very alarming ...

WESTJET
15JAN13 FLT/VOL 514

NARRAWAY/TREVOR MR

DEP: VICTORIA BC

ARR: EDMONTON INTL AB   10:40AM

8:10AM

BOARDING TIME/
HEURE D EMBARQUEMENT

7:35AM

ELECTRONIC/ELECTRONIQUE

STANDBY/D ATTENDE
BOARDING PASS/ CARTE D EMBARQUEMENT
NARRAWAY/TREVOR MR
15JAN13
FLT/VOL 514

GATE /PRT   2

SEQ 056
PNR CDXCZN

SEATLACE

DEP: YYJ
ARR: YEG

SEQ 056
PNR CDXCZN

SEAT/PLACE

8D

SEAT/PLACE

8D

8D

WESTJET

1-888-937-8538

We never saw the sun rise. There was a bank of fog also on top of the lower one.

We climbed up to 11,000 feet. It was hailing and snowing. The machine was covered with ice ... My radiator shutter and the water temperature indicator were covered with ice for 4 or 5 hours.

Brown had continually to climb up to chip off the ice with a knife ...

It was a terrible trip.[3]

Perhaps understandably, neither Alcock nor Brown, satisfied with having won the Northcliffe prize and knighthoods from King George V, showed any further interest in flying the North Atlantic.

In truth, Alcock and Brown were not the first to fly across the Atlantic by aeroplane. Two weeks earlier, on 31 May 1919, a United States Navy Curtiss NC-4 flying boat had arrived at Plymouth, England, having flown all the way from Rockaway, New York. The highly organized USN assault, however, had flown via Newfoundland, the Azores, and Portugal, with more than fifty warships carefully positioned at convenient intervals to provide navigational assistance and meteorological information. Following almost fifty-four hours of actual flying over a span of twenty-three days, only one of the three flying boats that started out completed the historic journey. Even so, the arrival of the six naval airmen in England was an epic achievement. While the Americans were on their way, there had been frantic – and unsuccessful – British attempts to beat them across from Newfoundland to the British Isles, despite the US government's waiving of any claim to Lord Northcliffe's prize.[4]

In the first week of July 1919, the British airship the R.34 quietly flew to New York and, three days later, back to England. This marked the first double crossing but, because the R.34 was an airship and because a heavier-than-air machine had already conquered the Atlantic, there was little attention paid to the accomplishment. The public's appetite for Atlantic adventure was temporarily satisfied and nobody could foresee any practical or commercial use for the route. After the race to be first across in the spring of 1919, little interest was shown in transatlantic flying for the next five years. Of four attempts in 1924, only one succeeded, and this was flown not over the direct route but in stages by way of Iceland, Greenland, and Labrador. The next try, in 1926, ended in tragedy, as did two attempts early in 1927.[5]

The other crossing that ranks with or even surpasses Alcock and Brown's as a landmark in transatlantic navigation is Charles A. Lindbergh's flight from New York to Paris during the night of 20/21 May 1927 in a single-engine monoplane, the now famous *Spirit of St. Louis*. Historically, these are two of the most important long-range flights of all time; Alcock and Brown's because it was the first to conquer the North Atlantic in a single hop, and Lindbergh's because it proved the practicability of the aeroplane as a means of bridging the ocean. Lindbergh's flight was inspired by Raymond Orteig of New York, who had offered $25,000 to the first pilot to fly from that city to his native Paris. It was the second non-stop crossing of the North Atlantic and the first from city to city, more than 1500 miles longer than Alcock and Brown's flight, and attempted after a series of highly publicized disasters that glamourized Lindbergh's courage in the eyes of the public. When the 'Lone Eagle' dropped from the skies onto Le Bourget airfield, he became an instant hero. Never has any pilot, including those who have ventured into outer space, been so widely and wildly acclaimed, a public reaction which must convey some measure of the barrier that the North Atlantic presented and the great daring of aviators who challenged it.[6]

Lindbergh's success reflected the steady progress that was being made in the design of aircraft and aero-engines as well as his skill as a pilot and navigator and his careful preparation. But the weather was a most important factor. It is interesting to compare his flight with that of Alcock and Brown. Although both crossings were made about the same time of year, one in May and the other in June, Lindbergh, in contrast to Alcock and Brown, was blessed with virtually ideal conditions. When he took off for Paris, a high-pressure system was centred over the North Atlantic, a most unusual occurrence – as Ferry Command pilots would later testify – and, while he encountered some fog patches and rain squalls and a little icing, he had good visibility most of the way. The wind was practically a negligible factor, greatly simplifying the problem of keeping the aircraft on track.[7]

Lindbergh's accomplishment triggered new interest in the desire to conquer the North Atlantic by air. Two other flights in various stages of preparation when the *Spirit of St. Louis* lumbered off from Curtiss Field on Long Island were also successful, and the great race to fly the Atlantic was on. Before the end of 1927, seventeen crews sought to emulate Lindbergh. Only four succeeded. Eight abandoned the adventure either before or after getting airborne, one was rescued at sea, and four were never heard from again – bringing the year's death toll to sixteen. The statistics for 1928 and 1929 were not appreciably different, but as the years passed there tended to be fewer flights with a slightly improving rate of success, no doubt an indication of more careful preparation and greater respect for the hazards of ocean flying, as well as the advances in machines and equipment. Yet each year the North Atlantic continued to exact its toll of would-be conquerors. All told, more than forty lives, including crew members and passengers, were lost in failed attempts to fly the Atlantic Ocean before the Second World War. And these depressing totals were the result of mostly spring and summer attempts – even the most foolhardy adventurers seldom dared to take off in the stormy winter months. One notable exception to this fear of the North Atlantic winter occurred on Christmas Eve, 1927, when a rich American, Frances Grayson, in an attempt to become the first woman across, took off in her Sikorsky amphibian with her pilot, navigator, and engineer, headed east, and vanished forever in the snow and ice over the ocean.[8]

Apart from the heroics, it is difficult to assess the significance of the pioneer flights to the later development of transatlantic flying. Some, including those of Alcock and Brown, Lindbergh, Commander Richard Byrd, Amelia Earhart (the first woman to fly the North Atlantic), and James Mollison (who flew it three times), made definite advances towards the ultimate goal of building an air bridge between the Old World and the New. At the same time, it must be kept in mind that many of the early flights were really glorified stunts that brought fame and fortune to a favoured few and tragedy to many more. By and large they were promoted by wealthy patrons of aviation, including some aircraft companies, who either put up attractive prize money or financed the flights of protégés. With the onset of the Great Depression, however, the financial awards began to dwindle and so too did the number of flights. Moreover, the US Commerce Department, in response to publicly expressed concern over the loss of life, decreed that only aircraft bearing licensed identification numbers could take off from the United States for foreign destinations.[9]

Flying between North America and Europe, the pioneer aviators used three main routes: the direct or great circle route followed by Alcock and Brown, Lindbergh, and most of the others; a northern route through Labrador, Greenland, and Iceland; and a southern route via the Azores. Interest centred on the direct routes, which presented the greatest challenge, offered the most prize money, and promised the greatest commercial potential. Its main advantage was that the curvature of the Earth's surface made it shorter than the other two. The great disadvantage, from the perspective of the 1920s and 1930s, was the long flight over the open sea. To span the ocean gap of almost 2000 miles, aircraft had to be fitted with extra fuel tanks. Indeed, the load was so heavy that the under-powered machines could barely stagger into the air. Crashes on takeoff were not uncommon. On the other hand, steady progress towards the development of more powerful engines and larger aircraft foretold that it was only a matter of time until the commercial possibilities of the great circle route could be exploited.[10] The incentives for success were considerable. The North Atlantic, as Robert Daley, biographer of Pan American Airways' founder Juan Trippe, has summarized,

was the busiest trade route in the world ... In 1925, out of about a million steamship passengers, a hundred and eighty thousand had crossed in first class, each one ... a potential customer if an airline could offer equal comfort and safety plus superior speed. In addition, ships had carried about 9 million pounds of precious merchandise (jewelery, art works, currency, precision instruments); about 28 million pounds of express packages, including cans of moving-picture film; and about 38 million pounds of letters and printed matter. This fraction of ship traffic suitable for air transport worked out to only eight-tenths of 1 percent but still added up to 75 million pounds. The potential profits were staggering.[11]

All this was of vital interest to Canada. At its western end the great circle route met the St Lawrence valley, placing Montreal closer to Europe than were the great cities on the American seaboard (see table 1). Looking to the future, Canadian aviation authorities visualized Montreal as the natural western terminus of the North Atlantic air route and the main distribution centre for air traffic, disgorging mail, passengers, and cargo to points across Canada and south into the United States. In 1927, in an effort to arouse public interest in Montreal's strategic location, the Government of Canada initiated an experiment known as the ship-to-shore airmail service. By using mail planes in conjunction with ocean liners in the Gulf of St Lawrence, it was possible to speed up the delivery of mail between North America and Europe by more than a day.[12]

The fledgling Royal Canadian Air Force flew the first flights. When the scheme proved practical and profitable, the service was taken over by a private company, Canadian Transcontinental Airways, later absorbed by Quebec Airways. Flying from Montreal, the mail planes made

TABLE 1
North Atlantic Air Routes

From	To	Route	Total distance (miles)	Flying time at 150 mph (hours)	Maximum over-sea flight (miles)	
Montreal	London	Northern	3785	25	780	Greenland to
New York	London		4000	26½	780	Iceland
Montreal	London	Southern (via	4425	29½	1350	Newfoundland to
New York	London	Nfld and the Azores)	4575	30½	1350	the Azores
Montreal	London	Southern (via	5250	35	2050	Bermuda to the
New York	London	Bermuda and the Azores)	4865	32½	2050	Azores
Montreal	London	Direct (or great circle route)	3250	22	1870	Newfoundland to Ireland
New York	London		3400	23	1870	

contact with incoming and outgoing ocean liners at Pointe-au-Père, near Rimouski in the Gulf of St Lawrence, for a transfer of mail. Incoming mail was flown on to Montreal and delivered about thirty hours before the ships docked. On eastbound flights, batches of mail for overseas collected in Montreal a day or so after the ships had sailed for the United Kingdom were flown ahead to Pointe-au-Père and transferred to surface vessels on their way out to sea. The delivery of letters and small parcels to Britain was accelerated by at least a day and sometimes by two or three days. During the Depression, budgetary cuts virtually eliminated intercity airmail service in Canada; the ship-to-shore operation survived, however, because it was seen as a link with the future, providing experience in organization and knowledge of weather conditions in the Gulf of St Lawrence which would prove valuable when transatlantic air operations got under way.[13]

In spite of the ship-to-shore mail service, which benefited parts of the United States as well as Canada, there was a danger that Canadians would be shouldered out of the North Atlantic route by their big, friendly, aggressive neighbour to the south. Of twenty-three successful North Atlantic crossing between 1927 and 1932, thirteen were by Americans and three others, including that by Canada's Errol Boyd, were made in US aircraft. In North America, while the embryonic Canadian intercity air services were being cut back, airlines in the United States were expanding with the support of government subsidies and even reaching into Canada with connections at Montreal, Toronto, Halifax, and Victoria. None did so more enthusiastically than Pan American Airways, where Juan Trippe pushed the US aircraft industry for bigger, better, and faster planes and aggressively sought out ever-expanding foreign routes. Determined to offer the first scheduled airline service across the North Atlantic, he had started working on the possibility long before other people thought such a development would ever be feasible. With single-minded purpose he pursued agreements for routes and landing rights with other airlines and even with foreign governments, including those in France, the United Kingdom, Newfoundland, and Canada.[14]

Trippe had first requested European landing rights for Pan American Airways in 1928. In November 1930 he signed an agreement with André Boilloux-Lafont and George Woods Humphery, representing Aéropostale of France and Imperial Airways of Great Britain, respectively. This was a remarkable development. These three individuals, quietly and without fanfare, negotiated a tripartite agreement to develop and share what was potentially the most lucrative air route in the world. Boilloux-Lafont and Woods Humphery at least spoke for government-owned airlines. Trippe represented no one but himself, or more correctly Pan American, which to Trippe was the same thing. And yet he appeared to get the best of the deal. All three companies agreed not to engage in transatlantic operations 'except jointly with each other.' The British and French governments, through existing international arrangements, could offer landing rights in London, Ireland, Paris, Lisbon, and the Azores; Trippe could legally offer nothing comparable. Nonetheless, Pan American would get 50 per cent of future air traffic on the route, while Imperial and Aéropostale would divide the other half equally.[15]

The aggressive founder of Pan American Airways quickly followed up this coup by negotiating landing rights in Bermuda (a 50–50 split with Imperial Airways) as well as in Canada and Newfoundland. Agreement with Canada came quickly, and a Pan Am subsidiary was soon flying mail to Halifax. Newfoundland was a more difficult problem, even for Trippe. His representative was in St John's when anti-government riots broke out, and he wired Trippe: 'Government routed by mob violence with prime minister and cabinet as refugees somewhere in backwoods ... My negotiations appear to be interrupted.[16] This message understated the case. The Dominion of Newfoundland – with control over its own air space – reverted in 1933 to the status of a crown colony, and anyone wishing to obtain landing rights there had to approach the British government and be prepared for long, hard talks. Despite all the fears of Pan American's expansionism, Trippe was temporarily stymied on the North Atlantic. He had purchased landing rights in Iceland, but lost those in the Azores when his French partner, Aéropostale, collapsed shortly after the signing of the tripartite agreement.[17]

Trippe, however, did not discourage easily. As a safety net, he had a good, even a special relationship with Woods Humphery, each agreeing informally that his airline would not begin transatlantic services independently of the other. Almost alone at this time, Trippe was convinced that the northern route was viable, and he devoted considerable money and effort to verifying his instincts. He studied reports on the Arctic and contacted every expert he could. In 1932 he sent two scientific expeditions of his own to Greenland – one in cooperation with the University of Michigan – to learn more about flying conditions in the region. He sent Charles Lindbergh on a survey of the potential route, and also on a goodwill tour of Newfoundland as a special representative of Pan Am. Trippe had already secured air traffic rights in eastern Canada; if he could gain special concessions in the strategically situated Newfoundland, Pan American would be in an ideal position to dominate the North Atlantic route. Governments in Canada and Britain might be outmanoeuvred by a private US citizen.[18]

Canada was not in a strong position to push its own policies in this area, because they were not clearly defined. Responsibility for directing Canadian civil aviation in these difficult times was shouldered mainly by Major-General A.G.L. McNaughton, chief of the general staff from 1929 to 1935, and by a civil servant, J.A. Wilson. The latter, an engineer by profession, had been closely associated with the development of Canadian aviation since 1918. Until the advent of C.D. Howe in 1935, Wilson was the most influential figure in civil aviation, which until 1936 was organized as part of the Department of National Defence. McNaughton's position in Canadian aviation is more difficult to determine. It was one of many causes he espoused in a lifetime of public service; as chief of the general staff, he should have been in an excellent position to further his views.[19]

As a member of the British Commonwealth, Canada looked to the United Kingdom to counter the American thrust. The mother country, however, was not concentrating on this area at this time. Between 1927 and 1932 only one British aircraft conquered the North Atlantic – a light de Havilland Moth type flown by James Mollison. He took off from Portmarnock Strand, near Dublin, at 11:00 a.m. on 18 August 1932 and landed thirty-three hours later at Saint John, New Brunswick. Mollison crossed again in 1933 and 1936, but his outstanding performance was no indication that the United Kingdom was about to stake a national or imperial claim on the North Atlantic airway. For the moment the British concentrated on two other areas and two special types of aeroplanes that were both singularly unsuitable for use on the North Atlantic: fast machines with short-range capability for European air routes, and medium-range flying boats for use on international and imperial air routes with links to Africa, Australia, and India. With respect to the North Atlantic, the British were thinking in terms of airships. This idea had been unveiled in London at the Imperial Conference of 1923 and again in 1926, when a plan for the construction of two 'great airships,' the *R.100* and *R.101*, was announced. The visiting prime ministers were asked to cooperate by providing airship stations. Prime Minister William Lyon Mackenzie King of Canada, apparently infatuated with the proposal, was the only Commonwealth first minister to make a firm commitment – an interesting response in view of his reputation for viewing British suggestions with extreme caution.[20]

Although the RCAF had misgivings about an airship project that would reduce the amount of money available for aeroplanes, there was no alternative but to go along with the government's decision. Plans went ahead for an airport at St Hubert, just east of Montreal, complete with a mooring mast and all the equipment required for docking and refuelling an airship. Subsequently, on 1 August 1930, the *R.100*, the biggest and newest airship in the world, arrived at St Hubert on its maiden voyage. This, the first airship flight to Canada, excited great public interest. An estimated one million people visited St Hubert for a close-up view, and at least another million saw the *R.100* in flight. About eight thousand fortunate individuals got a look inside. The ten-day visit raised great expectations about an imperial air connection.[21] However, by 1930 the idea that airships were the solution to transatlantic air travel and that aeroplanes were too small and too unreliable was no longer valid. Britain and Germany stubbornly clung to the outdated view, even though it was evident that aviation technology, especially in the United States, was moving steadily towards the development of larger and safer aircraft, while airships, in spite of many improvements, remained as fragile as during the First World War. In brief, the British airship program had been a costly mistake; it came to a sudden and tragic end with the loss of the *R.101*, sister ship of the *R.100*, on its first flight to India in October 1930. The *R.100* never flew again.[22] Although the possibility of an airship age did not finally die until the *Hindenberg* disaster at Lakehurst, New Jersey, in May 1937, it ended seven years earlier for Britain and the Commonwealth.

The Imperial Conference of 1932, held in Ottawa during July and August to find a solution to economic problems arising from the Great Depression, gave Canadians an opportunity to rekindle British interest in an air connection with Canada. On the economic front the conference solved practically nothing, but a scheme devised by Wilson, McNaughton, and P.T. Coolican, deputy assistant postmaster general, to speed up overseas mail during the conference had far-reaching results. The plan simply extended the ship-to-shore airmail service. Instead of transferring the mail at Pointe-au-Père, 400 miles northeast of Montreal, the exchange took place at Red Bay on the Strait of Belle Isle, about 600 miles further downstream at the entrance to the Gulf of St Lawrence. The flights, four inbound and four outbound, were flown by the RCAF and were timed to coincide with the summer sailing schedule of the SS *Empress of Britain*. Since the Canadian Pacific liner took about four days to reach Montreal after entering the Strait of Belle Isle, and the air force planes could cover the distance in fifteen hours, incoming mail arrived two to three days earlier than it normally would. The time saving for the outward mail was similar. Just as was hoped, the demonstration scheme impressed conference delegates, who were getting their dispatches to and from London in record time.[23]

Before the end of the conference, Canada succeeded in convincing the delegates from the United Kingdom, the Irish Free State, and Newfoundland to sign an agreement pledging to work together in developing a transatlantic air service over the direct or non-stop route. Canada insisted on the inclusion of a clause stipulating that the Commonwealth partners 'will not actively support the development of any other route, or give privileges to any foreign Government or its nationals in respect to the operation of trans-Atlantic air services ... or the establishment of air bases or air navigation facilities for the purpose of such services, without full and prior consultation with each other.'[24]

The restrictive wording reflects Canadian concern over the possibility that Pan American might obtain an operating base in Newfoundland. It also shows Canadian anxiety about the relationship between Pan American and Imperial Airways, the British company formed in 1924 to organize and operate the empire air routes. The two companies sometimes found it convenient to cooperate on various international routes. In Bermuda they combined their resources on the run to New York, with Pan American getting special privileges on the island and Imperial being granted concessions on the American mainland. They also planned to work together in extending their operations across the Atlantic via the Azores and Lisbon. Canadian officials had only a vague knowledge of the relationship between the British and the American companies, but feared it might extend to the non-stop route or perhaps to the northern route by way of Labrador, Greenland, and Iceland which Pan American was known to be investigating.[25]

The Commonwealth countries were finally becoming united in purpose. Although the British government had been slow to react to Pan American's North Atlantic ambitions and was not even aware that the American company had been lobbying for concessions in Newfoundland, it now came to view these developments as a serious threat to British prestige and the future of the imperial air connection. In June 1933 Newfoundland was strongly advised against granting air privileges to the Americans which could only lead to the creation of a United States' monopoly on the North Atlantic route and deprive the British of 'the opportunity to bargain with Pan American Airways for a share in the traffic which comes from the United States.'[26]

Paradoxically, neither the British nor the Canadians ruled out the possibility of cooperation with Pan American. On the contrary, interested officials from the two Commonwealth countries increasingly looked upon this course of action as the best means of gaining access to the rich US market. The immediate objective was to prevent the Americans from getting a head start. Commonwealth negotiators, therefore, proposed that the base of operations in Newfoundland be built by the United Kingdom and controlled by Newfoundland, with Pan American and Imperial Airways having equal user rights, on the condition that the Americans would not start operations until the British were ready. This arrangement became the basis for further exploratory talks.[27] The catch was that, while the American company was about to acquire a number of Sikorsky S-42 flying boats with sufficient range to cross the ocean non-stop, the C-class empire flying boats that were to carry the British flag were still in the early design stage. Thus the start of a summer mail and passenger service was still several years away.[28]

The delay gave the Commonwealth partners time to settle some of their own problems. At a conference held in Ottawa in November 1935, they reached agreement to create an imperial transatlantic service in three stages. In the first step, Imperial Airways would undertake a series of survey flights. Next, the British company would initiate an experimental airmail service. Finally, a passenger and mail service would be launched by 'a company nominated by the Commonwealth Governments concerned and a United States Company, with particular reference to the direct route via the Irish Free State, Newfoundland and Montreal.'[29] In essence, this meant Imperial Airways with Irish and Canadian support. A board of directors with representation from each country would oversee the joint venture, with the United Kingdom reserving the right to name the chairman and the manager. Britain would own 51 per cent of the new company; Eire and Canada, 24½ per cent each. Each of the three Commonwealth members would provide the necessary airports, as well as communications and meteorological systems. A conference in Washington, which followed the Ottawa gathering, confirmed the grant of privileges promised to Pan American.[30]

Weather forecasts for most of the transatlantic flights to this time had come from the Americans, who were quite willing to continue to provide this service and other facilities as well. However, the Ottawa conference of November 1935 decided that the ground organization should be the responsibility of the Commonwealth partners. The Canadian government agreed to provide weather forecasts for Newfoundland and the western half of the Atlantic, a gesture that gave Canada a vested interest in that part of the airway based in Newfoundland at very little cost. Canada took over existing weather stations in Newfoundland and added several others, including a central weather office at the Botwood seaplane base in the Bay of Exploits, a long arm of Notre Dame Bay on the north coast, for the immediate support of transatlantic operations. The man most involved in setting up the system was Dr P.D. McTaggart-Cowan, a Canadian Rhodes scholar who had studied meteorology in Britain. By the beginning of June 1937 his preparations at Botwood were well advanced and his staff, recruited primarily in Newfoundland, had made a good beginning in collecting, coordinating, analysing, and distributing weather data.[31] By the time war broke out in September 1939, McTaggart-Cowan was widely recognized as one of the foremost authorities on North Atlantic weather. His expertise in this field became highly valued by the crews of Ferry Command.

With the slow but steady preparations for transatlantic experimental flights, plans for a trans-Canada airway, dropped in 1930 after the completion of the prairie section, were revived. The rest of the route had been planned and most of the sites chosen, but little else had been done. In 1933, under the inspiration of Wilson and McNaughton, construction of the airway began in earnest, using unemployed men in government relief camps set up in British Columbia, northern Ontario, Quebec, and the maritime provinces. More than 170,000 labourers cleared the sites in exchange for food, clothing, and shelter, and twenty cents a day. When the scheme came to an end in 1936, some fifty intermediate airfields had been built.[32] More or less complete from Vancouver to Halifax, the next step was to link the airway with sites in Newfoundland, which Canadians had come to look on as the natural extension of their own system.

Soon after its return to office in the election of October 1935, Mackenzie King's new Liberal administration found itself under pressure to put the trans-Canada airway into operation without delay. Otherwise, when Imperial Airways began its experimental mail service, all the incoming mail would flow into the American airline system. As a preliminary step in this direction, the new government transferred the Civil Aviation Branch from the Department of National Defence to the newly formed Department of Transport, an amalgamation of the Departments of Marine and of Railways and Canals, under the dynamic leadership of C.D. Howe. Wilson retained his position as controller of civil aviation, but henceforth Howe was the dominant figure and chief civil aviation policy-maker in Canada.[33]

Howe's first major decision centred on the nomination of an airline company to operate over the trans-Canada airway and to link up with Imperial Airways on the North Atlantic route. Prior to his arrival on the scene it had been assumed in Canadian and British aviation circles, and in political circles as well, that Canadian Airways, by far the largest aviation company in Canada, would be the chosen instrument. It was also expected that the two railway companies, the government-owned Canadian National (CNR) and the privately owned Canadian Pacific (CPR) each of which held a 10 per cent interest in Canadian Airways, would be associated as the main source of capital. At first Howe appeared to accept this ready-made solution. In 1936 he gave a good deal of encouragement to James A. Richardson, president of Canadian Airways, who gained the impression that his company would be the prime carrier across Canada and would work with Imperial Airways on the North Atlantic route. In preparation for this role, Canadian Airways began to upgrade the qualifications of its best pilots to the highest airline standards and also undertook the operation of a commercial run between Vancouver and Seattle to provide crews with airline experience.[34]

Richardson was in for a disappointment. Other airlines, some of them only paper organizations backed by strong financial interests, were anxious to participate. None of their offers were accepted. However, as a result of their lobbying, opposition developed within the Cabinet to naming Canadian Airways as the operating company. Richardson, whose expertise was valued by Howe, was offered a position on the board of directors of Trans-Canada Air Lines (TCA), the new company formed by act of parliament on 6 April 1937, and the option of becoming a shareholder. This was not what he wanted and he withdrew from the scheme. Sir Edward Beatty, president of the CPR, likewise met with disappointment. Although expected to provide half the capital, about $2,500,000, he was allotted a minority position on the board of directors. Of the nine members, three were to be named by the government, three by the CNR, and three by the CPR. Since, in Beatty's view, Canadian National was an instrument of the government, he felt he would be outvoted on major issues. As soon as he was informed of the details of the proposed Trans-Canada Air Lines Act, he declined the invitation to participate.[35]

As a result of these negotiations, Trans-Canada Air Lines came into existence under complete government ownership and direction. The CNR acted as the government's agent in underwriting the cost and, while the way was left open for private companies to buy shares in the airline, none took up the offer. Howe recruited the top executives for the TCA in the United States, but ironically the company looked to Canadian Airways for its first aircrew and first aircraft.[36]

An interesting sequel to these events came in 1939, following the death of James Richardson, when the CPR bought Canadian Airways and all its affiliated companies. In 1940 Beatty became president and, with these resources at his command, he was able to provide valuable assistance in the organization of the British Commonwealth Air Training Plan and the establishment of the transatlantic ferrying organization.[37]

With plans agreed upon to move towards a transatlantic air service, all the countries involved had considerable work to do to prepare the necessary ground organization. The development of the Newfoundland sites was to be subsidized by the United Kingdom but, in theory at least, they were to remain under the jurisdiction of the colony. In practice this meant British control. In late 1933 Newfoundland, on the verge of bankruptcy, surrendered its dominion status and right to self-government for rule by a commission of six men appointed by the UK parliament: three commissioners from Britain and three from Newfoundland. All were basically administrators accountable to Westminster.[38] Thus, while the United Kingdom planned to finance the construction of the new facilities by a combination of grants to the colony and direct outlays, and Newfoundland would hold operational control, the constitutional arrangements protected British interests.

The commitment to build the airport for wheeled aircraft represented a certain leap of faith and a confidence in the continued improvement of landplanes. Those in service in 1935, while faster and more efficient than the flying boats used by the British and Americans for their longer routes, lacked the necessary range for a transatlantic passenger flight. There did not exist any land-based aeroplane capable of crossing the North Atlantic non-stop with a payload of mail and passengers. Nonetheless, aviation technology was moving in that direction and giving every indication that landplanes would eventually supersede flying boats on ocean routes. Several companies were feverishly working on long-range transport aircraft suitable for transoceanic operations. The Douglas Aircraft Company had launched its preliminary development studies for a four-engine transport, which would eventually become the DC-4, for use by Pan American and other US airlines on the Pacific and Atlantic routes. Boeing designers and engineers were working on a machine with similar capabilities. Spurred on by all these developments, the British government placed an order with the de Havilland Aircraft Company in 1936 for a fast mail plane capable of flying from Ireland to Newfoundland. The end product, defined as the DH91 Albatross, was to meet an Air Ministry order for an aircraft 'capable of transporting 1,000 lb. payload for a range of 2,500 miles against a 40 m.p.h. headwind.'[39]

Canadian aviation officials took more than a passing interest in the Newfoundland airport, which in their view could be the eastern terminus of the trans-Canada airway. In July 1935 Ottawa began to press for permission to send a Canadian officer to Newfoundland to conduct a survey for a suitable airport site. Thomas Lodge, commissioner of public utilities in the new Newfoundland administration, opposed this proposal on the grounds that it would give Canada a vested interest in the airport. The British government likewise hesitated to grant the request, but eventually gave permission in October, primarily to keep peace in the imperial family.[40] Later in the month, Squadron Leader L.F. Stevenson, an air force officer seconded to the Canadian Civil Aviation Branch, was instructed to carry out the survey. Working with two meteorological officers, one Canadian and one British, he examined about fifteen potential sites in the north-central part of Newfoundland. A location on the Gander River known as Hattie's Camp was recommended as the most suitable. Nearby Gander Lake was chosen as a suitable flying-boat base.[41]

The proposed airport site lay close to the great circle route. Located on a rocky plateau that offered good aircraft approaches, it was said to be reasonably free from fog. Although quite isolated, almost fifty miles southeast of Botwood and more than two hundred miles west of St John's, it was accessible by the main branch of the Newfoundland Railway. The British accepted the recommendations and the airport was built in the midst of the Newfoundland wilderness. Officially referred to as the Newfoundland Airport, it later, largely through the impact of wartime transatlantic ferrying operations, became known throughout the world simply as Gander.[42]

The British spared no expense in the construction of the airport, designed from the beginning as a major terminal on a route that expected a high volume of traffic. When completed, it would be one of the largest and technically most modern airports in the world. Because it was in an isolated region with practically no identifiable landmarks, it was equipped with an extensive system of boundary lights, a 36-inch rotating beacon visible in good weather for eighty-five miles, and flush-mounted sodium vapour lights down the centre of the runway.[43]

No comparable project had ever been undertaken in Newfoundland. In 1937, with the work under way but falling behind schedule, the British, determined to have the airport completed for the Albatross to use on transatlantic service, appealed to Canada for an experienced engineer to take over direction of the construction. J.A. Wilson recommended F.C. Jewett, who had worked as a superintendent engineer on the Welland ship canal. Jewett accepted the challenge on the condition that he could take with him Robert Bradley of Toronto, who had previously worked as his assistant engineer.[44] The British agreed and in April 1938 Jewett and Bradley moved into their new positions, the latter as resident engineer and with Jewett making policy decisions and conferring with Newfoundland authorities. Their contract called for the paving of the runways to their full length and to half their width by 1 September 1938, in case the Albatross was ready to fly, and to their full width a year later. All construction, including the terminal building, a hangar, living quarters, and a power house, was to be finished by 30

November 1939. In fact, the airport was usable early in 1938, and crews wrapped up construction at the end of October 1939.[45]

After the basic building program was completed and the construction camp emptied, life at the new airport moved at a leisurely pace. With the meteorological section under Patrick McTaggart-Cowan and the communication section under Tom McGrath, about fifty people in all moved from Botwood before Christmas 1938 and, from the new location, continued to service the flying boats on their experimental runs. The Newfoundland Airport itself, however, saw little flying activity. The Albatross, of which much had been expected, was being used by Imperial Airways on European routes, and at the beginning of the war was commandeered by the Royal Air Force. Nor did the Americans have any landplanes ready for transatlantic operations before the war; Pan Am was still making do with flying boats, staging through Botwood. Prior to the war only four aircraft were based at the huge new airport at Hattie's Camp: a de Havilland Fox Moth used for taking weather observations, a Fairchild 71C, and two obsolescent Handley Page Harrow bombers that had been converted to aerial tankers to refuel the flying boats *Cabot* and *Caribou*.[46]

Flying boats undertook what little transatlantic flying there was in the late 1930s. When the Second World War erupted in Europe in September 1939, the Newfoundland Airport lay idle in splendid isolation in the wilderness. In time it was to become a springboard for launching thousands of military aircraft on their way across the North Atlantic while also serving as an important base for Canadian and American anti-submarine squadrons. However, for months after the outbreak of hostilities, nobody demonstrated any awareness of the new airport's potential or of its strategic importance in the coming struggle. In fact, McTaggart-Cowan claims that the staff received, and ignored, orders to mine the runways.[47]

Before the war the Canadian government, notwithstanding its interest in the Newfoundland Airport, studiously avoided any discussion about the defence of its island neighbour strategically located on its eastern flank. After the declaration of war, Ottawa took a more realistic view and instructed the RCAF to extend the sweep of its defensive air patrols to include Newfoundland waters. Canada also expressed an interest in obtaining bases in Newfoundland.[48] Governor Sir Humphry Walwyn offered full cooperation. He proposed to the dominions secretary in London that the RCAF take over the new airport as well as the marine base at Botwood.[49] The British government was reluctant to let these facilities pass out of its control and at first objected strongly to Walwyn's proposal. However, pressed by the realities of the war, it had no alternative but to acquiesce. Even so, the RCAF took its time in moving to Newfoundland. Canada learned during the winter that it had free use of the airport facilities. Still, it was not until 17 June 1940 that 10 (Bomber-Reconnaissance) Squadron sent an operational detachment of Douglas Digbys to Gander.[50] The formal agreement transferring control of the airport to the Canadians was not completed until April 1941. It provided, among other things, that any changes at the airport had to be approved by the Newfoundland government, which would regain full control after the war.[51]

Meanwhile, as the work on the western landplane terminus progressed before the war, other aspects of the 1935 transatlantic air agreement proceeded somewhat as planned. The date set for the beginning of the experimental transatlantic flights by Imperial Airways and Pan American was 5 July 1937. At 2100 hours (Greenwich Mean Time or GMT) McTaggart-Cowan's weather forecasters briefed the crew of the Pan Am flying boat; at about the same time those at Foynes in Ireland were doing the same for the crew of the *Caledonia*, an empire flying boat fitted with extra fuel tanks to give it the requisite range. The two aircraft passed in mid-ocean. As the *Caledonia* crossed 30 degrees west longitude, it moved into the Botwood zone of control and landed at 1000 hours (GMT) on 6 July, taking just over fifteen hours to complete the 1900-mile flight. On 8 July it went on to Boucherville, the Montreal marine base, and then on to New York. A sister ship, the *Cambria*, made a flight over the same route at the end of July and another on 27 August. *Caledonia* made its second round trip on 15 August and a third, the last of the season, on 13 September. During the summer Pan American Airways ran three round trips, two by the direct route and one by way of Bermuda and the Azores.[52]

These flights marked the beginning of a new era in transatlantic aviation, but as yet no mail or passengers had been carried. For the British this resulted from the range limitations of the empire flying boats, which had no room for cargo when carrying the required fuel for the long ocean hop. To overcome this problem, the British first turned to the expediency of pick-a-back launching developed by the Mayo Composite Aircraft Company. In the early evening of 20 July 1938, *Mercury*, a small but powerful four-engine seaplane, was carried some distance out over the coast of Ireland on top of the flying boat *Maia* before disengaging and flying on under its own power. Piloted by

Captain D.C.T. 'Don' Bennett of Imperial Airways, an experienced pilot/navigator who was to play a vital part in the development of the transatlantic ferrying organization, *Mercury* flew non-stop to Montreal with a load of mail, newspapers, and photographs, the first commercial cargo flown across the North Atlantic.[53]

Although the British Air Ministry announced a program of eight transatlantic flights for 1938, Bennett's was the only one carried out. The failure of the others to materialize reflects the problems the British encountered in trying to keep abreast of the Americans in the production of long-range aircraft, while simultaneously preparing for a virtually inevitable war. In 1938 Imperial Airways received new empire flying boats with more powerful engines than *Cambria* and *Caledonia*, but the new machines could not lift off the water with a full load of fuel. To overcome this weakness, the two assigned to the North Atlantic, *Cabot* and *Caribou*, were equipped with the necessary equipment for the revolutionary new capability of mid-air refuelling. The first flight using this technique took place on 5 August 1939. After becoming airborne at Foynes with a cargo of mail and a partial fuel load, *Cabot* took on an additional 800 gallons from an aerial tanker and then set course for Botwood. The two aircraft made eight round trips during the summer of 1939. All but two were completed on schedule; one was delayed by weather and the other by the outbreak of war. From Botwood they flew on to Boucherville. There they connected with Trans-Canada Air Lines, which carried the mail across Canada.[54]

The Stars and Stripes did not appear over the North Atlantic in 1938. In that year, however, Pan American Airways acquired a fleet of Boeing 314 Clipper flying boats designed to carry forty passengers over distances up to 3100 miles. Pan Am first experimented with these advanced machines on its Pacific routes before the British, increasingly feeling the pressures of the international tensions in Europe, released the US airline from its obligation to wait for Imperial Airways before offering regular transatlantic flights to the paying public. Accordingly, Pan Am inaugurated a scheduled mail and passenger service in the summer of 1939, operating one flight weekly in each direction over both the direct route and the southern route by way of the Azores and Bermuda.[55]

Some idea of what it was like to fly in one of these aircraft was later related by a future prime minister of Canada, Lester B. Pearson. In August 1939 he was a senior official on the staff of the Canadian High Commission in London and enjoying a brief holiday at home in Canada.

Convinced that war was imminent, he felt he should return to London immediately. He decided to go by air – a course of action which O.D. Skelton, undersecretary of state for external affairs, considered unnecessarily rash. To discourage Pearson, he suggested that he would not likely get a seat on the plane on such short notice. 'I told him,' Pearson reported, 'I already had one, on a flying boat leaving the next day, thanks to a friend whom I phoned at Pan American headquarters in New York. Dr. Skelton gave up. He would take no responsibility for my decision.' He did, however, arrange for Pearson to fly on a Canadian government plane to Montreal, where the young diplomat caught a commercial flight to New York.

Early next morning I boarded a Boeing Clipper plane which deposited me on Southampton Sound the afternoon of the next day. I shared a cabin [the long-range craft were fitted out like ocean liners] on this large, slow, flying boat with two men; one a German reserve officer and the other a Polish reserve officer, both going home to fight; and perhaps kill each other. They became very friendly during the flight.

Only once did I doubt my good sense in rushing back by air. We had to come down at Shediac, New Brunswick, because of engine trouble. When we took off again we ran into a fierce North Atlantic storm. I was in an upper berth in the plane, and feeling very miserable for I was then as prone to air-sickness as to sea-sickness. I looked out of a small oval window into the black night and found that we were flying only a few hundred feet above the wild waves. I hoped the engine had been well and truly repaired and I said to myself, 'What the devil are you doing here?'[56]

The flights by Imperial Airways and Pan American Airways marked the beginning of a new stage in intercontinental aviation. Yet on the eve of the Second World War the air connection between North America and Europe was on a very small scale. The ground organization provided a minimum of facilities, and there were practically no radio aids to navigation. Operations on the direct route came to a stop in October. To fly the North Atlantic later than that was considered too hazardous. At the outbreak of war, transatlantic flying attracted no military attention whatsoever. Pan Am planned to continue its service via the Azores, but the British flying boats *Caribou* and *Cabot* were taken into service by the RAF for use on other more immediately important duties, and British transatlantic operations came to a halt.[57] The uncertainty of further developments on the North Atlantic air route prevailed for about another year. Then, when the tide of war suddenly and dramatically turned against the Allies, the air link quickly became a vital factor in British survival, one that was utilized and developed to a degree and at a pace hitherto undreamed of by the wildest visionary.

2

Canadian Pacific Railway

British forces have traditionally emphasized home industry as their source of supply. Indeed, during the interwar period, the Air Ministry in particular was satisfied with British-designed and -built equipment. There was little confidence in the United States as a potential supplier of military aircraft. The Austrian and Munich crises of 1938, however, forced a reassessment, with the result that, by the outbreak of war in Europe, Britain had signed contracts for the delivery of 250 Lockheed Hudson reconnaissance aircraft and 400 North American Harvard trainers.[1] Delivery commenced in February 1939, the aircraft being crated and carried by ship. Most made it to the United Kingdom before war was declared, but 214 arrived between September 1939 and February 1940.[2] On the outbreak of war the American neutrality laws clamped an arms' embargo against all belligerents. The restriction was removed by President Franklin Delano Roosevelt's cash-and-carry amendment of November 1939, and the British continued to place orders for Hudsons and other aircraft. By mid-summer of 1940, more than two hundred Hudsons had been delivered by sea to replace aging Avro Ansons in RAF Coastal Command.[3]

With transatlantic flying still in its infancy, it seems not to have occurred to anyone that an aircraft with the Hudson's range might have been flown to Britain. Of course, prior to the start of the war, there was no shortage of shipping space – a luxury that changed with the increase in the number of orders for all types of North American–produced war materials at the same time that the German navy began a highly successful U-boat campaign against Allied shipping. Early in 1940 the demands grew, as summarized by Edward Stettinius, President Roosevelt's lend-lease administrator: 'Three times as many orders were placed for planes by the French and the British in the first half of 1940 as in all of 1939 – over 8,000 planes and 13,000 engines. This brought the total orders placed in the United States by the French and the British for military planes in the eighteen months between January 1st, 1939 and June 30th, 1940 to 10,800.'[4]

After the German victories in Belgium and France, the Air Ministry flooded American manufacturers with orders for aircraft. 'The British air supply programmes as formulated in the summer of 1940,' reports the official history, 'called for the delivery of the following quantities between July 1940 and June 1942: first, 8,200 planes representing the undelivered balance of existing contracts, plus 1,500 for which orders were then pending, plus 4,200 by way of continuation orders for the capacity set up under the Anglo-French project of March 1940, which was originally to terminate in October 1941; secondly 12,000 planes which were to be the first instalment of a great new expansion scheme. In all approximately 26,000 aircraft.' Totals continually increased: 'By the time of the fall of France arrangements had been made for the eventual supply to the Allies of aircraft at the rate of a thousand a month. In subsequent discussions with the United States Government the idea had been conceived of setting up new plant which would yield a further three thousand planes a month.'[5] Many trainers were needed in Canada for the new joint air training scheme, but most of the deliveries would be to Britain – an increasingly difficult proposition.

The sudden and tremendous surge in aircraft purchases[6] coincided with a shortage of shipping space and a renewed intensity in Germany's campaign of submarine warfare. At the best of times, surface delivery of aeroplanes was slow and expensive. Many made the long trip to the United Kingdom lashed to the decks of merchant vessels. Others had to be partially disassembled, and many crated, before being loaded into the cargo hold of a freighter. And, of course, each of these had to be reassembled on reaching its destination. After the outbreak of hostilities, veritable squadrons of planes awaited the availability of shipping and the formation of convoys. German U-boats claimed many before they reached their destination. All filled limited cargo capacity increasingly in demand for other crucial war supplies. Overall it was a slow, expensive, and wasteful way to deliver aeroplanes. Nevertheless, feeling that the department was already burdened with too many commitments, and believing that in any case flying the North Atlantic regularly – especially in winter – was out of the question, Air Ministry officials clung to the policy that aircraft could not be flown across from North America. They must all be shipped.

Don Bennett of Imperial Airways, who was soon to become a key figure in the formation of the ferry organization, explained in his memoirs the emphasis with which the RAF denounced the whole idea:

It was, perhaps ... quaint to remember that when dear old Ginger [Air Marshal Sir Frederick Bowhill] had been C.-in-C. Coastal, he had been emphatic denouncing the idea of the creation of the Atlantic Ferry Organization – before it was formed. In fact, at one meeting Coastal Command maintained that it would be absolute suicide to attempt to fly aircraft across the North Atlantic from the American continent in winter, and, indeed, he was one of the more important influences in the R.A.F. which were opposed to the idea. It must be remembered that the Air Ministry and the R.A.F. consistently fought against the creation of the Atlantic Ferry. It was the Beaver and M.A.P. who established it. In saying this, I do not hold it against those who were of the opinion - at that time they knew no better.[7]

'The Beaver' was William Maxwell Aitken, first Baron Beaverbrook, the Canadian-born press magnate who became British prime minister Winston Churchill's minister of aircraft production in May 1940. In his personal history of the war, Churchill recalled that Beaverbrook presented something of a controversial figure and that some people objected to his appointment to the Cabinet. In fact, this particular choice gave the new prime minister his 'greatest difficulty.' However, he wrote of Lord Beaverbrook: 'I believed he had services to render of a very high quality. I had resolved, as the result of my experiences in the previous war, to remove the Supply and Design of Aircraft from the Air Ministry, and I wished him to become the Minister of Aircraft Production. He seemed at first reluctant to undertake the task ... I felt sure, however, that our life depended upon the flow of new aircraft; I needed his vital and vibrant energy, and I persisted in my view.'[8] The new minister did not disappoint. 'Lord Beaverbrook rendered signal service ... This was no time for red tape and circumlocution ... All his remarkable qualities fitted the need. His personal buoyancy and vigour were a tonic.' Churchill admitted: 'I was glad to be able sometimes to lean on him. He did not fail. This was his hour. His personal force and genius, combined with so much persuasion and contrivance, swept aside many obstacles. Everything in the supply pipeline was drawn forward to the battle. New or repaired airplanes streamed to the delighted squadrons in numbers they had never known before.'[9]

While he is often credited with supplying fighter squadrons with the requisite numbers of Hawker Hurricanes and Supermarine Spitfires to prevail in the crucial Battle of Britain in the summer of 1940, Beaverbrook's most important innovation possibly was his decision to initiate arrangements for North American-built aircraft to be flown across to Great Britain. It is hardly likely that the idea originated with him, but when it was presented to him it captured his imagination. After consulting experts on the feasibility of the project, he used his extensive power and influence to put it into effect without delay. This action was consistent with his reputation, personality, and drive. It was also typical that he took this momentous step without seeking the approval of the War Cabinet or consulting with the Air Ministry.[10]

Veterans and students of Ferry Command remember the Air Ministry for its opposition to the ferrying of new aircraft across the Atlantic. However, the department had proposed just such a venture in 1919 when it sponsored a plan to ferry Handley Page bombers from North America. In the event, nothing came of the scheme. As is so often the case in bureaucracies, it appears that the entire episode was lost to the corporate memory and remains nothing more than an interesting, if aborted, episode in the history of British air power.[11]

In its prewar planning, the Air Ministry sent a special mission to Canada in 1938 with instructions to encourage the Canadian aviation industry to develop a capacity capable of producing two hundred large bombers a year in peacetime, and five hundred in the first year of a war. 'Delivery was to be by air across the Atlantic.'[12] The order would include Handley Page Halifaxes and Short Stirlings, heavy four-engine bombers which, with extra fuel tanks, had the range for transatlantic flight. None was ordered, perhaps because Canadian industry was not yet prepared to produce such large aircraft. Thus the need to ferry them never arose. Moreover, officials at the Air Ministry seem to have had second thoughts about the virtues of flying bombers across the North Atlantic, apparently feeling that the hazards of war, added to the natural hazards of Atlantic weather, would result in an unacceptably high loss rate.

It is interesting to note that, in early April 1940 before the fall of France, an RCAF officer, Air Commodore N.R. Anderson, air officer commanding (AOC) Eastern Air Command, clearly foresaw the probable need for the transatlantic ferrying of bombers via the embryonic airfield at what later became known as Gander, Newfoundland. 'If Germany conducts a terrific Air Bombardment of aircraft factories and aerodromes in England and France and destroys a large number of Allied aircraft a very urgent demand may be made by England and France for the quick delivery by air of long range reconnaissance and bomber aircraft manufactured in Canada and the United States. These aircraft could be flown to the Newfoundland Airport and then across the Atlantic to England and France.'[13] It is unlikely that Beaverbrook saw Anderson's letter. No evidence has been discovered that the idea went beyond Air Force Headquarters (AFHQ) in Ottawa.

In his memoirs, *Ferryman*, Air Commodore G.J. 'Taffy' Powell, closely associated with the wartime ferrying organization from beginning to end, calls it a 'minor mystery that the idea of air ferrying the much needed Hudsons took such a long time to be born and even longer to be developed.' He does, however, throw new light on the origins of the scheme:

It was a firm of London export merchants, Hunt & Holditch Ltd., which seems to have put the first suggestion on the Ministry of Aircraft Production files when a director, Mr. Oakes-White wrote to Lord Beaverbrook, then Minister of Aircraft Production, to say that he had contact with a group of airline pilots and proposed a convoy system whereby each group of Hudsons would be shepherded by a flying boat. The scheme had some unworkable features and was turned down. It did however bring the suggestion to air ferry out into the open and to the front of Lord Beaverbrook's mind; so much so that by mid-1940 there were extensive exchanges for and against the proposal.[14]

Another suggestion came from 'the Lockheed representative in London, Mr. Yost, who persuaded his California superiors to have long-range kits designed and ready for the outstanding Hudsons for the RAF and proposed factory-engaged personnel to ferry them.' This was turned down 'by a senior Air Marshal on the grounds that US civilian pilots would be very expensive and that half the aircraft would be lost anyhow! Another commented that the idea was woolly but conceded that we had better try it.' British representatives in Washington also discussed the idea. The breakthrough came when Air Commodore George Pirie, the British air attaché, asked the opinion of G.E. Woods Humphery, recently retired as managing director of Imperial Airways, who was living in the United States. He agreed 'to take the job on if he could get sufficient of his old Atlantic team' and if he could work through an existing organization. Powell reports: 'He suggested the CPR in Montreal where he then had business interests.'[15] Don Bennett, a captain with BOAC (or British Overseas Airways Corporation, the new company that replaced Imperial Airways to carry the Union Jack on all overseas air routes in the fall of 1939) and a member of 'the old Atlantic team,' was approached and gave his support to the scheme.[16]

The idea of working through the Canadian Pacific Railway must have appealed to Beaverbrook. It provided the opportunity for just the type of ad hoc arrangement he loved. Moreover, the CP president, Sir Edward Beatty, was an old and trusted friend who had already been asked by the British government 'to coordinate Canadian shipping and rail transportation for the war effort.'[17] Even so, it seems strange that no one appears to have questioned this direct approach to a private citizen without going through C.D. Howe, by then minister of munitions and supply but still the key figure in Canadian aviation, or some other government official. The move seems to have been accepted, at least in part, because so many people respected Beatty. Bennett later described him as 'one of the finest men I have ever met.'[18]

No one questioned Beatty's patriotism. Indeed, he worked himself to death in volunteer war service. David Cruise and Alison Griffiths, in *Lords of the Line*, a book about the men who built the CPR, describe the effort he devoted to his wartime responsibilities: 'A huge task, it involved moving thousands of troops and hundreds of tons of cargo by sea, rail and air from Canada to Europe. Beatty placed himself on call twenty-four hours a day, breaking off CPR meetings to dash to Ottawa, and frequently eating his meals on the run as he shuttled back and forth. His evenings were filled with long phone calls that often lasted past midnight and his paperwork increased so much that he tripled his secretarial staff.' Normally a strong, robust man, he lost strength, came out of hospital after a bout of tonsillitis looking like 'an old man – pallid, haggard and humiliatingly frail.'[19] Following a period of recuperation he soon returned to work, but his productive days were numbered. He suffered a massive stroke in March 1941 and died two years later.[20]

At the start of the war, overlooking earlier misunderstandings with Howe when minister of transport, Beatty had offered to place all his railway's air facilities at the government's disposal. Howe had declined on the grounds that it was most important to Canada's overall war effort to keep all domestic air lines intact and functioning.[21] Beatty accepted this explanation, but at the same time he assisted the RCAF by arranging for Canadian Pacific Air Lines and its smaller affiliated companies to operate seven of the air observer schools and one elementary flying training school for the British Commonwealth Air Training Plan.[22] Whether he saw the proposed ferry service as an opportunity to break into transatlantic aviation, then virtually monopolized by Pan American Airways and BOAC, with Trans-Canada Air Lines waiting in the wings, it is impossible to say. Whatever his long-term goal, his immediate objective was to assist the Allied war effort by getting aircraft across to Britain as quickly as possible.

In the first instance, the idea of CP's involvement in the air ferrying scheme appears to have been suggested orally. A more formal approach came on 8 July 1940 when Morris G. Wilson, general manager of the Royal Bank of Canada and Beaverbrook's personal representative for the Ministry of Aircraft Production (MAP) in Canada and the United States, wrote to Beatty: 'I have heard through the British Air Attache in Washington and Mr. Woods Humphery that you have very generously offered to place the experience and facilities of your Company at our disposal to enable us to ferry those aircraft which are being constructed in the United States for the British Government and which have the necessary range to be flown to England instead of being sent by sea. Needless to say, we are very grateful for this offer and glad to accept it.'[23] Most people with whom he came in contact praised Wilson as a good businessman, but Bennett was unimpressed: 'No doubt he must have been a very capable man – but so far as I was concerned I can only say that I have never met anyone so devoid of qualities either good or bad.'[24]

Discussion or previous communication must have already brought an agreement in principle even before Wilson wrote to Beatty, for on the same date, in a letter from the British Purchasing Commission in New York to Woods Humphery, it was implied that the CPR had already agreed to help: 'I understand that as a result of your and Pirie's (Air Commodore Pirie, Air Attaché to the British Embassy, Washington) conversation with Sir Henry Self recently, it was agreed, subject to confirmation from Canada and England, that you will be responsible for flying across the Lockheed Hudsons, working with an organization in conjunction with the Canadian Pacific Railway.'[25]

Formal talks appear not to have been difficult and an agreement was reached that took effect on 30 July 1940. It was signed on 16 August by Beatty, Wilson, and Woods Humphery, representing the Ministry of Aircraft Production and the embryonic ferry organization. The agreement created an operating company called the CPR Air Services Department, 'for the purpose of manning and despatching aircraft on account of the Ministry [of Aircraft Production] from North America to the British Isles and elsewhere as may be agreed upon hereunder.' The designation was in some ways misleading, as the primary function of the CPR was to provide a framework of administrative services for what was essentially an operation of the British government. The CPR agreed to engage and pay all personnel and to procure the necessary supplies. The Ministry of Aircraft Production agreed to 'provide at least two competent and experienced officers who shall report to the Chairman and President of the Company in Montreal, and who shall thereupon be added to the staff of the Air Services Department.' The ministry also agreed to 'monthly, upon receipt of accounts duly certified by the Auditors of the Company, pay all expenses incurred by the Air Services Department in the carrying out of this agreement, excluding only the salaries of any executive officers of the Company, but including the travelling expenses of such officers.'[26]

The connection between the Government of Canada and the ferry service appears at first to have been an informal type of arrangement. Although Canadian support was absolutely essential, there is no evidence that Canada was formally approached by the Ministry of Aircraft Production or by any other branch of the British government. The oversight is not altogether surprising, for Beaverbrook, though a minister of the crown himself, tended to avoid official channels and red tape, preferring instead to work through individuals of his own choosing 'on a business man's kind of basis.'[27] The ferrying organization he treated much as he did his own private enterprises. Having issued orders for its establishment, he gave Beatty and Wilson a free hand, financially and otherwise, as long as results were forthcoming. They had to arrange for any assistance needed from the Canadian government in Ottawa.

The two Canadian ministers most directly involved, Howe and C.G. 'Chubby' Power, minister of national defence for air, expressed a willingness to help in whatever way they could, but, in the absence of any kind of agreement or understanding between the governments of Canada and the United Kingdom, they were sometimes in doubt as to what priority to attach to requests from the CPR Air Services Department. For instance, at St Hubert just east of Montreal, where the RCAF made room for the ferrying organization to set up its main centre of operations, it had to compete with No. 13 Service Flying Training School for hangar space, and at Gander, where there was only one hangar and more were already needed, Canadian and American requirements were looked after first.[28] On the other hand, in publicizing the need for ferry pilots and in recruiting them in the United States through the Clayton Knight Committee, the RCAF made a key contribution to the success of the enterprise.[29]

Besides assisting the CP Air Services Department in a general way, the Department of Transport made a number of noteworthy contributions. It made available its meteorological section at Gander, including the services of Patrick McTaggart-Cowan, who became the ferry service's chief weatherman in North America; it recruited some of its best radio operators for the transatlantic flights; it provided technicians to assist with the inspection of aircraft after delivery at Montreal and to service them for the flight across the ocean; and it constructed an airport at Dorval which became the headquarters for overseas ferry operations. It also built a rudimentary landing strip at Emerson, Manitoba, adjacent to an American facility at Pembina, North Dakota. There US planes, which by virtue of the American neutrality laws could not be flown beyond the territorial United States, were towed across the border by horses. (This practice ceased after the passage of the Lend-Lease Act in March 1941 when there appeared to be less political danger from isolationist sentiments. Moreover, the Roosevelt administration's legal staff, giving a new interpretation to the neutrality legislation, declared that the fiction of observance at border points was unnecessary.)[30]

The essentially informal nature of the arrangements is illustrated by the fact that several individuals began work on the Atlantic ferrying scheme more than two weeks before the agreement was actually signed. Assistance and key personnel were provided quickly by the Ministry of Aircraft Production, BOAC, the Canadian Department of Transport, the RCAF, and private business and industry in Canada. Beatty was chairman of the Air Services Department, Woods Humphery vice-chairman, and Lieutenant-Colonel H. Burchall, a representative of the Air Ministry, was general manager. As expressed by Don Bennett, who was to take a leading part in establishing the ferry service, 'the arrangement was that Woods Humphery, who lived in New York, would keep a general supervisory eye on the proceedings and the Canadian Pacific Railway would provide all administrative facilities such as we might need.'[31] The inclination towards informal arrangements persisted throughout the war. For example, the RCAF, Trans-Canada Air Lines, and Ferry Command cooperated extensively in the provision of radio and teletype facilities and radio range charts. And many nations contributed bases, equipment, information, and personnel.[32]

Beatty recruited a number of top-ranking executives as 'dollar-a-year men' to manage and advise on such matters as financing, purchasing, and publicity. They included J. Schofield, chief architect of the Canadian National Railways; G.M. Smith, chartered accountant: F.B. Walls, director and general manager of the T. Eaton Company; John G. McConnell, president, Montreal Standard Publishing Company; A.D. Dunton, editor of *The Standard*; B.W. Roberts, general purchasing agent of the CPR; and J.H. Norris, president of Wilder Norris Ltd, Realty Investments. More names were added to this list as time went on. While some of the volunteers acted in an advisory capacity, others served fulltime without asking any remuneration.[33]

The managers of the operation played an important role, but attracting and selecting competent aircrew was a constant and crucial problem. Although the Air Services Department urgently sought Canadian and American pilots, its mainstay in the formative period came from BOAC. In its agreement with the CPR, the Ministry of Aircraft Production was required to provide 'as many first class pilots, navigators and wireless operators, up to a total of twenty-five, as can be secured from England.'[34]

Don Bennett and A.S. Wilcockson, widely recognized for their work in pioneering the North Atlantic route from 1937 to 1939, the former as captain of the seaplane *Mercury* and the flying boat *Cabot* and the latter as captain of the *Caledonia* and *Caribou*, were sent to Canada as flying superintendent and superintendent of operations, respectively. Two other BOAC captains, R.H. Page and I.G. Ross, the latter a Canadian who had flown as a bush pilot before joining Imperial Airways, were appointed Bennett's assistants. While Bennett, Page, and Ross had served only in a flying capacity, Wilcockson had previously been in charge of Imperial's Atlantic division. Another veteran of the same airline came on loan from the RCAF. A squadron leader and chief navigation officer of Eastern Air Command, Taffy Powell also had a wealth of useful and relevant experience. A seasoned flying-boat captain with Imperial Airways, he had been in charge of the Bermuda division when the war broke out. Although not a Canadian, he had elected to join the RCAF. With the new air ferrying service he was assigned to lay the groundwork for the dispatch of aircraft from the Newfoundland Airport, was later to take charge of ferrying operations in Bermuda, and eventually ended up in a key position back in Montreal.[35] These five men, all of them first-class navigators as well as accomplished pilots, were responsible for the formation of the delivery unit within the framework of the Air Services Department, and to them must go the credit for the successful launch of the ferrying operations.

Work got started at the beginning of August 1940. Burchall and Wilcockson arrived in Montreal on 30 July and set up operations in offices provided by the CPR in the Windsor Station. Bennett, Page, and Ross arrived two days later, after crossing the Atlantic in a blacked-out liner with a group of women and children being evacuated from Britain. By this time the Lockheed Aircraft Corporation had agreed to deliver fifty Hudsons, ordered for the RAF, between August and October. This twin-engine medium bomber, already in service with Bomber Command and Coastal Command, would be the trial machine to determine if the transatlantic delivery scheme was feasible.[36]

After five days in Montreal, Bennett and Page left for Burbank, California, to visit the Lockheed plant. To this point all the RAF Hudsons had been delivered by ship. The primary objective of the trip was to determine if the modified, long-range version of the aircraft could indeed safely fly the Atlantic. Bennett recalls that they were met by Wing Commander Jimmy Adams, the RAF representative on the west coast, 'a personal friend of the majority of the stars.' The BOAC captains avoided Adams's habit of entertaining 'people from England by introducing them to the film community in a big way.'[37] Instead, they went right to work at the Lockheed factory and demanded a test flight as soon as possible, with Bennett at the controls and in charge of the readings. Despite being somewhat taken aback by the request and the impatience shown by the British representatives, Lockheed officials expedited the arrangements.

When Bennett found that the Hudson III fell 8 per cent short of its estimated performance figures, it was fitted with an additional fuel tank in the fuselage. He says that his hosts were initially sceptical of his reports, but moved quickly when they confirmed his findings. This critical perfectionist was very impressed with the people he dealt with at Lockheed. 'The speed with which American manufacturers implemented the demands made on them was an object lesson I shall never forget. Their spirit of co-operation was simply wonderful ... once one had convinced them on a particular point the speed with which they acted was simply fantastic.'[38] Satisfying themselves that the Hudson III could make the transatlantic crossing, and arranging for a number of small changes in the aircraft ordered (such as the installation of improved compasses and Bendix radio equipment), Bennett and Page learned that the first of the long-range Hudsons would not be ready until the middle of September, with fifty more scheduled for delivery within two months.[39]

The trip back to Montreal from Burbank bears special mention. The British airmen returned in two Hudson IIs, earmarked for use as trainers by the Air Services Department. However, to observe the legal and diplomatic niceties occasioned by the American neutrality laws, they had to travel as passengers. As qualified pilot-navigators, they were fascinated by the different procedures in use in the United States from those they had experienced throughout the British Empire. Bennett recalls: 'We went through the States, sticking always strictly to "airways," which added considerably to the distance and nothing to safety – in fact, to the contrary. These two American pilots would not leave the beam for any reason whatsoever. Thus we unnecessarily went through heavy thunderstorms to our great discomfort, and remained in the thick of the airline traffic, to our considerable danger – but that was, and is, American aviation.'[40]

Perhaps the highlight of the return trip was the stop at Pembina, North Dakota, on the Canadian border about sixty miles south of Winnipeg. Here, 'we solemnly stopped the engines, and had a horse hitched on to the front to pull the aircraft across the border, which was in fact, in the middle of a piece of farmland and was hard to define in any case. This most vital formality having been completed, we took off and flew on to Winnipeg, where we night-stopped.'[41] From time to time one hears stories like this about the early months of the war. They are often ignored as being too preposterous. In fact, many aircraft destined for both the RAF and the RCAF were towed across the border in a similar fashion. From Winnipeg, the flight continued on to St Hubert, with an overnight stop in Kapuskasing, Ontario.

While Bennett and Page had been checking out Hudsons at the Lockheed plant in California, recruiting and training had got started in Montreal. As soon as they reached St Hubert, the new aircraft were put to work to check out prospective aircrew, familiarize them with the Hudson, and train them in long-distance flying and navigation. Those who exhibited the requisite degree of skill in instrument flying and navigation, and were otherwise suitable, were offered contracts as first or second pilots. Officially, these two Hudson trainers were borrowed from the RCAF, with maintenance provided by Trans-Canada Air Lines. The two planes flew night and day, accumulating almost three hundred engine hours in a month. With spares in short supply, it took an imaginative and herculean effort by the TCA maintenance staff, as well as the instructors, to keep them serviceable.[42]

Neither the RAF nor the RCAF, with heavy training and operational demands, could spare aircrew to loan to the fledgling organization. It fell to civilian crews to man the machines for the historic transatlantic delivery flights. It had been assumed that American and Canadian airmen could supplement a nucleus of BOAC flying personnel. No real advertising was undertaken, but word went out through the various aviation grapevines that experienced pilots were required in Montreal to fly new bombers to Britain. Advantage was taken of a quasi-clandestine Canadian organization currently engaged in recruiting experienced airmen in the United States.

For several months the RCAF had been quietly attracting pilots from south of the border to help staff the British Commonwealth Air Training Plan schools sprouting across the dominion. Under the leadership of Clayton Knight, an American aviation artist and First World War flyer, and Homer Smith, a Canadian-born businessman, the Clayton Knight Committee maintained offices in various major US cities. Cultivating contacts in aviation circles and communicating with flying clubs and schools, this committee directed instrument-rated commercial pilots with more than three hundred hours on their logbooks to the RCAF. Particularly in the early years of the plan, most found employment as staff pilots and instructors at various BCATP schools. However, some managed to land a more lucrative position with the new ferry service. Of the 197 civilian pilots recruited by the Clayton Knight Committee by September 1940, forty-four eventually became transatlantic ferry pilots. This was undoubtedly a plum job. Beaverbrook had arranged for civilian aircrew to be well paid by the standards of the day: $600 per trip for group leaders, $500 for aircraft captains, $400 for co-pilots, and $300 for radio operators, with two trips per month guaranteed, plus expenses.[43] Few navigators or radio operators were expected to be available because of the use of radio ranges for long-distance flying in North America. Here airliners flew without navigators and radio operators; the pilots simply followed radio signals from point to point.

Many British officials felt that the generous pay rates were necessary to entice flyers from secure regular jobs to a short-term enterprise, which might be dangerous and which offered no pension or fringe benefits.[44] Others believed these 'extremely high rates of pay ... caused no end of friction.' Bennett went on to claim that many of the pilots had already been fired by American airlines. He singled out one candidate, admittedly rejected, who 'proudly sat on his [Wilcockson's] desk and said: "I'll show you how to fly the Atlantic – I've been thrown out of every airline in America for drunkenness. I'll show you how to fly the Atlantic!"' Bennett seemed to resent the disparity in remuneration, because

it meant that those of us from England were working for a fraction of the money which the American 'rejects' were to receive. Admittedly, those of us already in executive positions in Montreal were not unduly worried about this, but there were others, some of whom were the pilots from the U.K. who arrived subsequently. We also ran into the rather difficult comparison when British subjects from Canada and Newfoundland, or even from Australia, turned up for engagement in Montreal as ordinary civilian ferry pilots. They had heard of the rates of pay that were offered, and naturally resented any suggestion of unfair discrimination against themselves. This situation was one of the greatest causes of friction in the Atlantic Ferry and became worse as more and more outside authorities pushed their noses into our affairs. In fact, we could have got all the pilots we wanted and, probably, some better ones, had we not attempted this pathetic piece of bribery.[45]

The recruits came from a variety of backgrounds. George Lothian, a Trans-Canada Air Lines captain who spent some time seconded to the ferry service, notes: 'the crews consisted of as wide a mixture of backgrounds, experience, and cultures as had been gathered together outside the French Foreign Legion.'[46] Some were airline pilots. Others boasted of a wealth of experience in other fields of aviation, from many countries and from many walks of life. This has been summarized in the brief official account, *Atlantic Bridge*:

all the professions of the sky soon were sending their candidates. There were bush pilots – men who were opening up the lonely northern territories of Canada, skilful, instinctive fliers who rode unmapped country for trade and for development, remote from the crises of Europe. There were barn-stormers – men who would fly you for a dollar, thrill-makers, spell-binders, or taxi-men who from belief in flying and for bread and butter were teaching the men in the street the ways of the air. There were crop-dusters – those whose job it was to fly low, spraying crops by contract to counteract blights. There were sky-writers. There were amateurs who flew, business men who piloted themselves, pilots who worked for companies or commercial magnates. These and many others came. They came in the fall of 1940 and in 1941 from the United States, Canada, Britain. The wanted to do a flying job. They wanted to help the war.[47]

From downtown Montreal, the volunteers who survived a credentials check of their qualifications, logbooks, and licences, and an interview with Wilcockson, were sent out to St Hubert 'for a flight check by Captain Page or one of his colleagues.'[48] After they had passed this scrutiny, newly engaged pilots went to work learning the idiosyncrasies of the Hudson, not an easy aircraft to master. Bennett was the authority to whom difficult cases were referred. However, he recalled that 'Humphrey Page and Ian Ross did the donkey work of instruction. They certainly worked. Day after day, for all hours, they carried out dual instruction on an aircraft which had some very tricky characteristics, including an ability to drop a wing if bounced and quite a nasty stall if one was so stupid as to get too slow. It is not being unduly rude to say that the Hudson was a fine performer, but a handful, which could be extremely dangerous if one were careless.'[49]

An American pilot later wrote about his period as a trainee. The experienced BOAC veterans doing the instructing took nothing for granted. After passing Wilcockson's initial check, the new pilot headed to the classroom for a week studying navigation. 'Most of it he probably already knows, although the brushing-up brings to light many points he has forgotten or is not too clear on. From dead reckoning at which he is expected to be proficient from the start, he progresses to radio navigation and use of the flight computer. Many things are new to him. Unless he has been a Naval or boat pilot he probably has not used mercator charts. He must learn to think in knots, nautical miles, in degrees of latitude and longitude.' Americans had to learn completely new systems. 'Here he finds that, when we speak of radio navigation, we do not mean beam flying. If he has been an airline pilot in the U.S. he will miss that beam ... There are many groans from the American pilot who, after flying for years on "compass headings," finds suddenly that there is no such thing. Instead he must learn to navigate by the British system and the terminology is quite different.'[50]

The recruit also spent the second week on the ground at technical training, learning about the aircraft he would be expected to deliver to the United Kingdom.

Here he must draw the complete fuel and oil systems of the Lockheed *Hudson*. He also must chart the hydraulic system and the workings of the automatic pilot, the flaps, landing gear, etc. He is taken out into the hangars where he has opportunity to put his hands on the gadgets he has been sketching. Every *Hudson* to be ferried across carries an extra gasoline tank in the cabin and another in the bomb bay, in addition to the four regular tanks in the wings. The two special tanks carry the necessary extra fuel for the long flight and are taken out when the ship reaches its destination. So, in the hangar he is shown how to use fuel from the tanks so as to keep the ship balanced. He learns how to use the oxygen equipment, the Aldis signalling lamp, Very pistols, emergency escape hatches, and how to operate the automatic pilot. He is shown how to properly operate and make use of every bit of equipment in the aircraft.[51]

If the trainee passed the ground instruction, he reported for flying training. Following an introduction to the controls, instruments, and peculiarities of the Hudson, he finally got a chance to fly it. 'The [first] morning's flying consists of practising take-offs and landings. After lunch he goes up to 3,000 or 4,000 feet where he is shown the correct procedure in the event of an engine failure. This is important because if one engine fails with a full transatlantic load, only a correct procedure will bring the ship safely to port.' When the pilot exhibited enough competence he soloed, 'to get the feel of the ship.' However, he had not yet been accepted by the ferry service. He faced more checks before he could be entrusted with the delivery of a new aircraft. At this point, 'an instrument hood is put up and the pilot's ability to fly by instruments is checked. He must be able to steer a straight course within 5° and within an altitude variation of 100 feet. Precision turns, climbing and gliding turns – all must be accomplished satisfactorily, both with and without the use of the artificial horizon and directional gyro.' When this hurdle was cleared, there remained one final test at the end of the week of flying:

He plots a course to a point 100 miles away and return. He starts off assuming a dead calm, flying contact. After 15 or 20 minutes he must find a wind by visual fix, using his computer. After setting a new course for his turning point he is put under the hood. He now must fly by instruments to his turning point, then back to Montreal. At some point on the return trip the instructor cuts an engine. Upon his skill and accuracy in computing, and in his flying generally, depends whether he is made a captain, first officer or washed out.[52]

Initially there was no serious problem attracting pilots for such an exciting, well-paying project. As already mentioned, the shortages were in the area of navigators and radio operators. The planners intended to get around the first deficiency by dispatching the delivery flights across the Atlantic in loose formation, with only the lead aircraft including a navigator (provided by BOAC) in the crew. Some radio operators had been promised by BOAC. Finding others required more imagination in recruitment and training. On 6 September the Department of Transport transmitted a signal to its radio stations across Canada:

The Canadian Pacific Railway Company on behalf of the British Ministry of Aircraft Production require[s] operators for purpose of ferrying aircraft from Montreal to United Kingdom. Applicants are invited from our radio operating staff who are good code men with technical ability. Six men are required by fifteenth instant and others at intervals later. Volunteers selected on trial will on arrival in Montreal be interviewed, also tested in the air. Any found unsuitable will be returned to present position and will receive pay at their existing rates during their absence, together with transportation. Operators found suitable will be granted leave without pay from our services. Please get in touch with all operators under your jurisdiction immediately and wire in names of volunteers and date they can leave.[53]

As soon as these experienced ground radio men arrived in Montreal, they were put to work learning the radio procedure to be used on the ferry routes. On a more basic level, they also had to learn to do the job in the air rather than on the ground. Few of these men had any flying experience. None had ever spent much time in an aeroplane. For all these volunteers, their first long-distance flight would come with their first delivery. The training took place 'in a small shack at St. Hubert with Morse keys and telephones.'[54] The instructors were experienced BOAC radio operators, Jimmy Jubb and G.C. 'Jock' Cunningham. Jubb had read of the plans for ferrying North American aircraft in his newspaper in England. He volunteered for the operation and, within days, found himself joining an old Imperial Airways colleague, Cunningham, in the flying boat, *Clare*, heading for America. Cunningham 'barely had time to change out of the khaki uniform in which he had been instructing signallers in the British Army for nearly a year.'[55]

Art Stark, one of the first Department of Transport radio operators to arrive in Montreal, remembers Cunningham's early teaching techniques. The civilians had to learn the new wartime procedures they would be using with the ferry service. 'Much of our time for the first week was spent in memorizing new "Q" signals – such as "QUG – I am going to ditch" and others of a similar nature which were considered would be helpful – military message format and the coding and decoding of cyphers, since all weather data was classified and could not be sent en clair.'[56] Quite understandably, Cunningham was not familiar with the high level of expertise of his new recruits. At any rate, he had to ensure that they had the requisite skills. Stark told a story about a Morse code test that vividly demonstrates the high standards brought by the Canadian volunteers:

A new group of D.O.T. operators had arrived and were gathering around the operating table for their code test. Some of us who had been through the drill a few days before were sitting around kibitizing [sic] and passing uncomplimentary remarks about the operating abilities of the new-commers [sic]. Jock came in, settled himself at the key and after a few preliminary dits and dahs, looked around the table to see if everyone was ready. Receiving affirmative signs from the 'students' Jock started sending, but almost immediately stopped. He had noted that one of the chaps (R.W. 'Dusty' Weaver) seemed more interested in rolling a cigarette than in copying the test. A direct enquiry if he was ready brought a reply from Dusty, 'Sure, – go ahead.' Jock started sending again, but after a couple of words stopped again as he had noted Dusty was still busy with his cigarette. A further enquiry from Jock as to whether he intended to take the test, brought a somewhat surprised reply from Dusty of 'Yeah, sure – go ahead.'

Jock by this time was understandably getting somewhat exasperated, but started sending again. This time he did not stop although he noted that Dusty had still not started to write but was busy lighting his cigarette. Having no doubt mentally noted that there was one D.O.T. operator who wouldn't be around for long, Jock finished the test and collected the papers. Imagine his surprise when Dusty handed in a precisely printed perfect copy. That was the last code test given to any radio operator from the D.O.T.[57]

Weaver went on to make many delivery flights before he left the transatlantic ferry organization at the end of the war.[58]

Few of the recruits had any experience with visual signalling, a skill required by the ferry service. Consequently, they had to learn to use the Aldis lamp. This led to an amusing incident:

It was found that a good visual 'circuit' could be set up from our fourth floor class room to a service station lot about a block away. So with one party at the service station and another at the window on the fourth floor we became familiar with the Aldis Lamp. This practice went on quite successfully for several days until it was brought to an abrupt end one afternoon by the sudden appearance [of] the police in simultaneous raids at both ends of the 'circuit.' During explanations which followed it was learned that a keen-eyed and patriotic citizen had reported seeing a flashing light coming from an office building which he was convinced was the secret hide-out of German spies. In order to avoid further reports of espionage or revealing the true purpose of our activities (at that time Ferry Command [as veterans of the service refer to the organization] was very much under wraps) alternative training tactics were devised.[59]

Finally, Stark reported that they received a cursory introduction to more than just communications techniques and procedures. 'We were also given instruction – one two-hour lecture – in aircraft hydraulics and servo systems, to enable us to perform in-flight repairs! Luckily, I never had to prove my knowledge (?) and capabilities in these matters.' With that, the training finished, and the survivors were admitted to the ferry service. 'Then came the great day when we were taken out to St. Huberts [sic] airport, south of the city. There we were issued with a parachute and a pair of head-phones fitted into a soft leather flying helmet and then introduced to a Hudson V bomber ... There was only one short familiarization flight and after that we were on our own.'[60]

It all sounds rather casual. Yet from these informal beginnings the ferry service acquired many of the radio operators who played an important role in the operation for the rest of the war. Even when military pilots and navigators arrived later, the radio job continued to be done primarily by civilians. Cunningham stayed as chief signals officer and Jubb rose to manage these and other radio operators who joined the ferry service in ensuing months and years. Most of his original volunteers remained. They flew over and flew to all the inhabited continents. At least seventy-five of them gave their lives to the ferry service and lie buried in many far-flung corners of the globe.[61]

While the recruiting and training proceeded in Montreal, Beaverbrook and his representatives scoured the aviation world looking for aircraft that could aid the war effort. Thus it was that the first aeroplane flown across the Atlantic by the Air Services Department was not a new military craft but a second-hand flying boat, a commercial version of the Consolidated PBY (or Catalina to the British), with thousands of hours on its logbook. It was purchased by the British Air Commission in Washington from an American scientist, Dr Richard Archibald, who had used it extensively over the South Atlantic and the Indian Ocean on scientific expeditions and aerial surveys, the latter work undertaken for the government of Australia. In the course of its travels the flying boat had earned a reputation for endurance and had acquired the nickname *Guba*, after an equatorial squall peculiar to New Guinea. The decision to buy it and fly it to the United Kingdom, where it was put into service on the run to West Africa, may be taken as a reflection of Britain's lack of long-range capability and Beaverbrook's passion to obtain whatever aircraft he could from the United States.[62]

Ian Ross was assigned to fly the *Guba*, with the experienced American pilot Grafton Carlisle as first officer, Flight Lieutenant G.P. 'Pat' Christie as second officer, and two radio operators, Jock Cunningham himself and J.L. Glover.[63] Christie, a Montrealer in the RAF, had already won a Distinguished Flying Cross as a fighter pilot in the Battles of France and Britain. He had been shot down and was returning to active duty following six weeks' leave at home to recover from his wounds. Later in the war he returned to Montreal to serve with Ferry Command, only to lose his life in a flying accident in a Hudson.[64] Glover made another trip on a Catalina delivery in a couple of months. He was later killed while flying an aircraft in the United Kingdom with the Air Transport Auxiliary.[65]

On 25 October 1940 the *Guba* lifted off from Botwood harbour in Newfoundland. It was rather late in the flying season and, to add to the normal hazards of Atlantic flying, the *Guba*, equipped for the tropics, had no de-icing apparatus, no cabin heating, and no oxygen supply. All went well for the first seven hours, but with about five hours of flying time left, ice began to form on the propellors which was so thick that chunks flew off, smashing one of the windows. Then the wings began to take on a coating of ice and, in Ross's words, 'We became worried.' The *Guba* plunged on, gained altitude, and at 15,000 feet got above the cloud and the icing. At this height the combined effect of cold and lack of oxygen was numbing, but Ross, who did his own navigating as well as flying, kept the aircraft on course. He made his first landfall over Mallin Head at the tip of Northern Ireland and then flew on to Stranraer in Scotland, where the flying boat was safely moored. Initial reaction at the destination was one of disbelief. *Atlantic Bridge* reports: 'Probably for security reasons, Stranraer had been kept in the dark, and only a few people had received instructions about the aircraft. "Fill the goddamned thing up with gas and we'll fly it back," said the Captain with pardonable exasperation, when Stranraer expressed surprise at their arrival.'[66]

Meanwhile, back in Montreal, preparations were well underway to deliver the first new Hudsons. Every detail was taken care of, because the decision to continue with the enterprise would depend on the success of the first delivery flights. The aircraft itself remained a question mark. Bennett and Page may have satisfied themselves that the Hudson could fly the Atlantic, but it had yet to be demonstrated. Range was not the only factor. It remained to be seen how well the aircraft could withstand the buffeting of the Atlantic winter storms. Hudson IIIs were to be flown on the first flight. They were similar to the Is and IIs already in service in the United Kingdom and Canada, but were powered by two 1200-hp Cyclone engines in place of the 1100-hp units in the earlier versions.[67] Overload fuel tanks were added for the ocean crossing, making the plane 'a flying gas tank.'[68] De-icing boots, mounted on the leading edges of the wings and control surfaces, were a regular feature of the Hudson's design; as an added precaution, Kilfrost, an ice-resistant compound, was smeared over other vital parts such as aerials.[69]

The Hudson IIIs were to have been ready in August but, perhaps inevitably, delays occurred and it was not until 8 October that the first were delivered to Montreal. Plans for the transatlantic flights called for the Hudsons to carry a crew of three, a first pilot, a second or co-pilot, and a radio operator. With navigators in scarce supply, the first deliveries would have to find their way to Britain without each aircraft carrying its own. Officials hoped they could make do with one experienced navigator in a formation of several planes. As has been seen, the volunteer radio operators from the Canadian Department of Transport had been learning the difference in working from the air after a career on terra firma. At the same time, pilots continued to come to Montreal from a variety of civilian flying operations and claiming a wide array of qualifications and experiences. When the new Hudsons arrived, a period of intensive operational preparation could begin. There seemed little doubt that the aircraft, thanks to its overload tanks, had the endurance required for the flight from Newfoundland to Northern Ireland, but an error in navigation or faulty engine handling, by wasting fuel, could lower the margin of safety to an uncomfortable level, or even wipe it out altogether.

Each new Hudson underwent a series of tests to ensure that it could make it across the broad expanse of the Atlantic. As soon as the delivery aircraft arrived at St Hubert from California, the airmen who had survived the elimination process of credentials check, interview, and ground and flying training went to work testing them. In particular, they carefully checked engine power and fuel consumption. As one of the first American pilots recalled:

Each plane was put through a thorough flight test program in Canada, under simulated trans-Atlantic load conditions, to determine actual fuel consumption precisely. I made one test run of about 900 mi., at an indicated air speed of 135 m.p.h., at altitudes of 7–11,000 ft., and established a fuel consumption of 67 gal. per hr. On another test run I climbed to 9,000 ft. with a crew of three in the plane and established an average consumption of 66 gal. per hour for a flight lasting 4 hr. and 7 min. Indicated air speed at level flight cruising was 137.5 nautical m.p.h., and true air speed 157 nautical m.p.h.[70]

Bennett, later described by Air Chief Marshal Sir Arthur Harris of Bomber Command as 'the most efficient pilot I have ever met,'[71] played the leading role in overseeing this work to prepare for the delivery of the first Hudsons. A ubiquitous figure, at work in his office in the Windsor Street CPR Station in downtown Montreal, planning and preparing for the flight, fussing over Hudsons delivered to St Hubert airport, and conferring with US aircraft manufacturers, he impressed everyone he met with his masterful knowledge of aeroplanes and aviation, his skill as a pilot, and his command and control of the whole operation. His obsession for detail sometimes tried the patience of others because he believed in leaving nothing to chance. He personally tested the pilots and radio operators selected and trained by his assistants, and drew up precise cruising cards for each aircraft. When the men and machines were pronounced ready to his demanding satisfaction, he sent them off to Gander (as the Newfoundland Airport at Hattie's Camp was now generally referred to) to continue training until he arrived. They flew the nine hundred miles with a full load of fuel and navigated by dead reckoning without use of radio aids, much as they would have to do on the transatlantic flight.[72]

Squadron Leader Powell, in overall charge of ground organization, was already at Gander, having arrived there on 8 October to set up a base headquarters. He travelled not by air but by sea ferry to Port-aux-Basques, and then continued his journey across Newfoundland to Hattie's Camp on the narrow-gauge railway, which in due course would become well known to all those who were stationed at Gander for any length of time. His first concern was to find accommodation for the Hudson crews. Although Gander was claimed to be the largest airport in the world, it had only one hangar and no proper housing except for the quarters occupied by the small civilian staff of meteorologists, flying control personnel, and telecommunication technicians. In June the airport had received its first RCAF presence. 'A' Flight of 10 (Bomber

Reconnaissance) Squadron had moved in and was actively engaged in flying anti-submarine patrols with its Douglas Digbys. Because of the lack of housing, the officers and men were squeezed into whatever space could be found and the 1st Battalion of The Black Watch (Royal Highland Regiment) of Canada, charged with the responsibility of guarding the air base, was living in tents. New construction, including a thirty-room transit hotel for ferry personnel, was just getting under way. Nothing would be ready in time to accommodate the crews of the first flight of seven Hudsons. But the ever ingenious Powell found an answer. Perhaps inspired by his railway trip, he appealed to the New-foundland Railway Company to run a couple of sleeping cars and a diner onto the siding at Hattie's Camp. These served as sleeping and messing quarters for the first three formation flights as well as office space for Powell.[73]

The first of the Hudsons touched down at Gander on 29 October. On the previous day an early winter storm had completely covered the runways with snow, heavy drifts, and slush. A crew from 10 (BR) Squadron cleared a narrow strip for the incoming Hudsons, but the conditions remained poor. 'What looked like bare spots in the snow on the runways was actually four to six inches of slush,' recalled C.M. 'Curly' Tripp, the radio officer. He added, 'when we hit, it was quite apparent that all was not well. Slush, snow and water came up over the cockpit in what seemed a solid mass and for a moment I was sure we would nose over. The skipper [Captain R.E. Adams] gunned her and we stayed ... down.'[74] The hard landing damaged the flaps and elevators. They were repaired by 10 (BR)'s groundcrew, who willingly aided ferry crews in readying their aircraft for the overseas delivery flight, only one example of the cooperation so common among Allied service personnel during the war. Two more Hudsons came in the next day, landing without mishap, although the runway was still not in good shape. A fourth Hudson arrived on 3 November, and two more on the sixth.[75]

Much to the relief of the six ferry crews who were anxious to leave on their first transatlantic delivery flight, Bennett flew in from St Hubert on the afternoon of Saturday, 9 November. He planned to leave for the United Kingdom that same night, but found the other Hudsons grounded by a heavy coating of ice, the result of the previous night's freezing mist. The rest of the day and part of the next were spent in chipping away at the ice 'with every type of tool.' The delay was not altogether unfortunate, for on Sunday they were able to prepare for the flight 'with reasonable time at our disposal.'[76] McTaggart-Cowan provided a favourable weather forecast – at least for the first part of the journey, as far as the equipment and expertise of the day allowed – and Bennett scheduled takeoff for 2230 hours GMT. He later praised the meteorologist for his key role in the pioneer flights: 'He certainly had an excellent grip on Atlantic weather at that relatively early stage of Atlantic aviation. In fact, he gave us forecasts for the first crossing with practically no ocean information at all at his disposal; and the result, although not perfect, was extremely valuable.'[77] Final hours were taken up with a minute check of all equipment. 'Parachutes and life preservers were carefully readied. Emergency rations were inspected and stowed away ... The emergency life-boats ... were examined, along with Very pistols and signal flares. But no fire arms were given out as we were not supposed to fight even if we ran into trouble.'[78]

Much depended on this first flight. And never before had the North Atlantic been flown this late in the year. Many sceptics said it could not be done. A measure of Britain's plight was one report that the safe delivery of at least three aircraft would signal the go-ahead for the Atlantic ferrying scheme. 'It is a terrible reflection on the extremity of the need at that period that those responsible for the new project would have faced a loss of over 50 per cent in deliveries.'[79]

3

From Triumph to Tragedy

As the twenty-two airmen gathered in the Gander control room for the
final briefing prior to the first transatlantic delivery attempt, the recently
recruited Canadians and Americans shared a feeling of adventure and
excitement. However, an American pilot felt the BOAC pilots 'were cool
as cucumbers.'[1] Don Bennett agreed: 'Many of the American pilots just
didn't believe us when we told them that everything was under control.
They regarded themselves as big heroes but that didn't go far for any
of the BOAC pilots who were professionals in the true sense.'[2] On this
flight the pilots and co-pilots were British or American, though Bennett
was Australian. Six of the radio operators were Canadian and two were
British. (The lead aircraft carried two because of the anticipated extra
work load.)

Ex-BOAC Captain Bennett, the leader and designated navigator for
the trip, gave instructions that the aircraft were to fly in loose formation, each keeping in touch visually as well as by radio with his leading
Hudson. 'We had station-keeping lights on each aircraft clearly visible
from behind, and quite bright.'[3] (In truth, Bennett was not the only
navigator on the flight. Captains Allan Andrews and S.T.B. Cripps came
from BOAC and, as such, carried navigator qualifications.[4] They should
have been able to find their way across without much difficulty.)

If heavy clouds were encountered, the pilots were to break formation
according to a carefully arranged plan and continue on their own. Up
to a pre-determined point, about four and a half hours out of Gander,
each pilot had the option of turning back if he ran into trouble. The
superintendent of flying operations had prepared with his usual thoroughness and attention to detail. 'I briefed all crews after I had prepared the flight plan, and I gave them all detailed instructions on a card

which we had prepared of courses to be steered and times for alteration of course, so that, in the event of separation due to bad weather, each aircraft was fully instructed on what to do thereafter. On the opposite side of the card were full cruising instructions, the use of which had previously been explained to all pilots.'[5] His crews were impressed that everything possible had been taken care of. 'When he had completed his explanation of our flight procedure none of the captains had either suggestions or criticism to offer. We were ready for take-off.'[6]

Every preparation possible seemed to have been made, but not everyone was completely confident. McTaggart-Cowan, the weather forecaster, was sceptical:

They were supposed to play follow the leader across the Atlantic. We knew it wouldn't work but the Air Ministry in Britain and Lord Beaverbrook didn't. They'd line up on the runway and take off one after the other. What we did for the pilots that were to follow was a very detailed flight plan with compass headings and everything for each zone. We would try and pick a route that kept them south of any centre of any depression, so if the storm was deeper than we anticipated, they would drift south and then drift back north. They never knew they had been off course because it was self-correcting. We had to get self-correcting conditions because, within the first hour, these were night flights too, they'd be off course; there just was no hope of following the leader. On no account could we get them north of the centre of the depression because if they ran into head winds they wouldn't get there; the planes were that marginal.[7]

As might be expected, in spite of the secrecy surrounding the historic flight, news of the night departure circulated throughout the air base. Shortly after the briefing, Mrs Pattison, wife of the airport manager, arrived to distribute poppies to all crew members, for the next day was Armistice Day, 11 November.[8] The Queen's Own Rifles of Canada, which had replaced the Black Watch in August, posted a full alert, an indication of the importance attached to the flight, and also turned out their pipe band for the occasion. Taffy Powell described the procedure:

The final weather briefing confirmed the decision to go at 8.00 p.m. local time so we lined the aircraft up for the quickest possible take-off sequence to avoid the first machines off having to circle unnecessarily. For me with the meagre ground crew of two engineers and a few Newfoundland labourers it was a hard job to get seven pairs of engines running in the intense cold with snow about, though practically none underfoot that night. We warmed up all the engines just before dark, topped up the tanks, positioned the aircraft in line abreast on the wide runway and when the great moment arrived the band struck up. Miraculously, or perhaps fortunately, all aircraft started without trouble as the starter trolley moved down the line. In that cold Christmas-tree setting the Hudsons were played away by the pipes in front of our small group of well-wishers.[9]

This historic event was recorded in published accounts by three of the airmen making the trip. Despite the wartime secrecy, one of the American pilots, V. Edward Smith, wrote a description of the experience for the May 1941 issue of *Aviation* magazine. Four years later, shortly before the end of the war, radio operator C.M. 'Curly' Tripp's version was included in *Atlantic Bridge*. Finally, Don Bennett published his memoirs in 1958. By carefully reading these writings, one can reconstruct this attempt to fly the Atlantic in loose formation, even though only three of the seven planes are represented.[10]

Smith, who claimed to have been the second American pilot to volunteer, and who brought airline experience in China, began his account with the preparations. He described Bennett's detailed briefing, mentioned above, and then moved to dinner, where he felt everyone was preoccupied, concerned with the importance of proving the project feasible. He personally felt 'on the spot,' with an obligation to his British employers, as well as to 'the honor and traditions of American pilots.' He noted that 'already there had been quite a few American volunteer pilots rejected after a flight test punctured their exaggerated claims of flying experience. And there had been some grumbling among the Canadians about these American pilots with padded log books.'[11]

Just before 1900 hours, local time, Smith collected his crew (G.R. Hutchinson, his American co-pilot, and A.M. Loughridge, the Canadian radio operator) and climbed into his Hudson, 'number six on the right leg of the Vee formation.' Half an hour later he watched Bennett in the lead plane gather speed down the runway, his lights reflecting off the patches of ice and in the snow piled alongside, and take off into the night. Four planes later Smith did the same. He reported 'visibility was good, we easily located the running lights of the other planes and were soon in position in the formation.'[12] It did not go quite so smoothly for all the participants. Curly Tripp's pilot, Ralph Adams, had trouble spotting the leader. 'For the first hour there seemed to be planes all around us, and which one was the leader was the question.'[13]

Smith had no problem: 'We reached an altitude of 9,000 ft., which we held for the first leg of the flight in order to gain the benefit of favoring winds, and also to top a thick cloud layer which hid the Atlantic as far as we could see. The moon rose and shimmered across the sea of clouds. The air was calm and clear and our plane behaved perfectly. We all followed the leader and let him do the navigating. It was an auspicious start for the flight.'[14] In the lead Hudson, Bennett felt, 'all went well and we set out for the long dark crossing which for the crews behind me was a complete novelty, and for me a considerable responsibility.' He handed over to his co-pilot and moved to the navigator's table to concentrate on that vital role. As he looked up from his chart he noted 'with considerable surprise that my second pilot [American E.F.] Clauswitz, was wearing Texas cowboy boots with fancy leather-work and high heels! For luck, I believe!'[15]

Meanwhile, things were not proceeding as well for at least one of the planes. Tripp reported that Adams passed the controls to their co-pilot, American Dana Gentry, and set out 'to check over the ship' with a flashlight. This revealed an oil leak that occasioned some alarm. They informed Bennett and kept a close watch on the situation but pushed on. As if that was not enough, 'my radio blew up by shorting in the Antenna switch box and giving us all a good scare. Ralph hollered to me "Shut the — thing off," but I had beat him to the gun. With that load of gas it isn't pleasant to have fire skipping around the cockpit, and the corona from that transmitter was really something.' This crew must have felt jinxed when, a little over half way across, 'both motors started cutting out.' It was simply the bomb bay tank running dry but Tripp, for one, was surprised. 'I was not expecting it, and even if Ralph and Dana were, the way they went for that hand pump and gas valve made me think they didn't like it any better than I did. I don't think anything ever sounded so good to me as hearing those big Wrights hit their stride again and settle down to a steady drone.'[16]

Tripp's problems were not over: 'The indicator on the radio compass broke and I really felt up the creek without a paddle. No transmitter or compass and out over the Atlantic Ocean.' He still managed to reflect on the situation: 'We were at 18,000 feet, and we must have looked funny sitting there with a rubber tube stuck in our mouths.' Hindsight made the experience more frightening: 'I sometimes get scared when I think of how we started out that first trip with one little tank of oxygen and nothing but a rubber tube to suck it through. Ralph did the regulating and knew what he was doing, as none of us suffered any ill effects, although at one time I felt my stomach would cave in and Ralph got down in the nose and had trouble getting up. I didn't know until afterwards why he turned the oxygen full on for a few seconds.' In these conditions, Tripp got the radio transmitter working again.[17]

With about a quarter of the journey remaining, the seven Hudsons encountered the anticipated front. It was somewhat further east and higher than McTaggart-Cowan had forecast. They attempted to climb over but, as soon as it became clear that that was impossible, Bennett gave the signal to separate. 'We were already well on our way and on the intended track, and therefore I had no particular worry about the navigational side of the flight for the other aircraft. The icing, however, was fairly severe, particularly as I endeavoured to climb over the front, and was still in the "thick" at 22,000 feet. I only hoped that the others had sufficient knowledge of icing and that their de-icing facilities all worked satisfactorily.'[18]

Bennett was right to worry about icing. On this trip, as on many ferry flights, it was a problem. Smith reported:

Within a few minutes after breaking formation we began to pick up a load of ice. Already I was feeling the effects of the altitude and my first officer ... was completely incapacitated by now. To get rid of the ice I had climbed rapidly to 18,000 ft. and we soon were free of the worst of it, though the storm continued unabated. It was reasonably warm inside the cabin, but the outside temperature had dropped to −23 deg. C. Our oxygen equipment was not elaborate and, what with the storm and darkness, I did not try going any higher, but held level at 18,000 ft. for the remainder of the flight until time to let down. Our weather map had indicated that we would be in the storm area for about an hour but it actually extended almost all the rest of the way across. Several low pressure areas had apparently jammed up together into one big disturbance and we droned along through the 'soup' at 18,000 ft. for hour after hour. Presently one of the engines began to roughen up and drop a few revs. Probably it was icing trouble as it soon steadied down to work again and did not bother us further.[19]

Flying the machine by himself, with no assistance from his incapacitated co-pilot, Smith found the job tiring, especially when the automatic pilot gave him trouble:

At this stage of the flight my mind, like the engine, was skipping a beat occasionally, I supplemented my breathing by drawing on the oxygen bottle and managed to keep fairly clear-headed. What worried me most was the behavior of the automatic pilot. The wing would dip in the rough air and then come up very slowly. I studied the instruments for some clue to this performance, afraid to trust my own senses against the automatic pilot and flew manually for about an hour. As I disengaged the pilot the hydraulic pressure gage [sic], which should have read 100, was wavering around 35. Since the servo motor is operated by this hydraulic pressure it was obvious that the low pressure was responsible for the sluggishness of the controls. Doubtless due to faulty maintenance some foreign matter in the hydraulic system had been causing valve leakage and consequent reduction of pressure. Permitting the hydraulic system to idle for a period seemed to solve the difficulty for after I re-engaged the control there was no more trouble with that source.[20]

After a number of scares, things had settled down for Adams and his crew. He had slipped down to 6,000 feet, where the temperature was much more pleasant. The crew were even able to remove their heavy clothing. Tripp reported that everything was going well and that the mood was relaxed. He credits the co-pilot: 'Gentry was a treasure, the way he fooled around as though we were just on a pleasant jaunt and didn't have a care in the world.' They even had time for philosophical musings: 'The one thing I won't ever forget is the look we had together at the moon, which was full, through the Astro hatch. It was a beautiful and awe-inspiring sight and made us realise what a very small part of the world one really is.' He was disappointed when the light they spotted turned out to be a star rather than one of the other planes. As the radio operator, he had little to do. 'All was quiet on the air, as we were keeping W/T [wireless telegraphy] silence east of 20 west. Control was trying to pass Met. traffic but no one could read him through the rain static. Once W/T silence was broken, it became a wild scramble. The Skipper casually mentioned that he could use a bearing but, after listening to the static, realised it was hopeless.'[21]

In fact, the early ferry crews could not count on obtaining a bearing. McTaggart-Cowan has pointed out: 'There was virtually no navigation aids for the approach to Britain. Britain at that time was suffering from German bombing raids and they just turned everything off. There was just one little marine beacon on Storrey Island, a little rock off the north coast of Ireland. It came on ... for two minutes every twenty minutes and that was the one navigation they could home on. That was just ridiculous.'[22]

Despite the difficulties, Tripp recorded success. Shortly after Adams had dropped down to 5,000 feet, he recalled:

Dana was down in the nose, and I don't know who was the most surprised when he casually stuck his head up and said, 'Say Captain, there's land down there.' It was a big moment. Ralph stuck her nose down to get a better look and reached for the map case ... We were over land, but there was water in the distance. It was a tense moment when Ralph pointed to a little spot on the map and said, 'That's it over there, Catlin Island.' It didn't take long to prove him right.

It was only a few minutes until we came over Lough Neagh which was really beautiful in the morning light. Suddenly the Captain let out a roar and shouted, 'There's Aldergrove right over there.' With that he shoved the throttles forward and the way that Hudson jumped was like a horse coming down the home stretch. After one circuit we were down, at 08.50 G.M.T. We were third in.[23]

They found Bennett awaiting their arrival. The experienced transatlantic flyer had 'descended through a fairly low cloud base with beautiful clear visibility below, and steamed round the north coast of Ireland at low level and into Aldergrove.'[24]

Things did not go as smoothly for Smith as for the first arrivals. He carefully recalculated his course to allow for the developments during the flight, as well as for the estimated winds. Believing he would arrive half an hour early, he started his descent an hour from touchdown.

It was still soupy weather and black as pitch but at about 11,000 ft. we broke out between two layers of clouds and could see faint daylight beginning to break ahead of us. We continued down until at 8,000 ft. the ocean was visible below us. I continued at this altitude for half an hour, keeping close to the cloud layer above me just in case those imaginary Messerschmitts should materialize. At 0806 Greenwich Mean Time I spotted a dark shadow on the water which soon turned out to be an island. We had made landfall 15 min. ahead of schedule.[25]

The worrying thing was, none of the crew knew what land it was. Had they known their location, they might have been the first to reach Aldergrove. As they circled the island trying to identify it and fix their position, 'a plane came out of the storm and after a few anxious moments I identified it as Bennett's ship, which later proved to be correct, as he reported making landfall at about the same time and place as I had, but before I could intercept him he had plunged into another cloud bank and was gone.'[26]

Smith was still not home free. Writing closer to the event than Bennett, he recalled the weather as rather unfavourable over Northern Ireland the morning of 11 November 1940. And he still did not know exactly where he was. Even dropping down to 1000 feet did not help. Running low on fuel but, with a non-functioning master gauge for his wing tanks, uncertain just how low, Smith 'decided to use emergency procedure and ask for a radio bearing, although we were under strict orders to avoid this if possible.' The bearing his radio operator received did not conform to Smith's best guess of their location. A request for a confirmation went unanswered. The crew was getting worried:

After circling the island for 45 min., with fuel running dangerously low, I authorized the sending of a 'priority' message, which demands immediate attention. This got us the proper bearing in short order and we flew on to our destination without further delay. However, I heard a great deal about this priority message later as it stirred up quite a protest in British radio circles. Apparently they differed considerably from my own estimate of the importance of landing the bomber in good and serviceable condition on British soil. I could have made a precautionary landing on most any piece of pasture land, but would have run the danger of damaging the plane.[27]

No other mention of this incident has been found. Bennett simply made the general observation that, 'in the latter part of the flight some of the formation had panicked a little and broke radio silence with a bang. My own W/T operator, Radio Officer J. Giles (ex-Imperial Airways) [who, according to one report, had to handle all the radio traffic for the entire flight when his relief operator suffered from air sickness] tried to cope with the resultant bedlam and to shut them up. I often wonder whether any German monitoring service picked up the signals!'[28]

Smith reported one more small adventure before reaching Aldergrove. For a few minutes he feared he might be shot down by friendly fire:

As I approached my destination it was necessary to fly across a small land-locked harbor at fairly low altitude, due to a combination of high hills and a low cloud bank. We had been instructed to let down our landing gear and fly below 1,000 ft. when crossing settled areas, in order to keep from being shot down by anti-aircraft crews. So I had the gear down as we approached the harbor, but even so spent several anxious minutes as a patrol boat in the harbor trained its guns on us. We dropped even lower, throttled back the engines as much as I dared, and circled over the boat while the radio operator signalled them our friendly intentions. No shots were fired and we straightened away for the landing field.[29]

He claimed to have landed 'on the 11th of November after 11 hr. and 11 min. in the air.' He was the fourth down. There are no first-hand accounts of the other Hudson crews, but Smith reported: 'All arrived safely within an hour. The first mass delivery flight had proved to be a complete success. Lockheed planes and Wright engines had come through with flying colors.'[30] If this was true of the US-built equipment, so, of course, had the Canadian Department of Transport radio operators, the pilots (both British and American), and especially the Australian-born leader, Don Bennett. So too, it appeared, had the idea of flying delivery aircraft across the Atlantic Ocean in loose formation.

This was a historic occasion but, given the wartime secrecy, no fuss was made of the accomplishment. Indeed, no special welcome greeted the civilian flyers. They simply tucked into a hot breakfast in the RAF mess hall. The seven crews must have presented quite a sight to the locals: 'Twenty-two unshaven men – nine Americans, six British, six Canadians and one Australian – tried to convince the receptionist at a Belfast hotel on the morning of 11th November 1940, that they had just arrived from England. It was a necessary security measure; but the ten-gallon hats, the high-heeled Texan boots, the Canadian hooded parkas, led by Bennett's inevitable black homberg hat and briefcase caused many penetrating looks.'[31] As Bennett summed up the Belfast episode: 'It was indeed ridiculous trying to make the hotel people believe that we were something which we were not. With about 80 per cent American personnel [in fact, it was only about 68 per cent, even if the Canadians were included], it was naturally hard to convince them that we had purely local interests.'[32]

The next day the Hudsons were flown to Blackpool for servicing prior to squadron delivery. Much to their chagrin, the crews were immediately hustled onto a ship sailing from Liverpool. *Atlantic Bridge* records:

'They wanted to look around and go places,' writes the officer who was in charge of their journey. 'But headquarters wanted the men back quickly. There was then no return air service, but there was a ship for Canada due out that day. The last of the seven aircraft landed at about noon, and the embarkation officials wanted all passengers to be on board at 3 p.m. Thoughts of "going places" were to be dashed to the ground; those pioneers of Atlantic ferrying stood only for about two and a half hours on the soil of England, and most of that soil was a hangar floor. They were on board just after three o'clock and the situation was saved by the Embarkation Officer producing a tray of whiskies and soda, this being the first liquid or solid refreshment these men had taken in England.

'It was evening before I had finished clearing up. We had just finished dinner when several of the men, whom we thought were safely on board, came into the hotel at the port. They were in much better spirits. Someone had tried to stop them leaving the ship, but when they found out it was not leaving until the early hours of the morning they replied, "O.K. we'll be back," and protests from police and sentries went unheeded.

'While they were walking into the centre of the town, an air raid had started; they told me how they had been in a shelter and Hank had led the kiddies in singing. They had seen and heard a few bombs exploding, and they began to think that things were turning out according to plan after all. Their only desire then was to take back some souvenirs. "What sort of town is this," one said, "where you can't buy anything after 6 p.m." But he got his souvenir by buying one packet of every kind of cigarette in stock at the hotel, many of them brands that I had never heard of, and at last he was satisfied and went back to the ship.'[33]

Cigarettes were important to many airmen, and Smith confessed that he had furtively smoked one during the flight over. He called it his 'most expensive cigarette. Smoking had been strictly forbidden while in the air, but during some of the anxious moments recounted above I sought solace and relaxation through a few hurried puffs. Somehow the organization learned of my fall from grace and I was officially informed that I had violated approved procedure, and was fined $100.' Writing at a time when it was clear that the ferry organization would grow and would be recruiting more aircrew, he added a cautionary note. 'Perhaps the most important lesson learned on that first ferry flight was: "Don't smoke while en route." I pass this advice along to all pilots aspiring to a place in the trans-Atlantic ferry service.'[34]

While his crews were hurried back to Montreal, paradoxically in a slow convoy, Bennett went to London to see the minister of aircraft production. The flight had been a complete success and Beaverbrook was overjoyed when its leader reported to him. Bennett found him 'smiles from ear to ear. And how the Beaver can smile!' The problem was that the experiment was almost too successful. Bennett was not happy with formation flying and wanted more navigators to enable aircraft to fly solo: 'In fact, nothing that I could tell him about the unsatisfactory nature of flying without navigators would convince him that there was anything wrong. Seven aircraft had set out, and seven aircraft had arrived: what more could I ask? Indeed, it was not until a later visit to Beaverbrook that I was able to deal with the situation.

Certainly the success of this, the first flight, was not a good argument to try to convince the Beaver that I should change the policy.'[35]

Meanwhile, back in North America, preparations proceeded to dispatch more formation flights. The *Guba's* crew had returned, allowing Humphrey Page to brief the airmen scheduled to make the second flight. With temperatures well below freezing and snow almost daily, winter had set in at Gander and, despite favourable conditions over the Atlantic, the takeoff had to be postponed twice because of 'impossible conditions on the ground'[36] and 'problems with cold engine oil.'[37] Taffy Powell had only two ground engineers and three labourers to prepare the Hudsons. He probably would not have managed without the assistance of the RCAF, which 'lent aircraft fitters for these early flights.'[38] 'Fortunately the airport equipment included enough snow-clearing equipment to deal with the main runway but drifts around the aircraft and ice deposits on the wings had to be tackled the hard way – by manual labour.'[39] Finally, on the night of 28/29 November, the planes were dug out of deep snow, the ice chipped away, and, with Captain Page leading the way, lifted off the compacted snow on the runway at Hattie's Camp and headed east. Hudson T9423 contributed three firsts on this trip. It was captained by an air force pilot, Group Captain F. Pearce of the Royal Air Force, returning from a mission to the United States; it carried the first passenger, RAF Squadron Leader Norris; and it made the quickest journey yet, 10 hours 12 minutes.[40]

One of the pilots, Imperial Airways' veteran Captain W.L. 'Geordie' Stewart, left a short account of this trip. He noted that fear of German interception caused the delivery flights to adhere to a blackout rule: 'We were not allowed navigation lights because there was a Fokker Wolfe [sic] Condor Meteorological flight past Scotland down the Atlantic to the Bay of Biscay at least once a day we were scared of.' The crews did not believe their secret was secure: 'We knew Gerry [sic] had a pretty good idea of what we were doing. They did not even have to send out fighters. A JU-88 or anything with a gun would have done because we dare not open up to maximum power to escape or we would have used too much fuel and never have reached the other side.'[41]

Stewart thought that crossing the Atlantic in formation with other aircraft, at night, was too dangerous:

Formation flying even in decent conditions in daylight is quite an art. At night, with no navigation lights, it's more than that …

I don't think, though, that navigation lights would have been a risk at all. As it was you had people coming over the top of you and people coming underneath you. Why they never hit each other I've never been able to understand. In formation flying you've got to anticipate all the time in three dimensions. To do it at night with all the rest of the people never having had any experience is hair-raising ...

None of the formation flights arrived as formations. Humphrey Page and I arrived together by sheer luck. I shot a star fix just before dawn, got my position, thought I saw Venus coming up and then it wasn't bright enough. The leader was allowed one little clear light on top of the fuselage. Watching, I saw that it did not come up on the horizon. Then I realized it was someone flying below me. I put on more power and tucked myself in formation alongside him. I think he was more surprised than I was.[42]

One of the second flight of Hudsons pushed on all the way to Prestwick in Scotland. Stewart alleged that it was not a navigational error: 'Pat Eves landed at Prestwick. He had left some golf clubs at Prestwick and his First officer (Donald Anderson) was Scottish with a wife at Crieff. Prestwick made a great bally-hoo about their arrival and used it to get Prestwick used as a terminal. Actually there was a lot to be said for Prestwick once we knew the Hudsons had the range to make it. They gave a dinner every year to celebrate Pat's arrival and presented him with a beautiful cigarette case.'[43] Whether this is true or not, it is a great story that became part of the Ferry Command mythology.

Bennett paid tribute to Humphrey Page for the success of this flight: 'He led it like a veteran, even though it was, in fact, his first flight in command across the Atlantic.'[44] The conditions of war prevented any celebrations or publicity. However, the successful delivery of fourteen aircraft in less than three weeks at a time of year when many experts had predicted it could not be done was a significant achievement. Many connected with the operation thought that the point had been made. *Atlantic Bridge* reports: 'With this successful follow-up to the first flight, trans-Atlantic ferrying was established beyond doubt. These airmen, backed by Canada's ground organisation, had overcome even the notorious weather conditions which hitherto had been regarded as making winter crossings impracticable. A great flow of traffic across the Bridge could now be planned.'[45]

On 17 December ex-BOAC Captain A. Gordon Store, accompanied by Jimmy Jubb as one of his two radio operators, led a third formation of Hudsons to Britain, with the same success rate as Bennett and Page. The international cast (including one each from South Africa and Norway in addition to airmen from Britain, Canada, and the United States) arrived without incident. Captain R. Allen carried the ferry service's second passenger, Sir W. Leyton, and along with Captains S.H. De Kantzow and J.N. Wilson reached Aldergrove in 10 hours 10 minutes. One Hudson, flown by Richard Stafford, landed at Prestwick.[46] Nonetheless, despite the safe passage of twenty-one aircraft, the superintendent of flying operations was unhappy. Bennett later wrote: 'Winter conditions were obviously far too severe on the North Atlantic crossing to make formation flying a practical arrangement with any degree of certainty.'[47] He had returned to Montreal from London (by ship, posing as 'a young man going to Canada for winter sports,' much to the disdain of his fellow passengers) and arranged to lead the fourth group himself.[48]

The fourth formation flight was notable for an example of American generosity and solidarity with the Allied cause. The almost 20,000 employees of Lockheed and Vega contributed to the purchase of a Hudson as a gift to the people of Britain. *The Spirit of Lockheed and Vega*, as it was christened, left California on 22 December and reached St Hubert on Christmas Day. Bennett flew it to Gander and thence to the United Kingdom, where it arrived on 29 December, only a week after leaving the factory. The record delivery time would not be improved upon for some time.[49] It was a far cry from the months consumed by surface delivery by ship.

This flight distinguished itself from its predecessors, for another reason – only four aircraft made it to the United Kingdom. Captain Smith crashed on takeoff, without fatality, blocking the runway for Captain N.E. Williams, while Captain W.C. Rogers turned back to Gander with engine trouble. A fourth Hudson, piloted by Allan Andrews on his second crossing, landed at Speke aerodrome near Liverpool, 12 hours 43 minutes after leaving Newfoundland.[50] The incidents may have been fortuitous, especially since Bennett led the formation himself. On reaching London, he reported to the minister of aircraft production 'that the flight had not gone too well ... By this time I had learned to speak to Beaverbrook in his own language, and was able to tell him that I was running the show as I thought best. He acceded to my request, therefore, that we should use RAF navigators trained in Canada.'[51] Henceforth all aircraft were ferried individually. Officials arranged for selected navigator graduates of the British Commonwealth Air Training Plan to receive additional instruction on transatlantic navigation from a BOAC navigator in Montreal and to make one delivery flight to Britain.[52] The system worked – a testimony to the quality of BCATP instruction. Soon aircraft were arriving in the United Kingdom in increasing numbers and some degree of regularity. In contrast to prewar transatlantic attempts, their safe arrival received no headlines; yet it was a significant leap forward – a continuation, or perhaps a culmination, of prewar dreams of establishing direct air communication between the New World and the Old.

This did not happen quickly. Slow delivery from the factory, as well as the need to make the new arrangements for BCATP graduates to make one trip and for Prestwick to become the eastern terminus, meant that no Hudsons were dispatched in January. The first solo flight did not come until 10 February 1941, when Captain Allen, along with A.B. Watt and Radio Officer F. Mitchell, flew to Prestwick in 10 hours 44 minutes. Allen and Mitchell thus joined the select company of individuals who had crossed the Atlantic by air more than once. This initial quick success with a solo flight may have been a little misleading. Subsequent attempts demonstrated that progress would come slowly and only after much hard work by all concerned, and perhaps a little luck as well. The next solo takeoffs came on the night of 14/15 February. Two pilots, Jim Allison and J.A.S. Hunter, had to turn back because of problems with an auto pilot and excessive gasoline consumption. Captain D. Anderson, Radio Officer Jim Fraser, and Flight Lieutenant M.L. Wells, RAF, flew Hudson T9453 to Prestwick in 11 hours 18 minutes.[53] The next batch of takeoffs would include a celebrity passenger.

Inevitably, as the perception grew in the air force community that the delivery flights were becoming reasonably frequent and reliable, VIPs and service personnel in a hurry to get to the United Kingdom requested space on the aircraft. One of the first was Major Sir Frederick Banting, co-discoverer of insulin and Canada's first Nobel Prize winner. Following his great achievement, Banting widened his research interests; as professor of medical research at the University of Toronto he encouraged others to do the same. When war threatened, he agreed to work with the National Research Council and was instrumental in bringing the research facilities of the university and the NRC to bear on medical problems of a military nature. One of his most successful endeavours came with the formation of the Associate Committee on Aviation Medical Research, which pioneered studies of the physical effects of high-altitude flying and aerobatic manoeuvres. Under the auspices of this committee, Dr Wilbur Franks developed the world's first anti-gravity flying suit, which became an immensely appreciated and essential part of the Allied airman's operational wardrobe. He and Banting even used themselves as guinea pigs, carrying out experiments in a decompression chamber and flying as passengers in an aircraft while the pilot put it through a succession of high-level aerobatics. In the apt words of his most recent biographer, Michael Bliss, Banting became Canada's 'Warrior Scientist' involved in the planning of a large number of projects, his interests reaching as far as atomic and biological warfare.[54]

Because of his involvement in such highly secret research, some have speculated that the Canadian government sent the famous doctor to Britain on a matter of great importance connected in some way to military operations.[55] Recent authors have suggested that Banting was needed more in Canada than he was overseas; most of his colleagues opposed his leaving the country at this time. But Banting would not be deterred. He justified his trip on the grounds that he had to bring more coordination between research in Canada and the United Kingdom. Yet he had visited his British compatriots in the winter of 1939–40 and had seen at first hand what they were doing, and was not greatly impressed. He had also brought them up to date on his own projects.[56] In 1941, although the experiments on the effects of high altitude were going well, there was really nothing new to report.

It now seems clear that Banting's overseas trip was motivated, at least in part, by an overwhelming desire of an old soldier to get as close as possible to the front lines. The scientific teams he had set up were now able to carry on by themselves. He could indulge his craving to free himself from his administrative duties. During the First World War Banting had served as a battalion medical officer. Swamped by the heavy burden he carried in this new war, he yearned for the simpler times of the previous conflict, when 'I was at all times under orders. There was no great responsibility. In this war all is different. I never feel free of responsibility. If I take time off I feel as though I were stealing. I miss the contact with soldiers. Effects of work are so remote that it is sometimes difficult to see any connection with the army.'[57]

With his influence and prestige, Banting had little trouble persuading higher authorities that he should travel to Britain. Armed with an offer from the Royal Canadian Navy for passage in a destroyer or corvette, he went to a cocktail party in Ottawa (a farewell reception for James Duncan, outgoing deputy minister of national defence for air, who was returning to the private sector) at the end of January. There he chatted with Air Vice-Marshal A.A.L. Cuffe, the RCAF's air member for air staff, who suggested flying over with the new ferry service on a delivery flight. Banting leapt at the idea. Authorization for the flight came through early in February. Shortly afterwards he bade farewell to friends and family and boarded the train for Montreal. He would be the third passenger carried by the ferry service.[58]

Banting was assigned to Hudson T9449, one of two aircraft dispatched from St Hubert to Gander on Monday, 17 February. It was flown by Captain Joseph C. Mackey, a thirty-three-year-old American from Kansas City who had joined the ferry service in September 1940 with a modest reputation as an air racer and stunt pilot. Most recently he had been employed by the United States Army Air Corps as an instrument flying training instructor and had accumulated 2700 hours on various types of aircraft.[59] After two months of training with the organization, he qualified as captain on 1 November, making his first delivery as part of the second formation flight. On returning to Montreal he was employed on local flying assignments while awaiting another transatlantic trip. His crew in Hudson T9449 consisted of his regular radio officer, William Snailham of Bedford, Nova Scotia, and Pilot Officer William Bird of Kidderminster, England, as co-pilot.[60] Initially Banting seems to have been regarded as something of a curiosity by the crew, and as a liability by Mackey. However, over the next few days, while the weather kept them at Gander, the attitude changed to one of comradeship and mutual respect. The old soldier in Banting must have loved the informal sessions with the various airmen and the army defenders of the thriving little military community.

The weather at Gander was already closing in as Mackey's Hudson touched down from St Hubert, causing the scrubbing of all night departures. For the next few days, several Hudson crews killed time waiting for the weather to break. Billeted in the recently finished Eastbound Inn, a transit hotel for transient aircrew, Banting received many impromptu briefings on the hazards of ocean flying and the characteristics of the Hudson. He enjoyed the light-hearted banter and the ribald stories, contributing a few of his own in the process. He made the acquaintance of most officers at the air base, including the medical officer and the meteorologist McTaggart-Cowan. While he spoke of eagerly looking forward to the transoceanic flight, he also expressed a fear of flying and some apprehension about his trip. Perhaps he learned for the first time how few aircraft had already been delivered and how few passengers had been carried. Whatever fear he may have had was overridden by a stern sense of duty. During his three days at Gander he took a special interest in the well-equipped new hospital, which was already in operation, although the installation of heating, plumbing, and other equipment was not yet completed. His informal visit was a special occasion for its staff. Eventually the facility would be named after him.[61]

On Thursday, 20 February, snow fell throughout the day. McTaggart-Cowan, however, forecast good conditions across the Atlantic. Five Hudson crews, under Captains Adams, Rogers, and Harmes, as well as RAF Flight Lieutenant Butler, along with Mackey and Banting, spent the afternoon preparing for a night flight across the ocean. Departure would be between eight and nine, timed for arrival at Prestwick in the morning. Enough snow had fallen to make it necessary to clear the runway. In the control tower Tom McGrath watched with some concern until all aircraft were up and away. In his diary he made a brief note on each takeoff: '(1) bumped at ridge [or high spot where the runways intersected] but up O.K. (2) hit ridge at speed & bumped 10 feet into air & mysteriously stayed up (3) bumped and swerved off strip into "Circus" & ran towards south ditch of No. 3 but stopped in time. (4) good take-off – (5) wavery take-off & did left turn very low but went up out of sight – used all runway & pulled up sharply altogether an exciting series of departures.'[62]

Aircraft 5 was Mackey, whole decision to use the whole length of the runway may have been taken out of consideration for his passenger, or perhaps simply necessitated by the extra weight. No. 3 also managed to get off. The next morning Adams, Rogers, Harmes, and Butler (with Tripp as his radio operator) touched down at Prestwick. That meant that six Hudsons had been delivered solo across the Atlantic.[63] Meanwhile Mackey, in what would have been the seventh, was experiencing some difficulty.

Mackey later recalled that 'everything worked perfectly at the take-off and continued to function properly for approx. twenty five minutes, at which time my left engine failed.' At this point, approximately twenty-five miles out over the Atlantic, he 'immediately turned back and requested radio bearings from the Newfoundland Airport.' What happened after Snailham received these bearings is best left in Mackey's own words:

The next thing that happened was severe smoke pouring out of control box at my side. Whereupon I ordered the entire crew to the rear to throw out baggage and don parachutes. Altitude at this time was about five thousand feet. At this point the right engine started to lose power. I lost altitude to twenty-five hundred feet and called my radio officer by name. It was impossible to look away from the instruments but I gave him orders for everybody to jump. I was then about five miles in from the coast. He acknowledged the order. This was the last I saw of any of them until after the crash. The right engine continued to lose power but it was impossible for me to get out of the seat to don a parachute to bail out; so I rode the ship in for the crash. I was conscious of hitting the first trees, so I shut off the engine that was still running and continued to try to keep the ship right. I do not remember the final crash and was unconscious approximately an hour. I was not strapped in the seat at the time of the crash.[64]

On regaining consciousness, Mackey wrapped his handkerchief around his head and got up to inspect the plane. He was shocked to find that the others had not baled out as he had instructed. Snailham and Bird were dead and Banting was severely wounded. Mackey helped the famous doctor to the bunk provided in the Hudson. The only obvious wounds were a broken arm and a gash to the head, which was bleeding. The pilot cut up one parachute to make a sling and used another to cover his patient. Mackey continued his testimony to the Newfoundland inquiry:

By this time he was talking completely incoherently. The rest of the night was spent in trying to keep him on the bunk and covered up. At no time was he conscious of having been in an aeroplane crash and he was constantly dictating letters of a medical nature. I tried to explain to him what had happened and bring him to, but was unsuccessful, so I continued to follow in his line of thinking and acted as though I were taking his letters in order to quiet him. He had a terrific desire to undress and my condition was such that I could not forcibly prevent him from doing so. He took off his flying suit and some of his clothing and each time he took off his clothing I persuaded him to let me help him put it on again. He would not keep his gloves or shoes on, so I endeavoured to hold his hands often enough to keep them from freezing. I was able in each case to get him to put his flying boots back on after he had removed them. He expressed the thought that he should undress and go to bed. He had the idea in his mind that he was home. His speech was plain but not in connection with the situation. He expressed no pain at any time, even when his arm might be inadvertently bumped. He wanted to get out of the aeroplane but not realizing that he was in an aeroplane. He slid on the floor with my help back to the door, and stood with my help, he attempted to take a step and would have fallen had I not caught him. His feet were on the ground and he was standing. I was able to seat him back in the doorway. With his help I was able to get him back in the ship and onto the bunk and covered up. This same thing happened many times during the night and after daylight. At about noon I was able to get him to sleep, covered him with parachute silk, two overcoats and started out in search of help.[65]

By this time everybody back at Gander felt concern about the overdue Hudson. It had obviously come down somewhere between the airport and the point at which Mackey had decided to abort his delivery flight. Preparations began to launch a search at first light. The next morning three Douglas Digby aircraft of the RCAF's 10 (BR) Squadron were made ready but were grounded by snow and fog until the afternoon. Carrying CPR representatives, they searched an area fifty miles out to sea and parallel to the coast, without sighting the lost Hudson. They were looking in the wrong area, but would have been hard pressed to sight anything in the poor visibility caused by snow and light rain.[66]

While the air force planes looked for him off the coast, Mackey slogged through the snow in a desperate attempt to save the world-famous doctor. 'In my opinion if he were to survive he needed immediate help and I had the hope that I might find that help nearby. By this time his face was terribly swollen and his eyes were swollen shut. I walked about two miles south on improvised snow shoes and finally arrived back at the plane, having found no help, at approximately six p.m. I [was] just barely able to crawl to the ship.'[67] In fact, while his injuries were mild compared to the others in the plane, Mackey had not escaped completely unscathed. He suffered a severely bruised left leg, a lacerated nose, and severe cuts to the head and forehead.[68]

There was no sign of Banting when Mackey reached the plane following his vain attempt to find help. After resting for about an hour, until he could struggle to his feet, he reported: 'I found Sir Frederick in the brush approximately twenty five feet from the doorway of the ship, in a half reclining position. One of his shoes was off. He was otherwise dressed but without a top coat. He had obviously been dead for some time. I returned to the ship and took his coat and put it over him. He remained there until found by searchers.'[69] In a cruel twist of fate, one of the world's great medical researchers had died while flying in an aeroplane, representing the new field of research in which he had taken such an intense interest. Any loss of life is tragic, but it was especially tragic for the ferry service that its first fatal delivery crash had to claim the life of one so famous, respected, and valued.

The next two days found the planes from Gander continuing and widening the search, flying further to the west. Mackey heard and even saw some of them, but was unable to attract their attention. Snow had fallen and partially covered the wreckage, making it almost impossible to sight from the air. And the Hudson had carried no axe. With not even a pocket knife, and the trees snow-covered and heavily frost-bitten, Mackey found it impossible to light a fire. He confessed later, not unnaturally, to have been in deep despair. However, he would not give up and resolved, if necessary, to walk out, believing he could find the railway about twenty-five miles to the west. He made a new set of snowshoes from the plywood map locker and prepared a makeshift toboggan from the metal cowling of one of the engines, loading it with two red flares and emergency supplies from the aircraft. If the flying conditions were good, he would give the search planes four days to find him before setting out on his own.[70] In the meantime, one little creature cheered him up:

I might put in here that on this second day, a small bird came and sat on a tree, the same twig of the same tree every time he visited me. He was twice the size of a sparrow and of a brown color, with a bill a little longer than the average bird. I do not know what species he was, to sing in mid-winter in Newfoundland, but sing he did, returning time after time. And he was the only living thing I saw in those four days, and as he kept reminding me, often in the most hopeless hours of life, I am most grateful to him.[71]

When Hudson T9449 went missing, Don Bennett was in San Diego, California, checking out Consolidated Aircraft's new four-engine bomber, the B-24 Liberator. He learned about the mishap on arrival in Washington, where he had business to attend to with the British Purchasing Commission. Returning immediately to Montreal, he telephoned Mackey's wife. 'I asked her the simple question – whether she believed that her husband was alive or dead. I had heard in my various experiences in aviation, of a number of occasions when through telepathic effects, wives had been able to tell when their husbands were alive in doubtful circumstances such as this. It was for this reason that I asked Mrs. Mackey whether her husband was alive, and on her answer I acted.'[72]

Bennett, furious that none of his ferry pilots had been asked to take part in the search for their missing comrades, flew through the night to Newfoundland. He sent a signal with instructions for all delivery aircraft to be made available for the search. 'Naturally I had intended that they should only do so after I had landed. To my surprise and, in fact, delight, I found that many of them were already off the ground before I arrived.'[73] He set right to work smoothing out things with RCAF and airport authorities and helping to organize a revitalized search pattern. As it developed, the plans did not have to be implemented.

About the same time that his boss was stirring things up at the airport he had tried unsuccessfully to return to, Mackey, sitting next to a pile of fallen trees dowsed in gasoline, heard a plane approaching. 'It was coming very near and very low. I hurriedly set light to my signal fire. Then I saw the plane. It was about 600 feet and coming straight over me. My fire blazed furiously and briefly. The plane flew steadily [sic], straight overhead without the slightest indication of recognition. It vanished into the distance.' The stranded pilot was crushed. He would never be discovered in the snowy wilderness. 'My decision was made at once,' he later wrote, 'I seized the hauling rope of the metal toboggan, made from the shrouds of a parachute, and started. I gave up, once and for all, any hope of being found by aircraft.' After trudging 200 to 300 yards, 'I heard the airplane engine returning. When I heard it returning, I did not stop walking. I remember that now with some pity and some humor. So complete was the feeling of lost hope that I did not even pause in my stride.' It must have been a tragi-comic exhilarating scene as the lone figure struggled through the snow:

Right overhead the plane flew, following exactly in reverse the route it had taken a few minutes before. As it passed over my head, I could not help looking up, and as I looked up, I saw the plane dip one wing and heel over, in a steep bank, to let the pilot look down.

I halted. I waved madly. I flung my arms and shouted, but it was not me the plane had seen. Round it banked, lower and lower. It was the wreckage it had seen. Close down it banked beside the wreckage, and then it saw me.

It was [Mackey's friend, Texan] Jim Allison in that plane. I did not know it but it was Jim and he came and flew within 30 feet of me and he knew it was I. I was waving madly.

He dropped a message … just a sheet of log paper, 'Bringing help, Jim and Dunny [Pilot Officer Dunnicliffe, Allison's navigator].'

Then he started to climb. Never for a minute did he leave sight of me. Up and up he climbed to get altitude and send his wireless message clear.

But he circled round and round and never left sight of the spot, and in it seems an instant, planes came from all directions as Jim Allison's signals were picked up. I was beside myself. Planes came rushing and diving and the first thing they dropped was a sleeping bag. The second was a box of provisions with an axe strapped to it. Food, clothing, bedding, medical kits, tools, saws, came raining down out of the sky as a regular air show developed.[74]

One of the planes that joined the show was flown by Bennett. He flew out from Gander as soon as he received Allison's message. He was struck by the difficulty of spotting the wreckage. 'The camouflaged Hudson had touched down on the edge of a frozen lake, and had swung into trees as its wing tip touched the edge. The only indication of it were the tracks in the snow and a small figure reclining disconsolately also in the snow.'[75] By this time Mackey had worn himself out collecting supplies and plodding through the snow to spell out a message, 'Three dead – Joe.'[76] As he circled, contemplating what to do next, Bennett spotted two men and a dog team crossing a lake nearby. The airmen got their attention and dropped messages. As soon as the sledge was seen to be heading towards the crash site, Bennett's Hudson headed back to the airport. Mackey rested in his new sleeping bag, right beside his toboggan where he had stopped when Allison recognized him. 'I did not know that as I crawled into the sleeping bag there were coming over those ridges and cliffs and gullies of snow and rock two of the greatest men I have ever known on snowshoes, flying like the wind.'[77]

One of the aircraft alerted for the rescue mission was a ski-equipped de Havilland Fox Moth, which was owned by the Newfoundland government and based at St John's. In earlier days it was the first aircraft stationed at the new Newfoundland Airport, used for making weather observations and well known locally by its call letters VO-ADE. At that time it was flown by Douglas Fraser, one of the first pilots in Newfoundland. When Bennett returned to Gander, he found the Fox Moth and Fraser waiting, ready and willing to fly him back to the scene of the accident. They landed close to the wrecked Hudson and spent some time trying to figure out what had happened, without coming to any conclusions. Mackey was already on his way to Musgrave Harbour, a few miles away, under the care of the two local men, Walter Hicks and Dalton Abbott. Soon another party would be on their way to collect the bodies of Snailham, Bird, and Banting. Unable to do anything except snap a few photographs, Bennett and Fraser returned to Gander with a feeling of regret that 'that great doctor, Doctor Banting, who had discovered insulin,' had been '"wished" onto the flight by Ottawa at the last moment.'[78] Ironically, as we now know, it was Banting who had wished himself onto the plane.

All that was immediately known about the cause of the crash was that it was a result of engine failure. Mackey himself suspected it was due to carburettor icing, a not uncommon problem. A thorough inquiry absolved him of any blame.

Immediate cause of the accident forced landing due to engine failure. Underlying cause of the accident (a) failure of the port engine oil cooling (broken tension adjuster ring in thermostatic unit) followed by failure of feathering motor on port airscrew and subsequent seizing of the engine (b) inability of the pilot to maintain height on the Starboard engine. In the absence of direct evidence but after obtaining expert opinion in evidence, the Court is of the opinion that the partial failure of the Starboard engine was due to ice accretion in the carbuettor [sic] system.[79]

Captain Al Lilly, a pilot of great technical ability who became Ferry Command's chief test pilot, discounted any sabotage theory. If that had been the case, 'the accident wouldn't have happened until the aircraft was further out instead of just a few minutes away from base. The pilot almost made it back to the airport. It just happened that Mackey – the pilot – hadn't been properly briefed on the possible faulty reading of the oil temperature gauge.' He explained what probably went wrong:

It was a question of oil congealing in the rads. As you know oil congeals in cold weather and in Gander it sometimes froze almost solid. Now when the engines on the Hudson started up oil bypassed the [oil cooler] shutters because it couldn't get into the oil rads, whatever oil is in there would congeal just as in a car radiator in winter. As the engine keeps running it gets hotter and the oil temperature gauge goes up. The natural thing to do would be to reach down and open the oil cooler shutters. But this would be the wrong thing to do. What you should do is close them and this allows the oil to gradually warm up. On the other hand if the shutters are left open the oil in the engine becomes so hot it goes out through the oil breather pipe and the engine seizes. This is what happened in the Banting crash. Mackey's other engine kept running long enough for him to turn around and find a snow covered lake – but he couldn't see the rocks. He hit these and swung the aircraft around. Banting should have been sitting down facing aft against the bulkheads but apparently he wasn't. He suffered concussion and was killed.[80]

In fact, Banting's friend, Professor W.L. Robinson, performed a post-mortem in the Department of Pathology at the University of Toronto. He doubted that the concussion killed him. 'I have a feeling that the injuries to the head would probably have knocked him unconscious and that the dislocated shoulder and fractured ribs, in themselves, were not serious, but the punctured wound of the lung no doubt led to the haemorrhage and, finally, his death.' He regretted the circumstances: 'It is hard to resist the thought that if Sir Frederick had had immediate expert medical attention his life might have been saved, but as he was out in the barren wastes of Newfoundland, there was not much hope for his recovery even though he was a strong, virile, healthy man.'[81]

It seems clear that the first delivery fatalities came as the result of a simple accident. Of course, there were then, and still are, rumours of sabotage, as there invariably were when an aircraft was lost during delivery. This belief may have been encouraged by the unfortunate recommendation of the Newfoundland court of inquiry that 'publication of report not in public interest.'[82] Given the hazardous nature of the enterprise, it is almost a miracle that the first delivery loss took so long to occur. It would not be the last.

Meanwhile, ferry service Hudsons flew the bodies of the victims back to Canada. Sir Frederick, eulogized in the press and in Parliament, was honoured with a huge public funeral in Toronto, while Snailham and Bird received more modest burials in Halifax.[83] Joe Mackey returned to Montreal, where he was hospitalized for a short time as a precautionary measure. Selling his exclusive story to the *Toronto Star*, he donated the money to Snailham's three children. Given leave until 1 July, he delivered a couple of Hudsons in late summer and resigned on 1 September 1941. He subsequently started his own airline in Florida, and died in 1982 at the age of eighty-two.[84]

4

From ATFERO to Ferry Command

Despite the tragic loss of two valued aircrew as well as a celebrity passenger, not to mention a much-needed bomber-reconnaissance aircraft, nobody considered cancelling the new transatlantic ferry scheme. The loss rate was well within acceptable bounds, given the precarious course of the war at the time. It must be remembered that when Lord Beaverbrook had first considered flying North American-built aeroplanes to the RAF, Britain still had a European ally. Since that time the remnants of the British expeditionary force had been withdrawn from the continent, France had fallen, and the Luftwaffe had subjected Britain to that great fear of the 1930s, aerial bombardment. The situation had deteriorated. Even worse, the Battle of the Atlantic was going badly, with U-boats claiming a frightening tonnage of merchantmen sunk every month.

If aeroplanes were desperately needed in the summer of 1940, they were even more desperately needed the following winter, especially by RAF Coastal Command, which received the bulk of the machines ferried over. The government's highest priority was to expand and improve anti-submarine coverage. To accomplish this goal, the Admiralty wanted more and longer-range air support. Coastal Command struggled to help the Royal Navy cope with the U-boat menace. When the ferry service delivered the first Hudsons to the command in November 1940, it had fewer than five squadrons of long-range aircraft. With little threat from the air, the U-boats were having a field day, severely threatening Britain's lifeline. By the end of 1940 the Germans had sunk 1281 British, Allied, and neutral ships. U-boats had claimed 585 of this total, while losing only thirty-two submarines.[1]

North America offered the great hope of overcoming the deficiency in long-range aircraft. And the ferry service provided the means of getting these aircraft where they were needed, quickly and without having to worry about German submarines sending them to the bottom of the sea before they had been put to work. Although American factories were not yet in full stride, in December 1940 674 Hudsons, 91 Consolidated PBY Catalinas, 58 Consolidated B-24 Liberators, and 20 Boeing B-17 Flying Fortresses were ready, or almost so, for delivery to the RAF over the next six months. An unknown number of twin-engine medium and light bombers, Martin Aircraft's B-26 Marauder and A-30 Baltimore, as well as the Douglas DB-7 Boston, would soon be available, too.[2] Canadian industry was mainly occupied with the aircraft needs of the BCATP, but as soon as the demand for trainers had been satisfied, Canada, too, would begin producing bombers for the war in Europe. By the end of the year it was evident that the mass delivery of aircraft, though practicable, was an undertaking of major proportions. It was not going to be easy.

Changes and innovations came in quick succession as the Air Services Department and the Ministry of Aircraft Production sought ways of speeding delivery. As has been seen, formation flights, which imposed an extra element of danger and entailed some aircraft being kept waiting until the rest of the flight was ready, were given up at the beginning of 1941 in favour of dispatching planes independently as soon as they were prepared and the weather was suitable.[3]

By the time of the Banting tragedy a basic routine had been established. Delivery of aircraft was carried out in two main stages. Crews employed by the manufacturers flew the machines from the factories, primarily in the western United States, via stations on the trans-Canada airway, to St Hubert. There the Air Services Department took them over and prepared them for the transatlantic flight, which required a number of modifications such as the installation of oxygen equipment. After testing, the aircraft were dispatched to Gander and took off for Prestwick, which had replaced Aldergrove as the eastern terminus, with the first favourable weather forecast. Weather, technical difficulties, and failure of factories to meet production schedules sometimes caused delay and irregularity in the delivery routine.[4]

Consolidated Catalinas, much desired by Coastal Command because of their long range, began to be delivered to Boucherville, on the St Lawrence River near Montreal, in December 1940, although promised for two or three months earlier. Contrary to Bennett's instructions, that in winter the flying boats should be dispatched from Bermuda, the first two Catalinas flew to Dartmouth, Nova Scotia, where they became coated with frozen spray. Their departure for Greenock on the Clyde in Scotland, the British reception base for flying boats, was delayed for more than two weeks while RCAF experts devised a way to keep them free from ice during engine run-up and take-off.[5] Bennett was furious over this incident, which he learned about while he was in Britain after shepherding the fourth group of Hudsons over. On his return to Montreal, 'there was a little matter of friction.'[6] Powell was immediately transferred to Bermuda to establish a base for delivering flying boats.[7] Both Beatty, whose problems mounted with the growth in the size and complexity of the operation, and Beaverbrook were also concerned over the delay and bad publicity. It led to 'something of a blow-up between Beatty on the one hand and Woods Humphery and Burchell [sic] on the other.'[8] The latter two resigned and Beatty, asked to provide 'a first-class transportation executive,'[9] selected C.H. 'Punch' Dickins, general superintendent of Canadian Airways. He had won a Distinguished Flying Cross during the First World War before becoming 'one of Canada's outstanding commercial pilots, winning considerable fame for aerial pioneer work in Western and Northern Canada,' and being awarded an OBE in 1936.[10]

On 1 February 1941 Dickins became vice-chairman of the Canadian Pacific Railway Air Services Department and deputy director of the British Air Commission.[11] He soon inherited Burchall's title of general manager and had responsibility for all ferry business – dealing with the Ministry of Aircraft Production on routine matters and coordinating air deliveries to Montreal through American manufacturers and the British Air Commission in Washington. Training, maintenance, and operations at the three bases – Montreal, Gander, and Bermuda – came under his jurisdiction. As flying superintendent, directly in charge of the dispatch of aircraft, Bennett, who demanded much from his superiors as well as his subordinates, managed to establish a good working relationship with the Canadian bush pilot, although the two men were distinctly different in background and temperament: 'I accepted him happily as the boss of the department, and he, on his side, gave me the assurance that he knew his own limitations and that he would let me get on with my part of the job without any interference, and that I had his complete support. In fact,' Bennett claimed, 'it worked perfectly – he looked after Ottawa and Washington whilst I looked after the technical and operational sides. "Wilkie" [Wilcockson] was appointed to be in charge of training, a post which he filled extremely successfully from there onward.'[12]

This reorganization was soon followed by another. In April, Beatty, gravely ill, resigned as chairman of the ferry service and was replaced by Morris Wilson, Beaverbrook's right-hand man in North America, who brought with him as chief executive officer H.M. Long, a young Canadian dollar-a-year executive active with the British supply organization in Canada and the United States.[13] Opinions on Long varied. Sir William Hildred of the Ministry of Aircraft Production called him a 'human dynamo ... a first rate business man and organizer.'[14] Bennett, in his usual critical fashion, disagreed. Referring to Long as the 'big shot' brought along by Wilson, he described him rather crudely:

He was extremely fat, extremely soft, and wore thick-lensed glasses which apparently were not sufficiently effective to prevent him from finding his range from his associates until he had walked up to them so closely that his tummy touched them. In my opinion he was a 'dead loss' in every way. He was, however, Morris Wilson's blue-eyed boy, and the latter called him a 'human dynamo' and words to that effect. As far as I was concerned, I had never known such a catastrophe at any stage of my career. However, we managed to get along in spite of him, and the operation was growing in strength.[15]

Bennett credited this growth with causing the next reorganization. He claimed that once the Atlantic ferry had become a success it became a '"political football" – everybody wanted to take it over.'[16] He said that many people suspected Canadian Pacific's motives, fearing that in the long run at least this commercial concern had much to gain from its involvement in the venture. In fact, the CPR, busy mapping out the future of its aviation interests in the north and northwest, may well have been happy to sever its connection with the ferry organization, then facing severe growing pains and becoming the target of national and international criticism. In 1941 CP completed the purchase of Canadian Airways and nine other companies, merging them in 1942 as Canadian Pacific Air Lines.[17] At any rate, Morris Wilson, the new chairman, wanted the business of ferrying more closely tied to the Ministry of Aircraft Production.

The latest reorganization necessitated a name change. Officially it became the Operating Division of the Ministry of Aircraft Production. For some time, however, the term ATFERO had been used by employees. 'At first we were called Canadian Pacific Air Services Department because Canadian Pacific provided all our facilities – but that was politically unpopular in Ottawa and so we simply called ourselves Atlantic

Ferry Organization or ATFERO for short. On our Craig Street Office we had ATFERO on our door … Things worked out well enough but we did have politics creeping in so little things like the name were very sensitive subjects.'[18] By this point ATFERO was too widely accepted by its 263 civilian personnel (counting all flying, ground, and administrative staff)[19] to be replaced.

ATFERO's biggest problem was the acute shortage of aircrew, especially pilots with the proper background and training for long-distance ocean flights requiring, among other abilities, a high degree of skill in instrument flying. The authorities therefore decided to use operational crews from Coastal Command to deliver an allotment of Fortresses which, along with Liberators, were being added to the program early in the year. The first of these RAF airmen arrived in Canada before the end of December 1940. After a couple of weeks in Montreal, some were sent to Kansas City to gain experience on the Boeing Stratoliner with Trans World Airlines. It was apparently thought that this four-engine airliner by the same manufacturer bore enough resemblance to the Flying Fortress to make the side-trip worthwhile. After some casual flying with TWA, this detachment joined their colleagues at March Field, Riverside, California. There the US Army Air Corp's 93rd Heavy Bombardment Squadron introduced the RAF airmen to the intricacies of the B-17. Taffy Powell refers to this group as 'the Fortress party and that is about what it was, because the planners in the UK who had thought up this delivery arrangement had not taken account of American neutrality, which meant that foreign personnel from the RAF were not allowed to take any active part in flying or operating the B-17s. There was therefore little training, some familiarisation, but lots of bonhomie.'[20]

Eventually the Fortress party collected the new aircraft in Portland, Oregon, not in Seattle, Washington, where Boeing had built them. This avoided the sales tax levied by Washington. (Lend-lease would not pass through Congress until the middle of March, and the British Treasury watched its pennies.) The Fortresses flew to Wright Field at Dayton, Ohio, where they received a camouflage paint-job and RAF roundels. From there they proceeded to Floyd Bennett Field on Long Island, because 'the spring thaw was playing havoc with the surface' of the runway at St Hubert.[21] It should be remembered that the United States was still about eight months away from suddenly being forced to declare war. The mysterious arrival of the latest in military hardware appears to have caused a sensation in the vicinity of the peaceful New York airfield. 'Obviously the control tower knew they were coming in, but the station personnel generally did not,' recalls Powell, 'so there was much excitement – even consternation – when these dark camouflaged B17s slipped into the airfield over the US navy barracks. Floyd Bennett was then a US navy station and in a fairly populated area so that many US citizens in the evening rush-hour traffic were also concerned at these strange aircraft and caused police cars with lights flashing and sirens wailing to converge on the airfield to tackle the intruders if necessary.'[22]

Any confusion was straightened out quickly and efficiently – so well, in fact, that ATFERO staged the next batch of Fortresses and some Liberators through Floyd Bennett Field. Geordie Stewart later praised the cooperation and support he received from the American authorities when he had the job of expediting these deliveries. With three or four engineers and another pilot to take delivery of Liberators and Fortresses, he was assigned some bare rooms in a hangar at Floyd Bennett Field. In no time he had telephones installed, had ordered 20,000 gallons of fuel, and had contacted suppliers such as Wright, Bendix, and Sperry. He was amazed with the American enthusiasm and willingness to help:

The co-operation which we received from the American industries and authorities such as Customs and F.B.I. and the hustle which we witnessed had to be seen to be believed – as they themselves put it, 'this is the emergency of war,' and they cut red tape right, left and centre. Sperry's gave me a 'phone number to call night or day and said any replaced part for any of their equipment on the aircraft would be brought to the field immediately by high speed car under 'speed-cop' escort! This sort of atmosphere was catching and I think it had a lot to do with the tremendous amount of work that my little band carried out without a single complaint.[23]

Stewart offered an example of American assistance above and beyond the call:

One day we were anxiously peering out of the window. Four Forts were coming in. Two landed, the third one landed a little high and when it touched one of the tyres burst. Before it had stopped rolling I was speaking to the Naval Commandant of Floyd Bennett and he told me the nearest U.S. Army Air Force Fort Squadron – it was at Olmstead Field, Middleton, Pennsylvania. I had no idea of the phone number but Bell telephone put me through to the C.O. in seconds. He said he'd have a tyre on the train within one hour – when I mentioned payment he just said, 'We often burst tyres!'

Then I realized that parked right in front of the window on the edge of the tarmac was a perfectly good Lib fully serviced.

Picking up the phone again I was put through to the C.O., Olmstead: 'Hold that tyre – I'll be over in an hour – by air.'

'What are you coming in?'

'A B-24.'

'Gee, that's swell, we've never seen one.'

Everyone at Olmstead was anxious to get in on loading the tyre so that they could see over the Lib. We were back at Floyd Bennett with the new tyre two hours and 15 minutes after the Fort tyre had burst on landing. The Fort was serviced that night. The compass was swung next morning and it left for Gander and the U.K. the same afternoon.[24]

Stewart had words of praise for the Federal Bureau of Investigation, describing an incident that particularly impressed him.

The F.B.I. took over security functions for our operation at Floyd Bennett. It was my first experience with this remarkably efficient organization. A Capt. Butler was in charge. One day Don Bennett telephoned from Montreal to the effect that he and Harold Long would be visiting me the next morning and I warned Capt. Butler that two strangers would be seeking admittance through the barbed wire next morning. I gave him all the details I could think of.

Harold Long and Don Bennett duly carried out an inspection next morning and before they left expressed grave dissatisfaction with the security measures as they had no difficulty in getting in. I was very upset about this as I had been very impressed with Capt. Butler and all his men. When Bennett and Long left I had a talk with Capt. Butler and it was only then I realized how super efficient the F.B.I. is. Butler, heaven knows how, in less than 24 hours, had obtained photographs of Bennett and Long, a description of the car they used, a log of its journey through Brooklyn to Floyd Bennett AND a photograph and history of their chauffeur![25]

Not only the Americans could move quickly and work hard. Stewart telephoned Long on the first day to let him know they had got established. In the process, he expressed doubt about the adequacy of the $300 he had been given in Montreal to do the job. Long 'arranged for me to borrow a cashier, a cash box, a safe and several thousand dollars from the C.P.R. in New York.' But ATFERO headquarters could be demanding. 'The same evening Don Bennett phoned and asked how many aircraft we had despatched!'[26] To this point no delivery aircraft had arrived. When they did, there was considerable work for the small detachment:

We had to remove the armor plate from the Fortresses, label it and put it on the Libs (the Forts were too heavy for the Atlantic trip with the fuel load, ammunition, dinghies and spares, etc.). The spark plugs had all to be removed and cleaned or changed and then every aircraft had to have its compass swung in flight.

Weather reports had to be decoded, flight plans made, crews briefed and the aircraft fuelled for the hop to Hattie's Camp (Gander).[27]

The ATFERO detachment worked hard, but must have found the sojourn in New York a strange contribution to the war effort. Bill Franklin, a navigator by trade, remembered living at the St George's Hotel in Brooklyn and going to war every day in a Yellow Cab.[28]

By the time ATFERO delivered the first Flying Fortresses, it had already dispatched a Catalina across the great expanses of the Pacific Ocean. The first, flown by a Royal Australian Air Force crew, left San Diego on 4 March 1941. Staging through Honolulu, Midway, Wake, and Guam, it reached Manila four days later, thanks to the cooperation of Juan Trippe's Pan American Airways. Throughout the spring, ATFERO crews, led by Captain Clyde Pangborn, one of the senior American pilots, ferried more Catalinas to Manila. There the RAAF took over to fly them to Singapore. Pangborn himself made three separate crossings. To illustrate the distances involved, Captain J.A. Webber, a co-pilot in the first group of Hudsons flown to Aldergrove, spent almost sixty-three hours airborne after he left San Diego on 19 April before he touched down at Manila.[29]

Delivery responsibilities were thus expanding on three fronts, Catalinas from San Diego and Bermuda, and Hudsons, Liberators, and Fortresses from Gander. (The first '"giant" bomber type' Liberator landed at Gander on 5 March 1941.)[30] Meeting with limited success in luring pilots from their regular employment, even with the high rates of pay offered, ATFERO officials were forced to widen their search for aircrew. Recruiting had begun in August 1940. By the end of November, when the rate fell off to one or two a week, the Clayton Knight Committee had obtained only sixty-two American volunteers approaching ATFERO standards.[31] While the committee had sent 380 pilots to Canada, few met the more stringent Atlantic ferrying requirements. Many found work with the BCATP.[32] After preliminary testing by ATFERO, a number were judged unsuitable and practically all those accepted had to undergo further training before they were ready for ferrying duty. In Canada, where Canadian Airways and Trans-Canada Air Lines formed the main source of supply, the number of recruits was proportionately smaller. The war effort had already absorbed nearly all pilots of military age and the airlines, while anxious to help and seeing an advantage in having their crews gain experience in ocean flying, could contribute only a few pilots if they were to remain in business. Individuals tempted by the money offered for transatlantic ferrying were encouraged to consider the advantages of security of employment and opportunities for advancement with the domestic air services.

On the whole the recruiting program fell far short of providing the number of pilots needed. As a temporary solution, in order to keep aircraft moving across the Atlantic, ATFERO had to ask for more pilots from BOAC, the Air Transport Auxiliary (the civilian organization in the United Kingdom charged with delivering aircraft from British factories to squadrons), and the reluctant RAF. This provoked some heated disputes between the Air Ministry and the Ministry of Aircraft Production and also magnified the impact of the irritating anomaly in pay. British flyers received about a third as much as their more fortunate Canadian and American colleagues. Radio officers, for example, most of them recruited and trained in Canada, got only $300 a crossing. However, at this rate they earned more than the experienced military airmen with whom they flew. S.A. Dismore of the Ministry of Aircraft Production admitted to Air Marshal Sir Christopher Courtney at the Air Ministry: 'Many of the R.A.F. men have had literally to stay in the hotel because they could not afford the "high life" outside. But it does not lead to a happy spirit when they see their civilian colleagues going out and about with the best cars, food, wine and etceteras.'[33]

Much more seriously, the recruiting shortfall threatened ATFERO's expansion. It would be unable to cope with the anticipated pace of deliveries without a much bigger pool of aircrew. The Americans were predicting a rapid increase in the production of four-engine aircraft (Liberators and Fortresses), flying boats, and Hudsons, as well as other smaller types such as Lockeed Venturas, Lodestars, and Douglas Bostons that could be flown across the Atlantic. Sir Henry Self, chairman of the British Air Commission in Washington, in close touch with American manufacturers, pointed out that a crisis in air delivery was rapidly taking shape. He urged a re-examination of the whole question of air delivery: 'It is evident that ferrying aircraft will shortly present [a] very big problem which in our view will be far beyond capacity of ATFERO to handle on civilian basis. Present situation that ATFERO have at the moment available 3 group leaders 35 first pilots and 11 second pilots. Provision of further crews from civil sources this side on any scale is highly improbable.' As a solution to this predicament Self proposed that 'the RAF must accept responsibility for provision of all crews either from home or Canada,' with ATFERO retaining responsibility for ground organization.[34]

Another interesting assessment of the problem, pointing to the vital need to find an early solution, was raised by Air Vice-Marshal J.C. Slessor, head of the Air Ministry planning section, who visited Canada and the United States at the end of 1940 to check out the progress of the BCATP and to discuss the general question of aircraft supply. After meeting with Canadian and American authorities and also with Sir Henry Self, Slessor outlined his observations in a letter to Sir Charles Portal, RAF chief of the air staff:

The enormous production programme over this side raises a point of great importance of which I think the implications may not have been fully realized, namely the tremendous size of the ferry pilot service that will be necessary if we are to get all these aircraft over ... The present system whereby we bribe a few American pilots to fly machines over will not touch the fringe of the problem when we begin to get deliveries in really big numbers. Ultimately we shall want something of the order of at least 1,000 pilots on this job, and that, as far as I know, is a commitment which we have never faced up to in our calculations. No doubt we shall be able to raise many of them in the USA but nothing like all, and there isn't the least doubt that the RAF will be called upon to find crews in very large numbers for this ferrying job. I know this is a matter for MAP [Ministry of Aircraft Production] but it has many direct implications for the RAF ... and I feel that we must be prepared to do it ourselves.[35]

Slessor's disclosure of the inadequacy of ATFERO came as something of a shock to the Air Ministry, suddenly faced with a commitment for which it had made absolutely no preparation. Initially it had harboured doubts about the wisdom of attempting to fly the Atlantic in winter months. Even after it had been shown that this could be done safely, the Air Ministry was content to leave the ferrying to Beaverbrook. Fearing that it might be asked to divert aircrew from air operations to ferrying duties, it held to the view that as many aircraft as possible should be brought across the sea by ship.[36] Slessor and Self, on the other hand, were now arguing that all aircraft capable of crossing the Atlantic under their own power should be flown.

Somewhat reluctantly Portal and Sir Archibald Sinclair, secretary of state for air, concurred in this assessment of the situation and agreed that sooner or later the Air Ministry would have to accept complete responsibility for transatlantic ferrying.[37] At the moment, however, the general shortage of aircrew made it impractical. For the time being the Air Ministry was content to leave the initiative with MAP, offering what assistance the RAF felt could reasonably be spared and advocating that all except four-engine aircraft be shipped by sea. The most immediate concern was aircrew, and thoughts naturally turned to the BCATP. There was admittedly some risk in using fledgling pilots to fly aeroplanes across the Atlantic. However, while in Canada, Slessor had already made informal proposals for the expansion of the BCATP to include a special operational training unit for ferry pilots. The RCAF was receptive to the idea, which was now further explored by the Air Ministry, but problems involved in finding a suitable training field in Canada and in determining the type of aircraft to be used and the numbers of aircrew to be trained were not easily solved.

An unknown factor in the Air Ministry's planning was whether Lord Beaverbrook would willingly surrender control over his ferrying organization. Although the Air Ministry and MAP were in communication on the problems facing ATFERO, cooperation was hampered by personality clashes at the top level between Beaverbrook, egocentric tycoon, and Sinclair, former leader of the Liberal Party and 'a suave politician of the old school.'[38] In appointing Beaverbrook to Cabinet and giving him control of MAP, a department taken, in the newspaper publisher's own words, 'out of the ribs of the Air Ministry,'[39] Churchill was well aware that he was creating a situation potentially charged with trouble; but, as he reflected later, 'I needed his vital and vibrant energy and I persisted in my view.'[40]

Beaverbrook, no ordinary administrator, cut through red tape with fiery dynamism and cleared bottlenecks to speed the production and repair of fighter aircraft during the Battle of Britain.[41] In doing so, however, he showed little concern for the carefully laid plans of the RAF and felt that it was his place to determine military priorities. The Air Ministry and 'the bloody air marshals,' with only a few exceptions, he regarded as rivals.[42] The feeling was mutual, for they in turn considered him 'a merciless critic and even enemy.'[43] In spite of the friendly and flattering 'Dear Archie' and 'Dear Max' salutations, correspondence between the two ministers consisted of a series of charges and counter-charges leaving little room for compromise.[44] Soon after the institution of the transatlantic ferry service, disputes arose over the amount of assistance to be provided by the Air Ministry. After the disclosures of Self and Slessor, this became a major point of contention, eventually requiring the prime minister's intervention: 'MAP will continue to be responsible for the Atlantic Ferry Service. The Air Ministry is to supply the desired personnel or their equivalent.'[45]

Churchill's directive ended one dispute, but another, which had been simmering for a few weeks, was on the point of boiling over. It concerned six B-24 Liberators, a legacy of French contracts taken over by the United Kingdom, which arrived in Montreal in the spring of 1941. In November 1940, anticipating an early delivery of these aircraft, the Air Ministry gave authority for one of them to be used for air communications with Sweden, and the others to be put into service on the North Atlantic run by BOAC. On westbound flights, full priority would be given to returning ferry crews to Montreal. Any additional passenger space could be allotted to government officials and military officers. On the eastbound flights from Montreal, the Liberators were to carry non-paying passengers on military business, air express, and mail.[46]

Beaverbrook never accepted the Cabinet decision allotting the Liberators to BOAC, which really meant to the Air Ministry, to operate a military air service in conjunction with a return service for ferry pilots. He persisted in his arguments that the aircraft rightfully belonged to his department and that they should be used for no other purpose than returning ferry crews from the United Kingdom to Canada. On eastbound flights, spare parts and other essential aircraft equipment could be carried, but no passengers. Sinclair was rigidly opposed to Beaverbrook's scheme and again Churchill had to intervene. On 16 March he pronounced in Beaverbrook's favour that the Liberators 'are to be employed on carrying ferry pilots across the Atlantic under MAP.'[47] The next day this ruling was upheld by the War Cabinet.

By this decision, Churchill added to his own difficulties. BOAC, a creation of Parliament, was a sensitive issue in British politics. There was a distinct possibility that the reversal of the original decision to put the Liberators at its disposal would lead to embarrassing questions being asked in the House of Commons about government tampering with the country's national airline. Moreover, several government departments had been counting on using the Liberators as a means of air communication with Canada and the United States. To avoid a debate, the Cabinet issued an order-in-council placing the Liberators under MAP control and, contrary to Beaverbrook's wishes, also required that services be provided for other government departments when space on the aircraft was available. This part of the arrangement was highly displeasing to Beaverbrook, who wanted to have the Liberators on his own terms without having to answer to anyone but Churchill. On 24 March he characteristically complained to the prime minister

that this document, in my judgement, does not carry out the intention of the Ministers.

Your decision, endorsed by the Cabinet, was that the Ministry of Aircraft Production should have the five B.24's for the specific purpose of ferrying pilots across the Atlantic. The Air Ministry was to give us their assistance to the utmost.

But the Order in Council proposes to hand over to us control of a portion of the BOAC and transfer to us the Air Ministry's responsibility for an Atlantic passenger service. This was not in your intention and it should not be within our responsibilities.

Instead of the Air Ministry helping us with our ferry, we would be helping the Air Ministry with their passenger service.[48]

Churchill, for once, did not agree with Beaverbrook's interpretation and, in reply, encouraged him to make the best of a situation he himself had created:

If these machines are to be managed by you, as you wish, the taking back of ferry pilots to America must be the first charge. But you must try to help other people and other interests as well, and on the homeward journey you should give all possible facilities to other interests. No one would think it right that the B.24's should carry [only] spare parts etc. when there are much higher needs upon their space. It is lucky that no legislation is needed, and that the order works immediately. Otherwise there would certainly be an unpleasant debate. I am afraid we are getting into a mess. I am relying on you to produce a good service to satisfy everybody.[49]

After all this, Beaverbrook submitted the latest in a long series of resignations (reportedly fourteen in all). This time, on 1 May, Churchill accepted it. Beaverbrook's motives are not altogether clear. Undoubtedly, constant friction with the Air Ministry was a factor, but not necessarily the main one. Following the Battle of Britain he found the challenges diminished. Even while seeking greater authority, he was seriously considering leaving the department. Churchill, who looked to Beaverbrook as a personal adviser in much the same way that President Franklin Roosevelt looked to Harry Hopkins, had long contemplated employing his unconventional minister in a higher capacity. With his resignation the prime minister persuaded Beaverbrook to accept an appointment as minister of state and, at the end of June, he became minister of supply, with general supervision over all military production in the United Kingdom. At the Ministry of Aircraft Production he was succeeded, at his own suggestion, by J.T.C. Moore-Brabazon, formerly minister of transport, whose orthodox approach to interdepartmental differences paved the way for a more stable relationship with the Air Ministry.[50]

The interminable quarrelling between Sinclair and Beaverbrook and the constant failure of the British government to develop a firm overall policy on ATFERO, or to communicate directly with the Canadian government on problems related to transatlantic ferrying, left Canadian authorities confused and frustrated. At first both C.D Howe and C.G. 'Chubby' Power, the ministers of munitions and supply and national defence for air, had felt a compelling obligation to assist the ferrying organization in whatever way they could. However, rumours that the RAF planned to take over ATFERO left them in doubt as to how far they should go in supporting Beatty and Wilson.[51] On the other hand, they could hardly give full credence to reports emanating from the Air Ministry while Beaverbrook controlled ATFERO.

A prime example of the uncertain situation can be found in proposals to use BCATP graduates to fly aircraft to the United Kingdom. In January 1941 Sinclair and other Air Ministry officials discussed this idea with Howe and J.L. Ralston, the Canadian minister of national defence, who were in London on a mission dealing with various military matters.[52] Back in Ottawa, Power reported to the Cabinet War Committee that the situation regarding the employment of BCATP-trained crews for ferrying was confused: 'The Air Ministry wanted the RCAF to take the matter over; the Aircraft Production Ministry was apparently unwilling that this should be done. The RCAF was prepared to make an aerodrome available for the training of ferry pilots but no request had yet been received.'[53] Eventually all parties agreed to the formation of a special operational training unit (OTU) at Debert, Nova Scotia, to provide additional training for selected aircrew from BCATP schools – pilots, observers (as navigators were still called in the RAF), and wireless operators – to enable them to ferry aircraft across the Atlantic. The RAF was to furnish the instructional and maintenance staff, but the OTU was to be placed under the administrative control of the RCAF, as were all other units of the RAF in Canada.[54]

Beaverbrook and Wilson approved this scheme in principle. The latter, however, felt that his needs would be better served if the training unit were made an integral part of ATFERO, free from control by the RAF or the RCAF. In the end, ATFERO lost this little battle.[55]

Throughout this difficult period, the confusion and uncertainty surrounding ATFERO was mingled with criticism, on both sides of the Atlantic. This is especially evident in the correspondence of Howe, who felt frustrated by British indecisiveness and expressed little confidence in ATFERO. In February he cabled Beaverbrook: 'Having been requested ... to enlist Canada's help in Trans-Atlantic ferrying problems, have discussed subject with my colleague Power, also with Beatty, Wilson, Slessor, Pirie and others ... consider present organization wholly inadequate and feel those directing here have no clear conception of magnitude of undertaking, with result that Canada may be blamed for delay of United States planes in Canada.'[56]

One of the 'others' with whom Howe discussed the problems of ATFERO was Arthur B. Purvis, a Scots-Canadian industrialist of international reputation and, until his death in August 1941, head of the British Purchasing Commission in the United States. Purvis, working closely with Henry Morganthau, US secretary of the treasury, was acutely aware of the repercussions that might follow in American policy if American aircraft began to pile up in Canada. Consequently he was keenly interested in ATFERO. On 25 April he and Howe talked in confidence and the following day Howe set down his own views:

The most competent man in Canada to handle the situation is, of course, D.B. Colyer, Vice-President of Operations for Trans-Canada Air Lines. Colyer tells me that all the civil transport organizations in the United States and Canada combined would not now have personnel enough to do the ferrying job as it will develop. The present organization is operating with cast-off personnel and without adequate ground facilities, and while young Long (who is a son of Dick Long of CNR) and Punch Dickins are working hard, neither has the experience or organizing ability to do the job.

If I were responsible for Atfero I would get Phil Johnson, President of the Boeing Aircraft Company in Seattle, back to do the job. I have already sounded out the principal shareholders of the Boeing Company in this regard, and I know that we can get Johnson if he is needed and the way is clear. Johnson is a driver and a most careful operator, and with him in charge our troubles would be over.

I feel I have gone as far as I can in trying to straighten out this organization. I have given them the use of two of our best airports, one in Montreal, and one near Truro, N.S. We are building facilities for them at these two airports, and at Botwood, in Newfoundland. I have induced Chubby Power to give them all the help he can from the Air Training Plan, even at the risk of a good deal of criticism from killing his pupils.

Confidential word from the other side is that the Ministry of Aircraft Production is not on speaking terms with the Ministry of Air. Certainly we cannot move to reorganize Atferro [sic] until Lord B. [Beaverbrook] gives his consent. Some time ago, pressure was brought on the Government to turn over the resources and personnel of Trans-Canada to this service. I would not hesitate, to break up Trans-Canada for that purpose if I thought it would solve the problem but I am not prepared to do so under present management.

This is the situation, and as I see it today. I hope that you can find the solution, otherwise both Canada and yourself are headed for serious trouble.[57]

The worries on Howe's mind may be understood by reference to the volume of aircraft received by ATFERO from American factories and the number flown to the United Kingdom. Until the end of June, planes were delivered almost as fast as they were received in Montreal. Owing to the pilot shortage, the need to make technical adjustments and modifications to aircraft received from the factories, and the unfavourable weather, which sometimes kept planes grounded for days at a time, there was always a backlog of undelivered aircraft. By the end of June it numbered 59. This was not serious, but the number arriving in Montreal rose from 52 in June to 168 in July. At the end of that month the backlog of undelivered planes totalled 133. If arrivals from the United States had continued at this rate, or if they had reached the 200 mark predicted by American manufacturers, it seems obvious that ATFERO would have been swamped with aircraft it could not deliver. Such a predicament would have embarrassed the Canadian government as well as ATFERO. But Howe's fears were not realized. Given production problems in American factories and the absorption of more aircraft by the military forces of the United States and other allies, including the Soviet Union, the number of aircraft delivered to ATFERO dropped to ninety-one in August, to sixty-nine in September, and then fell more sharply.[58]

On the whole, the criticisms discount ATFERO's real achievements. Whatever weaknesses there may been in management and organization, aircraft were being moved across the Atlantic with little delay. ATFERO had one of its best days on 16 July, when twenty-two aircraft departed. In addition to movements such as this, ATFERO had also expanded its training organization at Montreal and inaugurated the Return Ferry Service (RFS). The Liberators over which Sinclair and Beaverbrook had been in dispute arrived in the spring of 1941, and the return service began in May. The first east-to-west flight was made on 3 May, with a crew of five and two passengers on board.[59] This aircraft landed at Gander, but on 8 May Bennett, in the first non-stop flight from the United Kingdom to Montreal, brought back a full load of returning aircrew in the boarded over bomb-bay.[60] Henceforth, many crews returned to the starting point within a few days, or even hours, of delivering aircraft to the United Kingdom. This turnaround had the same effect as a large injection of additional flying personnel.

The performance of ATFERO was watched closely by the Roosevelt administration, which showed impatience with any delay in the delivery of aircraft. For example, General Raymond E. Lee, military attaché at the US embassy in London, while perusing the cables from Washington one May morning, found 'one very hot one from the Secretary of War' directing him to see Portal and tell him 'bluntly' that seventeen B-17s had been waiting for almost a month to be flown to Canada. Most aircraft destined for the United Kingdom were flown to Montreal by American factory pilots. For some reason, as we have seen, the B-17s were taken all the way by British crews. Something had to be done immediately in this case because a delay in delivery 'produces a profoundly bad impression on both civil and military opinion in the United States.'[61] Within days the Fortresses were on their way, flown by Coastal Command crews, apparently satisfying the Americans. Portal later discovered that the aircraft could not have left earlier, as certain items of equipment were missing.[62] Nonetheless, the incident illustrates the importance attached by the Americans to the expeditious movement of delivery aircraft.

The US government was concerned about the heavy drain that the ferrying operation was imposing on the operational strength of the RAF. Sinclair, finding J.G. Winant, the US ambassador, open to suggestions on the problem, 'put to him a proposal that the Americans might themselves help us by ferrying aircraft across.'[63] Beaverbrook had no objections, so the request was made.[64]

In considering Sinclair's appeal for assistance, Roosevelt and his advisers authorized a few US Navy pilots to fly as second pilots on Catalina deliveries to Scotland, and seriously considered having the Army Air Corps take over the entire ferrying operation. General H.H. 'Hap' Arnold, chief of the Air Corps, found such a plan overly ambitious, at least for the time being. After conferring with British officials, he suggested that the USAAC ferry all aircraft from American outlets to Montreal, thus leaving ATFERO the responsibility of flying them across the ocean. This arrangement was seen to have two advantages. In the first place, the civilian pilots previously engaged in ferrying aircraft from factories on the west coast to Montreal would become available to serve with ATFERO on transatlantic deliveries. Second, American military pilots would obtain valuable experience in long-range flying with various types of aircraft. The president accepted this plan and presented it to Churchill:

In spite of the best efforts of the organization now handling flight delivery of combat aircraft from this country to England, I am advised that substantial numbers of these planes are accumulating in this country, and that this condition is apt to grow worse as production reaches an accelerated rate over the next few months. In our common interest, and in order to relieve situation as much as possible, I am prepared to direct the army and the navy to assume full responsibility of transfer of American built aircraft from factory to point of ultimate take off, and to supply maintenance and servicing facilities along the way and at ultimate landing field. This should release a number of civilian pilots now delivering planes. Many such pilots can reasonably be expected to increase pool corps of Atlantic ferry pilots now engaged in this work. Since military and naval pilots and ground crews would be engaged in delivery of planes, I am advised that closest co-operation, necessary to carry through successfully this continuous operation, can best be obtained if responsibility for Atlantic flights could be undertaken by their sister services under Air Ministry, using, of course, the present civilian pilots and such additional ones as may become available. This procedure would enable planes to be brought under control and direction of Royal Air Force prior to scheduling of take off and approach to their designated landing field in England. The success of this operation would depend in large part upon provisions for adequate westbound aircraft transportation, but I am confident that with good will on both sides, such problems can be solved and greater assurances given of ability to handle delivery of increased quantity of combat aircraft anticipated during the summer months. I hope you will comment frankly on this proposal.

... the American Army and Navy could deliver planes ... ready and serviced for RAF to take them over and fly them across.[65]

The British government wasted no time in accepting the American offer. Churchill received the president's message on 29 May. On 30 May he discussed it with Portal,[66] and the same day the Air Ministry drafted a reply for the prime minister's signature:

Grateful acceptance. I must of course consult the Canadian Government but I have no doubt about their response. The Air Ministry has been instructed to plan the re-organization of the ferrying service in accordance with your suggestions. A senior officer will be sent out at once to study the problem on the spot and to consult your Navy and War Departments. We are bent on speeding the flow of aircraft from your factories to our squadrons and the Royal Air Force will welcome the opportunity of working with officers of the United States on this task.[67]

'Grateful acceptance' clearly reflected the sentiments of the Air Ministry, but Churchill substituted a more personal and diplomatic opening paragraph: 'I am deeply grateful to you for your proposals of May 29 which we at once accept in principle.'[68]

In drafting a telegram for the information of the Canadian government, the British were somewhat embarrassed by Roosevelt's failure to make any reference to Canada. After discussions between representatives of the Air Ministry and the Ministry of Aircraft Production (in complete agreement since Beaverbrook's departure in early May), as well as the Dominions Office, it was decided that the best course would be to send Ottawa a copy of the president's message in full with a summary of Churchill's reply 'and to end up with a request for Mr. Mackenzie King's general co-operation.'[69] This was done in a prime minister to prime minister message, the first such communication on the subject of transatlantic ferrying, in which Churchill made a direct appeal for King's help: 'I know you will recognize the vital importance of this matter to us. May I ask for your acceptance and count on your co-operation in putting into effect arrangements which President Roosevelt has proposed.'[70]

The Canadian government showed no resentment at being overlooked in Roosevelt's telegram. Although ATFERO was based in Canada and depended to a large extent on Canadian support and assistance, Canadian officials regarded it as a British organization for which the UK government was administratively and financially responsible. Moreover, there was general satisfaction in Ottawa that ATFERO had at last become the subject of top-level negotiation and that American assistance was pledged, even though this would mean the establishment of American maintenance crews and pilot pools at Montreal and Gander. Consequently, Prime Minister King was able to reply promptly and affirmatively to Churchill's message, assuring him that 'my colleagues and I will be glad to co-operate to the fullest extent in putting into effect the arrangements which President Roosevelt has proposed.'[71]

Nonetheless, the Canadians had certain reservations about the future shape of the ferrying operation. These views were made known to British representatives sent to Canada to report on the extent of the reorganization that would be required to meet Roosevelt's demand. On the whole, the Canadians felt that control by the Air Ministry was a satisfactory solution. They advised, however, against the militarization of ATFERO by the RAF. Any extensive reorganization would probably be greeted with a public outcry because ATFERO, though a British responsibility, had been built up by Canadians, some of whom were donating their services. Howe, who had recently been so critical of ATFERO, now came to its defence, describing it as 'a live affair, an excellent show.' Any attempt to dismantle it would be a mistake, throwing away much of what had already been gained, and Canada 'would get a black eye out of it.' If necessary, ATFERO might be given a military façade, enough to satisfy the Americans, but Howe advised that it would be best 'to stop right there.'[72]

The Air Ministry chose Air Chief Marshal Sir Frederick Bowhill to reorganize the ferry service in accordance with the president's wishes.[73] His appointment was not without a touch of irony, for as air officer commanding-in-chief Coastal Command he had advised against the scheme to deliver aircraft under their own power across the Atlantic and had opposed the assignment of Coastal Command pilots for the job. He preferred to have the aircraft sent by sea. This attitude, however, did not carry over into his new position.

Bowhill's appointment was made in June, but not announced until after he had made a preliminary visit to North America with instructions 'to determine what modifications are required in existing arrangements.'[74] Accompanied by W.P. Hildred, to provide financial advice, and J.B. Bickell, a Canadian industrialist whom Beaverbrook had recruited, Bowhill arrived at Gander on 15 June. After conferring with

A Lockheed Hudson with the propeller on the port engine feathered. NFB
photo for DND, NA, PA 114606

Crews of the first formation flight, Gander, November 1940. Standing: W.R. Lyons, D.L. Gentry, R. Adams, C.M. Tripp, W.C. Rodgers, J.A. Webber, J.D. McIntyre, S.T.B. Cripps, N.G. Mullett, A.M. Loughridge, A. Andrew, N.E. Smith, G.R. Hutchinson, J.W. Gray, D.C.T. Bennett. Kneeling: D.B. Jarvis, H.G. Meyers, J.E. Giles, E.F. Clausewitz, K. Garden, W.T. Mellor. DND, PMR 85-475

Hudson T9427 at Gander prior to its departure as the lead aircraft of the second formation flight, the night of 28/29 November 1940, with a crew of Humphrey Page, Joe Silverthorn, and radio officers James Howard and Arthur Finch. DND, PMR 77-430

The wreckage of Lockheed Hudson T9449 in which Major Sir Frederick Banting, Flying Officer William Bird, and Radio Officer William Snailham were killed when it crashed near Musgrave Harbour, Newfoundland, the night of 20/21 February 1941. NA, C 9703

The wreck of Hudson T9449 as seen from the air the following summer.
DND photo, NA, PA 191367

A Boeing B-17 Flying Fortress taking off. DND, PL 23355

Air Chief Marshal Sir Frederick Bowhill, GBE, KCB, CB, CMG, DSO, air officer commanding-in-chief RAF Ferry Command, at his desk in Montreal. NFB photo for DND, NA, PA 141355

Trans-Canada Air Lines captain Sheldon Luck, on loan to Ferry Command, with an air commodore, probably S.E. Storrar. Sheldon Luck Collection, NA, PA 124214

Radio operators at the Belmont Manor Hotel, Bermuda, April 1941, prior to takeoff for the non-stop twenty-four-hour flight to Greenock, Scotland. Back row (left to right): Glen McKay, Gene Fougere, Steve Tyson, Don Hannant, Wes Goddard, Lloyd Wheeler, Sammy Kenny; front row (left to right): Eric Hoyt, Cecil Foster, Pat Ryan, and Len McMann. Photo and identifications, E.L. Thompson, DND, PMR 94-133

Consolidated PBY Catalina at rest, possibly off Darrell's Island in Bermuda's Great Sound, from which it would have subsequently taken off for the long flight to Greenock, Scotland. DND, RE 23088-16

Flight engineer Flight Sergeant Thomas A. Bexter, of Manchester, England, sits in the righthand co-pilot's seat while First Officer Wilbur A. Morris, of Dallas, turns the propeller on the starboard engine of Catalina *Galloping Goose* in order to get oil distributed throughout the system prior to startup. NFB photo for DND, NA, PA 191342

This photo, taken by an RCAF photographer from 3000 feet on 24 September 1941, gives the pilot's view of the approach to Gander. DND photo, NA, PA 191248

Goose Bay, looking north, 22 June 1943. DND, RE 64-1720

Housing at Goose Bay, May 1943. NFB photo for DND, WRF 939

A major overhaul on a Hudson at Goose Bay, May 1943. NFB photo for DND, NA, PA 153982

A gas bowzer at Goose Bay refuels a Hudson prior to the continuation of a delivery flight. NFB photo for DND, NA, PA 160800

Meteorological Section, Goose Bay, 3 March 1942. DND photo, NA, PA 191249

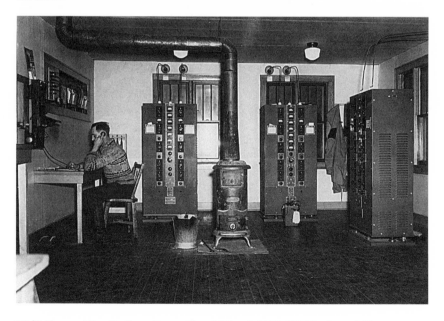

W/T Transmitter Station, Goose Bay, 3 March 1942. DND photo, NA, PA 191246

Busy tarmac at Dorval, 13 May 1942. NFB photo for DND, NA, PA 114763

Backlog of aircraft awaiting delivery at Dorval. NFB photo for DND, NA, PA 191374

Liberators, a Mitchell, Venturas, at Dorval. NFB photo for DND, NA,
PA 191375

Control Tower, Roberts Field, West Africa. NA, PA 187618

Bahamians unloading a Liberator at Nassau, January 1944. NFB photo for DND, NA, PA 191330

Douglas Dakota at Port Etienne, Senegal, West Africa, January 1944. Earl
Briggs Collection, NA, PA 187619

Groundcrew servicing a Liberator, Trinidad, October 1943. NFB photo for DND, NA, PA 114608

representatives of the Newfoundland government, who had an overriding responsibility for the efficient operation of Gander airport, he flew on to Montreal, Ottawa, and Washington, returning to London at the end of the month. In Canada he found 'a most difficult and delicate situation.' As for ATFERO itself, however, Bowhill found little to criticize. Problems of expansion had been surmounted and it 'is now in a very good state of efficiency.'[75]

The air marshal returned to Montreal on 19 July to assume control of the new RAF Ferry Command. With the cooperation of Wilson and Long, who served for another month or so, the transfer of authority was carried out gradually with no break in continuity. The Canadian leaders had first learned of the impending change through American newspapers and were under the impression that Bowhill was about to break up the existing organization. Highly indignant, the two top executives, and also the dollar-a-year men who had helped to build up the ferry service, were ready to resign. With the help of Bickell, a close friend of Wilson, Bowhill managed to persuade the Canadians that he had no intention of disturbing ATFERO. Wilson and Long agreed to stay on the job only until the transfer from civilian to military control had been carried out. However, feelings remained ruffled and an invitation to accept appointments as special assistants to Bowhill was firmly rejected. Long wrote to Howe:

Speaking personally and as a Canadian, I must express the bewilderment which I feel in attempting to understand the decision which has been made by our friends in England. After all, although ATFERO is to all intents and purposes a Canadian operation, based in Canada and, in the meantime at least, largely paid for by Canadian taxpayers, nevertheless a group of Canadian business men who have, without cost to the taxpayers, been giving their unstinted services in successfully building and operating this important war enterprise, are suddenly supplanted by a group from the United Kingdom, brought to Canada for that specific purpose. When it is so obviously apparent that the total manpower of the Empire is needed to successfully conclude the war effort, such a decision is, to say the least, disconcerting.[76]

In the end, most of the dollar-a-year executives remained – though uneasy as to how they would fit into a military organization. The only key figure to resign immediately was Bennett, who had been in charge of flight deliveries and training from the beginning. Having had personality clashes with Wilson and Long, neither of whom had any previous experience in aviation, yet somewhat disappointed that ATFERO was losing its civilian character, he felt that his position was impossible under either the old administration or the new. He requested a transfer to the RAF in the United Kingdom. Initially commissioned a wing commander and posted to Training Command, he eventually found a more satisfying outlet for his outstanding ability as a pilot and navigator in organizing and leading the famous Pathfinder Group of Bomber Command as an air vice-marshal. Bennett later claimed that Bowhill said, 'Bennett, my boy, there is no room for both of us here, you have got to go. They want you back in London anyway.'[77] He has written that Bowhill 'was extremely nice about it, but, of course, the position was an impossible one from my point of view.'[78]

There is no doubt that Bennett was the single most important individual in launching the transatlantic ferry service. He would be missed. However, not everybody regretted his departure. Some found his picky criticisms too much to take. One MAP official complained to Dickins that some experienced American pilots had resigned because of the perfectionist Australian's sarcastic comments.[79] Patrick McTaggart-Cowan remembered Bennett as 'one of the best navigators and pilots I've ever had the pleasure of knowing, but he had one bad habit, in that he assumed everybody else was as bright as he was.'[80]

Ferry Command, with Bowhill as AOC-in-C, came into existence on 20 July 1941. It was really a continuation of ATFERO, with a veneer of air force officers. The military component was purposely kept small and, besides Bowhill, included only one officer of air rank, Air Commodore F.P. Don, senior air staff officer and second-in-command. Four group captains, three wing commanders, and about fifteen officers of lower rank made up the balance. Only a few of these were located in Montreal, the others being stationed in Newfoundland, Bermuda, and the United States.[81] From ATFERO, Ferry Command inherited an organization of approximately a thousand personnel. About 400 were aircrew: 207 civilians, mainly Canadians and Americans, but also including 33 pilots on loan from BOAC and 36 from the Air Transport Auxiliary, 118 RAF, 18 RCAF, principally flying-boat pilots, and 3 from the Royal New Zealand Air Force. There were about 105 Canadian civilian employees located in Montreal, approximately another 300 at St Hubert, and others in Newfoundland and Bermuda. A number of CP personnel remained on loan with the new military organization, primarily in administrative positions.[82]

Thanks largely to Bowhill's leadership, and the example he set for his staff in tact and diplomacy, there was little friction between the British and the Canadians. The latter, proud of their accomplishments under ATFERO, were at first uncomfortable under military control. Hildred, Bowhill's civilian financial adviser, who went out of his way to establish friendly relations, reported that the dollar-a-year men were 'invaluable. They like F.B. [Frederick Bowhill] but do not overlook the hour when the RAF retire from the office.'[83]

The creation of Ferry Command increased the size of the aircrew pool. The Return Ferry Service had already had this effect, quickly returning crews to Montreal. Now more American civilians could be recruited after US military crews assumed responsibility for flying aircraft from the American factories. Soon the first BCATP graduates would join the pool. On graduation, some of the best students, pilots, observers, and wireless operator/air gunners, were selected for training in ferry operations at No. 31 OTU, Debert, Nova Scotia. This was the first of four OTUs established by the RAF in Canada. It was paid for and largely staffed by the RAF. One of its key staff members was RAF Squadron Leader W.H. Biddell from Coastal Command, who had already ferried a Fortress to the United Kingdom. Later posted to Ferry Command, he served with distinction until a Liberator he was flying disappeared between England and the Azores on 27 March 1945.[84]

Pilots coming from an OTU generally made two or three transatlantic flights with Ferry Command, occasionally more, before taking their place with a squadron in Coastal Command. Observers and wireless operator/air gunners however, usually made only one trip, remaining in the United Kingdom for squadron duty. Other 'one-trippers' included staff officers of the RCAF, flying instructors, and other experienced Canadian airmen posted to serve in an overseas theatre. Two of the first were Squadron Leaders N.B. Petersen and P.Y. Davoud, appointed to command 409 and 410 Squadrons, each of whom crossed the Atlantic on 26/27 May 1941 at the controls of a Hudson. Another was Squadron Leader K.L.B. Hodson. When posted from his position as chief flying instructor at No. 8 Service Flying Training School, Moncton, New Brunswick, in November 1941 to command 401 Squadron overseas, Hodson flew to Britain as co-pilot of a Liberator.[85] Many RAF officers, returning home on the termination of a tour of duty in Canada, similarly volunteered to serve as part of the crew on a delivery aircraft.

By July 1941 the ferry service, using mixed military and civilian crews from many nations, had delivered almost 200 aircraft and lost only one.

A series of accidents quickly shattered that good record. On 25 July a Hudson crashed at the Mull of Kintyre on the approach to Prestwick, killing the crew.[86] Barely two weeks later, on 10 August, a westbound Return Ferry Service Liberator failed to clear a mountain on the Isle of Arran at the mouth of the Firth of Clyde. All twenty-two civilian airmen on board were killed.[87] Four days later another heavily loaded westbound Liberator crashed without getting off the ground, again with no survivors. Among those killed was Arthur Purvis, a key figure in the purchasing of aircraft and other war *matériel* in the United States, whose death, in Churchill's words, 'was a grievous loss.'[88] The next accident involved a Liberator en route from Gander on the night of 31 August/1 September. It was the second Ferry Command crash at the Mull of Kintyre.[89]

Forty-three aircrew, some of whom had been recruited in the United States, were killed in the first two Liberator crashes alone, causing 'grave unrest' among American flyers and provoking accusations of incompetence against the BOAC pilots and administration of the Return Ferry Service.[90] To improve the atmosphere, Bowhill took steps to have some of his American aircrew trained for the Return Ferry Service. 'By doing so we will get thorough understanding between Americans and British crews and this feeling will then I hope, be eradicated.'[91] In addition to these crashes, Ferry Command also lost five more Hudsons in the summer and fall of 1941, killing fifteen men. One crashed on 24 August after leaving Gander, and three disappeared over the Atlantic, one on 20 September, one on the 26th, and the third on 10 October. Another crashed at Dundalk in Ireland on 27 September.[92]

The accidents, serious as they were, must be weighed against the safe delivery of 593 aircraft during the year. This total included 404 Hudsons, 89 flying boats (mostly Catalinas), 78 Liberators, 20 Fortresses, and 2 Lockheed Lodestar transports.[93] Nearly all the Hudsons and most of the Catalinas and Liberators, with the exception of those used for transport work, went to Coastal Command, which thus received the greatest benefit from the ferry service. That command viewed it as a mixed blessing. Owing to the shortage of regular ferry pilots, Coastal Command had to provide crews to fly some of these aircraft across the Atlantic. Many of the flying boats, as well as some of the Hudsons and Fortresses, were ferried by crews from Coastal Command. This drain on its operational strength led to the proposal that Hudsons be carried by ship. Fortunately this idea, understandable but most unimaginative, was ruled out by Churchill who, like Beaverbrook, saw the advantage of having all aircraft moved from factory to front line as fast and economically as possible, even at the risk of a temporary setback in military operations.

5

Flying Boats through Bermuda

To this point we have concentrated on the delivery of land-based aircraft. However, almost from the beginning, as we saw with the early Pacific deliveries, the ferry service also handled flying boats, especially Consolidated PBYs, or Catalinas to the British. Coastal Command eagerly sought these lumbering long-range reconnaissance machines to carry the anti-submarine campaign as far as possible out into the vast expanses of the ocean. The twin-engine Catalina cruised at a little over 100 miles per hour, with a total range of about 4000 miles and an effective patrol radius of 800 miles. It boasted tremendous endurance for its day, often remaining aloft for over twenty-four hours.[1] Ferry crews got a full taste of this performance feature.

One of the first new recruits to experience the Catalina's charms was Art Stark, last seen at St Hubert brushing up his radio operator's technique under the tutelage of Jock Cunningham. On Boxing Day, 1940, Stark signed his offer of appointment and formally became a radio officer with the CPR Air Services Department. Effective 1 January 1941 he would be paid $300 per delivery flight, with a guarantee of two trips a month, and could claim expenses, ranging from $8 to $10 per day, when away from Montreal.[2] For his first assignment he would 'replace one of the radio officers on one of the first two PBY (Catalina) flying boats delivered to the RAF from the USN [United States Navy].' He recalls his trip to Halifax:

Just before train time I was met at the Montreal station by Jock Cunningham, our Radio Superintendent, who presented me with two large packages of classified codes, maps, etc. for 'safe-hand' delivery to Halifax. What with my own personal kit I was somewhat loaded down and was wondering how I would ever fight my way to the dining car for meals, lugging the two bundles of secrets with me when I noticed a RCAF sergeant a few seats away. He was promptly co-opted as guardian of the bundles during my meals. I have often wondered since, what he thought of an obvious civilian requesting (almost ordering) him to take custody of two large parcels which were claimed to be highly classified material. I forget what cover story I gave him, but it must have been a good one for he accepted the job without murmur.[3]

Stark reported to Captain Ian Ross (of the *Guba*), who had charge of the party but would not make the crossing himself, and joined the two Catalina crews 'ensconced at the Lord Nelson Hotel' in Halifax. His team represented the cosmopolitan military-civilian mixture that so typified the transatlantic ferry service for the rest of the war. 'The Captain-cum-pilot-cum-navigator was F/L Gautrey, R.A.F.; Co-pilot D.L. "Dick" Gentry, ex-U.S. Navy; Flight Engineer AC-1 Riley, R.A.F.; Flight Radio Officers E.L.W. "Ted" Haggard, Imperial Airways and myself from D.O.T. Gautrey and Riley, of course, were R.A.F. professionals; Gentry was known as "Mr. PBY" – he had flown them for years with the U.S. Navy; and Haggart [sic] had been with Imperial Airways on their flying boats to the Far East as well as their ground stations in the Middle East.' Stark confesses, somewhat ironically, that he was not without some experience himself. 'Me – actually I had had some airborne operating experience – about an hour on an R.C.A.F. float plane when I was R.O. on the R.C.M.P. Cruiser "Adversus" on the West Coast and had, most unofficially, traded jobs with the R.C. Signal Corps operator for an afternoon flip.'[4]

The airmen received special flying kit to replace the 'Teddy Bear' suits and coveralls issued in Montreal. 'These were beautiful one-piece "jump suits" of goat skin with matching gloves and boots, all electrically heated. The theory was fine; they were light, flexible and not bulky like the "Teddy Bears" and kept one nice and warm until the electrical source packed it in, as it did on that first flight; then you just got colder and colder as there was no thermal insulation to retain body heat.'[5]

On New Year's Eve, three days after arriving in Halifax, Stark had his first flight in a Catalina, finding it much roomier than a Hudson and boasting a better view from the distinctive blisters on each side of the fuselage. The wing-span – more than 100 feet – particularly impressed him. With the flying boats lodged at Dartmouth across the harbour from Halifax, the crews had to ride to work in a small RCN tug, not always a pleasant experience. 'The only place on board where you didn't freeze to death in the sub-zero early morning temperatures was in the engine-room; but with the engineer there was only room for two, so there was always a rush to be the first on board.'[6]

It was so cold in Nova Scotia that holiday season that special precautions had to be taken with the flying boats:

When necessary to bring the bird on land, wheels were floated out and placed under the hull. With the likelihood of ice forming on the harbour at night our two aircraft were hauled out and parked on the launching ramp at Dartmouth. It was found that on take-off spray would freeze on the wind screen of the flight deck. There being no de-icer fitted it was necessary to improvise one. A hand-pumped fire extinguisher filled with de-icing fluid and a few feet of rubber tubing filled the bill. I found myself appointed 'chief de-icer' which involved crouching between pilot and co-pilot and pumping like mad as we made our take-off run down the harbour. It worked too![7]

The danger of icing on takeoff is confirmed by Don McVicar, a Ferry Command veteran with Catalina experience. He remembers the warning he received from Captain Charles MacDonald, the Australian pilot who checked him out on the flying boat a couple of years later: '"Well, I'll tell you something even *you* might not know. Even if Gander Lake doesn't freeze on the surface, the spray you kick up on take-off will freeze on your wings and props and the airfoil will be destroyed." Then the last shot. "And you won't be able to see through the ice on the windscreen either."'[8]

The flying-boat crews carried out the same type of meticulous preparations as the Hudson crews were doing at about the same time at St Hubert and Gander. Nothing could be taken for granted. Stark remembers that 'during our final pre-flight checks it was found that our oxygen bottles contained only compressed air. "Wrong bottles – sorry about that."'[9] With the need to climb over North Atlantic storms, it was crucial to have detected and corrected this deficiency.

When the icing problem appeared to have been resolved and when Catalina AM264 and its equipment were judged in proper working order, Gautrey and his crew were ready to set off across the treacherous skies over the North Atlantic Ocean. 'Finally,' radio officer Stark writes, 'late in the afternoon of January 16, 1941, we were off, with our scheduled landing at Greenock, Scotland. We roared down the ramp, dropped our wheels and at once got up on the step [hydroplaning] for our take-off. We lifted off at 1917 GMT. The delivery service of PBY's had commenced.' The flight plan took them over Gander where, four or five hours after lifting off from Halifax harbour, 'all the airport lighting had been turned [on] to wish us "bon voyage." We thanked them for their wishes and flew on eastward.'[10]

Gautrey then started to gain altitude in order to fly over a storm front predicted for mid ocean, but was unable to get high enough to avoid all the problems.

We climbed to 18,000 feet, our maximum altitude, but were not able to get on top of all the heavy weather. Flying through heavy rain at one stage we found that while the hull was watertight, the upper parts of the fuselage were most definitely not. Water poured in over, not only the radio equipment, but the main electrical control panel, eventually putting both generators out of service. We were left with only the batteries and these did not have sufficient capacity to provide for essential communications and navigational requirements *and* our electrically heated flying suits; so we just chattered our teeth and got cold.

It was also found that ice thrown off the propellers crashed most disconcertingly onto the plexi-glass of the flight deck just over the pilots heads. (Later models were fitted with metal protection plates.)[11]

About twelve hours after overflying Gander the crew of AM264 sighted land, but could not identify it. 'It was finally decided that we must be a bit south of our intended track and were off the coast of Ireland. So we turned north and started to coast crawl. Due to weak batteries we had been out of radio contact for some hours but finally managed to get a short report through to our ground station near Glasgow.'[12] As with so many ferry crews, particularly on their first delivery, these airmen discovered that reaching land did not mean they were home free.

We were wallowing along at about 1000 feet just off the coast when we sighted two destroyers below. They challenged this new and strange type of flying machine (PBY's were not in service in Europe at that time) by Very Light and we hurriedly thumbed through our code books and fired off an answer. It was only after landing and we [were] enjoying a cup of tea in the R.A.F. mess at Greenock that we discovered we had used the wrong reply! – apparently Halifax had got mixed up over GMT and provided us with the code table for the wrong day! Nobody was able to explain why we had not been shot down. We must have looked pretty helpless.

Leaving the destroyers behind we were still plugging along the coast when a Stranraer flying boat overhauled us. I was sitting in the port 'blister' at the time doing some sight-seeing and wondered why my welcoming wave caused a gunner to turn his machine gun towards us. The Stranraer had apparently been sent up to find out if we were for real – we were the first Catalina to be seen in those parts. Positive identification was eventually made when the Stranraer had closed close enough for its pilot and ours to recognize each other. They were old squadron buddies![13]

Now it was clear sailing: 'From there on in we had an escort until we landed at Greenock at 1340 GMT, January 17, 1941, 18 hours and 40 minutes after leaving Dartmouth. The first Catalina flying boat had been delivered by air.'

For the crew of AM264 the marathon was not yet over. Their arrival was too special to be ignored:

After the 'Cat' was safely moored to buoys in the river we were taken by launch to the R.A.F. flying boat base for tea. Then, with our kit, we were ferried across the river to where limousines of Scottish Aviation Ltd. were waiting to take us in style to the Central Hotel in Glasgow. (Scottish Aviation Ltd. was the organization appointed to receive the 'Cats' on their arrival, since they were still, at that stage of the war, supposed to be civilian aircraft – at least they had no armament aboard.) At the Central Hotel we found we were being feted to a dinner by the top brass of Scottish Aviation and the R.A.F. The main course was scrambled eggs – we found out later that they were sea gull eggs. While we were well aware of the honour being bestowed on us we were glad when it was over. All we wanted was to get to bed and sleep; we had been up for over 30 hours'[14]

If this reception differed from that accorded Don Bennett and the first Hudson crews to alight on British soil, that at the hotel would have been familiar to them:

Because of the security wraps under which Ferry Command was operating at that time we had been briefed not to say where [we] had come from or how. This caused a few confused moments and some consternation when we checked into the Central Hotel in Glasgow. Wartime regulations required that all civilian travellers state where they had spent the previous night when registering at a hotel; so when a group of oddly clad persons speaking with several different foreign(?) accents carefully left this question unanswered and declined to further enlighten the registration clerk he was ready to call the police. However, the arrival of an official from Scottish Aviation (or the Foreign Office, I never was sure which) hurriedly assured him that everything was in order and we were harmless enough if treated carefully.[15]

Unlike their compatriots who had delivered the first Hudsons, this pioneer ferry crew managed to spend a little time in Britain. The day after their arrival they 'were presented with travel warrants and proceeded to London by night train. The next day was taken up with various formalities, debriefings, etc.' Stark wondered about his status:

During a debriefing session my Canadian passport was picked up and then returned a few hours later with two fresh entries, both stamped by the Foreign Office; the first validated it for travel within the British Empire, while the second stated it was 'not valid for any military zone overseas.' Since it was a Canadian passport and, so far as I was aware, Canada considered Europe as a war zone, I was left in some doubt as to the legality of my stay in the U.K. However it was never questioned during my various visits across the pond.[16]

While he was in Britain, Stark wanted to do something about the useless flying gear he had been issued in Canada. 'Gentry and I found out our electrically-heated flying suits could be exchanged for regular R.A.F. "Irvine" sheep-skin two-piece thermal suits. So we found our way out to a supply depot at Wembley to pick up our new outfits. How two unknown civilians could walk into a supply depot unannounced and demand and receive full flying kits I never have figured out. But we came away with jackets, pants, boots, gloves, etc. – the works!'[17]

Don Bennett, in charge of delivery flights, was furious when he learned that the first Catalinas had staged through Canada so late in the year (see chapter 4). A special technical report had recommended against such an attempt, and Bennett had instructed that, in winter, the flying boats should go via Bermuda.[18] This incident led to much finger pointing in Montreal, and the reorganization of the CPR Air Services Department as the Atlantic Ferry Organization or ATFERO under direct Ministry of Aircraft Production control. But that did not solve the immediate problem of getting the much-needed flying boats to Britain.

Whoever was to blame for the Catalina delivery foul-up, arrangements had to be undertaken on short notice to prepare the Bermuda end – despite the fact that BOAC had formally loaned its base there in November 1940.[19] Fortunately, one of the key men knew the colony and its transatlantic flying-boat facilities. Squadron Leader G.J. 'Taffy' Powell had previously managed Imperial Airways' Bermuda operations. In

December 1940, however, he commanded the ferry detachment at Gander where, he now confesses, he wondered how he might amuse the bored airmen waiting to deliver Hudsons and how he could spend Christmas with his family in Halifax. He quickly forgot these concerns when told 'that a batch of Catalina flying boats had been released to the RAF and that I was to go to Bermuda to get a base established and to get them ferried to Scotland.' He admits in his memoirs:

To leave Gander in mid-winter to go back to Bermuda was a surprise almost too good to be true so after a quick call to my wife to say that we were off in three days by a Canadian National Steamship boat from Halifax I started on staff and planning. My wife claimed afterwards that in telephoning the short notice to get packed up I had ommitted [sic] to say where we were going! At Bermuda with so many old friends it did not take long to make my government calls and to take possession of the Imperial Airways base on Darrell's Island which had been my old domain. I had maintenance and office arrangements to make, moorings. to lay, motor boats to organize and crew accommodation to find.[20]

To facilitate this move and to allow him to work in civilian clothes, the RCAF posted Powell to Air Force Headquarters in Ottawa and placed him on leave without pay. He was also promoted to wing commander and, soon after, to group captain.[21]

Taffy Powell was the right man for the job of setting up the Bermuda base. Bennett praised him as one of the most valuable members of the organization.[22] Almost anyone else – without his connections, experience, and drive – would have encountered many difficulties. An ex-Royal Flying Corps officer, recruited from a local bank, described Powell's methods:

Bermuda's undercurrent gathered itself together and many rumours went the rounds. It was not till the first American-built ships [Catalinas] arrived that we knew what really was going to take place. For several days Powell had been in and around Hamilton, getting everyone to do something for him. He has that way, and it's a real satisfaction to have done something for him. After a good lunch and a good cigar is when he really gets things moving. Everyone else has been caught by the afternoon inertia, but that gets swept away without pain.

Practically overnight he had an organization ready to receive the ships; an office prepared, maintenance crews to get the ships ready and crews to fly them away. I switched overnight from banking. The amount of work to be done was incredible. Powell never seemed to sleep or get any time away. 'Where's everyone?' he would say about 7 p.m. after we had been up since 3.30 a.m. for an early departure. On being told they had gone home he'd say, 'I'll just do a few things and *we'll* go home.'[23]

With Powell's experience and Bermuda's wartime decline and isolation, the local arrangements proceeded quite smoothly. The lack of tourists during the war meant that accommodation presented no problem. 'The Belmont Manor on the shore of Warwick Parish close to the island base provided everything that we needed,' writes Powell, 'plus offices for signals and control and space for a branch meteorological station. As the hotel grounds included a golf course, swimming pool and tennis courts there were to be none of the highly charged "waiting for weather" periods that we endured at Gander where card games and various forms of fire water were the only distractions.' He also pointed out some additional attractions brought by the war. 'The British Government had installed a regional censorship office in two of the biggest hotels in Hamilton, the capital, which had meant the arrival of several dozen young ladies from the UK, a fact that brightened the lives of many Bermudians and ferry crews in the succeeding months.'[24]

Initially officials thought that a few Catalinas would be easy to handle. The UK high commissioner in Canada wired home: 'P.B.Y. boats do not present great problems as numbers limited and arrangements can easily be made for one or two experienced pilots to be polished at Bermuda and later Halifax to indoctrinate ferry crews.'[25] In fact, it was not quite so simple. The ferry organization was still in its infancy, with growing and interconnected demands. A change in one area inevitably affected the whole. Even ferrying a handful of Catalinas across the Pacific complicated the Bermuda startup. It left few experienced civilian aircrew for the Atlantic. The RAF and the RCAF had to loan pilots and co-pilots, and the Canadian Department of Transport assisted with the radio operators, leading to the enlargement of the informal school in Montreal.[26]

In January 1941 seven Catalinas arrived from the United States. Six were delayed at Darrell's Island, for a variety of reasons, ranging from unreliable weather forecasts, through technical problems, to a shortage of aircrew. One Catalina finally left for Greenock on 29 January. To say this, however, is misleadingly simple. The first Bermuda–UK delivery flight was a harrowing adventure for all involved – especially its crew, a typical international collection of servicemen and civilians. The pilot, Flight Lieutenant J.G. Fleming (RAF); the co-pilot, Flying Officer J.J. Meikle (RAF); and the radio operators, R.H. Hodgson and F.C. Eyre, were all Canadians. Flight engineers Latimer and Clark were on loan from the Royal Navy's Fleet Air Arm. The pilots came from Coastal Command and made several more deliveries before returning to their operational squadrons. Fleming was killed in action on 6 September 1944. Hodgson and Eyre, already ferry veterans, had numerous delivery flights in a variety of aircraft before the end of the war.[27]

The official Ferry Command account, *Atlantic Bridge*, records the ordeal suffered by the first Catalina crew out of Bermuda and is worth quoting in detail. The troubles began six hours into the flight.

Their automatic pilot suddenly jammed, the starboard aileron went full down, and the machine fell into a spiral dive. Immediately the ailerons began to flutter because of the steep angle at which they were meeting the flow of air.

'I was sitting at the radio table when the plane very suddenly went complete-ly out of control,' said one of the radio operators. 'The night was pitch black, so it was hard to tell what was happening, but we started some sort of spiral dive for the sea. On orders from Fleming I sent out an S.O.S., but just at that time our aerials gave way and wound themselves about the ship. This state of things lasted for several minutes as we had been flying at 20,000 feet. Our altimeter at one time showed 1,000 feet.' The pilots fought the spin. The crew jettisoned smoke flares, spare parts, tool kits, the £40 outfit just bought by one of the engineers. They recovered control when the Catalina was only a few hundred feet from the water. 'And sure enough,' continues the radio operator, 'when daylight came we were flying along with both ailerons completely torn away.' There was no lateral control. To remain airborne without lateral control, the pilot had to fly straight ahead, as use of the rudder without ailerons would be liable to put the machine into a fatal flat spin.

Although they were only six hours from their departure base, and hours and hours of Atlantic waste lay between them and Britain, Captain Fleming ordered no further S.O.S. From the trailing aerial, which was quickly fixed up, they simply signalled 'Both ailerons gone'; and flew on. The signal was received, but no one believed it. It seemed impossible that a Catalina weighing some fifteen tons could be handled under such conditions.

Fleming and Meikle sat side by side, using all their strength to keep the machine in the air. They dared not remove their hands from the controls to look at a map. They were flying due south. Fleming had memorised the course, and bit by bit they managed very gently to turn back on to it. Hour after hour they flew on with great fortitude and physical endurance. After weathering a storm they succeeded in coming down on the water at Milford Haven. They had been flying for twenty-eight hours, fifty minutes.

The sea was rough, and in spite of all that they had endured they could not face sea-sickness. So they actually took off again and flew skimming over the surface to within three miles nearer the moorings.[28]

If the first flight from Bermuda was more difficult than most, it does underline a problem endemic to wartime ferry operations – the constant fear of mechanical failure. Also crews believed that the Catalina would not fly on one engine until the fuel tanks were half empty.[29]

Despite the precarious beginning, the delivery of Catalinas continued. Even before the base was fully established, the frequency of arrivals and departures quickened. And, of course, so did the pace of training and checkout flights. The schedule was hectic, with everyone – often including office staff – frequently working seven-day weeks. Powell's first day off came in June. To keep the planes moving, assistant flight engineers were often recruited locally from sailors returning home, 'or members of the Bermuda volunteer regiment who wish to proceed to England to enlist.' They received a £10 honorarium for the flight.[30] Powell later recalled with pride the Bermudians who, anxious to join the British armed forces, volunteered to fly in this fashion. By resourcefulness and hard work, the base managed to deliver thirty-eight of forty-four flying boats received during its first four months; in June it passed fifty.[31]

The increased frequency of deliveries revealed deficiencies at the eastern terminus on the Firth of Clyde, which had been chosen because Scottish Aviation (Greenock) had the contract 'to equip these flying boats to operational standards.' Lack of experience in handling flying boats and poor communications, which often provided 'no information of the impending arrival of aircraft until they appeared overhead,' created problems. 'These shortcomings were accentuated by the exhausted condition of the crews at the end of the 24 hour flight and by the strong tide in the congested waterway in which the moorings were laid.' For a short time Coastal Command loaned marine-craft and crews to Scottish Aviation, but a more permanent solution came with the completion, adjacent to that firm's facility, of a new RAF base, Gourock. It assumed responsibility, in cooperation with Ministry of Aircraft Production staff, for receiving each new Catalina from North America.[32]

For most of the men who had just flown the Atlantic, an even longer, more circuitous journey remained. They had to return to Bermuda to pick up another flying boat. In the beginning, one veteran later reminisced, 'we'd fly here [Greenock], take a train to Liverpool, catch some banana boat convoy to Halifax, then a train to New York and then another ship to Bermuda. Some of the guys didn't get to see Montreal for months on end.'[33] The turnaround time improved tremendously in May when the Return Ferry Service began, employing used Liberators acquired from the United States. The MAP removed the armament and put a wooden floor in the bomb-bay. Thus 'converted,' the four-engine bombers flew crucial freight to Britain and equally essential aircrew back to Montreal.[34] The ferry service benefited as if the number of aircrew had taken a quantum leap. The passengers, however, suffered the indignity and discomfort of more than fourteen hours squeezed into a freezing bomb-bay, wearing the heaviest flying clothes available, possibly cocooned in a sleeping bag, and often sucking on an oxygen tube for much of the trip. Many ferry personnel considered the return to North America the worst part of the job.[35]

With a routine established and the size of the project growing, the administrative demands grew as well. In addition to arrangements with Bermuda authorities and businessmen, Powell and his staff also had to coordinate activities with the Americans. The US Navy began flying PBY patrols from Bermuda in November 1940, and on 7 April 1941 commissioned its own base in the colony.[36] With relatively small numbers of people involved, informal arrangements predominated. The various nationalities worked well together. There is even evidence that, as early as the last week of April and the first week of May 1941, a dozen officers of the officially non-belligerent US Navy flew as crewmen on ATFERO Catalina delivery flights from Bermuda to the United Kingdom.[37]

With more planes flying in and out of the colony, air traffic control became an increasingly complex problem. All users of Bermuda air space had to cooperate. Whenever they met to discuss the subject, American servicemen invariably outnumbered ATFERO or Ferry Command personnel. The British aircraft delivery organization fought from a minority position – particularly when the US Army Air Forces joined the talks.[38] Nonetheless, relations were courteous and everything functioned smoothly.

With the Bermuda station firmly established, Powell moved to ferry headquarters in Montreal. Accordingly, on 14 June 1941, a chartered accountant from P.S. Ross and Sons reported on the transfer of the cash balances to the new base manager, former BOAC captain A.G. Store. This document not only outlines the business and financial procedures established by Powell, but also describes other aspects of the operation, painting a detailed picture of how ATFERO functioned in Bermuda. Informality ruled, many items evidently borrowed or casually transferred from one government department to the next: payment for equipment, supplies, and services could wait until the war ended. Local businesses required cash for a variety of things, including hotel room and board and catering for the crews on their long flights. Cash was also needed for staff pay and allowances and some salary advances. Consequently, each week the Bank of Bermuda received $4500 (Canadian) and £200 (Sterling) from the Canadian Pacific Railway 'to meet current payments for expenses incurred at the base.'[39] The money went directly into two accounts, with the base manager as the signing officer. From that point the system became more informal:

As the banks in Bermuda do not maintain dollar checking accounts, it is necessary to make withdrawals from the Canadian dollar remittances in order to make cash payments of Canadian dollar liabilities. In order to reduce the amount of cash to be carried on his person, Mr. Higgs [the cashier-accountant] obtains from the bank a banker's cheque in his favour for the approximate amount of the weekly accounts of the Belmont Manor Hotel which he endorses over to the Hotel in part payment of its account. The balance of the withdrawal is carried by Mr. Higgs from the City of Hamilton to the Island base. Mr. Higgs is unaccompanied when transporting the money from the bank and no fidelity or hold-up insurance is in force in favour of the B.M.A.P. [British Ministry of Aircraft Production].[40]

The report also noted, with apparent concern, 'There is no insurance of any kind placed by Bermuda Base to cover fire, theft or damage.'[41]

Fastidious accountants must have been appalled at the casual approach. ATFERO kept its money in a small, borrowed safe in an unsecure building at the base. Operating on a cash basis only and paying hotel accounts and personal expenses of aircrew in Canadian dollars, but local bills and allowances for the airmen in Bermuda pounds,[42] separate statements were kept for the two currencies. However, the accountants found, 'the weekly petty cash statements do not reflect the expenditures for any definite period.'[43] They disliked the lack of checks and balances, particularly when it provided an opportunity for ferry crews to abuse the system.

Claims are made by returning flight personnel for subsistence and expenses incurred while away from Bermuda base and these items, if they appear correct, are paid although there is no means of the base knowing that claims had not been made elsewhere for the same expenses. Advances are also made in Montreal or England and if advice of these advances are not wired to Bermuda base there is no means of knowing whether all such advances have been deducted by personnel when filing claims.[44]

The transient nature of the aircrew and their job as well as the informality meant that there was 'no continuous record maintained of flight personnel from which it could be ascertained at any time just who were in Bermuda at any date.'[45] Even their local expenses were hard to keep track of. This placed hotel management in a precarious situation. On occasion some airmen left personal accounts unpaid when they took off for Britain before dawn and 'the Hotel was unaware of the departure.' By June the base informed the hotel 'of those members of the air base who are leaving the following day.'[46] ATFERO paid the basic hotel bills weekly, $5.00 per officer for room and board at the Belmont and $3.50 at the Rossdon, including the use of a conference room, telephone calls to the airport, and 10 per cent for gratuities.

On top of room and board, many of the staff also received tickets for use in the base lunch room at Darrell's Island. Some of the office staff, however, got a lunch allowance of ten shillings a week. The lunch room and the hotels failed to satisfy the catering requirements for the ferry flights, so this was arranged informally. The assistant office manager, John McMeeking, agreed to supply the food. 'Each ship is furnished with supplies for the flight to England at a fixed rate of £4-10, irrespective of what is furnished. The Captain designates beforehand what he would like to have supplied and as a rule his requests have been met ... this catering is looked after by Mrs. McMeeking and ... the assistant office manager ... brings the supplies to the airport so that they can be put on board for the flights which usually leave about 3.00 a.m.' The base put together its own emergency ration-pack, 'sufficient for the crew for six days,' because 'it was not considered that the tins of biscuits (Parlin) supplied with each aircraft were suitable.'[47] The containers of locally purchased 'food, cigarettes and chocolates' were made as air tight as possible but were not vacuum-sealed. After each delivery flight they were packed with other returnable equipment and shipped by sea back to Bermuda for eventual reuse.

The informality of the arrangements produced some inconsistencies. For example, in May BOAC billed MAP for airport facilities used in Bermuda, but had not done so for the previous months. Powell simply filed the invoice, because 'no definite arrangement has been made as to the amount to be paid for the premises and, in any event, payment would merely represent a transfer from one Government Department to another.'[48] In fact, BOAC freely helped the operation in many ways. It supplied its base, machine-shop and tools, and five motor-boats. (The coxswains at least were on MAP's payroll.)[49] Among materials from innumerable sources, Pratt and Whitney donated some spare parts,[50] and HMS *Malabar*, the Royal Navy's shore establishment in Bermuda, constantly helped out with such things as guy ropes and mooring equipment.[51] Other contributors included the Trade Development Board, Cable and Wireless Limited, and Watlinton and Conyers. Powell negotiated 'free use' of most of the borrowed items, 'with the exceptions of the safe [from the Glencoe Hotel] for which a rental charge is to be made.'[52]

ATFERO did own some things, including a Caterpillar tractor, six sets of beaching gear (to move aircraft from the water to the hangar), and nine buoys for anchoring flying boats. The report noted the way in which the staff sometimes had to adapt: 'The base has handled as many as fifteen planes at one time by using two buoys belonging to Pan-American Airways and having certain of the planes on land on beaching gear. It was necessary to anchor certain of the planes in the storage pool due to lack of space at the base.'[53] The inventory also included a number of smaller items, such as replacement radio parts, Aldis lamps, oxygen equipment, and navigation stores – compasses, sextants, and sixty-eight wrist chronometers remaining from an issue of seventy. The general supplies featured an accumulation of emergency ration biscuits, which continued to arrive despite no longer being used; Coston flares, which were ignored in favour of the regular RAF issue of pistols and flares; and twice as many flame floats as needed.[54]

The visiting accountants criticized the dispersed and cramped storage of supplies, as well as the lack of stock control – particularly regarding equipment loaned to ferry crews. No one was responsible, after a delivery, for packing equipment for return shipment to Bermuda, so it was done haphazardly. Often packing cases reached Bermuda after the crew concerned had already departed on another delivery flight. Base staff frequently found broken items, but no packing slips, so the contents could not be checked properly. Strange things happened. Of fifty flashlights issued, only five had been returned.[55] On the other hand, 'two binoculars in first class condition, never issued at Bermuda, were included with equipment returned to the base and these have been retained and are used by the base for observing planes in flight.'[56]

The difficulties delineated above should not be exaggerated. Despite the odd problem, in less than six months Powell had built the base and Catalinas were being dispatched to the United Kingdom as fast as the weather and arrivals from the factories would allow. It is unfair to dwell on observations made following a brief visit by a person looking for ways of improving the operation. ATFERO in general suffered from a shortage of manpower. Excluding aircrew, most of whom were transient, Powell had fewer than fifty people working for him when he handed over to Store.[57] Many performed double-duty and worked overtime. Nobody worried about job descriptions and frills like unnecessary paperwork, with the result that checks and controls were inevitably weak. After July, the birth of RAF Ferry Command brought service supply, accounting, and administrative procedures that ameliorated most of the weaknesses noted in the Ross report. In general, however, the station continued to function in essentially the same manner throughout the war.

Some problems were particularly persistent. One was communications, a key aspect of ferry operations. The first delivery flights from Bermuda highlighted certain difficulties: signals faded, necessitating several changes of frequency; equipment failed; power output was low; and there was a shortage of skilled operators. Consequently, ATFERO arranged for the installation of a new transmitter and increased cooperation with others in the signals business, in particular Cable and Wireless Limited and the Bermuda Meteorological Service.[58] After the RAF assumed responsibility for Atlantic ferrying, it assessed the signals facilities in Bermuda. Ferry Command inherited its own point-to-point transmitter and receiver on Darrell's Island and a partially installed transmitter at St George's. Cable and Wireless, which provided considerable assistance in both equipment and personnel, had transmitters there, controlled from its receiving station at Store Hill, the home of the company's medium- and high-frequency direction-finding facilities. Ferry Command also had unlimited access to the receiving station at the meteorological office behind the Belmont Hotel. The four receivers, one of which was described as 'obsolete' and 'of doubtful make and vintage,' were manned 'by five of our own R.A.F. personnel and one corporal of the Bermuda Volunteer Engineers.'[59]

Unfortunately, the setup was not as good as it sounds, and improvements came slowly. A misunderstanding with Dr Mackie, Bermuda's chief meteorological officer, hampered meteorological and signals arrangements for many months. At one point a Ferry Command signals officer wrote, in apparent exasperation: 'In the writer's opinion, Dr Macky [sic] is to blame for all the confusion, misunderstanding and all the difficulties which have arisen over this Met. requirement, – which should have been a very small problem involving about two signals and very little correspondence. Dr Macky is inclined to be somewhat obstinate, and it is difficult to convince him that the complete wireless facilities of the R.A.F. in Bermuda are not for his especial and exclusive use.'[60]

This question continued to bedevil the Bermuda base. Even the transfer of the meteorological service to the Air Ministry did not solve the problem. It merely placed Mackie in an awkward position:

The result is that the Director of the Met. Office who, up to the present has gone to the Colonial Secretary for decisions on all administrative matters, is now having to refer to the Air Ministry such questions as the rent to be paid for the new married quarters, the rates to be paid to temporary clerks, etc. As it is quite impossible to get decisions from the Air Ministry on these questions in the time available, the Director of the Met. Office has in fact had to go ahead on most questions in anticipation of Air Ministry authority, and he despairs of ever being able to convince the Air Ministry that the wages and the rents which he is paying are no higher than the standard under the new and highly artificial conditions prevailing in Bermuda.[61]

Other parts of the command had similar problems; many aspects of transatlantic weather forecasting were unsatisfactory. Air ferrying had grown so quickly that there was no infrastructure in place to support it. The answer decided upon was greater centralization. Early in 1942 Ferry Command established an Atlantic forecasting centre under Patrick McTaggart-Cowan at Dorval, the new headquarters on the western outskirts of Montreal,[62] and on 19 March Powell, now command senior air staff officer, saw it as the way to end a chronic weakness in the Bermuda operation. 'I am not satisfied with the weather service which we receive from Bermuda, although I admit that it is not the fault of the personnel but the poorness of communications. The Atlantic forecast centre at Dorval will, in the near future, issue Trans-Atlantic forecasts from Bermuda to the U.K.'[63] After a brief shake-down period, the new system functioned smoothly and served Ferry Command – including the Bermuda operation – extremely well.

After the summer of 1941, the story of ferry flights through Bermuda becomes relatively uneventful. The RAF assumed control through the new Ferry Command, and this change, along with systems already in place, allowed officials to deal with problems as they arose. Flying boats – late in the war four-engine Consolidated Coronados joined the Catalinas – departed regularly for the United Kingdom. With Coastal Command's pressing needs and increased US production, flying boats passed through Bermuda in the winter and through Boucherville and Gander Lake in the summer. The delivery took longer this way, but the crews benefited from the shorter legs, and light freight replaced the extra fuel. By 1942 Ferry Command maintained a detachment under Squadron Leader L.L. 'Slim' Jones at Elizabeth City, North Carolina, where crews picked up the flying boats, but Bermuda remained the principal Atlantic jumping-off point.[64]

Don McVicar, one of Ferry Command's experienced civilian captains, has left the only detailed account of picking up Catalinas at Elizabeth City, flying them to Bermuda, and subsequently on to Britain. It provides a good idea of how this part of the ferry service operated when it got up and running. McVicar, qualified as a navigator and radio operator as well as a pilot, joined Ferry Command in November 1941 at the age of twenty-six from the staff of No. 2 Air Observer School, Edmonton, Alberta. He had more qualifications than the average pilot, but was a free spirit disdainful of authority, not unlike the popular image of the typical Ferry Command airman. He had gained a measure of fame and made a significant contribution by participating in the northern survey flight checking out airfields in the northeastern Arctic. However, despite this record and having ferried a Liberator, a twin-engine North American B-25 Mitchell, two Hudsons, and two Martin B-26 Marauders, he had not been able to achieve his goal of seeing the world by flying boat. He had flown an amphibian version of the PBY, but only from land.[65]

McVicar's opportunity came in October 1942 when he was checked out on a Catalina and made the last flying-boat delivery of the season from Boucherville on the St Lawrence River. On his return to Montreal he flew some local communication flights and delivered a Douglas Boston to Prestwick. Squadron Leader Ed Coristine of crew assignments then matched McVicar up with a crew and sent them off to Elizabeth City to pick up Catalina FP280 and take it to Greenock. Crews often made this first leg of the journey by train. In this case they hurried down on Pennsylvania Central Airlines, only to find that their plane required major servicing and they would have a layover of a few days in Elizabeth City. With nothing much to do, McVicar got to know his crew who, except for his favourite flight engineer Bill Baker, were all unknown to him. The co-pilot, navigator, and one of the radio officers came from the RAF. Pilot Officers Alan Wilson and William James were young, but not as green as their captain remembers them. Each had made one Catalina delivery flight to the United Kingdom since graduation from the schools of the BCATP and each stayed with Ferry Command to make many more. Sergeant Howard Hill of the RCAF had just recently received his radio operator's wing, but he would be working under the eye of Eric Rush, an experienced man with many flights under his belt.[66]

On 27 November, a week after he had left Montreal, McVicar 'eased FP280 out of a light chop on Pasquotanic Bay' and set course for Bermuda. It was an uneventful flight, but the Catalina merited some attention. 'The engine on which they'd changed the cylinder was running hot and using too much oil. Baker and I decided we'd ask to have the oil filter screen pulled at Bermuda. Rush reported the direction-finding loop was out of calibration. That meant another test flight. But for a factory-new aircraft she was shaping up well.' After touching down in 'Great Sound, surely the most perfect flying-boat harbour in the world,' McVicar, undoubtedly like many of his compatriots, had some trouble tying up at the arrival buoy and was duly made 'an honoured member of the Royal Society of Bermuda Buoy Snatchers' by the 'ramp rats' led by King Parker, a mischievous American ferry pilot. He had moved east from the Pacific ferry and captained one of eleven boats ahead of McVicar in the queue waiting to take off for Scotland. Two others had left that day.[67]

The size of the backlog gave McVicar something else to brood about as the crew took the little ferry-boat to the jetty at the Belmont Manor Hotel, their home for at least several days. Wartime conditions had provided a unique opportunity for housing transient ferry crews.

The Belmont Manor was a prestige hotel which catered for rich Canadians and Americans who either had found a gold mine or needed the balmy Bermuda air to clear their lungs of tax problems. Pre-war, a section of high society made a point of making an annual visit. But now that was all changed for the rambling wooden structure with its swimming pool and ever-open bar. The Ferry Command had taken over as many rooms as needed. We appreciated the luxury and the landscaping, featuring a variety of sweet-smelling flowers of many colours. The kitchen had been world-renowned before the war, and still produced a fair meal under rationing. Liquor was cheap and available in unlimited quantities. Which made for an unbalanced diet for some people.[68]

Perhaps not surprisingly, McVicar claims that many of the aircrew stranded in Bermuda spent most of their time in the bar or gambling to while away the time. It was hardly the kind of wartime conditions endured by service personnel in operational theatres. Nonetheless, most airmen would rather have been getting on with the job of delivering Catalinas to Coastal Command. With poor weather, either in Bermuda or forecast over the Atlantic, moving up the queue was a slow process. The facilities were intended to handle two deliveries a day, but often dispatched more.[69] Every few days a few boats would take off for the long trip to Scotland, but a pall descended on the little community on 4 December when a Catalina failed to reach the United Kingdom. 'No trace of it was ever found.'[70] Ferry Command's losses were remarkably low, but high enough to act as a periodic sobering influence on the participants.

The monotony was then broken by the local weather station hoisting the gale warning signal. The station commanding officer, Wing Commander Maurice Ware, a veteran of half a dozen delivery flights, and Squadron Leader 'Paddy' Uprichard, the engineering officer, decided that crews should man the Catalinas tossing around in the Sound, using the engines to help the aircraft ride out the storm. A furious McVicar and his crew were taken out by a local coxswain, who strained to keep his craft alongside the blister of FP280 as the wind picked up. 'The next problem was that the crash boat seemed to bob up just as the Cat sank in a wave, so the climb up the flimsy ladder was pretty exciting. They threw in a box of sandwiches and a couple gallons of water and sped away to pick up other reluctant heroes.'[71] Twenty-four hours later the crash-boat picked them up, after a scary and, in McVicar's eyes, unnecessary adventure riding out the storm in a flying boat tethered to a buoy in the wind-swept harbour.

He may have been right. The official account of Ferry Command indicates that, as a rule, when a storm approached, the flying boats were 'brought ashore and lashed to the tarmac, head to wind.' Crews and maintenance staff pitched in to help. The same source notes that other Bermuda hazards included 'corrosion, which attacks vital parts of boats awaiting delivery, [and] the 4-foot swells which affect take-off.'[72]

The day after the storm, three Catalinas left for Gibraltar, an alternate destination, but not a popular one. There was reportedly a problem of swells in the harbour there and, even worse, the next leg involved flying around the Bay of Biscay, believed to be swarming with Luftwaffe aircraft. One of the boats, flown by Ralph Adams, got lost about fifty miles short of Gibraltar. Spotting a destroyer, he landed to learn his position. However, the Catalina's engines would not restart and the aircraft sank while under tow.[73] McVicar determined that he would wait for appropriate weather conditions to fly non-stop to Scotland when his turn came.

By 10 December five more Catalinas had made the direct flight to Greenock, and McVicar finally test-flew FP280:

I had devised my own method of swinging the compass now that our steel pay-load was on board. It worked. Quick and effective. Rush had the bottom off the DF loop and adjusted all the little compensating screws to give a good straight correction curve. But the temperatures of the left engine wouldn't come down. Baker and I had a conference, then we climbed to cool air at 10,000 feet and checked the feathering of the right engine. Perfect. Then I started it up and feathered the left engine. Of course the oil and cylinder head temperature started to drop immediately. I let it cool for almost ten minutes before I started it up again. This time all temperatures were normal. Baker scratched his head. It was a new one on him. I didn't worry too much about the method. Results were what counted.[74]

McVicar signed off the aircraft, moving up the queue to the next level, ready for dispatch. 'Which meant I'd have to attend the daily weather briefings at five a.m. Goodbye to late gambling and drinking nights.'

The drill at this point was quite simple. The crews waited for a weather forecast that seemed to promise good flying conditions for the more than 3000 miles between Bermuda's Great Sound and Greenock on the Clyde. This was not easy in these early days of transatlantic forecasting. As McVicar sums it up in his own inimitable style: 'There was one big problem. No matter how convincing the forecaster appeared we knew he was working with data which was already at least twelve hours old by the time it had been taken, coded, transmitted by wireless, decoded, then plotted. And we would be in the air for a full day, so his forecast had to be made for that far in advance. We would see the sun rise, set, rise again, and then we'd sure as hell better be down before it set once more.' He added: 'Theoretically our destination weather should have been an important factor, but in fact it rarely caused a cancellation. I suppose the general feeling was that if we ever got that far we'd get down somewhere, somehow.'[75]

Wing Commander Ware could cancel a departure, but each aircraft captain had to make his own final decision to go. Employing his veto power, McVicar passed on a reasonable forecast on 15 December, only to feel embarrassed when four other captains made it safely to Scotland. Four days later, over four weeks out of Montreal, he finally got the map he wanted. He filed a flight plan of 23 hours 35 minutes and, with his crew, climbed through the blister to start the first dangerous part of the long flight, getting the overloaded Catalina into the air. 'The Plimsoll line was buried, and I had worked out our all-up weight as almost 37,000 pounds. The operational curves in my US Navy Pilot's Handbook only went to 30,000 pounds.' They rode so low in the water that, 'as the speed built up with painful slowness the water started to pour over the cockpit.' It took over two minutes at maximum power to get airborne, at precisely 1300 GMT, and fifteen minutes to reach 3000 feet. McVicar decided to remain at that height, at 105 knots, until the weight decreased.[76]

McVicar disagreed with some of his colleagues about the best way of flying a Catalina such a long distance. 'I had spent a few sleepless nights before deciding 105 knots indicated was the best miles-per-gallon speed. There were other Captains who swore that the best way to get to the other side was to cut the engine power back so that the Cat flew just above the stall at, say, 80 knots. They believed the wind would blow them to the Promised Land. Some had managed to stay in the air for over 30 hours. I was convinced they were stupid.' However, McVicar and Baker worried about excessive fuel consumption, attributing it to the radar antennae fixed to the wing. To find better flying conditions, and hopefully a tail wind, they climbed (taking twenty minutes to do so) to 7000 feet. Without any outside help they would not reach Britain. Three hours out they had gone 380 miles and things looked better. A lunch of hot soup and 'sawdusty sandwiches' perked everybody up. 'Of course the new ground speed [125 knots] made a superb dessert.'[77]

FP280 droned on, with course corrections on the hour, until, after four hours, it was time to move gas from the overload fuselage tanks to the wings. After a few minutes, Baker reported that the fuel transfer pump would not suck. His pilot remembers: 'I guess we all thought the same: sabotage. I said to Baker, after I'd made a quick calculation, "I can give you an hour before we turn back. I sure as hell don't want a night landing at Bermuda." I didn't bother mentioning I'd never been trained for night water landings.' The flight engineer found the pump clogged with sand. He had to clean and grease it. 'A vital repair in mid-ocean. We agreed there'd be beers for Baker in Prestwick.'[78]

By 2100 GMT McVicar, considering their position, speed, and fuel consumption, calculated that there was a small reserve of fuel beyond that needed for the remaining 2000 miles. But they would have to rely on dead reckoning and radio bearings because of the increasing cloud cover. An hour later, as they approached the point of no return, McVicar briefly thought about retracing their steps. 'We had been airborne for nine hours and had flown 1,197 miles by my estimate. Our tail wind component had been 18 knots. If we turned back this would become a head wind making our groundspeed 98 knots for a flight time of 12.3 hours. So our total time airborne would be 21.3 hours, leaving plenty of reserve in case Bermuda weather went down. But after we returned we'd be facing another long, monotonous wait for the good forecast. The loss of astro was very serious but I decided to press on.'[79]

The biggest concern, as usual on long-distance ferry flights, remained the weather, notoriously unpredictable, especially over the North Atlantic. McVicar worried about a forecast deep, low-pressure area around the southern tip of Greenland, with an associated cold front, 'like a nasty blue worm across our track.'[80] Around midnight the plane suddenly began to bounce around and the crew noticed 'a light coat of rime on the wings.' They had reached the cold front a good three hours or 400 miles ahead of schedule. Despite a valiant attempt, McVicar could not get above the weather as the ice piled up on the outside of the aircraft and Baker backfired the engines to keep the carburettors from icing up. 'My problems were rapidly multiplying,' writes McVicar.

The Aldis lamp [used as a flashlight] now showed the bottom of the wing covered with rough ice resembling stalactites. I was flying by hand in accordance with the instructions that George should be disconnected just when most needed – in turbulent air. I felt a shudder. We were on the edge of the stall which would be followed by a spin taking us down to almost certain death. Over the roar of the engines I heard a rattling as if someone had thrown small chunks of gravel at us. The lethal clear ice composed of super-cooled water droplets had hit us. The ASV [radar] antennas were rectangular blocks of white and were vibrating dangerously. There was a loud crack as our wire antennas broke away from the wing. I could feel the elevators twitch as the wire tried to wrap itself around them. A hard pump on the yoke and they came free. Too late I realized I'd tried to stay high too long.[81]

As a last resort McVicar dove the aircraft in a desperate search for warmer air. 'There were flashes of lightning all around. Baker was still backfiring the engines and the turbulence was tossing us around hard against our safety belts. If that wasn't Hell, then it was a pretty good imitation. The long minutes passed and I levelled out at 35 degrees above zero, because I had no altimeter setting.' The extreme action worked. 'The ice started to slide off the wings in sheets and the engines smoothed out. The turbulence was still with us but I'd saved the Cat. I checked my watch. The whole terrifying episode had taken just twenty minutes.'[82]

The troubles had not ended. They had no idea of the wind speed or direction, crucial for navigation by dead reckoning. After carefully descending to about 100 feet, just below the clouds, McVicar set the automatic pilot, left Baker in the pilot's seat to help Wilson manhandle the controls in an emergency, and went aft to work with James on a drift reading. With great difficulty because of the poor visibility and high seas, after two failed attempts, they succeeded with the last flame float. Estimating the wind at 65 knots from 300 degrees, McVicar set course to use it by keeping the centre of the front to their left. The worst was over, though his navigating skills would still be tested because the unserviceable direction-finding loop prevented hearing a beacon from Ireland.[83]

Through the early morning hours McVicar slowly altered course around the low and headed for Scotland. The rain eased about dawn and the ceiling lifted. Shortly after a breakfast of sandwiches and coffee, they spotted land. McVicar brags: 'We were off Galway Bay right where we should be. James figured we'd flown 2,700 miles as of 0840Z, which made our ground speed 138 knots. This meant our elapsed time would be 20.5 hours, close to the record held by Bob Perlick of 19 hours and 50 minutes.' He steered around the north of Ireland, 'keeping well clear of a huge westbound convoy and those trigger-happy gunners,' past Ailsa Craig, and into Greenock. The other two Bermuda deliveries that day made it in 25 hours and 27 hours 30 minutes.[84]

After an evening of celebration with the international crowd in the Orangefield Bar, it was back to reality and to Montreal in the bomb-bay of Liberator AL528. Two days following McVicar's arrival in Montreal, 'a voice from Crew Assignments, loaded with the usual urgency, ordered me to report to the Bonaventure station. There I would board the Washingtonian. Departure 9.15 p.m. sharp. Ferry Command had reserved a whole Pullman sleeper just for the urgently needed Cat crews. At Washington D.C. the car would be tacked on to the Norfolk Southern Railroad express for delivery to Elizabeth City.' He thought he saw through this: 'By so doing they would leave more seats available on the airlines during the big holiday rush. And, more importantly, they'd be able to keep an eye on their precious flight crews.'[85]

On this trip, McVicar and three other captains escaped Elizabeth City just before a severe storm struck the Carolinas. They took off in six-foot waves, despite Consolidated's warning that three feet was the maximum for the Catalina. All four made the six-hour flight to Bermuda, only to sit there waiting for good weather. Several, including McVicar on two occasions when Bermuda control recalled him, set out only to turn back after several hours. In an ornery mood, McVicar claims that he and Bill Baker then took a hacksaw and removed the radar antennae from their Catalina in order to improve the speed and range. Following all the frustrating delays, 'for the first time in weeks I felt I'd done something constructive.'[86]

Finally, on 5 February 1943, the forecaster presented a favourable map at the morning briefing. Determined, after five weeks away from Montreal, to ignore any recall message, eight crews made the crossing, the biggest day yet for Bermuda deliveries. About four hours from the end of his flight, McVicar's radio operator received a bearing, ostensibly from Prestwick, to 'alter course almost 30 degrees to starboard.'[87] He ignored it as a false bearing from the Germans at Brest, and set down on the Clyde without further incident. Soon the Return Ferry Service had him back in Montreal to receive word that he was being taken off Catalina deliveries. He moved back to landplanes, chiefly Liberators and Fortresses. Ferry Command's permanent aircrew frequently changed aircraft types and routes, rarely having a chance to get bored with their jobs.

The Bermuda operation survived without McVicar. By the end of the war, Ferry Command had delivered more than 500 flying boats, mostly Catalinas and primarily through Bermuda, losing only a handful.[88] The best-known loss killed the noted Canadian pilot C.A. 'Duke' Schiller. On 13 March 1943 his Catalina developed engine trouble shortly after leaving Bermuda and came down heavily on the water.[89] Captain Ed Stafford and his crew were interned on 7 April 1943, after ending up in occupied France.[90] Most of the planes made it safely across and went to Coastal Command, where they contributed immensely to the campaign against the U-boat.

6

The Northern Routes

The shortcomings of Gander as the jumping-off point for transatlantic ferry flights quickly became apparent to many involved in the exercise. The airport, used by operational anti-submarine squadrons as well as Ferry Command, could not handle the massive air traffic anticipated when North American factories reached their peak production. And the long hop to the British Isles meant that only long-range aircraft could make the flight. Officials looked at Greenland and Iceland and saw a solution to both problems. Even before the war, some aviators had recognized the potential of these northern islands as stepping stones for a relatively easy flight across the North Atlantic. As early as 1930 the Atlantic had been bridged from Europe to North America in stages via the Faeroe Islands, Iceland, Greenland, and Labrador. It has been pointed out that the accomplishment of crossing by this route, 'while not extraordinary, indicated in its very ordinariness the ease of flying from the United States to England over a northern route that included a brief stopover in Greenland.'[1]

For a variety of reasons, the whole question of Greenland, officially owned by Denmark, took on some urgency following the successful Nazi blitzkrieg in the spring of 1940. The UK government wanted to take advantage of Greenland's strategic position and, by the same token, prevent the enemy from using it as a base for weather stations, and perhaps harbours, for its fleet of submarines. The United States had its own interest in Greenland, both as an outpost in the framework of continental defence and as a source of cryolite, a crucial component in the aluminum that was essential in the manufacture of modern aircraft. It soon became clear that the Americans would not only resist any attempt by Germany to take possession of Greenland, but would also not welcome the intrusion of any other European power, however friendly it might be. The British government felt that swift action on Canada's part, on the pretext of safeguarding Greenland and securing the cryolite mine at Ivigtut, might be overlooked in Washington. Urged on by the Aluminum Company of Canada as well as by the British, and persuaded that its intervention was justified, but still uncertain as to how far it should go, the Canadian government raised a small occupation force. Before taking the next crucial step, the Canadians consulted Washington. Prime Minister King cancelled the invasion plan when he learned that the United States strongly opposed the idea.[2]

British and Canadian officials continued to discuss the whole question, in particular the giant island's potential as a location for airfields. Indeed, they appear to have considered the feasibility of utilizing the Greenland–Iceland route even before the delivery scheme had proved workable. In the summer of 1940 the problem of establishing landing fields on the Greenland ice cap was the focus of discussions between the United Kingdom and Canada and, at the request of the British government, between Canada and the United States. A proposal to have the RCAF carry out a search for suitable airfield sites met with a request to postpone the Canadian plan until a similar survey had been completed by the Americans.[3] After this cool reception, the question lay dormant until early in December when, as we have seen, Air Vice-Marshal J.C. Slessor wrote to his chief of the air staff about the 'enormous' scale of aircraft production planned in the United States and urged, among other things, that 'the organization of the Greenland–Iceland route be tackled vigorously and soon.'[4]

The Empire Air Training Scheme Committee, responsible for overseeing all aspects of training for the RAF, took up the subject. The idea had its attractions. Some aviation experts recognized that the weather, while cold, was better for flying than the ubiquitous fog off Newfoundland. The relatively short distances between potential bases, all less than a thousand miles apart, would enable aircraft of medium range, such as Bostons, Venturas, and Hudsons, to be flown to the United Kingdom in easy stages, without the installation of overload fuel tanks. The air member for training also 'pointed out the value of any aerodrome facilities which could be provided in Greenland as emergency landing grounds for pilots experiencing difficulty on the Atlantic crossing by the Great Circle course.' His colleagues noted that the route would require wireless and meteorological facilities, along with the airfields.[5] All were available in Iceland, which the British had occupied following the Ger-

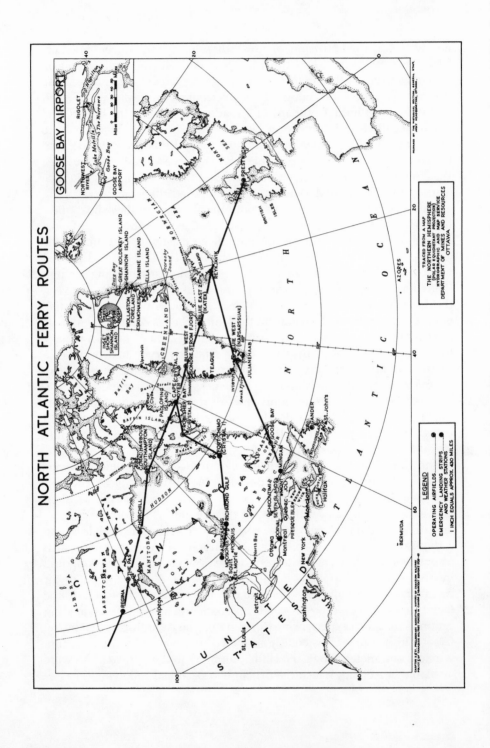

NORTH ATLANTIC FERRY ROUTES

man conquest of Denmark in April 1940. However, Greenland had no airports, apart from seaplane harbours, and obtaining suitable facilities there presented diplomatic problems as well as engineering difficulties.

Despite a certain lack of enthusiasm within the Air Ministry, Greenland was on the agenda when J.L. Ralston, Canadian minister of national defence, visited London in December 1940. On 16 December the British government asked Canada to undertake an expedition to Greenland to establish air bases, wireless units, and weather stations. On 7 January 1941, before any action had been taken, Air Ministry officials held talks with C.D. Howe and Ralston, pointing out that the utmost dispatch was necessary. Although the Canadian ministers promised to press the urgency of the problem on return to Ottawa, Howe felt that any such move on the part of Canada would encounter only opposition from the local inhabitants and the Danish representatives, not to mention the Americans.[6]

Later in the month the Canadians made a fresh approach to the United States urging that an air base be constructed by Canada, by the United States, or else by Greenland with American assistance. The Canadian government had no strong desire to develop airfields in Greenland. It was the British who saw an advantage in keeping the northern route in Commonwealth hands. The United States, however, long interested in a route to Europe via Labrador, Greenland, and Iceland, was working on its own plans for the development of a new network of northern airways. Indeed, it was preparing to.take Greenland under its protectorship through diplomatic means. In the American view, Canada's belligerent status made the dominion unacceptable as a partner in the project. Not surprisingly, it decided, with the consent of the Danish minister in Washington, to undertake the construction of the airfields on its own. In April this arrangement was written into an agreement by which the American government accepted responsibility for the defence of the Greenland.[7]

In fact, there was considerable cooperation between all the countries concerned, whatever their official status. The search for airbase sites in Greenland began in earnest in the spring of 1941 under the direction of the US Army Air Corps' Captain Elliott Roosevelt, the president's son. ATFERO's Don Bennett played a small but important role in the program, making the first aerial reconnaissance in a Liberator earmarked for the Return Ferry Service. He left Gander early on 22 April, accompanied by a crew of four, including a member of the RCAF, with the aircraft 'full of photographic apparatus and a great deal of film.'[8] By prearrangement, a small Danish vessel put out along the coast of Greenland to follow the movements of the aircraft, which was to drop messages giving the results of the search; this procedure, Bennett commented dryly, was 'to ensure that any information we ... obtained would not be lost in the unhappy event of our not returning to base.'[9] Erratic swinging of the compass complicated navigation, but some potential sites were picked out in the south near Julianehaab. These were marked on a large-scale chart, which was then placed in a water-tight container and dropped near the ship. After the survey, which lasted about nine hours, Bennett flew directly to Montreal, where photographs taken during the flight were developed and passed on to the Americans. The entire trip lasted about fifteen hours.[10]

As the survey flight demonstrated, the development of this northern route was facilitated by cooperation at different levels among Canada, Britain, and the United States. Progress, however, was not always smooth, and the pace was seldom fast enough for the Americans, who soon took the initiative almost completely into their own hands. Believing that ATFERO would be unable to handle all the American aircraft that would become available to the RAF as a result of the Lend-Lease Act and plans for greatly increased production, President Roosevelt felt that the Army Air Corps should assume responsibility for the entire North Atlantic ferry operation. General 'Hap' Arnold, commander of the Air Corps, while committing himself only to move aircraft to delivery points in Canada, was not totally opposed to the larger scheme that the president had in mind. Colonel Robert Olds, commander of the USAAC's new Air Ferrying Command, looked forward to taking the aircraft all the way to Britain. American planning thus proceeded on the assumption that eventually they would take over all transatlantic ferrying, 'lock, stock and barrel.'[11] They were soon working on a scheme of grandiose proportions, far beyond anything the British or Canadians had ever dreamed of, envisaging the construction of a vast network of northern airways, with new aerodromes projected in Labrador, northern Quebec, and the Northwest Territories, as well as in Greenland and Iceland. Using these routes, in addition to those through Gander and Bermuda, they intended to deliver all aircraft required by the RAF.[12]

While the British were somewhat taken aback by the scope of American plans for new airways, they continued to welcome this cooperation. In the spring of 1941, before the routes had been planned in detail, Air Chief Marshal Sir Hugh Dowding (of Battle of Britain fame), acting as a special emissary of Lord Beaverbrook, arrived in Ottawa with General

Carl Spaatz, assistant chief of the US Army Air Corps, to discuss American plans for ferrying aircraft via Greenland. A chain of airfields would be needed along the mainland of North America. Canada was asked to assist with a search in the Hamilton River area of Labrador for a site for an airfield to connect with Greenland. This meeting was followed by a visit from Captain Roosevelt, who expanded further on the surveys he proposed to make on the Labrador coast and Baffin Island.[13]

After examining its own files on Labrador and conferring with bush pilots and foresters familiar with the territory, the RCAF confirmed that the region around Northwest River, the location of the Grenfell Mission and a Hudson Bay post, was the area most likely to contain good airfield sites. In May, Eric Fry, a surveyor with the Dominion Topographic Survey who had worked with the RCAF on aerial surveys in the prewar years, was sent to Labrador.[14] On 17 June, after almost a month in the Labrador wilderness, Fry, while he was proceeding alone on foot, came upon an extensive sandy plateau along the shore of Goose Bay on Hamilton River not far from the Northwest Settlement. He saw at once that it was an ideal location for an airport. It needed little levelling, had good drainage, and was easily accessible from tide water. From local inhabitants he learned that it was known as Blake's Berry Patch, but he referred to it in his notes as Goose Bay. On 2 July, as Fry was completing his preliminary survey, he encountered a party of American surveyors sent out by Captain Roosevelt. They had made an extensive aerial reconnaissance of the Labrador coast without finding any suitable locations, but on comparing notes they agreed that the site Fry had chosen was ideal. On 14 July Air Commodore A.E. Godfrey, air officer commanding Eastern Air Command, flew in to examine the site and was likewise impressed.[15]

At the end of June, Chubby Power, the minister of national defence for air, and his chief of the air staff, Air Marshal Lloyd Breadner, had left on an air mission to the United Kingdom to discuss various matters relating to the BCATP. Before leaving Canada they had learned of Fry's discovery, but apparently were not aware of its full significance until Breadner received a telegram from Air Force Headquarters in Ottawa informing him that the Americans were pressing for the immediate construction of an airfield at Goose Bay. A hurried conference with Air Ministry officials on 9 July,[16] and another meeting the next day,[17] revealed that the British, while anxious for the development of airfields in Greenland linking up with Iceland and Gander, held a sceptical view of the possibilities of a route through Labrador and the Northwest

Territories, where climatic conditions would make construction extremely expensive in terms of manpower, material, and money. The cost of constructing an airport at Goose Bay was estimated at $20 million, and the Canadians were not sure what other commitments they would be asked to undertake. No consensus was reached at the two meetings, but Power and Breadner were left with misgivings about the feasibility of the Labrador route and the need for an airport at Goose Bay, at least 'within any reasonable period of time.'[18]

In the meantime, however, American pressure had begun to mount. On 17 July Arnold told Air Marshal Arthur Harris, best known as air officer commanding-in-chief Bomber Command but from June 1941 to February 1942 head of the RAF delegation in Washington, that he would like the Canadians to build an airfield at Goose Bay before the end of the summer. Harris felt compelled to comply with Arnold's request for 'vigorous support' and informed the Canadian air attaché, Air Vice-Marshal W.R. Kenny, that 'from the Air Ministry's point of view, such an aerodrome was a definite and urgent Air Staff requirement.'[19] Kenny was asked to take the matter up with Ottawa and to press for a favourable decision. Breadner, back in Canada after the discussions at the Air Ministry, was still apprehensive of being dragged into the larger American scheme of developing a network of bases in Labrador and the Northwest Territories, and was in no hurry to fall in with Arnold's proposal regarding Goose Bay. In any case, he felt that construction at such a northerly point could not begin so late in the summer, with the end of the navigation season only two or three months away, and Arnold was so informed.[20]

By this time, Air Chief Marshal Sir Frederick Bowhill, as well as Harris, had been brought around to the American point of view. The Canadians felt pressure from all sides, but especially from the south. On learning that Canada questioned the need for prompt action, the US government offered its assistance in order to expedite construction. At the same time it let it be known that, if necessary, Washington was prepared to undertake the entire project. Faced with this unpalatable alternative, the Canadian government had little choice but to comply with American wishes. On 29 July, at a meeting of the Canada–US Permanent Joint Board on Defence, the Canadian members concurred in a unanimous recommendation, 'That the Canadian Government undertake the construction of an air base in the vicinity of Northwest River, Labrador ... *as quickly as possible.*'[21] With the United States urging Canada 'to establish the aerodrome this summer to ensure uninterrupted ferrying of aircraft to the United Kingdom,' the Cabinet War Committee met on 13 August and 'approved, in principle, the granting of authority for the acquisition of property and the completion of the development of the air base at Northwest River, Labrador.'[22]

The Canadians now swung into action. An advanced party of surveyors and engineers were flown to the site by amphibian aircraft in August and work commenced under the supervision of the Department of Transport, responsible for the construction of all Canadian military airports according to plans and specifications laid down by the RCAF. In September the first ships, accompanied by an icebreaker, arrived carrying construction crews, supplies, and machinery of all kinds. Local sources cautioned that the bay froze solid by mid-November or possibly earlier, leaving a tight deadline for shipping in enough material to continue the project through the winter. Work went on by day and by night, under floodlights, and when the last boat left behind an icebreaker in early December, the airport had begun to take shape. Two blocks of offices and quarters and a large machine-shop had been built; a power-house, which later burned down, was nearing completion; and radio range towers had been erected, roads laid out, and the three runways graded and compacted with snow. The first landplane set down on 9 December. Thereafter visiting aircraft – Canadian, British, and American – arrived frequently. The station diary recorded: 'The drawl of Texans remarking on how cold it was ... was a foretaste of the future.'[23] One historian has, quite rightly, called the building of a major airbase in the northern wilderness in such a short time period 'one of Canada's remarkable wartime engineering feats.'[24]

The search for an airport site in Labrador and the quick construction that followed had proceeded with the informal permission of the Newfoundland government. All parties had agreed that formal documents could be signed at everyone's convenience. This turned out to be easier said than done. The Goose Bay lease negotiations between officials of Britain, Canada, and Newfoundland dragged on and on amid much acrimony. Finally, after three years of disagreements over a number of matters, not the least of which involved postwar rights to civil and military use of the airfield, a ninety-nine-year lease was signed on 10 October 1944. It gave Canada title to 120 square miles and granted wartime landing rights to aircraft of the three countries, as well as those of the United States. Civil and military use of the facilities would be negotiated following the war. Unlike the leases for US bases, it stipulated that the laws of Newfoundland would apply 'throughout the Air Base and to all persons therein or thereon.'[25]

At the same time as work had been progressing at Goose Bay, American military and civilian construction workers had been building landing fields in Greenland. Two sites had been chosen, one at Narsarssuak, known better by its codename, Bluie West 1 (BW-1), near the southern tip of Greenland, and Bluie West 8 at the head of Søndre Strømfjord, almost 500 miles farther north on the west coast. Another facility was developed, Bluie East 2, near Angmagssalik on the east coast. Construction of the airfield at Narsarssuak more or less paralleled that of Goose Bay. By the end of the year it was usable, though not fully developed until well into 1942. With British facilities in Iceland overcrowded, the Americans also started work on bases in the Keflavik area. The US Army Air Forces, as the Air Corps had been renamed in June, established base commands in Greenland and Iceland in September, leaving little doubt about the American commitment to transatlantic ferrying. The Japanese attack on Pearl Harbor on 7 December 1941 and the resulting declarations of war a few days later made it clear to all concerned that the United States would be heavily involved in the build-up of air forces in Britain.[26]

The essential spans of the air bridge were now in place. With airfields already available in Iceland, at Reykjavik and at Kaldaharnes, the construction of Goose Bay and Bluie West 1 bridged the gaps in what was generally known as the northern route. The Danes in Greenland provided meteorological services (until taken over by the USAAF) to complement those of the Canadians and the British at their bases. And the Americans helped with information from new weather stations they established in the Arctic (with Canada's permission), Crystal 1 at Fort Chimo in northern Quebec, Crystal 2 at the head of Frobisher Bay, and Crystal 3 at Padloping Island on Davis Strait, directly across from Greenland.[27] The relatively short distances between the airfields left little doubt about the feasibility of the route for ferrying shorter-range aircraft. 'BW-1, 495 statute miles from BW-8, lies roughly midway between Goose Bay and Reykjavik, Iceland, 777 miles from Goose Bay and 770 from Reykjavik. Goose Bay is 949 miles from BW-8, and BW-8 is 845 miles from Reykjavik. The distance from Reykjavik to Stornoway [in the Outer Hebrides] is 659 miles, to Prestwick, 844 miles.'[28]

Montreal remained the principal western terminus for the routes through Gander and Goose Bay, continuing to serve as the main transfer point where USAAF crews turned the aircraft over to RAF Ferry

Command. However, these activities no longer took place at St Hubert airport. Right from the start of the war, certainly from the advent of the CP Air Services Department, St Hubert had been hard pressed to cope with the heavy, and sometimes conflicting, demands of military and civilian flying. To overcome these problems, the RCAF agreed to give up its claim to a new airfield being built at Dorval just west of the city. It had been earmarked for use by the BCATP as a home for an air observer school and a wireless school. After the war the authorities planned to make it Montreal's civil airport. It looked ideal for ferrying, so on 1 September 1941 the command moved there. The BCATP schools went elsewhere. As it developed, the new base did indeed prove ideal for its wartime tenants, becoming the western hub of transatlantic ferrying and enhancing Montreal's growing reputation in the world of aviation. It housed Ferry Command's weather forecasting centre, extensive maintenance facilities, and a ferry training school. The operations centre kept in constant radio communication with Prestwick, the main eastern terminus, and all intermediate points on the various routes. A number of civil operations also transferred from St Hubert to Dorval, including Trans-Canada Air Lines, Canadian Colonial Airways, Northeast Airlines (formerly Boston Main Airways), and Québec Airways, but Ferry Command was the largest user. It built three of the original six hangars, operated the emergency services, and looked after its own security. Under the overall management of the Department of Transport, the new airport quickly became a very bustling place.[29]

As the job of delivering new aircraft grew, Dorval would sometimes get so busy that Ferry Command had to make arrangements to handle overflows. Once again, the Americans came to the rescue. On Friday, 13 March 1942, Bowhill led a delegation to the new USAAF Ferrying Command base at Presque Isle, Maine. As a result of this visit and the accompanying discussions, arrangements were made for the RAF to station a detachment at Presque Isle and later at Houlton, in the same state. A memorandum composed by Taffy Powell, now a group captain and Bowhill's senior air staff officer, illustrates the extent to which RAF and USAAF ferry operations were becoming intertwined. The Americans would provide accommodation for more than two dozen members of the Ferry Command detachment, as well as for up to fifty transient aircrew. At first 'two twin-engine aircraft a day' could be expected to use the Maine base. However, 'when the organization there is functioning smoothly we will increase the delivery rate through Presque Isle to five per day.' Ferry Command personnel would check a newly arrived aircraft 'for deficiencies and put on any equipment that is lacking.' After testing the plane and swinging the compass, they would hand it over to the USAAF maintenance staff at the base for further work. A Ferry Command inspector would then give the aircraft a final check and approve it for departure to the United Kingdom. The cooperation extended to meteorology, with weather forecasts provided over teletype from Dorval, and to cypher arrangements. Because the Americans agreed 'to provide sufficient staff, R.A.F.F.C. will not send any of their own personnel to do this [cypher] work.'[30] Similar arrangements were common wherever Ferry Command shared space with the Americans, who must therefore share much of the credit for the accomplishments of the enterprise.

With the opening of air bases in Labrador and Greenland and with arrangements ready for handling overflow, everything was in place for the second route across the North Atlantic, one suitable for aircraft of medium range. In addition, Goose Bay quickly assumed its own independent importance as a second jumping-off point for direct flights, to relieve congestion at Gander. Even these advances, however, did not satisfy the Americans. They pushed ahead with a plan for a chain of airfields a few hundred miles apart across the northern regions of Canada, to provide an easy route for ferrying short-range single-engine fighters from North American factories to the British Isles. To test the concept, to locate potential landing sites, and to check on the Crystal weather stations, the United States turned to Ferry Command. The job was entrusted to Louis Bisson, a well-known Canadian bush pilot.[31]

To accompany him on what was to be an expedition of about 2000 miles into the Canadian Arctic, Bisson chose Don McVicar, a recent arrival at Ferry Command. They had met when Bisson was flying down the Mackenzie River out of Edmonton, and they had a great deal of mutual respect. McVicar claims that he gave up a chance to ferry a Mitchell to Java to join this Arctic exploration flight. The maintenance engineer would be the much-respected Bill Baker, and the radio operator the experienced Lloyd Wheeler. Joining the expedition was Captain C.J. Hubbard of the USN, responsible for the Crystal weather stations. They left Montreal on 23 February 1942 in two ski-equipped Noorduyn Norseman aircraft borrowed from the RCAF, one piloted by Bisson, accompanied by Wheeler and Hubbard, and the other by McVicar, with Baker as his crewman. Because Hubbard also wanted to inspect weather stations in Greenland, a Hudson was added to the expedition. It was flown by Captain George Evans of St Louis, Missouri, with radio operator Gerry Pollock and flight engineer Gail Sweeney – all carefully chosen by Bisson.[32]

It was a hazardous, month-long adventure. The Hudson, which flew on ahead to Goose Bay and then to Greenland, experienced little difficulty. However, each of the Norseman crews encountered some of the worst hazards of winter flying in the Arctic. They ran into blizzards and had to make forced landings. They experienced radio blackouts and at times were completely lost. Their navigation instruments failed them and it was only through determination, skill, and perhaps a little luck that they managed to locate the three isolated weather stations. Nonetheless, all concerned considered the trip a success, even though one Norseman was wrecked. The main objective of locating the Crystal sites, ascertaining their problems, and integrating their weather reports with the North Atlantic network had been achieved. The expedition pinpointed suitable sites for landing strips, confirming the Americans in their belief that single-engine aircraft could be ferried over such a route.[33]

Spurred by the success of the exploration flight, the Americans pushed ahead with their grandiose plans, known collectively as the Crimson Project but generally referred to as the Crimson Route or the North East Staging Route. In reality, the plans involved not one route but three: an eastern route from Presque Isle or Montreal, staging through Chicoutimi or Mont Joli, Sept Isles (on the lower St Lawrence) and Goose Bay; a western route from San Francisco through Regina to The Pas and Fort Churchill in northern Manitoba, Southampton Island, and Baffin Island; and a central route from Detroit to North Bay, Kapuskasing, and Moosonee in northern Ontario, Richmond Gulf (on the eastern shore of Hudson Bay), Fort Chimo in northern Quebec, and Baffin Island, where it would link up with the western route. All routes would join in Greenland and Iceland.[34]

In May 1942 the United States presented a detailed outline of the Crimson proposals to the Permanent Joint Board on Defence. Mayor Fiorello LaGuardia of New York, chairman of the US section of the board, found the vast and imaginative scheme heady and exciting. However, he feared that his Canadian colleagues would reject the proposal. He wrote to President Roosevelt at the end of May:

I have just returned from Quebec where the Permanent Joint Board on Defense held its monthly meeting. I consider this meeting the most important we have had. The question of the new plans for Ferry Command came up. The plan itself challenges imagination. It is so gigantic and dramatic. It took our Canadian colleagues by surprise and frankly they have not yet recovered. We recessed until Monday and we must put it through on that day as every day now is precious.

We may encounter the usual difficulties because of pride and the little brother attitude with which you are familiar.[35]

Charles Stacey, the respected historian of Canadian defence policy, has observed: 'There was no impasse, but the later history of the scheme did a good deal to justify the little brother's cautious approach.'[36]

Asked for an opinion by their political masters, the Canadian chiefs of staff reported that 'the routes are practicable, but ... the problems of construction and transportation are very great.'[37] In spite of the misgivings reflected in this assessment and shared by the Air Ministry, the Canadians were carried along with the importance President Roosevelt attached to the Crimson Project. They felt they had no option but to support the 26th recommendation of the PJBD, calling on the Canadian government to construct 'or authorize the United States to construct these fields and inform the United States what, if any, Canada will construct.'[38] The wording reflects the problems that the scheme presented to Canada. On the one hand the government was concerned about the precedents that might be established if the Americans built and operated airfields on Canadian territory. On the other it had no desire to be drawn into such an enormous and costly undertaking, especially when unconvinced of the route's necessity or practicability. In the end Canada agreed to construct the base at The Pas, Manitoba, the most interior of the isolated sites. All the others were to be developed by the Americans, who also assumed responsibility for local defence, except at Fort Churchill where the Canadian Army already had a protective garrison.[39]

The Crimson Project was one of the largest military enterprises undertaken in Canada by the US government, costing roughly $39,500,000 and comparable to the Alaska Highway and the Canol project in the northwest. Ironically, as the work proceeded, the American combined chiefs of staff began to question the need for such a vast network of airways which, as the Canadians and the British had predicted, demanded an enormous expenditure of labour and material.[40] Many of these valuable and limited resources were needed for the military build-up preparing for the upcoming invasions of North Africa and Europe. Moreover, in the late spring of 1943 the crisis in transatlantic shipping had passed. Enemy submarines had been driven out of the North Atlantic, and new ships, together with improved techniques in loading and transporting fighter aircraft, made it simpler and less costly to send them by sea than to complete the Crimson Routes.

Interest in the northern bases gradually waned. Work already begun was continued, and the bases at Southampton Island and Frobisher Bay were completed but saw little use. Only a few bombers and reconnaissance aircraft passed through en route to the United Kingdom. Most of the planes flying into and out of these places were in support of supply operations, meteorological surveys, and photographic missions, of importance in the development of the Canadian north but of no real significance to military operations overseas. On 1 August 1944 Prime Minister King tabled an exchange of letters between Canada and the United States, and announced in the House of Commons that provision had been made for the northern bases to be transferred to Canadian control. The Americans were reimbursed more than $31 million for the cost of those facilities that were of a permanent nature, and the books were closed on the North East Staging Route.[41]

If the Americans had been overzealous in planning the Crimson Project, their insistence on prompt action in developing Goose Bay was fully vindicated by subsequent events. When the United States entered the war in December 1941, a good start had been made on the air base and, in line with the strategy of directing the main Allied effort against Germany, there was a rush to complete it as quickly as possible. Despite its unfinished state, there had been a steady stream of air traffic throughout the winter, but no planes destined for Britain. Who better to prove the new route than the men who had just spent more than four weeks flying around the eastern segment of the proposed Crimson Route? The day after McVicar arrived back in Montreal from his northern adventure he was summoned to Powell's office, along with Bisson and Evans. No sooner had they received congratulations from Powell and Bowhill than they were detailed to deliver the first aircraft via the Goose Bay, Greenland, Iceland route. 'We were stunned. This far northern route had not yet been scouted, let alone used to deliver aircraft. We had heard there was a bad jam-up at Gander because the usual westerly winds had died off, so we realized if we opened up an alternate delivery route it would be of immense value to the war effort.'[42]

Bisson was placed in charge of the first flight, in a Liberator, with McVicar and Evans accompanying him in Canso amphibians, the Canadian-built version of the Catalina. The idea was to have Bisson follow as a mother ship and fly the others back to Montreal as soon as possible after reaching Prestwick. McVicar recalls Powell saying, 'The quicker the round trip is made, the more we will impress the powers that be in Washington and London.'[43] Ever confident in his own abilities, McVicar talked his boss into letting him do his own navigating. To compensate, Powell assigned him two Czechoslovak fighter pilots, Sergeants Hubacek and Baillik, as co-pilots. Bill Baker and Eric Rush joined as flight engineer and radio officer respectively.[44]

Although the movement of aircraft in and out of Goose Bay was an almost daily occurrence, the arrival of Bisson, McVicar and Evans on 5 April with word that they were bound for Prestwick, in the words of the station diarist, 'caused a good deal of commotion.'[45] With the building program still unfinished, the transients spent the night in the construction company's bunkhouse. McVicar says they decided that the next leg should be to BW-8. 'Evans didn't like the winding, narrow approach up the fjord to BW-1, and Bisson and I agreed.' They wanted to get away the next night, aiming for a noonhour arrival in Greenland, after any ground fog would have been burned off. However, there would be no early departure: 'Dorval advised a twenty-four hour delay as they had got a rare weather report from the Greenland base.'[46]

During the layover McVicar confides that he and Baker helped themselves to a vitally needed part from a USN Catalina parked on the tarmac:

The next morning [6 April] Bill and I did a run-up to make sure everything was working. Bad news, one of our two voltage-regulators, a small unit consisting of relays and coils, was kaput. Now we were stuck. There was no way I would leave with just one generator charging. If it quit we could quickly run the ship's batteries flat. Bill looked at the defective unit and admitted he didn't have the facilities to repair it. It would probably take Dorval several days to send another unit. We looked over at a US Navy Cat that had wandered into Goose on some sort of sight-seeing trip for the brass. It contained two voltage-regulators. It wasn't worth the effort of asking for one of theirs – we knew the answer. Northbound, two were necessary, but southbound they could get by on one. We took our unserviceable unit and made a quick trip to the electrical panel of the ship with the big white star on its side. A deft flick of a screwdriver, then back to 533 [their own Canso], and soon we had two serviceable generators. As we shook hands Baker and I swore each other to eternal secrecy. Partners in Crime.[47]

There is no way of confirming the veracity of this tale. It is typical, however, of stories related by Ferry Command veterans to demonstrate their initiative.

That afternoon the proving flight received a favourable weather forecast, and the next day all three aircraft left for BW-8. The flight was without incident, except for a brief fright immediately after takeoff when one of McVicar's co-pilots unknowingly locked the undercarriage in the down position, ruining the climbing capability of the fully loaded Canso. The captain spotted the problem just in time to avoid running into a hill. Reporting that he 'felt like smashing him in the chops,' McVicar looked at the culprit. 'He was blissfully unaware of what he'd just put me through. I decided to hold my temper. After all he'd tried to do his best and soon he would be in a Hurricane or a Spitfire, intent on killing Germans. His life expectancy could probably be measured in weeks. But I made sure that on future take-offs he sat beside me with his arms folded.'[48]

With too much cloud cover for star shots, they navigated by dead reckoning. Flying across the Davis Strait they were impressed and relieved when the Greenland ice-cap appeared on the horizon. 'For such an inhospitable mass, a two-mile thick ice cube, it looked very welcome.' The problem was finding BW-8. Rush had not been able to raise it by radio, a not uncommon problem in the north. 'Over the indented coast,' writes McVicar, 'I tried to pinpoint our position. Not an easy job. All fjords look alike. Then I spotted what I at first thought was our own shadow proceeding up the fjord I'd identified as Sondrestrom. I looked again. It wasn't our shadow. It was the other Canso. I followed him onto the long gravel runway. We had just parked and shut down when the Lib appeared and scrunched down in a cloud of flying dust and gravel.' Their arrival was a complete surprise to the BW-8 staff, who had received no prior warning.[49]

Learning from the USAAF commander, the famous Norwegian pilot, Bernt Balchen, that his station was not yet directly connected by radio with Iceland, Bisson, Evans, and McVicar opted for a night departure 'so we could crawl into Iceland at high noon.'[50] The Canso crews experienced an eventful flight. McVicar lost his heating, causing the crew to put up with temperatures in the minus 40 degree range and freezing up the glass on the navigator's hatch. When he opened it McVicar could not take a star shot with fingers paralyzed from the cold and eyes running with frosty tears. A spectacular display of aurora borealis would have made the exercise extremely difficult, anyway. He continued by dead reckoning without any idea of the wind factor. Then a small fire in the electrical system took out all power in the aircraft. 'We had no radio, were almost frozen, were unsure of our position and were very frightened.'[51] McVicar let down to 300 and then to 100 feet over the Denmark Strait and peered anxiously ahead in visibility of a mile and less, aware that, at that height, he ran the risk of flying into a big iceberg. Finally, spotting seagulls and then a fishing trawler, he found Iceland and landed at Reykjavik.

Bisson followed a short time later. But there was no sign of Evans. Everyone worried. The RAF control tower fired rockets to help the missing Canso find the field, but still it did not appear. McVicar knew his American cohort was an excellent pilot, but he worried about his lack of experience away from the radio ranges of his native land. Finally, writes the Canadian:

Three hours after I had landed he showed up out of the snow and fog, coming in from the east, of all things. I ran out to greet him. The whole crew were quiet and grim. They had radio failure and Evans had not let down soon enough. His first sight of land was a mountain. Only a violent turn had saved their lives. Then he'd followed the rugged coast all the way round until he'd found Reykjavik. It had been a tough flight for both of us. Evans said if he never saw another Cat for the rest of his life it would be OK with him.[52]

The RAF squadron at Reykjavik lacked spare parts, but the Americans came through once again. By the following morning the maintenance section from the USN PBY squadron had both the Cansos in first-class shape. The final leg was anti-climatic. 'At Prestwick the crews of our three aircraft were given royal treatment. Ferry Command had pulled it off.'[53]

Bisson, McVicar, and Evans realized that their assignment had not ended. Powell wanted them back in Montreal as quickly as possible. This they attempted to do by taking off in the Liberator for BW-8 that night. However, a suspected engine fire forced them back to Prestwick. On their next attempt a day later they decided to refuel at Reykjavik, before stopping for the night at BW-8. This flight plan brought them into Goose Bay less than a week after they had left with the route's first two delivery aircraft. Continuing on to Dorval, with a dozen returning aircrew as passengers in the bomb-bay, they reported back to Powell. He was impressed with the nine-day turnaround since he had last spoken to them. Still wanting to prove the new route, he then had each of these senior captains take a Hudson from Goose Bay to Prestwick. He wanted to convince the authorities that there was a viable alternative to Gander. When that went well, Powell told them each to take a Liberator through Iceland. He really wanted to underline the value of the route. As it turned out, McVicar's Liberator was unserviceable, so he had to deliver another Hudson. Nonetheless, by the time the Return Ferry Service had deposited him back in Montreal, McVicar, Bisson, and Evans had each flown three aircraft across in twenty-seven days. In all, counting the exploration flights in the Norseman, McVicar records that he had devoted seventy-five days to the development of the new northern route, flying almost 200 hours.[54]

The new route had no sooner been proven than it was put to steady use. In May the flow of delivery aircraft through Goose Bay picked up momentum, with a Liberator, two Hudsons, and twenty twin-engine Lockheed Venturas touching down on their way to Prestwick.[55]

Air activity in 1942 at both Goose Bay and Gander climaxed with the movement of the USAAF's Eighth Air Force, as part of the Bolero plan to build up American forces in the United Kingdom. The first formations to go were the 97th Bombardment Group, the 1st Pursuit Group, and the 60th Transport Group. The aircraft, forty-nine B-17s, eighty Lockheed P-38 Lightnings, and fifty-two Douglas C-47s, were marshalled at Presque Isle. It was a daring enterprise, comparable to the first flights from Gander, and the American authorities were prepared to accept losses as high as 10 per cent. They were especially concerned about the twin-engine Lightnings, the first fighters to be flown across the ocean, and decided to dispatch them in groups of four, each led by a B-17.[56]

The leading elements of the Eighth arrived in late June, commemorated in the station diary as

a Big Day for Goose ... Records were established for the number of arrivals and also for the number of aircraft on the station at one time. Transport planes and Fortresses, USAAF, arrived all during the day. In the late afternoon ten small specks were located to the south. Seconds later, a mighty roar and eight American pursuit ships, P-38's with their B-17E attendants, dived and came over the field in perfect formation, a grand sight. The first of the 'Bolero' movement had arrived. Eight units, forty planes, came in forty minutes. A count of aircraft on the field showed ninety-one planes.[57]

The movement continued with little interruption, with the first planes reaching Prestwick on 1 July. There were mishaps. Of the first eighteen B-17s to take off for BW-1, six returned to Goose and three made forced landings on the Greenland coast. In mid-July six P-38s and two B-17s got lost and were forced down on the Greenland ice cap. Unfavourable weather and poor communications, a result of enemy radio interference, were blamed for these incidents. Fortunately, no crews were injured. Three other formations of the Eighth Air Force, the 92nd and 301st Bombardment Groups and the 14th Fighter Group, flew to the United Kingdom in July and August. The highlight of this operation was the non-stop flight from Gander to Prestwick of all four squadrons of the 92nd.[58]

Altogether in 1942, the USAAF flew 920 aircraft across the North Atlantic. A total of 882 reached their destinations safely, twenty-nine were wrecked en route, and nine were lost. Some 700 of these belonged to the Eighth Air Force and were flown by their regular pilots. The remainder were ferried over as replacements by USAAF Ferrying Command. Slightly less than two-thirds, about 650, took the northern route, staging through Goose Bay, the others flying non-stop from Gander.[59] In addition, the crews of Bowhill's command delivered almost 800 aircraft across the North Atlantic for the RAF. The greater number of these passed through Gander, whose log recorded the departure of 668 aircraft, while the diary for Goose Bay showed the dispatch of 123. There was a cost. Ferry Command lost more than twenty planes being delivered via the northern route in 1942, including four each of Venturas and Bostons, a Liberator and a Mitchell. The Hudson was the biggest loser statistically, with four crashing and seven disappearing somewhere over the ocean. One of the Venturas crashed between Gander and Goose Bay, and another crash-landed in Greenland, the crew escaping uninjured before it sank through the ice. Three RCAF airmen had a narrow escape after their Boston went down on the Greenland ice-cap. They were close enough to the coast to be picked up by a US Coast Guard vessel, but they suffered a harrowing adventure before being rescued. Most of the crews were not as lucky. Over seventy airmen – some military, some civilian – were lost on delivery during the second full year of ferrying aircraft across the North Atlantic to the RAF.[60]

By the end of 1942 the transatlantic ferry service was having an unmistakable impact on Allied military operations. Aircraft delivered for the RAF during the year more than equalled the number ferried across the ocean in the previous year and a half. In addition, the movement of complete formations of American fighters and bombers, backed up by replacement aircraft, added still another dimension to the war in the air. Admittedly, it was some time before the Eighth Air Force became really effective, but it is worth noting that twelve of the B-17s of the 97th Bombardment Group, ferried to the United Kingdom in June and early July, went into action on 17 August, against the Rouen-Sotteville marshalling yards, as part of the softening-up campaign before the Canadian assault on Dieppe two days later.[61]

It was in Coastal Command of the RAF that the importance of the transatlantic ferry service to the Allied war effort showed up most vividly. Aircraft delivered by Ferry Command, such as Hudsons, Venturas, Catalinas, Fortresses, and Liberators, made up one-half of Coastal's strength and the most important part of its long-range force.[62] The maritime air arm of the RAF did not always, however, boast a particularly good relationship with Ferry Command. There was some resentment over the need to loan operational crews to Ferry Command to help deliver much-needed aircraft. A good example came in October 1942 when eleven skeleton crews (pilot, navigator, flight engineer, and wireless operator/air gunner) from the RCAF's 422 Squadron returned to Canada to pick up new Catalinas. Led by Wing Commander L.W. Skey, a Canadian member of the RAF, the fifty-five officers and NCOs embarked on the *Queen Mary* on 7 October. The ship docked at Boston a week later and on 15 October the airmen arrived at Dorval for a briefing on their ferry assignment. They were divided into two flights and given one week's and two weeks' leave, respectively. On return from leave each group received training and lectures on ferrying procedures. On 28 October, after a delay of three days owing to unfavourable weather, the first flight of five Catalinas, minus one held back by engine trouble, left Boucherville for Gander Lake. On the 29th they crossed the Atlantic, landing at Lough Erne in Northern Ireland, where the fifth Catalina put down three days later. The second flight, going through the same procedure and following the same course, crossed the North Atlantic about a week later, one aircraft landing at Lough Erne, two at Greenock, and three at Beaumaris in Wales. En route ten of the Catalinas each carried about 1500 pounds of freight, 14,700 pounds in total, and one brought twenty-nine bags of mail for Canadians serving in overseas theatres of war.[63]

The employment of crews from 422 Squadron for ferrying duty provides an insight into the operations of Ferry Command, showing how its activities touched closely on those of other commands. While still facing a shortage of regular ferry pilots, it was able to take advantage of various opportunities to use military crews to keep the flow of aircraft moving. The reception of 422's Catalina crews at Dorval and the ease with which they fitted into the scheme of operations suggest that, by the end of 1942, Ferry Command had put most of its problems of administration and organization behind it.

Yet, inevitably, as old problems disappeared, new ones rose to take their place. As 1942 drew to a close, the ever-increasing number of aeroplanes flying the Atlantic made air traffic control one of the most pressing matters facing Bowhill. It also concerned the Americans. One aspect of the problem is vividly described by General Curtis LeMay. In the summer of 1941, then a major, LeMay was a pilot with the transatlantic transport service inaugurated by the USAAF Ferrying Command, similar in many ways to the British Return Ferry Service. Accustomed to flying over well-established airways with navigation beams to follow and strict traffic regulations controlling the flight of every aircraft from takeoff to landing, LeMay found transatlantic flying a new and challenging experience:

The lovely part about this career was the complete absence of traffic control. There just couldn't *be* any traffic control. It must be remembered that a great percentage of the traffic ... consisted of brand new airplanes which were being ferried over to England ...

Sometimes there would be as many as thirty or forty planes ganged up on the ground back in Newfoundland, waiting for halfway decent weather ... Then ... they would all take-off at five-minute intervals and head for Prestwick ...

We on the passenger ferry, on the other hand, were flying both ways across the Atlantic. These combat aircraft were coming one way only. But there were so many of them ...

There were no special altitudes assigned ... No restriction whatsoever: every pilot chose his own altitude. Thus when we went into a (weather) front we went in absolutely blind.

I suppose we would have had a hard time arranging to hit somebody on *purpose*. Mathematical chances were against ... it, but still there was nothing in our outlined procedure to prevent it.[64]

LeMay's statement requires some qualification. Flight plans were made out in the usual way providing for the aircraft to fly at a specific height, which might vary from one zone of the Atlantic to another depending on winds, temperatures, and cloud formations. Because of the great instability of Atlantic weather and the length of the flight, pilots were given some leeway to alter their courses on encountering unexpected conditions and, unlike pilots on regular airways, might choose to fly above, below, or around a weather front without knowing what action other pilots were taking. Only the neophyte BCATP graduates making their initial transatlantic flight had to hold to a fixed course, and they were not allowed to take off until favourable conditions could be predicted all along the route. Even seasoned pilots were permitted no undue risks with the weather and could not depart without clearance from the meteorological section. When conditions were marginal the final word rested with Patrick McTaggart-Cowan, whose extensive knowledge of North Atlantic weather earned him the nickname 'McFog.'[65]

With the increase in the numbers of American planes crossing the North Atlantic, the USAAF and the RAF adhered to the principle that each was responsible for the safety of its own aircraft and the control of its own operations. In line with this policy, the Americans soon took steps to instal their own transatlantic communications network and meteorological service paralleling those of Ferry Command. In Greenland the British were offered use of the American communication facilities, but the likelihood that in the event of a traffic overload the RAF would suffer led them to establish their own, linked with Iceland, Gander, Goose Bay, and Montreal. The need for cooperation was not overlooked in the development of the two separate systems. In the interest of safety and efficiency it was of vital importance to both air forces to have weather information passed quickly to all aircraft in flight, to know how many planes were en route along the main airways at any given time, to have a means of identifying each other's machines by codes and call letters, and to be in a position to assist any crew in distress.[66]

Bowhill and Major General H.L. George, commander of USAAF Air Transport Command, as Ferrying Command was renamed on 20 June 1942,[67] were very much aware of the overall need for closer liaison in air traffic control. On 16 November 1942, following a number of informal discussions on the subject, the two leaders held a conference in Montreal together with their specialists in meteorology, communications, and aircraft control. The British, who feared that if nothing were done their allies might press for a single system of control based on their own procedures, took the initiative by proposing the establishment of joint control centres at all the main airfields and staging points. In other words, members of Ferry Command of the RAF and Air Transport Command of the USAAF, using their own communications systems and in touch with their own aircraft, would work side by side in the same control rooms. In this way information on all aircraft movements would be immediately available to both users.[68] The acceptance of this solution by the Americans may be taken as a tribute to the diplomacy of Bowhill and the understanding of George.

A board of six officers, three appointed by Bowhill and three by George, was formed to implement the decision. Its immediate assignment was to draw up a plan for the organization of the combined operations rooms. The first meeting of the group ended inauspiciously with the members in complete disagreement. The Ferry Command representatives, Wing Commanders J.G.H. Jeffs and G.C. Cunningham, in charge of flying control and communications, and Patrick McTaggart-Cowan, chief meteorological adviser, could not forget that they had a good deal more experience in transatlantic aviation than their American colleagues. They felt that the USAAF representatives, Colonels I.J. Farman and A.F. Mereweather, and Lieutenant Colonel T.L. Boyd, were pushing, not for a combined control system, but for centralized control based on American standards. Bowhill and George were of one mind on the principle of combined control and, on learning that an impasse had been reached, sent their delegates back to the negotiating table with orders to get on with the job. Bowhill authorized a special entertainment allowance for his representatives and gave instructions that they were to win the confidence of their counterparts through generosity, charm, and good humour. Whether because of this approach or as a result of their official orders from above, or perhaps a combination of both, the six members of the new board were soon working together in an atmosphere of harmony and goodwill that continued throughout the war and provided the basis for a lasting circle of personal friendships.[69]

The board of officers, originally known as the Joint USAAF–RAFFC (Ferry Command) Board and later as the Combined Control Committee, began its work by making a survey of the disposition and organization of existing communications and weather reporting services. On its recommendations, these services were subsequently improved and reorganized to meet the needs of the British and Americans and also those of RCAF squadrons and detachments in the Newfoundland area. Traffic control centres, staffed by British, American, and Canadian personnel, were set up at the various staging points and provided with a set of British and American procedures drawn up by the control committee and published under the title *Joint Control Intelligence No. 1*. As time went on and amendments were made in these procedures, there was a definite trend towards the use of common terminology and uniform practices, though the principle remained that operational control must in all cases be exercised by the owner of the aircraft.[70]

McTaggart-Cowan was the first Canadian to serve on this unique committee and its only civilian member. Although an employee of the Department of Transport, he was closely associated with the ferry service from the time of its inauguration and, at Bowhill's request, remained on loan to Ferry Command to head up its weather forecasting centre. Bowhill had no hesitation in appointing him to the Combined Control Committee, where 'his experience and knowledge were an immense source of strength and guidance to all concerned.'[71]

With the passing of time the work of the Combined Control Committee became supervisory in nature. The six members frequently moved from base to base, with a mandate from Bowhill and George to settle all problems arising from the application of joint control procedures. In most instances they were able to overcome confusion, misunderstanding, and disagreement through persuasion and explanation, but in at least one case felt compelled to recommend the removal of a commanding officer who found it difficult to accept the concept of a jointly controlled operation centre.[72]

The committee also worked on developing a mid-Atlantic route. This received a boost from the Americans when their engineers, in Powell's words, 'literally pumped an airfield at Bermuda out of the sea. They made a land area that had not previously existed.'[73] The new airport, Kindley Field, provided the first leg of a new way for landplanes to cross the Atlantic. The next step was the establishment of facilities in the Portuguese-controlled Azores. Both the British and the Americans were anxious to obtain air bases in this strategically located archipelago. In June 1943, following a protracted series of negotiations with the Portuguese government, hesitant to take any action that might compromise its position of neutrality, the British, by virtue of their traditional friendship with Portugal and an alliance dating from 1380, were accorded landing privileges for military air transport and ferrying. All parties recognized that US military personnel would eventually be admitted, but for the time being the Portuguese government maintained a guarded attitude towards American service personnel, tolerating them only on the understanding that they were on loan to the British. Consequently, when the Combined Control Committee arrived to supervise the installation of a radio range, the three American members were given British insignia to wear on their uniforms, did their best to imitate British speech and mannerisms, and were introduced to Portuguese officials as being on attachment to the RAF.[74]

Slowly but surely a veritable ocean bridge was being put in place. A long tenuous span stretched across the Pacific and now a whole network of spans criss-crossed the North Atlantic. Soon no operational theatre of war would be out of Ferry Command's reach. If any of the men concerned stopped to think about it, they must have been amazed at what had been accomplished in only a couple of years. Flying the previously forbidding North Atlantic now seemed almost routine.

7

The Southern Routes

At the time the Air Ministry had been advising against ferrying aircraft across the North Atlantic in the summer of 1940, it had been frantically working to develop a ferry route across central Africa. Imperial Airways had pioneered this airway in 1936, running a weekly passenger and mail service from Takoradi in the British colony of the Gold Coast (now Ghana) to Khartoum in the Anglo-Egyptian Sudan, where it linked up with the main British Empire air route from South Africa to Cairo.[1] Authorities realized that this route had military potential, but did not fully recognize its value until the fall of France. In June 1940 Britain not only lost an ally; it also lost a secure supply route, via the Mediterranean Sea, to its forces in the Middle East. Henceforth everything they needed, from men to weapons and ammunition, had to be shipped around the southern tip of Africa to Suez – a distance of 13,000 miles. It took reinforcements over two months to reach Egypt this way.[2]

Realizing that the trans-Africa airway offered a shorter alternative, at least for aeroplanes, the RAF dispatched a party of technicians to prepare the basic facilities to off-load up to 120 aircraft a month at Takoradi, reassemble and test them, and ferry them to Egypt. On 20 September 1940 the first delivery flight of one Bristol Blenheim and six Hawker Hurricanes took off from Takoradi and, in a series of hops, made the long, difficult six-day trip to Egypt. They flew via Lagos (on the Nigerian coast), Kano (in north-central Nigeria), Maiduguri (in northeastern Nigeria), Fort Lamy (in Chad province of French Equatorial Africa, from 29 August under Free French control), Geneina (just across the border in western Sudan), to Khartoum, where they turned north to follow the Nile River to their destination. One Hurricane did not make it and the others required considerable servicing when they had completed the 3697-mile delivery flight through incredibly harsh and inhospitable conditions. The loss was slightly above the 10 per cent wastage rate experienced on the route over the course of the war.[3]

Facilities on this route, including hangar space, housing accommodation, maintenance workshops, and communication services, were at first most inadequate. The staging posts were little more than emergency fields laid out on the flat desert sand or in jungle clearings, prepared with the help of African workers. Only a few aircraft could be handled at a time. To avoid getting lost they flew in formation, as the first delivery flights across the North Atlantic had tried to do, with a mother ship as navigation leader and escort. Maps were scarce and meteorological stations few and far between. In December 1940 Air Marshal Arthur Tedder, newly appointed deputy air officer commanding-in-chief Middle East, flew over part of the route on his way to his headquarters in Cairo. He was impressed with the progress that had been made, but awed by the difficulties of navigation. Worst of all, he thought, was the stretch from Fort Lamy to El Fasher in the Sudan: 'Nearly seven hundred miles of sheer nothingness; brown country, streaked with dry water courses and dotted with brush; maps absolutely useless; nothing shown on them for the most part for two hundred miles at a stretch, and where something was shown it was obviously incorrect. I would have hated to do that trip without wireless.'[4] In fact, radio communications often failed, leaving crews completely out of touch with civilization.

While the British were developing the trans-Africa airway for delivering fighter aircraft to the RAF Middle East, Juan Trippe was reluctantly agreeing to a US government proposal for his company to expand its operations in Latin America. President Roosevelt himself, on behalf of the War Department, had asked the head of Pan American Airways to build a series of airports in countries to the south of the United States, as quickly and cheaply as possible, and in secrecy. Initially, Trippe turned Roosevelt down, no doubt stunned by the president's request. He could not understand how such a massive plan could be kept secret. Besides, as a businessman he sought profit, and the proposal for the string of airports for national security purposes precluded that. Finally, under constant pressure from Washington, Trippe gave in and signed a contract with the War Department on 2 November 1940. With the US Treasury paying the bills for the Airport Development Program, Pan American would build twenty-five airports, about 450 miles apart through Central America, the Caribbean, and as far south as Natal near the easternmost point on the coast of Brazil. Given the worsening international situation, in the words of Trippe's biographer, 'the bases were to form a shield, a kind of barrier reef extending from Miami to Brazil, behind which the United States could stand safe.'[5]

Trippe formed a new company, Pan American Airports, and put some of his best men to work on the program. In order to ensure secrecy, everybody had to think that the airports were simply part of Pan American's commercial expansion. 'Each was to seem a single, local project. No one was to know there were twenty-four others, or that the chain of airports was more than five thousand miles long. Each subordinate executive was given sufficient information to enable him to accomplish his own job, – and no more – and he was ordered to keep his own subordinates as much in the dark as possible.'[6] The government wanted the job done quickly, but it was not easy. Negotiations with the host governments were extremely tricky. Trippe insisted on an 'expression of sympathy' from each one. Since they were receiving free airport facilities, he also wanted certain favours – such as the elimination of customs duties on construction machinery and equipment for each of the airports, and no taxes on the land or on fuel and lubricants. He also wanted special arrangements regarding access roads, electricity, navigation beacons, and police protection. With negotiations carried on by the head of Pan Am subsidiaries, no one seems to have suspected that the whole thing was a US government project. The construction crews, mostly local citizens under American supervisors, worked in extremely difficult conditions. Nonetheless, in a matter of months a chain of rudimentary airfields appeared, often in isolated and wild locales.[7]

Meanwhile, the British asked the US government for fifty transport aircraft to facilitate the return of aircrew from Cairo to Takoradi. Just as in the case of the North Atlantic ferry service, it was essential to return ferry crews to the terminus to pick up new aircraft as quickly as possible. The Americans made twenty transports available and then, with the British, looked for a way to get them delivered across the South Atlantic. Everybody seemed to be short of pilots, navigators, and radio operators with long-range, multi-engine experience. Who better to turn to than Juan Trippe? He set up a company, Atlantic Airways, for the express purpose of getting these machines to Africa.

On 29 May 1941 the UK government signed an agreement with Atlantic Airways for the delivery of the twenty transports. The British would pay all expenses and supply the navigators. The Pan Am subsidiary would find the pilots, many on loan from Lockheed Aircraft. The first ten transports left Miami on 21 June for Port of Spain, Trinidad, and Belem, Brazil. There Brazilian police arrested the crews and held them for three days. The neutral government took exception to aircraft of a belligerent nation landing on its territory. Eventually things were straightened away and the planes proceeded to Natal, and thence across the Atlantic to Bathurst in Gambia and around the West African coast to Lagos. There the British put the transports to good use returning ferry crews from Cairo. Further problems with neutral Brazil were avoided by leaving future transfers of ownership until the aircraft reached West Africa. The British received the next batch of transports, seven in number, on 30 July. The final three of this allotment came in September.[8]

When they faced the problem of getting reconnaissance aircraft and bombers from the United States to the Middle East – even before the first ten transports had been delivered – British and American officials turned once again to Pan American Airways. While the Airport Development Program construction was just getting started during the summer of 1941, Juan Trippe reportedly dined with Prime Minister Winston Churchill at 10 Downing Street. The subject of conversation appears to have been the ferrying of aircraft across the South Atlantic and the trans-Africa route to British forces in the Middle East. Trippe had shared his views on this matter with several RAF officers earlier the same day, before receiving a summons to meet Churchill. Immediately after Trippe's return to the United States, Roosevelt called the aviation executive to the White House. The upshot was that Pan Am took on the job of delivering aircraft to British forces in the Middle East via the new southern airway, across the Atlantic at its narrowest point to West Africa, and then along the British trans-Africa route to Cairo.[9]

The USAAF official history reports: 'Preliminary plans were drawn up at a conference in General [Hap] Arnold's office on 26 June 1941, with representatives of the British Air Commission and the Pan American organization in attendance.' It was agreed that 'Pan American would establish both a ferry service and an air transport service to the west coast of Africa, and would also take over the British ferrying and transport operations across central Africa from Takoradi to Khartoum. The United States assumed the obligation of financing the contract services.' Contracts were signed by representatives of all parties on 12 August.[10]

As usual, Trippe established subsidiaries for the job. Pan American Airways-Africa Ltd, charged with upgrading the facilities on the trans-

Africa airway, was incorporated on 15 July and Pan American Air Ferries (PAAF), which would actually deliver the aircraft, on the 24th. The ferry operation began life with a skeleton staff of ten captains and two co-pilots, two radio operators, an operations manager and assistant, an engineer and a master mechanic, most from the parent company. Soon a school for ferry crews had been established in Miami and the first delivery aircraft began trickling down the unfinished Latin American airway and cross the South Atlantic to Africa.[11]

By September 1941 some 500 Pan Am personnel were at work in Africa. With the help of about 1500 local labourers, they began the tremendous task of transforming the trans-Africa route into a modern airway capable of handling hundreds of aircraft a day. The Americans installed up-to-date equipment and provided a ground organization at the staging fields along the route. All the airports, save Roberts Field in Liberia, were on British-controlled territory. Nonetheless, circumstances dictated that the Americans be given a large measure of control over the airway, including the scheduling of air traffic. In December 1941, however, when the United States declared war, the organization of the route was far from complete and few multi-engine aircraft had been flown over it.[12]

Some British officials had mixed feelings about Pan Am's intense involvement in the trans-Africa project. While admiring Trippe's ability to accomplish things, they suspected that his motives were commercial as well as military. Tedder used his influence to encourage BOAC to keep showing the British flag in Africa lest it be completely overwhelmed by the US giant. As a consequence, some Americans did not always feel completely welcomed. 'The British in Africa were not even totally cooperative,' an American complained, 'and one high official, Air Marshal Arthur Tedder, once termed Pan American-Africa Ltd. a naked grab by Pan Am for postwar air routes.'[13] In fact, although US air regulations prevailed along this route, most of the bases included both American and British establishments, in much the same way that Gander and Goose Bay had a Canadian, a British, and an American side.

In view of the demands for military aircraft by US forces, especially following the Japanese attack on Pearl Harbor, the program may have seemed overly ambitious. It was, however, most timely. Particularly significant was the progress made in developing the South Atlantic and trans-Africa routes to fly aircraft to North Africa, the Middle East, the USSR, and the Far East. These routes, sometimes referred to collectively as the southeastern, became a crucial supply line for the Allies. The western terminus was West Palm Beach in Florida. From there the airway passed in a southeasterly direction over the Caribbean Sea and along the coast of South America, with landing fields at Borinquen Field in Puerto Rico, Port of Spain in Trinidad, Atkinson Field (near George-town) in British Guiana, and Belem and Natal in Brazil. The last was the jumping-off point for the 1900-mile flight across the South Atlantic to West Africa. In the 1930s most of these places could boast of an air harbour for flying boats or a small landing field for wheeled aircraft. Under the Airport Development Program they all received facilities for handling large numbers of landplanes.[14]

Increasingly after Pearl Harbor, the USAAF, through its Ferrying Command and after June 1942 through its successor, Air Transport Command, gradually assumed control of the southeastern route, though Pan American Air Ferries continued to be very much involved. The USAAF history records: 'By the time the personnel and facilities of the organization were militarized at the end of 1942, some 464 planes had been delivered over the South Atlantic to the Middle East by PAAF crews.'[15] However, the rapid acceleration of American aircraft produc-tion following the entry of the United States into the war, plus the worldwide commitments of the RAF and USAAF, not to mention the in-creased demands of the USSR for more lend-lease machines, presented a problem in aircraft delivery of much greater proportions than pre-viously envisaged. Even with their combined resources, the USAAF, whose expansion was delayed by American assistance to the Allies, and Pan Am could not muster enough aircrew, particularly pilots qualified on four-engine aircraft, to keep pace with delivery requirements. It was thus natural that they looked to RAF Ferry Command at Dorval, with its strong core of experienced long-distance flyers, for assistance. As a result, Air Chief Marshal Bowhill and General George came to an ad hoc agreement for the loan of aircrew to ferry US-built aircraft over oceans and continents to distant battlefields.

It should be remembered that although Ferry Command had been concentrating its efforts on the North Atlantic, it counted among its achievements the delivery of nine Catalinas across the Pacific to Singapore early in 1941 to bolster British air defences in the Far East. The route flown led from San Diego to Honolulu, then by way of the islands of Midway, Wake, and Guam (which were to be scenes of fierce fighting during the war in the Pacific) to the US Navy base at Cavite in the Philippines – a distance of nearly 8000 miles. There the Catalinas were picked up by Royal Australian Air Force crews and flown to

Singapore, to join 205 (Reconnaissance) Squadron. The crews returned by Pan American Airways, which had opened the route in 1935 and ran a weekly return service from California.

The nine Catalinas were entrusted to three picked crews, each making three deliveries. The captains were J.A. Webber of Colorado, George Byars of New Mexico, and Bernt Balchen, the famous Norwegian flyer and explorer who had, among other accomplishments, flown across the North Atlantic from New York to Paris with Commander Richard Byrd in 1927. On the Catalina flight Balchen's co-pilot was Clyde Pangborn of Wenatchee, Washington, who had flown round the world in 1931. Both Balchen and Pangborn were also qualified navigators. The other members of the crew included two radio operators, Arthur Finch and A.F. Horn. Webber, also a navigator, was likewise accompanied by a co-pilot and two radio operators, E. Roberts and H. Severn. Byars's crew consisted of W. Hunt, co-pilot, W. Chitty, navigator, and radio officers R. Hughes and E.A. Aalmann.[16] Balchen's delivery of Catalina W8433 in June 1941 was his final flight with Ferry Command. On his return to the US, he was commissioned in the USAAF to develop bases in Greenland, where he was in command when the first Ferry Command deliveries passed through via the northern route, as we have seen in chapter 6. Byars joined the USAAF in 1942, while Pangborn and Webber carried on with Ferry Command and made many more deliveries.

The first aircraft the USAAF delivered using crews borrowed from RAF Ferry Command were five North American B-25 Mitchell medium bombers. They were intended for the Netherlands East Indies Air Force, which received minor concessions under lend-lease to facilitate its collaboration with a combined American, British, and Australian force in Java. This turned out to be a futile attempt to check a much larger Japanese force closing in on the Malay peninsula. The Japanese presence in the Pacific, and concern about the range of the Mitchell, brought a decision to fly eastwards across Africa and India to reach Java. By the time they reached Bangalore, India, after a flight of about 14,000 miles, Java had fallen. They went to No. 5 Photo Reconnaissance Unit of the RAF at Asand, India, where they were modified by removing gun turrets and armament. The surviving planes eventually ended up with 681 Squadron, RAF.[17]

The fall of Singapore to the Japanese in the middle of February 1942, and the Dutch East Indies about three weeks later, closed the southeastern route as the principal Allied line of air communication with the southwest Pacific area. Fortunately, American engineers had recently opened an alternative more southerly trans-Pacific route from the US west coast to Australia, stretching from San Diego, with intermediate landing fields in Hawaii, Christmas Island, Canton Island, Fiji, and New Caledonia.[18] In March 1942 Ferry Command loaned a number of crews to the USAAF to deliver planes along this new route to American forces in Australia.

One of the airmen sent from Dorval, Henry Flory, describes his tenure seconded to the USAAF. A qualified pilot and navigator, Flory was 'plying the Atlantic' when he 'received a thrilling assignment,' to deliver a Catalina from Elizabeth City to Australia. The crew mix differed from the Ferry Command norm: 'With two each of our senior personnel were combined four young Australian pilots, navigators and engineers who had to be returned to Australia after being trained in Canada.' Flory remembers it as 'a wonderful experience.' Three complete crews flew to New York's LaGuardia airport and, with Norfolk, Virginia, closed in by weather, they decided to take the train to Elizabeth City. They 'rode in to Pennsylvania Station and unceremoniously bumped off a whole Pullman carload of passengers with our high priority.' He claims: 'We were rated A1, which ranked second only to White House personnel in travel. The fact that we waited ten days for our planes to be made ready only showed how war works.'[19]

The first leg of the journey took them over Jacksonville, Florida, and along the Gulf coast to Corpus Christi, Texas. Flory relates a story of an adventure allegedly experienced by one of the other crews:

Capt. [Clyde] Pangbourne [sic], the real old timer who had covered about every inch of the States in his barnstorming days, refused to accept his (Australian) navigator's instruction to turn 90 degrees right to reach Corpus Christi Naval Air Base, where we were headed. They were flying at two hundred feet, just below cloud level, and Pang insisted he hadn't yet passed a bridge that joined the sandy coastal strand to the mainland. So they continued South till doubts arose in Pang's mind; he turned inland and decided to put the Catalina down and think things over! He landed in what was nothing but a shallow pseudo-swamp, and was stuck in watery mud. The plane's wings extended over cattails and other marshy reeds, and one of the Australians on board risked kingdom come by commenting what an extraordinary harbour Corpus Christi had!

Pang, realizing he was in real trouble, ordered the radio operator to get a bearing on the air base. To rev up the generators for power to send the signal the engines had to be opened up full, and sure as shooting the big fifteen ton plane began to hop and bounce along the mud; suddenly he hit a patch of water, Pang rammed the throttles against the stops, and in a few seconds was airborne again! He was about twenty miles from the air base and put the plane down there a few minutes later, as nonchalant as could be. He took a rough razzing from the rest of us, who had just finished our dinner, but took credit for being the only man ever to land and take off a Navy flying boat from a Texas cornfield! It turned out the bridge Pang was looking for had been washed away in a hurricane several years before.[20]

The rest of the trip was essentially uneventful, but Flory's explanation of how they managed 'the crucial trick' of finding tiny island air facilities in the vastness of the Pacific Ocean is instructive:

Finding those little dots in the ocean – Christmas Island, Palmyra, and Canton, was quite a trick, particularly as they made us fly by day, with only the sun available for taking sights. This made it impossible to pin-point one's position, and only to obtain a line of position on the ocean's surface, some spot on which you had to be. So what we did was make sure that our course would keep us one definite side of our target. We'd then run our distance till our line of position crossed over the island, and then alter course to move up the line till the island appeared. Thank God it always did, but the crucial thing was always to be sure on which side of it you were.[21]

Flory and his crew deposited the Catalina at Rathmines, north of Sydney, and, minus the Australian component, returned to North America in the USS *Tasker H. Bliss*.

The rest of Flory's Pacific flights were Fortresses and Liberators. On one occasion, during the summer of 1942 after delivering a Fortress from San Francisco to Australia, he reports being conscripted into emergency service using the plane to transport troops from Townsville in Queensland to Port Moresby in New Guinea, on the express orders of General Douglas McArthur: 'We flew continuously to New Guinea and back transporting troops for three more days without a moment's rest, and those were the only three consecutive days in which I never got into bed in all my life.'[22]

An incident on Flory's return trip to North America, if true, demonstrates the inventiveness of Second World War airmen. He was in a Liberator flown by a Consolidated Aircraft crew when the starter on one of the engines 'gave up the ghost.' Lacking a spare, the passengers resigned themselves to spending several days marooned on an isolated Pacific island.

But how we underestimated the resourcefulness of our Texan crew. In the early hours I heard an engine start up, followed by whoops and hollers around the tents that could only come from sons of the Lone Star State. The crew had started the engine by what they called the Texas rope trick. I still cannot vouch for it, but this is what they said. They started the engine by wrapping a long rope around the engine's propeller and tailing on to it; with one man in the cockpit to work the controls the rest had pulled on the rope which rotated the motor until, via the propeller, on the third attempt, it had burst into life and given the marvellous sound that woke us up. It wasn't ten minutes before we [were] all aboard, the other engines started, and very quickly we were airborne for Honolulu where spare starting motors were abundant. It was a great bit of work, and frankly I doubt that we ever would have thought of it.[23]

The US Navy guarded the Pacific route, but pilots were warned to be on the alert for marauding Japanese fighters. Ferry crews considered it safer to fly under cover of darkness, but the USN insisted on daylight flights, probably to help the crews spot the tiny island staging posts. According to one report, the veteran captain, Don Teel, left Canton Island for Fiji at midnight, despite the American policy. 'How, he said to the green lieutenant, do you intend to stop me? I'm an American civilian flying a Dutch aircraft for the Royal Air Force.' After a flight of a little more than six hours, Teel reached Fiji 'just in time for a nice hot breakfast.'[24] In April Ferry Command personnel delivered nineteen B-25s to the 3rd Bombardment Group after engine settings had been double-checked to ensure adequate ferry range. By the end of October the total reached eighty-seven. In November 1942 the crews were recalled to Dorval because they were needed on the southeastern route, where Ferry Command was becoming increasingly committed.[25]

The year 1942 was critical for the Allies. The Axis Powers were everywhere in the ascendancy; the Allies were badly mauled on all fronts. The Japanese were going from conquest to conquest in the Pacific. The Germans were driving deeper into the USSR, and in the Libyan desert the legendary General Erwin Rommel was chasing the British Eighth Army back across the desert to the Egyptian frontier. In June he dealt the British a stunning blow by capturing their main supply base at Tobruk, complete with an enormous store of munitions and weapons. Churchill, who received this piece of bad news in Washington where he was conferring with Roosevelt and who had assured his host that Tobruk would not fall, was deeply perturbed by this turn of events. So, too, was the American president. If Egypt fell to the Germans, the strategic advantage of the trans-Africa route would be wiped out and the Middle East with the rich oil resources of Iraq and Iran would be extremely vulnerable. If captured they could fuel Germany's war with the USSR. Without hesitation Roosevelt promised all possible aid, including guns, tanks, aircraft, and other war *matériel*.[26]

Most of the British requirements would have to be shipped via the long circuitous route around South Africa and up the east coast to the Red Sea. However, the Eighth Army was so desperately short of anti-tank ammunition it was decided to deliver it by air. Bowhill, Ferry Command's AOC-in-C, 'received instructions to arrange a massive airlift to Cairo.'[27] Henry Flory recalls bumping into Taffy Powell, the senior air staff officer, in Ferry Command headquarters on a Thursday and receiving an order to leave for Cairo the next morning. Since he needed immunization inoculations, he had to wait until after the weekend. When he showed up at Dorval early on Monday morning, he found 'the machine we were to take had gasoline dripping from its tanks on to the tarmac, which only meant fuel leaks. It would take days to cure them, and Powell leapt into action in the way I admired. He picked up the phone, got the superintendent of maintenance, and told him to get another plane ready by noon at latest, adding that if it wasn't ready he would no longer have a job!' Modifying a Liberator 'loaded for combat duty to the duty of carrying 4 tons of ammunition as freight was no mean undertaking.' Even so, 'that bomber was being towed into the line at five minutes to noon, with little men running alongside it receiving the last bits and pieces to come off!' At this point in his account, Flory digresses to pay tribute to the SASO: 'If we had had more Powells in our war effort it might have been over in two years!'[28]

Powell had a number of Liberators, scheduled for ferrying to the United Kingdom, removed from the delivery line and converted for transport operations. It was a big job. Groundcrew removed gun turrets and armour plating and installed floor boards across the bomb-bays in order to carry ammunition and other freight. Because the flight path lay across the southern route, they also stripped the de-icing gear. Each aircraft would be manned by a crew of five (including some of the command's most experienced personnel) – two captains, as pilot and co-pilot, a navigator, a radio operator, and a flight engineer. The Liberators would leave in groups of three or four and, on orders from General George of the USAAF's Air Transport Command, would receive priority clearance at all American bases. Since a number of accidents had occurred on the trans-Africa route, and since Ferry Command had little information about conditions likely to be encountered, a preliminary survey was carried out. This task fell to Captains Al Lilly (in Liberator FK214), Louis Bisson (FK227), and J. Bradley (FK243), three experienced Canadian senior pilots, and Squadron Leader Willie Biddell of the RAF in (FL911). They left Montreal on 2 July, stopping at the main bases to find out what communication facilities, weather forecasting services, emergency landing fields, aircraft maintenance arrangements, and crew accommodation were available and generally to ensure that the staging posts were ready to receive and service the Liberators and speed them on their way.[29]

The airlift proper got under way on Thursday, 7 July. On that day, Captains A.J. Burke (in FL913 with Flory as his co-pilot), E.W. High- tower (FL917), and T. Livermore (FL509), all Americans, left Montreal and flew to New York, where the ammunition, brought there by special train, was transferred to the Liberators. Other important items, includ- ing spare parts for aircraft and tanks, were also loaded. The next day Burke and Hightower set off on the 11,000-mile flight from New York to Cairo. Livermore was delayed and did not get away until the 12th. Although the Liberator had a range of more than 2000 miles, these hastily modified versions were so heavily loaded, each aircraft carrying about three tons, that the journey had to be made in relatively short hops, taking advantage of most refuelling stops. From New York their course took them to Trinidad, then to Belem and Natal on the Brazilian coast. With the new American airfield on Ascension Island not quite ready, the first of the airlift Liberators crossed directly from Natal to Liberia, where Pan Am had built a large modern airport, Roberts Field. From there a 700-mile flight along the coast brought the crews to the city of Accra in the Gold Coast, which served as the main western terminus of the trans-Africa airway for multi-engine aircraft.[30]

The next leg of the flight led on a northeast heading away from the Gold Coast and into the heart of Africa. The first stop was at Kano in north-central Nigeria – an ancient walled city with a modern airfield, equipped with 'a magnificent set of runways,' a unique combination of the old and the new. Although Kano boasted a regular control tower staffed by air controllers, it employed an unusual method of announc- ing the arrival and departure of aircraft, as described in the contempor- ary *RAF Middle East Review*: 'All day and every day a native clad in traditional costume – loose white cotton smock, drain-pipe trousers and large floppy straw hat – stands in the taxying apron and warns the locality of aircraft movements by blowing on a six-foot metal horn. He knows only two bars of four notes each but what he lacks in versatility he makes up for in lung power.'[31]

Kano to Khartoum in the Sudan, a distance of 1700 miles, was one of the longest legs of the flight and perhaps the most difficult. It included the section which Air Marshal Tedder had found so formidable when he flew over it eighteen months earlier. It offered only the barest hope of a safe forced landing. Although conditions had improved in the interim, especially in regard to communications, the endless stretches of desert and rugged grassland with no distinguishing landmarks, along with maps which, as Tedder had observed, were useless, added considerably to the problems of the navigators. A reminder of the difficulties that lay ahead on leaving Kano came with the 'Goolie Chit,' issued to crews before takeoff in case of a forced landing in this desolate region. Printed in English, Arabic, and French, it offered 'a generous reward if the Arabs deliver your warm, live body to the nearest outpost. Unharmed, of course.'[32]

At least one ferry crew, caught over the Sudan after dark with fuel tanks almost empty, got a demonstration of the Goolie Chit as a substitute for a regular system of search and rescue. Baling out over the desert, they were rescued by a Sudanese who led them on an eight-day camel journey to a British outpost. En route they lived mainly on camel's milk and goat meat – seven goats being killed and roasted. As they passed through one encampment after another, the four men in the crew maintained a polite deference to native customs. At the end of the journey their British host paid the guide for the use of the camels and the food consumed.[33]

The last leg, 1000 miles from Khartoum to Cairo, was the least difficult. The Liberators flying to the rescue of the Eighth Army now followed the green valley of the Nile River until a distant view of the Egyptian pyramids heralded the end of the long journey. Burke and Hightower landed at Cairo on 17 July, and Livermore touched down the following day. Captains G. Horsum (Liberator FL915) followed on the 21st, J. Bradley on 5 August, and R.M. Lloyd (FL914) two days later. Altogether about eighteen tons of anti-tank ammunition, plus spare parts for planes and tanks, had been delivered in record time.[34] Powell says that some of the aircraft made more than one trip during this emergency airlift. 'One Liberator piloted by Norman Williams made four crossings of the south Atlantic from Brazil to West Africa in 3 days 16 hours. To do this Williams and his crew flew 11,500 miles in 88 hours, which was an average speed of 135 mph including all refuelling and rest stops. In the course of this sequence they had breakfast at Ascension Island four mornings running.'[35]

The ammunition airlift is one of the earliest examples of the use of long-range aircraft as a means of supply for military forces in the field. How effective it was can only be surmised, for one will find no reference to it in the many historical accounts of the desert fighting. This is quite understandable because military historians have tended to focus on personalities, or on tactical and strategic considerations, overlooking more mundane matters such as globe-circling logistical requirements. Yet it would seem that the airlift did make a useful and timely contribution. When Rommel, after having forced the British back to Alamein, struck again on the night of 30 August, in what became known as the Battle of Alam Halfa, the Eighth Army had an ample supply of anti-tank ammunition. On 1 September the German Panzers were stopped by a steady bombardment from Montgomery's artillery and almost constant attacks from RAF aircraft. The next day Rommel decided to withdraw. By the 6th the Battle of Alam Halfa was over.[36] Ferry Command could rightfully claim a small share of the credit.

Soon after the Americans entered the war it became obvious that they would be unable to undertake the ferrying of British aircraft as earlier promised, at least not without borrowing more crews from Ferry Command. Rather than continue this arrangement, which could lead to some of its most experienced crews being absorbed into the American organization, the RAF decided that Ferry Command, in addition to its responsibilities on the North Atlantic, should undertake the delivery of all British aircraft slated to be flown across the South Atlantic, including those going to the USSR. (The Soviets received lend-lease aircraft directly from the Americans and also through the British from the latter's own allotment. Planes supplied from the United States reached the Soviet Union by the Northwest Staging Route through Alberta, the Yukon territory, and Alaska, and by sea, as well as by the South Atlantic route.) British deliveries over the southern route would, of course, be carried out in close collaboration with Air Transport Command of the USAAF, which continued to exercise overriding authority for the airway. To keep in touch with the progress of its crews, Ferry Command was permitted to operate its own communication channels between Dorval and Accra. It also established a base at Nassau in the Bahamas (replacing the detachment based for a time in Nashville, Tennessee), and liaison units in Trinidad, Belem, and Natal, where Ferry Command personnel wrote back to the northern hemisphere complaining about boredom and sunburn. Across Africa, No. 216 Group of the RAF monitored delivery flights.[37]

Under these arrangements Ferry Command began delivering Lockheed Venturas, Martin Marauders and Baltimores, and Douglas Dakotas, plus a few Hudsons, across the South Atlantic in the summer of 1942. Crews picked up the aircraft at West Palm Beach, Florida, the main dispatch centre for planes and air cargo. From there they flew to distant points sometimes halfway round the world. Ferry Command records show that 127 machines were delivered via this route in the last few months of 1942, over a thousand in 1943, 1689 in 1944, and 375 in the final year of the war.[38] Practically all of those delivered in 1942, and most of those delivered in 1943, went to North Africa, enabling the British Desert Air Force to maintain air superiority in that theatre. Most of the others went to more distant points in the Middle East for the RAF, or on to the Soviet Union. Those destined for the USSR passed through Cairo to Iran, where they were turned over to Soviet crews at Basra or Tehran. Planes bound for India went to Karachi, either across Arabia or through Iran.[39]

Except for a few BOAC Lockheed Lodestars operating between Cairo and Takoradi, the southeastern route at first had no return ferry service. When Ferry Command started pouring aircraft over the route, it was still being organized. Most of the available transports were busy hauling personnel and essential equipment, including spare parts, from West Palm Beach and Miami to the newly developed staging posts. Delivery crews, having completed their runs to Cairo or other distant points, had to make their way back to North America as best they could. The problems and possibilities were illustrated by the experiences of Don McVicar, once again involved in the embryonic stage of a new route. After landing in Cairo with one of the first Marauders delivered by Ferry Command across the South Atlantic to North Africa, he had to arrange to get home. He spent a few days sightseeing while billeted at 'the famous Shepherd's Hotel,' where 'without our spray gun to kill cockroaches we would have been eaten up alive.' Quite by chance he met the captain of a Pan Am Douglas C-47 transport returning to Accra who invited him to fly in the co-pilot's seat. Then came a wait of a day or so in Accra, where 'I fought my way to the top of the line for a seat on a Boeing Stratoliner flight to Ascension and Natal.' There McVicar transferred to another Pan Am C-47 that took him as far as Miami – a 4000-mile flight remembered for the 'heat, box lunches, discomfort, boredom.' With the high priority pass of a Ferry Command pilot, he obtained a seat on an

Eastern Airlines flight to New York. He finally arrived at Dorval aboard Canadian Colonial Airways on 22 August 1942, about three weeks after he had left for Cairo with the Marauder.[40]

McVicar's tale demonstrates how transportation on the South Atlantic was not well organized in the summer of 1942. Morale suffered from the long delay in getting ferry crews back to the starting point. It also restricted the number of aircrew available for duty at any given time. At the root of the problem was the shortage of four-engine transports, in great demand in all theatres of war. Occasionally, emergency runs were laid on to pick up stranded personnel. In March 1943, as aircraft production started to catch up to demand, five new lend-lease Liberators were placed on the South Atlantic run. Based at Nassau, they provided a return ferry service initially between that point and Accra and later between Accra and Dorval. The number of Liberators on this run increased as more became available. In 1944 the command had a fleet of fourteen shuttling back and forth across the South Atlantic, resulting in a much smoother flow of traffic and making it possible to run a weekly return ferry service from Cairo. On their eastbound flights, the Liberators carried freight to various points along the route.[41] If by chance they were coming back empty they were instructed to stop in Liberia for a cargo of crude rubber. As Al Lilly recalled, this was not a popular assignment: 'The rubber came in large two hundred pound cubes which often were just soaked with rain and gave off a most offensive odour ... For weeks afterwards the aircraft reeked with the smell. It seeped into your lungs and it seemed as if we could never get rid of it.'[42]

Of the twenty or so Liberator captains who served on the South Atlantic service, the most widely known was undoubtedly Don Teel of Odessa, Texas. Teel joined Ferry Command in October 1941 and, during his first months, he was employed mainly on the North Atlantic. In March 1942, as we have seen, he was one of those who delivered Mitchells to Australia. In September 1942 he moved to the South Atlantic route. For the next two years he flew out of West Palm Beach and Nassau, carrying heavy equipment, spare parts for engines and airframes, and even complete engines, to Accra and other staging points that had to maintain a full stock of aircraft replacement items. On return flights he often picked up aircrew who, for one reason or another, had become stranded at some isolated out-of-the-way place. Many of his passengers were Americans. Most of his flights were in Liberator FL919, inscribed with the nickname *Magic Carpet*. To those he rescued along the way it must have seemed most appropriate.[43]

Another captain who ended up on the southern return ferry was Henry Flory. He admits that it 'was considered the plum route of the whole ferrying business.' He flew 'from Miami, Florida, to Accra, West Africa, carrying V.I.Ps and freight to the East and bringing our own delivery pilots back to the West.' Regulations restricted crews to 150 flying hours a month, 'which opened up for us a great opportunity.' He explains:

A round trip from Miami to Accra and back took approximately seventy-five hours, which could be quite safely accomplished in one week. So the combined brains of the South Atlantic Ferry organization concocted the following formula. Each crew would make two round trips back to back, completing our permitted flying hours in two strenuous weeks exactly. We could do this because our planes had been fitted with a bunk bed aft of the cockpit and carried a steward who could cook us short order meals on a hot-plate. This gave every crew a fortnight of complete leisure during which we enjoyed golf, tennis, and sea bathing for which Florida is famous. We were given honorary membership at the best clubs in Palm Beach, where most of us lived.[44]

Usually flying with Norman Williams, who 'described himself as a Southwestern New York State hill-billy,' Flory gives the following account of their normal routine:

When we were to make a trip, his [Williams's] idea of Heaven was to spend the afternoon on the beach with his wife, get shaved, have a massage and a facial, and then get drunk at dinner. We'd get down to 36th St Airport at Miami, climb aboard the aircraft, and I would fly it from Miami to Trinidad while he slept it off in the bunk provided. We would get there in time for breakfast, after which he would fly the plane from Trinidad to Belem-Para, an airport at the mouth of the Amazon River in Brazil – during which period I slept soundly. By now both of us refreshed, we'd share the pleasant afternoon flight to Natal on the eastern tip of Brazil, where we spent twenty four hours. Then I would fly the machine to Ascension Island, arriving about dawn, he'd fly to Accra, West Africa, and we'd both collapse into bed until dinner time. That night we would take off with our load of passengers and share the duty until we were back in Nassau in two and a half days. Twenty-four hours later we would repeat the process, and there we were; one hundred and fifty hours of strenuous flying time done in two weeks, and fourteen days of freedom to do whatever we wished. I have to admit I had a pretty easy war.[45]

Flory also confesses that his wartime flying career in the South Atlantic allowed him to make a little extra money on the side with 'a lucrative boon-doggle.' He found that he could buy duty-free Scotch whisky for $44 a case in Nassau. He says that alcohol was scarce at the base opened by the USAAF on Ascension in July 1942. Individual bottles cost as much as $100 on the black market. Flory quotes an officers' mess official as saying, 'When someone has paid that price for a fifth of liquor, believe me, he is going to drink it all himself, usually in quite a hurry.' This led to problems of intoxication and two tragedies, 'one when a sergeant had shot and killed one of his mates, and another when a G.I. had deluded himself into thinking his jeep was an airplane; he had barrelled it down the runway and straight into the South Atlantic Ocean, where they later recouped the jeep but found no trace of the man's body.' Flory claims to have been offered 'any price at all' for any whisky he could bring with him on his visits. The only stipulation being that the product had to be 'dispensed through the bar, under some control.' They settled on a price of $84 a case, the going rate in New York City at the time. Our intrepid ferry pilot-cum-bootlegger recalls that the officer in charge of the officers' mess, 'practically swooned in my arms!' Under the circumstances, it was easy for an airman to rationalize. 'So,' Flory now admits, 'overcome by the chance to become a real public benefactor, I developed a smart trade in bootlegging Johnny Walker and Black and White from Nassau to Ascension Island. It was obviously in defiance of multitudinous regulations, both R.A.F. and Customs, but I was convinced of my rectitude in solving a serious problem for the boys stranded on that remote rock in the Ocean.'[46]

Flory describes how the smuggling was done:

Our Liberators had been converted to carrying freight and passengers, and one modification had been closing in the windows in the navigating compartment in the nose so that no one could see in. Experiments carried out surreptitiously in Nassau showed we could stash three cases into the nacelles that held our main landing wheels, and ten more cases in the navigator's compartment. Fairness, to say nothing of discretion, entailed that we share the bonanza with our crew members, and indeed, with the other crews; and so it was that distant base had ample supplies of whiskey for the duration, while we collected ample loose cash to lose in the numerous poker games that occupied our limited free time.[47]

In fact, the 'boon-doggle' does seem to have been taken advantage of by more than just Flory and his crew. H.R. 'Red' Syrett writes of his time on the South Atlantic route for twelve months from September 1943: 'We kept the Officers' Club in Ascension Island in booze that was purchased duty free in Nassau and delivered forthwith under the guise of paid entertainment. RAF Ferry Command arrivals at Ascension Island were heartily greeted by the base entertainment officer and his cheque book. To say the least, we were popular.' Syrett adds that they 'stowed the "entertainment" for Ascension Island Officers' Club under the safety equipment.'[48]

We should not leave this question of smuggling and bootlegging without noting that it involved an element of flying risk, as Flory describes:

Each time we flew a Liberator from Nassau to Miami to take on its load of military freight the plane was completely empty except for whiskey loaded right up in the nose. This put it completely out of balance – very nose-heavy, so that the pilots would have to send the rest of the crew back to the toilet (which was where the tail-gun had originally been), in an effort to smooth out the landing in which otherwise the plane would keep trying to dive into the ground. I guarantee that some of the hairiest landings in history took place at Miami airport during this period, while every tenet of weight and balance was being violated to the Nth degree. I shudder now when I think of it![49]

Flory remains amazed to this day that 'those Customs men in Miami never thought of looking in the nose compartment ... They never set eyes on a single case.'[50]

Flying along the coast of South America and across Africa, Ferry Command crews encountered challenges and experiences vastly different from those seen on the North Atlantic route. Every day brought a different diet and every night a new crop of insects adding to the ever-present possibility of contracting malaria or some other tropical disease. Icing presented no danger, but the tropical climate brought other hazards. In Brazil and on the west coast of Africa, heat and humidity were a constant problem. In the wet season crews had to be on the alert for violent squalls and thunderstorms that often arose so suddenly they were impossible to predict with any degree of accuracy. In Africa the desert equivalent of the squalls was the 'haboob,' or desert dust storm, which sometimes rose to a considerable height, reducing visibility to a dangerously low level. In contrast to the North Atlantic route, where the chief meteorologist told pilots when to fly and when not to fly, pilots on the southeastern route, where weather forecasting was less advanced, had to decide when to take off. They then hoped for the best, after basing their decisions on unreliable forecasts.[51]

There was little likelihood of encountering enemy aircraft on the southeastern route. Nonetheless, pilots were warned to keep well clear of French West Africa, particularly the Ivory Coast and Dahomey, which bordered British colonies and which remained under the control of the Vichy administration after the fall of France. In these territories, aircraft displaying British markings were considered hostile. Although there were reports of delivery aircraft straying into French air space and being chased into the clouds, there appear to be no records of any serious clashes. However, there were incidents. One involved a Hudson piloted by Flight Lieutenant George Phillips of Orangeville, Ontario.

Phillips was one of the few ferry pilots who had fought in the First World War. On returning to Canada, he was employed by the Ontario Department of Lands and Forests and acquired a reputation as an outstanding bush pilot. In 1931 he was awarded the McKee Trophy for his contributions to Canadian aviation. In 1940 he applied to join the RCAF and, although over age at forty-seven, he was accepted and assigned to training duties. Like most of his colleagues, he was anxious to get closer to the action and, in 1942, volunteered and was accepted for service with Ferry Command.[52] At this time Phillips was fifty years of age. Most of the regular pilots in Ferry Command were in their thirties. His acceptance for active flying duties over the long and difficult route to Cairo undoubtedly reflects how hard pressed the ferrying organization was for delivery pilots.

After training in long-distance navigation and ferry procedures, Phillips' first assignment was to deliver Hudson FK499 to British forces in North Africa for use in general reconnaissance operations. The other members of his crew were Flying Officer Bill Campbell, RCAF, navigator, and Sergeant G.A. Seward, RAAF, radio operator. Both were products of the BCATP. Seward already had one flight across the North Atlantic to his credit. Campbell, like Phillips, was on his first delivery trip. Picking up the Hudson at West Palm Beach on 26 September 1942 and following the usual route, they headed southeast over the Caribbean Sea towards the coast of Brazil, with stops at Borinquen Field in Puerto Rico, Port of Spain in Trinidad, and Georgetown in British Guiana, to Belem and Natal in Brazil. Thus far all went well, but on the nine-and-a-half-hour flight to Ascension the fuel pump began to give trouble. Maintenance staff at Ascension made repairs and the crew conferred about whether to leave right away or wait until morning. Seward recalled:

It was a question of daylight as we wanted to reach Accra before dusk. At any rate, we decided to take off and as we approached the coast of Africa there was not much daylight left. To make matters worse we ran into a bad storm which knocked out our radio. The navigator could not use his sextant because it was too late to get a shot at the sun and the stars were not yet visible. We finally saw land and then we knew if we turned north we would hit the African coast. Soon darkness started to fall and we felt that the best thing to do was to put the Hudson down on the beach. On looking for a spot we saw a landing strip up ahead in the dusk and felt that we were home free.[53]

Through some oversight, the crew had not been warned about the strip of French territory along the African coast. Approaching the landing strip it became obvious that they were by no means home free:

As we were coming in we saw that there were barriers across the runway. Ack-ack was fired at us and assuming that this was British territory I fired the colours of the day. It was too late to pull up. We crashed into the first of the barriers, the right tire blew causing the Hudson to ground loop ... We came to a standstill and got out through the windows of the aircraft. I had to get rid of the coding machine in a hurry and threw it into the jungle before anyone saw it. It was found the next day but by then the codes would have been changed. We were quickly surrounded by Senegalese soldiers – tall handsome fellows. They said, 'why did you land here? This is Vichy French territory and you are prisoners.'[54]

They were kept for a few days at Cotonou (in Dahomey), the place where they came down. Then, remaining in French West Africa, they were taken to Bamako (in Mali), travelling up the Niger River in a wood-burning paddle-wheel steamer. This was a gruelling trip of about 1500 miles 'and under more pleasant circumstances would have been most interesting ... along the way we saw alligators, lions and other animals of the jungle.'[55]

At Bamako, Phillips found himself the most senior officer in the camp. In spite of rather unpleasant conditions, including a steady diet of peanuts and considerable illness, malaria, dysentery and peritonitis, they managed to keep their spirits up. They planned escapes, but never carried them out. This may have been just as well, with the region infested with dangerous animals. Through sympathetic French workmen and newspapers smuggled into the camp, they learned of the Allied landings in North Africa in November, giving their morale a tremendous boost. Later in the month it was announced that French West Africa had joined the Allies. Phillips and his fellow prisoners were soon rescued and moved from Bamako to Freetown in the British colony of Sierra Leone. On 20 January 1943 they were moved to Accra and then flown to West Palm Beach in Don Teel's *Magic Carpet*. Later the three airmen learned to their great satisfaction that Hudson FK499, impounded at Cotonou, was eventually repaired and went into service with the RAF. Phillips made one more trip to Africa. He was then placed in charge of the RAF liaison unit at Natal. Seward and Campbell continued to make deliveries with Ferry Command.[56]

Following Portugal's grant of landing rights in the Azores in October 1943, the southern route began to lose some of its importance. At the end of that month, Taffy Powell flew to Lagens to discuss with other officers of the RAF and USAAF the arrangements for routing reinforcement aircraft through their newly acquired base in mid-ocean, once a rendezvous of Spanish treasure ships. It was now possible for planes to fly from Gander to Lagens, a distance of 1500 miles, and then on to North Africa, the Middle East, and the Far East with a substantial saving in time and distance and fuel. Similarly, flights originating in Miami could go to India and China by way of the Azores. However, because of the long leg from Miami to Lagens, over 2000 miles, this route was not practical for medium-range aircraft, which continued to go via the South Atlantic.[57]

A couple of months after Powell's visit to the Azores, Liberator EV843 passed through on its way to Karachi, then part of India. Members of the crew were Flying Officers Jack Uren of the RCAF as pilot, John Butler Wood, RAAF, navigator, along with co-pilot Pete Yaross from New York, radio officer Bill Neale from Vancouver, and flight engineer Jock McGee from Glasgow. Wood's detailed account of the flight gives a good idea of what a long trip across the mid-Atlantic route was like. They left Dorval early on 24 December 1943, but found themselves grounded at Gander by a blizzard. Leaving there two days after Christmas, Wood recalls trying to skirt a front, perhaps the same one that had caused the Newfoundland blizzard. The Liberator had just entered a menacing cloud, when suddenly there was a crack like a pistol shot and a dazzling, flaming chain of fire appeared suspended between the bulkheads of the crew compartment. It hung there for possibly a second – it seemed much longer – blinding in the intensity of its jagged animated brilliance; then it was gone. For a few moments we were too stunned to move, but the sickening lurches of the aircraft and the wild gyrations of the compasses demanded instant attention, and the next few minutes were among the most anxious of our lives, as pilot, co-pilot and engineer fought to regain control of the aeroplane. The pilot, Jack Uren, immediately switched off the automatic pilot, and slamming the four throttle levers fully forward, pulled back hard on the control column. Then as the maximum power of the four engines strove to drag the huge bulk of the Liberator ever higher, we sat tense and silent while the needle of the altimeter slowly revolved and we climbed up through the dark closeness of the storm, breathless lest the lightning should refute the old adage and strike again.

For, in fact, we had been subjected to a severe form of electrical discharge, commonly identified as lightning. Frequently on other occasions when passing through clouds I have seen sparks emanating from wings, windscreen and various other parts of an aircraft, but never before and, I trust never again, have I been in an aircraft when it has been struck by lightning. It was a most unnerving experience, and to this day I shudder to think of the result had one of us been in the path of that fiery chain of electricity.[58]

They continued on and set down on the 'interlocking steel plates' of Lagens airport with no further incident. In fact, the journey continued uneventfully, with stops at Rabat in Morocco, Biskra in Algeria, Cairo, and finally Habbaniya in Iraq, before reaching Karachi on New Year's Eve. In the week since leaving Montreal they 'had covered 8,350 miles (7,247 nautical miles) in just on forty-eight flying hours, an average speed of 174 miles per hour (151 knots).'[59]

Next came the trip back. Most agreed it was the worst part of flying for Ferry Command. On 3 January 1944 the crew of EV843 and 'some twenty other assorted "bodies" straggled out onto the tarmac and clambered up the three awkward steps into the fuselage which was to be our home for the next thirty-odd hours.' The 'home' was a USAAF ATC C-47, complete with 'bucket' seats, 'a fiendish device' used in many service transports:

The so-called 'seats' were actually impressions about 12 inches long, 10 inches wide and 3 inches deep, pressed one beside the other in a sheet of aluminium;

the sheets, each comprising about six seats or impressions, were attached to the interior walls along both sides of the fuselage. Presumably the original design envisaged the use of cushions in the impressions, but none were ever provided so that the unfortunate passenger was obliged to sit on the four edges of the impression, just like sitting in a square bucket.[60]

After takeoff, most opted for the floor.

The Dakota stopped, usually just long enough to refuel, at Masira Island (in the Arabian Sea just off the coast of Oman), Aden, Khartoum, El Fasher, Maiduguri, and Kano. At the last stop the passengers moved to an ATC C-87, transport version of the Liberator, and continued to Accra, Ascension, and Natal. From there a USAAF Stratoliner took them to Miami, via Belem, Georgetown, and Borinquen. They then flew Eastern Airlines to New York and Colonial to Dorval (stopping at Albany and Burlington). The return, more than 13,000 miles, took 74 hours 15 minutes flying time, spread over six days, using three different carriers in five different aircraft types. Wood summarizes the experience: 'Karachi and back; 21,500 miles in 122 hours; more than 25 landings in 18 different countries in 18 days.' Following three days leave, the airmen would be off on another delivery.[61]

In June 1944 Walter Jones was part a crew that made a similar trip in seven days, this time via Bermuda, Lagens, Rabat Sale, Castle Benito, and Cairo. His return came in an ATC C-54 via Abadan, Persia to Castle Benito, Casablanca, Lagens, and Stephenville, Newfoundland to New York.[62]

Not counting those that went via the mid-Atlantic, Ferry Command crews delivered a total of 3191 aircraft across the South Atlantic route for the use of the RAF. Americans delivered still more, both for the RAF and for their Soviet allies further on. These aircraft and the crews that flew them seldom made headline news, but their contribution to the fighting in North Africa and the Middle East won a tribute from Air Chief Marshal Tedder as AOC-in-C RAF Middle East: 'I would like ... to let the Ferry Pilots know ... that although they are not taking an active part in the battle, and may think their efforts pass unnoticed, this is not so. I take the keenest interest in their work and watch daily the progress of reinforcements along the route. Without their loyal, ever-willing and tireless assistance our recent successes would have been impossible.'[63] Similar sentiments no doubt applied to other theatres, in the USSR and in southern Asia.

8

One-Trippers

Generally speaking, there were two groups of aircrew in Ferry Command. The mainstay was a more or less regular staff of civilian pilots and radio operators whose numbers were reinforced as necessary by air force personnel attached to the command for a few months or a year or more. Credit for the success of the ferrying operation must be given to the staff of regulars but, as Air Commodore Taffy Powell has pointed out, the job could not have been done without the support of the 'one-trippers.'[1] As the name suggests, these were aircrew who for one reason or another made only one transatlantic delivery flight. Typical of this group were RAF and RCAF aircrew travelling across the Atlantic on leave or on duty. Instead of going by sea, the usual way, they might be assigned to fly as pilot or co-pilot of an aircraft being delivered by Ferry Command. Thus one more badly needed plane would reach an operational squadron and space would be saved in a crowded troop ship. On occasion, veteran air force navigators and wireless operator/air gunners also flew on single delivery missions. However, the largest number of one-trippers were recent BCATP graduates, or 'kids flying the Atlantic.'[2] Like all the one-trippers, they shared the same perils as the regular crews.

Many of these fresh young products of the air training plan, often no more than twenty years old and with remarkably few hours in their log-books, received their introduction to long-distance flying as well as to Ferry Command procedures at the new No. 31 Operational Training Unit that the British and Canadian authorities had agreed to set up in the winter of 1941. As soon as they decided to employ BCATP graduates on transoceanic ferry operations, they moved quickly. Everybody understood that the new crews would need further training, so the

Canadian government made available an airfield under construction at Debert, Nova Scotia. It was well located for the kind of instruction required and also to support the anti-submarine patrols of the RCAF's Eastern Air Command. The nucleus of the RAF OTU's headquarters staff arrived at the still unfinished Debert on 21 May 1941.[3]

At the end of the first week, the official daily diary described the new school's aims and objectives. The statement clearly stressed 'the importance and the urgency of the need for establishing on a sound basis the arrangements for the ferrying of American Aircraft across the Atlantic.' The diarist underlined the importance the British authorities placed on the venture by noting: 'The whole expense of providing DEBERT and adapting it to its altered purpose would be borne by the Air Ministry.' Notwithstanding its location in the new world, the school would be organized as RAF Station Debert, with two components: '(1) An Operational Training Unit for the training of pupils in operating the types of aircraft which are to be ferried across the Atlantic and (2) a short conversion course for J.A.T.P. [Joint Air Training Plan, as the British frequently referred to the BCATP] or R.A.F. pilots to enable them to carry out duties as second pilots.'[4]

With Ferry Command and its supporters banking on the success of the OTU, its training plan is worth looking at in some detail. The basic OTU course would last eight weeks, with staggered entries producing twenty pilots and twenty wireless operators qualified for transatlantic duty every four weeks. Where possible, pilots selected for training at Debert would already have graduated from a general reconnaissance school (invariably 31 GRS, Charlottetown), for the experience gained in long-distance flying over water. Those who succeeded at 31 OTU 'will gradually replace Atfero and loaned R.A.F. personnel as first pilots of Hudsons. They may be employed on ferrying duties for a period of six months (or less if Operational Training Unit and possibly conversion courses output in relation to aircraft production allow more rapid turnover).' If plans seemed rather imprecise for pilots, they were no less so for the rest of the crew: 'On account of the return passage problems wireless operators [who arrived at Debert from BCATP Bombing and Gunnery Schools in Canada] normally will only do one trip, unless Atfero's resources cannot cope with the balance, in which event it may be necessary for them to do additional trips or to organize a special course for additional operators.' Pilots and radio operators who had trained together for the first eight weeks were joined by navigators to complete potential ferry crews. Graduates of BCATP navigation schools were not thought to need the full course. They 'should be able to obtain sufficient additional experience during the last part of Operational Training Unit course [in essence a few hours in the air].' Like the wireless operators, 'normally navigators will only do one trip unless output proves insufficient.'[5]

The full OTU course at Debert was complemented by a conversion course, 'designed to fit pilots trained R.A.F. or J.A.T.P. schools to carry out duties as second pilots.' This course lasted for two weeks, with a minimum of ten hours' flying. 'Output is to work up to 50 pilots per month, i.e. with a peak pupil population at any time of 25.' BCATP schools supplied these students as well.

The 31 OTU training plans remained flexible, evolving to meet constantly changing ferry requirements. Initially, however, the goal of starting both courses early in June could not be met. The RAF did not even hoist its ensign for the first time until 11 June. The incomplete construction and the slow arrival of equipment and supplies frustrated the RAF staff:

The month of June has been rather an unhappy month for all personnel at the Station. The officers and airmen arrived full of energy and enthusiasm to start a most important job, but found that no actual work was possible, due to various causes. Before leaving England, it was understood the Aerodrome and Station at Debert was ready for use. This was not the case as although it was possible to use the runways in a very limited way, continual or hard work was impossible. During the month, a start was made by the Rayner Construction Company to tarmac and seal the runways and it is hoped the work will be completed in 60 days. Equipment, spares, stationery and the thousand and one other things necessary to start an O.T.U., had not arrived and it soon became evident that the operational plan would be late in starting. The target date for the opening of the first Course in both the O.T.U. and Conversion Course was June 4th. Up to date, training has not commenced, although the necessary personnel have arrived.[6]

The diary entry then goes on at some length about the problems of accommodating, and keeping 'reasonably happy and comfortable,' 725 airmen on a station built for 450.

A month later nothing had changed much: 'July has been another disappointing month as far as actual training work was concerned although a fair amount of flying was possible.' In fact, it may have been even more miserable for the RAF airmen already at Debert. The commanding officer used the delay to whip them into shape. 'Perhaps it was a fortunate thing,' the diary rationalized, 'that operational training could not commence immediately we arrived at Debert, as a large proportion of officers and airmen had come from Operational Stations at home [in Britain] and by the nature of things, had become slack in discipline and untidy in appearance.' A CO's parade was held each Friday. 'After two or three parades, a noticeable improvement in general appearance and deportment was evident.' Moreover, a series of Saturday morning inspections had a similar impact. The only consolation for the airmen was a full program of sports and social events. At least the diary could report that the paving of the runways and tarmac would be completed by 1 September.[7]

Finally, on 1 August, 'four Pilot Officers and sixteen Sergeant Pupils, all members of the R.C.A.F., reported from Halifax for the 1st Observers' Course.' By the 16th, the same day that the second observers' course (twenty RAF and ten Royal New Zealand Air Force) commenced, fifteen of these first students 'successfully completed' their course, after fourteen hours' flying, and left for Ferry Command headquarters in Montreal. 'Non-graduates' went to the 'Y' Depot at Halifax for embarkation for overseas by ship. In the meantime, bad weather, along with the incomplete facilities, made it difficult to cope with overlapping courses. Arrangements had to be made with Ferry Command to complete night training for some of the trainees. 'F/Lt. Whyte (At Ferro [sic]) has said that should it not be found possible to give the Observers a night flight during the short period they are on the camp, he was prepared to accept them, subject to there being facilities which will enable them to familiarise themselves with the interior lay-out of instruments in Hudson aircraft under night conditions.' Debert took up this offer when the second course graduated. 'Bad weather conditions again interfered with the completion of the Night Flying Navigation tests, and in consequence, H.Q.F.C. were notified that fourteen of the Observers reporting to them should preferably be given a night navigation exercise before proceeding on the Transatlantic flight.' This arrangement did not last long because the influx of partially trained aircrew put too great a strain on the facilities available in Montreal. However, it is a small example of the way in which 31 OTU and Ferry Command headquarters were in frequent communication discussing requirements and possible improvements in the curriculum.[8]

When the first graduates fell short of the standards expected by Ferry Command, Air Force Headquarters in Ottawa stepped in, sending the air navigation schools guidelines for selecting observer trainees for posting to 31 OTU:

(a) The Observer's ability at Astro Navigation must be above average, and under no circumstances should an Air Observer who has not completed an average amount of night work, be selected.
(b) The Observer should be keen and cool headed.
(c) Thoroughness, accuracy, and quick thinking are essential.
(d) Although difficult to ascertain, an airman with common sense is a very desirable type.
(e) Observers should be of good physique and not liable to exhaustion as a result of prolonged activity.[9]

No. 1 ANS, Rivers, Manitoba, replied that they were doing the best job possible of preparing the student observers. Group Captain A. Lewis, the CO, pointed out that his school had already requested longer-range aircraft like the Hudson. The Avro Anson did not have the performance to provide adequate long-distance training. As it was, 'the best graduates of this school are sent direct to Debert for trans-Atlantic ferrying duties.'[10]

The first several courses at Debert were for navigators, reflecting Ferry Command's greatest aircrew need at this early stage in its history. However, September saw the arrival of the first wireless operator/air gunner (WO/AG) and pilot trainees, creating a severe shortage of class-room accommodation. In fact, there was a miscalculation, and pilot training soon had to catch up with the navigators. The chief flying instructor, Squadron Leader Bradley, said that 'it was his ambition to give these pupil pilots 100 hours on Hudson before passing them out.' Ferry Command expressed satisfaction with this goal. This helps one understand where the term 'kids flying the Atlantic' originated to describe the young BCATP graduates sent to Ferry Command. The 31 OTU diary recorded, following a meeting the CFI had in Montreal, that Ferry Command's civilian pilots 'had done a minimum of 1,000 hours and in many cases, as much as 5,000 hours. The 4 pupils who have arrived so far, have done approximately 60 hours solo.' The OTU agreed 'to produce 30 pilots every 3 weeks for ferrying.' Training was rarely straightforward. Pilots arriving from a general reconnaissance school required sixteen hours per week of lecture-room instruction. Those who had not attended GRS needed 50 per cent more time in the classroom. When students with such varying degrees of prior preparation arrived for the same course, it made scheduling and instructing difficult for the Debert staff.[11]

The first wireless operator/air gunners also presented problems when their basic skills fell short of the level required by Ferry Command. Their standard of Morse reception was only about fifteen words per minute. The aim was to bring them up to twenty: 'It was decided to weight the instruction of these pupils as far as possible on the signals side, in view of the present absence of range facilities and armament equipment generally, and also because it was understood that these pupils will probably be required for Transatlantic Ferry duties before it is possible to complete the armament side of their training.' Not surprisingly, given the criticism and the importance placed on Morse proficiency, the students worked at improving their basic skills. The diary reported: 'The Morse room is very often filled until such a late hour as 21.00 hrs.'[12]

Whenever possible, the pilots and WO/AGs did their flying training together. For example, No. 1 pilots' course, to 29 September, 'included 16 cross country flights of approximately 2½ hrs each,' with the trainee pilots flying the planes while the WO/AGs worked on their own airborne exercises. Staff pilots were used for 'four additional cross country flights of approximately 2½ hours.' Finally, 'nine cross country flights of 10 hrs each were also carried out with a staff pilot in each a/c [aircraft].' The student pilots, 'however did all the work.' Training staff found these exercises 'of considerable value,' for the pilots flying the planes, the navigators charting the courses, as well as the wireless operators. The students benefited from the experience of an independent trip approaching the duration of a transatlantic delivery flight.[13]

OTU training was not without mishaps. The air force and its historians have long known that training was dangerous, especially in wartime, and claimed many lives. As Debert endeavoured 'to turn out the crews for the Atlantic crossing as quickly as possible,' its diary records numerous accidents, mostly on the airfield without any serious injuries. There were tragedies, however. On 23 and 25 October the first fatalities arrived with a vengeance. Three Hudsons crashed during long-distance flights, killing eleven airmen, three pilots, three observers, and three wireless operator/air gunners, as well as two Debert groundcrew. These were the first of at least ninety-three fatalities recorded at 31 OTU.[14]

No sooner had the first pilot and WO/AG courses received their postings, on 22 November after extensions due to weather and other complications, than a new training policy was implemented. Debert received word to extend the pilot and WO/AG courses to twelve weeks and the observer course to eight, with twenty-two new trainees starting a new course of each trade every four weeks. 'This change of policy differs considerably from that formerly in use, wherein pilots were given 8 weeks, WO/AGs 8 weeks and Air Observers one week's training.' The plan allowed pilots more advanced instruction and 'a minimum of 100 hours flying on Hudson aircraft before leaving operationally fit.' Henceforth the observers would arrive at the OTU better qualified, having first completed four weeks at a GRS. At Debert, 'they will crew up with pilots for the final two stages of training (i.e. elementary and advanced operational training).' The WO/AG course would be divided into three distinct phases: a conversion stage to meet Ferry Command standards and become familiar with the Hudson, an elementary operational stage where each trainee would be crewed with a pilot and an observer, and finally an advanced operational stage.[15]

The day the new training policy was announced, No. 3 WO/AG course commenced instruction. Among its twenty-two members was Sergeant Don Macfie of Dunchurch, Ontario, a young graduate of No. 1 Wireless School in Montreal and No. 1 Bombing and Gunnery School at Jarvis, Ontario, who set himself apart from his classmates by keeping a diary of his time at Debert. It allows us to get an idea of what 31 OTU was like for a trainee. Macfie's account of his first month reflects what the official record has already told us. He spent most of his time in the classroom practising Morse code. After a hectic, unexpected Christmas leave, much of it crammed in trains, Macfie returned to more boring Morse practice and finally had his familiarization flight in a Hudson on 5 January 1942: 'It was a navigation trip we ran into snow across the Bay of Fundy. Turned back and played around among the hills for a couple of hours. It is nice in the Hudson – I was in the turret to-day. They are slick.' If he was happy to get into the air at last, he expressed less pleasure with the RAF routine: 'We are made to go to three parades a day and also a daily Barrack inspection. They are making it hard as possible to live around here.'[16]

Once he had made his first Debert flight, Macfie found his time split between the air and the classroom, with occasional trips to the firing range. On 26 January he 'got crewed up at last,' with Pilot Officers Don Clark from Vancouver and Bill Randolph from London, England, as pilot and observer. Two days later Macfie found himself in trouble:

Was scheduled to fly at 7.45 A.M. I didn't see it on D.R.O. [daily routine order] Schedule in the mess until too late last night to get the W.T. equipment. Dashed over this morning to the section but nobody there. So I am in dutch with everybody up to Sqdn. leader. I got a pair of earphones and got into the A/C and when we came back they were all waiting for me. Had a hard time talking my way out of it all and getting things straightened up. We did some skeet shooting in the afternoon.

Macfie did not like the treatment the trainees received at Debert. 'Things are getting worse here. The C.F.I. has everybody after us like a gestapo. Continually getting warnings and told of new things to do to make us more miserable.'[17]

He was impressed with his crew. On 13 February they had a cross-country flight over southern New Brunswick and Prince Edward Island: 'After three hours the observer figured we should be over Summerside so we broke cloud and there we were over the middle of town. Mighty good observer we have.' The same day another crew had a less pleasant experience. Burt McNall took off at 5:00 p.m.: 'He got really lost and stayed up until 9 o'clock and circled a village. All the people came out and made a flare path with car lights and he finally landed on a little lake. Everything went well till he hit a cement pier on the shore and wiped off the undercart and knocked down the telephone and Hydro lines and drowned the plane in a river. He came out O.K. Fri 13th? or just bad luck?'

Exactly a month later Macfie's course graduated, most of its members heading off to Dorval to ferry a Hudson to Britain. He, however, was transferred with seven classmates to No. 6 WO/AG Course, 'in place of eight Norwegians who did not arrive.'[18] His disappointment at the prospect of remaining at Debert was assuaged by two weeks' leave, spent at home in Dunchurch. He unilaterally extended this by two days, without suffering any consequences, and returned to a new crew, Pilot Officers Bert Russell from Edmonton and Jack Ritchie from Windsor, Ontario, as pilot and navigator. He also learned that things had changed during his absence: 'Parade every morning for colour hoisting and no skipping lectures.' It must not have been too rough; Macfie confessed to his diary on 1 April that he had not yet made it up early enough for the flag raising and roll-call.[19]

April was devoted to flying, both long-distance and local, as well as to much waiting around, with a little boring time in the classroom as well. At one point our WO/AG commented, 'Surely is a haphazard organization this.'[20] Just as in his first course, Macfie and his crew made many flights of about three hours' duration over the Maritime provinces and adjacent waters. In each course they also went on a couple of longer trips, including one to Gander the first time and another to Montreal via Anticosti Island during his second stint. Although Macfie does not appear to have known about it, the staff at the OTU must have received a boost in April, when the station received an extract from a February Air Ministry signal: 'Wish to offer congratulations on successful ferrying of Hudsons by first three graduates of J.A.T.P., Pilot officers Syer, Triggs and Russ. Pilots have been interviewed and are enthusiastic regarding training received.' After quoting this accolade, the station diarist added: 'Unofficial information has been received that many more complete crews have made successful aircraft delivery flights to the United Kingdom.'[21]

The same month Debert 'first became operational, a request having been received from E.A.C. [Eastern Air Command of the RCAF] on the 18th, for aircraft to assist in patrols from Dartmouth. The first operational patrol was that done on the 20th, when following notification of a submarine in the Bay of Fundy, bombs were obtained from 16X [Explosives] Depot and two aircraft were sent in search of it.'[22] Macfie was one of the chosen few, although he did not see it that way. Before going to bed that night he scribbled in his diary: 'Around 10 P.M. I was told that I was getting up at 3 A.M. to go on a sub-patrol. I wonder who got this bright inspiration.' He and his crew, supplemented by staff pilot Flight Lieutenant McNeill, were one of a pair that took off just after 0600 to patrol the Bay of Fundy for a second day. 'It was raining and low cloud over the bay,' wrote Macfie. 'I put in 5 hrs in the turret as a gunner, sure is tiresome ... Nobody sighted any submarines. We now hear on the Radio when we got back that there was a big school of whales in the Bay of Fundy. Probably some fishermen mistook one for a sub & the result being us going out on a wild-goose chase.' The week following his first operational patrol Macfie turned twenty-one.[23]

Hudsons from 31 OTU continued to assist EAC's anti-submarine campaign. On Sunday, 3 May, Macfie and his crew flew out of Dartmouth to protect a large convoy sailing for the United Kingdom: 'After getting bombed up and briefed we did a zig-zag patrol past the [Halifax] harbour mouth and keeping an eye on the convoy going out. We were supposed to be out 6 hours but about 5.30 P.M. I got a message saying to return to base. We came in to shore and it was all covered in fog. Came in on the beam and made an awfully bumpy landing. Every time we hit I would think of the bombs.' No U-boats had been sighted.[24]

Five days later, Macfie spent his last day at Debert, but he was in no mood to celebrate. He called it a 'pretty glum day,' as he packed up while trying to recover from the previous night's party in the mess. 'Somebody got the grand notion to have a graduation parade for us. So out we went to parade Square about 2 P.M. Just as we marched out on the square it started to pour rain so the C/O didn't come out but sent one of his stooges who gave us a farewell speech. It quit raining just after we paraded off the square.' To this point they had no clear idea where they going: 'We got on train at 5.30 P.M. and set out for Dorval. It appears we are on Ferry Command alright but we didn't know till last minute.' Indeed, Macfie was one of eighteen WO/AGs dispatched to Dorval, along with a like number of pilots, and twenty observers. In addition, four pilots transferred to the US forces and one observer remained with 31 OTU as an instructor. May was the busiest month in the school's brief history, with almost 4040 flying hours, 334 at night.[25] At least from the perspective of training, the scheme to use young BCATP graduates to ferry aircraft across the Atlantic was well under way.

If Macfie had arrived in Montreal, he had not finished his training. Bunked at Lachine's No. 5 Manning Depot, he took the daily bus out to Dorval as he passed the next ten days practising Morse code and attending lectures on Ferry Command procedures. When he failed to get a weekend pass, his diary reveals that he simply took the time off and went home. On 18 May he wrote: 'Arrived back at Dorval around 10.30 AM and went up to Radio School expecting to be on charge for being A.W.O.L. but we were never missed I guess nobody said anything.' Two days later he passed his final examination and received four days' legitimate leave, which he again spent in Dunchurch with his family. Everyone realized that this leave was different, as Macfie put it: 'This time I'm away over.' Sunday night 'all but Dad drove up to N[orth] Bay to see me off [on the train].' Loaded down with goodies from home, he arrived back in Montreal on Monday morning, only to spend the week waiting to take off for Britain. The following Sunday the crew got the word that they would leave the next day.

On 1 June 1942, more than six months after he had started training to help ferry a new Hudson to Britain, Sergeant Don Macfie's big day arrived. He rose early, 'coaxed a breakfast out of the cook and caught an early bus and arrived at the airport with half an hour to spare before take-off.' However, there was a problem. 'The mad dash was halted when the dispatcher didn't have the right Syko cards to give me (For decoding purposes). At eight o'clock I was very near crazy and when at last I got squared around and dashed out to the A/C no one was around and it was called off a little later. This is what ages a man quick. It seems that the weather is bad around Newfoundland.'

The next day started as 'a repeat on yesterday morning.' Finally they got off early in the afternoon, arriving at Gander about 1930, catching up with all their classmates who had preceded them over the previous few days. Macfie had been impressed with that site during a training visit, and was not disappointed this time. 'We had a very good meal here and given an excellent bed. This is the best place to eat and sleep I've seen yet.' The stay was short. The next day, loaded down with 2400 cigarettes (for barter on the other side), he and his crew prepared for their trip. The young airmen made the key decisions together: 'Weather report for the Atlantic is cloudy with a little ice and although it is entirely up to the crew if they go or not everybody decided to go.' Macfie made sure that food and thermoses were loaded. Then, at about 2100, Hudson FH444 taxied out to take off. 'Had quite a job getting off but did O.K. sure a heavy load. The A/C seemed to be just up there kind of rolling back and forth and about like a water soaked log about to sink. I was quite confident of my job and not worried. Checked our course as we crossed the coast of Newfoundland a half hour after take-off and headed out over the Atlantic for Ireland. We had to start to climb immediately to get over the cloud.'

Macfie thought that, as the radio operator, all he had to do was 'send call sign every two hours and keep my ears open in between.' However, few transatlantic ferry flights were completely uneventful. 'The first thing to happen was with the oxygen. We turned it on about an hr and a half out and in doing so Bert [Russell, the pilot] turned his valve out too far and couldn't get it back in again and so the oxygen was blowing out at a great rate and we could have lost it all soon so I had to figure out a way of regulating it with the main valve at the back. It was a delicate business and sometimes we weren't getting enough and would feel a little woozy.' Jack Ritchie, the navigator, had the biggest oxygen problem: 'He didn't know he had to turn a valve to get his and just put his mask on and let it go at that. We wondered after awhile what was the matter with him as he seemed to be acting funny. Came up out of the nose once in awhile and looked around but couldn't speak to us with his mask on. He said afterward that he got awfully sleepy and unconcerned about everything and gave up navigating and just sat there and left everything up to us. That is the way lack of oxygen gets you.' Despite making light of it in the diary, Macfie must have recognized that an incapacitated navigator presented a problem for a crew out over the Atlantic, because Ritchie could not help them much. 'He went back once and tried to take a shot of the stars through the astro dome but breathed on the glass of the sextant and it immediately frosted over rendering it useless for the rest of the trip. Of course at the time he didn't know what he was doing and blamed the sextant for being faulty.'[26]

Oxygen was not the only problem: 'After about three or four hours out a tank ran dry and the motors quit and we went into a dive for the sea. Me not knowing what it was had a great scare and thought all was up with us. But Bert woke up out of his half stupor from lack of oxygen and seeing the big red light blazing at him switched over and got us going again. This happened three times on the way.' Macfie 'had to pump 110 gal of fuel up from the bomb-bay at the rate of 6 pulls up on the pump per gallon. This was pure hell and agony when you are oxygen shy and freezing.'

Fuel and oxygen may have been under reasonable control, but the crew did not know where they were. Fortunately for the inexperienced airmen now entrusted with deliveries, Bowhill and McTaggart-Cowan had convinced the British authorities to provide more radio aids to navigation since the first delivery flights.[27] 'After nine hours and still over cloud we figured we should be getting somewhere,' Macfie wrote, 'but weren't sure of our position we just went by what I could get in Radio bearings after awhile we saw a hole in the clouds and came down through and there was land. We breathed a great sigh of joy but weren't sure what country it might be. I had trouble getting the low frequ. set tuned up but finally got contact and with the D/F or Direction finding station and got a fix which put us on the biggest lake in Ireland.' With great relief the radio operator 'got a QDM (course to steer) from Prestwick and in Half an hour we were over Scotland. I'll never forget the pretty sight Ireland and Scotland made.'[28]

The youthful crew did not yet feel totally comfortable. 'We cut into the circuit and landed without permission because all tank gauges were reading empty. We had about 15 gallons left. Our time for the trip was 10 hrs and 45 minutes.' Just like the first arrival of Hudsons on 11 November 1940, this one by a crew of young BCATP graduates brought no fanfare. Macfie expected 'it would be quite a ceremony taking the first step on foreign soil.' As it was, 'I didn't even realize it at the time and until half an hour later. We had a lunch and went through customs and everything finally in order. Tried a beer a Guinness – peuh! At 7 P.M. we were on a bus for Glasgow and headed by train for Bournemouth England.' Nonetheless, as he sat on the train and reflected on what he had accomplished, Macfie bragged to his diary: 'Well it is all over and at last I feel as though I have done something. I guess I have eh?'

In fact, Sergeant Macfie's real war had not yet started. He remained at the Aircrew Reception Centre in Bournemouth until 18 July, when he was posted to 423 Squadron, flying Short Sunderland flying boats on anti-submarine patrols out of the picturesque town of Oban in western Scotland.[29] His stay with Ferry Command had been short, but it was typical of the hundreds of BCATP graduates who passed through Dorval during the war.

Young students like Macfie were not the only men that ferry Command got from the BCATP. It was decided quite early that navigation instructors should be given the opportunity to broaden their experience by acting as navigators on delivery flights to Britain. When word went out to the schools about this policy, it was explained as having a two-fold benefit: 'It is the intention that this Trans-Atlantic flight be used to further the experience of the instructors and to give them an opportunity, while in the United Kingdom, of visiting an operational unit so that they may observe actual war conditions and bring back useful information on current navigation practice.'[30]

Flight Lieutenant Harold A. Wills, a good example of this other type of one-tripper, differed from the student those experiences we have just chronicled. If Don Macfie was young, fresh, and impressionable, Hal Wills was older and more experienced. A schoolteacher by profession, when war erupted in September 1939 he was assistant principal of an elementary school in Kitchener, Ontario. Thirty-seven years of age, married, with a young daughter, Wills could have sat out the war advancing in his education career and satisfying his patriotic feelings with some form of volunteer work. But he had a strong urge to serve in a more active role. Of the three services, the air force held the greatest attraction. Had he been younger, Wills would undoubtedly have volunteered for aircrew duty. The upper age limit for pilots, however, was twenty-seven and for other aircrew, thirty-three.[31]

Another avenue beckoned for someone keenly interested in flying. Under the BCATP, the largest air training plan in the history of the Commonwealth, Canada agreed, among other things, to establish ten air observer schools for training navigators, or air observers as they were known until 1942. They were to have a combined output of about 4000 air observers a year. Finding enough instructors to open them on time was an urgent matter. In the small prewar RCAF, pilots did their own navigating. If a particularly long or difficult flight required a navigator, the job went to the co-pilot. With the development of bigger and faster aircraft with longer range, the need for specialist navigators arose, but plans to introduce them were still on paper when war was declared. Thus, in setting up a navigation training program, the RCAF was starting from scratch. No other part of the BCATP began under a greater handicap.[32]

To fill the gap the RCAF recruited a number of university graduates with majors in mathematics (a good background for navigators), gave them an intensive two-month course at No. 1 Air Navigation School at Rivers, Manitoba, and sent them out to open the air observer schools. The RCAF recruited 28 potential instructors in 1939, 107 in 1940, and 77 in 1941.[33] More were recruited in 1942, but by that time the training organization was capable of producing its own instructors from among the top graduates of the air observer schools.

Although Wills had been working towards a degree by attending summer sessions at the University of Western Ontario in London, he had not yet completed all the required courses. In the summer of 1940, instead of continuing the regular program of studies, and most likely after some advice from air force recruiting authorities, he enrolled in special courses in air navigation, astronomy, and spherical trigonometry at Western. In September, after completing his studies, he was tentatively accepted by the RCAF, even though he was above the preferred age, and told to hold himself in readiness.[34] Meanwhile, No. 1 ANS was expanding month by month and working full out in training navigator instructors.[35] There were still quite a few ahead of Wills and he was not called up until mid-May 1941.

Before going to Rivers, Wills was ordered to report to No. 1 Manning Depot, in the Coliseum on the grounds of the Canadian National Exhibition in Toronto, which housed more than 5000 RCAF trainees. Here, where new recruits were introduced into the ways of service life and taught how to march and salute, he spent four weeks on a daily routine of '2 hourly lectures and one hour drill morning & afternoon.'[36] On 19 June he left Toronto by train for Rivers. On the 23rd Pilot Officer Wills began training with fifteen other officers as No. 10 Air Navigation Course.[37]

No. 1 ANS was the principal centre for air navigation training in Canada, with the overall purpose of establishing and maintaining a high standard of navigation in the BCATP and throughout the RCAF. It was located at Rivers because of the clear prairie sky, ideal for studying stars and practising astro navigation. In 1940 and 1941, No. 1 ANS's main function was to turn out instructors. Renamed Central Navigation School in 1942, it became a research centre as well as a training school.[38]

The most challenging task for the potential instructors was to master the art of dead (or deduced) reckoning – determining the position of an aircraft in flight and plotting its course from point to point by means of compasses, air speed indicator, and drift recorder. They also had to become proficient in the use of radio aids to navigation and in celestial navigation, not as substitutes for dead reckoning but as methods of checking their DR calculations and ensuring the greatest degree of accuracy. Air training, where the navigators had to make practical application of what they learned in the classroom, was carried on concurrently with ground instruction.[39] After the usual couple of familiarization flights, Wills's first training flight, on 2 July, was a map-reading and pinpointing exercise. On his second, three days later, he flew as first navigator on a cross-country trip responsible to the pilot for plotting the course and keeping the aircraft on track. 'Did O.K.,' he jotted in his diary.[40]

On completing the course, the new instructors were sent to various air observer schools to impart their newly acquired knowledge and skills to raw recruits. Wills went to No. 1 AOS, Malton, Ontario, where he arrived on 2 September 1941, the same day he learned of his promotion to flying officer.[41] Malton was an average-size school with a population, including civilians, instructional staff, and trainees, of close to one thousand. Like No. 1 ANS it was extremely busy, with Avro Ansons, the aircraft used for navigation training, taking off and landing at all hours of the day and night. A steady stream of recruits flowed through the school. A group of approximately forty arrived every two weeks for the twelve-week air observer course. There were always six or seven courses in various stages of instruction, including the new arrivals and those preparing to leave. Each course was in the charge of a senior instructor, with two or three others assisting.[42]

During his stay at Malton, Wills worked with three different courses, including one made up almost entirely of Australians. He had a reputation for taking a fatherly interest in his pupils, following their progress carefully and corresponding with some after they went overseas. He was also known for setting up difficult air exercises. One student wrote: 'That popular officer named Wills / Made our course a series of thrills / Each day that we flew / He would give a route new / Till we damned near went blue at the gills.'[43]

In September 1942 Wills was posted to No. 4 AOS, London. It was a straight exchange posting – Wills going to London and Flight Lieutenant William L. Halperin leaving there for Malton. Halperin, in his mid-twenties, had graduated from the University of Toronto in mathematics and was lecturing at St John's College in Winnipeg when war was declared.[44] This was the first time that the paths of the two men had crossed, but the fortunes of war would bring them together again.

The navigation instructors with whom Wills and Halperin worked have a unique place in RCAF history. They were the first navigators in the service, apart from pilots, and made a noteworthy contribution in getting the air training program under way. It is curious, however, that although during training and instructing they were required to fly, they were shown in the official air force list as 'non-flying.' The uncertainty of their status is further revealed in their not being given a navigator badge, or a flying badge of any kind, in a service where aircrew badges counted for so much.

In 1942, navigators came into their own. That year brought sweeping changes in the structure of the RAF and other air forces of the Commonwealth, following the appointment of Air Marshal Arthur Harris as commander-in-chief of Bomber Command in February. Harris quickly came to the conclusion that, despite valiant efforts by the aircrew, targets were being missed because of faulty navigation. The main problem was that the air observer, who was responsible for navigating to the target and back home again, was also responsible for dropping the bombs and, if necessary, taking a turn at the guns. Harris's solution was to replace the overworked observer with two men – a full-time navigator and a bomb-aimer who, in spare moments, would serve as assistant to the navigator.[45]

These decisions had a significant impact on the strategic bombing offensive and, on another level, other interesting results. They led directly to the designing of two new aircrew badges – for navigators and for bomb-aimers. This in turn focused attention on navigators 'non-flying.' Were they entitled to wear the new badge? Although the training of navigators, in place of air observers, began in March 1942, Air Council did not hand down a decision on this question until November. In a long-overdue gesture, it was announced that 'officers employed in the navigation branch (Non-Flying List)' might be awarded the navigator's badge, provided they had completed a minimum of six months on instructional duties and had at least one hundred hours of day flying and fifty hours by night.[46] With more than 400 hours in his logbook, Wills met the conditions and entered a terse note in his diary: 'Awarded "N" Wing.'[47]

The order also stated that navigation instructors could apply for service overseas, provided they were of aircrew age – not over thirty-three. This left Wills out, and more or less meant that he would be employed as a navigation instructor for the duration. Many of his associates, for instance Halperin, were able to qualify for overseas postings.

In the meantime, Wills steadily progressed in the service. In July he was promoted to flight lieutenant and placed in charge of all the even-numbered classes in the school, supervising both ground instruction and flying exercises. His cheerful disposition, enthusiasm, and determination to succeed made him well liked by his fellow officers and the navigator trainees. In off-duty hours this popularity was enhanced by his talent at the piano and a good baritone voice. He took readily to service life and, in so far as he thought about the future, he seemed to be attracted by the prospect of a career in the navigation branch of the RCAF after the war.[48]

As a senior instructor, there were opportunities for flying that Wills readily accepted. In September 1943 he went on a special course at No. 31 OTU. While there he flew on anti-submarine patrols in the Gulf of St Lawrence and Halifax area.[49] The course lasted only two weeks, but the experience enabled him and the instructors working with him to bring more realism into navigation training at No. 4 AOS. Three weeks after returning to London from Debert, Wills was on his way to Montreal for a delivery flight with Ferry Command to study at first hand the techniques used in transatlantic navigation. For anyone involved in aviation, Montreal was an exciting place during the war. Wills was very impressed. 'This is a great spot,' he wrote to his wife, Gladys, 'every type of aircraft imaginable and you're talking & working with real "gen" men – Men who have been places & done real things.'[50]

As soon as he reported to Dorval on 22 October, Wills, like every other new arrival, wanted to know what type of aircraft he would be assigned to and what route he would be taking. However, as he explained to Gladys, to whom he wrote every two or three days without fail, usually enclosing a note for his daughter, Gale, there was no simple answer to these questions.

There are several possibilities as to routes we may take. Dorval to either Gander in Newfoundland, or Goose in Labrador. Then to Greenland (maybe not land there) – then to Iceland – to the United Kingdom. If we go to Gander may go directly across with no stops. Or we may go to Elizabeth City (somewhere on east coast of U.S.A. – am not sure where – New Jersey I imagine [sic]) and from there to Montreal – Goose & directly over, or Gander & directly over, or to Bermuda and directly over. This is the case only if we take a flying boat (Catalina or Canso). They make it in one leap – about 25 hours – are rather slow but can carry loads of gas ... The type of ship & the weather determines the route you take. I'll take the Iceland trip if possible. It is broken up over 3 days and the hops are fairly short.[51]

Regardless of his experience, on reporting to Dorval a navigator had to undergo a series of ground classes and air tests at the Ferry Command instructional school before being accepted for transatlantic duty. The course lasted about two weeks. If successful, he then received a definite assignment. In Wills's case, training began on 25 October and ended on 10 November. 'Our day consists of 9.30 to 4.30,' Gladys learned. 'Get the 9 bus out of Montreal if we have breakfast in town or an earlier bus if we eat at the station.' During the day there were lectures on meteorology, the location of transatlantic radio stations and their signals and codes, dinghy drill and pyrotechnics (use of flare signals in event of distress), and star recognition. There were also plotting problems to work out, computing airspeed and headings for a given set of conditions 'just like an Atlantic flight.'[52]

High-altitude flying was another subject on the curriculum, for on crossing the Atlantic they would be flying at a greater altitude than they were accustomed to at AOS. It included an ascent in the decompression chamber, which Wills described in some detail:

Wednesday morning [3 November] we had lectures on Altitude flying & in the afternoon went through the decompression Chamber at McGill [University]. It was quite an experience. About 10 get into the chamber at once with an M.O. [medical officer]. They take us to 24000 ft very quickly – in about 4 minutes & there you stay. You first notice your breathing is heavier. Then you get sluggish. They ask you to write your name & address & give you a simple multiplication problem. At first you can do it. As time progresses you write more poorly & make more & more mistakes in multiplying. You know you aren't doing it correctly but can't figure things out. You get dopier & hazier. It becomes difficult to write at all. Then your memory goes & you may do things you don't remember. I did. I wrote things I have no memory of doing. Finally your writing ends in an unintelligible scrawl & finally you pass out ... When you are practically out the M.O. puts on your oxygen mask & you revive very quickly with no ill effects. I was the *last* one to need oxygen ... After the last man has his oxygen mask on you go up to 33000 ft. You find no difference than atmospheric pressure with oxygen.[53]

Towards the end of the first week, Wills had a familiarization flight in a Mitchell. 'It looks as if that's what I'm going to draw,' he informed Gladys. 'If I do it means Labrador, perhaps Greenland, definitely Iceland & then ... on to the U.K.'[54]

On air exercises Wills was paired with Flight Lieutenant Stewart Ferguson, an instructor from No. 5 AOS, Winnipeg. They went up for their 'checkflight,' a cross-country trip to assess their navigation skill, on 1 November. After two years of instructing they both found it rather routine, although the start was a bit hectic. At 10 o'clock on a Monday morning, without any prior warning, they were told they had ninety minutes to get ready. 'We didn't have any maps, charts, flying clothes etc. Believe me, we hustled around. By the time of take-off we had our equipment gathered together but didn't have a lick of flight preparation done. At any rate away we went.' The flight, in a Lockheed Ventura, took them from Montreal to Blissville, New Brunswick, and then north to Presque Isle, Maine, and back again – a round trip of about five hundred miles. 'Stew navigated down and I did it coming home ... Navigated entirely by radio. Tried the sun but it was too low, ... On ETA [estimated time of arrival] I was directly over Mt. Royal, so that was pretty good.'

Montreal was a good place to meet other aircrew, some just back from a flight to Britain, Africa, or India and some, like Wills, just arriving on the scene. All had stories to tell or questions to ask. One of the first persons Wills ran into was Halperin. 'We traded jobs when I went to London,' he reminded Gladys. A few days later he noted that 'Halperin got his check flight yesterday and he's ready to go.' He was especially pleased when he met 'Pritchard and Calladine,' former students from course 70 at London. 'They each have a trip to Africa to their credit – via Brazil. They expect to do the North trip next.' From the officer in charge of navigation he learned that 'Calladine is rated extremely highly down here. So was Syrett.' The latter, another ex-pupil, had recently been posted from Dorval to No. 111 OTU at Nassau in the Bahamas. 'The OIC [officer-in-command] Navigation couldn't remember Pritchard's trip, but his pilot asked for him permanently, so I feel rather good about the 3 of them.' Flight Lieutenant W.G. Heslop, whom he had seen at No. 4 AOS just a few weeks earlier, arrived on 1 November: 'Had 3 days in England ... a good trip.' A few days later Flight Lieutenant Dave Bruce, another acquaintance, showed up at Dorval. 'Came up with his crew from Nassau. They are getting genned up & are taking a Liberator to India where they are posted to a Coastal Command Squadron.'[55]

Wills was so taken with Ferry Command that he appears to have tried to wangle a permanent posting. 'The O.I.C. Navigation here is going to try to get a new set up here – about 20 F/Ls each sort of O.I.C. a certain group of pool navigators & act as their instructor. Have a pretty good hunch if it goes through he is going to ask for me – maybe. – It's a long shot, but it might happen – who knows. It would be swell.'[56]

In a letter dated 6 November Wills said that he was nearly finished the course, 'but was told today it may be a week or 10 days before we actually get away. Apparently, quite a few are stalled in Goose Bay by weather, and we will have to wait until they clear out. Of course, that can happen very quickly if some good weather comes along.' One of those held up at Goose was Halperin, navigating a Mitchell and flying the same route that Wills was to follow. With a slight improvement in the weather on the 6th, he and his crew took off early in the morning, but by evening they had not reached their destination and were reported missing. Somewhere between Goose Bay and Greenland the aircraft simply disappeared.[57]

Wills may or may not have learned of Halperin's fate. Even if he did, although it would have saddened him, it would not have altered his own plans. Flying the North Atlantic was a challenge as well as an opportunity and he accepted it as such. At the moment he was preoccupied with the bad weather. On the 6th he told Gladys that he 'was supposed to do a night flight to-night but weather washed it out. Am now supposed to do it to-morrow night.' Two days later he wrote: 'As usual, it's raining ... Out around the station it's one big mud puddle with young lakes everywhere ... Couldn't fly last night nor tonight.' On the 10th he lamented, 'Things are just the same here. Have been supposed to do a night flight every night, but the weather has been terrible ... However, if we don't get the night flip in, it won't hold us up.'

Training ended on Tuesday, 9 November, with 'a Met. lecture by the World's leading Met. Authority on Trans-oceanic flying [obviously

McTaggart-Cowan]. The next step was a visit to 'Crew Assignments' to find out what aircraft he would be flying in and to meet his pilot and either crew members. He hoped for a Dakota. In this regard, Wills had developments to report on the 15th: 'I am going as far as Goose Bay (Labrador) to-morrow morning – Tues. Nov. 16 ... Am going over in a B-25 (Mitchell).' His crew was a typical Ferry Command cosmopolitan mix: 'The pilot is a Norwegian [Lieutenant Erik Bertil Palm] – has had considerable experience – so has the W.A.G. [Pilot Officer Gerald Raymond Styles, RCAF, from St Thomas, Ontario] Also have a Co-Pilot – English [Sergeant Eric Hanway Swanston, RAF, Watford, Hertfordshire]. We are going by way of Greenland – Iceland to the United Kingdom ... It may take as long as a couple of weeks – or even longer. Depends on the weather. Fellows have been held up in Greenland for as long as 3 weeks. Also in Goose & Iceland.' Then on a more optimistic note he added: 'If we have good weather we'll be there Friday.' In a note to his daughter, he promised, 'I'll do my best to be home by Christmas.' He also promised to write from every stop, partly to keep the family informed of his progress and partly because letters from these out-of-the-way places would be treasured as souvenirs.[58]

The weather along the northern route was usually at its worst in the last two months of the year. In November 1943 it lived up to its reputation. Owing to a prevailing flow of warm air over southern Greenland, that area had persistent fog and a combination of fog and snow. Other parts of the route, the leg from Dorval to Goose Bay and Goose Bay to Greenland, were unfavourable, but Greenland appeared the most vulnerable. Strangely, at this time the direct route from Gander non-stop to the United Kingdom was not plagued by these conditions. Aircraft using it were experiencing few delays.[59]

Wills's next letter did not come from Goose Bay but from Mont Joli, a small town on the south shore of the St Lawrence River in the Gaspé region of Quebec, where he was billeted in the Hotel Chez Donat. Mont Joli housed No. 9 Bombing and Gunnery School, which served as an alternate airfield when weather closed Goose Bay. 'Will be able to leave in the morning for Goose, I think,' Wills wrote over-optimistically on the evening of the 16th. The next day they were still at Mont Joli. 'Just as we were thinking of getting on our way to Goose, Dorval sent in a weather report for us to stay as Goose was closing in ... In fact other ships came in here to-day. The station is overcrowded & so are the hotels.'

They reached Goose Bay on the 18th. 'Arrived here yesterday afternoon after a lovely trip. Hit the place dead on,' Wills boasted in a letter written the next day. 'My ETA was exact to the half minute. ' He expected to be at Goose Bay 'a couple of days, at least,' but was stranded there for almost a week. He wrote several letters, noting 'I've been away a month now, but will see you before another month rolls around.' During the delay he also 'met a few chaps I met at Dorval,' including Stew Ferguson. They had arrived a day or two earlier and were now waiting for a break in the weather. Some of them, including Wills and his crew, finally got airborne again on 23 November on a heading that took them across the Davis Strait towards Greenland.[60]

'Well, I'm at —.' A conscientious censor had cut out the missing word, but Wills nevertheless managed to give a subtle hint of his whereabouts. 'Remember the old hymn about this place? It really is true.' Looking through her hymnary, Gladys undoubtedly spotted the old missionary hymn, 'From Greenland's Icy Mountains.'[61] More precisely, he was at Narsarssuak near the southern tip of the giant island, at the head of a long mountainous fjord, where the Americans had built BW-1, little more than a narrow landing strip of steel mats sloping down to the sea.

Waiting for the weather to clear, Wills found time hanging heavily on his hands. 'All we do is play ping-pong, Chinese Checkers, read, write letters and sleep.' However, as guests of the Americans they were well looked after. At Goose Bay Wills described the meals as 'O.K. On a par with what Crumlin [the airbase at London, Ontario] used to be like. No fancy stuff, but quite O.K.' At BW-1 he had 'the best meals ... since I've had one at home – better than any service meals I've ever had. Uncle Sam sure looks after his doughboys – in every way in fact.' He also appreciated the dazzling display of northern lights. 'The Aurora Borealis ... reached from West horizon to East – really beautiful ... huge waves & colours. I thought what I saw in Rivers was something – it was nothing to the Northern Lights here.'[62]

On Saturday, 27 November, Wills wrote: 'Well, we are still here. Thought we were going to get away this morning, but no go. It looks as if we should make it to-morrow. If so we should be at our destination Monday – one more stop to make.' Although it was late in the year, he felt that if they reached the United Kingdom soon he could still get home by Christmas, especially if he was able to fly back to Canada.

Sunday morning the four men climbed into their Mitchell and prepared to leave on the third leg of their trip. Most takeoffs from BW-1 were spectacular, and their's was probably no exception. The normal procedure was to roar down the runway with the noise of the engines re-echoing deafeningly from the mountains on either side. The aircraft would lift off right at the water's edge and climb to about 12,000 feet to clear the mountain peaks. They then set course for Iceland some 750 miles away. An hour out from Reykjavik, wireless operator Styles called for a radio signal, probably a routine position check. The signal was given and acknowledged. Then, somewhere over the North Atlantic, some unknown tragedy struck. Nothing further was heard from Mitchell FV990. As soon as Reykjavik reported it overdue, the RAF in Iceland initiated a search. No trace of the missing plane was ever found. On 1 December Gladys received word that her husband was missing.[63]

Ironically, according to Taffy Powell, the Mitchell was the best-liked aircraft in Ferry Command.[64] It was fast and, under good conditions, promised a quick trip overseas. But in November 1943 conditions along the northern route were not good. Besides the aircraft in which Wills and Halperin were flying, another Mitchell, FR203, was lost between BW-1 and Iceland, and yet another went into a spin from 11,000 feet, the pilot recovering just in time to prevent another tragedy. Two more were lost in December.[65]

When an aircraft disappeared over the Atlantic without leaving a trace, as in the cases of Wills and Halperin, it is impossible to say exactly what happened. Given the conditions prevailing over Greenland in November 1943, the most likely explanation is carburettor icing, one of two types of icing hazards confronting the crews of Ferry Command. The other was the accretion of solid ice on the wings, tail, and propellers. Both types, especially the former, were virtually unpredictable and frightening when they occurred. Ice accretion could be prevented, or at least lessened, by smearing exposed surfaces with a de-icing compound or by building special devices into the wings and propeller mechanism. Sometimes the problem could be overcome by climbing or descending into warmer air. Carburettor icing was a more insidious thing. A freak of nature, it developed without any visual warning, making itself evident to the pilot by a sudden loss of power or perhaps an engine failure. It occurred, not in extremely cold weather, but at temperatures near freezing in conditions of high humidity. If the moisture-laden air flowing into the carburettor became cooled, ice crystals were deposited in somewhat the same way that hoar frost is deposited in nature.[66]

In most aircraft, carburettor icing was prevented by preheating the air intake. The Mitchell was an exception. Its Holley carburettors employed a device that automatically compensated for variations in the temperature and humidity of the air. The conventional preheaters were eliminated.[67] Don McVicar explains that, although he liked the Mitchell, the

Holley carburettors were known for their ice-collecting tendency. On one occasion, flying between Goose Bay and Greenland, he had a dramatic demonstration as one engine suddenly cut out. There followed some anxious moments until 'I got straightened up.'[68] This happened in June. In November the possibility of icing was much greater and the effects more severe.

Whatever happened to Mitchell FV990, whether its disappearance was caused by ice forming in the carburettor or by something else, its loss was a tragic illustration of the hazards faced by Ferry Command crews. Back in Canada, No. 4 AOS mourned the loss of one of its most experienced and best-liked instructors, 'one of nature's noblemen, with a cheery smile and a kind word for every one.'[69] For Gladys and Gale, and for the families of all the others lost, it was a sad Christmas.

9

No. 45 Group

By the time Flight Lieutenant Harold Wills made his tragic attempt to cross the Atlantic as a one-tripper, Ferry Command had technically ceased to exist – at least by that name. The entire operation had undergone its fourth and final major reorganization. Now, officially, it had a new name, as well as demotion in status to group level from command. In March 1943, reflecting the expanded role of the aeroplane in the supply and communications role, the RAF created Transport Command, giving it responsibility for all transport operations, including ferrying. Initially it comprised three groups: No. 44 at Gloucester in England, No. 45 at Dorval, and No. 216 in the Middle East. By September 1945 it had added six more, stretching all the way to Delhi, India. Air Chief Marshal Sir Frederick Bowhill was made air officer commanding-in-chief, with headquarters at Harrow in Middlesex, England. Air Vice-Marshal R.G.L. Marix, lately second-in-command to Bowhill at Dorval, became head of No. 45 Group. Notwithstanding its downgrading from command status, this group remained the most important strategic air supply arm of the RAF. Its primary function continued to be aircraft ferrying, but more attention came to be focused on air transport in its broader sense. Members of the ferry service, however, then and since, continued to refer to the operation as Ferry Command, regardless of the period of the war.[1]

The reorganization followed a similar development in the USAAF, where Ferrying Command had become Air Transport Command under General H.L. George in June 1942.[2] These changes stemmed from the increased production of long-range cargo aircraft, which revolutionized the role of air transport in military operations, as well as from a growing appreciation by commanders of how the new tool could be used to maximum effect. We have already seen in chapter 7 that a fast resupply by Ferry Command Liberators undoubtedly had an impact on the campaign in North Africa.

Besides obvious war materials like ammunition and spare parts, the cargoes carried by the aircraft of Ferry Command and its successor, Transport Command's 45 Group, reflected the intricate character of the war itself. Medical supplies, mail, food, and technical equipment needed in a hurry generally received a high priority. After the Normandy landings there was a marked increase in the amount of penicillin flown from Montreal. In mid-1943 penicillin shipments averaged about thirty pounds. By the end of August 1944 the drug, highly valued in the prevention of infection in open wounds and the treatment of communicable diseases, was being airlifted in lots of several thousand pounds each. Live frogs, carried from South Africa to Canada, presumably for pregnancy tests on women members of the forces, and Satin Moth parasites flown from Canada to South Africa, were two more interesting items of cargo.[3] Others included 'theodolites, chloroform ampoules, serum, fishing kits, canned fish, artificial eyes, louse powder, colour films, portable cookers, buttons, hexachlorethane, dehydrated pork, garden seeds to be sent to Axis countries for our prisoners of war.'[4]

In 1942, material for the Dieppe raid was rushed to the United Kingdom, and in September 1944 twenty-eight tons of vitally needed supplies were flown from Cincinnati, Ohio, to the battlefront in northern France in Liberators and Dakotas of 45 Group.[5] The planes, it seems, might have been asked to carry almost anything. Henry Flory, flying on the South Atlantic return ferry service, particularly recalls 'one load of grass seed destined to Malta, that heroic island in the Mediterranean that had been bombed to near extinction and needed grass planted to prevent its being completely blown away. But for the most part it was grass seed and penicillin and spare parts going East, and returning ferry pilots coming West. We got this down to a real routine.'[6]

The newly created No. 45 (Transport) Group functioned through two arms, 112 (North Atlantic) Wing at Dorval and 113 (South Atlantic) Wing at Nassau in the Bahamas.[7] The operations of these two wings encompassed more than a score of staging posts and miscellaneous units along the strategic air routes spanning the North and South Atlantic. Two Pacific wings, No. 280 at San Diego, California, and No. 300 at Sydney, Australia, were formed in December 1944 and January 1945 to supervise 45 Group's operations in the South Pacific over a route staging through Honolulu, Canton Island, and Fiji.[8] In February 1945 fourteen Dakotas, the first aircraft delivered to Australia by 45 Group, were flown over this route.[9] The pilots were brought back by the trans-Pacific service, which henceforth operated on a schedule of roughly two flights in each direction every week. The number of aircraft ferried to Australia by 45 Group was not large, approximately sixty-four, primarily Dakotas. The deliveries and the return service depended on a good ideal of assistance from the Americans, who had shouldered the responsibility for the development of the trans-Pacific route. A significant aspect of 45 Group's Pacific operations was the establishment of regular air communications with Australia and New Zealand. Political officials and high-ranking military officers from these countries were now able to travel to North America in RAF aircraft.[10]

The reorganization leading up to the formation of No. 45 Group included the establishment of 231 (Transport) Squadron at Dorval. This unit flew regular transatlantic flights, including a return service to Cairo and sometimes as far as Karachi, and also ran shuttle services from Montreal to New York, Washington, and San Francisco. However, perhaps the foundation of its service to the group was the schedule of flights it provided between key stations like Dorval, Gander, and Goose Bay, known as 'milk runs' to the staff. Whenever called upon, it was available to fly VIPs at short notice to almost any corner of the globe. The fleet of aircraft included Dakotas, Liberators, and Consolidated Coronados, four-engine American patrol-bomber flying boats converted to the transport role. During the summer months the Coronados were based at Boucherville and provided a freight service to Iceland. In winter they were transferred to Bermuda and used on the South Atlantic.[11]

Probably the best-known individual aircraft in 231 Squadron's fleet was Liberator AL504. A standard bomber, it was taken off the delivery line in the summer of 1942 and hurriedly converted to a passenger configuration in order to take Lord Louis Mountbatten to Britain following his appointment as chief of combined operations. Taffy Powell reports, 'I flew the aircraft myself and received his permission on arrival to name it *Commando*.' In July 1942 the Air Ministry signalled Ferry Command to supply an aircraft and crew to fly Prime Minister Churchill on a special mission (to Cairo). Powell chose *Commando*, with a crew headed by 'a young American Captain Bill Vanderkloot, who had been with us for a year having been recruited by the Clayton-Knight organisation in Washington D.C. He was equally well qualified as a navigator and had made a special study for us of radio facilities in the United Kingdom, so that we could publish approach diagrams and facilities for alternative airfields when Prestwick Airport was closed or difficult. His instrument flying was superb and he was quiet and unassuming.'[12]

Even though this episode in *Commando*'s life predates the birth of 45 Group, the subject of this chapter, it bears telling here because this particular aircraft was such an integral part of the history of the group and its main communications arm, 231 Squadron.

Officials in the United Kingdom at first had reservations about a young American civilian flying the wartime prime minister. However, an interview with Sir Charles Portal confirmed Powell's choice. The twenty-seven-year-old Vanderkloot, from Lake Bluff, Illinois, not only impressed the chief of the air staff, he also offered an alternative to the planned route through Gibraltar to the Gold Coast and the trans-Africa airway to Cairo. Churchill himself takes up the story:

Vanderkloot, who had already flown a million miles as a civilian pilot, asked why it was necessary to fly all round by Takoradi, Kano, Fort Lamy, El Obeid, etc. He said he could make one bound from Gibraltar to Cairo, flying from Gibraltar eastward in the afternoon, turning sharply south across Spanish or Vichy territory as dusk fell, and then proceeding eastward till he struck the Nile about Assiout, when a turn to the northward would bring us in another hour or so to the Cairo landing-ground northwest of the Pyramids.[13]

To this point, many British officials had opposed the idea of the prime minister's trip because the trans-Africa route would take five or six days and also would require 'a whole series of protective injections.' Vanderkloot's bold suggestion 'altered the whole picture.' The prime minister realized he 'could be in Cairo in two days without any trouble about Central African bugs and the inoculations against them. Portal was convinced.'[14]

Since this would be Churchill's first flight in an unpressurized aircraft, possibly flying at high altitude, he went to Farnborough during the night of 31 July to get briefed on what to expect. During a special oxygen-mask test, his biographer, Martin Gilbert, writes that he asked 'if the mask could be adapted so that he could smoke his cigar while wearing it.' Strangely enough, 'the mask was duly adapted.'[15] A couple of days later, accompanied by the chief of the imperial general staff, General Sir Alan Brooke, Churchill left England in *Commando*.

This was a very different kind of travel from the comforts of the Boeing flying-boats. The bomber was at this time unheated, and razor-edged draughts cut in through many chinks. There were no beds, but two shelves in the after cabin enabled me and Sir Charles Wilson, my doctor [later Lord Moran], to lie down. There were plenty of blankets for all. We flew low over the South of England in order to be recognized by our batteries, who had been warned, but who were also under Alert conditions. As we got out to sea I left the cockpit [where the PM liked to spend considerable time in the co-pilot's seat] and retired to rest, fortified by a good sleeping cachet.[16]

Flying through the night and skirting the Bay of Biscay to avoid contact with any roaming German planes, *Commando* reached Gibraltar in the morning. That evening it left on the long flight to Cairo, 'a hop of two thousand miles or more, as the détours necessary to avoid the hostile aircraft around the Desert battle were considerable.' Churchill continues his account of the voyage:

Vanderkloot, in order to have more petrol in hand, did not continue down the Mediterranean till darkness fell, but flew straight across the Spanish zone and the Vichy quasi-hostile territory. Therefore, as we had an armed escort till nightfall of four Beaufighters, we in fact openly violated the neutrality of both these regions. No one molested us in the air, and we did not come within cannon-shot of any important town. All the same I was glad when darkness cast her shroud over the harsh landscape and we could retire to such sleeping accommodation as 'Commando' could offer. It would have been very tiresome to make a forced landing on neutral territory, and even descent in the desert, though preferable, would have raised problems of its own. However, all 'Commando's' four engines purred happily, and I slept sound as we sailed through the starlit night.[17]

Four days later Churchill learned that General W.H.E. Gott, his choice to replace Claude Auchinleck in command of the Eighth Army, had been killed when his plane was intercepted by the Luftwaffe. The incident must have struck home with the PM. Only two days earlier he had flown in the same area himself to inspect Eighth Army positions at El Alamein and to talk to Gott. Having to make a quick decision, Churchill chose General Bernard Montgomery. He assumed command and inspired the Eighth Army to great heights in North Africa.[18]

On 10 August *Commando* left Cairo for Tehran and Moscow, so Churchill could confer with Joseph Stalin. The party grew, including the high-ranking American diplomat, Averell Harriman. Following three days of intense discussions between Churchill and Stalin, *Commando* retraced its steps, again with stops at Tehran, Cairo (for more talks with the generals), and Gibraltar. The prime minister was back home in Britain on 24 August, after three weeks and many tiring miles of flying in distinctly non-luxurious conditions. He says of his Ferry Command pilot's contribution: 'It was a fine performance.'[19] In fact, Churchill returned to his own accolade. His biographer quotes the US general Douglas MacArthur, then in Australia awaiting his opportunity to retake the Philippines from the Japanese. 'If disposal of all the Allied decorations were today placed in my hands,' he reportedly said to a senior British officer, 'my first act would be to award the Victoria Cross to Winston Churchill. Not one of those who wear it deserves it more than he. A flight of 10,000 miles through hostile and foreign skies may be the duty of young pilots, but for a Statesman burdened with the world's cares it is an act of inspiring gallantry and valour.'[20]

Five days later, on Saturday, 29 August, *Commando* arrived back at Dorval, eight weeks after having left, ostensibly just to fly Lord and Lady Halifax to Britain. Unlike other accomplishments of the ferry service, which were clothed in secrecy, the Montreal papers fêted the achievement of Vanderkloot and his crew, co-pilot Jack Ruggles from San Francisco, radio operator Russell Holmes from Toronto, and flight engineers Ronald Williams and John Affleck from Centreville, New Brunswick, and London, Ontario. Photographs of the civilian crew in front of *Commando* and ample quotations on their impressions of their important passenger, as well as the exotic regions through which they passed, filled several columns beneath such headings as 'Home from Historic Flight to Moscow' and 'Churchill Plane Crew in Montreal after Trip of Some 50,000 Miles.' Montrealers were even treated to photographs and interviews with the wives of the two pilots.[21] Vanderkloot flew *Commando* for Churchill again, to Casablanca, Cairo, Adana in Turkey, Tripoli, and Algiers in January-February 1943.[22] The young American may have been Ferry Command's most famous pilot, even becoming the first one immortalized in a published biography, *The Man Who Flew Churchill*, by Canadian author Bruce West.

On its return to Dorval, *Commando* received its scheduled maintenance and some improvements to the rudimentary interior appointments, as it usually did after a trip, and carried on performing heroically, often on special missions with the same crew that went to Moscow. However, other Ferry Command airmen did serve in AL504. Powell himself, for example, flew *Commando* when he took Bowhill on a tour of the South Atlantic Route and the trans-Africa airway. Powell was again the pilot when the famous aircraft made the first ever London-to-Ottawa direct flight on 7 September 1944.[23]

By the time that historic trip took place, *Commando* was quite a different aeroplane. In August 1943 Consolidated Vultee in Tucson, Arizona, modified it extensively. A tall single tail replaced the rounded twin-tail assembly, 'a distinctive feature of a conventional Liberator.' The fuselage was stretched by several feet to permit the installation of seven sleeping berths, a great improvement over the two makeshift bunks available when Churchill used *Commando*. After Al Lilly, 45 Group's chief test pilot, had checked out the virtually new aircraft, it went back to work with 231 Squadron, inaugurating the regular service between Canada and Australia and carrying VIPs over the North and South Atlantic. Performance and comfort were improved over the original configuration. The high cost, however, precluded modifying any more of the group's Liberators to this special C-87 transport version. *Commando's* glorious history came to a tragic end on 27 March 1945, when it disappeared near the Azores with the loss of all fourteen on board. The missing crew was headed by Wing Commander Willie Biddell, officer commanding 231 Squadron. The seven passengers included Air Ministry officials flying to Canada to attend the final BCATP wings parade, amongst them H.A. Jones, author of *The War in the Air*, the official history of the RAF during the First World War. No cause could ever be found for *Commando's* disappearance.[24]

The increase in transport requirements on top of the host of other wartime flying jobs, including ferrying, necessitated an expansion of the RAF's transport training capabilities. With only two transport operational training units in the United Kingdom, in December 1943 transport training began in Canada at No. 32 OTU, Patricia Bay, British Columbia. This RAF school had originally moved from West Kirby in Cheshire, England, late in 1941 to carry on its torpedo-bomber training off Vancouver Island. It became an integral part of the BCATP in 1942 and turned out crews for squadrons of both the RAF and the RCAF. Initially it concentrated on torpedo-bomber instruction, producing replacement airmen for Coastal Command. With many of the graduating crews temporarily engaged to ferry aircraft to Britain, the course included the necessary skills required for this task. In time the transport job gained the ascendancy.[25]

Some of the instructors came from 45 Group and others, who lacked the necessary experience in long-range flying, did a short tour of duty at Dorval and made two transatlantic deliveries. The training syllabus, based on the one in use in Britain, stressed long-distance flying. The course lasted twelve weeks, after which the graduates went to 45 Group for a period of transatlantic ferrying before being posted to a transport squadron. To enable the RAF to recall more of its personnel, Canadians were progressively added to the training staff. In June 1944 the unit was redesignated No. 6 (RCAF) OTU, but continued to function as part of the BCATP. Concentrating on turning out Dakota crews, the school moved to Comox to escape the congestion at Patricia Bay. On the urging of Air Marshal Robert Leckie, who replaced Lloyd Breadner as the RCAF's chief of the air staff in January 1944, the quota of Canadian pupils was increased and, in the autumn of 1944, sixteen RCAF aircrew and sixteen RAF graduated each month. Despite the BCATP agreement, which placed all graduates at the disposal of the Air Ministry, the RAF permitted the RCAF to use as many of the Canadian OTU graduates as it needed to meet the aircrew requirements of its own transport squadrons.[26]

After the Canadian needs were met, RCAF graduates, along with those from the other Commonwealth and Allied air forces, were available for transport operations in the United Kingdom and other theatres of war. Since only three transport squadrons of the RCAF were located outside the western hemisphere, No. 435 and 436 in India and No. 437 in Britain, most of the Canadians wound up in RAF squadrons. By the end of the war 32/6 OTU had sent more than 700 aircrew overseas for service with RAF Transport Command. The intake included a large proportion of former flying instructors and other experienced pilots who became available for transport work after the rapid curtailment of the BCATP. About one-quarter of the overall output were Canadians and the others were mainly British, but included a number of Poles, Norwegians, and a few members of the Free French air force. Most of them saw service with 45 Group, some as one-trippers; others remained long enough to make four or five deliveries. Few stayed more than a few months.[27]

Other operational training units, No. 5 at Boundary Bay, British Columbia, and No. 111 at Nassau also provided 45 Group with one-trippers. Both of these schools trained selected BCATP graduates for bombing and coastal operations in India on Liberators, giving them enough additional training to deliver an aircraft to their new theatre of operations.[28] Although 111 OTU at Nassau did not form part of the BCATP, it was closely associated with air training in Canada and there was a constant interchange of students. In March 1945 the unit was home to 172 Canadians.[29] There were many more among the estimated 3000 officers and men of the RAF in Nassau, not only at 111 OTU, but also stationed at 113 (South Atlantic) Wing, at the colony's RAF Hospital, and at No. 250 Air-Sea Rescue Unit.[30]

Final instruction for most aircrew assigned to deliver aircraft came from the staff of Ferry Command, or 45 Group, as we have seen in the cases of Sergeant Don Macfie and Flight Lieutenant Harold Wills in the previous chapter. Originally this was all done in Montreal, first at St Hubert and then at Dorval. However, by the spring of 1942 even the impressive modern facilities of the new airport were overcrowded, shared as they were with civilian airlines. As a consequence, Ferry Command sought a new base for its training function. It settled on North Bay, Ontario, a staging station for RCAF ferry traffic and home for a detachment of the RCAF's 124 (Ferry) Squadron. By the first week of June 1942 an advance party from Dorval was operating the Trans-Atlantic Training Unit out of tents and other makeshift facilities with five Hudsons. Courses started almost immediately and, by the fall, it was in full operation. Eventually the unit added Mitchells and Dakotas, as well as de Havilland Mosquitoes and Avro Lancasters to its inventory. During a course that lasted from three to four weeks, crews became familiar with the type of aircraft they were likely to deliver and with the flying control procedures followed in oceanic flying. In February 1944 the station was named No. 313 Ferry Training Unit.[31]

Whatever the school was called, the training remained basically unchanged throughout its history. BCATP graduates arrived full of confidence, only to find out how little they really knew. 'At North Bay, over a beautiful and wild countryside, they do a specialist course to fit them for the long distances of the ferry routes. They are crewed-up half way through the course, and to pass out they have to fly a rigorous cross-country trip over Lake Huron, Lake Ontario and the typical bush country of northern Canada.' The official account continues, 'When they reach Montreal they have to do a further ten hours on the current delivery type; then they are ready for routine delivery work.' The best candidates were much like those favoured by Coastal Command. 'They must be steady, assured, very patient, and capable of sitting for long hours methodically carrying out the job. There are also special characteristics which have to be developed. They must be "jacks of all trades," ready to cope with unforeseen circumstances in outlandish places. They must understand loading problems in various types of aircraft. They must be tactful, and able to handle passengers.'[32]

The new crews passed through a final checkout at Dorval, which also conducted courses for regular ferry pilots, navigators, and radio operators to acquaint them with new types of aircraft and to keep them abreast of recent changes in flight procedures.[33] Experienced service aircrew making a single delivery, and graduates of the OTUs, sometimes went straight to Dorval. The general policy, however, was for North Bay to carry as much of the training load as possible.

Even if the growth of the ferry service had forced the delegation of responsibilities to outlying stations, Montreal remained the hub, increasingly recognized as one of the most important aviation centres in the world. In addition to its own requirements, and as part of its continuing cooperation with the USAAF, the RAF provided training and experience for selected American airmen at Dorval. This also helped fill gaps in the pool of available aircrew. One USAAF trainee, Sergeant Robert Byrne from Minnesota, has left his impressions of a sojourn in Montreal. Recently posted to the 315th Bombardment Squadron at Mac-Dill Field, Tampa, Florida, and expecting to be sent overseas, Byrne received orders instead, in early January 1943, 'to take a course of study on British Aircraft radio.' He considered this 'a good deal,' informing his sister, 'Will be living almost as a civilian.' On 15 January he told her, 'I've really hit the jackpot this time.' At the end of the course, 'I am told that upon reaching capability as an operator we will have a practice flight with the ferry command; presumably to England.' Byrne expected to be worked hard. 'I know I am going to have to study like hell but I'm also going to have the time of my life. There are only two hundred American soldiers in this city of a million and a half. All the girls practically fall into your arms.' He could live anywhere he wished, but decided to stay at the YMCA for a while because it was economical. Montreal was 'an expensive town.'[34]

The young American sergeant later wrote, 'I can't tell you anything about my work because they seem to consider it highly confidential.' However, he had little trouble praising the city's cosmopolitan nature, enhanced by meeting airmen from many nations, as well as its plentiful, attractive, and eminently available women. By the end of February he was looking forward to the possibility of a secondment to the RAF command. 'We are entering the final stages here and when spring breaks we are led to believe that we will make more than one trip if they can possibly keep us here.' He had obviously picked up some gossip from the base and the bars: 'From the stories the old experienced operators tell, it is a good thing my insurance is paid up. I can see what they mean – There is a helluva lot of water in ye olde Atlantic!'[35]

On 14 March Byrne proudly wrote: 'I am no longer a student – At the moment my time is occupied in flying in twin engined bombers as a radio operator ... I'd like to stay in the Ferry Command. With ships being sent to all points in the world I'd certainly see a lot of the country.' No wonder he wanted to remain at Dorval. The routine he described was not very onerous, particularly for wartime: 'I'm going to be an awfully spoiled boy when I leave here. Starting this week we will report to the field only every other day and alternate Sundays. What a racket – Up one morning at six and sleep till noon the next. I hope they don't decide to change the whole schedule because the present schedule appeals to my lazy nature.' His serviceman's conscience did bother him a little: 'I can't help but think of how the boys in Africa would react if they could only see us. If I were to tell the average soldier what kind of a military life I'm leading he'd call me a damn liar.' He mentioned only one drawback to his current posting: 'After the "newness" wears off, flying is one of the most monotonous things in the world. Same old deafening roar of engines, same old ground below, and same old sensation every time you hit an air pocket.'

Considering wartime secrecy, it is surprising what information correspondents sometimes passed on. Byrne, for example, related the following tale:

The first one of our guys to start for the U.K. got as far as Newfoundland, got lost, and ended up on an iceflow. The story has a happy ending though. The entire crew is back at Dorval, each blaming the other for losing their direction. The crew setup was sort of screwy anyway. This is a very cosmopolitan base and the crew on this particular ship proves it. The pilot – Polish (spoke very, very little English). The navigator – Norwegian (spoke English and French, both poorly) – Our radio operator spoke nothing but good old U.S. jargon. How in hell is an outfit like that supposed to know what the other guy is doing?

It is probably only the lack of names that got that letter past the censor.

Despite this misadventure by one of his USAAF colleagues, Byrne looked forward to a transatlantic delivery. 'We have been slated to go for some time but something has always come up. I'd hate to go back to Tampa without making the trip,' he wrote on 26 April. Finally, almost a month later he reported from his room in the Ford Hotel (where he had moved early in February): 'I'm leaving for Bermuda tomorrow morning. We'll be in England very shortly. – Don't tell Mom; she worries too much. – Never thought I'd be chasing dots and dashes all over the Atlantic.' Three days later, after a train trip to Elizabeth

City, he wrote from the Virginia Dare Hotel (popular with ferry crews) that they had tested their plane and would be leaving in the morning. On 22 June he returned to Tampa. 'Since I last wrote I have been in Bermuda, Newfoundland, Scotland, and made a return trip by boat. Both trips were uneventful and most of the details cannot be given out. Tell you more someday ... I really hated to come back. I have had the best deal possible in military life. Now it's back to the old routine.' As if to underline this last point, on 10 July he complained, 'I'm bored to tears.'

Subsequent to his brief period with the RAF at Dorval, Sergeant Byrne served with various USAAF units in the United States and ended the war with the 414th Fighter Squadron on the island of Iwo Jima in the Pacific.[36] It is not clear exactly how many American personnel saw service with RAF Ferry Command or 45 Group. However, there were a number of others as the Allies worked together to defeat the Axis powers, in this case by delivering as many planes as necessary to operational theatres. In fact, at least six USAAF airmen died while delivering aircraft with the British command.[37]

Sergeant Byrne was in Montreal when the organization was ferrying increasingly large numbers of planes across the Atlantic. A survey of the delivery history of the ferry service reveals that large movements of aircraft did not begin until well into the war. Predictions by American manufacturers in 1941 that ATFERO would be required to move at least two hundred aircraft per month across the Atlantic, predictions that heaped a good deal of criticism on the struggling ferry service, did not materialize until much later. There were two main reasons for this delay: one was that American production did not develop as quickly as expected, and the other, that the expansion of the American forces absorbed a large part of the output. Consequently, it was not until mid-1943 that monthly receipts of two hundred were reached. Thereafter, the delivery rate rose considerably above this figure. It is worth noting that mutual-aid aircraft from Canada made up 10 per cent of the total deliveries in 1944, and 30 per cent in the first four months of 1945.[38]

By and large the ferrying operation was concerned with three main categories of aircraft, each of which contributed in an important way to a particular phase of military operations. The first, and perhaps most outstanding, were the long-range machines, Hudsons, Liberators, Catalinas, and Fortresses, which were employed by the RAF with such decisive effect in the Battle of the Atlantic. The second group comprised light and medium bombers, Bostons, Mitchells, Marauders, and Baltimores, which provided much of the daylight bombing in support of British operations in North Africa, the Mediterranean, and Middle East. There the policy of the RAF was to equip and maintain its squadrons with American aircraft which, with the exception of the fighters, were flown to the United Kingdom in substantial numbers in 1943 and 1944.[39] Six squadrons were equipped with these planes for day bombing and, after the invasion of Normandy, provided close bombing support with the Second Tactical Air Force. The third group were the Dakotas, used on every front as transports for personnel, mail, and freight, and as air ambulances. They also towed gliders and carried paratroops in airborne operations. In RAF Transport Command, twenty-five squadrons, including Nos 435, 436, and 437 of the RCAF, were equipped with Dakotas.[40]

Apart from the distinctive contribution of the long-range aircraft, the medium and light day-bombers, and the Dakotas, it is difficult to assess the precise impact of the transatlantic ferry service on air operations. The Canadian-built Avro Lancasters and de Havilland Mosquitoes arrived too late to have a pronounced effect, though the former were not without importance in the operations of No. 6 (Bomber) Group. The equipment policy of Bomber Command in regard to the RCAF's 6 Group was to supply it with Lancasters built in Canada and to reserve British Lancasters for British squadrons. This meant that, until Canadian-built Lancasters became available, the Canadian group had to be satisfied with Handley Page Halifaxes.[41]

Thus, two of the ferrying tasks carried out by 45 Group involved the delivery of Lancasters and Mosquitoes manufactured in Canada – altogether more than a thousand aircraft.[42] The government chose to focus considerable public attention on the first Lancaster Mark X built in Canada by Victory Aircraft in Toronto. The prototype, KB700, flew on 1 August 1943 and was pronounced airworthy. It required more work on the electrical system, but 'Ottawa officialdom' went ahead with the celebration anyway, despite the company's protests.[43] On the 6th it was christened Ruhr Express by Mrs C.G. Power, wife of the minister of national defence for air, in a special ceremony at Toronto's Malton Airport. For maximum publicity, Squadron Leader R.J. Lane, RCAF, veteran of fifty-one bomber missions, many with the élite Pathfinder Group, accompanied by an experienced bomber crew, had been sent home to fly the aircraft across the Atlantic for 45 Group.[44]

As soon as the crowds left the tarmac, Lane and his crew climbed into KB700 to fly it to Dorval, the first stop on the way to the United Kingdom. 'We soon found out about the electrics; none of the engine instruments was working and we had to make a decision whether to press on to Montreal, as planned, or return to Malton. In view of the publicity, we decided it would be politic to head for Dorval. There the aircraft was quickly wheeled into a hangar.'[45] A team of technicians was quietly sent from Toronto to complete the work. KB700 remained in the hands of these specialists from Victory Aircraft for the rest of the month. At that point the Ministry of Aircraft Production insisted on a full test program, as it always did with the first plane from a new manufacturer, before the new Lancaster could be dispatched across the Atlantic. The landmark bomber, the first four-engine aircraft built in Canada, finally reached Prestwick in the middle of September, with the veteran civilian captain, Clyde Pangborn, accompanying Lane for the crossing. Taffy Powell explains his choice: 'Number one from Canada had to go over as a quick and efficient job, nothing daft had to happen, and I knew I could count on Pangborn.'[46]

In the United Kingdom, the *Ruhr Express* was put on display at a number of Canadian bomber squadrons as a reminder of what was being done on the home front. It was finally delivered to 405 Squadron with No. 8 (Pathfinder) Group and on the night of 22 November made its first operational sortie in a raid on Berlin, undoubtedly for publicity purposes. Ultimately, like other Lancaster Xs, it served in 6 (RCAF) Group, with 419 Squadron. It survived many missions over Germany and occupied Europe, until 2 January 1945 when it overshot the runway and burst into flames on the return from a raid, fortunately with no injuries to the crew. All the Lancaster Xs flown on operations with overseas squadrons were delivered, without any losses en route, by 45 Group.[47]

The Mark X Lancasters from Victory Aircraft began arriving in the United Kingdom in the fall of 1943, but only six had been delivered by the end of the year. Squadrons of 6 Group began exchanging their Halifaxes for Lancaster Xs the following spring. The conversion process continued as aircraft became available. However, by the end of the war several Canadian squadrons were still flying Halifaxes. When European hostilities drew to a close, the squadrons earmarked for operations in the Pacific, as part of 'Tiger Force,' flew their Lancaster Xs back to Canada, staging through the Azores and Gander.[48]

Like the Lancaster, the Canadian-built Mosquitoes reached their production peak too late in the war to influence military operations to any great extent. Moreover, the first to arrive required extensive modifications before being accepted for operations. Even so, some were in use with Bomber Command before the end of 1943, and in 1944 four squadrons of the RAF were flying Canadian Mosquitoes in attacks on Berlin and other distant targets. By the end of May 1945, 357 Canadian Mosquitoes had been put into service by the RAF, while about a hundred more were still being modified or remained in storage in Britain.[49]

The most serious problem with the long-range ferrying program was the difficulty of obtaining spare engines and spare parts. The emphasis centred on whole aeroplanes. In an emergency some spares could be moved in transports or stowed in delivery aircraft, but the great bulk was shipped by sea. The time lag caused shortages of spark plugs, instruments, and other such items. The British found it difficult to get spares for their Canadian Mosquitoes, for example, which suffered from a lack of part compatibility with those built in Britain.[50] The problem was often much worse in remote theatres, where aircraft serviceability frequently depended on the expedient of stripping some machines – 'cannibalizing' them – to keep others operational, and also on the ingenuity of maintenance crews in manufacturing parts from material at hand.

While the primary job of the ferry service was delivering new aircraft from North America to operational theatres, it also flew a few old machines in the other direction. The battle-worn RAF Lancaster used for demonstration purposes in North America, flown over in 1942 by Clyde Pangborn, had been one of the first. Others, in 1944, included four Halifaxes for use by BCATP instructors in training flight engineers, and about three dozen Mitchells returned to the United States.[51]

Perhaps the best-known 'reverse ferry' was the delivery of twenty obsolete Handley Page Hampden twin-engine bombers from operational squadrons in Britain to Patricia Bay near Vancouver, for use in training by 32 OTU. The first of these deliveries was made by Don McVicar, who seized it as an opportunity to try out the western leg of the Crimson Route. After depositing a Dakota at Prestwick on 29 July 1943, he and his radio operator, Fred Johnsen, picked up a Hampden in Wales and flew it to Patricia Bay via Prestwick, Reykjavik, BW-8 on the west coast of Greenland, Crystal 2 on Frobisher Bay, Coral Harbour on Southampton Island, and Edmonton. The battle-worn Hampden held up surprisingly well, though much of the trip was made with the radio unserviceable. After the longest leg, from Coral Harbour to Edmonton, No. 2 AOS maintenance crews inspected the aircraft. 'They found a lot of loose nuts and bolts and a cracked exhaust stack which could have caused a fire later, but otherwise the old bomber had shaken down in good order.'[52] After 28 hours 10 minutes total flying time, McVicar set down at Patricia Bay, 'where there was quite a gathering to welcome the first Hampden from overseas. Even the CO [commanding officer], Group Captain Wurtele, was there to greet us ... It seemed as if the whole station was anxious to entertain the crew of the first English Hampden who had made the first-ever Polar flight from Europe to Canada.' McVicar could not help but reflect that, if he had chosen to fly via Montreal, he would only then be reaching Winnipeg.[53]

McVicar and Johnsen returned to Dorval via Trans-Canada Air Lines, ferried a Marauder – 'the widow maker' in McVicar's mind – 'to Britain, and returned with another Hampden. McVicar was proud of his role in helping to open up northern staging posts and chose a slightly different route on this trip, stopping at Prestwick, Reykjavik, BE-2 on the east coast of Greenland, BW-8, Fort Smith in the Northwest Territories, and Fort St John in northeastern British Columbia. On landing at Patricia Bay, after overcoming a problem with his undercarriage, McVicar claims: 'None of the other aircraft which had stopped at Dorval had made it to the West coast yet.' He adds: 'After the festivities at Pat Bay the hangover set in and I had plenty of time as TCA whirled me back to Dorval to realize how lucky we'd been. An obsolete aircraft with no de-icing and no single-engine performance over a route where rescue would be almost impossible. No one in their right mind would have done it. You can stretch your skill and knowledge just so far. After that just plain luck has to be on your side.'[54]

One of the Hampden crews was not so fortunate, although in their own way its members became more famous than McVicar. Captain Robert E. Coffman from Louisiana, RCAF Flying Officer Norman E. Greenaway from Alberta, and radio officer Ronald E. Snow from Digby, Nova Scotia, suffered an engine failure just off the east coast of Greenland. After Coffman had ditched on the sea, they grabbed the emergency kit and clambered into the dinghy. It took about twenty hours of struggle through an ice field before they could reach a great black rock some fifty yards off shore. Their refuge had nothing to offer in the way of food or shelter or, if truth be known, hope. They apportioned their meagre emergency rations – forty-five malted-milk tablets, four squares of barley sugar, twelve sealed pints of water, and a small quantity of chewing gum – to last a week. After an often stormy nine days in bitterly cold conditions, they were in bad shape. They had seen two high-flying aircraft and one distant ship. In each case their desperate shots with the Very (flare) pistol were wasted in cloudy conditions of poor visibility. On the tenth day, when all three were in a very weakened state and resigned to their fate, they were miraculously rescued by a small Norwegian vessel, the last ship of the year through those waters. Had the *Polar Bjorn* not had to stop to make engine repairs, and had an American major not come up on deck to check out the Greenland scenery through binoculars, Coffman, Greenaway, and Snow would probably not have been saved.[55]

Possibly spurred by McVicar's choice of the trans-Arctic route for his part of the Hampden reverse ferry, 45 Group undertook a second survey of the Crimson Route in the fall of 1943. Powell chose McVicar to captain the aircraft because of his experience and interest in Arctic flying. On 8 October he left Edmonton with Bill Baker and John McGrail as flight engineer and radio officer, along with Squadron Leader George Wakeman and Flight Lieutenant Norman Vaughan from 45 Group headquarters as passengers. The only serious incident occurred the next day at Churchill. It was described in a report that appears to have been composed by Wakeman:

The aircraft did not perform normally on the take-off[;] the captain cut off power after being airborne and made an endeavor with brakes to hold direction on the runway, but the aircraft took up a violent right swing crossed a 120 ft. gravel apron adjacent to the concrete runway passed through a large open ditch 20 ft. wide and 6 ft. deep to crash on its belly on the far side of this ditch at a distance of 3000 ft. from the position of take-off at the north end of the runway. No fire occurred although 230 gals. of high octane gas escaped as the bomb bay tank broke open. There was evident a thick coat of hoar frost on the wings and other surfaces of the aircraft. This accretion of hoar frost had occurred during the one hour layover. The captain and flight engineer admitted seeing the hoar frost on the aircraft before take-off and said they had often seen worse conditions. Perhaps they overlooked the high wing loading of a Hudson type aircraft, as I believe this aircraft was stalling on the take-off, with its all up weight of 21,000 lbs., and the accretion of hoar frost was a contributory cause of the trouble.[56]

Fortunately, all on board escaped serious injury and, after a delay of ten days, the flight resumed in a new Hudson flown in from Dorval. With stops at Crystal 2, BW-8, and Reykjavik, the party arrived in Prestwick on 19 October, after about twenty-four hours flying time from Edmonton. On the return trip they stopped at Reykjavik, BW-8, Crystal 2, and Coral Harbour, and flew low over Crystal 3 on Padloping Island to observe airport approaches and facilities.[57]

The report on the survey flight described the various bases that could be used as staging posts and emergency fields, as well as the northern geography and map deficiencies. It also outlined the advantages and disadvantages of the route. For the former the report noted that Prestwick and Vancouver were more than a thousand miles closer via this route, as opposed to the one through Montreal and the trans-Canada airway. The route required 'a series of four short over water flights compared to the (1760 n. miles) ocean crossing, Derrynacross, Ireland to Gander, Nfld.' The shorter distances allowed aircraft to carry greater payloads and less fuel. Finally, good flying weather was common in the high latitudes. On the other hand, the report enunciated even more disadvantages for the Crimson Route. The northern waters had very little shipping 'to aid with weather reports, navigation, or sea rescue.' In fact, there were 'only a limited number of weather reporting stations.' Radio communications in the north were extremely difficult. The report also noted 'a lack of any prepared emergency landing areas between the principal airports.' There was concern about twin-engined aircraft making it over the Greenland icecap in event of an engine failure and, generally, about the rugged terrain around BW-8 and BE-2. Finally, the Greenland and Iceland airports 'are not in British Territory.'[58] Given the tone of the report, it is not surprising that 45 Group chose not to use the route.

A number of Catalina flying boats were delivered via another northern route. In May 1944, 45 Group airmen assisted crews from the Soviet Union in flying these aircraft from Elizabeth City to Murmansk, via Gander and Reykjavik. Taffy Powell assigned an experienced pilot and radio operator to each plane:

It was unbelievably difficult to sort out. They were not well trained by our standards and tried to make up for deficiencies by a much too eager approach to all tasks as if they were afraid of being found wanting. They looked competent enough, all leather-coated and rather older than our crew members. I do not think that our first impressions changed much in the months ahead. Although our command status was clearly laid down, there was an element of split responsibility that our people never liked and we were glad that the whole 48 passed out of our hands in Iceland without mishap for the last lap to Murmansk.[59]

The Soviets were not as lucky after they took over for the final leg. At least one of the flying boats 'flew into the sea approaching Murmansk.'

One of Powell's captains involved in this operation agrees with the SASO's account. Flight Lieutenant Arthur Teulon, an American in the RCAF, came to 45 Group from an operational squadron and made many deliveries from late 1943 until the end of the war. His logbook and his recollection indicate that these particular boats were PBN-1s, an improved US Navy version of the Catalina. He remembers meeting the Soviet airmen at Elizabeth City and coping 'with no interpreter on board for the flights, just sign language and some sheets of paper with phonetics on it.' This was the least of the problems.

To make matters worse we weren't to be in the pilots' seats for take-off or landing because the chaps were such expert pilots; also they insisted on formation flying in flights of three. Remember now, we were in command of the flight even under these strange conditions. Our flight of three took off for Gander: F/L Green, Capt. Bach and myself. Prior to our take-off we three had a plan that when we went on instruments that would end this folly of formation flying and each of us would go to our predetermined altitude. It wasn't very long into the flight before this took place. The Russian proficiency wasn't any thing like we had been led to believe: by the time we arrived at Gander, my log book shows a flight of 10 hrs 45 mins; I was well established in the pilot's seat. I found out later both Green and Bach had come to this same conclusion. After our rest in Gander we again took-off, not in formation this time, for Reykjavik in Iceland. My log shows this was a 13 hr leg. From Iceland the Russians went on their own to Murmansk, an over-the-pole flight.[60]

From December 1944 to April 1945 Teulon helped ferry another allotment of PBN-1s for the USSR, in the same fashion (but with the addition of a 45 Group flight engineer) across the southern route, from Natal to West Africa, up to Morocco, and across to Iraq, where the Soviet crews took them north to the Caspian Sea. The final deliveries were taken by the Soviets themselves directly from the Consolidated plant in San Diego to Alaska and then across the Bering Sea to Siberia. Little can be found on this aspect of the aircraft supply story. Powell was happy that 45 Group's contact with the Soviets was limited. 'I do not know how they fared but I was glad, when the third and fourth batches came along in 1945, that we were relieved of our safety crew responsibility and were only asked for base and control facilities within our area. So far as I know we received not one word of thanks from our Russian allies. It was a very dreary and frightening experience for our crew members and even my own staff and Crew Assignments got very snappy about the Russian aid program.'[61]

A novel operation in air transport was carried out by 45 Group in the summer of 1943 when a Waco CG-4A glider carrying one-and-a-half tons of freight was towed across the North Atlantic behind a Dakota. The flight marked the culmination of a freight-carrying experiment that began in February 1943, when two Waco gliders were delivered to Dorval. After a number of non-stop trips, gradually increasing to almost 1200 miles, were made without mishap, permission was granted by Transport Command for the unprecedented transatlantic flight. Tug and glider, accompanied by a Catalina lest they come down in the ocean, left Dorval on 24 June. With stops at Goose Bay and BW-1, Prestwick was reached on 1 July. The total time spent in the air was 28 hours, about double that normally taken by a Dakota from Montreal to the United Kingdom. It was by no means a normal journey. At the end of its towline, the glider bounced about violently in the turbulent air; there were times when the crew feared it was coming to pieces. The pilot could not relax or take his eyes from the tow plane for even a moment. Even so, the flight was considered a success and, by any standard, it must be rated as a remarkable achievement. But no attempt was made to repeat it. There was little point in risking crew and cargo in a heavily loaded glider when the freight could more safely be carried inside a Dakota. Moreover, unfounded rumours that the glider was to be used on the return ferry service caused some disquiet among aircrew and gave good reason to terminate the experiment. The adventurous nature of the exploit is reflected in the award of the Air Force Cross to three of the crew involved, Squadron Leader R.G. Seys (RAF) of Montreal, pilot of the glider; Squadron Leader F.M. Gobeil (RCAF) of Ottawa, co-pilot; and Flight Lieutenant W.S. Longhurst (RAF) of Montreal, who flew the Dakota.[62]

The constant flow of personnel through 45 Group makes it difficult to determine the strength of the formation at any given time. Available statistics must therefore be accepted as approximations only. They do, however, reveal quite clearly that Canadian aircrew made a substantial contribution. At the end of June 1944, out of a given total of 1330 aircrew employed on transatlantic ferrying, 634 were members of the RCAF. At any time, RCAF personnel accounted for between one-third and one-half of the service aircrew strength of 45 Group. In addition, RCAF airmen were engaged in ground capacities at Dorval, Gander, Goose Bay, and the numerous out-stations.[63] And, of course, many of the RAF personnel posted to the group were Canadians – so-called CANRAF types, the lost legion, as they have called themselves since the war, because their identities were swallowed up in the mass of Air Ministry personnel records. As members of a foreign service there is no record of their military careers in their own country.

Since 45 Group, like Ferry Command before it, was an RAF formation operating in Canada by virtue of the Visiting Forces Act, RCAF personnel attached to it would, under normal circumstances, be legally subject to British military law even though on Canadian soil. To avoid this anomalous situation, as embarrassing to the British as to the Canadians, members of the RCAF employed with 45 Group at Dorval were shown on their personal documents as being posted to the RCAF's No. 3 Training Command at Montreal and attached to the RAF for duty only. As a result of this formality, they remained subject to Canadian air force law. Similarly, those at Gander were placed on the strength of the RCAF's No. 1 Group in St John's, Newfoundland. On the other hand, in Bermuda and stations in the South Atlantic where there were no conveniently located Canadian formations, RCAF members serving with 113 Wing were formally attached to the RAF and governed by its regulations as provided for in the Visiting Forces Act.[64]

Although military personnel dominated 45 Group, it was, like Ferry Command, ATFERO, and the Air Services Department of the CPR, a hybrid organization in which civilians played a significant role. Most of these were Canadians. Some remained with the ferry service from beginning to end. While, with a few exceptions, military aircrew were seldom retained on ferrying duty for more than a few months, the civilian pilots, navigators, radio officers, and flight engineers formed a more permanent attachment, though there were some, mainly from the United States, who left after completing only a few flights.[65]

It should also be noted that the flying personnel were all men. Contrary to a popular myth about women ferry pilots, and notwithstanding their admirable work with Britain's Air Transport Auxiliary and the USAAF's Women Airforce Service Pilots, no woman ever captained an aircraft on a wartime transoceanic delivery, although a handful attached to the ATA did make one trip with Ferry Command as supernumerary co-pilots.[66] Early on an attempt was made to have Jacqueline Cochran, the famous American 'aviatrix,' ferry a plane to the United Kingdom. However, some ATFERO aircrew rebelled at the proposal and threatened to withdraw their own services if she did. As a compromise, it was agreed that she could fly as Captain Grafton Carlisle's co-pilot in a Hudson, as long as she did not take off or land the plane. This still allowed newspapers to write that Jacqueline Cochran had flown a bomber to the boys overseas.[67] As a corollary to this restriction against women pilots, it might also be mentioned that all aircrew had to be of the white race. Even the involvement of the National Association for the Advancement of Colored People could not overcome this hurdle for Gordon M. Ashe, a particularly well-qualified and persistent black American pilot.[68]

Initially, the civilian crews of the first delivery flights wore whatever clothes they wished. However, early in 1941 concern about the treatment civilians could expect, especially if they happened to be forced down in enemy-controlled territory, brought the development of a uniform. At first it was simply service-style khaki with hats sporting an ATFERO badge, hastily designed in Taffy Powell's office 'with no thought of heraldic significance and took the form of a lion standing astride the northern hemisphere, but centred on the north Atlantic. Theoretically the lion had an aeroplane in his mouth to symbolise the delivery function between the two continents, but in spite of having a good artist on the staff the aeroplane looked like a dart or a cigar and was deleted.' After the birth of Ferry Command the civilians were issued uniforms combining the organization's brief heritage with that of the RAF. Air force badges, including wings, 'were worn with chrome buttons on dark-blue winter uniforms and khaki in summer. Standard RAF-stripes were used for senior captains, co-pilots and other aircrew.' With the advent of 45 Group the old ATFERO badge was resurrected. 'Admittedly it was polished up a bit but it was approved by the College of Heralds in London.'[69] The crews were proud of the uniform. Don McVicar welcomed an opportunity to show it off.[70]

Between September 1941 and September 1945, the ferry organization employed a monthly average of about 400 civilian aircrew. The greatest number serving at any given time was 547.[71] No official nominal rolls have come to hand, but unofficial lists show that at least 328 Canadian civilians flew on ferrying and transport operations.[72] The number of pilots was not great, probably not much more than a hundred, since most Canadian flyers of military age joined the RCAF and many of the older pilots were persuaded to remain with the domestic airlines whose operations were an important factor in the national economy. Moreover, to be accepted by the ferry service, civilian pilots had to have a commercial licence, 1000 hours in the air, and a high instrument rating.[73] Canadian pilots possessing these qualifications were relatively scarce, and the airlines employing them were reluctant to let them go. At least fifty-five of the Canadian pilots flew as captains, and the others as first officers. (Throughout its history the ferry service followed the civilian method of pilot ranking. Captains were the most senior; first officers flew as first pilots without carrying that title. Second officers flew as co-pilots.)

Among the most senior of the Canadian captains was Al Lilly, formerly a prewar pilot with the Royal Canadian Mounted Police. He made his first crossing of the North Atlantic on 11 July 1941 as captain of Hudson AM757. Most of his flights were across the North Atlantic, but he also ferried aircraft and flew transport planes over the South Atlantic and the Pacific. Eventually he became the chief test pilot for 45 Group. The first Canadian civilian to pilot a Hudson for the ferry service was Duke Schiller, who took Hudson AM735 from Gander to Prestwick on 22 May 1941.[74]

Another outstanding pilot was Louis Bisson, who was part of the first survey flight of the North East Staging Route, but who generally flew more on transport operations than on ferrying. He was also air chauffeur to prime ministers and ambassadors. He and Don McVicar were the only Canadians to be awarded the OBE for their services to Ferry Command. OBEs also went to American pilots Bill Vanderkloot, Grafton Carlisle, George Evans, and Dana Gentry. MBEs were received by Captain Jack Ruggles, flight engineer John Affleck, and radio officers Russell Holmes and J.W. Gray. In addition, fourteen civilian captains, twelve radio officers, two flight engineers, and traffic officer D.F. McPherson got certificates of commendation.[75]

The Canadian radio officers may have been the most interesting group employed by Ferry Command. At the beginning of the war these men worked for the Department of Transport. Volunteering for duty with the ferry organization, they showed up in Montreal with no previous flying experience and, after a brief course in air procedures, they soon found themselves in aircraft flying to all corners of the globe. Records compiled at the end of the war show that 220 of the 326 civilian radio operators who served with the ferry organization came from Canada. Most of the others were drawn from the United Kingdom, about half a dozen were from the United States, and two or three were from other countries. No fewer than seventy-five members of this group, most of them Canadians, lost their lives along the air routes of the world. Some have no known graves, a few were brought home for burial, and others rest in Iceland, Greenland, Bermuda, Brazil, Scotland, Newfoundland, and Labrador.[76]

Aside from the globe-circling extent of its operations, one of the most intriguing features of the ferry service was the mixed character of the organization, part military, part civilian, part British, part Canadian, with Americans, Norwegians, Poles, and at least fifteen other nationalities also participating. The role of the Canadians is most difficult to define. By sheer weight of numbers, they made a distinctive contribution in both flying operations and ground support. Yet the ferry service was entirely a British enterprise designed to deliver aeroplanes from North America for use by the RAF. Though based in Canada, it was controlled and financed by the British government. Despite the large number of Canadian servicemen involved, only one member of the RCAF, Taffy Powell, served in an executive capacity. Yet he, temporarily a British expatriate, was in no sense a Canadian representative. He had been asked for at the beginning because of his background as a captain with Imperial Airways. Eventually he transferred to the RAF.

It is evident, however, that from the beginning the operation depended to a large extent on Canadian cooperation. In a sense the arrangement was based on the partnership in transatlantic aviation formed in 1935. While the Canadian government viewed it as a military undertaking essential to the conduct of the war, it also realized that the routes followed by the bombers would one day become the highways of commerce. Canadian officials and politicians were thus doubly motivated in their support of the British organization. If content to play the role of silent partner, the Government of Canada watched developments with consuming interest, always with an eye on the future of the North Atlantic route. It is significant that the sector of government most directly involved and in closest touch with Bowhill and Marix was the Department of Transport.

The motives that influenced the government were also felt by Canadians who served in 45 Group. Though generally far from the scene of enemy action, they had the satisfaction of contributing to an operation that was a vital factor in winning the war. Moreover, with transatlantic flying still in the experimental stages when the war began, it was a unique and exciting challenge to help usher in a new age of routine transoceanic air travel.

10

Mosquito Deliveries

As the story of Ferry Command has unfolded in the preceding chapters, we have encountered most of the aircraft that were delivered in significant numbers. Almost ignored to this point, however, is the de Havilland Mosquito, one of the most exciting aircraft of the war – and, from the perspective of the ferry crews, one of the most controversial. Conceived independently by de Havilland aircraft, it had been developed, despite a lack of interest by the Air Ministry, in a remarkably short period of time. The first deliveries to the RAF came in July 1941, only 'nineteen months from the start of design.'[1] The RAF was quickly impressed with its performance and soon found many uses for its remarkable versatility – most notably as a night-fighter; a high-speed unarmed bomber, particularly with No. 8 (Pathfinder) Group; and in the crucial, unsung photo-reconnaissance role. Able to outrun German fighters, it was even used by BOAC to maintain a regular air service with Sweden for the duration of the war.[2]

Airmen tended to fall in love with the sleek aerodynamic lines and impressive performance of 'the wooden wonder.' Employing expertise built up during the development of its Comet racer and Albatross airliner before the war, de Havilland was able to avoid putting pressure on the already overburdened British metal industries by building the Mosquito of wood. It featured a double birch plywood skin over a balsa and spruce frame. The fuselage was made of two halves joined after the wiring and controls were installed. The wing was a simple and light one-piece construction. Even the two 40-gallon drop tanks were made of moulded plywood (with an internal plastic coating). They supplemented the 539 imperial gallons of fuel carried in the wings. Powered by two Rolls-Royce Merlin engines, it was a powerful, robust, and manoeuvrable aircraft.[3] Performance obviously differed in the fifty-one official variants of this versatile machine, but it began with a top speed of 388 miles per hour for the prototype and a range of more than 1000 miles. Some of the reconnaissance versions were capable of considerably more than 400 mph.[4] The Mosquito remained the fastest aircraft on either side until late in the war.

Most of the almost seven thousand wartime Mosquitoes were built in the United Kingdom. More than a thousand, however, were constructed in Canada in what was called 'the most audacious and ambitious program of aircraft production yet attempted in this Dominion.'[5] The task of delivering them overseas fell to 45 Group. In order for the planes to make the crossing to Britain, de Havilland Canada installed extra fuel tanks in the bomb-bay. The additional 121 imperial gallons extended the range to 2430 miles. Unfortunately, exciting as the aircraft may have been, it had a disturbing habit of going missing on delivery flights from North America.[6]

Initially there was no hint of any problems with the new type. The first Canadian-built machines, powered by Packard-built Merlins, went to operational training units of the BCATP in Canada. No. 45 Group delivered its first two Mosquitoes, christened *New Glasgow* and *Acton*, in August 1943. Taking the northern route with its short hops, they staged through Greenland, Iceland, and Prestwick before arriving at de Havilland's Hatfield facility in Hertfordshire on the 12th. Three more arrived from Canada in November. After rigorous testing and some modification by the parent de Havilland engineers, not to mention the RAF, the first one, KB161, went into action with 139 Squadron, RAF, on 2 December 1943 as part of a raid on Berlin. Coincidentally, it was flown by Flight Lieutenant G.W. Salter, a Canadian in the RAF, who piloted it for more than two hundred hours before it was wrecked on landing by another pilot.[7]

Deliveries of Mosquitoes gradually increased in frequency through the spring and summer of 1944. As they did, transatlantic records tumbled, even though ferry crews were instructed to fly at the most economical cruising speed. For some unknown reason, the section on record-setting flights in the brief official history of the ferry service does not mention any records by Mosquitoes. These new machines made the crossing from both Goose Bay and Gander in less than seven hours. Even so, *Atlantic Bridge* ascribes the fastest Newfoundland–UK crossing to a Liberator, piloted by Captain W.S. May, at 7 hours 47 minutes.[8] Such a time would have been slow for a Mosquito. In May

Aircrew who flew with Ferry Command were the first to admit that most of their experiences lacked the hardships and dangers that other airmen had to endure during the war. Here Pilot Officer J.F. Fewell (Vancouver), Pilot Officer A.E. Herber (Minneapolis), Pilot Officer F. Hawthorn (Brantford, Ont.), and Pilot Officer G. Strathon (Weyburn, Sask.) enjoy a drink in the garden of the Royal Victoria Hotel, Nassau. NFB photo for DND, NA, PA 191338

Ferry crews return to North America from Africa in a Liberator. 'The boys talk, sleep and sign each other's short snorters. This one is made up of bills from the different countries the pilot has visited.' NFB photo for DND, NA, PA 114612

George Phillips (on right) as a bush pilot in northern Canada. NA, PA 90219

In a scene familiar to many aircrew, six airmen sit in a decompression chamber with an 'MO' (medical officer) for a simulated ascent to high altitude. NFB photo for DND, NA, PA 140655

North American B-25 Mitchell. NFB photo for DND, NA, PA 191381

The usual mix of civilian and military aircrew are briefed by an officer of Ferry Command prior to their transatlantic delivery flights. NFB photo for DND, NA, PA 114611

Consolidated Coronado flying boat, JX494, of No. 45 Group's 231 Squadron, out of the water on the ramp at Darrell's Island, Bermuda. Sheldon Luck Collection, NA, PA 124231

Not your average Liberator – *Commando* after acquiring its single tail,
stretched fuselage, and interior improvements. DND, PL 34144

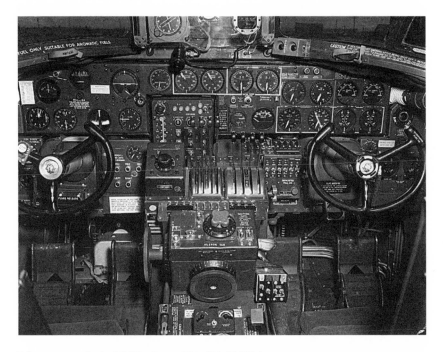

Liberator cockpit. DND photo, NA, PA 136726

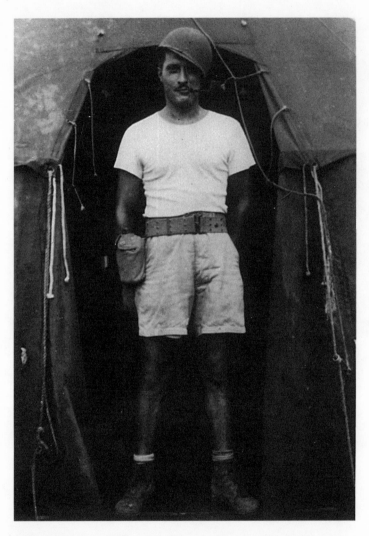

Sergeant Robert Byrne, USAAF, on Iwo Jima, long after his stint
with RAF Ferry Command. Gerald Forrette, DND, PMR 94-204

Douglas Dakota with port propeller feathered. NA, PA 187617

Avro Lancaster Mark X, KB700, the *Ruhr Express*, rolled out at Malton as the first four-engine bomber built in Canada. DND, RE 20283-1

A Handley Page Hampden drops a torpedo during a training flight, Patricia Bay, British Columbia. DND photo, NA, PA 14776

Waco CG-4A glider, *Voo-Doo*, at Dorval. NFB photo for DND, NA, PA 191328

De Havilland Mosquito. DND, PL 14567

Mosquito (foreground) being ferried through Trinidad, October 1943. NFB photo for DND, NA, PA 114609

Lord Beaverbrook emerges from a Return Ferry Service Liberator at Gander in August 1941. DND photo, NA, PA 132644

The funeral at Lamlash Cemetery, Isle of Arran, of the victims of the
Liberator that flew into Goat Fell on 10 August 1941. DND, PMR 94-124

Given the way in which the Return Ferry Service Liberator AL591 broke up on impact, it is a miracle that anyone survived the 9 February 1943 crash ten miles short of the Gander runway. DND photo, NA, PA 191279

Montreal citizens and an RCAF band join Dorval staff at Christ Church Cathedral on 30 October 1942 for the funeral of seven of the victims of the crash of Ventura AE729. *Montreal Star*, NA, PA 151225

Firemen on the scene where Liberator EW148 crashed in downtown Montreal on 25 April 1944. *Montreal Star*, NA, PA 116061

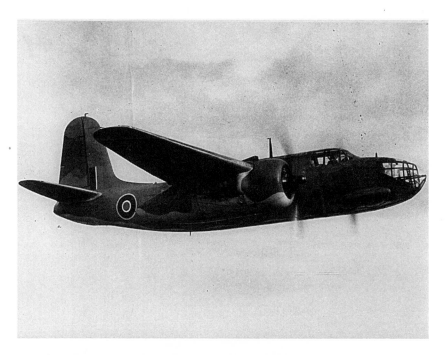

Douglas DB-7 Boston. DND photo, NA, PA 115098

Julie Lavergne overpaints the US insignia with the RAF roundel on a Dakota at Dorval prior to dispatch overseas. NFB photo for DND, NA, PA 141357

Mechanics work on a Ventura, Dorval. NFB photo for DND, NA, PA 191378

In September 1940, the Air Services Department of the C.P.R. was formed in Montreal to ferry bombers most urgently required in Great Britain. In May 1941, this organization was taken over by the Ministry of Aircraft Production and later by the Royal Air Force Ferry Command. When the Royal Air Force Transport Command was formed in April 1943 the Montreal formation became the headquarters of No 45 Group.

From this early date very large numbers of multi-engined aircraft were ferried from Canada, Bermuda and the Bahamas across the North and South Atlantic to many parts of the world by a team of civilian aircrew in support of the Royal Air Force. This team was disbanded when victory in Europe was won, and

This Certificate is Presented to

P. Laurin

to record his most meritorious services to the war effort as.....

First Officer

between *March* 1944 and *June* 19 45

G.J. POWELL (AIR COMMODORE)

Certificate of service awarded to Pierre Laurin, a civilian ferry pilot from Quebec City, when he left 45 Group of RAF Transport Command in June 1945. DND, RE 18923

1944 Wing Commander John D. Wooldridge, an RAF one-tripper working his way home after a mission in North America, and his radio navigator, Flying Officer C.J. Burns, RAAF, flew from Goose Bay to Prestwick in 6 hours 46 minutes. Five months later Captain Ernest M. Gill, from Caterham, Surrey, and crewman W.E. Francis, from Windsor, Ontario, landed at Prestwick 6 hours 44 minutes after taking off from Gander. The next month Gill flew from Goose Bay to Prestwick in 6 hours 8 minutes. In May 1945 Captain J.G. Naz and radio navigator Fred G. Plaxton of Saint John, New Brunswick, made the Gander trip in 5 hours 37 minutes. The same day another. Mosquito, piloted by Flight Lieutenant H.C. Graham from Glasgow, with Flying Officer F.C. Seidenkranz, RCAF, of Hamilton, as his radio navigator, took only a minute longer for the same delivery. The quickest known transatlantic flight by a Mosquito came on 23 October 1945 when a photo-reconnaissance version of 540 Squadron, RAF, flew from Gander to Mawgan in Cornwall in 5 hours 10 minutes at an average speed of 445 mph, helped by a tailwind of 70 mph.[9]

Despite the impressive appearance and performance of the Mosquito, many ferry crews tried to avoid having to fly one. It quickly developed a reputation as a dangerous aircraft. Don McVicar, with thirty deliveries,[10] ferried only one Mosquito to Britain, but he checked out other pilots on the type during his stint as an instructor at Dorval.[11] He has left little doubt about the problems with the plane and the prevailing attitude towards it. Initially he was eager to try his hand on the hot new machine.[12] He got his chance in April 1944 at Elizabeth City when he squeezed into the right-hand radio operator/navigator's seat beside the checkout instructor, Flight Lieutenant Rust. He realized right away that this was a much different aircraft from anything he had been flying. It was not simply the British instruments and controls, so different from the American ones he was used to; it was also the realization that this was a very powerful aeroplane, requiring far more boost than he had ever used. Even the instructor had difficulty keeping the plane on a straight path during the takeoff. 'Rust opened both throttles slowly, then, as we began to swing off the runway to the left, he opened the left throttle way ahead of the right and kicked on right rudder. I was glad to see he hadn't used the air brakes which were controlled by a short lever on the control column. I had a feeling they'd be just as touchy as that damn hand-bar which controlled the differential brakes on the Hudsons and the Ventura. I found out later I couldn't have been more right on that one.'[13]

The checkout aircraft lacked dual controls, but McVicar got a good idea of what it was like:

Once airborne the Mossie showed its thoroughbred characteristics, even with the power at normal cruise power settings. We were soon steaming along at 10,000 feet in the clear air over the Atlantic showing an impressive 300 mph on the clock. Rust let me feel the controls. The ailerons were as light as my pocketbook after a night on the town, and the elevators were sweetly sensitive. I presumed the rudders were the same. Now Rust slowly pulled one throttle fully off, then pushed the red feathering button. He pointed at his right foot which was easily holding the aircraft straight with just a few inches of rudder pedal. He didn't even have to crank in trim like all the other aircraft I'd flown. I was astonished. As the speed slowly decayed to around 250 he unfeathered and fed power to the simulated failed engine. The airspeed needle climbed rapidly. It was all very impressive.[14]

Returning safely to the ground was another matter: 'The airspeed was hard to kill until he [Rust] got the landing gear down.' McVicar found the high-speed landing a little hairy and was happy to call it a day. After shutting down, 'I rigged the little ladder in the escape hatch in the belly and climbed down. I felt a silly urge to kiss the ground.'[15] His own turn came a few days later, with an RAF wireless operator/air gunner, Sergeant Perrin, in the right-hand seat:

As I buckled on my seat parachute and my shoulder restraining straps I looked down at the entrance hatch. I wondered how I would ever get out of that small hole with a bulky parachute strapped to my ass. I'd had enough trouble scrambling through it without the jump-sack. I tried to forget it and turned my attention to the business at hand. The gas cocks were behind my seat, and I had to get Perrin to turn them on as I looked awkwardly over my shoulder. I found the throttles were cramped up against the fuselage wall and figured it would be difficult to lead the left one on take-off. When we cranked up I found they were short-coupled and a small movement released a lot of those horses out of the Merlins. There was no mixture or supercharger control. Apparently some sort of magic brain took care of all those details. I hoped the magic brain never failed.

On the take-off I found I was overcontrolling, and the torque was just as severe as Rust had demonstrated. The first circuit was a little ragged but we all arrived in one piece, which some pilots say is the mark of a successful landing. I did two more, each a little smoother, before I gave myself the pleasure of air work at 10,000 feet.[16]

Like many pilots, McVicar found the Mosquito great fun to fly. It took him back to his aviation roots:

This was the first aerobatic aircraft I'd flown since another de Havilland product, the Moth, many years before. The contrast was terrific. The little Moth's entry speed for a loop with a roll off the top was a shaky, vibrating 100 mph. The Mossie roared smoothly as I pushed the taps forward to an indicated 380. Up and over we went, the horizon spinning. It was exhilarating and I felt like a young fighter pilot. Then a couple of barrel rolls. I suddenly felt that a squadron pilot could love his Mossie over all other aircraft, in spite of its hot take-off and landing speeds.[17]

However, he had enough experience to realize that this aeroplane should be treated with respect: 'it would always be a tough taskmaster, forcing its pilot to be on his toes, but always delivering the best performance of any aircraft in the world.' As he completed his checkout flight, McVicar 'shot up a Lib, just to keep my new-found fighter pilot's hand in. Then three more landings, the last two three-pointers for a total of 180 minutes. I felt I was competent. It had been a marvellous day.' Nonetheless, he ends this story with a proviso: 'I was to find out later that a Mossie at light weight and a Mossie fully loaded were two different machines.'[18]

McVicar did not have to wait long to learn about the characteristics of a loaded Mosquito: it was his next delivery. On 29 April 1944 he and Clayton Eby, also from Saskatchewan and 'a Radio Navigator of unflappable attitude and great skill,' departed Dorval for Goose Bay, the first leg of the trip to Prestwick, 'with all the pride of a Mosquito crew with ready-to-boil Packard Merlin engines.' They went right up to 20,000 feet to check fuel consumption and levelled out at 300 mph:

We had donned our uncomfortable, smelly oxygen masks to make sure that the system worked, and then it was time to check the bomb bay long-range fuel tank, which was essential for our longest legs. I told Eby to shut off his radio to avoid sparking, then selected the valve position that would transfer the volatile fuel into the wings where it could then be fed to the engines. Now came the part the flight crews were wary and worried about. There always seemed to be a faint odour of gas in the bomb bay, and the electric fuel transfer pump, which didn't appear to be fully enclosed, was fixed near the bottom of the tank. One little spark and the aircraft would instantly become our fiery coffin. I flicked the switch, hoping that Eby had better connections with the Lord than

I, then shut my eyes, which I realized was a rather primitive reaction against impending doom.

When I opened them again I could see the wide blue St. Lawrence far below and I mentally promised God I'd try to reform.[19]

With a favourable weather forecast for the next leg to Greenland, McVicar and Eby continued their journey the next morning. As they hurtled along, high above the Davis Strait, the captain was amused at the USAAF radio stations: 'Eby called them and I smiled as I heard them, as before, calling themselves *Blondie* and *Dagwood*. I wondered what the unsmiling Germanic minds of the U-boat monitoring stations made of this comic-page humour.' As they came in for a landing at BW-1, the 'black, forbidding cliffs' on either side of the fiord seemed particularly menacing in a Mosquito. 'As the end of the runway flashed below,' McVicar recalls, 'I chopped the power and the Merlins made their usual barrage of popping protest. The tail was trying to swing around under the impetus of a 15 mph quartering tail wind, and I was glad when I got the three wheels firmly planted, because beside the runway were wrecks of aircraft that had not been able to stay on the concrete.' As he parked he spotted five other Mosquitoes obviously awaiting a suitable weather forecast to proceed.[20]

The next morning a USAAF major assured us that we could top everything at 20,000 feet on a direct flight to Prestwick, and I guess that is where the trouble started. Because I couldn't top the cloud, which was full of ice, even at 29,000 feet. The engines wanted to jump out of their mounts and as I changed course and let down I thought I'd had it. So I had plenty of time to think about the self-assured Met man who'd got me into the mess. One of our guys arrived on one engine and one was lost and I did a lot of hollering and screaming about the quality of the Met coverage to the de-briefing bloke. He seemed to think it was all part of the job, which did nothing to calm me down, so I guess they could have heard me right across Scotland in Edinburgh. The de-briefing officer told me he would put me on report.[21]

In fact, 45 Group lost a number of Mosquitoes for unknown reasons, some simply disappearing. However, because of the lack of archival sources on aircraft losses, it is impossible to confirm McVicar's recollection that a Mosquito went missing over the North Atlantic at this time. A file of miscellaneous 45 Group losses does indicate that KB220 disappeared a week later. Flight Lieutenant George Henry Wood, RAF, and his radio navigator, Flying Officer John Owen Klippel, RAAF, went missing somewhere between BW-1 and Iceland.[22]

Ferry crews knew there would be losses. Initially, therefore, nobody appears to have taken much note of the occasional problem with the new Canadian-built Mosquito. Gradually, however, word filtered through 45 Group that the problems with this plane were more serious than usual for machines fresh off the assembly line. More notice was taken of oil temperature gauges failing, of reports of gas fumes in the cockpit, and even of radio failures, not to mention the odd loss. Rumours suggested that mechanical troubles were happening with increasing frequency. Maintenance staff at the various staging posts had been simply fixing any faults rather than taking the trouble to submit a report. Each complaint was looked at in isolation, as a natural occurrence, so that neither headquarters nor the manufacturer was aware of the overall picture. Nonetheless, their faith in the Mosquito shaken by what they heard, many aircrew feared drawing one for delivery, and tried to avoid the assignment.[23]

A.G. Sims, a pilot who joined Ferry Command in 1941, said that 'some pilots refused to fly Mosquitoes. They were a good aircraft and the R.C.A.F. operated them without any trouble but the modifications required for the trans-Atlantic flights gave rise to serious problems.' He mentioned the special bomb-bay tanks as being particularly worrisome: 'This was a sort of tied on affair and the modifications sometimes caused things to go wrong with the fuel system. I clearly recall one flight with a Mosquito when petrol was swishing about in the fuselage by the time we got to Prestwick.'[24]

Concern mounted as the problems multiplied. On 20 May Robert Adkison, from Watsonville, California, and his radio operator, Paul Francis Zyvitski, from Oshawa, Ontario, disappeared somewhere between Dorval and Gander.[25] At the end of August a Mosquito 'disintegrated in the air' at Goose Bay, probably on a test flight. John Matheson Brown, a civilian engineer, was killed; the pilot, Tex Roberts, baled out successfully.[26] During the summer, a number of delivery crews suffered engine failure. When power from the right engine was lost it could also kill the radio, a frightening experience over the vast, cold emptiness of the North Atlantic. Headquarters took notice and began to monitor the situation more closely. The captains of thirty-eight Mosquitoes delivered in September reported mechanical problems of varying severity, the most common involving oil leaks or gas fumes.[27] It does not appear to have been until almost the end of October that 45 Group was jolted into action. The chief engineer officer, Group Captain Gordon Best, later reported:

It was soon discovered, however, that we were living in a fool's paradise. As weather became colder, reports of low operating oil temperatures were received and increasing instances of oil cooler failures occurred. Failures resulting in complete engine failure occurred on:-

KB 452 on 18/10 and
KB 489 on 25/10.

These failures were the cause of some concern amongst the Ferry crews and on more than one occasion propellers were feathered due to oil pressure gauges being u/s [unserviceable] and giving false readings, the pilots taking it for granted that the engine was about to fail. The engine failure (starboard) on KB 489 also resulted in the loss of radio as the battery was exhausted during the feathering operations. This aircraft was fortunate in reaching its destination.[28]

No. 45 Group engineering officers and de Havilland experts met and worked to rectify the problem. Instructions were issued to preheat aircraft prior to startup and, according to Best, 'the Packard Merlin representative and the Chief Maintenance Foreman from Dorval were sent over the Northern route to give special instruction on the handling of Mosquito aircraft.'[29] This was not enough. After Oklahoman Thomas Campbell and his radio navigator, Pilot Officer George Daniel Boyd (RCAF, from Lachute, Quebec), in KB504, disappeared on 12 November between Gander and BW-1, and Captain Oliver Huss (Wahpeton, North Dakota) and Earl Ecklin (White Rock, British Columbia), in KB535, did likewise between Goose Bay and BW-1 eighteen days later,[30] the experts, redoubled their efforts. There had been six accidents, including the two disappearances, and eighty-two incidents involving mechanical troubles during the September–November period alone.[31]

With no solution in sight, all 45 Group Canadian-built Mosquitoes on the northern route were grounded after KB536 crashed near Summerside, Prince Edward Island, on 10 December, killing the Norwegian pilot, Sub-Lieutenant Sigmund Breck, and the radio navigator, Pilot Officer Francis Edward Sorensen, RAAF.[32] The initial cause of the accident was judged pilot error, but officials decided to take no more chances. Deliveries would go via the southern route (Natal to Dakar, French West Africa, then to Rabat Sale, and up to Britain) until it was determined how to deal with cold-weather operations. Engineering staff were sent from 45 Group and de Havilland to Nassau, Natal, and Rabat Sale, the key points on the route.[33]

Unfortunately, cold weather did not appear to have been the problem. On 15 December Dorval dispatched twenty-two Mosquitoes via the southern route, leaving half a dozen stranded at various points in the north. Two, KB626 and KB620, 'disappeared without trace within 40 minutes flying of Belem,' on the 16th, claiming four more civilians, Captains Ray Garver (from Ohio) and Truman Clay Henderson (Texas) and radio officers Joseph George Shelfoon (Tignish, Prince Edward Island) and Alan William Harding (Edmonton).[34] The following day KB634 landed at Zandery Field in Surinam on one engine, while KB378 did likewise at Caicos. Best concluded:

As no indications of bad weather were at that time forthcoming and the pilots of KB 626 and KB 620 were very experienced and not in the least affected by the general apprehension towards this type of aircraft, it was assumed that some sudden mishap such as an explosion must have occurred which would prevent an S.O.S. being sent. If this was so, it was also reasonable to assume that the disappearances over the Northern route might have been due to similar cause. In addition, as no Maintenance personnel experienced on Merlin engines were available either at Caicos or Zandery, no report on the cause of engine failures was immediately forthcoming, and it was assumed that the cause was primarily due to cold starts having been made at de Havillands or Dorval which had done damage to the oil coolers, but such damage had not become apparent until the aircraft were operating in hot weather.[35]

Given these tragic developments 'and the mental attitude of the pilots towards Mosquitoes in general, S.A.S.O. [Senior Air Staff Officer, Air Commodore Powell] stopped further deliveries, and grounded all aircraft en route pending a full investigation.'[36] He called a meeting on 19 December at which representatives of 45 Group, the British Air Commission, de Havilland, and Packard tried to decide what action should be taken before resuming delivery of Canadian-built Mosquitoes. Judging by the minutes, which fill four-and-a-half legal-size pages, it appears to have been a full, frank, and wide-ranging discussion. The participants concluded that something – such as an explosion – had happened very suddenly to prevent the disappeared aircraft from sending a radio message. Or, alternatively, the starboard engine had failed, killing the radio in the process, and the plane had subsequently failed to reach its destination. They felt any explosion could have been caused in a number of ways, a short circuit or static spark setting off fuel or hydraulic fumes, a defective immersion pump in the bomb-bay tank, or severe boiling of the battery.[37]

Group Captain Best reported that the conference agreed to take the following action:

(i)   Install an additional battery on a separate circuit from the aircraft battery to ensure radio communication in the event of a starboard engine failure.

(ii)   Extension of F.A.Z. valve vent from the bomb bay to atmosphere and incorporation of suction venting through the camera hatch covers. It was considered that this venting would be sufficient to prevent explosive mixtures accumulating in the aircraft.

(iii)   Either replacement or modification of the amphenol plug of the oil temperature gauge, in order to provide a gauge of the required reliability.

(iv)   Removal and test of all oil coolers presently installed in aircraft ex-production line.

(v)   Fitment of perforated blanking plates to oil coolers to raise operating temperatures to minimum of 60° centigrade in sub-zero outside air temperatures.

(vi)   The adoption of oil dilution subject to clearance in respect of frothing.

(vii) Exhaustive tests of the immersion pump to determine whether it could cause an explosion in the bomb bay tank. After discussion, it was agreed that the possibility of explosion from either the battery or hydraulic fumes was negligible and need not be considered further.[38]

The responsibility for undertaking the tests and modifications was divided equally between de Havilland and 45 Group, with both agreeing to do experiments on oil dilution.

Air Commodore Powell signalled Transport Command headquarters summarizing the decisions of the conference and the steps being taken. After outlining the tests and modifications ordered before delivery of Mosquitoes could be resumed, the SASO zeroed in on the question of possible explosions: 'With regard to unexplained losses only satisfactory solution is leakage of fuel into bomb-bay emersion [sic] pump, one of which on test definitely demonstrated dangerous symptoms.' He reported, 'no further flights in Group will be made until bomb-bay pump either removed or tested. Secondly, approximately, 60 aircraft will be ferried southabout as soon as minor modifications incorporated. Thirdly, reversion to northern route will be made when cooler modifications completed and oil dilution fitted.' Powell demonstrated his concern about the possibility of explosions in Mosquitoes when he concluded his message: 'We urgently suggest that general warning be issued at once covering suspected internal leakage bombay pump.'[39]

Arrangements were made for each Mosquito to be flown for five hours before it was dispatched overseas, in order 'to overcome the numerous minor faults and to re-establish the pilots' confidence in the aircraft.' This new requirement, on top of the modification work, would be 'far beyond the capacity of Dorval – both as regards hangar accommodation and maintenance personnel.' To undertake this work, 45 Group established a detachment, the Mosquito Preparation and Despatching Unit, at Crumlin Airport, London, Ontario. It opened with five officers, four airmen, and six civilians, in addition to eight permanent aircrew, on 10 January 1945.[40]

The engineering staff obviously worked hard, because deliveries resumed on the southern route on 23 January 1945. However, 'due to shortage of personnel and numerous technical difficulties, the output was very low and it was not until the end of February that a reasonable output was reached.' Initially there were no accidents or serious incidents, though 'numerous minor difficulties arose due to lack of spares and lack of experience of the Maintenance personnel over this Southern route in servicing Mosquito aircraft.' Group Captain Best cited one case of a 45 Group pilot reporting a minor engine problem at an American base. The next time he saw his Mosquito it was all in pieces. 'On enquiring the reason, he received the reply "if we are going to service these aircraft, we might as well find out what makes them tick."'[41]

Many considered the question of oil dilution the key one to be resolved before the northern route could be used again for Mosquito deliveries. Considerable testing and experimenting was undertaken by engineers of 45 Group, de Havilland, Packard, and even No. 8 OTU at Greenwood, Nova Scotia.[42] Finally, 'it was decided that sufficient oil dilution if used in conjunction with pre-heating could be attained without modifying the breather system through the camshaft covers and final instructions with regard to its use, based on results of the experiment, were issued to Units together with clearance of the aircraft for the Northern Route on the completion of the Chief Engineer Officer's inspection of this Route.'[43]

The first three Mosquitoes were cleared for delivery via the northern route at the beginning of February, 'coincidental with the Chief Engineer Officer's inspection.'[44] One of them was KB370, which had arrived at Dorval on 3 December, only to be stranded there pending the results of the deliberations and the oil dilution experiments, not to mention any needed modifications. Captain E.H. Moody gave it a complete test flight on 1 February 1945, and a departure check was done two days later. On 4 February departure inspector J. Rutledge did a pre-flight inspection and certified the aircraft serviceable for delivery.[45] Meanwhile, Squadron Leader Ed Coristine's crew assignments department had assigned two BCATP graduates, Flying Officers J.M. Squance, RAF, and G.L.M. Maxon, RCAF, to take KB370 to the United Kingdom. Their backgrounds may have been different but, by February 1945, they were both ferry service veterans. However, this would be the first Mosquito delivery for each of them.

At thirty-two, Gunn Maxon, from Selkirk, Manitoba, was the senior of the two in terms of age and ferry experience. He had reached Dorval on 26 March 1943, direct from No. 3 Air Observer School at Pearce, Alberta, and had subsequently completed a dozen transatlantic deliveries as navigator on Catalinas, Liberators, and Baltimores. Judged an average navigator, he had started training as a radio operator in June 1944. A number of navigators were cross-trained in this way to help make up the two-man crews required for Mosquitoes.[46] It appears that, while he was proficient enough to undertake the job of radio navigator on a Mosquito delivery, Maxon was only an average radio operator. Richard W. Haigh, deputy chief radio instructor at 45 Group's Dorval radio school, said of Maxon: 'He ranked 19th in a class of 22 on Flight Procedure and 16th on Technical Examinations. His assessment on graduation was low, his report reading: "Reliable, steady worker. Rather slow and nervous."'[47]

John Squance, from Durham, England, eleven years Maxon's junior, appears to have been rated as slightly better at his specialty than was his crewman. He had reported to 45 Group from No. 34 OTU, Pennfield Ridge, New Brunswick, on 17 January 1944. After completing the full captains' course in the Training Wing, he had delivered Mitchells, Bostons, and Lancasters via the northern and the mid-Atlantic routes. At the end of December Pilot Officer Bradshaw, a staff instructor, had checked Squance out on the Mosquito, judging him 'a high average pilot. O.K. for Delivery on Mosquito Aircraft.'[48] He flew one more Lancaster to Prestwick, via Goose Bay, for his eleventh delivery, and then was teamed with Maxon on KB370.[49]

The plan was to fly to Goose Bay via Mont Joli. Squance and Maxon took off near midday on 4 February but, for some unknown reason, returned to Dorval ninety minutes later. Following two-and-a-half hours on the ground they tried again to reach Mont Joli, finally arriving after a flight of about an hour and forty minutes. On 8 February they resumed their journey with a flight of just under two hours to Goose Bay. While the leg from Dorval to Mont Joli appears to have been uneventful, at least after the abortive first attempt, that to Goose differed from the norm in one, possibly significant, way – Maxon did not acknowledge or initiate any communications with Goose Bay during the flight. As it developed, the radio navigator reported a broken key, which was replaced before the next part of the trip.[50]

Strangely, with his radio navigator seated beside him in the Mosquito, Squance did not seem to have been aware of the communication problem. Flight Lieutenant Cyril Minchinton, RAF, the operations control officer at 84 Staging Post, Goose Bay, said that Squance 'was satisfied with his aircraft's performance on the trip.' Minchinton reminded him of 'the advisability of keeping in contact with radio stations during flight.'[51] Squance asked the maintenance staff to check the superchargers and fuel booster pump. He also reported 'a slight oil leak at port and starboard engines.' This was found simply 'to be due to the oil tanks being over-filled.' Oil dilution was not used, but the plane was kept in a heated hangar overnight. On the morning of the 10th, KB370 received a daily inspection and was prepared for departure.[52] The flight to BW-1 appears to have been uneventful. Evidently the lack of contact between Goose Bay and the aircraft during the previous leg had indeed been due to the problem with the key. After repairs were made, Maxon kept in touch during the next stage of the trip.

On arrival at the USAAF base in Greenland, Squance and Maxon were met by Alfred Elkin, employed by RAF Transport Command as its liaison engineer there. He fixed a small oxygen leak reported by Squance and then left the plane outside overnight. He later said: 'The only reason for putting an aircraft in the hangar here is for engine change or retraction tests. There is no hangar space at Bluie West 1 for accommodation.' He was not convinced that it was necessary anyway: 'I would rather leave the aircraft outside. My reason for this is that due to quick change in temperature, condensation is more liable to form in fuel, oil and coolant lines.' The next morning KB370's 'engines, oil coolers and cockpit were heated for about six hours.'[53]

Meanwhile, Squance and Maxon spent the night with twelve other 45 Group crews. Some had been waiting for some time for a weather report that would allow them to continue their journeys. One of the pilots was Squance's friend, Flying Officer Alan Dixon, RAF, in the middle of a delayed Mitchell delivery. After three crossings as a Mitchell captain, and two as co-pilot on Liberators, he had departed Dorval on 27 November 1944, only to be stuck at Goose Bay. He finally flew Mitchell KJ713 to BW-1 on 4 February. He recalled talking to his friend after the weather briefing on the morning of the 11th. They felt they had a similar problem. 'Neither Mitchells nor Mosquitoes are supposed to fly in cloud, and we agreed that it was worth a try to make the flight round the tip [of Greenland] and if we found the opening as forecast, we considered the flight could be made quite safely.'[54]

Following the formal briefing, Squance questioned the USAAF meteorologist, Second Lieutenant George C. Krewson. 'He told me that he was flying the Mosquito and asked if I could be certain of no ice on course,' the American later recalled.

I said I could assure him that in the clouds there would be light to moderate turbulence and light to moderate rime ice. I further stated to all pilots that any aircraft that could not take ice to try 50 to 100 miles south of the tip of Greenland, and if no breaks were seen, then to turn around and come back. Several aircraft checked out after the briefing and did not take off. They were all RAF Mitchells (B-25). That was a day not at all sure for ships fearing ice, and the crews were so told on briefing.[55]

Dixon, perhaps frustrated by the slowness of his delivery, decided to chance it. Squance seems to have hesitated, hanging around the operations room. He told Flying Officer William Edwards, the RAF liaison officer at BW-1, that 'he was waiting for a report from pilots who had already taken off. He mentioned that Mosquito aircraft were to avoid cloud flying and I understood his take off would depend on reports received back from aircraft enroute.' Edwards left to attend to some duties. When he returned to the operations room, Squance had gone.[56] Whether he had received the reassurance he sought would be pure conjecture.

Whatever the reason, he had obviously decided to take off for Reykjavik. As always, the aircraft captain had the final say. The maintenance staff pronounced KB370 'serviceable and fit for flight.' Elkin, the civilian half of 45 Group's representation at the isolated Greenland staging post, later testified: 'The crew ran up the engines for about ten minutes, taxied to the ramp leading to the hangar, ran the engines up at that point for about fifteen minutes and then went to the end of the runway, staying there for about a minute and took off at about 1300Z [GMT].'

Elkin watched the take-off, pronouncing it 'normal ... in every way' with the engines 'functioning perfectly.'[57]

To this point Squance and Maxon had been experiencing a relatively uneventful delivery, and one with fewer delays than often occurred over this route. Even by February 1945, however, despite more than four years of experience by the ferry service, such trips could never be taken for granted. The North Atlantic skies could be very unforgiving – particularly to the crews of de Havilland Mosquitoes. A few minutes after taking off Maxon reported, on schedule, that KB370 was over BW-3 (at Simiutak, south of BW-1) at about 10,000 feet.[58] No further position signals were received.

At 1437 GMT, Staff Sergeant Robert L. Kress, USAAF, an experienced radio operator with the U.S. Army Airways Communications System, picked up a faint SOS from an unidentified aircraft.

I heard only the SOS given once followed by a long dash, the length of which I estimate to be about 15 seconds. It did not fade away, but was of the same weak strength throughout, then it stopped abruptly. I heard no other distress signals. At the time, I was guarding 6500, 500 and 4575 frequencies. The line was clear when the SOS was given, no position was received and it was pure luck that I caught the SOS as the signal was so weak. I stood by to hear more, no one else was sending. As the signals were so weak, I thought that someone else may have heard the SOS, therefore, waited for somebody else to take action. At 1441Z [GMT], Prestwick commenced sending weather, and Reykjavik, also commenced sending weather. I called net and reported an SOS from an un-known aircraft. Net then took control and from a process of elimination, came to the conclusion that the SOS was from KB-370.[59]

The distress signal had been too weak for bearings to be taken. However, Kress noted: 'Approximate position of 60/20 N, 36/30 W, was determined based on aircraft's flight plan.' The American radio operator also reported that 'ATC (Air Transport Command [of the USAAF]) Flight Control received a QTE bearing of 42 degrees on HAYY [KB370's call-sign] from Winter Harbour, Maine, taken at 2142Z on 6440 KC. Considering that the bearing was taken seven hours after the distress call, the crew were possibly on a life raft, but nothing was heard at this station.'[60] An air-sea search was initiated as soon as possible, but nothing more was ever heard or seen of Squance or Maxon.

Flying Officer Dixon had spotted the gap in the clouds predicted by the BW-1 forecaster and made it successfully to Reykjavik. So too did

the Dakota in which Group Captain Best was flying as co-pilot. However, the other three aircraft that had taken off from the Greenland strip
– all Mitchells – had returned, apparently deterred by the flying conditions.

Wing Commander K.C. Rappell of the RCAF's Accident Investigation
Branch looked into the disappearance of Mosquito KB370, probably
because one of its crew was a member of the RCAF. As with many
ferry losses, he found that 'the cause of this accident is obscure.' After
hearing from a score of witnesses representing all the bases visited by
Squance and Maxon during their flight, he concluded: 'In view of the
weather conditions on the probable track taken by the aircraft, together
with the pilot's comparative inexperience on this type, it is considered
that these two factors "weather and inexperience" may reasonably be
presumed to be joint causes of the aircraft being missing.' He recommended that Mosquitoes be ferried in formation and that a commission
or board of inquiry be established 'to thoroughly investigate and report
on: Firstly: The problems of trans-Atlantic flights as it affects Mosquito
aircraft as now equipped ... Secondly: The standard of training given
Mosquito crews.'[61]

Not surprisingly, 45 Group staff did not completely agree with everything Rappell wrote. Wing Commander L.L. Jones from RAF Station
Dorval, after concurring with the findings of the investigation, took
issue with the recommendations:

Firstly – a number of conferences called by this Headquarters have been attended by technical experts, pilots of Test Dept., ferry pilots and manufacturing
representatives. The recommendations of whom was to incorporate certain
modifications in the aircraft, and to lay down strict despatching orders; this has
been done. It is considered, therefore, that no useful purpose will be served by
taking further evidence from individual ferry pilots.

Secondly – Mosquito crews are made up of some of our most experienced
personnel who have completed a number of Atlantic crossings in various types
of aircraft, and have for the purpose of ferrying Mosquito aircraft been given a
conversion course on this type.[62]

Group Captain A.W. Fletcher agreed with the investigation report as
modified by Jones's remarks. He wrote: 'Cannot agree that a pilot's
comparative inexperience on Mosquito aircraft is a contributing factor,
when the pilot in question is experienced and has 9 trans-oceanic crossings as captain of aircraft to his credit. Although there is no proof, it

appears from the evidence that the pilot deliberately or inadvertently must have flown in cloud, contrary to the most definite briefing instructions.'[63]

Notwithstanding the official denial of the need for action, the loss of KB370 does seem to have caused 45 Group authorities to redouble their efforts in the ongoing attempt to make Mosquito deliveries safer and more reliable. Group Captain Best had changed his mind about the problem, undoubtedly influenced by his recent experience as a delivery co-pilot: 'During discussions with pilots, both en route and at Prestwick, and as a result of this last accident [KB370], the Chief Engineer Officer decided that these disappearances were in all probability caused by some entirely different causes to those originally assumed. It also appeared that there was every possibility that each disappearance had been in the vicinity of bad weather.'[64]

While he was in Prestwick, Best discussed the Mosquito problem at length with the de Havilland representative there, G.E. Ferguson. At the end of February, Ferguson sent Best a detailed report based on conversations with nine Mosquito delivery crews following their arrivals at Prestwick. Six had taken the southern route, two the northern, and one had staged through the Azores. None arrived without mechanical complaints. Most had experienced a variety of difficulties, some of them quite serious and worrisome to the company representative as well as to 45 Group, not to mention the crews. There appeared to be no discernible pattern. At one point Ferguson reported, 'Generator trouble as mentioned on KB520 has occurred at S.A.L. [Scottish Aviation Limited] as well. In this respect I feel quite sure that someone must be tampering with the generator wiring after it has been assembled at the factory. I base my statements on the fact that there are at least four Inspection Department tests on this service prior to delivery.' He seemed to be groping towards a charge of sabotage. 'There was one other aircraft rendered u/s [unserviceable] and was in the hands of S.A.L. [which did the daily inspections at Prestwick] due to the fact that the elevator horns were severely flattened and punctured, supposedly from ice somewhere on the Northern route.'[65] Neither he nor anyone else ever mentioned sabotage officially, but ferry personnel had their suspicions. It appears, however, that Mosquitoes simply required more careful monitoring of the manufacturing, testing, training, and delivery processes.

March brought a series of meetings, considerable testing, and more correspondence on Mosquitoes for the engineering staff at Dorval, de

Havilland Canada, and even the British Air Commission.[66] The procedures were improved and the situation somewhat ameliorated, but the problem of Mosquito technical faults and mysterious losses was never completely resolved. Even as the investigative work was proceeding, the losses continued. On 20 February a Polish pilot, Flight Lieutenant Mierczyslaw Goldhaar, and Sergeant Thomas Henry Monson, from New Zealand, died when KB475 crashed at Lagens en route to the United Kingdom.[67] Two weeks later Woodrow Walden and Thomas Scotland disappeared on their way to the Azores. Best put it down to bad weather: 'KB 593 was lost without trace on 6/3/45 between Gander and Lagens in the approximate vicinity of a front. This added further weight to the theory that all the accidents were connected with poor weather conditions even if this condition might be locally on the route.'[68]

The latest disappearance probably influenced 45 Group's chief engineer officer when he offered a brief analysis of the problem. Best wrote:

Considering losses in bad weather, wing icing was discarded as a possibility due to the two accidents on the Southern Route [KB620 and KB626 in December].

The other possible causes resulting in loss of control and, therefore, failure to send an S.O.S. could be caused by

(i) Sudden carburettor icing
(ii) Toppling of the gyro horizon due to:-
    (a) Poor condition of the instrument.
    (b) Failure of the Vacuum Pump.
    (c) Poor installation of the Instrument Panel.
    (d) The aircraft being too light on the aileron control, resulting in the pilot overbanking in a turn bank sufficient to topple his gyro. This latter point had been raised by No. 8 Group Bomber Command.[69]

On 7 April Best summed up the Mosquito problem in a full report covering delivery of the type over the previous five or six months. He was now satisfied that the disappearances were 'due to failures of accessories ... and not the airframe or engine. These failures are approximately equally divided between poor design and poor workmanship.' Improvements in the inspection system should look after this aspect of the problem. He also noted a couple of secondary causes, already singled out, especially in the case of KB370. Even though flights were restricted to clear weather, 'investigations into the disappearances revealed that in every instance a front or high cloud existed in the vicinity of the disappearance.' Unexpected poor weather and a 'technical failure' could be a deadly combination when 'coupled in certain instances with comparative inexperience of the pilot.' Best cautioned that he was not criticizing his colleagues: 'The above comment is not intended to be a criticism of the Air Staff or Meteorological organisation, but it does indicate that there is difficulty in accurately forecasting weather over the North Atlantic routes.' This was very true. Flying the Atlantic had come a long way since the start of the war, but those who tried it still had to exercise extreme caution. Even so, the chief engineer was happy with the Canadian-built Mosquito and satisfied that the worst of the problem had been solved. 'During the period March 6th to April 7th, 1945, a total of 128 Mosquitoes have been delivered without a major accident and it is felt, therefore, that the Canadian built Mosquito may now be considered as a reliable aircraft with the exception of the oxygen system and ... this could be cleared up in the very near future.'[70] It is not clear when this was finally resolved.

Not all the problems were gone. Mosquitoes still went missing and crashed. Captain A.G. Sims and his radio navigator were lucky. On 17 April they managed to reach Prestwick after an explosion blew a hole in the fuselage of KA970. Martin Sharp and Michael Bowyer, in perhaps the definitive book on the Mosquito, describe what happened:

Seventy-five miles from Prestwick, on descending, the pilot heard a loud explosion. His feet were knocked from the rudder pedals, and as the starboard engine ran roughly he feathered the propeller. Despite twenty minutes hand pumping he failed to lower the undercarriage. A belly landing at Prestwick followed, a small fire soon being put out. On examination Nos. 3 and 4 bulkheads were severed for about twelve inches of their circumference, No. 5 was torn in half, the hydraulic oil tank smashed, No. 6 bulkhead and rudder lever distorted. A hole about seven by two feet had been blown in the rear starboard fuselage skin, yet the crew escaped unhurt.[71]

All they lost was their personal luggage.

Al Lilly, the Dorval test pilot, explains how it happened:

One of the problems was that the Mosquitoes had an air bottle that was connected with the pneumatic brakes. A compressor on one of the engines kept this bottle up to a given pressure. When the pressure built up to a certain point, say six or seven hundred pounds, the release valve would open so that the pressure would stop building up. If the aircraft came out of a condition of high humidity the release valve would sometimes freeze. The compressor would then go on charging until the bottle blew up and this would knock out a chunk of the fuselage. In some cases we suspect it carried the tail away and put the aircraft out of control, or it may have blown up the whole aircraft.

There was one case, I think Tim Sims was the pilot, where the crew had placed their luggage in the aft stowage compartment before taking off. After landing at Prestwick they got out of the aircraft and saw that a large chunk had been blown out of the fuselage. Their luggage was gone and they suddenly realized what a close call they had had. However, by removing the air bottle from the fuselage and putting it in one of the engine nacelles where it was warm we overcame this problem.[72]

Sims had obviously had a close call. The incident may also have provided a clue about some of the mysterious disappearances. Unfortunately, we shall never know.

With all the meetings and testing, along with the improved inspection systems put in place, 45 Group thought it had eliminated the worst of the Mosquito problem. However, it still was not a safe aeroplane. On 16 April KA968, with Flying Officers W. Wielondek and M. Zajac, left Gander and was never seen again. Ten days later KA153 crashed at Reykjavik, killing Flying Officer Ferwley William Clarke, RAF, and Flight Lieutenant Kilburn William Grist, RAF. On 10 June Captain Howard Stanley Wright and James Douglas Woodyard, in KA237, were lost out of Goose Bay.[73]

On 17 June 1945, eight crews gathered for a morning preflight briefing at Crumlin Airport in London, Ontario. They heard that, while the weather was not ideal, it looked good enough for a flight to Goose Bay, the first leg of their trip to Prestwick. The briefer, Francis Innes, a meteorological assistant with the Department of Transport, had placed a dawn telephone call to the duty forecaster at Dorval, prior to preparing his own forecast. He had learned that a low-pressure front centred just south of James Bay 'was causing an area of precipitation extending along the route from Montreal to near Mont Joli.' Discussions with the operations officer, Flying Officer Stanley Thompson, RAF, as well as with some of the pilots, resulted in the decision to fly at 7000 feet, between cloud layers. Innes anticipated no icing at that height, but there would probably be rain 'of moderate intensity.' He warned the crews that 'there was a possibility that in some sections they would have to fly in cloud.'[74]

One of the pilots who attended the briefing that morning and decided to go was New Zealander Brian James Duigan. He had joined Ferry Command in February 1943 and had become a captain after two trips as co-pilot. He then delivered twenty-three aircraft, including Baltimores, Marauders, Dakotas, Liberators, and nine Mosquitoes. He had taken the full range of technical courses and passed these and his refresher flight checks with above-average results. Captain Thomas Givens Smith, chief flying instructor at Dorval, considered Duigan 'one of our most experienced Mosquito captains.'[75]

For the delivery of Mosquito KA260, Duigan's radio navigator was another civilian, James Stanley Tegart, from Collingwood, Ontario. He had even more experience with the ferry service than his pilot on this flight. Tegart had joined the organization in June 1941 from his previous job as an operator for Trans-Canada Air Lines at St Hubert Airport. Prior to that he had served with the Royal Canadian Corps of Signals at Kingston, Ontario. He had completed twenty-two deliveries, including Pacific flights early in 1942. He had also worked with the Test Department at Dorval. Since April 1943, when he had checked out as a radio navigator, he had completed five Mosquito deliveries. Jimmy Jubb, responsible for the radio operators in 45 Group, found him 'one of the most efficient Radio Officers, both technically and practically, on this Command, and his work as both Radio Officer and Radio-Navigator was always of the highest standard.'[76]

As Duigan lifted KA260 off the Crumlin runway at 1333 GMT, the aircraft came under the control of Flying Officer Frederick George Slaght, RAF, flying control officer at 45 Group headquarters, Dorval. At 1345 Tegart reported their departure and gave the estimated time of arrival at Goose Bay as 1741 GMT. He confirmed the flight plan at 1428. One hour 6 minutes later Slaght heard from Tegart again, indicating that the Mosquito was on course northeast of Quebec City at 9000 feet.[77] At 1600 Joseph LeRoy Dunn, a civilian DOT radio operator at Mont Joli, thought he had received something from Tegart. He later recalled, 'At 12.00 hours Local Time I heard a signal which sounded like a "260," giving a position report. The remainder of the transmission was blocked by a transmission from KA 276 (Mosquito). I called this unknown aircraft seven times but was unable to raise it.' Dunn said there were inexplicable problems with communication that day. 'From signals which I received from other aircraft it seemed that some of them were having difficulty in reading the Range Station. These aircraft reported that wet cloud static was causing difficulties encountered. I have been stationed here for ten months and this is the first time that I have known aircraft to have difficulty in reading our signals.'[78]

The other Mosquito calling the Mont Joli station was flown by Flying Officer Bruce Montgomery Smith, RCAF, who had left Crumlin at about the same time as Duigan. He had been 'flying between layers at 9,000 feet. The gap finally closed at about 8,000 feet approximately 40 miles West of Mont Joli.' He reported 'moderate carburettor icing in the cloud but was dealing successfully with it by means of the carburettor alcohol in the "Low Flow" position.' He confirmed Dunn's opinion regarding conditions. 'All radio reception was very poor due to the rain, and I was experiencing particular difficulty with the liaison receiver.' Because he was cleared only CFR, or contact flight rules, meaning he must fly within sight of the ground, he requested and received clearances from Mont Joli to let down to 3500 feet and then to land. This he did a couple of minutes before noon local time. During his exchanges he recalled overhearing 'a routine exchange between Mosquito KA 260 and the Mont Joli Range Station.'[79]

About the time Smith was landing, Wilfred Ross, a farmer near St Irene in Matepedia County south of Mont Joli, was telling his neighbours about the plane crash he had just witnessed. Ross had been in his barn just before noon when he 'heard an aeroplane flying very low, the engine of which sounded as though it was in trouble.' He went outside in time to see the aircraft coming towards him from the northeast. 'It circled my farm three times and then flew away in approximately a North West direction towards the hills. Just before it disappeared from view over the first hill, I saw smoke coming from it and then flames, and then it disappeared and I saw a big cloud of smoke and heard an explosion.' He said: 'The weather at the time was heavy rain with low clouds at about 500 feet. The tops of the mountains were covered.'[80]

Ross told a local trapper, George Thomas, and another farmer, Noel Belanger, who was on his way home from church. Thomas set off to find the crash site, while Belanger had his dinner before driving six miles to ask Philip Belanger (no relation) to telephone RCAF Station Mont Joli about the crash. The call was taken by Flying Officer John Watson Moore, the flying control officer at 6 Reserve Equipment Maintenance Unit [REMU], Mont Joli, at about 1400. He immediately dispatched a rescue crew and guards. The ambulance stopped at the home of a local civilian doctor, Dr René Adrien Lepage, because the air force did not have a medical officer at Mont Joli. By this time Thomas had found the wreckage, scattered over about half a mile of hillside. When

Dr Lepage arrived on the scene between 1430 and 1500, he confirmed that two occupants of the plane had been killed on impact.[81] While the doctor was making this assessment, Flying Officer Moore received a call from Eastern Air Command, Halifax, 'enquiring about an overdue Mosquito KA 260 en route to Goose from London, Ontario.' When a call to Sept Iles confirmed that the plane had not checked in there, and when Sergeant Pelletier told him it had called the Mont Joli radio range, Moore concluded, correctly, that KA260 was the aircraft that had crashed.[82] This was verified from personal documents from the crash site by the RAF Transport Command liaison officer at Mont Joli, Douglas Stewart.[83] The Duigan-Tegart delivery had ended suddenly, prematurely, and tragically.

Within days Squadron Leader Henry Cobb arrived from Air Force Headquarters in Ottawa to investigate the accident. He determined that the Mosquito 'had crashed on the eastern slope of a heavily wooded hill.' The starboard engine had struck 'two fairly large birches.' When he checked the broken branches of the trees, he found 'no evidence of damage such as would have resulted from a rotating propeller.' As the plane hit the ground, it 'had cartwheeled and disintegration had been complete.' He said: 'Very little remained of the airframe structure and this comprised only small pieces scattered over a wide area. Fragments of both wing tips were recovered and the positions of these, coupled with the tree damage, indicated that the mainplane had been complete up to the moment of impact.' It was clear that 'there had been fire at several points where fuel tanks or pieces of these had fallen but no evidence of extensive fire. There had, however, been fire at the rear of the starboard engine and the adjacent firewall which was lying at the rear of the engine, after these parts had come to rest, but it could not be established that there had been fire previous to impact.'[84]

This was a difficult accident to investigate and the court of inquiry, made up of Flight Lieutenants John Battison and D.R. Thoday, did little more than state the obvious. They could not account for Duigan being thirty miles south of Mont Joli, but felt 'an order instructing pilots to land if the radio equipment fails ... may have influenced the pilot.' Proper procedures having been followed from the initiation of the flight, and no mechanical faults having been discovered by the investigator, the court's diagnosis was simple: 'Primary cause was flying at a low altitude in bad visibility.' Why Duigan was so low was more difficult to ascertain. Perhaps he had a problem with carburettor icing, 'known to have been present.' If that were the case, he may have 'descended either to find a clear region or because he had no option. Once out of cloud, the ice cleared and he flew low endeavouring to pinpoint his position.' Battison and Thoday felt that the circling of Ross's farm indicated the Mosquito 'was under control at that time.' Alternatively, he may have lost contact with Mont Joli, 'or not have been sure of his position and – against good flying sense – broken cloud without knowing where he was and having broken cloud without an accident, continued on, looking for a pinpoint.' Another possibility was that 'he may have tried a Range descent, and due to extremely poor reception, wandered off the Leg and broken cloud, and having done this decided to continue Contact with Mont Joli.'[85]

The court speculated that after circling the farm, Duigan carried on towards Mont Joli, flying 'over the first hill and up the valley ... Finding the cloud base was lowering as the floor of the valley rose, the pilot attempted a tight 180 degree turn to port, intending to fly down the valley. It is quite possible the pilot was half on instruments and half on contact flying and found he had to tighten his turn considerably to clear the South West hillside.' At this point one of two things might have happened. Duigan 'may have failed to increase power sufficiently and flicked over in a high speed stall and struck the hillside as already described.' On the other hand, if the evidence of Squadron Leader Cobb was correct that 'the starboard engine may not have been under power at the moment of impact, the stall may have been caused by engine failure, which would have resulted in the aircraft flicking over in the same manner.' In the end, Battison and Thoday could only conclude: 'Since there is no evidence to show why the aircraft descended so low in the first place, the cause of the accident must remain obscure.' Any possible recommendations were 'covered by existing flying regulations.'[86]

Taffy Powell signed the report for the air officer commanding 45 Group: 'I agree with the conclusions and the possible causes which have been advanced. The pilot was known to be steady and reliable, and it is reasonable to conclude that at the time of the accident he was trying to overcome mechanical or flying difficulties additional to the weather and radio conditions existing on the ground; however, it is impossible to decide why he was unsuccessful in this.'[87]

Six weeks after VE Day, Duigan and Tegart, civilian volunteers, were killed in an accident of obscure cause while delivering a warplane to Britain where it was no longer needed. And this was not the last Mosquito loss. Two more crashed on the northern route. On 28 June Flight

Lieutenant G.F. Ayton perished and his radio navigator, Flying Officer H.R. Anderson, was seriously injured when KA317 'crashed and burnt out.' Three days later Warrant Officer S.G. Witherspoon, RAF, and Flight Lieutenant Vladimir Joseph Sopuck, a Czech member of the RCAF, died when KA316 made an unsuccessful attempt to land on one engine.[88] With the end of the war in Europe, deliveries across the Atlantic gradually ended. Many aircraft recently arrived in Britain were simply parked or placed in storage in case they might be needed while the authorities concentrated on Japan.

The Mosquito was an exciting, versatile aeroplane that made a valuable contribution to the Allied victory in virtually all facets of the air war. It could also be a dangerous aircraft for ferry crews to deliver. As such it was treated with respect, and even fear, by many airmen with 45 Group. At the same time administrative and engineering staff laboured long and hard to make the plane as safe as possible to fly across the Atlantic. Even so, a number were lost. Incomplete records make it impossible to say exactly how many were flown across successfully and how many failed to make it. K.M. Molson and H.A. Taylor, in the definitive volume, *Canadian Aircraft since 1909*, list the serial numbers of twenty-eight Mosquitoes apparently lost between assembly line and delivery to Britain, in spite of the special precautions that had been taken.[89] Don McVicar quotes the same figure.[90] Research for this book has identified the serial numbers of nineteen Canadian-built Mosquitoes lost by 45 Group, along with the names of the crews, as related in this chapter.

Perhaps the last word on ferrying Canadian-built Mosquitoes should go to the anonymous bard who summed up a radio operator's attitude to the plane. It seems to catch the mood of many aircrew.

THE HAVE I LANDED JITTERS

Oh, don't send my boy in a Mossie,
For he is my favorite son,
Oh, don't send my son in a Mossie,
What dreadful thing has he done?

For he is my only boy, sir,
The best son a mother e'er had.
Oh, don't send my boy in a Mossie,
For they make him feel ever so sad.

They give him the shakes and the shivers, sir,
He tosses all night in his bed,
And if you give him another, sir,
T'will send him right out of his head.

He's taken to drinking and girls, sir,
He comes home stewed up to the gills.
Oh! please don't give him a Mossie,
'Cause the thought of them gives him the chills.

Sometimes he talks in his sleep, sir,
And as he lies tossing his head,
I hear him muttering and groaning
'Please, give me a Boston instead'![91]

11

No Piece of Cake

Mosquitoes were not the only planes lost by Ferry Command. While the statistical summary of the delivery story is quite good on the whole, a number of tragic losses did occur, taking the lives of valuable aircrew and depriving the RAF of desperately needed operational aircraft. The records of many of these incidents appear to have been lost or destroyed since the war, but enough documentation has survived to give us a good idea of the darker side of the Ferry Command story.

We have already seen, in chapter 3, that Sir Frederick Banting was a passenger in the first delivery loss and was killed, along with the co-pilot, Pilot Officer William Bird and radio officer William Snailham, when Hudson T9449 suffered engine trouble and came down on a frozen lake near Musgrave Harbour, Newfoundland. In fact, none of them can be counted the first fatality of the ferry service. On 19 February 1941, the day before Banting took off from Gander on his ill-fated attempt to fly to Britain, two civilians, Captain Leigh Allyn Jackson (from the United States) and Canadian radio operator Sherman H. McCaughan, were fatally injured in a crash at St Hubert.[1] Just as Snailham and Bird would not be the last aircrew lost on a delivery trip, nor Banting the only passenger, Jackson and McCaughan would not be the last killed on a non-delivery flight. The records do not always supply many details, but it is clear that some losses came during training and communications flights. Most, of course, came during delivery across the Atlantic.

It is easy to forget when reading the historical documents, with their brief entries recording the comings and goings of aircraft, that flying the Atlantic was not a routine assignment. Occasionally there are hints. On 26 May 1941 Captain Daniel Duggan (who had made one trip as a first officer at the end of December) left Gander with a Hudson at 2151 GMT and headed for Prestwick. The Gander airport log notes curtly what happened next: 'Sent QAC 2350 GMT & SOS at 0022 GMT. Aircraft went into spin but control regained. Became lost while returning – finally landed here at 0555 GMT.'[2] Those few words undoubtedly mask several hours of anxiety, and perhaps terror, for Duggan and his crew, Sergeant Turner and radio officer Laing.[3] Their Hudson finally made it to the other side on 1 June. It is rare for the curious researcher to find even this sparse information about aborted flights, but there were many, usually recorded simply as 'returned' in the airport log. Tom McGrath worked as a flying control officer at Gander. On one occasion during this early period he jotted in his diary that an unidentified Hudson had 'returned after 6 hours out – 13 hrs. flying!'[4] We can only speculate on the horror of the seven-hour return to Gander against the prevailing winds, with the fuel gauge getting closer and closer to the empty mark.

This pioneering effort to fly across the Atlantic on a regular basis and on a massive scale had to struggle with the vagaries of the weather as well as with equipment and expertise that, in many ways, was barely adequate for the task at hand. Notwithstanding these problems and some initial setbacks, the ferry service had proven the sceptics wrong. Aircraft were being delivered to Britain at an accelerating pace. On 11 June 1941 Air Chief Marshal Sir Charles Portal, chief of the air staff of the RAF, was informed of the civilian organization's accomplishments to date: sixty-five Hudsons had been delivered, sixty-four Catalinas (five across the Pacific), twenty-two Liberators, and nineteen Fortresses. There was a downside: 'Casualties have been 1 Hudson (2 crew and 1 passenger killed) on Atlantic Flight and 1 Hudson (3 killed) on training flight. 2 other Hudsons crashed taking off – no casualties.'[5]

Not all the crashes occurred on takeoff. On 14 June captain Alton Chester Earl (from Huntington, West Virginia), with Pilot Officer Victor Hall (from Quebec City) as navigator and Alexander Albulet (from Regina) as radio operator, short of fuel after almost twelve hours in the air, crash-landed at Port Ellen on the Isle of Islay, just short of the Firth of Clyde.[6] If this Hudson crew survived, that of Flight Lieutenant Keith Fergus Arnold (a member of the RAF, but born in Saskatchewan) was not so lucky. Along with his navigator, Sergeant Percy Keast, RAF, and radio officer Wilfred Bratherton of New Westminster, British Columbia, he made it across the Atlantic, only to perish when their Hudson crashed at the Mull of Kintyre on 25 July 1941.[7] Barely a week later, another Hudson did not even reach Gander. The British captain, Alfred

Williams, and his radio operator, Frank Godfrey, from Glencoe, Ontario, were killed in a crash at Moncton, New Brunswick, on 3 August. Their navigator, Flying Officer G.A.L. Webby, RNZAF, survived.[8] These losses reminded all involved in the ferrying project that the Atlantic still presented a formidable obstacle to any who wished to cross it in an aeroplane. In the vernacular of the day, it was no piece of cake. Events in the next few days were to hammer this home with a vengeance.

As mentioned in chapter 4, the Ministry of Aircraft Production had managed to acquire some Liberators to transport aircrew back to Montreal in order to speed up the delivery process. Since the first flight in May, an irregular service had been carrying important passengers and freight to the United Kingdom and returning ferry crews to the western terminus. Known as the Return Ferry Service, it was crucial to the success of the whole delivery scheme. Administrators appear to have come to view the service as routine. This was not so for the aircrew. Whatever the hazards of the delivery flight, they invariably looked upon the trip back to North America as even worse.[9] If they had to come by ship, they worried about being torpedoed by a German U-boat and also about the waste of time. If they had to fly as passengers with the Return Ferry Service, they worried about the discomforts of the long, cold journey packed into the modified bomb-bay of a Liberator. The prospect of reclining on the hastily installed wooden floor, bundled up against the subzero temperatures and sucking on an oxygen tube offered little attraction. They also worried whether the heavily laden aircraft would get off the ground. With the benefit of hindsight, many of their fears appear to have been prescient.

The tragic events of August 1941 have already been touched upon, but they merit closer scrutiny. On Sunday, 10 August 1941, at about 2030 hours British Daylight Time, Captain E.R.B. 'Herbie' White, an experienced veteran of Imperial Airways, took off into the rain from Heathfield Aerodrome in Ayrshire for a flight back to Montreal with a load of ferry crews, one of two Return Ferry Service flights departing that evening. (The second, by Captain S.T.B. 'Trevor' Cripps, carried Lord Beaverbrook for a meeting with Winston Churchill and Franklin Roosevelt off Newfoundland.) Watching the departure was a group of aircrew awaiting their turn to be carried back to the western terminus, so they could pick up another aircraft for delivery to Britain. Some of them were bothered by White's habit of making a slow climb towards Goat Fell, a mountain on the Isle of Arran. Captain Ed Wynn reports that this particularly rankled one his colleagues: "'Why in hell doesn't the guy sneak out over that flat firth in this mess," blurted out Joe Silverthorn, an able American who learned his ferrying business down in Central America.'[10] Concern mounted when the Return Ferry Service Liberator made no radio contact to report its progress, a usual occurrence on the homeward-bound trip. With no word of the plane after eighteen hours – longer than a Liberator could remain aloft – everyone knew that something terrible had happened. (In the meantime, Cripps had long since deposited his VIP passenger safely at Gander.)[11]

Some thought White's plane had disappeared over the broad expanse of the Atlantic; others believed it would be found much further east, on the mountainside that White had to clear so soon after takeoff. As events unfolded, the latter view proved correct. On Monday a farmer tending his sheep on the Isle of Arran discovered the wreckage near the top of Goat Fell. His dog brought him a piece of an aeroplane, and a little exploring revealed a horrible scene. He quickly took word down the mountain, and soon about 150 police and service personnel were scouring the desolate terrain. Newspaper accounts said that the plane 'had evidently crashed into the hillside with terrific force and the debris was scattered over a considerable area.'[12] The search for bodies lasted two days and included a party of sailors from the aircraft carrier HMS *Argus*. One of the seamen remembered it as difficult work: 'We had an awkward trek down, four men to a stretcher, and slipping and sliding.'[13] After losing only a handful of aircrew in its first eight months, Ferry Command had suddenly lost twenty-two in one terrible crash, eleven pilots, ten radio operators, and the flight engineer from the crew. All civilians, seven came from the United States, five from Britain, nine from Canada, and one from Australia.[14]

Ed Wynn thought about 'the messages that must have been trickling back to the apartments in Montreal where the wives of those kids were waiting, as they did from trip to trip.' Even while mourning his departed comrades, he paid tribute to their wives: 'Those courageous girls are real heroes of his war. Their husbands were flying a new, pioneering route over the Atlantic. Nothing but water and danger, and no ballyhoo about it. It was those girls, always waiting and never hinting how they feared our trips, that made the whole job easier.'[15]

The task at hand left little time for mourning – aircraft had to be delivered. On 14 August Ferry Command personnel at Gander dispatched nineteen Hudsons and two Return Ferry Service Liberators across the Atlantic.[16] That night, on the eve of the funeral for the twenty-two airmen killed when White flew into Goat Fell, seventeen more clambered into the bomb-bay of another Return Ferry Service Liberator for the trip back to Montreal. There was one less airman on this flight because they were joined by a VIP passenger, Arthur Purvis of the British Purchasing Commission in the United States, who had been conferring with government officials in London, but was needed by the prime minister during his meeting with the US president. Still, with the crew of four, there were again twenty-two men on board when BOAC Captain Richard Stafford taxied out to take off. Once again, Ed Wynn and some of his buddies watched the departure. They were astounded when Stafford turned the big four-engine kite onto the shortest runway. They were even more astounded when 'he started revving his motors for the take-off into a slipping cross wind. It was almost elementary, I thought, not to do such a thing.' Wynn adds that he was not alone in his concern: 'Several weeks later, the RAF officer in the control tower confided to me that he started to give Stafford the red light but thought that an old-line, noted pilot knew what he was doing.'[17]

The onlookers stared in disbelief as Stafford picked up speed and 'suddenly veered off the runway and roared across the grass.' The plane bounced over the slight rise where two runways intersected and careened wildly across the field. Yelling fruitless advice to cut the engines, Wynn was forced to watch the inevitable end to a virtual suicide run:

I didn't want to look, but I did. Stafford apparently made no attempt to stop the plane. There was no application of brakes. Its speed must have been 150 miles an hour when it rushed into the edge of the field and the six-foot embankment loomed ahead. Stafford did the instinctive thing – nosed it straight up to clear the embankment. The nose wheel left the ground, but the plane didn't follow. It crashed into the barrier and broke in two. The nose end hurtled crazily about sixty feet in the air and collapsed over a railroad track. Flames towered toward the sky. We had to stand and watch it.[18]

The only survivor of the impact, the young American Earl Wellington Watson, who had proudly drawn the co-pilot assignment for this flight, lived for just a few hours.[19] Twenty-two men were killed. One of them was Purvis; the remainder were Ferry Command civilian aircrew.

Witnesses could not believe what they had seen. Wynn reports that some talked about sabotage. He disagreed: 'Sabotage, hell! Nothing can sabotage a man's mind and make him keep all four engines wide open without a chance of taking off.' Still, the American could not understand why an experienced multi-engine pilot with several thousand hours on his logbook could have acted the way he did: 'Stafford was a right guy. I don't know what happened to him. When he pushed the Liberator down the runway maybe he was thinking of Herb White and the mountain – as we were on the ground.'[20]

The circumstances of the second Return Ferry crash have remained a mystery to this day. Henry Flory, however, has a theory that he believes explains the tragedy. The morning following the accident he arrived from Gander as navigator of Captain Oscar Jones's Liberator: 'Circling to land, we noticed tell-tale tracks of airplane wheels running off the concrete, across the grass infield, and ending at an embankment that bordered the airfield.' They could not miss seeing the smoldering remains of a Liberator against the railway embankment. Their worst fears were confirmed as soon as the flight engineer, Vic Sharpe, beat the rest of the crew out onto the tarmac.[21] A great admirer of Stafford, whom he had met when both were instructing at St Hubert, Flory pieced together fragments of information and rumours to formulate his own explanation for the previous day's tragic events. He believes that there were psychological overtones 'of unique interest in flight history, but which, due to strict censorship were never aired.'[22]

Flory says that Stafford was under great stress. He had been working extremely hard at St Hubert training newly arrived pilots. 'That was nerve wracking in itself, and I can give testimony to his unselfish dedication to this job. He would be at the field each morning at seven, make endless "circuits and bumps" with his pupils till dinner time, and then often continue into the night with night-flying tests until midnight or later.' However, he was not a happy man: 'Something was bothering him terribly – this separation from his wife in Scotland. The other Imperial [Airways'] pilots had by hook or by crook wangled passage for their wives to Canada, but Staff was by nature no wangler, and repeated requests for his wife's transport had bogged down in the bureaucracy.' His loneliness seemed to drive him to work harder and harder. 'I personally had a very high regard for Staff and his selfless dedication to his job,' writes Flory, 'while other pilots were making trips and enjoying the free days to relax between them he was grinding it out, day after day and night after night in his training duty.' One of his favourite pieces of advice is tragically ironic in light of what happened on that Scottish airfield the evening of 14 August 1941: 'He was the one who instilled into me and the rest "For God's sake, Flory, if the bloody thing starts swinging on take-off, stop it, and start again." The Hudsons we trained on were apt to swerve badly ... but the principle of aborting any shaky take-off was paramount, whatever the aircraft. Hence Stafford's ... instruction.'[23]

Finally, after months of instructing, Stafford was told, according to Flory, that he could make the next round trip to Scotland and bring his wife back to Montreal with him. 'Ecstatic is insufficient to describe how Staff felt at this great turn of events. He took the flight over, brought his wife to the airport, and next night was ready to bring the flight back to Canada with his wife aboard, and sundry other flight delivery crews. Then Fate played its part.'[24] Stafford's wife was struck from the passenger list:

An emergency arose requiring Sir Arthur Purvis, [sic] the head of the British Purchasing Mission in Washington to be flown over that very night. The R.A.F. officer in charge of traffic that night, instead of off-loading some obscure wireless operator who would have been happy to spend another day in Scotland, bumped-off, instead, Capt. Stafford's wife! It was a dreadful mistake. Stafford pleaded with this bureaucratic cretin to have his wife put back on the flight to no avail; and when he failed something cracked up in his mind. To have the Air Ministry's decision to bring Staff and his wife together after a year's separation shot down by this officious Flight-Lieutenant of a Traffic Officer was too much, too much.[25]

Flory contends that the loneliness and stress under which Stafford had been working caused something to snap when he suffered the sudden, intense disappointment of having to return to Montreal without his wife:

Reconstructing the event I can only believe Stafford entered the cockpit of that plane, with its load of delivery crews and Sir Arthur Purvis, O.B.E. M.B.E. etc. [sic] in a cold but driven fury. He taxied the plane out, and never even turned right to get to the end of the runway he was going to use. He swung left and rammed open all four throttles; before he covered a hundred yards the plane had swung off the runway, and instead of respecting his endless behest to start again he kept his hand on those throttles come what may ... Well he did not pull them back, but barreled across the wet soft grass, never attained take-off speed, and immolated the whole group, including the head of the British Purchasing Mission in America, on the railway embankment that bordered the runway. Although questions were asked in Parliament about the loss of that invaluable man Purvis I doubt seriously whether the full story of that fateful night has before been told. And the particular Traffic Officer on duty that night has probably had years to reflect that at times the consideration of human feelings should override following the book![26]

We can probably never know if Flory's theory is correct. However, his observations and his hypothesis are consistent with Wynn's eyewitness account.

Whatever the cause of the latest crash, it took the lives of eleven more civilian airmen from the United States, eight from Canada, and two from Britain. In two terrible accidents Ferry Command had lost forty-three aircrew – twenty-three pilots, eighteen radio operators, and two flight engineers – a sizeable portion of the roster.[27] (There were no navigators included in the list because recent delivery flights had used one-trippers in this vital role.) The command had had its heart ripped out, literally as well as figuratively. All of the dead were already experienced transatlantic flyers who would have made up the nucleus of the ferry service for the rest of the war. To say that two crashes of this magnitude within five days was a crushing blow would be an understatement. To this day the news of these tragic accidents remains the blackest memory of the war for many Ferry Command veterans.

The day after the second crash, the survivors in Scotland buried the victims of the first. As the closest military unit, the Royal Navy handled the service, providing an honour guard and pallbearers. The Reverend F.W. Hadfield, Church of England; the Reverend A.W. Kennedy, Church of Scotland; and Father E. West, of the Roman Catholic Church, conducted the burial services. The Lord Lieutenant of the County of Bute, the Duke of Montrose, represented King George VI. The villagers of Lamlash turned out en masse as the procession wended its way to the local cemetery. There the twenty-two caskets were laid side by side in a long grave as an RN contingent fired volleys and as buglers sounded the last post and taps. Two carloads of floral offerings were laid at the gravesite, including wreaths from Ferry Command, the Trans-Oceanic Pilots' Association, and the Trans-Oceanic Radio Operators' Association, as well as flowers from the Ministry of Aircraft Production, BOAC, several aircraft manufacturing companies, friends and relatives of the deceased, and local citizens.[28]

The same day Protestant and Roman Catholic memorial services were held in Montreal at the Church of St Andrew and St Paul and at the Church of the Ascension. With relatives and friends joining military and civilian officers of Ferry Command, the Ministry of Aircraft Production, and the RCAF, the services were conducted by the Reverend Gordon Taylor, assisted by Squadron Leader Gilbert Oliver, MC, Protestant chaplain of the RCAF's No. 3 Training Command, and Squadron Leader George Hamel, Roman Catholic chaplain of No. 3 Training Command, assisted by the Reverend Donald J. Ferron. Squadron Leader Oliver undoubtedly summed up the feelings of many when he said in his eulogy:

We feel a deep, sincere and abiding sorrow for these men of courage, these men of endurance, who, without hesitation, when the call came gave their services to the cause of truth ... That men of the United States were with others of Canada and the Empire ... meant that there was one more tie that bound the people of Canada to their neighbours to the South. We owe a tremendous debt of gratitude to these men and to those others who day by day are carrying out similar duties. We should gain a real sense of inspiration. These men were doing something they felt should be done. When we think of their sacrifice, it can do nothing but inspire us to follow them in paths of courage and sacrifice. For each of us there is a task to do. These men are saying to us: 'We are handing you the torch. You must carry on.' That is what they would have us do.[29]

Four days later the ceremonies were repeated on both sides of the Atlantic; a second funeral for twenty-two victims of a plane crash took place in Scotland, and twenty-one more airmen were mourned in Montreal.[30]

As soon as possible, the survivors met to reflect on what had happened and to decide what to do next. It may not have been clear at the time but, with the benefit of hindsight, it is no surprise that they followed Padre Oliver's advice. They seized the torch and resolved to continue their work. Henry Flory boasts, proudly and correctly, that 'they overcame this morale shatterer very bravely ... At a rallying get-together held in Montreal a few days later we were addressed by the High Brass, and the unanimous decision was to carry on. This showed an uncompromising spirit, and pride in our pioneering trade of flying bombers across the oceans.' Still, he remembers, 'We had all lost many close friends.'[31] (Flory himself lost a friend and room-mate only days later when the British BOAC first officer, Geoffrey Llewellyn Panes, was killed with Captain Kenneth Garden (from Australia), radio officer Samuel Walter Sydenham (from Swift Current, Saskatchewan), and flight engineer Charles Alvan Spence (from Long Island, New York) as Liberator AM915, carrying six passengers, crashed 'at Achinhoan Head' during the night of 31 August/1 September.)[32]

As Ferry Command, and later 45 Group, carried on delivering aircraft across the oceans of the world, not many weeks were to pass without some story of a crash, a disappearance, a near miss, or a heroic and miraculous survival flashing through the rumour mill that flourished among the staff fanning out almost around the globe. As the first anniversary of the first deliveries drew near, four more Hudsons were lost. Three disappeared somewhere over the North Atlantic, on 21 and 27 September and 11 October, and another crashed at Dundalk in Ireland on 27 September, killing the crew.[33] By the time the new year dawned, the Canadian Pacific Air Services Department, the Atlantic Ferry Organization (ATFERO), and Ferry Command had lost a total of seven Hudsons (eight if the training accident at St Hubert on 19 February was a writeoff), three Liberators (counting those of the Return Ferry Service), and, most importantly of all, sixty-eight aircrew (sixty-nine if the message to Portal of 11 June was correct that three, not two, had been killed in the St Hubert crash). This number included thirty-four pilots and twenty-seven radio operators. The routine seemed well established: a few weeks of uneventful deliveries, followed by a series of losses in quick succession.[34]

Given the state of the archival record, it is impossible to quote accurate and definitive figures. However, there followed at least thirty-three aircraft lost in 1942 (including the first Baltimores and Marauders on the southern route, as well as Bostons, Catalinas, Mitchells, and Venturas), thirty-nine in 1943 (including the first Dakota loss), thirty-six in 1944 (as the Mosquito joined the list of lost aircraft), and twenty-seven in 1945. This meant that more than 500 military and civilian aircrew were lost to Ferry Command and the Allied cause (more than 200 pilots, 100 navigators, 140 radio operators, and a score of flight engineers). Civilians accounted for at least 180 of the aircrew killed while serving with Ferry Command. Of the military personnel, at least 125 were RCAF, 125 RAF, 21 RAAF, 6 RNZAF, 7 USAAF, and 6 from the Royal Norwegian Air Force. Of nationalities that could be identified, more than 200 appear to have come from Canada, 135 from Britain, 69 from the United States, 23 from Australia, 8 from New Zealand, 7 from Poland, 6 from Norway, 3 from Newfoundland, and 1 each from South Africa and Egypt. If passengers are included, the overall total jumps to 560. These figures represent conservative estimates. There were occasions during the research on losses where it appeared a plane or an airman may have been lost. However, only documented cases have been used for this statistical summary and for the list of losses in appendix B, as well as for the descriptive accounts in this chapter and elsewhere in the book.[35]

Despite the occasional loss of delivery aircraft, the less frequent incidents involving the return of crews made the greatest impact on the operation. As we have seen, a westbound trip in a Return Ferry Service Liberator was not a pleasant experience. Sometimes it could be downright frightening. On Tuesday, 9 February 1943, two Liberators left Scotland within a few minutes of each another loaded with returning aircrew. Don McVicar was a passenger in AL529, flown by Geordie Stewart, and he remembers the flight that night as a particularly harrowing one. The jet stream, though not yet known as such, was strong, radio communications were poorer than normal, and unknown to the crews of the lumbering Liberators and their human cargo freezing in the bomb-bays, the weather at Gander was closing in with the approach of a winter storm. By the time Gander control finally established radio contact with the two aircraft, conditions at the airport had deteriorated to a frighteningly dangerous degree. With a ceiling of only about 200 feet, Gander control directed both aircraft to Sydney, Nova Scotia. In AL591, Pat Eves, the captain credited with having shown the way to Prestwick, after the difficult flight and with his fuel gauge frozen, feared that he lacked sufficient fuel for this diversion and opted to stick with Gander. Stewart managed to make it to Sydney and got down on his first attempt in quickly deteriorating conditions. His passengers had no idea where they had landed. A local Trans-Canada Air Lines worker told them: 'You're in balmy Sydney, you lucky guys.'[36] He was more right than he could ever know.

In the meantime, the staff in the Gander control tower 'were astounded when 591 said it was coming in here. Emergency procedure was put into operation.' The Gander Ferry Command diary records that 'aircraft was overhead for approximately one and a half hours.'[37] However, McVicar claims that Eves, with his perceived narrower margin of safety than Stewart after having used up more fuel by flying higher and faster in the early stages of the crossing, had decided on a straight-in instrument approach to Gander. According to this version of events, neither Eves nor any of his crew could locate the runway as he approached the airfield. McVicar claims that the ground staff had placed flame pots along the wrong one.[38] If this indeed happened, the crew no doubt noticed the problem as they passed over the field and went round again for another attempt to land. In the end, whichever version is correct, AL591 ran out of fuel on the final approach and went down like a rock ten miles short of the runway. As soon as the radio went dead, the Gander staff must have known what had happened. However, with the blizzard increasing in ferocity, they could not even mount a search. After midnight the next night a Norseman got off during a break in the storm 'and flew for an hour and a half in an endeavour to find flares or lights from the missing aircraft. The weather was not at all pleasant and no lights were seen.'[39]

On Thursday, with the weather having cleared, the Norseman, the old reliable Fox Moth (VO-ADE), and three Hudsons started a proper search. The wreckage of AL591 was quickly located ten miles northeast of the airfield. The Norseman and the Fox Moth 'landed alongside the crash & found three survivors, Pilot Officer [C.N.] Abelson [RAF], Sgt. [Graham Pritchard] Pollard [RAF] & Capt. [A.E. 'King'] Parker. The remainder of the 21 crew & passengers were dead.'[40] The survivors were flown to Gander and admitted to the Sir Frederick Banting Memorial Hospital, where Pollard later died. The fatalities included one non-Ferry Command passenger, British Army Lieutenant-Colonel L.T. Grove, and eighteen aircrew: nine pilots, and three each of navigators, radio operators, and flight engineers. Ten of the victims came from Britain, five from Canada, and three from the United States. Twelve were civilians and four were members of the RAF, with two from the RCAF.[41] It was a bad crash, but not quite 'the worst ever to occur in North America,' as at least one newspaper account alleged. (That dubious distinction went to the accident that claimed twenty victims when an American Airlines plane went down near St Thomas, Ontario, on 30 October 1941. Two years later, twenty-four died when a Liberator of the RCAF's 10 (BR) Squadron crashed near St Donat, north of Montreal.)[42]

Old hands no doubt recalled the terrible events of August 1941 when Return Ferry Service crashes took the lives of forty-three of their colleagues. Perhaps old fears returned. Once again the view that they were really paid for the trip back proved well founded. Great losses seemed to come in close proximity. Less than a month earlier, on 17 January, a dozen of their number had been lost when a westbound USAAF Air Transport Command aircraft disappeared over the South Atlantic.[43] In between these two large losses, Ferry Command lost at least six men when Catalina FP309 went missing out of Bermuda on the night of 6 February, and two more two days later when an aircraft crashed at Whiteface Mountain, New York. The body of the Catalina pilot, Samuel Howard McCawley of Alhambra, California, was subsequently found floating in a liferaft in the Atlantic.[44]

Later that year, in the early hours of 7 September 1943, ten more aircrew from Ferry Command (by then officially No. 45 Group and part of RAF Transport Command) were lost when a USATC C-87 transport version of the Liberator crashed and burned about two miles from

Accra in the Gold Coast. The aircraft had just taken off with a load of passengers travelling to North America, including the 45 Group aircrew who had delivered planes to West Africa. Some had arrived from Ascension only hours before. The group's fatalities included one civilian American captain, an RAF pilot, and eight members of the RCAF (two pilots, three navigators, and three wireless operators).[45] This constituted the last loss of aircrew as they were returning from a delivery trip. Had 45 Group personnel known this at the time, they would undoubtedly have heaved an immense sigh of relief. The three Return Ferry Service crashes, two in Scotland and one in Newfoundland, plus the two USATC losses on the southern route claimed the lives of eighty-four Ferry Command/45 Group aircrew.

In fact, returning airmen were not the only ones to die in large-scale crashes. On 26 October 1942 a Ventura piloted by Captain Carl Frederick Kaiser (from Roseville, Michigan) went down shortly after taking off from Dorval. Witnesses said it seemed to develop engine trouble and plowed into a farmer's field 200 yards from Cote de Liesse Rd, about two-and-a-half miles from the end of the runway. Leaving a crater 5 feet deep, the plane exploded in flames, preventing rescuers from approaching the wreckage. At any rate, press reports stated that the crew and passengers would have been killed on impact. Kaiser and his radio operator, Arthur Harold Down from Tillsonburg, Ontario, and their passengers, four civilians from the Department of Transport and private firms, and ten members of the RCAF were killed.[46] The second worst air tragedy to that point in Canada's history, the crash of AE729 climaxed a bad month that claimed another Ventura, a Boston, a Mitchell, and Tom Livermore's Liberator, along with sixteen aircrew.[47]

Henry Flory claims that Captain Livermore crashed because he took off from Piarco airfield in Trinidad 'on the emergency tanks installed for the Atlantic crossing instead of the regular ones. As they only had a short leg to Belem, in Brazil, these tanks had only fifty gallons in them, just to keep them wet. The plane got only a hundred feet into the air before all engines quit cold. The flight engineer's fault it undoubtedly was, but remembering the complexity of that particular fuel system I can see exactly how it happened.'[48]

A Liberator accident that may have been the worst one yet, because it resulted in the death of ten innocent civilians on the ground in Montreal, occurred on 25 April 1944. Three Polish airmen – the pilot, Flying Officer Kazamierz Burzinski; the co-pilot, Pilot Officer Andrzej Kuzniacki; and the navigator, Flight Lieutenant Adolf Nowicki – along with an RCAF wireless operator and an RAF flight engineer, Pilot Officer James Smith Wilson (from Trenton, New Jersey) and Flight Sergeant Islwyn Jones (from Swansea, Wales), had just taken off from Dorval on a delivery flight to the United Kingdom and were heading over the city when something went wrong. Eye-witness accounts differed on whether the plane burst into flames before or after it hit the tenements on Ottawa Street in the Griffintown area behind the Canadian National Railways Bonaventure station. They all agreed that it seemed to be struggling to stay in the air. Some thought that Burzinski, one of the most famous airmen from his homeland, was trying to make it to the St Lawrence River to avoid coming down in a populated neighbourhood. In the end he failed. The crash and ensuing fire, fueled by the full tanks in the delivery craft, killed ten local citizens, including women and children and a popular policeman, Constable Philippe Lemieux, overcome while trying to rescue people trapped in a burning building. The entire crew died, too. The Polish airmen and Jones took with them a wealth of ferry experience. Wilson's only delivery flight had lasted about six minutes. He had arrived from his training course at North Bay only two days earlier.[49]

A more famous Polish citizen died in July 1943 when a Transport Command Liberator crashed off Gibraltar. General Wladyslaw Sikorski, prime minister of Poland's government-in-exile in London, was returning from a visit to Polish troops in the Middle East. His entire entourage and all the crew, save the Czechoslovakian pilot, Flight Lieutenant Edward Prchal, were killed when the plane was seen, quite inexplicably, to fly into the sea just after leaving the runway. The cause of the accident remains a mystery, partly because many people believe it was an assassination. Among the arguments advanced to support the theory of sabotage are the series of incidents that seemed to plague General Sikorski during his wartime travels. One of them happened at Dorval on 30 November 1942, when a Ferry Command Hudson was forced to make a wheels-up landing only seconds after taking off to fly the Polish statesman to Washington. Both engines of the aircraft had mysteriously cut out. This was one of many occasions in which sabotage was suspected but never proven, at least not in any documents this author has been able to find.[50]

The losses described above were not the last of the major crashes. The closing months of the war brought a series of 45 Group Liberator accidents that took a big toll. On 13 March 1945 eighteen airmen died when one crashed at Lagens. We have seen, in chapter 9, that the famous Liberator, *Commando*, went missing on 27 March 1945 with seven crew members and a like number of passengers. Not all the accidents were total disasters. On 9 April, Captain George Voorhees literally lost No. 3 engine when it caught fire and then fell off shortly after taking off from Dorval. He then struck high tension wires during his attempt to crash-land in a field near St Simone. Two passengers and a civilian on the ground were killed. An officer of the RCAF's Accident Investigation Branch, in the course of looking into the incident, wrote: 'No. 45 Transport Group have been somewhat unfortunate recently. You will remember only too well the loss [on 27 March] of the Air Ministry delegation to the B.C.A.T.P. ceremony. On March 13th a Liberator crashed on take-off from Lagens, in which 18 persons were killed, including one R.C.A.F. officer, F/L L.F. Jarvis, Flying Control.'[51]

The large-scale losses still were not finished. On 4 July George Peter Evans (from Marlboro, Massachusetts), one of the most famous civilian captains, who had helped survey and pioneer the northern route and who had flown Lord Beaverbrook on the first nonstop flight from London to Washington, went missing on a flight from Dorval to Northolt in England with five other highly experienced crew members and nine passengers from the UK civil service on their way home from the United Nations' San Francisco Conference. The 45 Group monthly accident summary sums up all that anyone has ever known about the incident: 'This aircraft took off from Dorval on a flight to the United Kingdom and after a few routine messages were received, nothing further was heard from the aircraft.'[52] Despite an exhaustive search, neither the plane nor the people in it were ever found. Almost a month later, on 3 August 1945, only three days before the first atomic bomb was dropped on Hiroshima, the ferry service suffered its final wartime loss. Thirteen airmen died when their 45 Group Liberator crashed on takeoff at Lydda in Palestine.[53]

This may not have been the last fatality of the ferry scheme. As a kind of epilogue, and a reminder of the hazards of flying the Atlantic, a Return Ferry Service Liberator on its way to Montreal from Lagens, struggling in severe icing conditions, landed in a raging snowstorm at Charlottetown on 20 February 1946. It 'exploded and burst into flames ... as its wheels touched ground at 9.06 p.m. [local time] and within seconds was a mass of flames.' Fortunately, the military and civilian passengers and most of the crew managed to escape. The co-pilot, D.W. Ray of Montreal, was killed in the crash. Other crew members, including the captain, E. Poole of Montreal, and some of the eight passengers, suffered burns before they got out of the aircraft.[54]

Notwithstanding the dangers of flying the Atlantic, obvious to anyone connected with the enterprise, there was rarely a shortage of people willing to make the trip. On occasion some even did so illegally. Leading Airwoman Marion Darling, from Massachusetts, while stationed at RCAF Gander, hid behind some baggage on a flight to Britain in an attempt to join her husband overseas. She reportedly ended up with a job at RCAF Overseas Headquarters as a reward for her initiative, but her husband was posted to another theatre of war.[55] Elizabeth Drewery, a British civilian, took a greater risk by climbing into the nose-wheel compartment of a Return Ferry Service Liberator just before it took off from Prestwick. By some miraculous stroke of good fortune, she picked one of the few flights to come all the way at a low enough altitude that the crew and passengers did not need oxygen. She remained standing (in a narrow gap between the wheel-well and the back of the instrument panel) throughout the flight and the stopover at Gander. A security guard spotted her when she climbed out after the plane was stowed in a hangar at Dorval. She eventually got the pilot training she had been seeking in North America, but too late in the war to join the Air Transport Auxiliary or the Women Airforce Service Pilots of the USAAF.[56]

Even if one subtracts those lost in the massive accidents of planes returning aircrew and on communications flights from the overall totals, there were still too many airmen – both civilian and military – killed while serving with the ferrying organization. Many of the losses occurred when aircraft simply disappeared during a delivery. The cause of each such incident was then, and remains today, unknown. As we have already seen, weather forecasting lacked sophisticated knowledge and equipment. Some of the disappearances may have been caused, as was generally believed at the time, by unexpected weather conditions, such as a localized unforeseen storm. On the northern route, as mentioned in chapter 8, the experience of Flight Lieutenant Hal Wills and his crew in their Mitchell on 28 November 1943 suggests that icing conditions may have been an all-too-common problem. Similarly, our look at the problem of Mosquito deliveries showed the same concern with that type of aircraft. In fact, no plane was immune from environmentally caused difficulties or mechanical troubles. This was particularly troublesome when the aircraft were being flown extremely long distances over inhospitable regions, often by quite inexperienced crews. We will never know how many of the men lost on their first trip, or with little experience on the type, may have known how to get out of their initial difficulty if they had had more hours on their logbooks.

With many of the lost aircraft disappearing in this manner, one cannot help but wonder how many men died because of poor search and rescue (or SAR to use the current Canadian Forces' terminology) techniques and equipment. The Second World War did see some miraculous rescues;[57] usually, however, if a plane went missing over the sea or barren regions, its occupants were never seen again. With the exception of anecdotal evidence, there is generally little information available on this subject. However, following the loss of Dakota KN271[58] and Mosquito KB370, described in chapter 10, somewhere between Greenland and Iceland on 6 and 11 February 1945, Flying Officer R.R. Alexander, air/sea rescue officer with 112 (North Atlantic) Wing, RAF Transport Command, visited the Goose Bay and Greenland staging posts to look into SAR arrangements and procedures. His detailed memorandum on the matter, filed with the investigation report into the loss of KB370, makes interesting – if depressing – reading. If the findings are accurate, one can only conclude that some lives were lost on the northern route, and perhaps in other regions as well, because of poor procedures and lack of equipment.

Alexander arrived at 84 Staging Post, Goose Bay, on 21 February. He learned that, with the exception of 'Flap Maps' for the routes between Goose and Dorval, the staff there had little equipment to aid in searching. He reported that they had 'dropping kits' (without indicating what they contained), but no other SAR supplies. Beyond a Norseman assigned to SAR duties by the RCAF, there were no other aircraft regularly available for this crucial emergency role. No. 45 Group and USATC delivery aircraft could be used in searches, and indeed they were on many occasions. However, Squadron Leader Thomas, acting commanding officer of the RAF Transport Command detachment at the isolated Labrador base, pointed out the obvious, that 'there may be no delivery aircraft at Goose Bay' just when a search had to be initiated. The situation was much too informal: 'There is at present no ASR [Air/Sea Rescue] Committee embracing the three units [RAF, USAAF, and RCAF] concerned at Goose Bay and no flap procedures laid down.' Alexander reported that 'S/Ldr. Thomas suggested that any co-ordinated action would have to come from Dorval or Manchester for deep or prolonged sea searches.'[59]

When he reached 81 Staging Post at BW-1 on 25 February, Alexander appears to have found the SAR situation only slightly better than that at Goose Bay. He reported to the RAF Transport Command liaison officer who introduced him to USATC control officers. Over the next couple of days he also spent some time with the USN captain in charge of naval operations and his staff, with the communications officer, and with the acting officer commanding (OC), 1st Arctic Search and Rescue Squadron, USAAF. He found all the Americans 'most co-operative' and willing to discuss any matter in great detail, ranging from SAR in general to 'the recent cases of Mosquito KB 370 lost on 11th Feb. and Dakota KN 271 lost on 6th Feb.' Regarding the incidents that had precipitated his visit, Alexander wrote: 'A dense sea search was put forward in both cases and evidence of this indicated that the U.S. Navy not only can, but does do a workmanlike job and are willing and able to co-operate in every way.' He summarized the arrangements: 'Apparently 1st Arctic is responsible for air search out of BW-1, their own airfleet [a couple of OA-10s, a version of the Catalina, as well as Norseman and Beechcraft aircraft] being supplemented by delivery aircraft of USATC, RAFTC and aircraft of U.S. Navy where required. The U.S. Navy provide surface search and rescue at sea, diverting necessary surface craft, Weather Ships and cutters where required.'[60] However, the rest of his report on the visit to BW-1 leaves the impression that he thought more could be done. What he learned in his various formal and informal meetings in Greenland was not reassuring.

Perhaps the biggest problem came from the same type of informality that prevailed at Goose Bay. There existed no 'organized control to provide the co-ordinated efforts of USN, USATC and 1st Arctic Search & Rescue [Squadron] for instant action in an emergency, notably in the manner to contact Weather Ships.' Despite the presence of additional resources in Greenland, SAR received no more priority than it did in Labrador. The USAAF airmen given this responsibility had received little or no direction. Alexander's report of his meeting with the man responsible for air searches out of BW-1 was revealing: 'The O/C [of 1st Arctic Search & Rescue Squadron] stated that our paper was the first he had had covering search at sea. He stated that neither himself [sic] or his staff had received any instruction or manuals covering this subject, although the main search and rescue work in that area would be sea search. Prior training consisted of a course in arctic survival and little else.' This officer obviously cared deeply and asked that his squadron be placed on the distribution lists for all rescue bulletins and similar material.[61]

When he discovered the search procedures followed in the recent incidents, Alexander concluded that 1st Arctic's planes may have been flying too high. They had flown 'at an altitude of 1500 feet with a visibility of 15 miles in a modification of creeping line ahead search, i.e. tracks to be flown would be at intervals of 15 miles with 7½ miles to be covered on either side.'[62] The height may have been only a small part of the problem, if current Canadian Forces' SAR practice is any guide. Depending on the sea state and visibility, 1500 feet is the maximum altitude recommended for such searches today. Under certain conditions, in which visibility is poor or a liferaft could be hidden behind a sea swell, an altitude as low as 800 feet would be preferable. And even at 1500 feet the searchers would not have been able to spot a liferaft bobbing around at anything near the extreme edge of the intervals flown by 1st Arctic. Current Canadian SAR instructions give the search visibility at 1500 feet as a mile and a half.[63] This would mean flying at intervals of three miles, a fifth that flown by 1st Arctic. It is difficult to avoid concluding that the crews in Mosquito KB370 and Dakota KN271, if they survived any crash-landing, had virtually no chance of being found. Such an assessment probably applies to most of the aircraft that disappeared during the war.

Alexander, speaking of his visit to BW-1, but probably echoing the views of most airmen at the time, wrote in a somewhat understated fashion: 'Aircrew of all units appear not to have confidence in safety measures provided for them and all concerned appear to be cognizant of that fact.' Even so, he remained hopeful: 'The impression gained at BW1 was that equipment is at hand for an efficient Air Sea Rescue Organization but that closer liaison will have to be maintained between the services concerned.' He recommended that the British and American authorities be approached to improve coordination. He proposed that 'An Air/Sea Rescue Committee comprised of U.S. Navy, USATC, 1st Arctic Search & Rescue Squadron, Communications and RAFTC be assembled, and that Standing Orders for ASR be Promulgated.' In addition, he urged that 'a training program for 1st Arctic Search & Rescue Squadron and laid down procedures adopted for its use be immediately promulgated. Sea search by aircraft should bulk the subjects required [sic].' If this could not be done, he had another suggestion:

It is alternatively recommended that, if no further effort is to be made to bring the unit up to efficient standards of air search, particularly over water search, RAFTC should provide a small ASR Flight for its own protection. The maintenance of RAFTC aircraft is at present handled by one civilian engineer at BW1 and the supply of an ASR Flight with its engineers might serve two problems, providing additional engineers, with advantage of air search to cover the large numbers of our aircraft using BW1 as a Staging Post and further for aircraft proceeding to and from the mainland and Iceland, over the routes to the south of Greenland.[64]

Alexander also made detailed recommendations that steps be taken to facilitate communication between weather ships and aircraft in need of assistance.

If Flying Officer Alexander's report on search and rescue on the northern route was acted upon, it is a very important document. Unfortunately, no evidence has been found to indicate that any of his recommendations were officially adopted. If no steps were taken to improve the situation, more lives must inevitably have been lost. On 28 March, two weeks after Alexander wrote his memorandum, Dakota KN409 disappeared between Reykjavik and Prestwick.[65] At 1047 GMT on 16 April, Mosquito KA968 left Gander for Prestwick and was not seen again.[66] Then on 10 June another Mosquito, KA237, was lost between Goose Bay and BW-1. Perhaps not surprisingly, in the only mention of an actual search for any of these aircraft, the diary of RCAF Station Goose Bay recorded about the last case: 'An intensive search instituted by the A.S.R. unit at BW1, together with the R.A.F. A.S.R. Canso FT999, captained by F/L Forbes, failed to sight any trace of the missing aircraft and crew.'[67] Despite the lack of success, there appears to have been an improvement in the region's SAR commitment. Still, it seems clear that the absence of an adequate search and rescue capability undoubtedly cost the lives of aircrew on the northern route and probably on others as well.

Occasionally crews, or some members, survived a crash and made it back to civilization. On 8 May 1942 the crew of Ventura AE747 were saved after they had crash-landed in Greenland and seen their plane sink through the ice.[68] Six months later, on 10 November, the diary of the Ferry Command contingent at Gander reported: 'Boston BZ 215 failed to reach Reykjavik and is presumed lost.' On the 12th it recorded hopefully that the missing plane had been 'heard transmitting S.O.S. from Greenland coast. Catalina FP 532 standing by to join in search when weather permits.' The weather did not permit any movement for a several days. BW-1 was closed in, and each day's entry noted that Gander's Catalina was 'standing by to join in search' or that 'Bad weather still prevented amphibian PBY FP 532 from searching for Boston BZ 215.' On 15 November, with Gander's aircraft still grounded by the weather, a report was received from BW-1 'that one boat and more than twenty planes were searching. Rumour that flares were seen.' Finally, on 26 November with their own aircraft still stuck at home base, Gander reported that 'an American ship had picked up crew of Boston B.Z. 215, stranded on ice cap since November 10th. Stated to be all well.'[69] In this case the crew had had a good chance of being found because they had been able to send out an SOS signal.

Their Ferry Command colleagues, and indeed the world, learned more details about this 'Arctic ordeal,' as it was popularly termed, after the RCAF crew, Pilot Officer David Goodlet (pilot, from Simcoe, Ontario), Pilot Officer Alfred Nash (navigator, from Winnipeg), and Flight Sergeant Arthur Weaver, (radio operator, from Toronto), returned to Canada. Stories detailing their adventure appeared in various newspapers, and *Maclean's* carried a feature account that was later reprinted in slightly abridged form by *Reader's Digest*. Tens of thousands of readers learned a great deal about this particular unsuccessful delivery flight. This was certainly different treatment from that which the first ferry crews had received only two years earlier.

It seems that Boston BZ215 had left Gander at 0800 local time and run into fog a couple of hours out. Heavy overcast prevented Nash from taking sun shots and the radio died, so Weaver could not reach any ground station to find out where they were. Goodlet 'kept her pretty steady at 15,000 ... since there was a chance we might have drifted over Greenland where the mountains are pretty high.' However, they could not remain at that altitude for long. The pilot told the writer from *Maclean's*:

With half an hour's gas left, I knew I had to start letting down. If there was any chance for a landing I wanted to have some power. We passed through heavy clouds, wondering all the time if we were going to bump into a mountain. We came out of it at 3,800. Al relieved things a little. All the way down he kept yelling into the intercom mike, 'Fifth floor, ladies' wear, lingerie and fancy hosiery.' Stuff like that. He was down to the bargain basement when we came out of it.[70]

They were over a snow-covered plateau between a range of mountains and the coast about fifteen miles away. Goodlet managed to avoid the numerous crevasses and made a perfect wheels-up landing.

With the snow almost waist deep, the temperature around 40° below zero, and the wind showing at 62 miles per hour on the plane's airspeed indicator, the three airmen remained in the aircraft for the next several days. They supplemented their clothing by ripping up their parachutes and wrapping the silk around themselves. Weaver said, 'We looked like Egyptian mummies but the silk helped a lot.' They also stuffed parachute silk into cracks in the fuselage to keep as much as possible of the wind out. They took turns stretched out on top of one another in a desperate attempt to keep warm, and never slept for more than a few minutes at a time, afraid they would freeze if they fell asleep. 'We stayed like that all night, shuffling around like a deck of cards so we'd take turns on being middle man which was the warmest spot. About every half hour we'd all get up and slam our feet against the sides.' The only food in the plane was a 'box of iron biscuits' which they decided to ration at one each every 24 hours, later cut to a half and then to a quarter. 'These biscuits were about half an inch square and were supposed to be full of vitamins but they tasted like sawdust.' Weaver 'monkeyed with the radio' from time to time, as much as his frozen hands would allow, and eventually got it operating long enough to send out an SOS with their position and to receive an acknowledgement. This buoyed their spirits and they made plans to drag the dinghy to the coast and paddle the estimated 100 miles to the nearest settlement.[71]

Weaver recalled, 'On the sixth morning the weather cleared and we inflated the dinghy with the carbon-dioxide cartridge. We destroyed the bombsight and burned all the papers as required in crash orders. It wasn't much of a fire but we stuck the frozen coffee flasks into it and got about a cup melted before the papers burned up.' They learned very quickly that it would be a very difficult trek: 'We started moving about one o'clock. It was tough going even with the snowshoes. The dinghy pulled harder than the devil and we couldn't go more than 50 yards without getting winded. In two hours we covered about a quarter of a mile and then the snow started again. We knew we couldn't last long in that stuff so we started back for the plane and holed in again and smoked cigarettes and talked and pounded each other all night.' The next day they tried it again, in almost tropical conditions (relatively speaking) as 'the temperature shot up 54 degrees and rain started falling.' They pushed on until darkness fell and then spent seventeen hours crouched in frozen flying suits, with their dinghy propped up for a little protection from the wind. Worried about stumbling into a crevass in the dark, they waited until sunrise to resume their circuitous route to the coast around the numerous crevasses blocking the route.[72]

They were in the process of negotiating their way around a crevass when they heard an aeroplane engine. Only one of the marine signals in the dinghy worked, but the crew in the search-plane spotted it and soon had dropped 'small parachutes with food, clothing, sleeping bags, a bottle of Scotch, snowshoes, 100 feet of rope and a note of instructions.' After putting on dry clothes and eating the equivalent of several meals, they crawled into the sleeping bags 'and went to sleep for the first time in nine days.' They were not yet home free. Following the written instructions, 'to rope ourselves together and keep on toward the coast in as straight a line as possible,' they made their way across ever more difficult terrain in the direction of the coast. There, they had been informed, 'a U.S. Coast Guard patrol boat was smashing its way through the ice toward us.' When they reached the coast after a few more extremely difficult days, their feet painfully frost-bitten and their clothes frozen, they saw a ship about ten miles out. 'With Dave's lighter, which he'd refilled with alcohol from the plane's radiator, we tried to set our parkas on fire. But they were too damp.' Searchlights from the ship played along the shore all night, without picking out the flyers. When daylight came a plane took off from the vicinity of the ship and flew over them, but it too failed to spot them jumping around and waving their parkas. All they could do was stand and watch when the ship turned and started to sail away. Weaver took up the story:

We didn't say anything. We just stood there and watched it until darkness blotted it out.

We thought we were gone then. Our food was gone. We knew we didn't have enough strength left to make it back to the plane and we knew we couldn't stand even one of those 40-below nights in the open.

About an hour after dark Dave said he thought the parkas might burn all right now because the day had been clear and the wind had dried them out. We tore part of them into strips so they'd catch fire easier. Dave spun his lighter but it was getting very low on fuel and it took a lot of sparking to get it going. But when it did, the parkas caught fire nicely and we had a good, bright blaze.

As soon as the flames went up there was a burst of flares from out in the ice field and the ship's signal lamp started blinking. I read the Morse: 'Move back from the edge of the glacier and bear south to meet landing party.'[73]

Six hours later they were plucked from the shore and taken to the US Coast Guard cutter *Northland*.

As a postscript to this tale of survival, Weaver had $120 in pay stolen from the Toronto home of his in-laws while he was staying there during the twenty-eight days of leave he was granted following his ordeal. The thief also took the piece of hardtack biscuit from the emergency pack that the radio operator had saved as a souvenir of his Greenland adventure.[74]

Not all searches took place so far from home. On Tuesday, 8 December 1942, less than a month after BZ215 went missing out of Gander, the Ferry Command detachment's diary recorded that two other Bostons, BZ294 and BZ319, 'circled over Gander for considerable period due to snowstorm after flight from Dorval. BZ 319 eventually landed at Stephenville. BZ 294 reportedly force landed near Benton, 8 miles East of Gander, at approximately 2015 local time.' Having an idea of where the plane went down was no guarantee that it would be found quickly. After a series of misadventures involving both ground and air searchers, an RCAF Harvard two days later 'located a man in the bush about three miles South East of the Radio Range station. The man spelled out in the snow the word "EAT." Shortly afterwards, a small packet of food wrapped in a blanket was dropped from a Harvard, then a larger parcel by parachute from a Norseman.' By Friday, Flight Sergeant Fred Coates, RCAF, the Boston's radio operator from Winnipeg, had been 'admitted into hospital suffering from nothing worse than minor bruises and reaction.'[75]

The Ferry Command diary recorded the story, as related by Coates: 'They were coming in to land and could see the lights of the airport when suddenly he felt a series of ever increasing shocks culminating in a terrific crash.' It was later confirmed that the altimeter read 1500 feet. Extricating himself with some difficulty from the wreckage, 'he saw that the aircraft was already beginning to burn. He shouted out and heard groans coming from the pilot's cockpit.' He did not recall how he did it, but somehow Coates got the pilot, Flight Lieutenant Douglas Gordon Chown, RCAF, also from Winnipeg, out of the plane before 'one or more tanks exploded.' He thought the navigator, Pilot Officer Kenneth Herbert Wells, RCAF, from Victoria, British Columbia, must have been killed. He looked but could find no trace of his body. With Chown suffering from two broken legs and internal injuries, Coates 'lit a fire and tried to keep him warm with his own body.' After failing to attract the attention of a Canso that flew overhead, 'he decided to try and walk for help but very shortly found he was back on his own tracks in the snow. He, therefore, returned to the pilot and stayed with him until he died at 1100 hrs in the morning.' The diarist commented: 'It is tragic to think that there was a doctor and rescue party within a mile of them from about 0100 hours onwards.' With nothing to keep him near the plane, Coates started walking towards the radio range station, only to find that he kept going around in circles. While this was going on he was finally spotted from the air and took shelter by some trees on the side of a brook, from where he was rescued Friday afternoon. The wreckage itself was not located until 19 December. The bodies of Chown and Wells were brought back on the 21st and buried at Gander two days later.[76]

A more harrowing Newfoundland survival story began on 8 May 1943 when Sheldon Luck was piloting Ventura AJ164 on the milk run from Goose Bay to Gander. With smoke entering the passenger compartment from a malfunctioning heater, four passengers panicked and jumped from the plane just after it had crossed the Strait of Belle Isle. RCAF and Ferry Command aircraft spent the ensuing weeks in a fruitless search for the missing men. Two of them eventually made it to civilization. After the ground and air searches had been suspended, the diary of RCAF Station Gander recorded in late June, 'Corporal [Eric] Butt [RAF] and Mr. [John] Hogan – a civilian Forest Ranger, who bailed out of an aircraft about the first of May, 1943, along with two other men, when the aircraft caught fire [sic], were brought to the station by air from Port Saunders.' In fact, Hogan was a member of the Newfoundland Rangers, a constabulary force responsible for all manner of government business throughout Newfoundland and Labrador. Not mentioned in the air force account was the information that the rescue came as the result of a chance meeting between Hogan and a survey party. Nor did the diary do justice to their sorry physical condition: 'The two men had spent forty-nine days in the bush of Newfoundland, subsisting on snared rabbits and herbs. They were suffering from malnutrition – in addition, Corporal Butt was taken to the hospital suffering from frost-bite and exposure.'[77]

Another source indicates that Hogan had lost 80 of his 205 pounds and Butt 60 of his 165. In addition, when they were found, 'Butt's feet were still black and swollen to the calves. A horrible odor of rotting flesh came from them and puss dripped through the crude bandages that covered them.' In the end he lost only 'a couple of toes.'[78] It was probably Hogan's experience in the bush that had saved them. Still, they had had a terrifying experience. They were lucky; the other two passengers who had panicked and jumped from the plane were never found, despite a resumption of the search following the miraculous rescue of Hogan and Butt.[79]

Occasionally there were rescues on the southern route as well. On 1 February 1944 Baltimore FW640, piloted by Gene Hamilton Rowe of Nashville, developed engine trouble short of Belem, Brazil. As one engine quit and the other showed signs of doing the same, Rowe ordered his crew to bale out and held the plane steady for them to do so. After sending an SOS and releasing a carrier pigeon with a note giving the plane's position, the navigator and radio operator, Flying Officers F. Bruce Clark of Hudson Heights, Quebec, and Jack G. Doherty of Cornwall, Ontario, jumped from the plane and landed safely in the jungle. There are conflicting accounts of Rowe's fate. One says he 'apparently struck the plane and his body was found some distance from the plane's wreckage.' Another, not inconsistent with the first explanation, suggests he jumped too late for his parachute to open. A third claim, that he rode the aircraft down to his death, can be discounted; searchers spotted three parachutes in the area. However it happened, the American civilian died after ensuring that his RCAF crewmates had cleared the stricken bomber. Four days after landing in the 'snake and crocodile-infested jungle' near the mouth of the Amazon River, Clark and Doherty were rescued by a USN blimp 'which made a daring landing on the only clearing in the jungle.'[80]

Not everyone who left a Ferry Command aircraft in flight did so on purpose. On 21 December 1942 Torontonian Harry Griffiths, employed as a drift-sight reader, and Captain John 'Syd' Gerow were testing a Boston prior to its delivery flight. Griffiths squeezed into the nose to check the compass. Forty years later he told a *Toronto Star* reporter what happened next: 'I'd taken off my parachute because there was so little room up there, and I was just beginning to take a reading when the hatch fell out from under me ... I grabbed the first thing I could hold on to, but soon I was being sucked out the hole by the rush of the wind, barely hanging on. I was flush with the body of the aircraft, and my hands were starting to freeze.'[81]

Gerow sensed something was wrong when he felt a rush of cold air, obviously from an open hatch. He also thought he could hear Griffiths's faint cries for help. Knowing he had removed his parachute, and sensing a disturbance to the airflow, Gerow came to the correct conclusion. He guessed immediately what must have happened. However, with no automatic pilot on the aircraft, he could not leave the controls. His options were limited. Therefore, flying as steadily as possible, he flew as slowly and as low as he dared over Lac St Louis. Griffiths, his fingers frozen to the hatch, could not let go, even when he realized what his friend was doing. It was when Gerow started to climb, after flying across the lake as low as ten feet or less, that Griffiths was flung free. Thinking his young life was over, he said 'Goodbye,' flew though the air for a few feet, fell to the ice, and slid along the surface. A local farmer, Oliva Vallée, who witnessed the entire scene over the lake, assumed the plane had simply dropped a bundle of some kind, and later said: 'I thought it was a bag ... I went out to investigate, and as I got nearer I saw the "bag" move and realized it was a man. I shouted to another man who was passing and together we carried him to my house.' Only partially conscious, Griffiths had frozen hands but no other apparent injury. Ferry Command rescue personnel arrived on the scene and took him to hospital, where he spent a few days recovering from minor bruises, frostbite, and exposure.[82]

Meanwhile, Gerow had his own problems to contend with. He had been flying so slowly that he almost stalled the Boston as he climbed away from the lake. He made another pass over the area without seeing any trace of Griffiths, so he returned to Dorval. As Griffiths later told the story, the pilot 'landed the plane and just left it at the end of the runway ... He crawled out of the plane and sat there, shaking like a leaf. They had to go out and get him.'[83] In the end, Gerow and Griffiths became two of Ferry Command's biggest heroes, even being lauded in a comic strip, 'Real Heroes,' under the subtitle, 'R.A.F.F.C. Bomber Trapeze Team.'[84]

Lac St Louis, essentially a widening of the St Lawrence River just south of Dorval on the western part of the island of Montreal, was the scene of other Ferry Command flying incidents, often with less happy endings than in the Griffiths-Gerow adventure. One of the best known came shortly after noon on 5 July 1942, when a popular Montreal member of the RAF, Squadron Leader George Patterson Christie, already a war hero for his exploits with Fighter Command and a veteran of several deliveries with Ferry Command, flew into the lake during a training flight. Wing Commander Brian G. Carr-Harris, RCAF (from Picton, Ontario), being checked out on the Hudson by Christie in his role of chief flying instructor, and Leading Aircraftman Clement Stewart Llewellyn, RAF wireless operator (from Wales), were also killed in the crash. This is one accident that may have been avoidable. A newspaper report says the crash occurred 'when their Ferry Command Hudson bomber touched a wing tip to rough water, looped and smashed its nose into a claybank seven feet under the surface of the lake.'[85] Henry Flory, who knew and admired Pat Christie, calls it 'a foolish accident,'[86] which happened when his friend was 'doing a slow roll in a Hudson too low over the St. Lawrance River.'[87] This version rings true, not only with the press account, but also with air force experience during the war.

The RAF's flight safety publication *Tee Emm* is replete with warnings about unauthorized low flying. All the commands found it a perennial problem and issued periodic memoranda imploring pilots not to engage in the practice. Obviously certain operational circumstances required that a plane fly at a very low altitude. However, it could be extremely dangerous, especially in training, and it claimed the lives of many men. Even so, pilots often found it too much fun to resist.[88]

Not only was low flying fun; pilots could also be accused of doing it to impress people. On 24 June 1943, local inhabitants and vacationers around Lac St Joseph, near Ste Agathe north of Montreal, were treated to a Hudson buzzing the lake. Corporal S.G. Helleur, RCAF, on leave at a cottage, saw the whole show. 'The object of its low-level attention,' he later recalled, 'appeared to be the YMCA mixed camp, OTEREKE, hidden from my view by a knoll to the south east.' The plane circled the lake and flew low over the camp for about ten minutes, before it 'glided behind the knoll from east to west and on its reappearance a second later was belching flame and thick black smoke from its starboard wing.' The pilot was obviously in trouble, particularly at an altitude estimated by the witness as 'little more than 200 feet.' Helleur watched the Hudson as it 'made a climbing bank to the left, the pilot obviously intending to circle and fly back north for a landing in the lake.' The airman on the ground thought that 'he negotiated an extremely tight turn for a Hudson and headed directly up the lake.' It looked as if the plane would miss the lake and crash into the cottage. 'However, when about 300 yards away and at about 200 feet up, the plane's starboard tailplane appeared to disintegrate and fall away from the aircraft which went completely out of control, starting a spiral dive to starboard. Its engines still functioning, the plane more or less drift-dived over the highway bordering the lake and crashed vertically at the base of a hill about 75 yards beyond the road. With the crash came a terrific blast of flame and billows of heavy, black smoke.' Helleur and his wife 'drove to the spot' with another couple and, running across a field, joined a number of other people doing the same thing. The crew probably died instantly, but nothing could be done for them anyway: 'it was impossible to get within more than 50 feet of the actual scene because of the intense heat. Within three minutes, all that had escaped the flames were wing tips and tail-wheel.'[89]

The pilot, Sergeant Peter Alan Naylor, RAF (from London, England), had had one trip to the United Kingdom as co-pilot of a Hudson. Recently returned on the *Queen Mary*, he was preparing for his first delivery as an aircraft captain when he died. Also killed in the crash were the navigator, Pilot Officer Donald Morrison McLennan (from Vancouver), and the radio operator, Sergeant Edward Lloyd Barrett (from Merritt, British Columbia). With two members of the crew from the RCAF, 45 Group informed Ottawa. At Air Force Headquarters, Air Vice-Marshal W.S. Stedman phoned Air Commodore Powell at Dorval and commented afterwards: 'A Court of Enquiry is being held, but there is no doubt about the findings because it is a clear case of unauthorized low flying, in which the Pilot dived on a cottage where he spent his holidays and hit a tree.'[90]

As a postscript to the Lac St Joseph crash, Corporal Helleur claimed that he had trouble getting through on the telephone with word of the accident. The operator required his name before she would connect him with No. 3 Training Command headquarters in Montreal as he requested. He said that he 'heard her say: "I have an emergency call from a Corporal Helleur in Ste. Agathe. Will you take the call and accept the charges?" "Who is calling?" "A Corporal Helleur from St. Agathe. He says it's an emergency." "Well, I'm sorry but If the call is not from an Officer it's not an emergency." "I'll tell him then, that you can't take the call?" "Yes. If it's not from an Officer, it's not an emergency call."' The officious voice on the other end of the line hung up. However, before the operator had a chance to do the same, the frustrated corporal blurted out that there had been a plane crash. After about five minutes he was finally 'connected with a Flight Lieutenant who took down particulars.' The office of the chief of the air staff at AFHQ in Ottawa took an interest in this little matter, but let it drop after receiving a brief conciliatory note from No. 3 Training Command.[91]

Among the unsung heroes of Ferry Command, and indeed of all the Allied air forces, were the groundcrew and support staff who kept the planes and the aircrew flying. For every man who flew, there were many more men, and women, engaged in a myriad of support functions. A vast infrastructure had rapidly grown up and stretched half-way round the globe. Its administration required a staff of thousands, mostly civilians, doing the countless jobs one finds in such large organizations. They laboured long and hard, not only at Dorval where they had modifications as well as basic maintenance to do on aircraft, but also at staging posts stretched out along the various routes where Ferry Command flew. They frequently worked and lived in difficult, uncomfortable, and isolated conditions. Like their aircrew colleagues, their job was often no piece of cake.

If the records are sparse for the aircrew and the aircraft, they are even more rare when it comes to the groundcrew and their work. One sees occasional hints, however, of their pride and dedication. Not content to prepare planes for delivery, they also worked to salvage as many as possible after they had crashed. If that proved impossible, they rescued as many parts as they could, knowing how valuable and needed they all were. For example, after Baltimore FA140 force-landed on the beach at Triacao in northern Brazil, on 19 December 1942, technicians dismantled it to remove it from the beach. (More than two years later the British and Canadian governments were still arguing over who was responsible for paying the Brazilian claim for £1.5.6. Was it for services to the British plane or the Canadian crew?)[92]

There is little mention of such activities in the historical record that has survived, but for several months after the crash of the Return Ferry Service Liberator AL591, the Gander Ferry Command diary mentions salvage parties working at the crash site to save what they could of the aeroplane. Similarly, the same diary, as well as that of the RCAF at Gander, periodically records trips to various points around Newfoundland to salvage a plane that had been forced down, or whatever parts could be saved from the wreck. In many cases the mechanics and technicians involved had to struggle to get to the site, and then endure considerable hardship while there. Usually they accomplished much more than could ever have been reasonably expected. On one occasion they took so much pride in what they had achieved that a special report was prepared and filed with the Ferry Command diary. It is worth looking at in some detail as an example of the kind of work done by the groundcrew.[93]

During the night of 25 July 1942, a Hudson Mark V, AM844, flying from Reykjavik to Goose Bay, 'got off course and eventually ran out of petrol and crashed on a hill-top some four miles from the railway at Main Dam, Grand Lake, about one hundred and twenty miles from Gander. The crew were unhurt, and the aircraft, though seriously damaged, was not a "write off."' After a local contractor quoted a figure of $15,000 'for the salvage and delivery, with engines, wings and all components packed in crates F.O.B. Cornerbrook,' the Ferry Command maintenance staff at Gander decided to try to repair the plane and fly it out. They reasoned that, 'allowing for subsequent shipping and rail charges, also the risk of damage or loss in transit ... unless the aircraft could be repaired "in situ" and flown off, the only parts worth salving were the engine, instruments and the radio equipment.' In October a preliminary survey from the air and a subsequent check on foot suggested that it could be done: 'The replacements required proved to be one engine, two airscrews and one Pitot Head Mast.' The aero-engine mechanics already had an engine from a Mark VI Hudson that had been taken from another crash site. This would work, 'provided airscrew and wiring differences between Mk. V and Mk. VI Hudsons could be reconciled.' When this was worked out, 'the engine was sent in to the crash on Oct. 18th with a party of five men.' They took a bulldozer with a winch attachment. 'The latter is invaluable in the bush and enables the bulldozer to pull itself out of the bog.' Even with hard work, the Hudson was not ready for takeoff until 19 January 1943, 'the unduly long time taken being due to two main factors: 1. Lack of air transport, 2. Delay in getting the airscrews.'[94]

When the repairs were completed, groundcrew specialists from each of the aircraft support trades, such as aero-engine and airframe mechanics, as well as instrument and electrical technicians, had to undertake a thorough inspection to ensure that the plane would safely fly. Only then was it ready to be flown out of the wilderness. 'The first task, however, was to clear a track for the take-off, and this was done by the bulldozer which prepared a track about 450 yds. × 10 yds.' They tried to take off on 19 January, 'but when the aircraft had proceeded about 100 yds. down the snow-covered improvised runway, the port wheel broke through the crust of snow, into a hole, snapped the left leg off at the root, and the aircraft, spinning around, smashed the port wing and bent the airscrew.' This must have been a near crushing blow to the mechanics who had worked so hard to make the plane flyable. They wanted to carry on the project, but first had 'to concentrate on the salvage of Ventura AJ 471 which, in the meantime, had force landed on the frozen Birchy Lake.' This put the Hudson work in jeopardy: 'By the time the Ventura was salved the spring thaw had started, thus adding to the difficulty of the party which, on March 23rd, resumed salvage operations.'[95]

The mechanics had to haul a new port wing into the site by bulldozer. They then started work, they proudly proclaimed, 'on a repair which, in the hangar at Gander, took T.C.A. experts ten days to carry out on one of their aircraft. Under the direction of Mr. Gilmour, who flew in with the Menasco Moth, the repair was finished in three days, a remarkable achievement.' Now, however, the changing of the seasons presented a real threat to the success of the enterprise. The climax is best left in the words of the anonymous writer of the report:

By this time, however, day temperatures were so high that the runway was only useable early on some mornings, depending on the previous night's tempera-ture. Skids were then prepared on which the Hudson could be towed down to a frozen lake, half a mile below the runway, from which the take-off would have been simple, if the ice continued to hold. However, the skids were not required, for on April 17th, the Gander Staff Canso was flown from Dorval by Capt. Thompson, and today [19 April 1943] Capt. Thompson left for Deer Lake at 6.00 a.m., as passenger in a R.C.A.F. Norseman. The Canso, piloted by G/C Anderson followed at 8.00 a.m.; being delayed by a flat tyre in the nose wheel; and landed on the frozen lake, just after Capt. Thompson had made a success-ful, and very skillful take-off down the narrow runway.[96]

The report proudly concluded with an assessment of the cost-ef-fectiveness of this venture: 'It is difficult to assess the actual extra cost to the Government of these salvage operations. The wages of the men are in any case paid, so that beyond a few hundred dollars for local labour, petrol, railway charges etc., it would seem highly unlikely that the cost has exceeded $2,000.00.' At that point an additional clause was added in longhand: 'which for an aircraft valued at over $100,000.00 is very encouraging.'[97]

The maintenance staff obviously took great pride in their achievement, as well as in other salvage operations. It must be remembered that, as they worked on these special projects, they kept their primary duty firm-ly in mind, preparing delivery aircraft for the next leg of the trip to Britain. In this case they had managed, by adapting and fitting parts from planes that had been written off, to recover a valuable aeroplane for future use. Captain Thompson took Hudson AM844 up on a test flight on 1 May. After a couple more such tests over the following week, the salvaged aircraft returned to Dorval, and to the Ferry Command inven-tory, on 10 May 1943, almost ten months after it had crashed.[98] For the next few months it was used for miscellaneous communications flights. It survived until the fall, when Don McVicar, undertaking his second survey of the Crimson (or North East Staging) Route, crashed it on takeoff from Churchill. He then had to await the arrival of a new

Hudson from Dorval before he could continue his flight.[99] There is no evidence that AM844 ever flew again. For the second time it joined almost two hundred aircraft lost by the ferry organization.[100]

Most, but by no means all, of these losses occurred during delivery flights. Statistically the loss rate was good, much more acceptable in fact than what had originally been projected when the Atlantic ferry scheme was first launched. With almost 10,000 aeroplanes delivered overseas, the authorities could live with 2 per cent wastage. This should not detract from the difficult nature of the job. Nobody would claim that it was as dangerous as flying on operations over enemy territory; on the other hand, as the loss of over 500 aircrew shows, it was clearly no piece of cake.

12

Lasting Legacy

Given the use of Montreal as the headquarters, and the heavy involvement of Canadians in all aspects of British ferry operations, we should make special mention of the host country's role in the enterprise. This review will also give us an opportunity to look at wartime arrangements that led to the tremendous growth of international aviation in the postwar world. Many lessons learned in military air-ferrying operations were carried forward into peacetime for the benefit of travellers on civilian commercial airlines. Canadian efforts to share in the wartime burdens of transatlantic air transport operations are intertwined with the story of RAF Ferry Command and its important adjunct, the Return Ferry Service operated by BOAC.

No country played a bigger role in the story told in this book than Canada. Beyond providing the headquarters and various other key physical facilities, Canada was involved in the ferry service from the very beginning. Hundreds of its citizens ferried aircraft from Montreal to the United Kingdom and other operational theatres, flew cargoes of war materials from North America to various battlefronts, and worked in innumerable ground support jobs wherever Ferry Command extended its reach. Even so, there was no distinctive Canadian air presence on the North Atlantic route until 1943. In that year two Canadian services, modest in comparison to those operated by the British and the Americans, made their appearance, one established by Trans-Canada Air Lines (TCA) and the other by the RCAF. Their creation helped catapult Canada into a key position in the development of postwar international aviation. Improvements in infrastructure and cooperative control procedures, necessitated by these and other developments, affected No. 45 Group of RAF Transport Command and subsequently all international air carriers.

Participation by TCA in the Return Ferry Service, in association with BOAC, was first seriously discussed in August 1941, shortly after the official formation of RAF Ferry Command. Previously, control of the Return Ferry Service had been in the hands of Morris Wilson and Harold Long, Lord Beaverbrook's Canadian lieutenants in the organization and direction of ATFERO. Although BOAC crews were employed, Beaverbrook opposed the direct involvement of the airline itself, contending that the Return Ferry Service was inseparable from ATFERO. As we have seen in chapter 4, in the spring and summer of 1941 Beaverbrook, Wilson, and Long ended their association with transatlantic ferrying and the civilian ATFERO was replaced by RAF Ferry Command under Air Chief Marshal Sir Frederick Bowhill.

Shortly after taking up his new post, Bowhill learned that BOAC would operate the Return Ferry Service as an agency of Ferry Command. This, the Air Ministry explained, was based on the consideration that while the primary purpose of the Return Ferry Service was to facilitate the ferrying of aircraft by returning pilots to Montreal on westbound flights, on eastbound flights it should carry passengers, mainly government officials and military officers, mail, and freight, which was a job for an experienced airline. Undoubtedly, another factor was that Britain had a vested interest to protect on the North Atlantic route. Before the war, the UK government had chosen BOAC as its transatlantic carrier. Experience gained in air transport during the war would enable the British airline to keep abreast of its chief competitor, Pan American Airways.[1]

The proposal held little appeal for Bowhill. He felt that it could embroil him in controversy with the Americans, who would undoubtedly protest the use of lend-lease Liberators by BOAC, and possibly with the Canadians, who might suspect that the British were attempting to steal a march on the Atlantic routes: 'It must be remembered,' he wrote in a report to the Air Ministry, 'that Mr. Howe is very anxious to start a service organized by Trans-Canada Airways [sic] over to the UK. I am afraid there are going to be political repercussions if we allow BOAC to start as an agency service to the BFC [British Ferry Command].'[2]

Bowhill also pointed out, on another occasion, that there was still some discontent surrounding the Wilson and Long resignations. He feared that the proposed change would aggravate old wounds: 'I feel by leaving things as they are for the present an opening [for offence] will not be given and later on when the [Ferry] Command has been working for some time we can reconsider the position.'[3] The Air Ministry accepted this argument and agreed to a transitional period during which Ferry Command would continue to operate the Return Ferry Service: 'It is, however, Air Ministry policy as you know that BOAC should assume formal responsibility as soon as possible since from parliamentary angle this is air transport service under British Overseas Airways Act. Please let us know when friction has died down and time is ripe for BOAC to take over,'[4]

Air Ministry officials were by no means blind to the ramifications of their decision. The chief danger lay with isolationist elements in the United States. The use of lend-lease Liberators by a British airline would play directly into their hands, providing them with a fresh opportunity to criticize the Roosevelt administration. There was nothing to fear from the American government itself, for both the president and General Arnold emphasized the military importance of good air communications between North America and the United Kingdom. Nor was Pan American likely to object. Not only was Juan Trippe's company expanding its services in the North Atlantic, but it was making inroads on the trans-Africa route at the expense of BOAC.[5]

The British were also concerned about the Canadian reaction, because Canada and the United Kingdom had entered into a prewar agreement to cooperate in the development of a transatlantic service. The Air Ministry 'had it in mind to safeguard the British-Canadian partnership ... by inviting Canada to take a hand in the operations of the BOAC.'[6] It fell to Harold Balfour, undersecretary of state for air, to remove any bitterness the British might have created by their pre-emptive move and to promise C.D. Howe that Canada would not be left out of the picture. After a discussion with the powerful Canadian minister in August, Balfour reported to Sinclair:

I suggested to Mr. Howe that Trans-Canada Airways [sic] might be associated in some way or other with BOAC, as and when the Corporation took over the running of the (return) ferry service. It might be that Trans-Canada could give a valuable contribution by the supplying of crews even if they could not provide aircraft. It might be that when we had an adequate number of B.24's we could hand one or two of these over to Trans-Canada, to be operated in association with BOAC under the Trans-Canada flag and of course, under the same general direction of Ferry Command as BOAC.

This was only a 'sweetener' and whether or not it had any effect I do not know, but the fact remains that Mr. Howe ... was not unfavourable to BOAC taking over responsibility for the (return) ferry service.[7]

About the same time, Beaverbrook, who though no longer associated with the ferry service maintained an interest in it, reported to Sinclair: 'Mr. Howe tells me he is willing to divert the organization now carrying on an air line from East to West in Canada to ferrying pilots across the Atlantic. The Canadians would do the job at their own expense, but you would have to hand over the transport aircraft to them without crews. What do you say to this proposition?'[8] In his reply Sinclair gave two reasons why the suggestion was impractical: 'The resources of Howe's Trans Canada Air Lines are very limited, both in aircraft and flying personnel and they could not possibly take over the whole show.' Moreover, from a political point of view the move would be premature: 'The Americans are very touchy about air-line developments and this would only arouse their suspicions.'[9]

The decision to make BOAC responsible for the management and operations of the Return Ferry Service was implemented in September. The change was less drastic than Bowhill had feared it might be. The operation of the Liberators, the management of passenger traffic, as well as the loading and unloading of mail and freight were entrusted to the airline. The final authority in regard to times of departure and loads to be carried rested with Bowhill, and, in general, BOAC had to meet the requirements of Ferry Command.[10]

At Bowhill's request, no publicity was given to the new arrangements, but it was widely known that a change had taken place. Indeed, rumours had run ahead of the event itself. In August, for example, a journalist from the *New York Times* protested that commercial practices were creeping into Ferry Command: 'Evidence is at hand here that for a $600 contribution to the British Spitfire fund, private passengers can cross the Atlantic on the British ATFERO service, and mail is reaching individuals in the United States marked "Per North Atlantic Service." The marking is British. At the same time Pan American's mail portage is off 10 per cent, and there is a developing difficulty for the American line in getting air passengers in Europe.' The Toronto *Globe and Mail* reprinted this article, with the editor expressing 'grave disquietude' at what the British were reported to be doing. Such activities would only add to 'a rising tide of criticism of the British war effort' and erode public support of President Roosevelt's defence program. While admitting that the charges might have been maliciously concocted, the editorial was inclined to the view that there must be a large measure of truth behind them or else a prompt denial would have been forthcoming from the British embassy.[11] On the whole, however, it was a piece of bad reporting and represented the type of publicity the British wished to avoid.

Whatever the newspapers might say, they could not accuse ATFERO of operating a luxurious passenger service. BOAC, very likely at Bowhill's insistence, had carefully avoided any comparison with Pan American Airways. Return Ferry Service flights offered few amenities. Some aircraft eventually received seats, but on others passengers made themselves as comfortable as possible on mattresses placed on the floor. George Lothian, a TCA pilot who spent time on secondment with Ferry Command, describes a return trip:

There was a well justified saying in Ferry Command, 'You don't get paid for the trip over. You get paid for the ride back.' This was no reflection on the crews which were responsible for the trip home but on the means of transportation. In one case it meant boarding a ship in a slow convoy travelling through sub-infested waters for two or three weeks or making the return in the bowels of a converted Liberator bomber on a two-stage trip, enduring as much as twenty hours in cabin temperatures of twenty-five to thirty degrees below zero ...

Somehow the evening for departure always seemed to make a good setting for a ghastly murder. The Liberator sat, dimly visible through the falling rain and mist, admidst [sic] darkly glinting puddles on the blacked-out tarmac. It is easy to tell yourself that other people in other places are going through much more harrowing experiences but somehow this one becomes very personal. The reluctant passengers, or 'bodies' (a distasteful term used by the R.A.F.), got into the bomber through a hatch in the bomb bay area. Inside, the floor of the bomb bay had been lined with plywood and was strewn with sleeping bags. Most people preferred to take their places on one of the long wooden benches running along each side during the early stages of the proceedings. There were no windows and the twenty-two bodies tended to sit and stare morosely at the far wall. All talking ceased the instant the engines were started and the Lib began to rock as it taxied to the runway. Twenty-two pairs of ears pricked up and listened closely as the engines were run up for the magneto checks. When they were opened up for the endless take-off run people could be seen crossing themselves and some sadist would start to intone a count-down. There was a theory – when he got to a certain number if the Lib was not off the ground you had had it. I never knew what the final number was as we were always airborne while he was still counting. Once launched into the sluggish climb, the bodies began sorting themselves out on the floor for the endless twelve or thirteen hours until the next stop at Gander. In what seemed like a hundred years the aircraft finally arrived at Dorval.[12]

VIPs flying on the Return Ferry Service suffered the same indignities. In March 1944 Vincent Massey, Canadian high commissioner to the United Kingdom, flew home in a Liberator, the passengers 'being packed into it in sardine fashion, head to feet on the mattresses.' In commenting on the flight in his memoirs, Massey remarks: 'Many people crossed the Atlantic in this way – I was glad of the experience but I would not have liked to make a habit of it, although we were in excellent hands and the crew inspired confidence in all of us.'[13]

Pre-boarding instructions drew attention to the lack of heating in the Liberators:

The crossing is very cold and special flying kit is essential. On request a regulation RAF flying suit will be loaned ... to each passenger for the flight. Helmet and flying boots are provided. A large over-size flying suit and over-size flying boots are better protection against the cold than those which fit snugly. To prevent frostbite it is essential that no constricting clothing of any kind should be worn. Socks, boots, etc., should be loosely fitted. Garters should not be worn. If you do become frostbitten do not rub the part as this will increase the chance of infection. Consult the Medical Officer at the port of arrival if you have been frostbitten. The aircraft is very noisy and earplugs or cotton wool are an advantage.[14]

Frostbite was not uncommon. On one occasion a passenger reportedly lost consciousness when his oxygen supply failed and had both his hands so badly frozen that amputation was necessary.[15] Obviously, Pan American had little to fear in the way of competition from the Return Ferry Service. None of its aircraft had heating or passenger seats installed until January 1944. Even then, four of the eight Liberators on this service remained 'equipped with mattresses and sleeping bags.'[16]

Generally speaking, the only passengers carried by the Return Ferry Service were military personnel and government officials on urgent business which, like the limited freight accepted, could not wait for the slow crossing by ship. As a rule, women were excluded because of the lack of facilities for them. Exceptions were occasionally made, however, for the wives and families of Ferry Command personnel. They could fly on a military transport, 'entirely subject to space and load being available,' if 'the period of temporary duty of the husband or father concerned will exceed three months.'[17]

Whatever their rank or status, people who flew the Atlantic became eligible for a 'short-snorter,' a piece of paper currency signed by a fellow traveller and prized as evidence of the accomplishment. On 29 and 30 June 1943, Churchill and Roosevelt exchanged wires on the subject, the British prime minister raising the matter on behalf of King George VI: 'Former Naval Person to President Private. Will you kindly fly a short-snorter dollar bill signed by yourself and Harry [Hopkins] over here to me at earliest convenience for the King to join the Club upon? Repayment and subscription will be made in due course apart from Lend-Lease.' Roosevelt replied less than twenty-four hours later: 'For the Former Naval Person from the President Personal and Secret. The short-snorter dollar is on its way. Please welcome the King into the Club with adequate initiation and tell him I hope to catch him without his certificate some day. Harry and I are charging the account to a fund to give the Congress a long recess.' It appears that celebrities at this level may have taken some liberties with the generally accepted short-snorter procedures. 'The "short-snorter" club was for persons who had flown over the Atlantic,' Warren Kimball, editor of the Churchill-Roosevelt published correspondence explains. 'The rules varied, but generally consisted of the initiate either paying a fee (one dollar per short-snorter club member) or buying a round of drinks for the members. The new member's dollar bill (other currencies were occasionally used) was then signed by those present. Thereafter, if a short-snorter was found without his or her bill (Eleanor Roosevelt was a member), he or she had to either buy a round of drinks or pay each short-snorter present a fine, usually a dollar.'[18]

Special efforts were occasionally made to improve the comfort and amenities for government dignitaries flying with the Return Ferry Service. Early in August 1941 Bowhill was asked by Long, now a representative of the Canadian government, to ensure that all proper arrangements were made 'for the comfort of a very important person who is going to fly over to England shortly in a Liberator.'[19] The very important person was none other than the Canadian prime minister, who was planning his first wartime visit to the United Kingdom. Accompanied by Norman Robertson, undersecretary of state for external affairs, Georges Vanier, secretary of the Permanent Joint Board on Defence, and members of his staff, Prime Minister King left St Hubert (Ferry Command not yet having moved to Dorval) at 11:45 a.m. on 19 August. The aircraft arrived at Gander at four in the afternoon and departed about an hour before midnight. It was a warm evening, and King found it comfortable enough in a small unheated section that contained two reclining chairs. It was his first flight and he wrote about it at length in his diary. Like most Atlantic air travellers, he was fascinated by the experience of flying towards the sunrise and enchanted with his first aerial view of Scotland.[20]

The prime minister's discussions with Churchill, and other government business, kept him busy until 6 September. He left for Canada early the next day. Vincent Massey accompanied him to the airport and afterwards left in his diary a vivid memory of the early morning departure: 'Up at 4:15 a.m. Breakfast at 5:00 and over to the Ayr aerodrome by 5:30 when it was still dark. An extraordinary scene – the vast aeroplane warming up its engines which emitted blue flames as they roared at full throttle; black figures moving about in the murk; white coated figures working at the aircraft, etc. At 6 they took off – just at daybreak, rising like a bird off the tarmac. Breakfast in Ayrshire – dinner in the Gatineau Hills!'[21]

The feeling of exhilaration that King experienced on his flight to the United Kingdom appears to have been lacking on the return journey, possibly as a result of strong headwinds and turbulent air. In his diary, he recorded that he 'thanked God with all my heart as we reached the airport safely, and I saw the ground once again solid beneath my feet.' Yet he appreciated the convenience and speed of air travel as compared with a sea voyage, only '15 hours and 10 minutes straight across from Ayr to Montreal without a stop.'[22]

The best Return Ferry Service time for a direct flight from the United Kingdom to Montreal was 13 hours 30 minutes. The record was set on 10 June 1941 by Captain E.R.B. White, the pilot who flew into Goat Fell on the Isle of Arran two months later. Flying with the wind, Captain S.T.B. Cripps once flew the 3100 miles in the opposite direction in 12 hours 51 minutes.[23] These record times are for BOAC only and do not include flights made by delivery aircraft or by American or Canadian machines. It should be noted that transatlantic pilots were officially discouraged from making record attempts.

In October 1941 the omnipresent Beaverbrook, again thrusting himself into the affairs of the Return Ferry Service, informed Sinclair that he had recently received a letter from Howe regarding Canadian cooperation in the transatlantic service: 'Howe says that … if our personnel became impaired to a point that would involve difficulty in operating the taxi Service taking pilots back to Canada, he would be prepared to take over that operation and use Trans-Canada crews … He has always felt it strange that Trans-Canada Air Lines have not been asked to help to any great extent.'[24] Since the British were experiencing no great difficulty in keeping the Liberators flying on schedule, and were in touch with Howe regarding Canadian participation, Sinclair attached little importance to Beaverbrook's letter, but his reply was cordial and to the point: 'As soon as the time is ripe, we intend to ask Trans-Canada to participate. And C.-in-C. (Commander-in-Chief) Ferry Command has arranged with Howe to take three or four Trans-Canada pilots for a few months at a time, in order to give them trans-Atlantic experience ... Bowhill will renew our assurance that we hope for Trans-Canada co-operation in the future if Howe approaches him on the matter.'[25]

Although it was not too difficult for Canadian officials to obtain air passage to the United Kingdom, getting home again often presented problems. Few merited the priority given to the prime minister. As a rule, space on westbound aircraft was reserved for aircrew on their way back to Montreal. Diplomats, military officers, and others frequently had to return by boat, with all the attendant dangers and delays, unless a place could be found for them on a Pan Am clipper or an American military transport – reputedly more comfortable than those flown by BOAC. Not at all pleased with this situation, Vincent Massey proposed to his home government in December 1941 'that in the present circumstances and the production of larger planes in Canada, consideration be given to the establishment of an air line between Canada and the United Kingdom.'[26] The high commissioner's letter did not provide an immediate solution to the problem, but it does reflect something of the frustration that Canadians were beginning to feel because of their dependence on the British and the Americans for air transport across the Atlantic – a feeling that added to Howe's determination to make a start on the North Atlantic route.

Another incentive in this direction sprang from the opening of TCA service to Torbay, Newfoundland, on 1 May 1942. Terminating in Newfoundland, the Canadian airline presented an unfinished picture to Howe and H.J. Symington, president of TCA, who could not help but compare it to BOAC and Pan American Airways. American airlines, already expanding before the United States entered the war, experienced a new period of growth after Pearl Harbor. Responding to military requirements, Pan Am expanded its New York-to-Lisbon schedule, while continuing to use Botwood in the summer season. Two other American companies, Transcontinental and Western Air, and American Export Airlines, both under contract to the USAAF's Air Transport Command, had opened regular runs across the North Atlantic, also staging through Botwood.[27] No revenue from passengers or freight was involved, but, as in the case of BOAC, the experience gained would place these airlines in a strong competitive position after the war. Consequently, for reasons of prestige, as well as in consideration of what would be at stake in postwar commercial concessions, the urge for TCA to spread its wings over the Atlantic was great.

This could be done in one of two ways. One was for TCA to operate one or two of the Liberators of the Return Ferry Service in association with BOAC, already accepted in principle. The other was to take up Massey's suggestion and form a distinctive Canadian service. Anxious to get a foot in the door, and convinced that the Americans were no longer in a position to complain if TCA showed the flag on the Atlantic, Howe pursued both policies at the same time. On 27 May, in informal discussions with Balfour, he asked what the British reaction would be if Canada acquired some Douglas DC-4s and put them into service between Canada and the United Kingdom. Whether Howe was in earnest, or merely engaging in wishful thinking, it is difficult to tell. However, both he and Balfour must have known that it was most unlikely that TCA could obtain any DC-4s, among the largest and most sophisticated transports produced in the United States during the war.[28] Pointing to the great scarcity of transport aircraft, Balfour brushed Howe's idea aside as impractical and steered the conversation towards the proposal 'that TCA should co-operate with BOAC in manning one ... and perhaps two Liberators with TCA crews.' After further discussion, it was agreed that this idea should be explored further with Bowhill and representatives of TCA. Meanwhile, Canadian officials from several interested departments met to discuss the question.[29]

Despite developments during the next month, the plan was not destined to get beyond the paper stage. By 1 June Howe and Balfour jointly decided to go ahead with the scheme and, after spelling out the broad outlines, left the details to be worked out between Symington and W.L. Runciman, director general of BOAC. TCA crews were to man two Return Ferry Service Liberators carrying TCA markings. As far as possible, passenger space would be allotted to Canadians travelling to and from the United Kingdom. However, like the Liberators operated by BOAC, they were to conform to the requirements of Ferry Command, which determined the schedules to be followed and the loads to be carried. Because they were regarded as British property, not Canadian, and remained part of the Return Ferry Service, the British agreed to accept the entire cost of the operation, including payment of the

Canadian crews.[30] In commenting on the proposed arrangement in a letter to Malcolm MacDonald, the British high commissioner in Canada, Balfour remarked: 'I shall be delighted when TCA are on the route, as it will be another concrete piece of evidence of the close working between Canada and ourselves for the war effort and will help to lay the foundation for continued post-war co-operation.'[31]

Howe, Symington, and other TCA officials viewed the agreement in a somewhat different light. For them it was neither the beginning of a new partnership nor the continuation of an old one, but simply the most convenient way of gaining entrance to the North Atlantic route. According to one official, who was otherwise not too well disposed towards the association with BOAC, 'our participation will serve a useful purpose and has to some extent placed the foot in the door with respect to things ahead.'[32] Howe entertained similar views. He felt certain that sooner or later TCA would acquire long-range transports; as he told Symington, 'When that time comes we will have the advantage of being in the trans-Atlantic business.'[33] While the Canadians saw the association with BOAC as a means to an end, this did not mean that they were closing the door on cooperation with the British. The need for such cooperation was taken for granted, but in the Canadians' view it must take a form that would leave them free to make their own policy decisions, particularly in regard to the United States, whose air relationship with Canada was becoming increasingly complex.

Notwithstanding the apparent desires of Howe and Balfour to implement the agreement, it never got off the ground, the only positive achievement being the training of three TCA crews by Ferry Command. Bowhill, a key figure in the arrangement, professed a desire to make it work, yet continued to feel that it would be criticized by the Americans and might impair the good relationship he had so carefully nurtured with Lieutenant General Harold George, commander of the USAAF's Air Transport Command.[34] The British ferry commander was 'a little perturbed' by rumours that TCA, which according to the agreement were to operate under his general orders in the same manner as BOAC, 'are trying to work up a complete little unit of their own and say what passengers they will carry, what freight they will carry, and that any Canadian officials should travel by them.'[35]

Bowhill, who did not like BOAC putting its distinctive markings on its Liberators or showing the flag in any way, also objected to the display of TCA insignia. He made it clear that planes allotted to TCA would not be Canadian-owned, but were to be pooled with other Liberators at his disposal. On the other hand, the Canadians were somewhat disillusioned to learn that the so-called TCA Liberators would not necessarily be flown by Canadian aircrew or made available for Canadian passengers.[36] Although overseas air mail for Canadian forces had not yet become an issue, Massey was disappointed to learn that only a limited amount of troop mail would be carried, 300 pounds on flights to the United Kingdom and none at all on the return journey.[37]

On 21 October 1942 Howe brought the question of Canada's participation in the Return Ferry Service before a meeting of the Cabinet War Committee, where he put on record 'that the United Kingdom would do nothing to meet our needs. They insisted upon control over all presently available [aircraft] space and had, so far, refused to allocate planes for operation by Canadian crews.' He added, 'This was most unsatisfactory, both as regards present and post-war needs.' Consequently, in a proposal approved by the committee, Howe recommended that Canada take unilateral action to establish a government-operated transatlantic air service to carry Canadian personnel and Canadian mail between Canada and the United Kingdom. He was optimistic that three aircraft, enough to make a beginning, could be obtained from the United States.[38]

As it developed, Howe's confidence about procuring American transport aircraft was misplaced. When none were available, the British came to the rescue. Although they often appeared to be thwarting Canadian aspirations for a position on the North Atlantic air route, British authorities on this occasion paved the way for TCA to make its long-delayed debut in transatlantic aviation by making available a retired Lancaster bomber – a gesture that reflects the curious complexities and contradictions in the Commonwealth relationship. The aircraft in question was Lancaster III R5727, used on operations by 44 Squadron of the RAF and flown to Canada in August 1942 by the veteran Ferry Command captain Clyde Pangborn for demonstration in North America.[39] It was scheduled to be returned to the United Kingdom, but Howe, after trying unsuccessfully to purchase transport aircraft south of the border, asked permission for it to remain in Canada for the use of TCA. Welcoming the opportunity to have the transport potential of the Lancaster fully explored, the Air Ministry and the Ministry of Aircraft Production gave their consent. In March 1943, after Victory Aircraft in Toronto removed military equipment, the plane was used to move freight to Goose Bay. The success of this operation and other experimental flights prompted Howe to have the aircraft further modified to carry passengers and mail to the United Kingdom. With the minister of munitions and supply aboard, R5727 was flown back to Britain in May for modification by its original manufacturers. New engines, long-range fuel tanks, and a more pointed plywood nose gave it a cruising range of 4000 miles. Now designated TCA-100, on completion of the work, R5727 was registered as CF-CMS.[40]

On 16 June 1943 Howe rose in the House of Commons and announced the immediate establishment of a Canadian government wartime air link with Britain: 'The new war service is not a commercial or a permanent one. It will carry no fare paying passengers. Space on the aircraft will be allotted by the deputy minister of transport in Ottawa; space on the aircraft westward by the Canadian high commissioner in London.'[41] Bowhill, who had cooperated with Howe by providing airmen to ferry R5727, now returned the TCA pilots trained by Ferry Command to help the new Canadian venture put together a cadre of experienced crews.[42]

Pilots, of course, were not enough; qualified navigators were particularly hard to find for this line of work. In order to start the service, arrangements were made for the RCAF to 'loan to T.C.A. three first class navigators until they can train their own men and qualify them for Trans-Atlantic work.'[43] The three originally posted to TCA were Flying Officers J.R. Gilmore and D.S. Florence and Flight Lieutenant B. Priestman. In early October, Priestman was returned to Ferry Command and replaced with Pilot Officer H.F. Thomas. After considerable discussion about how to handle pay and allowances, as well as any possible liability or pension claims, the navigators were posted to No. 3 Training Command for duty with TCA. Even before all the details were finalized for these arrangements, TCA-100 made the inaugural flight of the Canadian Government Trans-Atlantic Air Service on 22 July 1943 carrying a handful of passengers and several thousand pounds of mail from Montreal to Prestwick.[44]

Two more Lancasters, transport versions of the Canadian-built Lancaster X, were obtained in the fall, and another four were added in the final year of the war.[45] These aircraft, one of which was lost, were manned by TCA pilots and radio officers, with navigators supplied by the RCAF. They maintained a schedule of three round trips a week and in 1944 carried one million pounds of mail and 2000 passengers between Canada and the United Kingdom. Canada's decision to go ahead with its own air service elicited neither surprise nor objections from the British, even though it cast doubt on their plans for a British-

Canadian partnership in transatlantic operations after the war. At the time, they accepted Howe's explanation that the Canadian Government Trans-Atlantic Air Service was not permanent, but simply an essential part of Canada's military effort – which indeed it was. The temporary nature of this venture was illustrated by its stationery: throughout its brief history it used Trans-Canada Air Lines letterhead, with 'Canadian Government Trans-Atlantic Air Service' added by the same typewriter on which each letter was typed.[46] Still, both sides recognized that the small fleet of Lancasters was evidence of the Canadian government's intention, as the House of Commons was informed, 'to press vigorously for a place in international air transportation consistent with Canada's geographical position and progress in aviation.'[47]

As Howe had surmised, and contrary to earlier British prognostications, the Americans raised no objection to the appearance of TCA on the North Atlantic route. Indeed, with three of their own civil carriers operating across the North Atlantic in conjunction with the USAAF's Air Transport Command, they had no cause for complaint. Moreover, at the time the Canadian Government Trans-Atlantic Air Service was inaugurated, and for some months before, the governments of Canada, the United Kingdom, and the United States, and those of other countries as well, were carefully studying the whole question of international air transport and its postwar organization. With the need for intergovernmental discussions generally accepted, no nation was prepared to press its views too forcefully, despite the suspicious way they viewed one another's air transport operations.

The development and growth of military transport during the war is reflected in the expansion of the RCAF. There is no need for a detailed look here in what is essentially a discussion of the British ferry service. Suffice it to say that, at the start of the war, the Canadian air force had no transport aircraft of any size. The only unit devoted to transport duties used light passenger planes to fly senior staff officers between Ottawa and the various commands.[48] The heavy transport needs of the BCATP and the RCAF's Home War Establishment were adequately met by rail and road communications. However, when the RCAF accepted the responsibility for the construction of an airfield at Goose Bay, it was faced with an entirely different situation. Much of the required material could be taken in by water but, from the onset of winter until the heavy shore ice disappeared in late spring or early summer, the site was accessible only by air. To keep the base operational and to continue the construction program, Air Force Headquarters estimated that 80,000 pounds of freight would have to be flown in every week. The responsibility fell to the RCAF, though the USAAF's Air Transport Command and RAF Ferry Command kept the cargoes moving until the Canadians were in a position to do the job.[49]

The RCAF formed a special unit for the purpose. No. 164 Squadron was so successful that another, No. 165, was created for similar transport duties in Western Air Command. The expertise gained in these operations, and by many RCAF aircrew with Ferry Command, allowed Canada to expand its own international transport service with the formation of 168 Squadron in the fall of 1943, when the buildup of Canadian forces overseas brought an increasing demand for improved mail delivery. Starting with used USAAF Flying Fortresses and later adding Liberators and Dakotas, No. 168 (or Bomber Mail as it was nicknamed) delivered over 125 million letters to Canadians in the United Kingdom and operational theatres before it was disbanded in March 1946. The regular and speedy movement of mail between service personnel overseas and their families and friends at home was an immeasurable boost to morale.[50]

The RCAF's bomber-mail squadron established a reputation for safe and reliable transport both at home and among the countries of Europe, while assuming a burden that may otherwise have at least partially been thrust upon Ferry Command. Along with the Canadian Government Trans-Atlantic Air Service, it was Canada's main flag carrier on international routes, and continued flying after the end of hostilities until TCA was able to complete the change from a quasi-military service to a full-fledged commercial operation. Most of the flying done by 168 Squadron was of the workhorse variety, but a tone of sophistication crept into its operations, as it did into virtually all air travel by the late stages of the war. One of its Liberators, No. 574, was modified to provide government dignitaries and high-ranking military officers with a standard of comfort commensurate with that offered by the RAF, USAAF, and civilian airlines. Prime Minister King was pleased with this aircraft, which he used to travel to the United Nations' Conference in June 1945 and which he found 'met every requirement of comfort and convenience.'[51]

By the end of the war in Europe, almost five years had elapsed since the ferrying of the first Hudsons across the North Atlantic in November 1940. Forced along by the stimulus of war, air transport between North America and Europe had matured rapidly. Even before the conflict was over, flights across the Atlantic were being carried out with a degree of regularity and safety and in numbers scarcely thought possible by the pioneers of the 1930s. From Montreal a well-regulated network of airways – a veritable ocean bridge – reached out across the North and South Atlantic, the Pacific, and to virtually all parts of the world. Established to transport bombers to air battlefronts, the transoceanic airways and the chain of ground facilities that served them were now available for peaceful purposes in the postwar world.

All involved in wartime ferry and transport operations – from government officials to the airmen themselves – realized that the change from war to peace would bring new problems as well as new opportunities. During the war, long-range air transport had emerged as a new force in national policy. How to avoid cut-throat competition, how to obtain the maximum benefits from international aviation with minimum international restrictions, how to reconcile the principle of freedom of the air with the demands of national sovereignty and independence were questions given serious consideration by the Allied nations while the war still raged.

Mackenzie King offered the first concise statement of the Canadian approach to these problems in April 1943. The prime minister directed the attention of the House of Commons to the 'remarkable expansion of Canadian aviation' and to the country's unique location 'that will enable us to play an important part in the development of international air transport routes.' Understandably, he said that, for the present, military considerations took precedence over everything else and 'by agreement with our allies military transport in the northwest had been undertaken by the United States Army and in the northeast by the ferry commands.' Looking to the future, he gave assurances of the government's intention at the end of the war to terminate 'all concessions and privileges that have been granted by Canada as part of the war effort.' Stressing the basic theme of Canadian war aviation policy, he said, 'We are determined, however, that our influence in the course of events will be in the direction of international co-operation and collaboration.'[52]

King apparently intended his speech to give some indication of the approach the government planned to take at forthcoming discussions to be held in the United Kingdom and the United States on postwar aviation problems. Its main thrust, however, was directed towards allaying fears arising from the American penetration of Canadian air space, particularly in the northwest corner of the country embracing the northern parts of Alberta and British Columbia as well as the Yukon Territory. In this area, as King explained to the House of Commons, the American military had been given free use of the Northwest Staging Route, a chain of airfields reaching from Edmonton, Alberta, to Fairbanks, Alaska, an air distance of about 1700 miles.[53]

Although Ferry Command had nothing to do with this airway, it must be mentioned here because activities in the west eventually impinged on those in the eastern part of North America. Decisions made by US and Canadian commanders in the west and the northwest came to have an effect on transcontinental and transoceanic flying during the last stages of the war and ultimately contributed to the postwar systems and procedures adopted internationally by civil aviation authorities.

Canadians found it easy to believe that their neighbours from the south were seeking to entrench themselves permanently in certain parts of the dominion. For example, American behaviour in parts of the north – particularly the northwest – convinced many Canadian officials that this was indeed the case. Vincent Massey, who from his distant post in the United Kingdom kept his own watch on events in Canada, confided to his diary: 'The American government clearly have in mind the use of the air routes for commercial purposes. All they have to do is to repaint their planes and change the clothes of their crews and they will have their civil routes in being directly peace is declared.'[54]

Feeling it necessary to dispel such fears, King had already made a brief statement in the House of Commons on 1 February 1943 on the status of the American military undertakings in Canada. He pointed out that the arrangements were properly authorized by an exchange of notes as part of the program of wartime cooperation between the two countries and did not give the United States 'any continuing rights in Canada after the conclusion of the war. Indeed, in regard to most of the projects … agreements have already been made which make the post-war position completely clear.'[55]

One of the agreements to which Mackenzie King referred was the 28th recommendation of the Permanent Joint Board on Defence, approved by the Canadian and US governments on 27 January 1943. Introduced by the Canadian section of the board, the recommendation dealt with the disposition of facilities established by the Americans or constructed for them by the Canadian government. The relative ease with which agreement was reached suggests that considerations of residual

American rights entered into the deliberations in a very minor way, if at all. In general terms the recommendation specified that permanent defence installations constructed by the United States in Canada would revert to the Crown within one year of the end of hostilities. The Americans had the option of selling movable facilities to Canada or removing them to the United States. Details were handled through an exchange of notes between the two governments delineating the reimbursements due to the United States for permanent improvements to airfields in the northwest. The agreement was later extended to the rest of Canada, as well as to Goose Bay in Labrador.[56]

Although the Americans were quite willing, even anxious, to terminate their air operations in Canada as quickly as possible after the war, there was no doubt in the minds of Canadians that their neighbour would press for new concessions in the postwar period. As a result of the war, the impact of long-range aviation on the future Canadian-American defence relationship stood out clearly. The air approaches to Canada from the north, northeast, and northwest were also air approaches to the United States. The air bases that served them, particularly those along the Northwest Staging Route, Goose Bay, and, to a lesser extent, the Crimson Route in the northeast, remained of strategic importance to the United States. The significance of the situation was carefully examined by the Advisory Committee on Post Hostilities Problems set up in December 1943 as part of the machinery designed to keep the Cabinet War Committee informed about the anticipated new situation in the postwar world and to facilitate the requisite policy planning. In a report submitted on 23 January 1945, the PHP Committee observed that 'the possibility ... of the United States being moved to exert undue pressure on Canada, particularly as respects matters of defence, should not be overlooked.'[57]

Mackenzie King appears to have felt uneasy about the future air relationship with the United States. Notwithstanding his reassuring words to the House of Commons, he revealed an altogether different attitude in a private conversation with Vincent Massey approximately a year later. The prime minister, the distinguished diplomat recalled,

raised the subject of future relations between the USA and Canada and spoke apprehensively of the process of disentanglement which must follow when the Americans must withdraw and leave us in full control of our own bases and their wartime installations. The P.M. showed that he had grave doubts as to whether the international agreements on this which Canada had secured from the United States provide any practical guarantee against the United States' claims and pretensions. When I suggested that the Americans although undoubtedly friendly, did not take us seriously enough as a nation, King said that Canadians were looked upon by Americans as a lot of Eskimos. This was a striking observation made by a man who had been so often accused of being subservient to American policy.[58]

Mackenzie King apparently spoke more from emotion than from intellect, and may well have been playing up to the anglophile inclinations of Massey. There can be little doubt, however, that the scale of American air activity in Canada during the war had made a deep impression on his mind.

A more positive result that came about from the proliferation of American aircraft on Canadian airways was the standardization of rules and regulations on matters essential to the orderly movement of aircraft. The wisdom of such an arrangement is obvious enough in view of the volume of air traffic between the two countries; it would undoubtedly have developed in its own time had it not been fostered by pressures built up during the war. On the whole, the differences between American and Canadian procedures were not great, but they were magnified by the rapid growth of aviation during the early war years. When large numbers of aircraft were involved, most of them flown by newly trained pilots, the differences could be confusing and hazardous. With all the North American flying done by Ferry Command, it both contributed to the problem and benefited from the solution.

At the start of the war, air traffic control in Canada was the responsibility of the Department of Transport. However, with the massive increase in the number of military aircraft and military operations, the RCAF became more and more involved. In the summer of 1942 the Department of Transport and the Department of National Defence for Air reached agreement on plans for a system of control embracing military and civil procedures. As a result, the RCAF opened a school of flying control at Patricia Bay, British Columbia.[59]

The problem of coordinating Canadian and American military traffic appears to have been tackled first in the west. Although the idea of a unified command of the Pacific Coast region had been turned down by the Canadian government, military cooperation was facilitated by the 22nd recommendation of the PJBD, agreed to on 20 December 1941 and approved by the US government four days later and by Ottawa on 14 January 1942. The purpose of the recommendation was to decentralize defence functions to the command level, a measure apparently deemed desirable by the urgency of the situation following the Japanese attack on Pearl Harbor and by the distance of the Canadian and American commands from their respective parent headquarters. Accordingly, the regional commanders were authorized 'to effect by mutual agreement any arrangements they deemed necessary ... for the common defense including but not limited to, the installations of accessory equipment in the territory of either, the transit of armed forces, equipment or defence materials into or through the territory of either, and the utilization by either nation of the base and military facilities of the other.'[60]

With these terms of reference as a guide, the RCAF's Western Air Command, Western Defence Command of the US Army, and the US Navy shared the air defence of the west coast of North America. Under the shadow of Pearl Harbor, there was little difficulty in reaching agreement on the need to set up an interlocking system of air patrols, to provide protection for vulnerable points, and to make the air forces of Canada and the United States mutually supporting. The commands exchanged information on such matters as aircraft routing, codes and call signs, meteorological services, and flight procedures. Cooperation, at first effected through oral and written communications between operational headquarters and an exchange of liaison officers, proceeded in piecemeal fashion.[61]

Gradually the focus of attention shifted from purely defensive measures to transport operations. The first important step was an agreement signed on 6 November 1942 between Western Air Command of the RCAF and Northwest Sea Frontier of the US Navy to establish 'procedures, methods and communications to be used jointly by the two commands.'[62] The agreement contained instructions on methods to be adhered to in preparing flight plans, briefing pilots, and dispatching aircraft in the two commands. This was followed by another more comprehensive agreement involving Western Air Command, Northwest Sea Frontier, Western Defence Command, and Air Transport Command of the USAAF. Signed on 1 February 1943, it came into effect on the 15th. Known as the JAN-CAN (Joint Army, Navy-Canadian) Agreement, it was perpetuated by a JAN-CAN Committee that met regularly to study and analyse existing procedures in order to provide for fuller coordination of the movements of Canadian and American aircraft in the western command areas. It stressed the urgent necessity of improving the quality of flight control along all routes and at all stations. It

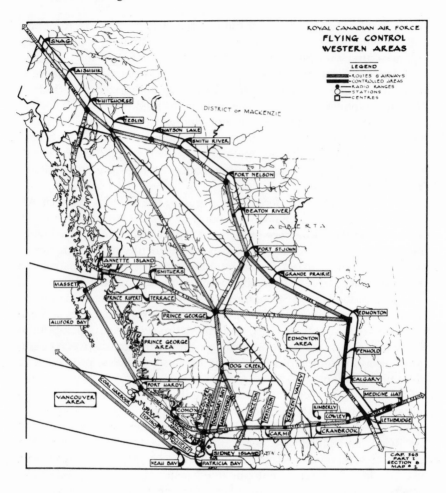

urged that this should be done through 'a single centralized traffic control agency,' but stopped short of designating an agency to accept the responsibility.[63]

Working at the command level hindered the JAN-CAN Committee in its efforts to coordinate air traffic. For example, the agreement applied to the route through the BC interior but not to the Northwest Staging Route, which came under the jurisdiction of No. 4 Training Command of the RCAF (despite its primary user being the USAAF to ferry aircraft for the Soviets and supplies to Alaska). Both these routes were used extensively by American aircraft; the anomaly reflects the problems that were developing in the control of Canadian airways and airports.

The progress made by the JAN-CAN Committee was favourably received in Ottawa. Looking forward to an important role in postwar civil aviation, as evidenced by the prime minister's statement in the House of Commons in April, the Canadian government was anxious to establish full control over its airways. The Northwest Staging Route was the main trouble spot. Since it was intended to be used primarily for military purposes, the RCAF had assumed the control function from the Department of Transport in October 1942. This change in responsibility from civilian to military authority brought little, if any, improvement. Flight plans were not always properly filed, aircraft en route frequently went unreported, and when reported could not be identified. All concerned were aware of the need for improvement, but the Canadians wanted to avoid the embarrassment of asking the Americans to control the airways, even as an interim measure.[64]

Ottawa developed a plan that was simply an enlargement of the JAN-CAN Agreement. The most significant point had the RCAF taking over the principal Department of Transport facilities at Vancouver and Edmonton and assuming control over the airways in Western Air Command as well as the Northwest Staging Route. In other words, the RCAF became the controlling authority advocated by the JAN-CAN Committee. Despite the apprehension of some civilian officials that this might herald a return to the days before 1935 when the RCAF regulated all air movements in the country, the Department of Transport supported the changes.[65]

The significance to our story of these seemingly tangential arrangements in the west becomes clear when we see the agreements developed there widened to include other areas in which the Canadians and Americans had to cooperate to control air movements. The scheme first developed on the Pacific Coast was soon extended to the east.

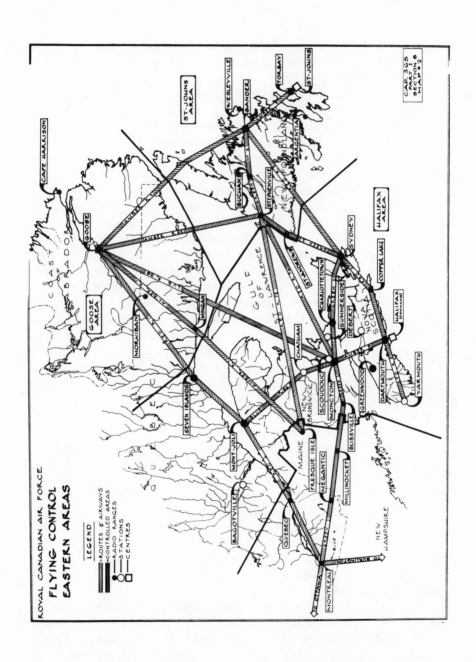

In August 1943 a committee composed of Canadian and American air force personnel and Department of Transport officials considered the way in which the type of cooperation found in the west could be adopted throughout the northern half of the continent. The committee, chaired by Air Vice-Marshal N.R. Anderson, senior air staff officer at Air Force Headquarters and earlier in the war air officer commanding Eastern Air Command, met under the jurisdiction of the Permanent Joint Board on Defence. Its report occasioned the board's 32nd recommendation, approved by both countries in September. The recommendation dealt mainly with the question of control, maintenance, and defence of airfields in the Canadian north, control in this case referring to administrative responsibilities as well as the direction of air traffic. Although recognition was given to the principle that the main user should be generally responsible for the airfield in question, it is not surprising that the Northwest Staging Route remained under Canadian jurisdiction. Eight flight strips along the Alaska Highway, fifteen others related to the Canol oil pipeline project from Norman Wells to Whitehorse, plus those on the Crimson Route in the Northeast, all used almost exclusively by the Americans, were to be controlled in all respects by the USAAF.[66]

The most significant feature of the recommendation, however, was a clause which provided 'that regulations applicable to airway and airport traffic control shall be prepared jointly by the using services.' This clause gave rise to many important questions that became the subject of discussion for the rest of the war. While the main recommendation was still in draft form, a subcommittee of RCAF officers and Department of Transport officials, headed by Wing Commander Z.L. Leigh, commanding officer of the awkwardly named Directorate of Air Transport Command at Air Force Headquarters, met in Ottawa. After reviewing the existing problems of air traffic control in Canada, it prepared a new draft of procedures and reached agreement on the transfer of authority over airways in Eastern and Western Air Commands from the Department of Transport to the RCAF for the duration of the war.[67]

American authorities then examined the work of Leigh's subcommittee to ensure that airway traffic control procedures were identical for Canada and the United States. The RCAF promulgated the amended draft as CAP (Canadian Air Publication) 365, 'Regulations for the Control of Aircraft Movements in Canada.' In December 1943 it became effective in the operational areas of Eastern and Western Air Commands and was issued to American agencies using Canadian airways. However, there was a delay in gaining the full advantage of the new regulations. In Eastern Air Command, new control centres were required at

Goose Bay, Halifax, and St John's, which, owing to the shortage of the complex communications equipment used in airway control systems, were not completed until the war was nearly over.[68]

Although not involved in the negotiations, the British welcomed the introduction of a uniform set of procedures in Eastern Air Command. Not only would this promote safety and efficiency, it would also strengthen the hold of Canada, and thus of the Commonwealth, on Goose Bay and Gander. Still, the fear of the British and the Canadians that their ally would dominate these two strategically located airports was not dispelled until the United States withdrew its forces at the end of the war.[69]

In February 1944 the RCAF gave official notice to No. 45 Group of the RAF and to Air Transport Command of the USAAF of its intention to take over control of all airports in the Atlantic area, with the exception of those on the Crimson Route. At the same time it requested that the regulations previously laid down by the Joint Control Committee be amended to comply with CAP 365, where the North Atlantic routes merged with the control zones of Eastern Air Command. The RCAF also asked for representation on the Joint Control Committee. With the acceptance of these proposals, Canada achieved complete control over its own airways and at last stood as an equal partner with the United States and the United Kingdom on the North Atlantic routes. The RCAF emerged from the negotiations as the controlling authority on Canadian airways, responsible for regulating the movements of all civil and military aircraft.[70]

The Canadian-American cooperation in air traffic control had a sequel of worldwide significance. In early February 1945 at the Trans-Atlantic Air Control Board, a new name given to the Joint Control Committee, the USAAF proposed that air regulations based on the Canadian-American system be adopted for the North Atlantic and other world routes. Canada's support of this proposal, accepted in spite of some opposition from the British, who understandably favoured their own procedures, was in keeping with the policy of the government in regard to the control of international aviation. In explaining the Canadian position in March 1944, Howe emphasized: 'It is obvious that air regulations dealing with such matters as traffic rules, safety and navigational aids should be as nearly as possible, uniform throughout the whole world and that an international authority must be set up and given the power to prepare regulations which would be accepted as standard by the members of that authority.'[71]

Because of its strategic location in respect to transatlantic air routes and its ranking among the air powers of the world, Canada exerted considerable influence in the discussions and conferences leading up to the formation of the Provisional International Civil Aviation Organization. The choice of Montreal as the location for PICAO's headquarters is a tribute to the part Canada played in bringing the organization into existence and also to the key role that the city played during the war as headquarters for the worldwide network of air routes developed by the British ferry service. One of the major Canadian contributions was in the development of a universal system of air traffic control. Since a proposal by the United States was more likely to be regarded with suspicion, it fell to Canada to argue the merits of the Canadian-American system. Although most countries were reluctant to give up their own diverse practices, the Canadian proposal, with some changes, was accepted for international air routes, and Canadians went on to play a significant part in the improvement of practices and procedures in international aviation.[72]

While steps were being taken to extend the Canadian-American system of traffic control to the air routes of the world, 45 Group continued to deliver aeroplanes overseas. As the war dragged on into 1945, many of the staff, particularly the civilians, grew restless. This was increasingly the case as it became obvious that not all the aircraft deposited on the other side were desperately needed. Taffy Powell admits: 'It was quite clear by early 1945 that the aircraft ferrying race had been run on both the north and south Atlantic. This was in [the] sense that the urgency had gone. Nothing damaged the moral and enthusiasm of a ferry crew more than arriving at Prestwick, Cairo or elsewhere to find an aircraft still there that they had delivered a month or more ago and which showed no sign of being moved.'[73] At the same time, some ferry crews delivering Lancasters to Britain reportedly heard about the return of the RCAF's Lancaster squadrons to Canada and questioned the coordination of the war effort.[74]

Civilian personnel began to drift away as they succumbed to job offers of every description. Many pilots found positions with airlines or fledgling aviation companies hoping to take advantage of a postwar flying boom. Don McVicar, for example, flew for a few months with British West Indies Airways before branching out on his own. In February 1945, age, and the RAF's regulations, caught up with Sir Frederick Bowhill and he retired as air officer commanding-in-chief of Transport Command. Sir Ralph Cochrane moved from No. 5 Group of Bomber

Command to replace him at Harrow. In June, Reggie Marix followed his chief into retirement and was succeeded by Air Vice-Marshal George Beamish at Dorval. A month later Air Commodore Taffy Powell flew back to Britain with his family, relinquished his RAF commission, and started a new career in the aviation insurance industry.[75]

Jimmy Jubb had a standing job offer from an American businessman, so he felt confident in remaining at Dorval to ensure that his radio operators were all launched on their postwar careers. He remembers the winding-down period:

I had about 600 men reporting to me at that time, many in different parts of the world. These men kept coming in very spasmodically and I had made up my mind I was going to stay in Montreal until the last one arrived home and I had to sign pay slips for the civilians and, of course, the RAF took care of their people. Most of the men coming home and those currently in Montreal wanted character and recommendation letters and I also wrote those. I made arrangements also to get them back to their homes, some in the United States, some Canada and many in England. There were no parades of any kind. Of course, VJ Day was an excuse for many parties to be held, but the push was to get these people home as fast as we possibly could. Senior RAF officers were there one day and not the next and there was a general orderliness of helping everyone to leave and get home as promptly as possible.[76]

After all his radio operators had been returned from the staging posts through which they had been passing when hostilities ended and safely sent home, Jubb knew that his job was done. 'I recall very clearly,' he says, 'making one last trip to Dorval Airport, visited my office in Hangar #2, and there was hardly anyone at the airport and certainly no one I knew, so I closed the door, drove home and the next day moved to the United States where I already had a job waiting for me.' While 'this sounds uninteresting,' he adds, 'it is in actual fact what really happened. Great relief, great joy and I want to go home was the general feeling among the ranks, service and civilian.'[77]

After the surrender of Japan on 2 September 1945, all overseas deliveries stopped and the staff of 45 Group was rapidly reduced. BOAC, which had made more than 2000 Return Ferry Service crossings of the Atlantic on behalf of Ferry Command and 45 Group, and TCA arrivals and departures increasingly made up the bulk of the traffic at Dorval. Finally, on 15 February 1946, in a small ceremony at what had become Canada's busiest airport, the RAF ensign was officially lowered for the last time. Perhaps fittingly, photographs of the occasion reveal snow piled behind the guard of honour and the official party, in a similar manner to that described by the witnesses to an earlier small ceremony at Gander on the evening of 10 November 1940, when Don Bennett's formation of seven Hudsons was sent on its way in the first transatlantic delivery attempt. More than five years after that historic event, Air Vice-Marshal Beamish, as air officer commanding No. 45 Group of RAF Transport Command, presented a bronze plaque to Lieutenant-Commander C.P. Edwards, deputy minister of the Canadian Department of Transport, to commemorate the work done at Dorval during the war by various RAF and civilian formations. The departing AOC noted that these organizations had delivered more than 11,000 warplanes to operational theatres overseas. A local reporter commented: 'Montreal needs no bronze plaque to remember the R.A.F.T.C. for its men made the city their own. They brought something of Karachi, Cairo, Scotland, Trinidad and the Azores to homes here and the roar of their Mosquitoes and Liberators is strangely absent from the skies.'[78]

The transfer of Dorval Airport and its facilities to the Department of Transport took effect at noon on 16 February. At midnight 45 Group, the last organizational manifestation of the wartime transatlantic ferry service, officially ceased to exist.[79]

Thus ended, in rather an anticlimactic fashion, a key contribution to the Allied war effort. The more than 10,000 people involved in the enterprise,[80] whether remembering it as the Canadian Pacific Railway Air Services Department, the Atlantic Ferry Organization (or ATFERO), Ferry Command, or No. 45 Group of RAF Transport Command, carried home great pride in a good job well done. While their work had been, and would continue to be, unsung, each knew that the job had been important, even crucial, to winning the war. Hailing from virtually every belligerent Allied nation, the personnel of Ferry Command worked well together towards the common goal of delivering aircraft, supplies, and passengers where and when they were needed to help defeat the Axis Powers. The tendency of higher officials on occasion to think of national (and perhaps postwar commercial) interests was rarely demonstrated by those preparing and flying the planes. They left for new, peacetime, adventures, confident they had been part of an operation originally labelled impossible by many experts.

Long-distance flying, particularly across oceans, was in its infancy when war broke out. The most treacherous of the potential routes, that over the North Atlantic, had not been flown in the fall or winter. And, even in the summer months, it had only been conquered by the most experienced of aviators. The pioneers of the ferry service and the 'one-trippers' of Ferry Command and 45 Group had proven the feasibility and practicability of transatlantic flying. In so doing they had delivered desperately needed warplanes to the battlefronts of the world. They had also carried important freight and passengers over many airways that they helped open up around the globe. They had, in fact, done their small part to revolutionize modern warfare. After their unsung contribution to victory, military commanders could not ignore long-range air transport in their strategic and tactical planning.

The contribution of the ferry service, in spite of its bewildering changes in organization, cannot be measured solely by the 10,000 aircraft delivered across the oceans of the world. Its value lies as much in the transformation of the Atlantic route, pioneered before the war, into an airway for the mass movement of bombers, reconnaissance aircraft, and transports and the development of the concept of long-range strategic air supply which the Allies employed so effectively in every theatre of the war.

At the same time, the routes flown to deliver planes and *matériel*, and the meteorological, communications, and control procedures established in the process, formed the basis of the international grid of civil air routes throughout the world. During the Second World War, the military air transport services developed the routes and procedures that evolved into the postwar aviation systems we all take for granted. We not only owe the veterans of Ferry Command our thanks for the part they played in winning the war, but also for helping to lay the foundations of today's worldwide aviation network.

Aircraft Delivered: CPR Air Services Department, ATFERO, Ferry Command, and No. 45 Group

TYPE	PRINCIPAL RAF USER COMMAND(S)
Avro Lancaster	Bomber Command
Boeing B-17 Flying Fortress	Bomber and Coastal Commands
Consolidated PBY Catalina	Coastal
Consolidated Coronado	Transport
Consolidated B-24 Liberator	Coastal
De Havilland Mosquito	Bomber and Fighter
Douglas DB-7 Boston	Middle East and Bomber
Douglas DC-3 Dakota	Transport
Douglas DC-4/C-54 Skymaster	Transport
Lockheed Electra	Transport
Lockheed Hudson	Coastal
Lockheed Lodestar	Transport
Lockheed Ventura	Bomber and Transport
Martin A-30 Baltimore	Middle East
Martin B-26 Marauder	Middle East
Martin PBM-3 Mariner	Coastal
North American B-25 Mitchell	Middle East and Bomber

Losses: CPR Air Services Department, ATFERO, Ferry Command, and No. 45 Group

In the absence of any definitive listing or statistical summary, it has generally been accepted that two to three hundred airmen lost their lives flying with Ferry Command. A careful check of the crew assignment cards, unit diaries, incomplete accident files, and other related records has revealed that the figure is over five hundred. It grows to approximately 560 if passengers in the command's aircraft are included. The names of individuals identified as killed during service or travel with Ferry Command are noted in the following chronological list of crashes and disappearances. Given that many delivery aircraft flew during the night, and also that losses were often recorded several days after the event, numerous small discrepancies occur in the precise dates of occurrences.[1]

DATE/ PLANE	NAME/SERVICE/ NATIONALITY	SEAT	REMARKS
19 Feb. 41 Hudson T9450	Leigh Allyn Jackson, Am civilian Sherman H. McCaughan, Cdn civ	Pilot RO	St Hubert (training flight?), possibly 1 additional fatality
20 Feb. 41 Hudson T9449	P/O William Bird, RAF William Snailham, Cdn civ Maj Sir Frederick Banting, Cdn	Pilot RO Pass	Nr Musgrave Harbour, Nfld [radio operator] [passenger]
25 July 41 Hudson AE640	F/L Keith Fergus Arnold, RAF (Cdn) Sgt Percy Keast, RAF Wilfred Bratherton, Cdn civ	Pilot Nav RO	Crash, Mull of Kintyre [navigator]
3 Aug. 41 Hudson AE657	Alfred James Williams, Br civ Frank George Godfrey, Cdn civ	Pilot RO	Crash, Moncton, NB

DATE/ PLANE	NAME/SERVICE/ NATIONALITY	SEAT	REMARKS
10 Aug. 41 Liberator AM261	Josiah James Anderson, Cdn civ Francis Delaforce Bradbrooke, Cdn civ Daniel Joseph Duggan, Am civ Watt Miller King, Am civ George Thomas Harris, Am civ Hoyt Ralph Judy, Am civ John Evan Price, Aus civ John James Roulstone, Am civ Harold Clifford Wesley Smith, Cdn civ Ernest Robert Bristow White, Br civ Jack Wixen, Am civ Ralph Bruce Brammer, Cdn civ John Beatty Drake, Cdn civ Henry Samuel Green, Br civ Wilfred Graves Kennedy, Cdn civ George Laing, Cdn civ Hugh Cameron McIntosh, Cdn civ William Kenneth Marks, Cdn civ Albert Alexander Oliver, Br civ George Herbert Powell, Br civ Herbert David Rees, Br civ Ernest George Reeves, Am civ	Pilot Pilot Pilot Pilot Pilot Pilot Pilot Pilot Pilot Pilot Pilot RO RO RO RO RO RO RO RO RO RO FE	Return Ferry Service crash, Isle of Arran, off west coast of Scotland [flight engineer]
14 Aug. 41 Liberator AM260	Elbert Beard Anding, Am civ Murray Benjamin Dilley, Am civ Alton Chester Earl, Am civ Edward Hamel, Am civ Gerald Hull, Am civ John Joseph Kerwin, Am civ Philip Francis Lee Jr, Am civ James John Moffat, Cdn civ Richard Charles Stafford, Br civ Walter L. Trimble, Am civ Earl Wellington Watson, Am civ Martin Joseph Wetzel, Am civ Richard Coates, Cdn civ Joseph Patrick Culbert, Br civ Robert Arnold Duncan, Cdn civ Wesley Francis James Goddard, Cdn civ Donald Norman Hannant, Cdn civ John Joseph MacDonald, Cdn civ Glenwood McKay, Cdn civ	Pilot Pilot Pilot Pilot Pilot Pilot Pilot Pilot Pilot Pilot Pilot Pilot RO RO RO RO RO RO RO	Return Ferry Service crash, Ayr, Scotland

DATE/ PLANE	NAME/SERVICE/ NATIONALITY	SEAT	REMARKS
	Albert Tamblin, Cdn civ	RO	
	Roland Fulford Davis, Am civ	FE	USN Reserve pilot
	Arthur B. Purvis, Cdn civ	Pass	Head, Br Purchasing Commission
1 Sept. 41	Kenneth Garden, Aus civ	Pilot	Crash, near Campbeltown,
Liberator	Geoffrey Llewellyn Panes, Br civ	Pilot	Kintyre, Scotland
AM915	Samuel Walter Sydenham, Cdn civ	RO	
	Charles Alvan Spence, Am civ	FE	
	Dr Benjamin	Pass	
	Count De Bailler-Letour	Pass	
	Professor Mowatt	Pass	
	Capt Pickering	Pass	
	E. Taylor	Pass	
	Col Wrongham	Pass	
21 Sept. 41	F/L R.F. Leavitt, RAF (Cdn)	Pilot	Lost out of Gander
Hudson	Sgt Elwood Wallace McFall,		
AE545	RCAF	Nav	
	Robert Desmond Anderson, Cdn civ	RO	
27 Sept. 41	F/O Harold Wilson Oldham,		
Hudson	RCAF	Pilot	Lost out of Gander
AM940	Sgt William Ronald Lance, RCAF	Nav	
	Cyril Harvey Small, Nfld civ	RO	
27 Sept. 41	F/L Louis Romeo Dubuc, RCAF	Pilot	Crash, Dundalk, Eire
Hudson	Sgt Frederick James Goodwin,		
AE577	RAF	Nav	
	Samuel Raymond Kenny, Cdn civ	RO	
11 Oct. 41	William James Guy, Br civ	Pilot	Lost out of Gander
Hudson	William Allen Herron, Am civ	Pilot	
AM951	Clinton Lloyd Larder, Cdn civ	RO	
9 Jan. 42	F/L James Lee Mitchell,		
Hudson	RCAF (Am)	Pilot	Lost out of Gander
V9125	P/O Keith Percival Squire O'Donnell, RAF (Aus)	Nav	
	Sgt Francis Garrity RAF (Cdn)	RO	
19 Jan. 42	Louis Edouard Adels, Am civ	Pilot	Lost on the SS *Lady*
	Henry Edward Fausett, Am civ	Pilot	*Hawkins,* en route to
	AC1 Edward Ernest Charles Snell, RAF	FE	Bermuda

DATE/ PLANE	NAME/SERVICE/ NATIONALITY	SEAT	REMARKS
24 Jan. 42 Hudson AM932	Baha Eldin Hosny, Egyptian civ Robert Warren Whitmore, Am civ S/L Edward Dan Chantler, RAF Horace Gayzal Meyers, Cdn civ	Pilot Pilot Nav RO	Lost out of Gander
8 April 42 Hudson FH246	Richard G. Miller, Am civ F/O William Murray, RAF Nathan Frenkelson, Cdn civ	Pilot Nav RO	Lost out of Gander
12 April 42	Frederick Andrew Matson, Am civ	Pilot	Lost, local flight, Prestwick
22 April 42 Hudson FH335	S/L Joseph Theodore Gutray, RCAF Sgt Patrick Albert Beavis, RAF Sgt Robert Richard Kember, RCAF	Pilot Nav RO	Crash, New Carlisle, Que.
25 April 42 Liberator 41-1119	G/C Herbert Reginald Carefoot, RCAF W/C Mervyn John Cameron Stanley, RAF P/O William George Jack Woodmason, RAF Leo Benedict Doherty, Cdn civ Hamish Ian Douglas, Cdn civ	Pilot Pilot Nav RO FE	Lost out of Gander
3 May 42 Ventura AE711	Leon Segal, Am civ P/O James Watson, RCAF Martino M. Paggi, Br civ	Pilot Nav RO	Crash, nr Bradore Bay, Que.
10 May 42 Hudson FH269	W/C Charles Francis Herington, RAF P/O Richard John Sotham, RNZAF P/O Alexander Rental Montgomery, RCAF	Pilot Nav RO	Lost out of Gander
10 May 42 Ventura AE740	Leonide B. Long, Cdn civ	RO	Crashed on landing, Reykjavik, Iceland; other 2 crew slightly injured

DATE/ PLANE	NAME/SERVICE/ NATIONALITY	SEAT	REMARKS

23 May 42
Hudson
FH233
	F/L James Constabaris, RCAF
	P/O Kenneth Bushbridge Dyer,
	   RAF
	Sgt Donald Eugen Engemoen,
	   RCAF
		Pilot
		
		Nav
		
		RO
			Crashed into sea nr Ire-
			land

29 May 42
Hudson
FH465
	P/O Raymond Purdy Dezall,
	   RCAF
	P/O David George Gatehouse,
	   RAF
	Sgt Arthur Scarth, RCAF
		
		Pilot
		
		Nav
		RO
			Lost out of Gander

5 July 42
Hudson
FH395
	S/L George Patterson Christie,
	   RAF (Cdn)
	W/C Brian G. Carr-Harris, RCAF
	LAC Clement Stuart Llewellyn,
	   RAF
		
		Pilot
		Pilot
		
		RO
			Crash, Lac St Louis, nr
			Montreal, during training
			flight

12 July 42 Hudson FK413	F/L Robert Denis Crofton, RAF Sgt Raymond Edgar Wylie, RCAF Sgt Elton Duncan Brabender, RAAF	Pilot Pilot RO	Lost out of Gander

15 July 42
Hudson
FH386
	F/L Hubert Hamish Gilchrist,
	   RCAF
	P/O John Basil Maitland Bryson,
	   RAF
	Sgt Thadde Ignace D'Hondt, RAF
	Sgt Raymond Earnest Mole, RAAF
	Sgt John Marshall Sales, RCAF
		
		Pilot
		
		Pilot
		Pilot
		RO
		RO
			Training flight, crashed 2
			miles NW of Dorval, Que.

22 July 42
Hudson
FH317
	F/L John Kingsley Rhodes, RAF
	Sgt Brian Joseph A. Burdon-
	   Murphy, RCAF
	Sgt John Lionel Anderson, RAAF
	Sgt Ronald Eldred Richards,
	   RAAF
	P/O Francis Gabriel McInnis,
	   RCAF
		Nav
		
		Nav
		Nav
		
		Nav
		
		RO
			Navigation training flight,
			crashed and burned nr
			Dorval

14 Aug. 42
Catalina
FP151
	QM Jens Arnold Veiersted, RNAF
	Frederick Orin Anderson,
	   Swed civ
	Harry Thomas Moores, Nfld civ
	Joseph Henry Kitchen Parker,
	   Br civ
		Pilot
		
		Pilot
		RO
		
		FE
			Crash, Cape Charles,
			Virginia, en route Eliza-
			beth City, NC, to Boucher-
			ville, Que.

DATE/ PLANE	NAME/SERVICE/ NATIONALITY	SEAT	REMARKS
17 Aug. 42 Marauder FK119	S/L Geoffrey Robinson, RAF Sgt George Frederick Lyman-Dixon, RAF P/O J.J. Doran, RCAF Gordon Henry Randle, Cdn civ	Pilot Pilot Nav RO	Lost out of Natal, Brazil
27 Aug. 42 Ventura AE917	P/O Charles De Cardonnel Findlay, RAF Sgt Rhys Maelswyn Alexander, RAF P/O John McCubbin, RAF Sgt Francis Augustine Weaver, RNZAF	Pilot Pilot Nav RO	Lost out of Gander
8 Oct. 42 Ventura AJ450	Sgt Derrick Wallsh, RAF Sgt Thomas Geoffrey Knowles, RAF Sgt Dennis Frederick John Jupp, RAF Sgt John Robert Weldon Grant, RCAF	Pilot Pilot Nav RO	Lost out of Gander
14 Oct. 42 Liberator 41-23882	Thomas Leonard Livermore, Am civ William Campbell Chitty, Am civ George Frederic Johnston, Am civ Clarence Victor Atkinson, Cdn civ Charles Frederick McDougall, Cdn civ	Pilot Pilot Nav RO FE	Crash, Trinidad
15 Oct. 42 Mitchell FR369	F/L Ronald Laurence Moss, RAF P/O Francis John Pook, RAF Sgt Michael John Gardner, RAF Leonard R.J. Vine, Br civ	Pilot Pilot Nav RO	Lost out of Gander
26 Oct. 42 Boston BZ200	QM Nils Bjorn Rasmussen, RNAF	Pilot	Force-landed in a bog, 5 miles west of Crossmolina, Eire; pilot drowned after he was trapped when the plane flipped over
26 Oct. 42 Ventura AE729	Carl Frederick Kaiser, Am civ Arthur Harold Down, Cdn civ LAC D.A. Abbott, RCAF John T. Barry, Civ	Pilot RO Pass Pass	Crashed shortly after takeoff from Dorval

DATE/ PLANE	NAME/SERVICE/ NATIONALITY	SEAT	REMARKS
	LAC K.D. Campbell, RCAF	Pass	
	LAC J.F. Carr, RCAF	Pass	
	Cpl C.T. Christopherson, RCAF	Pass	
	Charles Herbert Cole, civ	Pass	
	LAC W.B. Danielson, RCAF	Pass	
	Cpl M.J. Kasey, RCAF	Pass	
	LAC B.E. Malone, RCAF	Pass	
	H.S. Millan, civ	Pass	
	Morris S. Myles, civ	Pass	
	LAC V.F. Peebles, RCAF	Pass	
	AC1 L.V. Sparkes, RCAF	Pass	
	LAC P.J. Tennant, RCAF	Pass	
11 Nov. 42 Catalina FP209	Robert Hugh Malcolm Sandeman, Br civ	Pilot	Crashed nr CNR wharf, Mulgrave, NS, on Strait of Canso, on flight from Bermuda; 2 crew survived
	P/O Stanley Frasier Fairbairn, RCAF	Nav	
	Devereux Lionel Doria DeBretigny, Cdn civ	RO	
	Sgt Norman James Cheny, RNZAF	RO	
20 Nov. 42 Baltimore FA179	John A. Morrison, Am civ	Pilot	Burst a tire taking off at Geneina, Sudan; 2 crew injured
28 Nov. 42 Hudson FK693	P/O Albert Moore Carey, RCAF	Pilot	Lost out of Gander
	Joseph Kiernan, Am civ	Pilot	
	P/O Norman Alexander Allen, RCAF	Nav	
	F/O Irwin Edward Stillwell Robinson, RCAF	RO	
3 Dec. 42 Hudson BW384	F/L John Henry Prentice, RCAF	Pilot	Crash, Halifax harbour; RCAF aircraft
	Chail, civ	Pass	
	M.R. MacCaulay, civ	Pass	
5 Dec. 42 Hudson FK687	P/O George Newell Harrison, RNZAF	Pilot	Crash, Houlton, Maine
	Sgt August Leroy R. Beckwall, RCAF	Pilot	
	Sgt Arthur Gordon B. Gibson, RCAF	Nav	
	Sgt Henry Bordewick, RCAF	RO	

DATE/ PLANE	NAME/SERVICE/ NATIONALITY	SEAT	REMARKS

5 Dec. 42
Hudson
FK690
	P/O Ronald George Stanley
	   Burrows, RAAF
	Sgt Douglas Percy Chas. Simmons,
	   RAF
	P/O Graeme Hamilton Thomson,
	   RAF
	Sgt Jack Eric Fazel, RAAF
		Pilot
		
		Pilot
		
		Nav
		RO
			Crashed and burned after
			takeoff at Gander

8 Dec. 42 Boston BZ247	Arnold Cowitz, Cdn civ P/O Raymond Reginald Hustwait, RAF Robert Leslie Abernethy, Cdn civ	Pilot Nav RO	Lost out of Gander

8 Dec. 42
Boston
BZ294
	F/L Douglas Gordon C. Chown,
	   RCAF
	P/O Kenneth Herbert Wells,
	   RCAF
		
		Pilot
		
		Nav
			Force-landed nr Benton,
			Nfld; RO survived

10 Dec. 42 Boston BZ287	F/L Svend Wessel, RNAF Sgt Orville Russell Ballantyne, RCAF	Pilot RO	Crashed during a night landing at Reykjavik; navigator survived

24 Dec. 42
Catalina
FP266
	Benson Hutches Pierce, Am civ
	Sgt Roy Harding, RAF
	Sgt Douglas Oliver Bevan, RCAF
	Sgt George Edward James Craven,
	   RAAF
	James Hamilton Auld, Cdn civ
	Sgt Reginald Edwin Thompson,
	   RAF
		Pilot
		Pilot
		Nav
		
		RO
		RO
		
		FE
			Lost out of Bermuda

30 Dec. 42 Boston BZ238	John Robert Scribbins, Am civ P/O John Robert William Craig, RCAF Sidney George Wells, Br civ	Pilot Nav RO	Missing between George- town, British Guiana, and Belem, Brazil
11 Jan. 43 Mitchell FR377	P/O Victor Lewis Martin, RCAF	RO	Crashed onto prison farm nr Jacksonville, Florida; 3 crew members survived
17 Jan. 43 USATC C-87 41-11708	F/O Geoffrey Addison Clegg, RAF Paul Blecker Makepeace, Am civ F/L Herbert James Martin, RCAF William Richard Nixon, Cdn civ	 Pilot Pilot Pilot Pilot	USAAF ATC transport disappeared over South Atlantic between Accra Gold Coast, and Natal, Brazil

DATE/ PLANE	NAME/SERVICE/ NATIONALITY	SEAT	REMARKS
	Sgt John Lowery Bell, RAF	Nav	
	P/O William Thomas Wright Smithson, RAAF	Nav	
	Sgt John Henry Warman, RCAF	Nav	
	F/O Peter Charles Zoephel, RCAF	Nav	
	Clinton Blackwell Berry, Cdn civ	RO	
	FSgt Norman Patrick Drury, RCAF	RO	
	Sgt Harold Victor Lamb, RAAF	RO	
	Otway Cecil McCombie, Cdn civ	RO	
6 Feb. 43 Catalina FP309	Samuel Howard McCawley, Am civ	Pilot	Lost out of Bermuda
	Andrew Eugene Bleau, Am civ	Pilot	
	P/O Edward Dennis Markham, RAF	Nav	
	Sgt Thomas Clarence Judiesch, RCAF	RO	
	Stephen Francis Whatmore, Br civ	RO	
	Sgt Cecil Stanley Rumble, RAF	FE	
8 Feb. 43 Hudson FH235	Sgt Antony Manderson Harris, RAF	Pilot	Training flight, crashed at Whiteface Mountain, NY, during a local snowstorm
	FSgt Ronald Charles Brooks, RCAF	RO	
9 Feb. 43 Liberator AL591	Fortune Anthony Dugan, Am civ	Pilot	Return Ferry Service crash, nr Gander; 2 survived
	Sgt James Robert Elding, RAF	Pilot	
	G.P.M. Eves, Br civ	Pilot	
	T.R. Harmes, Br civ	Pilot	
	Sgt Howell Leonard Benjamin Lewis, RAF	Pilot	
	Robert Marvin Lloyd, Am civ	Pilot	
	Sgt David Jervis Owen, RAF	Pilot	
	Sgt Graham Pritchard Pollard, RAF	Pilot	Died in hospital
	Jack Stagner, Am civ	Pilot	
	Sgt Wilton Henry Kyle, RCAF	Nav	
	P/O Robert Irving Scott, RCAF	Nav	
	Frederick Joseph Brown, Br civ	RO	
	John David Jones, Br civ	RO	
	Frederick Scrafton, Cdn civ	RO	
	Reginald Wadsworth, Br civ	RO	
	Ernest Graham Longley, Cdn civ	FE	
	J.B. Merriman, Br civ	FE	
	Ivan Wilmot Wilson, Cdn civ	FE	
	Lt-Col L.T. Grove, Br Army	Pass	

DATE/ PLANE	NAME/SERVICE/ NATIONALITY	SEAT	REMARKS

22 Feb. 43
Hudson
BW615
	John Macdonald Dame, Cdn civ
	F/O Ernest William Hyland,
	   RCAF
	Sgt Charles Baxter Simpson,
	   RCAF
	Cecil Charles Lane, NZ civ
		Pilot
		
		Nav
		
		Nav
		RO
			Crashed at Nashville,
			Tenn.

23 Feb. 43 Mitchell FR148	Donald Lee Annibal, Am civ F/O Leslie Edward Triplett, RCAF (Am) Clifford Donald Saugstad, Cdn civ	Pilot Nav RO	Lost out of Gander
10 March 43 Boston BZ385	Kenneth W. Quayle, Am civ P/O Andrew Seton Campbell, RAAF Albert Befus, Cdn civ	Pilot Nav RO	Crashed at Goose Bay, Labrador
12 March 43 Hudson FK621	F/O H.J. Crowe, RCAF	Nav	No record of other 2 crew members, who may also have perished
12 March 43 Hudson FK722	Sgt Percy Philip Fahie, RCAF FSgt G.E. Somerville F/O L.H. York	Nav RO RO	
13 March 43 Catalina FP116	Clarence Alvin 'Duke' Schiller, Cdn civ Sgt David Wilkie, RAF J.C. Ford, USAAF (rank unknown) William Bradley Collins, Nfld civ	Pilot Nav RO RO	Crash, nr Bermuda
17 March 43 Boston BZ396	Alexander Edward Dame, Cdn civ George C. Denton, Cdn civ LAC W.A. Hale, RAF	Pilot Nav RO	Test flight, crash, St Urbain de Chateauguay, Que.
18 March 43 Baltimore FA354	P/O Donald Terence Hollowell, RCAF	 Pilot	Crashed and burned on landing at Nassau
25 March 43 Baltimore FA340	Sgt Ian Simpson Glen, RAF	Pilot	Crashed and burned on landing at Nassau; rest of crew survived
28 March 43 Baltimore FA427	Elwood Palmer Walmsley, Am civ William Frederick Morris, Cdn civ	Pilot RO	Crashed and burned on takeoff at Nassau.

DATE/ PLANE	NAME/SERVICE/ NATIONALITY	SEAT	REMARKS
13 April 43 Baltimore FA314	Lennox Dale Faulkner, Cdn civ Sgt Douglas William Perry, RAF Sgt Geoffrey John Hamilton 　　Carter, RAAF	Pilot Nav RO	Crash, Georgetown, Brit- ish Guiana
19 April 43 Baltimore FA330	Jack Groover Durham, Am civ F/O John Dickson Grant, RCAF Harold Alfred Picher, Cdn civ	Pilot Nav RO	Lost out of Natal
29 April 43 Hudson FH365	Robert Venable Anderson, Am civ Albert Harris, Br civ George Somerville Thomson, 　　Br civ	Pilot Pilot RO	Stalled at low altitude and crashed at Nassau
8 May 43 Ventura AJ164	Cpl M. Maley, RAF LAC F.A. Moore	Pass Pass	Four passengers panicked and jumped from a/c when smoke entered cabin from faulty heater; 2 res- cued after 50 days in the wilderness
20 May 43 Baltimore FA520	FSgt Francis Arthur Robert 　　Milbury, RCAF Sgt Hugh Dennis George Ward, 　　RCAF	 Pilot Nav	Crashed at Georgetown, British Guiana
22 May 43 Mitchell FL209	S/L Charles Robinson Elgar, RAF M. Koshuta, USAAF (rank 　　unknown)	Pilot RO	
28 May 43 Hudson FK742	P/O Donald Eugene Woodfield, 　　RCAF P/O Andrew Fleming Lavery, 　　RAF P/O John Barber Taylor, RNZAF P/O Gordon Douglas Hay, 　　RCAF Sgt L.C. Medhurst, RAF	 Pilot Pilot Nav RO Pass	Crash, Reykjavik
30 May 43 Baltimore FA227	Henri Chouteau Jr, Am civ J.P. Lyons Cyril John Somerville, Cdn civ	Pilot Observer RO	Test flight, crashed at Nassau
22 June 43 Marauder FK129	Burton Craig Miller, Am civ Lowell Luther Burchfield, Am civ	Pilot Pilot	Crashed 35 miles W of Borinquen, Puerto Rico

DATE/ PLANE	NAME/SERVICE/ NATIONALITY	SEAT	REMARKS
	WO2 Reginald Edward Mudie, RAAF	Nav	
	Philip Arthur Vickery, Cdn civ	RO	
22 June 43 Boston BZ272	Lt Fritz W. Svenson, RNAF P/O John Everlyn Wreford Birkett, RCAF WO2 Walter Jesse Thurlow, RCAF	Pilot Nav RO	Crashed nr Mingan, Que.
24 June 43 Hudson FK442	Sgt Peter Alan Naylor, RAF P/O Donald Morrison McLennan, RCAF Sgt Edward Lloyd Barrett, RCAF	Pilot Nav RO	Crashed at Ste Agathe, Que.
11 July 43 Baltimore FA137	Sgt Richard Alderton, RAF Sgt Charles Edward Bake, RCAF	Pilot RO	Crashed during landing at Piarco, Trinidad; navigator survived
19 July 43 Mariner JX101	LAC L.L. Scott crew uninjured	Pass	Drowned when a/c sank while taxiing out for takeoff at Bermuda, because of an unsecured main hatch
6 Aug. 43 Hudson EW898	John M. Smithers, Am civ Leland Cooper Lloyd, Am civ Sgt George Stanley B. Newman, RCAF	Pilot Pilot RO	Crashed at Martintown, Ont.
7 Sept. 43 USATC C-87 41-24140	John Kilby Cummings, Am civ FSgt David Gale, RAF P/O William Alexander Gardner, RCAF P/O Eric Ogilvy Smith, RCAF Sgt John Samuel Cram, RCAF Sgt Samuel Jacob Donen, RCAF F/O John Scott MacLean, RCAF Sgt Ronald Cyrus Lounsbury, RCAF Sgt John MacRae, RCAF FSgt Erle Donald Rennick, RCAF	Pilot Pilot Pilot Pilot Nav Nav Nav RO RO RO	USAAF ATC transport, crashed at Accra, Gold Coast, West Africa
13 Sept. 43 Baltimore FW395	Sgt Donald Goodman, RAF Sgt John Leslie Edward Blake, RAF	Pilot Nav	Crash, Nassau

DATE/ PLANE	NAME/SERVICE/ NATIONALITY	SEAT	REMARKS
	FSgt Cedric Gardiner Rafuse, RCAF	RO	
17 Sept. 43 Baltimore FW377	P/O Peter Raymond Colls, RAF	Nav	Engine failed on takeoff and crashed into parked Baltimore FA114; both a/c burned out
13 Oct. 43 Marauder FB454	F/O Roland Henry Barber, RAF P/O Douglas Waitt Cormack, RCAF F/O Denis Durwood, RAF F/L John Griffith Owen, RAF	Pilot Pilot Pilot Pilot	Crash, Nassau; caught fire in the air during training flight
24 Oct. 43 Baltimore FW472	P/O Douglas James Bullock, RAF	Nav	Died after crash at Trinidad

6 Nov. 43
Mitchell
FW138
	F/O Aleksander Cezary
	    Monkiewicz, PAF
	F/O Derrick Joseph Oswald Pyne,
	    RAF
	F/L William Lionel Halperin,
	    RCAF
	F/O Stewart James Hansen, RAAF
		Pilot
		
		Pilot
		
		Nav
		RO
			Lost out of Goose Bay

7 Nov. 43
Ventura
FP647
	Leonard Sylvester Lumb, Cdn civ
	P/O John Allen Ovens, RCAF
	Eugene Gilbert Antoine Young,
	    Cdn civ
	LAC Charles Ewart Conroy,
	    RCAF
		Pilot
		Nav
		
		RO
		
		Pass
			Lost out of Trinidad
			
			Radar mechanic

8 Nov. 43 Mitchell FR203	Guy Record, Cdn civ F/O Frederick Avery Beyer, RAAF Owen Geraint Davies, Br civ	Pilot Nav RO	Lost between BW-1, Greenland, and Reykjavik, Iceland
22 Nov. 43 Ventura FP645	Amor Meade Deemer Jr, Am civ FSgt Russel Graham Wilson, RCAF WO2 Laurie Burke, RCAF LAC L. Winkler, RCAF	Pilot Nav RO Pass	Crash, Trinidad
28 Nov. 43 Mitchell FV990	2/Lt Erik Bertil Palm, RNAF Sgt Eric Hanway Swanston, RAF F/L Harold A. Wills, RCAF FSgt Gerald Raymond Styles, RCAF	Pilot Pilot Nav RO	Lost between BW-1, Greenland, and Reykjavik, Iceland

DATE/ PLANE	NAME/SERVICE/ NATIONALITY	SEAT	REMARKS

6 Dec. 43
Mitchell
FW159
	Harold Nigel Egerton Salmon,
	  Br civ
	P/O William Frederick Forster,
	  RCAF
	P/O Robert Donisthorpe Darling,
	  RAF
	F/O Eric Anthony Richardson,
	  RAAF
		Pilot
		
		Pilot
		
		Nav
		
		RO
			Lost out of Goose Bay

19 Dec. 43 Mitchell FW165	William Verne Walker, Cdn civ F/O Melvin Henry Ramsay, RCAF Allan Parker Cann, Cdn civ	Pilot Nav RO	Crash, Reykjavik

16 Jan. 44
Ventura
JT801
	Preston Krumbhaar Herndon,
	  Am civ
	F/O Robert Archie Wilkins, RCAF
	WO2 George Andrew Flood,
	  RCAF
		Pilot
		Nav
		
		RO
			Lost between Trinidad
			and Zandery Field,
			Surinam

18 Jan. 44 Dakota FZ632	P/O Thomas Davidson Thomson, RCAF	Nav	Ditched in sea 15 miles from Lagens, Azores; rest of crew saved by A/SR
1 Feb. 44 Baltimore FW640	Gene Hamilton Rowe, Am civ; other 2 crew members baled out and were rescued by USN blimp	Pilot	Crashed short of Belem after engine failure
18 Feb. 44 Baltimore FW680	Sgt Philip Clarke, RAF; other 2 crew members survived	Pilot	Crashed and burned on landing at Belem

22 Feb. 44
Baltimore
FW693
	P/O David William Whiffin,
	  RAF
	F/O Ronald Thomas Cochrane,
	  RAF
	P/O John Richard Hutchins,
	  RAAF
		Pilot
		
		Nav
		
		RO
			Lost out of Zandery Field,
			Surinam

1 March 44 Liberator BZ935	1/Lt C.M. Dorsett, USAAF 2/Lt O.E. Hess, USAAF 1/Lt G.L. McBride, USAAF SSgt J.W. Wiant, USAAF Sgt R.F. Mennig, USAAF	Pilot Pilot Nav RO? FE	Lost out of Stephenville, Nfld. No explanation has been found why this USAAF crew was flying an RAF Liberator out of a US base

DATE/ PLANE	NAME/SERVICE/ NATIONALITY	SEAT	REMARKS
5 March 44 Dakota KG396	P/O Lester James Tingle, RCAF P/O Donald Keith Nelson, RCAF P/O Philip Joseph Asseff, RCAF	Pilot Nav RO	Crash, Meeks Field, Iceland
7 March 44 Dakota KG446	Sgt James Gerard Bruen, RAF P/O Kenneth William Raper, RCAF Sgt Andrew Thorpe, RAF	Pilot Nav RO	Lost out of Reykjavik
7 March 44 Dakota FZ676	Sgt Bernard Vincent Arney, RAF P/O John Nisbet Thomson, RCAF Sgt Noel Arnold Thomas, RAF	Pilot Nav RO	Crashed into mountain, 15 miles from Reykjavik
11 April 44 Marauder HD419	Howard Cleylon Weiben, Cdn civ P/O Stanley Blackburn, RAF P/O Kenneth Frederick Probert, RCAF P/O Richard Frank Stubner, RCAF	Pilot Pilot Nav RO	Crash, Atkinson Field, Georgetown; one engine cut out on takeoff
13 April 44 Dakota KG508	Sgt Ronald Jack Uden, RAF P/O Gwilym Deinol Morris, RAF Sgt William John Poling, RAAF	Pilot Nav RO	Crashed and burned 3 miles S of Assu, Brazil, en route to Natal
25 April 44 Liberator EW148	F/O Kazamierz Burzynski, PAF P/O Andrzej Kuzniacki, PAF F/L Adolf Jan Nowicki, PAF P/O James Smith Wilson, RCAF FSgt Islwyn Jones, RAF	Pilot Pilot Nav RO FE	Crashed into tenement building in downtown Montreal, killing 10 people on the ground
8 May 44 Mosquito KB220	F/L George Henry Wood, RAF F/O John Owen Klippel, RAAF	Pilot RO/Nav	Lost between BW-1, Greenland, and Reykjavik, Iceland
19 May 44 Baltimore FW828	F/O Francis George Raine, RAF; rest of crew survived	Nav	Crashed into sea 4 miles N of Trinidad
19 May 44 Ventura JT846	Clarence Wheeler Perry, Am civ Sgt Leslie George Bradbury Ambler, RAF	Pilot Nav	Crashed into sea, 4 miles SW of Reykjavik, after takeoff

DATE/ PLANE	NAME/SERVICE/ NATIONALITY	SEAT	REMARKS
	P/O Harold Edwin Hutchings, RCAF	RO	
20 May 44 Mosquito KB230	Robert Adkison, Am civ Paul Francis Zyvitski, Cdn civ	Pilot RO/Nav	Crashed into Grand Lake, Nfld, during flight, Dorval to Gander
24 May 44 Mitchell HD352	P/O Piotz Glydziak, PAF F/L Josef Rojek, PAF WO2 George Simon Streisel, RCAF	Pilot Nav RO	Lost between Gander and Lagens
28 May 44 Marauder HD417	P/O Denis Clement Farmer Perkins, RCAF P/O Norman Joseph Bernard Hodgins, RCAF P/O William Grant Cantlay, RCAF FSgt Robert Gerald Huxtable, RCAF	Pilot Pilot Nav RO	Crash, 10 miles E of Khartoum, Anglo-Egyptian Sudan (one source gives the a/c no. as HD548 and some date the crash, 3 June)
2 June 44 Liberator KG847?	F/O Wojciech Jan Dolewski, RAF	FE	Accident at Gander
16 June 44 PBN-1 02826	Col V.N. Vasilyov, USSR; Soviet delivery crew; other names unknown		Lost between Reykjavik and Murmansk, USSR
22 June 44 Hudson FK736	P/O Donald William Adams, RCAF P/O William Perry McLaren, RCAF WO2 Cyril Harold Thomas, RCAF FSgt Amos Rowe Dobson, RCAF	Pilot Pilot RO RO	Crashed at Ellenberg Depot, NY, during training flight
25 Aug. 44 Mitchell KJ588	F/O J.S. Szybka, PAF F/O Archibald Donald Doner, RCAF WO K.A. Chlopicki, PAF	Pilot Nav RO	Crashed in heavy timber, 5 miles NE of Matawek Lake, Que., 22 miles from RCAF Stn Seven Islands, Que.
26 Aug. 44 Mosquito KG398	John Matheson Brown, Cdn civ	Engineer	Disintegrated in the air, Goose Bay; pilot baled out

DATE/ PLANE	NAME/SERVICE/ NATIONALITY	SEAT	REMARKS
29 Aug. 44 Mitchell KJ584	Vladimir John Kabin, Cdn civ Sgt David Flood, RAF Sgt Thomas Tweed Sheldrick, RAF	Pilot Nav RO	Crashed during a night takeoff at Gander
17 Oct. 44 Marauder HD664	F/O Maurice Francis O'Neill, RCAF F/O John Walter Wood, RCAF	Pilot Pilot	Crash, Nassau
17 Oct. 44 Boston BZ593	F/O William George Preston, RCAF	RO/Nav	Ran out of fuel and ditched in sea, 15 miles W of Rabat Sale, Morocco; Nav drowned; pilot rescued after 21 hrs in dinghy
3 Nov. 44 Dakota KJ986	F/O Lewis Turner Morris, RAF F/O Archie Whitelaw, RCAF Thomas Victor Woods, Br civ F/O Morley Douglas McLaughlin, RAF	Pilot Nav RO Pass	Crash, nr Goose Bay
7 Nov. 44 Boston BZ549	F/O Kenneth David Clarson, RAAF	RO/Nav	Crash, Reykjavik
12 Nov. 44 Mosquito KB504	Thomas Franklin Campbell Jr, Am civ P/O George Daniel Boyd, RCAF	Pilot RO/Nav	Lost out of Gander, en route to BW-1
30 Nov. 44 Mosquito KB535	Oliver Huss, Am civ Earl Ecklin, Cdn civ	Pilot RO/Nav	Lost between Goose Bay and BW-1
10 Dec. 44 Mosquito KB536	Sub/Lt Sigmund Breck, RNAF F/O Francis Edward Sorensen, RAAF	Pilot RO/Nav	Crashed into sea off Summerside, PEI
10 Dec. 44 Mitchell KJ721	F/O Fred Charles Bower, RCAF F/O James Boe Cuthbertson, RAF Sgt William Frederick Pywell, RAF	Pilot Nav RO	Crash, Lac St Louis, nr Montreal

DATE/ PLANE	NAME/SERVICE/ NATIONALITY	SEAT	REMARKS
16 Dec. 44 Mosquito KB626	Sylvan Ray Garver, Am civ Joseph George Shelfoon, Cdn civ	Pilot RO/Nav	Lost between Georgetown and Belem
16 Dec. 44 Mosquito KB620	Truman Clay Henderson, Am civ Allan William Harding, Cdn civ	Pilot RO/Nav	Lost between Georgetown and Belem
23 Dec. 44 Mosquito KB563	J.E. Rogers, civ A. Copp, civ	Pilot Observer	Crashed on test flight at Downsview, Ontario, when aileron jammed
26 Dec. 44 Mitchell KJ735	FSgt Roy Alan Freeman, RAF FSgt John Roch Smith, RCAF Sgt Francis John Wholey, RAF	Pilot Nav RO	Lost between BW-1 and Reykjavik
3 Jan. 45 Mitchell KJ751	P/O Francis Gerald Physick, RCAF F/O James Parsloe Jenkins, RCAF Sgt Norman Charles Wagstaffe, RAF	Pilot Nav RO	Lost between Reykjavik and Prestwick
12 Jan. 45 Catalina 02915	Peter Harry Nataros, Cdn civ 4 Soviet airmen also killed	RO/Nav	Crashed during a night takeoff, Elizabeth City, NC
1 Feb. 45 Dakota KK194	F/O F. Bishop, RAF P/O Thomas Brown Milne Alexander, RAF WO1 Gilbert Nichols, RCAF	Pilot Nav RO	Flew into high ground on Isle of Mull on approach to Prestwick
4 Feb. 45 Mosquito KB313	John Frederick Bradley, Cdn civ John Donald McIntyre, Cdn civ	Pilot RO/Nav	Crash, Amherst, NS
6 Feb. 45 Dakota KN271	S/L Zozislaw Waclaw Hirsz, PAF P/O Denis Washer, RAF FSgt William Roy Gregory, RAF F/L Herbert Bond Clarke, RAF (Nfld)	Pilot Pilot Nav RO	Lost between BW-1 and Reykjavik
6 Feb. 45 Liberator KL386	Hugh Murray Martin, Cdn civ Edward Craig Talbot, Cdn civ P/O William Arnold Coott, RCAF Jean-Pierre Lagadec, Cdn civ Sgt A.C.A. Grace, RAF	Pilot Pilot Nav RO FE	Crash, Bermuda

DATE/ PLANE	NAME/SERVICE/ NATIONALITY	SEAT	REMARKS
11 Feb. 45 Mosquito KB370	F/O John Martyn Squance, RAF F/O Gunn Lauger Marino Maxon, RCAF	Pilot RO/Nav	Lost between BW-1 and Reykjavik
20 Feb. 45 Mosquito KB475	F/L Jerzy Mierczyslaw Goldhaar, PAF P/O Thomas Henry Monson, RNZAF	Pilot RO/Nav	Crash, Lagens
6 March 45 Mosquito KB593	Woodrow Walden, Cdn civ Thomas Scotland, Br civ	Pilot RO/Nav	Lost between Gander and Lagens
13 March 45 Dakota KN345	FSgt Peter Antrobus, RAF WO2 Floyd Eugene George, RCAF FSgt Frank S. Holmes, RAF FSgt Edward Watkins, RAF	Pilot Pilot Nav RO	Lost between El Paso, Texas, and Sacramento, Cal.; a US aviation cadet was also lost on this aircraft.
13 March 45 Liberator EW626	F/O V. Jilek F/O A.P.R. Walker F/L A.J. Volek F/L A.K. Murdock WO2 D.E.J. Bouchard FSgt L. Kondziolka LAC W. Bridges, RAF Sgt G.A. Cain, RAF S/L A.J. Davey, RAF LAC C.S. Hubbard, RAF F/L L.F. Jarvis, RCAF Cpl F. Jeckells, RAF Sgt J.H. Lawrence, RAF Cpl W. McKenzie, RAF F/O C.G. Montgomery, RAF F/L J.E. Yarnell, RAF	Pilot Pilot Nav Nav RO FE Pass Pass Pass Pass Pass Pass Pass Pass Pass Pass	Crashed on takeoff, Lagens

Plus one more unidentified passenger |
| 27 March 45 Liberator AL504 *Commando* | W/C William Hugh Biddell, RAF FSgt Aubrey Norman Brodie, RAF F/L Kenneth George Shea, RAAF F/L David Buchanan, RCAF Frederick Walter Williams, Br civ P/O Douglas James Spence, RCAF Victor Ian Claude James Bannister, Br civ | Pilot Pilot Nav Nav RO FE Steward | Lost between Northolt, England and Lagens |

DATE/ PLANE	NAME/SERVICE/ NATIONALITY	SEAT	REMARKS
	Sir John Abraham, Br civ	Pass	Air Ministry
	Commander R.A. Brabner, MP	Pass	US of S for Air
	A/M Sir Peter Drummond, RAF	Pass	Air member for training
	H.A. Jones, Br civ	Pass	Air Ministry
	S/L E.G. Plum	Pass	Air Ministry
	E. Robinson, Br civ	Pass	Private secretary to US of S
	E. Twentyman, civ	Pass	Ministry of Food
28 March 45 Dakota KN 409	F/L H.R. Hannaford F/O John William Newman, RCAF FSgt Alex D.C. Jamieson, RAF WO2 Patrick Lavin, RAF	Pilot Pilot Nav? RO	Crash, approach to Prestwick on leg from Reykjavik
9 April 45 Liberator AM929	crew safe; 2 passengers and a civilian on the ground killed		Struck high tension wires, nr St Simone, Que.
16 April 45 Mosquito KA968	F/O W. Wielondek, PAF F/O M. Zajac, PAF	Pilot RO/Nav	Lost out of Gander

26 April 45
Mosquito
KA153
	F/O Ferwley William Clarke,
	    RAF
	F/L Kilburn Howard Grist,
	    RCAF
		Pilot
		
		RO/Nav
			Crashed trying to land on
			1 engine at Reykjavik

28 April 45 Mitchell FV987	F/O Leslie William Laurence Davies, RAF FSgt William Gribbin, RAF	Pilot RO	Crash, North Bay, Ont. 2 civilian passengers survived
1 May 45 Norseman FR405	John Joseph Gilmour, Br civ S/L Frank Latham Ratcliffe, RAF	Pilot RO	Crash, Charlottetown, PEI, oic wireless, Gander
10 May 45 Mosquito LR503	F/L Maurice Briggs, RAF F/O John Baker, RAF	Pilot RO/Nav	Flew into control tower during demonstration flight at Calgary, on a tour under 45 Group control
10 June 45 Mosquito KA237	Howrad Stanley Wright, Cdn civ James Douglas Woodyard, Cdn civ	Pilot RO/Nav	Lost between Goose Bay and BW-1

DATE/ PLANE	NAME/SERVICE/ NATIONALITY	SEAT	REMARKS
15 June 45 Liberator JT985	F/L Saxon Millis Cole, RCAF	Pilot	Crash, Dorset, England
	F/O Donald Angus Twaddle, RCAF	Pilot	
	F/O Joseph Craig Todd, RCAF	Nav	
	F/O George Everett McPherson, RCAF	RO	
	Sgt George Frederick Wyke, RAF	FE	
17 June 45 Mosquito KA260	Brian James Duigan, NZ civ	Pilot	Crash, nr Mont Joli, Que.
	James Stanley Tegart, Cdn civ	RO/Nav	
28 June 45 Mosquito KA317	F/L G.F. Ayton	Pilot	Hit a pile of stones and burned during precautionary landing nr Galway, Eire
30 June 45 Liberator KN768	F/O Derrick William Southwell, RAF	Pilot	Crash, Dorval
	P/O J.A. Winkley, RAF	Pilot	
	Sgt Geoffrey Frank Buers, RAF	RO	
	Sgt A.T. Furness, RAF	AG	[air gunner]
	Sgt Ivor Ralph Platt, RAF	AG	
	Sgt G.R. Chappell, RAF	FE	
1 July 45 Mosquito KA316	WO1 S.G. Weatherspoon, RAF	Pilot	Crashed and burned 6 miles SW of Mont Joli airfield while trying to land on one engine
	F/L Vladimir Joseph Sopuck, RCAF (Czech)	RO/Nav	
4 July 45 Liberator JT982	George Peter Evans, Am civ	Pilot	Lost between Dorval and Northolt
	John Weldy Ross, Am civ	Pilot	
	F/O Roy Holden Marshall Patterson, RCAF	Nav	
	Cyril Paul Joseph Meagher, Cdn civ	RO	
	Gayle Burton Swaney, Cdn civ	FE	
	LAC W.T. Keates, RAF	Flight clerk	
	Col D.C. Capel-Dunn	Pass	Ministry of Defence
	Miss J.M. Cole-Hamilton, civ	Pass	Foreign Office
	Miss A.M. Collard, civ	Pass	Foreign Office
	Miss B. Hibberd, civ	Pass	India Office
	Sir William Malkin, civ	Pass	Foreign Office
	Roland Tennyson Peel, civ	Pass	India Office
	Miss M.J.C. Scupham, civ	Pass	Foreign Office

DATE/ PLANE	NAME/SERVICE/ NATIONALITY	SEAT	REMARKS
	Miss D. Smith, civ	Pass	Foreign Office
	Miss P.M.S. Spurway, civ	Pass	Cabinet Office
3 Aug. 45 Boston BZ478	WO1 James Brown, RCAF	WAG	Lost en route to Africa
3 Aug. 45 Liberator KN826	F/O Kenneth Hugh Leslie Houghton, RAF	Pilot	Crashed on takeoff, Lydda, Palestine
	F/O Stanley Albert Bennett, RAF	Pilot	
	F/L J.A. Sprigge	Pilot	
	Sgt E.F. Rogers, RAF	Nav	
	Sgt R.R. Gibson	RO	
	Sgt M.A. Hammond	RO	
	Sgt Dennis Gordon Longhurst, RAF	AG	
	Sgt Robert Reade Milligan, RAF	AG	
	Sgt Terence Phillip Pipe, RAF	AG	
	Sgt W.F. Reeks	AG	Two more unidentified
	Sgt Ralph Meanley, RAF	FE	casualties
20 Feb 46 Liberator AL528	D.W. Ray, Cdn civ	Pilot	Caught fire during emergency landing due to severe icing conditions; Return Ferry Service co-pilot only fatality

RAF Transport Command and No. 45 Group at Peak Strength, Summer 1945

TRANSPORT COMMAND
(Headquarters, Bushy Park, Teddington, Middlesex, England)

No. 4 (Transport Group)	York
No. 38	Marks Hall
No. 44	Gloucester
No. 45	Dorval
No. 46	Harrow
No. 47	Hendon
No. 87	BAFO
No. 216	Heliopolis
No. 229	Delhi
No. 300	Melbourne

Plus more than two hundred numbered staging posts around the world

NO. 45 GROUP

No. 112 (North Atlantic) Wing	Dorval
No. 231 Squadron	Dorval
No. 5 Aircraft Preparation Unit	Dorval
No. 6 Aircraft Preparation Unit	Bermuda
No. 6 Ferry Unit	Dorval
No. 313 Ferry Training Unit	North Bay
RAF Station	Reykjavik
RAF Hospital	
No. 9 Mechanical Transport Company	

No. 113 (South Atlantic) Wing	Nassau (Bahamas)
No. 7 Ferry Unit	
No. 7 Aircraft Preparation Unit	
No. 280 Wing	San Diego

Staging Posts Controlled by 45 Group

No. 74	Lagens, Azores
No. 80	Bermuda
No. 81	Bluie West 1
No. 82	Elizabeth City
No. 83	Gander
No. 84	Goose Bay
No. 85	Boucherville
No. 86	Reykjavik
No. 88	Nassau
No. 89	Jamaica
No. 90	Ascension
No. 95	Piarco, Trinidad
No. 96	Borinquen, Puerto Rico
No. 97	Miami
No. 98	Natal, Brazil
No. 99	Belem, Brazil
No. 100	Dorval
No. 139	San Diego
No. 140	Los Angeles
No. 141	Honolulu
No. 142	Canton Island
No. 143	Fiji
No. 144	Auckland, New Zealand
No. 145	Sydney, Australia

Notes

CHAPTER 1 Atlantic Pioneers

1 Kenneth McDonough, *Atlantic Wings* (Hemel Hempstead, Eng. 1966), 116–
23; David Beaty, *The Water Jump: The Story of Transatlantic Flight* (New
York 1976), 4–78; Charles Dixon, *The Conquest of the Atlantic by Air* (London [1930]); Basil Clarke, *Atlantic Adventure: A Complete History of Transatlantic Flight* (London 1958), 14–108; and F.H. and E. Ellis, *Atlantic Air
Conquest* (Toronto 1963). See also an intriguing series of files (roughly
1008-1-32 to 1008-1-164) in the National Archives of Canada (NA) holdings of Department of National Defence (DND) records, Record Group
(RG) 24, vols 4888–96. These concern numerous pioneering aviation projects of both Canadian and foreign origin, including many transatlantic
attempts – successful and unsuccessful, real, aborted, and still-born. The
references in this account are not meant to provide a bibliography of
early transatlantic aviation. There are many books on the subject that
were not consulted for this introductory chapter, which is simply an attempt to give the reader an idea of the first tentative steps towards con-
quering the North Atlantic by air.

2 Sir John Alcock and Sir Arthur Whitten Brown, *Our Transatlantic Flight*
(London 1969), 74–92; Beaty, *The Water Jump*, 25–32; Clarke, *Atlantic Adventure*, 23–8

3 Quoted in Alcock and Brown, *Our Transatlantic Flight*, 173 and 175. See
also a brief logbook kept during the flight, as well as a notebook used by
the airmen to communicate. Copies are in the John Alcock biographical
file at the Directorate of History, National Defence Headquarters, Ottawa
(DHist).

4 For an excellent account of the USN operation, see Richard K. Smith,
First Across! The U.S. Navy's Transatlantic Flight of 1919 (Annapolis, Md

1973), and for a good brief treatment, see Beaty, *The Water Jump*, 9–23. See also Wayne Biddle, *Barons of the Sky: From Early Flight to Strategic Warfare, the Story of the American Aerospace Industry* (New York 1993), 125. For this and other early attempts, see also Percy Rowe, *The Great Atlantic Air Race* (Toronto 1977). Clarke, in *Atlantic Adventure*, 14–28, does a nice job of telling the story of the race to win Lord Northcliffe's prize.

5 Beaty, *The Water Jump*, 32–42; Dixon, *The Conquest of the Atlantic by Air*, 77–100; Clarke, *Atlantic Adventure*, 29 and 67–75

6 Richard J. Beamish, *The Story of Lindbergh, the Lone Eagle* (np 1927); Beaty, *The Water Jump*, 43–7; McDonough, *Atlantic Wings*, 6, 25; Clarke, *Atlantic Adventure*, 30–3; Biddle, *Barons of the Sky*, 151–4

7 John P. Heinmuller, *Man's Fight to Fly* (New York 1944), 74; Beaty, *The Water Jump*, 45–6; Henry Ladd Smith, *Airways: The History of Commercial Aviation in the United States* (1942; Washington 1991), 122–3

8 McDonough, *Atlantic Wings*, 116–18; Beaty, *The Water Jump*, 50–78; Robert Daley, *An American Saga: Juan Trippe and His Pan Am Empire* (New York 1980), 214; Clarke, *Atlantic Adventure*, 37

9 McDonough, *Atlantic Wings*, 88; Clarke, *Atlantic Adventure*, 48, 50–6, 58, 61, 63; Nick A. Komons, *Bonfires to Beacons: Federal Civil Aviation Policy under the Air Commerce Act, 1926–1938* (1977; Washington and London 1989), 112–14

10 J.H. Parkin, 'North Atlantic Air Service, London-Montreal' (paper presented to the semicentennial meeting of the Engineering Institute of Canada, Montreal, June 1937), 11–13, DHist 74/704; Clarke, *Atlantic Adventure*, 88–91

11 Daley, *American Saga*, 105. See also Marylin Bender and Selig Altschul, *The Chosen Instrument: Pan Am, Juan Trippe: The Rise and Fall of an American Entrepreneur* (New York 1982), 182–3.

12 Parkin, 'North Atlantic Air Service,' 8; Canada, DND, *Report on Civil Aviation and Civil Government Air Operations for the Year 1927* (Ottawa 1928), 35

13 Fred John Hatch, 'Ship-to-Shore Airmail Service in the 1920's,' *Canadian Geographic* 97 (Aug.–Sept. 1978), 56–61; J.R.K. Main, *Voyageurs of the Air: A History of Civil Aviation in Canada, 1858–1967* (Ottawa 1967), 91–2; W.A.B. Douglas, *The Creation of a National Air Force*, Official History of the Royal Canadian Air Force, vol. 2 (Toronto and Ottawa 1986), 84

14 Wilson to Woods Humphery, 28 Dec. 1932, A.G.L. McNaughton papers, NA, Manuscript Group (MG) 30 E 133, vol. 102; Fred Hatch, notes of an interview with Sir Leonard Outerbridge, 31 Aug. 1974; Daley, *American Saga*, 105–10; Beaty, *The Water Jump*, 82–4

15 Henry Ladd Smith, *Airways Abroad: The Story of American World Air Routes* (1950; Washington 1991), 38; Daley, *American Saga*, 107; Beaty, *The Water Jump*, 90–1; Bender and Altschul, *Chosen Instrument*, 198–201

16 The Pan Am representative, Alan Winslow, took no further part in negotiations. Tragically and inexplicably, he was killed in a fall from his hotel-room window in Ottawa a few months after sending Trippe the cable quoted. Daley, *American Saga*, 107–8; Bender and Altschul, *Chosen Instrument*, 210–12

17 Daley, *American Saga*, 126, 134; Robin Higham, *Britain's Imperial Air Routes, 1918 to 1939: The Story of Britain's Overseas Airlines* (Hamden, Conn. 1961), 184–5. For Newfoundland's situation at this time, see Peter Neary, *Newfoundland in the North Atlantic World, 1929–1949* (Kingston and Montreal 1988), 39–44.

18 Daley, *American Saga*, 126–7; Frank H. Ellis, *Canada's Flying Heritage* (Toronto 1962), 220, 229; Beaty, *The Water Jump*, 79ff; Bender and Altschul, *Chosen Instrument*, 212–14; Wilson to Woods Humphery, 28 Dec. 1932, McNaughton Papers, vol. 102; notes of an interview with Sir Leonard Outerbridge, 31 Aug. 1974

19 John Swettenham, *McNaughton, 1: 1887–1939* (Toronto 1968), 254–68, 286–99; Robert Bothwell and William Kilbourn, *C.D. Howe: A Biography* (Toronto 1979), 104–14

20 Canada, Imperial Conference 1926, Appendices to the Summary of Proceedings (Ottawa 1927), 149–69, DHist 934.009 (D208); DND, *Report on Civil Aviation and Civil Government Air Operations for the Year 1930* (Ottawa 1931), 67–71; Clarke, *Chosen Instrument*, 51–5, 58, 63

21 Main, *Voyageurs of the Air*, 135–6; Swettenham, *McNaughton*, 1: 245–8; Clarke, *Atlantic Adventure*, 72

22 Main, *Voyageurs of the Air*, 137; Swettenham, *McNaughton*, 1: 250; Clarke, *Atlantic Adventure*, 73. The history of St Hubert as an airship 'harbour' – and particularly the dismantling of the tower, used only for the *R.100* – is documented in 'Airports, Construction & Mntce. – Airport Development, Mooring Mast St. Hubert Airport,' Department of Transport file 5158-Q173 pt 1, NA, RG 12, vol. 2358.

23 Strait of Belle Isle to Montreal Air Mail Service, vol. 2, July 1932–June 1933, DHist 181.009 (D15); Swettenham, *McNaughton*, 1: 257–9; Canada-Newfoundland correspondence in Alex I. Inglis, ed., *Documents on Canadian External Relations (DCER)*, 5: *1931–1935* (Ottawa 1973), 613

24 Draft International Agreement, McNaughton Papers, vol. 102. Quoted in Swettenham, *McNaughton*, 1: 260.

25 Secretary of state for external affairs to dominions secretary, 25 April

1932, *DCER*, 611; Wilson to Woods Humphery, 28 Dec. 1932, McNaughton Papers, vol. 102; Swettenham, *McNaughton*, 1: 260–2

26 'Confidential note of views expressed at meetings on 9th and 12th June 1933 as to the application of Imperial Airways and Pan American Airways for a concession to operate air services to and from Newfoundland,' Newfoundland Provincial Archives (NPA), GN 1/3, 201-800, 229/23. See also Canada-Newfoundland correspondence, June–August 1933, *DCER*, 614–16.

27 High commissioner to secretary of state for external affairs, 27 July 1935, *DCER*, 622, and other correspondence on transatlantic service, 616–28.

28 C.H. Grey and Leonard Bridgman, eds and comps, *Jane's All the World's Aircraft 1934* (London 1934), 87a; C.H. Barnes, *Shorts Aircraft since 1900* (London 1967), 312–17; Daley, *American Saga*, 207

29 Acting secretary of state for external affairs to chargé d'affaires in the United States, 27 Nov. 1935, *DCER*, 634

30 Chargé d'affaires in the United States to secretary of state for external affairs, 5 and 12 Dec. 1935, ibid., 635–6; under secretary of state for air, extract from a Report on Transatlantic Air Service, 30 July 1936, in Paul Bridle, ed., *Documents on Relations between Canada and Newfoundland, 1: 1935–1949, Defence, Civil Aviation and Economic Affairs* (Ottawa 1974), 1063– 6; Higham, *Imperial Air Routes*, 186; Harald Penrose, *Wings across the World: An Illustrated History of British Airways* (London 1980), 94; Bender and Altschul, *Chosen Instrument*, 260–1; and A.M. Fraser, 'History of the Participation of Newfoundland in World War II,' 100–1, old DND DHist file 290NFD.013 (D1), now in NA, RG 24, vol. 10,995

31 Air Ministry, 'Progress Report on Transatlantic Air Service,' 1 Aug. 1936, Bridle, *Documents*, 1066–7; Canadian Meteorological Service, 'An Interview with Dr. Patrick D. McTaggart-Cowan,' transcript (excerpt), 3–7, copy in P.D. McTaggart-Cowan biographical file, DHist; Fraser, 'Newfoundland in World War II,' 101–3, NA, RG 24, vol. 10,995; P.D. McTaggart-Cowan, 'Transatlantic Aviation and Meteorology,' *Journal of the Royal Astronomical Society of Canada* (May–June 1938); Clarke, *Atlantic Adventure*, 92; and Penrose, *Wings across the World*, 96

32 Main, *Voyageurs of the Air*, 269–85; Swettenham, *McNaughton*, 1: 286–99

33 Bothwell and Kilbourn, *Howe*, 104–14

34 Ibid.; K.M. Molson, *Pioneering in Canadian Air Transport* (np 1974), 183–98

35 Main, *Voyageurs of the Air*, 144–7; Bothwell and Kilbourn, *Howe*, 108–9

36 Bothwell and Kilbourn, *Howe*, 110

37 F.J. Hatch, *The Aerodrome of Democracy: Canada and the British Commonwealth Air Training Plan, 1939–1945* (Ottawa 1983), 164; Main, *Voyageurs of the Air*, 157

38 Neary, *Newfoundland*, 44–108

39 C. Martin Sharp, *D.H.: A History of de Havilland* (Shrewsbury, Eng. 1982), 163. See also *Jane's All the World's Aircraft 1936*, 42c, 277c, 280c; A.J. Jackson, *DeHavilland Aircraft since 1915* (London 1962), 349–51; and *The Aeroplane* 56 (March 1939), 704.

40 Batterbee to Lodge, 28 July, 16 Aug., and 5 Oct. 1935, NPA, GN 1/3, 441-570/35

41 'Memorandum Relating to Canadian Terminal Bases for a Trans-Atlantic Air Service,' 7 Nov. 1935, and 'Memorandum Relating to the Establishment of Bases on the Atlantic Coast for the Operation of a Trans-Atlantic Air Service,' nd, L.F. Stevenson biographical file, DHist

42 Neary, *Newfoundland*, 110–11; T.M. McGrath, *History of Canadian Airports* (Ottawa 1992), 103–4

43 William C. Brown, 'The Newfoundland Airport,' summer essay, third-year electrical engineering, McGill University, 1939; Fred Hatch, interview with J.D. James, general airport manager, Gander, Newfoundland, Sept. 1974; McGrath, *Canadian Airports*, 104

44 Wilson to Holmes, 30 March 1938, and Jewett to Floud, 1 April 1938, NPA, GN 1/3, 7-10, 10/38

45 Fred Hatch, notes of an interview with Robert Bradley, 14 June 1974; McGrath, *Canadian Airports*, 105

46 McGrath, *Canadian Airports*, 105–6; McTaggart-Cowan interview, 7, biographical file, DHist; excerpts from T.M. McGrath diaries, DHist 74/635; Fraser, 'Newfoundland in World War II,' 103, NA, RG 24, 10,995

47 McTaggart-Cowan interview, 9, biographical file, DHist. For apparent confirmation of this claim, see 'W' Force file WFS 2-0-0-10, 'Preparation of Aerodrome Runways for Demolition,' DHist 355.009 (D8). For lack of defence coordination between Canada and Newfoundland, see C.P. Stacey, *Arms, Men and Governments: The War Policies of Canada, 1939–1945* (Ottawa 1970), 92–4. One report claims that A/V/M George M. Croil, the RCAF's chief of the air staff, feared 'that the Newfoundland Airport might become "a positive menace" since it could possibly be captured by an enemy landing party or by planes operating from a raider.' Fraser, 'Newfoundland in World War II,' 116, NA, RG 24, vol. 10,995

48 Secretary of state for external affairs to governor of Newfoundland, 5 Sept. 1939, and reply, 6 Sept. 1939, Bridle, *Documents*, 42–3. For more on

the strategic value of Newfoundland, see Fraser, 'Newfoundland in World War II,' 441–6, NA, RG 24, vol. 10,995.

49 Governor of Newfoundland to dominions secretary, 15 Sept. 1939, Bridle, *Documents*, 45–6; Fraser, 'Newfoundland in World War II,' 104–6, NA, RG 24, 10,995

50 Fraser, 'Newfoundland in World War II,' 106–19, 121–2, NA, RG 24, 10,995; Douglas, *National Air Force*, 381; Neary, *Newfoundland*, 131; McGrath diary, DHist 74/635; 10 (BR) Squadron, daily diary and operations record book, DHist

51 'Memorandum of Agreement between Canada and Newfoundland Respecting the Transfer of Air Bases,' 17 April 1941, Bridle, *Documents*, app. E, 1049–13; Fraser, 'Newfoundland in World War II,' 123–40, NA, RG 24, vol. 10,995

52 Higham, *Imperial Air Routes*, 191–3; Clarke, *Atlantic Adventure*, 94–7; Penrose, *Wings across the World*, 100–1. Daley gives the date as 3 July for the start of the experimental flights. *American Saga*, 216

53 D.C.T. Bennett, *Pathfinder* (London 1958; reprinted 1983), 65–72; G.R. Duval, *British Flying-Boats and Amphibians, 1909–1952* (London 1966), 203–4; *The Aeroplane* 45 (July–Dec. 1938), 121; Clarke, *Atlantic Adventure*, 97–105; Smith, *Airways Abroad*, 41–2; and Penrose, *Wings across the World*, 111

54 Duval, *British Flying-Boats*, 191–2; Higham, *Imperial Air Routes*, 195–7; Clarke, *Atlantic Adventure*, 98–9; Penrose, *Wings across the World*, 91, 95, 112, 114; and Ministry of Information, *Merchant Airmen: The Air Ministry Account of British Civil Aviation, 1939–1944* (London 1946), 6–9, 12, and 21; Smith, *Airways Abroad*, 41

55 *Jane's All the World's Aircraft, 1939*, 99a, 229–30c; McGrath diary, DHist 74/635; Daley, *American Saga*, 225, 228–9, 242ff

56 Lester B. Pearson, *Mike: The Memoirs of the Right Honourable Lester B. Pearson, PC, CC, OM, OBE, MA, LLD*, 1: *1897–1948* (Toronto 1972), 134–5

57 Smith points out that 'Up to the end of 1939 only thirty-odd commercial aircraft had ever flown across the Big Pond.' *Airways Abroad*, 64. See also Duval, *British Flying-Boats*, 192–3; Higham, *Imperial Air Routes*, 197; Penrose, *Wings across the World*, 118 and 121. The Luftwaffe destroyed *Cabot* and *Caribou* at their moorings a few miles south of Narvik on 5/6 May 1940 during the German attack on Norway. *Merchant Airmen*, 23

CHAPTER 2 Canadian Pacific Railway

1 H. Duncan Hall, *North American Supply* (London 1955), 105–9. See also H. Duncan Hall and C.C. Wrigley, *Studies of Overseas Supply* (London 1956),

4; and Jeffrey Davis, 'ATFERO: the Atlantic Ferry Organization,' *Journal of Contemporary History* 20, 1 (Jan. 1985), 71–2. Sholto Watt, *I'll Take the High Road: A History of the Beginning of the Atlantic Air Ferry in Wartime* (Fredericton, NB 1960), 3, gives the totals as 200 and 400.

2 'Aircraft Arrivals in United Kingdom from North America,' table 135 in *Statistical Digest of the War: Prepared in the Central Statistical Office* (London 1951), 156n

3 Owen Thetford, *Aircraft of the Royal Air Force, 1918–1957* (London 1957), 318

4 Edward R. Stettinius Jr, *Lend-Lease, Weapon for Victory* (New York and London 1944), 22

5 Hall and Wrigley, *Studies of Overseas Supply*, 109–10. See also Hall, *North American Supply*, 170–3; and Davis, 'ATFERO,' 72.

6 Here Hall uses the subheading 'The Beginning of Extravagance,' in *North American Supply*, 115. See also Watt, *High Road*, 5–13.

7 D.C.T. Bennett, *Pathfinder* (London 1958; reprinted 1983), 121. Bowhill commanded Coastal Command at the start of the war, moving to Ferry Command when it was created in 1941. See also 'Transcript of a recorded interview by F.J. Hatch, Directorate of History, with Air Vice-Marshal D.C.T. Bennett C.B., C.B.E., D.S.O. regarding the inauguration of the North Atlantic Ferry Organization and the formation of the Pathfinder Force in Bomber Command, taped in Montreal on 17 June 1976,' 1, D.C.T. Bennett biographical file, Directorate of History, National Defence Headquarters (DHist).

8 Winston S. Churchill, *Their Finest Hour*, The Second World War, vol. 2 (Boston 1949), 13

9 Ibid., 325

10 A.J.P. Taylor, *Beaverbrook* (London 1972), 428. See also Watt, *High Road*, 8 and 14; and S.A. Dismore's report, 'Atlantic Ferrying Organization (ATFERO): The Past,' 22 May 1945, in Public Record Office (PRO) AIR 8/474, AIR 2/7508 and AIR 20/6090

11 See Louise M. Dawe, 'The Air Board, the Air Ministry and the Handley Page Proposals for Transatlantic Flight, 1917–1919,' paper presented to the annual meeting of the Canadian Historical Association, 1985.

12 Hall, *North American Supply*, 30. See also W.J. McDonough, 'Canada's Aircraft Industry,' address by the president of Central Aircraft Mfg Co. Ltd before the Canadian Section, Society of Automotive Engineers, Royal York Hotel, Toronto, 15 Nov. 1944, 7, copy in A.G. Sims Papers, National Archives of Canada (NA), Manuscript Group (MG) 30 A 76.

13 Anderson to Sec. DND (Department of National Defence), 6 April 1940, RCAF file S.3-5-2, 'Distribution of Units – Air Defence – East Coast,'

DHist 181.003 (D4095). In fact, the Air Ministry may have considered flying some US-built aircraft to the United Kingdom. See the Associated Press story, 'U.S. Aircraft to Cross Seas in Freighters; Britain Drops Plan to Fly Machines because of Technical Plans,' *Globe and Mail* (Toronto), 3 Nov. 1939, clipping in the *Hamilton Spectator* collection, DHist 81/531, box 4, file 'War: European: 1939 Britain.'

14 Griffith Powell, *Ferryman: From Ferry Command to Silver City* (Shrewsbury, Eng. 1982), 19–20

15 Ibid., 20–1

16 Ibid. See also interview, D.C.T. Bennett biographical file, DHist.

17 David Cruise and Alison Giffiths, *Lords of the Line* (Markham, Ont. 1988), 353. See also J.R.K. Main, *Voyageurs of the Air: A History of Civil Aviation in Canada, 1858–1967* (Ottawa 1967), 163.

18 Interview, 8, D.C.T. Bennett biographical file, DHist

19 Cruise and Griffiths, *Lords of the Line*, 353

20 Ibid., 356 and 359

21 K.M. Molson, *Pioneering in Canadian Air Transport* (np 1974), 233

22 'History of Civilian Flying Training Schools in the BCATP,' DHist 181.003 (D3); F.J. Hatch, *The Aerodrome of Democracy: Canada and the British Commonwealth Air Training Plan, 1939–1945* (Ottawa 1983), 209–10

23 Wilson to Beatty, 8 July 1940, quoted in D.H. Miller-Barstow, *Beatty of the C.P.R.* (Toronto 1951), 170–1. On 14 June 1940 Beatty had written to Prime Minister William Lyon Mackenzie King proposing an emergency transatlantic airmail service for the duration of the war. He made no allusions to any plans to deliver aircraft to the United Kingdom – nor did King in his replies of 18 and 27 June (the latter after Cabinet had considered and rejected the mail idea). Beatty had other correspondence with his prime minister that summer and fall, with nary a mention of the ferry scheme. See the King Papers, NA, MG 26 J 1, vol. 283, particularly 239417–22 (microfilm reel C-4566).

24 Bennett, *Pathfinder*, 97

25 British Purchasing Commission, New York, to Woods Humphery, 8 July 1940, quoted in [John Pudney], *Atlantic Bridge: The Official Account of R.A.F. Transport Command's Ocean Ferry* (London 1945), 7

26 H. Burchall, general manager CPR Air Services Department, to S.A. Dismore, DCPA, MAP, 7 Oct. 1940, enclosing an unsigned copy of the agreement, DHist 74/799. Note particularly paragraphs 1, 4, 3, and 5. See also Watt, *High Road*, 20; and Davis, 'ATFERO,' 73.

27 Quoted in Watt, *High Road*, 9. See also Taylor, *Beaverbrook*, 415–45. The latest biography of Beaverbrook has only a brief mention of the North

Atlantic ferry service. Its description of his tenure as minister of aircraft production does, however, tend to support the interpretation offered here of the way he operated. See Anne Chisholm and Michael Davie, *Beaverbrook: A Life* (London 1992), 387–8 and generally, 374–97. See also Tom Driberg, *Beaverbrook: A Study in Power and Frustration* (London 1956), 251–64.

28 Memorandum for the Commission of Government, 16 June 1941, attached to Woods to Machtig, 16 June 1941, PRO, AIR 2/7508. The earliest date discovered on a Canadian government file relating to the Atlantic ferry scheme is on a letter from Burchall to the chief of the air staff (CAS), Ottawa, 17 Sept. 1940. Air Force Headquarters (AFHQ) then arranged for Eastern Air Command (EAC) to work informally with CP as the latter required, at first primarily on aircraft movements and radio procedures. See EAC file 30–12, 'Operations – Ferrying of Aircraft from Canada to United Kingdom,' DHist 181.002 (D167).

29 For records of the Clayton Knight Committee, see DHist 80/68.

30 *Atlantic Bridge*, 8–9; Powell, *Ferryman*, 22–4; Watt, *High Road*, 24; Main, *Voyageurs*, 163–4. It is not clear exactly how many aircraft were towed across the border. See correspondence with Fred Hatch from Lockheed Corporation and from the US National Archives in June 1974 in DHist 81/748.

31 Bennett, *Pathfinder*, 99. See also interview, 2, D.C.T. Bennett biographical file, DHist. Bennett, an Australian, later established and commanded No. 8 (Pathfinder) Group of RAF Bomber Command, ending the war an air vice-marshal.

32 The inclination towards informal arrangements persisted throughout the war. See, for example, correspondence on RCAF, TCA, and Ferry Command cooperation on radio and teletype facilities and radio range charts in file HQ 1008-1-166 pt 4, NA, Record Group (RG) 24, vol. 4896.

33 Watt, *High Road*, 103–4

34 Agreement, paragraph 3, DHist 74/799

35 Major R.H. Mayo, 'Report on Technical Aspects of Scheme for Delivery of Aircraft by Air to Great Britain,' 8 Oct. 1940, PRO, AIR 38/1

36 Watt, *High Road*, 23; Bennett, *Pathfinder*, 97

37 Bennett, *Pathfinder*, 98. This account of the visit to Lockheed is based on ibid., 98–100; Powell, *Ferryman*, 21–2; Watt, *High Road*, 24; and *Atlantic Bridge*, 7–8.

38 Bennett, *Pathfinder*, 99

39 *Atlantic Bridge*, 8

40 Bennett, *Pathfinder*, 99–100

41 Ibid., 100. See also *Atlantic Bridge*, 8; Watt, *High Road*, 24; and Powell, *Ferryman*, 22.

42 Bennett, *Pathfinder*, 101; Mayo, 'Report on Technical Aspects,' PRO, AIR 38/1; interview, 3, Bennett biographical file, DHist. The agreements made appear not to have been written down until 7 March 1941. See 'Memorandum of understanding reached at meeting between Mr. W.K. Trower, Mr. E.P. Wells and Mr. W.H. Hobbs regarding procedures in connection with the maintenance and overhaul of aircraft on loan from the R.C.A.F. at Malton and used for training pilots for British ferry service, the said understandings having been reached after consideration of Mr. DeCarteret's letter to Mr. Trower of March 5th, 1941,' and related RCAF–TCA correspondence in HQ 1008-1-166 pt 2, NA, RG 24, vol. 4896.

43 W.A.B. Douglas, *The Creation of a National Air Force*, Official History of the Royal Canadian Air Force, vol. 2 (Toronto and Ottawa 1986), 635; Fred Hatch, 'Recruiting Americans for the Royal Canadian Air Force, 1939–1942,' *Aerospace Historian* (March 1971), 12–18; V. Edward Smith, 'North Atlantic Ferry,' *Aviation* (May 1941), 132

44 Powell, *Ferryman*, 22–3

45 Bennett, *Pathfinder*, 100–1

46 George Lothian, *Flight Deck: Memoirs of an Airline Pilot* (Toronto 1979), 75

47 *Atlantic Bridge*, 8. See also Henry Ladd Smith, *Airways Abroad: The Story of American World Air Routes* (1950; Washington 1991), 72.

48 Powell, *Ferryman*, 22. See also Edgar J. Wynn, 'Bombers Across,' *Flying Aviation* (Feb. 1942), 15.

49 Bennett, *Pathfinder*, 101. See also Geoffrey P. Jones, *Attacker: The Hudson and Its Flyers* (London 1980), 10; and Andrew Hendrie, *Seek and Strike: The Lockheed Hudson in World War II* (London 1983), 28 and 36.

50 Wynn, 'Bombers Across,' 15

51 Ibid.

52 Ibid.

53 Quoted in *Atlantic Bridge*, 9

54 Watt, *High Road*, 28. See also Powell, *Ferryman*, 23–4; and *Atlantic Bridge*, 9.

55 *Atlantic Bridge*, 9. Jimmy Jubb has confirmed the account of his own start with the ferry service in conversations with the author.

56 Art Stark, 'Off to Ferry Command,' unpublished memoir, 1, A.P. Stark biographical file, DHist

57 Ibid., 2

58 *The Transat; Bulletin of Trans-Oceanic Radio Officers' Association* 2, 2 (Oct. 1945), 32; RAFFC crew assignment cards, DHist 84/44
59 Stark, 'Off to Ferry Command,' 3
60 Ibid.
61 *Transat* (Oct. 1945), 4–8; crew assignment cards, DHist 84/44
62 *Atlantic Bridge*, 9–11. For more on the *Guba's* career in New Guinea, see 'Exploratory Flying Boat: Experiences of the Consolidated PBY2 "Guba" in New Guinea,' *Flight* 37, 1620 (11 Jan. 1940), 33. Technically, this was not the first 'Guba,' Dr Archibald having bought an earlier PBY1. He sold it to the USSR in August 1937 and took delivery of a newer model later in the year. Both aircraft carried the same registration, NC-777. This was not the first PBY the Air Ministry received from the United States. A modified PBY4 was purchased, entered in the RAF registry as P9630, and flown from San Diego to Felixstowe (for evaluation) via Botwood in July 1939. This was probably the first transatlantic delivery flight by a military aircraft. William E. Scarborough, 'The Consolidated PBY – Catalina to Canso,' *Journal American Aviation Historical Association* 16, 1 (spring 1971), 29–31. A.M. Fraser may be referring to P9630 when he says that a Consolidated PBY flying boat 'had been delivered via Gander, before the outbreak of war [in July 1939].' 'History of the Participation of Newfoundland in World War II,' 140–1, old DND Directorate of History file 290NFD.013 (D1), now in NA, RG 24, vol. 10,995
63 [Ferry Command], 'Record of Operations – PBY,' DHist
64 Hugh Halliday, *No. 242 Squadron, the Canadian Years: The Story of the RAF's All-Canadian Fighter Squadron* (Stittsville, Ont. 1981), 95 and 103n; *The RCAF Overseas: The First Four Years* (Toronto 1944), 8 and 38; Leslie Roberts, *There Shall be Wings: A History of the Royal Canadian Air Force* (Toronto 1959), 143 and 147; A. Mowatt Christie's unpublished biography of his brother, George Patterson Christie, typescript, 96–7 and 114–18, copy, DHist
65 'Record of Operations – PBY,' DHist; *Transat* (Oct. 1945), 5, 8, 10, 13, and 26
66 *Atlantic Bridge*, 11; 'Excerpts from the Diaries loaned to DHist by Mr. T.M. McGrath, M.O.T., concerning operations at Gander and Botwood from 1939 to 1945,' 10, DHist 74/635
67 Mayo, 'Report on Technical Aspects,' PRO, AIR 38/1; Smith, 'North Atlantic Ferry,' 132
68 'Address by Dr. P.D. McTaggart-Cowan on Early Trans-Atlantic Aviation

in Newfoundland given at the CAHS Meeting, 18 November 1975,' transcript, 24, DHist 80/350

69 Bennett, *Pathfinder*, 103; Smith, 'North Atlantic Ferry,' 131
70 Smith, 'North Atlantic Ferry,' 132
71 Sir Arthur Harris, *Bomber Offensive* (New York 1947), 25
72 Interview, 8, Bennett biographical file, DHist. Everyone who was with the ferry service at this embryonic stage speaks or has written of Bennett's total involvement in every aspect of preparing the aircraft and crews for the first delivery flights.
73 No. 10 (BR) Squadron, daily diary, DHist; Powell, *Ferryman*, 25–6; Fraser, 'Newfoundland in World War II,' 119, 143, NA, RG 24, vol. 10,995
74 Quoted in *Atlantic Bridge*, 12. See also Watt, *High Road*, 36–7; 10 (BR) Squadron, daily diary, 28 Oct. to 1 Nov. 1940, DHist; McGrath diary, DHist 74/635; and Fraser, 'Newfoundland in World War II,' 144, NA, RG 24, vol. 10,995.
75 Newfoundland Airport Watch Log, copy, DHist 79/1 LG; 10 (BR) Squadron, daily diary, DHist
76 Bennett, *Pathfinder*, 104
77 Ibid.
78 Smith, 'North Atlantic Ferry,' 132
79 Watt, *High Road*, 45. See also 'Address ... by McTaggart-Cowan,' 24, DHist 80/350; Davis, 'ATFERO,' 75.

CHAPTER 3 From Triumph to Tragedy

1 V. Edward Smith, North Atlantic Ferry,' *Aviation* (May 1944), 134
2 Interview transcript, 5, D.C.T. Bennett biographical file, DHist
3 D.C.T. Bennett, *Pathfinder: A War Autobiography* (London 1958; reprinted 1983), 103. See also A.S. Jackson, *Pathfinder Bennett: Airman Extraordinary: Air Vice Marshal D.C.T. Bennett, CB CBE DSO* (Lavenham, Eng. 1991), 40.
4 Newfoundland Airport Watch Log, copy, Directorate of History, National Defence Headquarters (DHist) 79/1 LG; RAFFC crew assignment cards, DHist 84/44
5 Bennett, *Pathfinder*, 104
6 Smith, 'North Atlantic Ferry,' 132. Each pilot was issued 'Special Instructions to Captains of Aircraft,' which he was to hand 'to the *meteorological officer* at the airport of destination immediately upon arrival.' The document, providing primarily information about weather and communications and related procedures, was under no circumstances to be allowed to fall into enemy hands. See two copies

sent by S/L Pattison, aerodrome control officer, Newfoundland Airport, to AOC (air officer commanding), EAC (Eastern Air Command), on 19 October 1940, in EAC file 30-12, 'Operations – Ferrying of Aircraft from Canada to United Kingdom,' DHist 181.002 (D167).

7 Morley Thomas, 'Oral History Project: An Interview with Dr Patrick D. McTaggart-Cowan,' 16–17, excerpt from transcript in McTaggart-Cowan biographical file, DHist

8 Bennett, *Pathfinder*, 104. 'Squadron Leader Pattison, an RAF signals expert, had been seconded to the Newfoundland Government as Air Adviser and was in charge of the airport with his two highly professional assistants, Messrs Ratcliffe and McGrath, looking after the wireless and control sides.' Griffith Powell, *Ferryman: From Ferry Command to Silver City* (Shrewsbury, Eng. 1982), 26

9 Powell, *Ferryman*, 27. There is disagreement about the time of departure. Smith says 1930, half an hour earlier than Powell ('North Atlantic Ferry,' 134). The airport watch log records 2233 GMT (DHist 79/1 LG). Most commentators say it was the Black Watch Regiment that provided the ground defence force at Gander. However, Professor A.M. Fraser, in his unpublished narrative, 'History of the Participation of Newfoundland in World War II,' says that this unit was replaced by the 1st Battalion of the Queen's Own Rifles of Canada on 10 August 1940 (119). See old Department of National Defence (DND) Directorate of History file 290NFD.013 (D1), now in National Archives of Canada (NA), Record Group (RG) 24, vol. 10,995. This is supported by C.P. Stacey, *Six Years of War: The Army in Canada, Britain and the Pacific*, Official History of the Canadian Army in the Second World War, vol. 1 (Ottawa 1966), 179.

10 Smith, 'North Atlantic Ferry,' 132–6; and Bennett, *Pathfinder*, 102–6. For other secondary accounts of the first, pioneering transatlantic flight of new aircraft, see also Sholto Watt, *I'll Take the High Road: A History of the Beginning of the Atlantic Air Ferry in Wartime* (Fredericton 1960), 34–45; and Reader's Digest, *The Canadians at War, 1939/45* (np 1969), I, 114–16; [John Pudney], *Atlantic Bridge: The Official History of R.A.F. Transport Command's Ocean Ferry* (London 1945), 13–16; and Jackson, *Pathfinder Bennett*, 41–2.

11 Smith, 'North Atlantic Ferry,' 132–4

12 Ibid., 134

13 Quoted in *Atlantic Bridge*, 13. Tripp's account is also quoted in Watt, *High Road*, 38–44.

14 Smith, 'North Atlantic Ferry,' 134

15 Bennett, *Pathfinder*, 105

16 *Atlantic Bridge*, 13–14

17 Ibid., 14

18 Bennett, *Pathfinder*, 105–6. Smith says that the formation climbed to only 16,000 feet in attempting to fly over the front. 'North Atlantic Ferry,' 134

19 Smith, 'North Atlantic Ferry,' 134

20 Ibid.

21 *Atlantic Bridge*, 14–15

22 McTaggart-Cowan interview, 17, biographical file, DHist

23 *Atlantic Bridge*, 15

24 Bennett, *Pathfinder*, 106

25 Smith, 'North Atlantic Ferry,' 134

26 Ibid.

27 Ibid., 134–6

28 Bennett, *Pathfinder*, 106. For the air sickness, see *Atlantic Bridge*, 15–16.

29 Smith, 'North Atlantic Ferry,' 136

30 Ibid. According to the Newfoundland Airport Watch Log (DHist 79/1 LG), the elapsed flying time from Gander to Aldergrove was 11 hours 12 minutes for the first three aircraft and 12 hours 47 minutes for the last to touch down. Two sources, however, give Bennett's flying time as 10 hours 17 minutes. (*Atlantic Bridge*, 16; interview, 3, Bennett biographical file, DHist). Signals notifying EAC of the safe arrival of all seven aircraft make no mention of the time required to make the trip. DHist 181.002 (D167)

31 *Atlantic Bridge*, 16

32 Bennett, *Pathfinder*, 106

33 *Atlantic Bridge*, 16

34 Smith, 'North Atlantic Ferry,' 136

35 Bennett, *Pathfinder*, 107. For more on this meeting, see interview, 4, Bennett biographical file, DHist.

36 *Atlantic Bridge*, 16

37 Powell, *Ferryman*, 29

38 *Atlantic Bridge*, 17

39 Powell, *Ferryman*, 38

40 Watch Log, DHist 79/1 LG. Powell writes: 'Group Captain F. Pearce proved to be an excellent Hudson pilot and an industrious snow shoveller at Gander when he had to disengage his aircraft from the drifts.' *Ferryman*, 72

41 Quoted in Watt, *High Road*, 48

42 Ibid., 48–9

43 Ibid., 49. See also Watch Log, DHist 79/1 LG. It took Eves only 10 hours 35 minutes to fly to Prestwick, less time than Captains Joe Mackey and

Sweet took to get to Aldergrove. David M. Smith also reports Eves's landing at Prestwick, but gives the time of his flight as 10 hours 45 minutes. See *Action Stations, 7: Military Airfields of Scotland, the North-East and Northern Ireland* (Cambridge 1983), 173.

44 Bennett, *Pathfinder*, 109
45 *Atlantic Bridge*, 17
46 Ibid.; Watch Log, DHist 79/1 LG; Bennett, *Pathfinder*, 109. Ted Beaudoin, in his biography of Sheldon Luck (who joined Ferry Command as a pilot in 1942), claims that there was an accident on this third formation flight. It has allegedly been expunged from the historical record. *Walking on Air* (Vernon, BC 1986), 183
47 Bennett, *Pathfinder*, 109. See also Jackson, *Pathfinder Bennett*, 42.
48 Bennett, *Pathfinder*, 107
49 *Atlantic Bridge*, 17; Watt, *High Road*, 46–7. Ted Beaudoin again thinks there was a coverup on this flight. He claims that the *Spirit of Lockheed and Vega* had to be written off after it crashed on takeoff at Gander. *Walking on Air*, 183–4
50 Watch Log, DHist 79/1 LG; crew assignment cards, DHist 84/44
51 Bennett, *Pathfinder*, 109
52 Ibid., 110
53 Watch Log, DHist 79/1 LG
54 Michael Bliss, *Banting: A Biography* (Toronto 1984), 254–97; Lloyd Stevenson, *Sir Frederick Banting* (Toronto 1946), 377–406; Peter Allen, 'The Remotest of Mistresses: The Story of Canada's Unsung Tactical Weapon, the Frank's Flying Suit,' *CAHS Journal* 21, 1 (spring 1983), 110–16; Ralph Barker, *Survival in the Sky* (London 1976), 49; and clipping, *The Telegram* (Toronto), 25 Feb. 1941, copy, Frederick Banting biographical file, DHist. See also John Bryden, *Deadly Allies: Canada's Secret War, 1937–1947* (Toronto 1989), passim; and W.R. Feasby, *Official History of the Canadian Medical Services, 1939–1945, 1: Organization and Campaigns* (Ottawa 1956), 340. One might have thought that Banting would have been enrolled as at least a colonel, if not at a general officer rank. It was his own decision to join the militia and accept the lower rank.
55 See, for example, Watt, *High Road*, 113–14; and Barker, *Survival*, 49.
56 Bliss, *Banting*, 259–68. Stevenson supports the personal liaison theory. *Sir Frederick Banting*, 405–6
57 Quoted by Bliss, *Banting*, 273. See also Bryden, *Deadly Allies*, 56.
58 Bryden, *Deadly Allies*, 56; Bliss, *Banting*, 294–7; Watch Log, DHist 79/1 LG; Thomas M. McGrath, 'The Crash of Hudson T9449,' *CAHS Journal* 25, 1 (spring 1987), 23

59 Crew assignment cards, DHist 84/44; Stevenson, *Sir Frederick Banting*, 410–11; and Joseph C. Mackey's testimony, 'Enquiry into the Death of Sir Frederick Banting, Wireless Operator William Snailham and Navigator William Bird,' Newfoundland Provincial Archives (NPA). I am indebted to Tom McGrath for sharing his copy of this important document. Barker says that Banting flew from Montreal to Gander with Captain 'Penny' Rogers. No archival evidence has been found to support this contention. *Survival*, 50

60 Watch Log, DHist 79/1 LG

61 Bliss, *Banting*, 301–4; Stevenson, *Sir Frederick Banting*, 409–10; interview, McTaggart-Cowan biographical file, DHist; and McGrath, 'The Crash of Hudson T9449,' 23

62 Tom McGrath, diary, copy, DHist 74/635. See also Watch Log, DHist 79/1 LG; and Mackey's testimony, 'Enquiry,' NPA.

63 Watch Log, DHist 79/1 LG

64 Mackey's testimony, 'Enquiry,' NPA. See also Stevenson, *Sir Frederick Banting*, 411; Bliss, *Banting*, 305–6; Watt, *High Road*, 113–14; and M.D. Banks, 'Night of Tragedy,' *Legion* (July 1971), 15 and 53. The airport watch log records the request for radio bearings as coming thirty-two minutes after takeoff. This source adds: 'unheard after 0103 GMT [5 minutes later].' DHist 79/1 LG

65 Mackey's testimony, 'Enquiry,' NPA. See also Stevenson, *Sir Frederick Banting*, 413–15; Bliss, *Banting*, 307; and Barker, *Survival*, 53–5.

66 McGrath diary, DHist 74/635; 10 (BR) Squadron, daily diary, DHist; and McGrath, 'The Crash of Hudson T9449,' 23

67 Mackey's testimony, 'Enquiry,' NPA

68 Editorial insertion in ibid.

69 Ibid.; Stevenson, *Sir Frederick Banting*, 416–17

70 Mackey's testimony, 'Enquiry,' NPA; Stevenson, *Sir Frederick Banting*, 419; McGrath diary, DHist 74/635; 10 (BR) Squadron, daily diary, DHist; [Joe Mackey], 'Survivor's Story,' *CAHS Journal* 25, 1 (spring 1987), 24–5 (reprinted from *Toronto Star*, 17 Feb. 1982)

71 'Survivor's Story,' 25

72 Bennett, *Pathfinder*, 113–14

73 Ibid., 114. See also Jackson, *Pathfinder Bennett*, 44–5.

74 'Survivor's Story,' 25. See also Stevenson, *Sir Frederick Banting*, 420; and Barker, *Survival*, 57.

75 Bennett, *Pathfinder*, 114

76 No. 10 (BR) Squadron, daily diary, DHist; Barker, *Survival*, 58; and McGrath, 'The Crash of T9449,' 23. Mackey recalled the message in reverse

order: 'Joe. 3 dead' ('Survivor's Story,' 25; Stevenson, *Sir Frederick Banting*, 420). Bennett just reported seeing the 'Three dead' (*Pathfinder*, 114).

77 'Survivor's Story,' 25. See also Bennett, *Pathfinder*, 114–15.

78 Bennett, *Pathfinder*, 115. See also McGrath, 'The Crash of Hudson T9449,' 24; and Fred Hatch's interviews with various people relating to the Gander airport and transatlantic ferry operations, DHist. Hicks and Abbott are named in Stevenson, *Sir Frederick Banting*, 421.

79 Governor of Newfoundland to secretary of state for external affairs, Ottawa, secret no. 19, 2 April 1941, NPA, and W.L.M. King Papers, NA, Manuscript Group (MG) 26 J 1, vol. 305, 258103 (microfilm reel C-4863)

80 F.J. Hatch, interview with A.J. Lilly, 27–28 Oct. 1975, transcript, 16, Lilly biographical file, DHist. George Lothian says that 'some scuttlebut' claimed that the crash happened because an anti-icing fuel additive caused scales on the interior of the tank to lift off and clog the system. See the draft of this memoirs, 154, in NA, MG 30 A 81. This comment did not survive the editorial process of his *Flight Deck: Memoirs of an Airline Pilot* (Toronto 1979).

81 Quoted in Stevenson, *Sir Frederick Banting*, 430–1.

82 Governor of Newfoundland to secretary of state for external affairs, 2 April 1941, NPA, and NA, MG 26 J 1, vol. 305, 258103 (microfilm reel C-4863). For more on the persistence of the sabotage theory, see Beth Gorham, 'Plane in which Banting died is recovered,' *The Gazette* (Montreal), 21 Oct. 1990 (copy in Lillian Hanson Wheeler scrapbook, DHist); and Bliss, *Banting*, 305.

83 Watch Log, DHist 79/1 LG

84 Crew assignment card, DHist 84/44; 'Survivor's Story,' 24; Bliss, *Banting*, 308; interview by F.J. Hatch with Lillian Wheeler, secretary, Ferry Command Association, 27 Oct. 1975, Lillian Hanson Wheeler biographical file, DHist

CHAPTER 4 From ATFERO to Ferry Command

1 W.A.B. Douglas, *The Creation of a National Air Force*, Official History of the Royal Canadian Air Force, vol. 2 (Toronto and Ottawa 1986), 471; John Terraine, *The Right of the Line: The Royal Air Force in the European War, 1939–1945* (London 1985), 223, 235, and 244

2 F/O Hodgins, 'O.T.U's under the B.C.A.T.P.; No. 31 O.T.U.,' unpublished manuscript, [1945], 1, citing AFHQ (Air Force Headquarters) file 192-10-22/31 pt 1, Directorate of History, National Defence Headquarters (DHist) 74/13

3 'Paper dealing with the past functions of ATFERO [Atlantic Ferry Organization] under the Ministry of Aircraft Production [MAP] and the future functions of the Royal Air Force Ferry Command,' 2 Aug. 1941, Public Record Office (PRO), AIR 2/8135

4 Ibid.

5 S.A. Dismore, 'Atlantic Ferrying Organization (ATFERO): The Past,' 22 May 1945, 1, PRO, AIR 8/474, AIR 2/7508, and AIR 20/6090; and D.C.T. Bennett, *Pathfinder: A War Autobiography* (London 1958; reprinted 1983), 107–8

6 Bennett, *Pathfinder*, 107

7 Griffith Powell, *Ferryman: From Ferry Command to Silver City* (Shrewsbury, Eng. 1982), 29. See below, chapter 5, for more on the Bermuda operation.

8 Bennett, *Pathfinder*, 108

9 BAC (British Air Commission, Sir Henry Self), 17 Jan. 1941, PRO, AIR 8/474; BAC to MAP, 17 July 1941, PRO, AIR 19/247

10 K.M. Molson, *Pioneering in Canadian Air Transport* (np 1974), 173 and 207; 'Summary of Information covering the organization of the Atlantic ferry bomber service by the Canadian Pacific,' unpublished account, 25 March 1942, 5. I am indebted to Matthew Rodina for providing a copy of this document, apparently written by Punch Dickins or at his direction.

11 Dismore, 'Atlantic Ferrying Organization (ATFERO): The Past,' 2, PRO, AIR 2/7508; [Wilcockson], 'General Report,' PRO, AIR 38/2; 'Summary of Information,' 5–6

12 Bennett, *Pathfinder*, 108–9

13 Dismore, 'Atlantic Ferrying Organization (ATFERO): The Past,' 2 and 4, PRO, AIR 2/7508; Sholto Watt, *I'll Take the High Road: A History of the Beginning of the Atlantic Air Ferry in Wartime* (Fredericton, NB 1960), 102–3. Watt says, not unreasonably, that Wilson gradually assumed control as Beatty's health failed. See also 'Summary of Information,' 8.

14 Hildred, 'Report on ATFERO,' paragraph 5, PRO, AIR 2/7508. See also Watt, *High Road*, 102–3, for claims of similar reactions by British visitors.

15 Bennett, *Pathfinder*, 118

16 Ibid.

17 Molson, *Pioneering*, 237. CP Air ultimately became Canadian Airlines International.

18 Interview transcript, 8, D.C.T. Bennett biographical file, DHist

19 [John Pudney], *Atlantic Bridge: The Official Account of R.A.F. Transport Command's Ocean Ferry* (London 1945), 23; Watt, *High Road*, 105

20 Powell, *Ferryman*, 74. See also Watt, *High Road*, 107–8; and *Atlantic Bridge*, 22–3.

21 Powell, *Ferryman*, 74.

22 Ibid., 75. See also Watt, *High Road*, 108.

23 Quoted in Watt, *High Road*, 109. The author has been unable to locate the original source of this quotation.

24 Ibid., 110–11

25 Ibid., 111

26 Ibid., 109–10

27 Ibid., 110. See also Powell, *Ferryman*, 75.

28 Powell, *Ferryman*, 75. See also Henry Flory's unpublished memoirs, excerpt, 115–17, in his biographical file, DHist.

29 Watt, *High Road*, 106; *Atlantic Bridge*, 23. No part of the Ferry Command story is well documented. For some reason, however, there is a particular shortage of information about the Pacific ferry.

30 Newfoundland Airport Watch Log, DHist 79/1 LG; RCAF Station Gander, daily diary, DHist

31 Air Member for Personnel Division, progress reports, 12 Feb.–3 Nov. 1940, DHist 73/1174, vol. 1B

32 Clayton Knight Committee, 'Financial Statistical Report,' 31 Dec. 1940, DHist 80/68, file 12; 'General Report,' PRO, AIR 38/2

33 Dismore to Courtney, 6 June 1941, PRO, AIR 8/474

34 Self to Westbrook, 1 Jan. 1941, PRO, AIR 19/247

35 Quoted in Sir John Slessor, *The Central Blue: Recollections and Reflections* (London 1956), 335–6

36 CAS (chief of the air staff) to secretary of state for air, 6 Jan. 1941, enclosure dated 7 Jan. 1941, PRO, AIR 19/247

37 'Plans of a Meeting held on 14 January at 5 p.m. to Consider the Atlantic Ferry Situation,' ibid.

38 James Leutze, ed., *The London Journal of General Raymond E. Lee* (Toronto 1971), 13

39 Beaverbrook to Balfour, 16 Feb. 1942, quoted in A.J.P. Taylor, *Beaverbrook* (New York 1972), 429

40 Winston S. Churchill, *Their Finest Hour*, The Second World War, vol. 2 (Boston 1949), 12–13

41 Ibid., 325

42 Taylor, *Beaverbrook*, 414–19; B.H. Liddell Hart, *History of the Second World War* (New York 1970), 92

43 PM to Beaverbrook, 15 Dec. 1940 (private), appendix to Churchill, *Finest Hour*, 699

44 Taylor, *Beaverbrook*, 429–30. See their correspondence in Beaverbrook Papers, copies in DHist 74/527, folder A and A1; and PRO, AIR 19/247 and AIR 19/248.

45 Churchill to secretary of state for air, 1 March 1941, PRO, AIR 19/248
46 Summary of correspondence, MAP to S of S (secretary of state for air), 14 Jan. 1941, ibid.
47 Bridges to secretary of state, 16 March 1941, ibid.
48 Beaverbrook to PM, 24 March 1941, ibid.
49 Churchill to Beaverbrook, 29 March 1941, ibid.
50 Taylor, *Beaverbrook*, 467–9 and 477–8; Winston S. Churchill, *The Grand Alliance*, The Second World War, vol. 3 (Boston 1950, 349 and 870–1; Churchill, *The Hinge of Fate*, The Second World War, vol. 4 (Boston 1951), 62; and Anne Chisholm and Michael Davie, *Beaverbrook: A Life* (London 1992), 397, 399, and 403–4
51 Cabinet War Committee (CWC) minutes, 29 Jan. and 3 Feb. 1941, in Paul Bridle, ed., *Documents on Relations between Canada and Newfoundland*, 1: *1935–1949; Defence, Civil Aviation and Economic Affairs* (Ottawa 1974), 329–30 and 331
52 'Minutes of a Meeting held at 5 p.m. on 7th January, 1941, in the Air Council Room to discuss with Representatives of the Canadian Government: (I) The proposal to establish the Greenland Route (II) The Atlantic Ferry Pilot Situation,' PRO, AIR 19/247
53 CWC minutes, 11 Feb. 1941, Bridle, *Documents*, 1: 332
54 'Requirements of Canadian Pacific Air services in Canada and Newfoundland to cope with trans-Atlantic flight deliveries of aircraft,' 20 Feb. 1941, and CWC minutes, 27 March 1941, ibid., 335–6 and 339; Dominions Office to acting UK high commissioner in Canada, 7 March 1941, Empire Air Training Scheme Committee, extracts of notes from the 30th meeting, held on Friday, 14 March 1941, PRO, AIR 19/248
55 McKean to Air Ministry, 3 April 1941, ibid.; Wilson to Moore-Brabazon, 29 May 1941, PRO, AIR 2/7508
56 Howe to Beaverbrook and Balfour, 16 Feb. 1941, Bridle, *Documents*, 1: 333. See also Howe to Beaverbrook, 31 Jan. and 3 March 1941, ibid., 330 and 337. In the last telegram Howe suggested that the question 'should be handled between Government and Government as there is possibility of danger arising out of so many people being involved.'
57 Howe to Purvis, 26 April 1941, Bridle, *Documents*, 1: 340
58 'Cumulative Monthly Receipts and Deliveries, Sept. 1940 to Dec. 1942,' PRO, AIR 38/23; Bridle, *Documents*, 1: 1407–8
59 Watch Log, DHist 79/1 LG
60 Bennett, *Pathfinder*, 120. Bennett claims to have brought back twenty-four aircrew on this flight. The usual limit, however, was eighteen.
61 Portal to Lee, 16 May 1941, PRO, AIR 19/249

62 Ibid. This was the second batch of Fortresses delivered by Coastal Command crews. Some of the first group had staged through Floyd Bennett Field on Long Island, as discussed above.

63 Sinclair to Beaverbrook, 25 March 1941, PRO, AIR 19/248

64 J. Eaton Griffith, principal private secretary to MAP, to R.H. Melville, PS to SOPS, 26 March 1941, Melville to Air Ministry officials, 28 March 1941, enclosing Air Ministry memorandum, 'Delivery by Air of Aircraft Produced in USA,' 25 March 1941, ibid.

65 President to former naval person, 29 May 1941, PRO, AIR 2/7508. See also PM to PM, 2 June 1941, and CWC minutes, 3 June 1941, Bridle, *Documents*, 1: 342–3; and 'Report Minister of National Defence for Air Mission to United Kingdom (30-6-41 to 24-7-41),' DHist 80/525.

66 Rowan to CAS, 30 May 1941, PRO, AIR 8/1369

67 Draft reply to signal from president to PM, attached to Melville to Martin, 30 May 1941, ibid.

68 Former naval person to president, 31 May 1941, ibid.

69 'Notes of a meeting held on 2.6.41 to discuss the Future Organization of Trans-Atlantic Ferrying in the Light of the Telegram from the President of the USA,' ibid.

70 PM to PM, 2 June 1941, HQS 7410-7, National Archives of Canada (NA), Record Group (RG) 24, vol. 2791, printed in Bridle, *Documents*, 1: 343

71 PM to PM, 4 June 1941, PRO, AIR 2/7508 and AIR 8/1369

72 Quoted in report on ATFERO, attached to Hildred to Street, 3 July 1941, PRO, AIR 2/7508

73 Dominions secretary to governor of Newfoundland, 9 June 1941, Bridle, *Documents*, 1: 346

74 Directive to Bowhill, 12 June 1941, PRO, AIR 2/7508

75 Report on ATFERO signed by Bowhill, 28 June 1941, ibid.

76 Long to Howe, 28 July 1941, Bridle, *Documents*, 1: 356

77 Interview, 5–6, Bennett biographical file, DHist; Bennett, *Pathfinder*, 124

78 Bennett, *Pathfinder*, 120

79 Bickell to Dickins, 2 May 1941, PRO, AIR 8/474

80 'Address by Dr. P.D. McTaggart-Cowan on Early Trans-Atlantic Aviation in Newfoundland given at the CAHS Meeting, 18 November 1975,' transcript, 16, DHist 80/350

81 Memo by A.W. Street, 15 Aug. 1941, PRO, AIR 2/7509

82 Hildred to Street, 29 Aug. 1941, ibid.; *Atlantic Bridge*, 24; 'Summary of Information,' 8

83 Hildred to Street, 29 Aug. 1941, PRO, AIR 2/7509

84 No. 31 OTU, daily diary, DHist; crew assignment cards, DHist 84/44; Powell, *Ferryman*, 75 and 94

85 Watch Log, DHist 79/1 LG; P.Y. Davoud and K.L.B. Hodson biographical files, DHist; crew assignment cards, DHist 84/44

86 The pilot of Hudson AE640 was F/L Keith Fergus Arnold, RAF (born in Kinderley, Saskatchewan); the navigator, Sgt Percy Keast, RAF (Cornwall, England); and the civilian radio operator, Wilfred Bratherton (New Westminster, British Columbia). Crew assignment cards, DHist 84/44; 'Statistics of the "Silent Keys,"' *The Transat: Bulletin of the Trans-Oceanic Radio Officers Association* 2, 2 (Oct. 1945), 8. The figure 200 is admittedly an estimate, but 165 had been delivered across the Atlantic and 5 across the Pacific by 11 June. RSC PS to CAS, 11 June 1941, PRO, AIR 8/474

87 Watch Log, DHist 79/1 LG; Bennett, *Pathfinder*, 122. Ralph Barker claims that but for two pilots changing flights for personal reasons, Lord Beaverbrook, on his way to meet Churchill at Placentia Bay, 'would have perished ... on Arran.' *Survival in the Sky* (London 1976), 101. For more on this accident, see below, chapter 11.

88 Churchill, *Grand Alliance*, 446. Churchill wrote that Beaverbrook left Prestwick on a different Liberator within a few hours of Purvis. It was only a stroke of fortune that saved him (ibid.). See also Bennett, *Pathfinder*, 122; and Bowhill to Sinclair, 15 Aug. 1941, PRO, AIR 2/7509.

89 Watch Log, DHist 79/1 LG; Bennett, *Pathfinder*, 122

90 Bowhill to Street, 16 Aug. 1941, PRO, AIR 2/7509; Powell, *Ferryman*, 69

91 Bowhill to Street, 21 Aug. 1941, PRO, AIR 2/5340

92 Watch Log, DHist 79/1 LG; crew assignment cards, DHIST 84/44; T.M. McGrath diary, DHist 74/635; computer listing of RCAF casualties compiled by Hugh Halliday from various sources (mostly at DHist), including casualty cards and Part II Air Force Routine Orders ('the green sheets'), DHist 90/19; 'Statistics,' *Transat* (Oct. 1945), 8; Bennett, *Pathfinder*, 123

93 'Aircraft Receipts and Deliveries by RAF Ferry Command and RAF Transport Command from September 1940, to April 30, 1945,' PRO, AIR 38/23, Bridle, *Documents*, 1: 1407

CHAPTER 5 Flying Boats through Bermuda

1 John Terraine, *The Right of the Line: The Royal Air Force in the European War, 1939–1945* (London 1985), 243–5; Alfred Price, *Aircraft versus Submarine: The Evolution of Anti-Submarine Aircraft, 1912 to 1980*, rev. ed. (London 1980), 73–4; K.M. Molson and H.A. Taylor, *Canadian Aircraft since 1909* (Stittsville, Ont. 1982), 204 and 209; and David W. Wragg, comp., *A Dictionary of Aviation* (New York 1974), 87. W.A.B. Douglas

appears to be conservative in giving the Catalina's range as 2400 miles. *The Creation of a National Air Force*, Official History of the Royal Canadian Air Force, vol. 2 (Toronto and Ottawa 1986), 480. His figure may apply to operational as opposed to ferry range.

2 Letter of appointment, signed by H. Burchall, for 'The Company,' and A.P. Stark, 26 Dec. 1940; 'Off to Ferry Command,' unpublished memoir, 3, A.P. Stark biographical file, Directorate of History, National Defence Headquarters (DHist)

3 Stark, 'Off to Ferry Command,' 4

4 Ibid., 5. The makeup of the crew is supported by 'Record of Operations, PBY,' DHist. It does, however, give the other radio operator's surname as 'Hagger,' the same way it is spelt on his employment record card, DHist 84/44.

5 Stark, 'Off to Ferry Command,' 5

6 Ibid., 4. Stark gives the wing-span of the Catalina as 102 feet, but Molson and Taylor say 104 feet for the Canso, the Canadian-built version of the PBY. *Canadian Aircraft*, 209

7 Stark, 'Off to Ferry Command,' 5

8 Don McVicar, *North Atlantic Cat* (Shrewsbury, Eng. 1983), 6. McVicar does not give the first name of his PBY checkout pilot. Charles Avery MacDonald appears to be the only Australian MacDonald in the Ferry Command crew assignment cards with the requisite experience to have been the man McVicar refers to. DHist 84/44

9 Stark, 'Off to Ferry Command,' 6

10 Ibid. The departure date is confirmed in 'Record of Operations, PBY,' DHist

11 Stark, 'Off to Ferry Command,' 6

12 Ibid.

13 Ibid., 7

14 Ibid.

15 Ibid., 8

16 Ibid.

17 Ibid.

18 Major R.H. Mayo, 'Report on Technical Aspects of Scheme for Delivery of Aircraft by Air to Great Britain,' 8 Oct. 1940, Public Record Office (PRO), AIR 38/1; D.C.T. Bennett, *Pathfinder: A War Autobiography* (London 1958; reprinted 1983), 107–8

19 'Paper dealing with the past functions of ATFERO under the Ministry of Aircraft Production and the future functions of the Royal Air Force Ferry Command,' 2 Aug. 1941, 3, PRO, AIR 2/8135

20 Griffith Powell, *Ferryman: From Ferry Command to Silver City* (Shrewsbury, Eng. 1982), 29
21 Ibid., 39–40; *Royal Canadian Air Force List*
22 Bennett, *Pathfinder*, 109
23 Quoted in [John Pudney], *Atlantic Bridge: The Official Account of R.A.F. Transport Command's Ocean Ferry* (London 1945), 18. For a general confirmation of this testimonial, see McVicar, *North Atlantic Cat*, 89.
24 Powell, *Ferryman*, 29–30
25 UK high commissioner in Canada to Dominions Office, secret cypher message G.4288, 4 Jan. 1941, No. 21 secret, PRO, AIR 8/474
26 S.A. Dismore, 'Atlantic Ferrying Organization (ATFERO): The Past,' 1, PRO, AIR 8/474, AIR 2/7508, AIR 20/6090; 'Past functions of ATFERO,' 2, PRO, AIR 2/8135; *Atlantic Bridge*, 18
27 Crew assignment cards, DHist 84/44; 'Cumulative Monthly Receipts and Deliveries ... North & South Atlantic – U.K.,' PRO, AIR 38/23, Paul Bridle, ed., *Documents on Relations between Canada and Newfoundland*, 1: *1935–1949; Defence, Civil Aviation and Economic Affairs* (Ottawa 1974), 1407–8; 'Bermuda – report on Communicatons, Situation as at 12th February, 1941,' PRO, AIR 38/9. A statistical summary indicates that two 'Boats' were delivered in January. This would, however, include the Catalina flown by Gentry and his crew from Dartmouth.
28 *Atlantic Bridge*, 19; Powell, *Ferryman*, 31; Les Allison, *Canadians in the Royal Air Force* (Roland, Man. 1978), 136 and 170; crew assignment cards, DHist 84/44
29 McVicar, *North Atlantic Cat*, 46
30 Report by P.S. Ross & Sons, Chartered Accountants, [July 1941], 12–13, PRO, AIR 38/31
31 Powell, *Ferryman*, 38; 'Receipts and Deliveries,' PRO, AIR 38/23; Dismore to A/M Sir Christopher Courtney, Air Ministry, 6 June 1941, PRO, AIR 8/474
32 All the information in this paragraph is from 'Past functions of ATFERO,' 4, PRO, AIR 2/8135.
33 Quoted in McVicar, *North Atlantic Cat*, 103
34 Dismore, '(ATFERO); the Present,' 2, PRO, AIR 8/474; 'Past functions of ATFERO,' 4, PRO, AIR 2/8135; *Atlantic Bridge*, 23; Sholto Watt, *I'll Take the High Road: A History of the Beginning of the Atlantic Air Ferry in Wartime* (Fredericton, NB 1960), 138; Powell, *Ferryman*, 67–8
35 George Lothian, *Flight Deck: Memoirs of an Airline Pilot* (Toronto 1979), 83. Lothian follows with a graphic description of his first trip in a Return Ferry Service Liberator. Other interesting accounts, all in substantial

agreement about the horrors of the experience, include Don McVicar in *Ferry Command* (Shrewsbury, Eng. 1981), 30, 90–2, and 211, and in *North Atlantic Cat*, 26, 34–5, and 104–15; and Harold Balfour, *Wings over Westminster* (London 1973), 161–4 and 208–9. Even VIPs received similar treatment. For more on the Return Ferry Service, see chapter 12, below.

36 Samuel Eliot Morrison, *History of United States Naval Operations in World War II*, 1: *The Battle of the Atlantic, September 1939–May 1943* (Boston 1947), 16 and 83

37 They were Ensigns Harper, Hill, Nolen, Robinson, and Smith, and Probationary Lieutenant Rheinhart. 'Record of Operations, PBY,' DHist. See also crew assignment cards, DHist 84/44, which also include a card for United States Navy [USN] Lieutenants Riggs, Sutherland, Swanson, Thorburn, and Zimmermann, as well as Sub-Lieutenant Wagner, USN.

38 'Bermuda Airport Control Tower; Notes on Meeting Held at U.S. Naval Operations Base Bermuda on Monday, 11th October [1941], 2.00 P.M.,' PRO, AIR 38/9. The USAAC became the USAAF, 20 June 1941. Carroll V. Glines, *The Compact History of the United States Air Force*, rev. ed. (New York 1973), 152

39 P.S. Ross and Sons to Ministry of Aircraft Production, 14 July 1941 (hereafter Ross report), 1–2, PRO, AIR 38/31. The paymaster at HMS *Malabar* informally provided a 'float' of £150, 'to make salary advances to R.A.F. and R.C.A.F. personnel.' These advances were limited to pilot officers, £15; flying officers, £20; flight lieutenants, £25; and squadron leaders and above, £30.

40 Ross report, 1, PRO, AIR 38/31

41 Ibid., 20

42 Ibid., 19. A Currency and Exchange Control Board regulated exchange rates. At the same time, 'the rates were stabilized at $4.04 U.S. and $4.47 Canadian for one pound.' Airmen wishing to change Bermuda pounds into Sterling had to apply to the board.

43 Ibid., 3

44 Ibid., 4–5

45 Ibid., 22

46 Ibid., 14

47 Ibid., 15

48 Ibid., 8

49 Ibid., 26

50 Ibid., 38

51 Note, 13 Sept. 1941, PRO, AIR 38/31

52 Ross report, 29

53 Ibid.

54 Ibid., 30–4

55 Ibid., 35

56 Ibid., 37

57 Ibid., 21–3

58 'Report on Radio Communications,' 12 Feb. 1941, PRO, AIR 38/9

59 'General Report and Appreciation Signals Situation, Bermuda,' [Sept. 1941] (hereafter 'Signals Situation'), PRO, AIR 38/9; chief signals officer, RAFFC, to A/C Don, 2 Sept. 1941, PRO, AIR 2/8135. In addition to the signals facilities directly used by or for Ferry Command, the Royal Navy maintained transmitting and receiving stations at the west end of the island.

60 'Signals Situation,' PRO, AIR 38/9

61 F.H. Sandford, 'Memo on Visit to Bermuda,' 9 Dec. 1941, PRO, AIR 38/31

62 A/C/M Sir Frederick Bowhill to Sir Arthur Street, permanent undersecretary of state, Air Ministry, 19 Feb. 1942, PRO, AIR 38/31. McTaggart-Cowan, or 'McFog' as he was reportedly known throughout Ferry Command, probably did more than any other individual to advance the science and art of Atlantic forecasting. See draft histories of the Canadian Meteorological Service, DHist 80/548. All who reminisce about their Ferry Command experiences have nothing but praise for McTaggart-Cowan. For more on Dorval, see below, chapter 6.

63 Powell, 'Notes on Proposed Operations through Bermuda,' 19 March 1942, PRO, AIR 38/9

64 Powell, Ferryman, 43 and 100. He indicates that the Command delivered 169 Coronados (81). Many statistical returns simply list 'boats.'

65 McVicar, Ferry Command, 12–13, 32, 212–13, and, generally, passim. McVicar's claims about flights and crew members have been checked in other sources, notably the crew assignment cards, DHist 84/44. For the northern survey flight, see below, chapter 6.

66 Crew assignment cards, DHist 84/44; McVicar, North Atlantic Cat, 27–51

67 McVicar, North Atlantic Cat, 51–6

68 Ibid., 56

69 Atlantic Bridge, 44

70 McVicar, North Atlantic Cat, 59. No reference could be found to this loss in the admittedly incomplete archival record. On 11 November 1942 Catalina FP209 left Bermuda and crashed at Pirate Harbour, Strait of Canso, Nova Scotia. Two civilians, pilot Robert Hugh Malcolm Sandeman (from London, England) and radio officer Devereux Lionel Doria De Bretigny

(from Montreal), and two Commonwealth airmen, the navigator Pilot Officer Stanley Frasier Fairbairn, RCAF (from Calgary), and second radio operator Sgt Norman James Cheney, RNZAF, were killed. On 16 November 1942 Catalina FP273, initially reported missing, was located at Lough Gill, Ireland. The only recorded loss in December came when Catalina FP266 disappeared on Christmas Eve. Its crew was Benson Hutches Pierce (civilian pilot from Booklyn, New York), Sgt Roy Harding (RAF pilot from London, England), Sgt Douglas Oliver Bevan (RCAF navigator from Cayley, Alberta), Sgt George Edward James Craven (RAAF wireless operator from Brisbane, Australia), James Hamilton Auld (civilian radio operator from Toronto), and Sgt Reginald Edwin Thompson (RAF flight engineer from Birmingham, England). Crew assignment cards, DHist 84/44; RCAF casualties, DHist 90/19; Gander Ferry Command diary, PRO, AIR 38/3; 'Statistics of the "Silent Keys,"' *The Transat: Bulletin of Trans-Oceanic Radio Officers Association* 2, 2 (Oct. 1945), 8

71 McVicar, *North Atlantic Cat*, 59–61
72 *Atlantic Bridge*, 44
73 AOC-in-C, report for Dec. 1942, PRO, AIR 24/506; McVicar, *North Atlantic Cat*, 61; crew assignment card, DHist 84/44
74 McVicar, *North Atlantic Cat*, 61
75 Ibid., 62
76 Ibid., 63–5 and 66
77 Ibid., 67 and 69
78 Ibid., 71
79 Ibid., 73
80 Ibid., 70
81 Ibid., 74
82 Ibid., 75
83 Ibid., 75–7
84 Ibid., 77–8
85 Ibid., 84
86 Ibid., 93. See also 84–6 and 92.
87 Ibid., 98. Other Ferry Command veterans have also claimed, in conversations with the author, to have received false bearings during delivery flights.
88 'Cumulative Monthly Receipts and Deliveries,' PRO, AIR 38/23. The table in this file totals 550 flying boats, but for the early period the types are not identified, nor were they all flown via Bermuda. Powell gives a total of 472 for Catalinas (*Ferryman*, 80). Documentary evidence has been found for seven Catalina losses: 14 August, 11 November, and 24

December 1942, 6 February, 13 March, and 7 April 1943 (crew interned in France), and 12 January 1945. Crew assignment cards, DHist 84/44; RCAF casualties, DHist 90/19; Tom McGrath, diary, DHist 74/635; Newfoundland Airport Watch Log, copy, DHist 79/1 LG; Ferry Command Gander diary, PRO, AIR 38/3 and AIR 38/4; 'Statistics,' *Transat* (Oct. 1945), 8

89 Bowhill to undersecretary of state for air, 9 April 1943, PRO, AIR 24/506; Watch Log, DHist 79/1 LG; *Atlantic Bridge*, 44. Other crew members killed in the crash were Sgt David Wilkie (RAF navigator from Perth, Scotland), J.C. Ford (USAAF radio operator), and William Bradley Collins (civilian radio operator from St John's, Newfoundland). Crew assignment cards, DHist 84/44; McGrath diary, DHist 74/635; 'Statistics,' *Transat* (Oct. 1945), 8; unidentified clippings, Lillian Hanson Wheeler scrapbook, copy, DHist

90 Ferry Command Gander diary, 7 April 1942, PRO, AIR 38/3; Powell, *Ferryman*, 33; Griffith Powell, *Per Ardua Ad Astra: A Story of the Atlantic Air Ferry* (Montreal nd), np; 'R.A.F.T.C. Flier Arrives Here after Escaping from Germans,' *Montreal Star*, 14 April 1945, Wheeler scrapbook, DHist. Other members of the crew of Catalina FP138 were Harry Les Abrin (civilian pilot, like Stafford, from New York), Pilot Officer Keith Thompson (RAF navigator from Doncaster, England), Sgt Howard L. Covert (USAAF from Lakeside, Michigan), Roslyn Lloyd George Browne (civilian radio operator from Ottawa), and Sgt Alan Rodgers (RAF flight engineer from Cumberland, England). Crew assignment cards, DHist 84/44

CHAPTER 6 The Northern Routes

1 Nancy Fogelson, 'Greenland: Strategic Base on a Northern Defence Line,' *Journal of Military History* 53, 1 (Jan. 1989), 57–8. See also Basil Clarke, *Atlantic Adventure: A Complete History of Transatlantic Flight* (London 1958), 44, 47, and 50.

2 C.P. Stacey, *Arms, Men and Governments: The War Policies of Canada, 1939–45* (Ottawa 1970), 367–70; C.P. Stacey, *Canada and the Age of Conflict: A History of Canadian External Policies, 2: 1921–1948: The Mackenzie King Era* (Toronto 1981), 308–9; James Eayrs, *In Defence of Canada, 2: Appeasement and Rearmament* (Toronto 1965), 167–72. The weather station fear is not far-fetched. We now know that the Germans established an automatic weather station in northern Labrador. See Alec Douglas, 'The

Nazi Weather Station in Labrador,' *Canadian Geographic* 51 (Dec. 1981–Jan. 1982), 42–7.

3 Stacey, *Arms, Men and Governments*, 369; Stanley W. Dziuban, *Military Relations between the United States and Canada, 1939–1945* (Washington 1959), 149–52

4 Quoted in Sir John Slessor, *The Central Blue: Recollections and Reflections* (London 1956), 335. See above, chapter 4.

5 Empire Air Training Scheme (EATS) Committee minutes, Public Record Office (PRO), AIR 20/1379A

6 'Minutes of a meeting held at 5 p.m. on 7th January 1941, in the Air Council Room to discuss with Representatives of the Canadian Government: (1) the proposal to establish the Greenland Route, (2) the Atlantic Ferry Pilot Situation,' PRO, AIR 19/247

7 Stacey, *Arms, Men and Governments*, 369; Dziuban, *Military Relations*, 152; Cabinet War Committee (CWC) minutes, 29 Jan. and 11 Feb. 1941, in Paul Bridle, ed., *Documents on Relations between Canada and Newfoundland, 1: 1935–1949; Defence, Civil Aviation and Economic Affairs* (Ottawa 1974), 330 and 332. Air Ministry officials may have had their interest in a northern route of short hops – and consequently in Greenland – stimulated by a memorandum written by an RAF officer in Iceland. On 18 March 1941 S/L Leeroy L. Brown wrote 'An Appreciation on the Delivery of Aircraft from the U.S. and Canada via the Trans-Atlantic Route Direct and via Iceland' and sent it to the undersecretary of state for air at the Air Ministry. It may be simply a coincidence, but some of his ideas appear to have been adopted on the northern route. A contemporary carbon copy of this seven-page memorandum is in National Archives of Canada (NA), Manuscript Group (MG) 30 E 177. No evidence has been found that it influenced RAF policy, but the timing was right.

8 D.C.T. Bennett, *Pathfinder: A War Autobiography* (London 1958; reprinted 1983), 116. The Newfoundland Airport Watch Log, copy, Directorate of History, National Defence Headquarters (DHist) 79/1 LG, lists the RCAF representative as 'Sgt. Major Wiseman.' For Captain Roosevelt's role, see CO (commanding officer), Gander, to CAS (chief of the air staff), 29 May 1941, Bridle, *Documents*, 341.

9 Bennett, *Pathfinder*, 116

10 Sholto Watt, *I'll Take the High Road: A History of the Beginning of the Atlantic Air Ferry in Wartime* (Fredericton, NB 1960), 121–2; interview transcript, 7, D.C.T. Bennett biographical file, DHist; [John Pudney],

Atlantic Bridge: The Official Account of R.A.F. Transport Command's Ocean Ferry (London 1945), 26–7

11 Harris to secretary of state for air, 6 July 1941, PRO, AIR 2/7509; Samuel Milner, 'Establishing the Bolero Route,' *Military Affairs* 11, 4 (winter 1947), 215

12 Milner, 'Establishing the Bolero Route,' 213 and 215

13 'Report, Minister of National Defence for Air, Mission to the United Kingdom (30-6-41 to 24-7-41), Construction of staging aerodromes in Greenland–Iceland Ferrying Route, note of a meeting held at the Air Ministry on 10-7-41,' DHist 181.003 (D132); CAS to undersecretary of state for external affiars, 18 June 1941, Bridle, *Documents*, 347

14 'Development of RCAF Station Goose Bay, Lab,' 26 May 1942, in 'RCAF Station Goose Bay, Labrador, Transportation, 12 Jan. 1942–19 June 1944,' RCAF file 5-17-4, DHist 181.009 (D2941); Kenneth Wright, 'How Goose Bay was Discovered,' *The Beaver* (June 1946), 44; Jane Finlayson, 'How Eric Fry Beat the US to Arctic Base,' *Saturday Citizen*, 3 Feb. 1973, 17; 'North Atlantic Ferry Routes,' HQS 15-24-30 (particularly pt 1), NA, Record Group (RG) 24, vol. 5201; Eric Fry, 'Search for the Goose,' in Judy MGrath, ed., *'On the Goose': The Story of Goose Bay* [special edition of *Them Days Magazine*, Happy Valley, Goose Bay, Labrador, 12, 4 (June 1987),] 5–11

15 Eric Fry, 'Copy of the Story Written at the Request of F/lt Shepherd, Adjutant of Goose Bay Airport in September 1942, for Insertion in the Airport "Archives,"' J.D. MacDonnell, 'A Quarter-century of History in Goose Bay to 1967,' and 'Goose Bay, Lab. Information Folder Prepared for visit of P.J.B.D. 1 June 50 by RCAF and USAF,' all in Goose Bay permanent reference file (PRF), DHist; R.R. Wall, 'RCAF Station Goose Bay, Labrador,' *Among the Deep Sea Fishers* (International Grenfell Association), April 1947, 7–9, and July 1947, 45–6; W.A. Browne, 'Stations of the RCAF: Goose Bay,' *The Roundel* (Dec. 1960), 8–11; W.J. McFarlane, 'Report on the Establishment of the RCAF Detachment at Goose Bay, Labrador, from September 1941 to March 1942,' in RCAF Station Goose Bay, daily diary, DHist; *Atlantic Bridge*, 28; Eric Fry, 'Report on Investigation for Landing Areas near Northwest River, Labrador,' 10 July 1941, Bridle, *Documents*, 349–51; T.M. McGrath, *History of Canadian Airports* (Ottawa 1992), 113

16 'Record of Conference held at the Air Ministry on Wednesday 9 July 1941,' PRO, AIR 2/7509

17 'Report ... Mission to the United Kingdom,' DHist 181.003 (D132)

18 'Record of Conference ... 9 July 1941,' PRO, AIR 2/7509. See also

'Minutes of a Meeting to Discuss the Construction of Staging
Aerodromes for Ferry Command,' 10 July 1941, Bridle, *Documents*, 352–3.
19 '6th Weekly Letter from Air Marshal Harris to C.A.S. week ending 1800
hours Saturday, 2 August 1941,' PRO, AIR 45/12
20 Ibid.
21 'PJBD, Journal of Discussions and Decisions,' 29 July 1941, Bridle,
Documents, 357; Dziuban, *Military Relations*, 183, app. A, Seventeenth
Recommendation of PJBD, 353–4; Stacey, *Arms, Men and Governments*,
34–5 and 374
22 Minister in United States to secretary of state for external affairs, 2 Aug.
1941, and CWC minutes, 13 Aug. 1941, Bridle, *Documents*, 359 and 361.
Professor A.M. Fraser says: 'On 3rd August, Canada requested Newfoundland's permission to make an immediate survey at a point south of
Goose Bay on Terrington Basin with the object of locating a suitable site
for an air base in the North West River area of Labrador. Canada pointed
out that the possibility of establishing such a base had been discussed at a
meeting in Montreal of the United States Canada Permanent Joint Defence
Board, which had been attended by the Newfoundland Commissioner for
Justice and Defence. Permission was granted ...' 'History of the Participation of Newfoundland in World War II,' 155, old Department of
National Defence DHist file 290NFD.013 (D1), NA, RG 24, vol. 10,995
23 McFarlane, 'Report on the Establishment of the RCAF Detachment at
Goose Bay,' RCAF Station Goose Bay, daily diary, DHist. See also Bridle,
Documents, 361–72; and *Atlantic Bridge*, 28–9.
24 Peter Neary, *Newfoundland in the North Atlantic World, 1929–1949*
(Kingston and Montreal 1988), 161
25 Paragraph 10 of agreement, Bridle, *Documents*, 1416. For the negotiations,
see ibid., 482–549 and 1414–16; Neary, *Newfoundland*, 197–201; David
MacKenzie, '"A Fog of Misunderstanding": The Anglo-Canadian
Negotiation of the Goose Bay Agreement, 1941–1944,' paper delivered to
the annual meeting of the Canadian Historical Association, May 1985;
David MacKenzie, *Inside the Atlantic Triangle: Canada and the Entrance of
Newfoundland into Confederation, 1939–1949* (Toronto 1986), 87–114,
chapter 5, 'Goose Bay: "A Fog of Misunderstanding"'; Stacey, *Arms, Men
and Governments*, 377; and Fraser, 'Newfoundland in World War II,'
156–69, 442, 447–65, NA, RG 24, vol. 10,995.
26 Wesley Frank Craven and James Lea Cate, *The Army Air Forces in World
War II*, 1: *Plans and Early Operations, January 1939 to August 1942* (Chicago
1948; reprinted 1983), 333–44; Milner, 'Establishing the Bolero Route,'
215–16

27 Stacey, *Arms, Men and Governments*, 374
28 Milner, 'Establishing the Bolero Ferry Route,' 215
29 McGrath, *Canadian Airports*, 147–8. For the implications of the overcrowding at St Hubert, see the Department of Transport (DOT) file, 5404-Q173 pts 1 and 2, 'Air Traffic Control, Airport Control, St. Hubert, Que.,' 1937–40, NA, RG 12, acc. no. 84-85/073, box 29.
30 Senior air staff officer, RAFFC, to United States Army Air Corps [sic] liaison officer, Dorval, 17 March 1942, DHist 181.009 (D2939)
31 Stacey, *Arms, Men and Governments*, 374; Milner, 'Establishing the Bolero Ferry Route,' 215–16; Don McVicar, *Ferry Command* (Shrewsbury, Eng. 1981), 35–6; Griffith Powell, *Ferryman: From Ferry Command to Silver City* (Shrewsbury, Eng. 1982), 49
32 Air Staff Memorandum No. 102, 24 Feb. 1942, RCAF file 5-33-5, DHist 181.009 (D4461); 'Notes sur Louis Bisson par Rév. Père Ferranque, OMI,' in Lorenzo Cadieux, *De l'avion à l'avion: Joseph Marie Couture, s.j.* (np 1959), 141 (translation, 3, Louis Bisson biographical file, DHist); Powell, *Ferryman*, 49
33 McVicar, *Ferry Command*, 34–65
34 Stacey, *Arms, Men and Governments*, 374–5; Dziuban, *Military Relations*, 224, 324, and 334; K.C. Eyre, 'Custos Borealis: The Military in the Canadian North' (PhD thesis, University of London 1981), 112–20; and Powell, *Ferryman*, 47. For a mass of detail on the route and the individual stations on it, see the files 'North Atlantic Ferry Routes,' HQS 15-24-30 (particularly pts 1-6), NA, RG 24, vol. 5201, and 'Inspection and Facilities reports,' HQS 15-24-30A pt 2, ibid., vol. 5202.
35 Quoted in Stacey, *Arms, Men and Governments*, 375
36 Ibid.
37 Chiefs of staff to the ministers, 30 May 1942, RCAF file 15-24-30 pt 1, NA, RG 24, vol. 5201
38 Dziuban, *Military Relations*, 387; Stacey, *Arms, Men and Governments*, 346 and 375
39 Stacey, *Arms, Men and Governments*, 376
40 Dziuban, *Military Relations*, 186–7. DHist holds a number of kardex files on the Northeast Staging Route. See, for example, 181.009 (D1062), 193.009 (D12), (D17), (D22), (D32), (D36), (D43), and 314.009 (D17).
41 Canada, Parliament, House of Commons, *Debates*, vol. 61 (1944), 5706–8; Setson Conn and Byron Fairchild, *The Western Hemisphere: The Framework of Hemisphere Defense*, United States Army in World War II (Washington 1960), 408; Stacey, *Arms, Men and Governments*, 376. For a detailed description of the facilities of the NE Staging Route, see DOT file, 5150-

31 pts 1 and 2, 'Airports and Airharbours, General Correspondence, Northeast Staging Route – Inspection of August, 1944,' NA, RG 12, vol. 1405; and DHist 181.009 (D1062).

42 McVicar, *Ferry Command*, 66–7

43 Ibid., 67

44 Ibid., 70

45 RCAF Station Goose Bay, daily diary, DHist

46 McVicar, *Ferry Command*, 70

47 Ibid., 70–1

48 Ibid., 72

49 Ibid., 73

50 Ibid., 74. For Bernt Balchen's career at BW-8, see his autobiography, *Come North with Me* (New York 1958), 215–56.

51 McVicar, *Ferry Command*, 75

52 Ibid., 77

53 Ibid., 77–8

54 Ibid., 79–83. See also RCAF Station Goose Bay, daily diary, DHist, and the crew assignment cards, DHist 84/44.

55 RCAF Station Goose Bay, daily diary, DHist

56 Craven and Cate, *Plans and Early Operations*, 638–45; Milner, 'Establishing the Bolero Ferry Route,' 213 and 218–20; F/L E.P. Wood, 'Northern Sky-trails, Part X,' *The Roundel* 1, 10 (Aug. 1949), 8–9

57 RCAF Station Goose Bay, daily diary, DHist. Craven and Cate are probably in error when they give 23 June as the date on which the first aircraft of the Eighth Air Force arrived at Goose Bay. *Plans and Early Operations*, 644

58 Milner, 'Establishing the Bolero Ferry Route,' 220–2; Craven and Cate, *Plans and Early Operations*, 644–5

59 Craven and Cate, *Plans and Early Operations*, 645. The statistical picture is slightly different in Milner, 'Establishing the Bolero Ferry Route,' 222.

60 Newfoundland Airport Watch Log, DHist 79/1 LG; RCAF Station Goose Bay, daily diary, DHist. Although such records seem to have noted accidents that occurred after aircraft were dispatched, it cannot be assumed that all losses are mentioned. The diaries are barely adequate sources of information about the various types ferried. No archival record has been found that provides good and reliable information about Ferry Command's losses of either aircraft or personnel. These statistics were taken from a special file prepared from a number of sources during research for this book. The file has been deposited at DHist. The key sources consulted, besides the unit diaries, were the crew assignment

cards (DHist 84/44) and the RCAF casualties list consolidated by Hugh Halliday as DHist 90/19. Civilian radio officers are listed in 'Statistics of the "Silent Keys,"' *The Transat: Bulletin of the Trans-Oceanic Radio Officers Association* 2, 2 (Oct. 1945), 8. For more on losses, see below, chapter 11 and appendix B.

61 Milner, 'Establishing the Bolero Ferry Route,' 222

62 Denis Richards and Hilary St George Saunders, *Royal Air Force, 1939–1945*, 2: *The Fight Avails* (London 1954), 375 and 378. Three RCAF squadrons operating with Coastal Command were equipped with aircraft that had been delivered by ATFERO and Ferry Command – No. 407 with Hudsons and Nos 413 and 422 with Catalinas.

63 No. 422 Squadron, operations record book (ORB), app. A to form 540 for Oct. 1942, DHist; L.W. Skey biographical file, DHist

64 General Curtis LeMay with Mackinlay Kantor, *Mission with LeMay: My Story* (New York 1965), 203–4

65 Watt, *High Road*, 134–5

66 Milner, 'Establishing the Bolero Ferry Route,' 220–2

67 Wesley Frank Craven and James Lea Cate, *The Army Air Forces in World War II*, 6: *Men and Planes* (Chicago 1955; reprinted 1983), 66–7

68 'Minutes of a Discussion held between Ferry Command, RAF Delegation, and Air Transport Command at Dorval, 16 November 1942,' NA, RG 24, vol. 5420

69 'Notes of an Interview with Mr. (G/C ret'd) J.G. H. Jeffs, 9 October 1973,' Jeffs biographcial file, DHist

70 Ibid.; 'Notes of an Interview with Dr. P.D. McTaggart-Cowan on 4 July 1973,' McTaggart-Cowan biographical file, DHist

71 Bowhill to Patterson, 1 April 1943, NA, RG 12, vol. 645. See also interview, McTaggart-Cowan biographical file, DHist.

72 Interview, Jeffs biographical file, DHist

73 Powell, *Ferryman*, 99

74 Interview, Jeffs biographical file, DHist; Llewellyn Woodward, *British Foreign Policy in the Second World War* (London 1962), 374–83. At least one ferry crew, forced to land in neutral Portugal, was interned there.

CHAPTER 7 The Southern Routes

1 Robin Higham, *Britain's Imperial Air Routes, 1918 to 1939: The Story of Britain's Overseas Airlines* (Hamden, Conn. 1960), 207–12; *Jane's All the World's Aircraft, 1937*, 28a; John Terraine, *The Right of the Line: The Royal Air Force in the European War, 1939–1945* (London 1985), 305

2 Terraine, *Right of the Line*, 305

3 Ibid., 305–6

4 Lord Tedder, *With Prejudice: The War Memoirs of Marshal of the Royal Air Force Lord Tedder G.C.B.* (London 1966), 37. For more on the job of ferrying aircraft across Africa, see Tony Dudgeon, *Wings over North Africa* (Shrewsbury, Eng. 1987).

5 Robert Daley, *An American Saga: Juan Trippe and His Pan Am Empire* (New York 1980), 306, and generally 302–6. See also Marilyn Bender and Selig Altschul, *The Chosen Instrument – Pan Am, Juan Trippe: The Rise and Fall of an American Entrepreneur* (New York 1982), 331–3.

6 Daley, *American Saga*, 306

7 Ibid., 306–9; Ford G. Daab, 'The Brazilian Air Force in World War II,' *Air University Review* 37, 5 (July–Aug. 1986), 68–9

8 Wesley Frank Craven and James Lea Cate, eds., *The Army Air Forces in World War II*, 1: *Plans and Early Operations, January 1939 to August 1942* (Chicago 1948; reprinted 1983), 320–2

9 Daley, *American Saga*, 310–11; W. Donald Thomas, 'Flight Radio Navigator: Adventures with Pan American Air Ferries – 1942,' *Journal American Aviation Historical Society* (summer 1984), 118. For the president's concern about assisting the British to improve the trans-Africa airway and to ferry bombers via this route, see Warren F. Kimball, ed., *Churchill and Roosevelt: The Complete Correspondence*, 1: *Alliance Emerging, October 1933–November 1942* (Princeton, NJ 1984), 206–7 and 209–11. The scheme is explained in a three-page memorandum from the secretary of state for dominion affairs, London, to the secretary of state for external affairs, Ottawa, 29 Aug. 1941. A copy was fowarded to the minister of transport by Norman Robertson, undersecretary of state for external affairs, and 'LBP' [Lester B. Pearson], on 1 September 1941. See file 11-52-10 pt 1, 'Defence Measures and Regulations, United States, Ferrying of Aircraft across the South Atlantic,' National Archives of Canada (NA), Record Group (RG) 12, vol. 643.

10 Craven and Cate, *The Army Air Forces*, 1: 322–3

11 Daley, *American Saga*, 311; Thomas, 'Flight Radio Navigator,' 119–20; Craven and Cate, *The Army Air Forces*, 1: 323–4. Some of the airmen with the PAAF, such as Joe Mackey, claimed previous experience with the British transatlantic ferry service.

12 *Jane's All the World's Aircraft, 1941*, 68b; Craven and Cate, *The Army Air Forces*, 1: 324 and 328–9; Henry Ladd Smith, *Airways Abroad: The Story of American World Air Routes* (1950; Washington 1991), 80 and 132–3. For a copy of the agreements, as well as the related contracts and

correspondence, as printed by the Air Ministry, see Department of Transport file 11-52-10 pt 1, NA, RG 12, vol. 643.

13 Daley, *American Saga*, 312. See also Vincent Orange, 'Tedder and the Americans,' paper delivered to the annual meeting of the Society for Military History, Kingston, Ontario, May 1993; and Smith, *Airways Abroad*, 80 and 132–3. Shortly after Pearl Harbor, the United States received permission from the British 'to establish a regular air ferry service between Washington and Cairo via Brazil, Gold Coast (Accra)[,] Nigeria and Anglo-Egyptian Sudan (El Fasher) ... to transport Government officials and possibly diplomatic mail.' Secretary of state for dominion affairs to secretary of state for external affairs, 23 Dec. 1941, file 11-52-10 pt 1, NA, RG 12, vol. 643.

14 Craven and Cate, *The Army Air Forces*, 1: 120, 131, 329

15 Ibid., 324. See also Kimball, *Churchill and Roosevelt*, 1: 369–70. In fact, one source indicates that the route was militarized on 1 November 1942. See secretary of state for dominion affairs to secretary of state for external affairs, 21 Nov. 1942, file 11-52-10 pt 1, NA, RG 12, vol. 643.

16 Interview by Fred Hatch with E.A. Aalmann, 19 June 1976; Bernt Balchen, *Come North with Me: An Autobiography* (New York 1958), 211. The identity of the flight engineers could not be discovered.

17 Public Record Office (PRO), AIR 38/23; Don McVicar, *Ferry Command* (Shrewsbury, Eng. 1981), 94–5; Geoff Thomas, 'Eye of the Phoenix,' *Aircraft Model World* (a series of thirteen articles, Feb. 1985 to May 1987). I am indebted to Bob Smith for providing this detailed information about the fate of these aircraft.

18 Craven and Cate, *The Army Air Forces*, 1: 331; and Craven and Cate, *The Army Air Forces in World War II*, 7: *Services around the World* (Chicago 1958; reprinted 1983), 174. The US government asked for and received British permission 'to establish an air route between the west coast of Africa via Pointe Noire, Leopoldville, Bukama, Mbeya, Mombasa, Seychelles, Coetivy, Chagos Archipelago, and Cocos Island to Fort Hedland in Australia.' Secretary of state for dominion affairs to secretary of state for external affairs, 4 March 1942, file 11-52-10 pt 1, NA, RG 12, vol. 643

19 Henry Flory, unpublished memoir, 123–4, excerpt held by Directorate of History, National Defence Headquarters (DHist)

20 Ibid., 124–5

21 Ibid., 126

22 Ibid., 126–7

23 Ibid., 128

24 McVicar, *Ferry Command*, 99

25 Bowhill to undersecretary of state for air, 10 Nov. 1942, PRO, AIR
   24/506; reports from Sept. 1941 to March 1943, table 2, PRO, AIR
   24/5493; McVicar, *Ferry Command*, 98–100
26 Kimball, *Churchill and Roosevelt*, 1: 516–19; Winston S. Churchill, *The
   Hinge of Fate*, The Second World War, vol. 4 (Boston 1950), 383 and 422
27 Griffith Powell, *Ferryman: From Ferry Command to Silver City*
   (Shrewsbury, Eng. 1982), 88
28 Flory memoir, 132, DHist
29 Powell, *Ferryman*, 89–90; crew assignment cards, DHist 84/44; Fred
   Hatch interview with Al Lilly, 27–28 Oct. 1975, DHist
30 Flory memoir, 132, DHist
31 'Takoradi to Cairo,' *RAF Middle East Review* (May–Dec. 1942), DHist
   181.003 (D1023)
32 McVicar, *Ferry Command*, 191
33 'Baling Out over the Sudan,' Transport Command Notes on the Middle
   East, DHist 181.003 (D2713)
34 Flory memoir, 132–3, DHist; crew assignment cards, DHist 84/44
35 Powell, *Ferryman*, 88. The United States had received permission to build
   the airport on Ascension early in 1942. See secretary of state for
   dominion affairs to secretary of state for external affairs, 11 Feb. 1942,
   file 11-52-10 pt 1, NA, RG 12, vol. 643. For the air supply of British
   forces in North Africa, see Smith, *Airways Abroad*, 102–3.
36 Major-General F.W. Von Mellenthim, *Panzer Battles, 1939–1945: A Study of
   the Employment of Armour in the Second World War*, trans. H. Betzler
   (London nd), 140; Terraine, *The Right of the Line*, 378–83; Tedder, *With
   Prejudice*, 347; B.H. Liddell Hart, *History of the Second World War* (New
   York 1970), 291–7
37 Telegram to RAFDEGATION, Washington, 26 Sept. 1942, PRO, AIR 8/474.
   For opinions of personnel stationed along the route, see the letters and
   postcards sent to Lillian Hanson Wheeler, Jimmy Jubb's popular
   secretary. Copies at DHist
38 PRO, AIR 38/23
39 Major Kenny Allred, 'The Persian Corridor: Aid to the Soviets,' *Military
   Review* 65, 4 (April 1985), 15, 19, and 22–3; Craven and Cate, *The Army
   Air Forces*, 1: 329
40 McVicar, *Ferry Command*, 194–201
41 Marix to AOC-in-C (air officer commanding-in-chief), Transport
   Command, 7 Aug. 1944, PRO, AIR 25/648
42 Lilly interview, DHist
43 Crew assignment cards, DHist; Powell, *Ferryman*, 91

44 Flory memoir, 133, DHist

45 Ibid., 133–4

46 Ibid., 134. For the US responsibility for Ascension's facilities and defence, see secretary of state for dominion affairs to secretary of state for external affairs, 10 March 1942, file 11-52-10 pt 1, NA, RG 12, vol. 643

47 Flory memoir, 134–5, DHist

48 H.R. 'Red' Syrett, '45 Atlantic Crossings,' *Airforce* 6, 3 (Sept. 1982), 9 and 24. John Butler Wood, an RAAF navigator, also mentions Ferry Command facilities on the island, in '"Overseas" with the Royal Air Force Transport Command,' unpublished wartime memoir, copy at DHist.

49 Flory memoir, 135, DHist

50 Ibid.

51 Syrett, '45 Atlantic Crossings,' 9, 24–5, and 39–42; McVicar, *Ferry Command*, 180–93; Wood, '"Overseas",' Part 3, particularly 158 and 184, DHist

52 George Phillips biographical file, DHist

53 'Notes of an Interview by F.J. Hatch with Mr. G.A. Seward regarding his operations with Ferry Command of the R.A.F. and in particular the circumstances under which he and his crew were captured in Dahomey French West Africa and held prisoner by the Vichy French,' Seward biographical file, DHist

54 Ibid. See also Bruce West, *The Man Who Flew Churchill* (Toronto 1975), 85–6.

55 Seward interview, biographical file, DHist

56 Ibid.; Phillips biographical file, DHist; crew assignment cards, DHist 84/44

57 Powell, *Ferryman*, 102–3

58 Wood, 'Overseas,' 206, and generally 201ff

59 Ibid., 248, and generally 206–48

60 Ibid., 252

61 Ibid., 260, and generally 252–60

62 Walter Jones's letter home [addressed 'Dear Folks & Geo' from 'Ike'], 11 June 1944, copy in his biographical file, DHist. For US airlines flying these routes as a service to the military, see Smith, *Airways Abroad*, 73.

63 Quoted in 'Takoradi to Cairo,' *RAF Middle East Review* (May–Dec. 1942), DHist 181.003 (D1023). The same sentiment is evident in Roderic Owen, *The Desert Air Force* (London [1948]).

CHAPTER 8 One-Trippers

1 Griffith Powell, *Ferryman: From Ferry Command to Silver City* (Shrewsbury, Eng. 1982), 56

2 [John Pudney], *Atlantic Bridge: The Official Account of R.A.F. Transport Command's Ocean Ferry* (London 1945), 25

3 No. 31 Operational Training Unit (OTU), Debert, NS, daily diary, Directorate of History, National Defence Headquarters (DHist); F/O Hodgins, 'O.T.U.'s under the B.C.A.T.P.: No. 31 O.T.U.,' unpublished narrative [1945], DHist 74/13

4 No. 31 OTU, daily diary, entry for 27 May 1941, DHist

5 Ibid.

6 Ibid., 30 June 1941

7 Ibid., 31 July 1941

8 Ibid., Aug. 1941

9 Director of airmen personnel services to CO [commanding officer], 1 ANS (Air Navigation School), 28 Oct. 1941, ANS training file, DHist 76/221

10 CO, 1 ANS, to director of airmen personnel services, 5 Nov. 1941, ibid.

11 No. 31 OTU diary, 7 and 8 Sept. 1941, DHist

12 Ibid., 3 Sept. 1941

13 Ibid., 29 Sept. 1941

14 Ibid., 13 Sept., 23 and 25 Oct. 1941; RCAF casualties, DHist 90/19. This source lists fifty-five members of the RCAF, six RAF, six RAAF, one RNZAF, and a civilian noted as 'prop hit.' Another source indicates that the 'wastage rate' was unacceptably high in 31 OTU's early days, 18.8 per cent for 1942, but gradually fell to 13.9 per cent for 1943 and ultimately to 5.8 per cent when it switched to Mosquitoes in 1944 under a new designation, No. 7 OTU. See F/O Hodgins, 'O.T.U.'s under the B.C.A.T.P.: No. 31 O.T.U.,' 11–12, DHist 74/13. In all, 856 aircrew were killed or seriously injured during the life of the BCATP. Fred Hatch, *Aerodrome of Democracy: Canada and the British Commonwealth Air Training Plan, 1939–1945* (Ottawa 1983), 150 (citing BCATP Supervisory Board minutes, DHist 73 1558, X, 55)

15 No. 31 OTU diary, 24 Nov. 1941, DHist

16 Don M. Macfie, diary, especially 5 and 6 Jan. 1942, copy in his biographical file, DHist. All the Macfie references on the following pages are from this document.

17 Ibid., 30 Jan. 1942

18 No. 31 OTU diary, 13 March 1942, DHist

19 Macfie diary, 13, 29, and 30 March, and 1 April 1942, DHist

20 Ibid., 22 April 1943 and passim

21 No. 31 OTU diary, April 1942 summary, DHist

22 Ibid.

23 Macfie diary, 20, 21, and 27 April 1942, DHist. See also 'Operations

Record,' attached to 31 OTU diary, DHist; and W.A.B. Douglas, *The Creation of a National Air Force*, Official History of the Royal Canadian Air Force, vol. 2 (Toronto and Ottawa 1986), 490.

24 Macfie diary, 3 May 1942, DHist. See also 31 OTU 'Operations Record,' DHist, which gives the time up and time down simply as 1530 and 2130 hours; and Douglas, *National Air Force*, 496. It was not only while at an OTU that ferry crews assisted with the anti-submarine war. Occasionally delivery crews reported sighting U-boats and relayed the word to operational commands.

25 No. 31 OTU diary, 31 May 1942, DHist

26 Macfie diary, 4 June 1942, DHist

27 'Oral History Project: An Interview with Dr. Patrick D. McTaggart-Cowan,' transcript, 17, McTaggart-Cowan biographical file, DHist

28 Macfie diary, 4 June 1942, DHist

29 Ibid. For more on BCATP graduates at Bournemouth, see Ted Barris, *Behind the Glory* (Toronto 1992), 261–3; Murray Peden, *A Thousand Shall Fall* (Stittsville, Ont. 1979), 110–27, and Spencer Dunmore, *Wings for Victory: The Remarkable Story of the British Commonwealth Air Training Plan in Canada* (Toronto 1994), 235, 305, and 341, which briefly tells the story of 31 OTU and Don Macfie on 303–4. Don Macfie's short stint with Ferry Command may have been over, but not his love affair with the aircraft he helped deliver to the United Kingdom. He has tried, unsuccessfully, to track its wartime career, most recently by writing to *Airforce* (17, 2 (July 1993), 35): 'All I know is that the aircraft went to India and was struck off strength 5 Feb. 1945. I would like to know what it did for the war effort. It was a good "kite." So look into your log books you Hudson men and see if FH444 is there.'

30 AOC (air officer commanding) No. 2 Training Command to CO 1 ANS, 22 Sept. 1941, ANS training file, DHist 76/221

31 Hatch, *Aerodrome of Democracy*, 120 (citing DHist 74/7, 130, and 188–9)

32 Ibid., 163–73; Douglas, *National Air Force*, 224–5 and 264–6

33 *Royal Canadian Air Force List*

34 H.A. Wills, 'Diary of RCAF Service,' copy in Wills biographical file, DHist

35 No. 1 ANS diary, DHist

36 Wills diary, DHist. For more on No. 1 Manning Depot, see Barris, *Behind the Glory*, 48–56; Hatch, *Aerodrome of Democracy*, 33, 47, 121, 125; and Douglas, *National Air Force*, 278.

37 No. 1 ANS diary, 23 June 1941, DHist

38 Hatch, *Aerodrome of Democracy*, 40 and 171

39 Ibid., 164–5; Douglas, *National Air Force*, 245
40 Wills diary, 2 and 5 July 1941, DHist
41 Ibid. See also *RCAF List*.
42 No. 1 ANS diary, passim, DHist
43 H.A. Wills, scrapbook, copy, DHist. See also 1 AOS (Air Observer School), daily diary, DHist; Wills diary, DHist; and Red Syrett to Fred Hatch, 1 Oct. 1983, copy in Wills's biographical file, DHist.
44 Wills diary, DHist; W.L. Halperin biographical file, DHist
45 Sir Arthur Harris, *Bomber Offensive* (New York 1947), 96–7; Douglas, *National Air Force*, 264; Hatch, *Aerodrome of Democracy*, 169
46 *Air Force Administrative Orders*, A.51/28, 30 Nov. 1942
47 Wills diary, 'Feb or March/43,' DHist
48 Ibid.; and Wills correspondence, copies in H.A. Wills biographical file, DHist; and Syrett to Hatch, 1 Oct. 1983, ibid.
49 Wills diary, DHist; 31 OTU diary, DHist
50 Wills to his wife, 27 Oct. 1943, H.A. Wills biographical file, DHist. The quotations which follow are also from this collection of photocopied letters.
51 Ibid., 25 Oct. 1943
52 Ibid., especially 25 and 27 Oct. and 1 Nov. 1943
53 Ibid., 4 Nov. 1943
54 Ibid., 27 Oct. 1943
55 Ibid., 22, 25, and 27 Oct. and 1 and 4 Nov. 1943
56 Ibid., 27 Oct. 1943
57 No. 45 (Atlantic Transport) Group, 'Operational Activities for the Month of November 1943,' Public Record Office (PRO), AIR 25/647. Other members of Halperin's crew were F/O Aleksander Cezary Monkiewicz (Polish Air Force pilot), F/O Derrick Joseph Oswald Pyne, RAF (pilot, from Hitchin, Hertfordshire), and F/O Stewart James Hansen, RAAF (wireless operator/air gunner, Queensland, Australia). Crew assignment cards, DHist 84/44; and RCAF casualties, DHist 90/19
58 Wills to his wife and daughter, 10, 15, and 20 Nov. 1943, Wills biographical file, DHist. See also crew assignment cards, DHist 84/44; and RCAF casualties, DHist 90/19.
59 No. 45 (AT) Group, 'Operational Activities for the Month of November 1943,' PRO, AIR 25/647
60 Wills to his wife, 19, 20, 22, and 23 Nov. 1943, Wills biographical file, DHist
61 Ibid., 23 Nov. 1943. The censor also cut out Wills's casual reference to the times that he saw Mars, the sunset, and the aurora borealis.

62 Ibid., 19, 23, 24, and 27 Nov. 1943

63 Crew assignment cards, DHist 84/44

64 Powell, *Ferryman*, 78. See also A/M C.R. Dunlap, 'Memories of 139 Wing,' *High Flight* 2, 5 (Sept./Oct. 1982), 189.

65 PRO, AIR 25/647

66 J.H. Parkin, 'North Atlantic Air Service London–Montreal' (paper presented to the semicentennial meeting of the Engineering Institute of Canada, June 1937), 37–8, DHist 74/704. For notes on ice-accretion problems encountered by Ferry Command pilots over the North Atlantic, see National Research Council file 4-A3-22, in National Archives of Canada (NA), Record Group (RG) 77, vol. 237; and papers of the De-Icing Research Committee in A.G.L. McNaughton Papers, NA, Manuscript Group (MG) 30 E 133, vol. 232.

67 *Jane's All the World's Aircraft, 1943/44*, 66d

68 Don McVicar, *Ferry Command* (Shrewsbury, Eng. 1981), 114

69 *London Air Observer* (Feb. 1944), 7, in No. 4 AOS diary, DHist

CHAPTER 9   No. 45 Group

1 [John Pudney], *Atlantic Bridge: The Official Account of R.A.F. Transport Command's Ocean Ferry* (London 1945), 37. Griffith Powell, *Ferryman: From Ferry Command to Silver City* (Shrewsbury, Eng. 1982), 117. For the composition of the various formations, see Air Ministry, *Confidential Air Force List* (CD 200/1943/3 to CD 200/1945/9; [London 1943–5]).

2 Wesley Frank Craven and James Lea Cate, *The Army Air Forces in World War II*, 7: *Services around the World* (Chicago 1958; reprinted 1983), 14

3 AOC (air officer commanding) 45 Group to AOC-in-C (air officer commanding-in-chief) Transport Command, 10 Oct. 1944, Public Record Office (PRO) AIR 25/648. These were undoubtedly the same type of South African frogs purchased by the Royal Canadian Medical Corps 'for diagnostic [pregnancy] tests on C.W.A.C. personnel,' and flown to Canada by the RCAF's 168 (Heavy Transport) Squadron. See A/C J.W. Tice, director of medical services (air) to AMS, 10 May 1944, and DMS (Air) to CO (commanding officer) RCAF HQ, Cairo, secret signal, 3 June 1944, in file HQC 45-17-28, National Archives of Canada (NA), Record Group (RG) 24, vol. 5372.

4 *Atlantic Bridge*, 56

5 AOC 45 Group to AOC-in-C Transport Command, 10 Oct. 1944, PRO, AIR 25/648

6 Henry Flory, unpublished memoir, 133, excerpt in his biographical file, Directorate of History, National Defence Headquarters (DHist)

7 Command Routine Orders by A/C/M Sir Frederick Bowhill, serial no. 15, 7 April 1943, PRO, AIR 24/506; Air Ministry, *Confidential Air Force List; July 1943* (CD 200/1943/7; [London 1943]), 193

8 Marix to AOC-in-C, 18 Jan. 1945, PRO, AIR 25/648

9 Marix to AOC-in-C, 8 March 1945, ibid. For an account of the early plans to fly freight and passengers on the Pacific route, see R.B. Jackson, chief traffic officer, 45 Group, to A.G. Maitland, Office of the High Commissioner for the United Kingdom, Earnscliffe, 21 Nov. 1944, copy on Department of Transport (DOT) file 5252-10 pt 1, NA, RG 12, vol. 599. A copy of the operations order for the delivery of Dakota KN347 to Sydney, Australia, in Feb. 1945 is in the J.U. Stephens biographical file, DHist.

10 Powell, *Ferryman*, 96. For discussion of priorities, especially for Canadian passengers, on the Pacific route, see DOT file 5250-9 pt 1, 'Air Traffic, General Correspondence, Trans-Pacific,' which includes a copy of 45 Group traffic notice no. 115 of 21 Oct. 1944, describing the nature of the new service, the route, and the regulations. NA, RG 12, vol. 599

11 Powell, *Ferryman*, 81; 45 Group Organization Orders and Traffic Notices, DHist 181.009 (D3077)

12 Powell, *Ferryman*, 91

13 Winston S. Churchill, *The Hinge of Fate*, The Second World War, vol. 4 (Boston 1950), 453

14 Ibid. See also Bruce West, *The Man Who Flew Churchill* (Toronto 1975), 1–11 and 56.

15 Martin Gilbert, *Churchill: A Life* (London 1991), 725

16 Churchill, *Hinge of Fate*, 455–6. There is disagreement about the departure date. The PM says 'after midnight on Sunday, 2 August ...' (ibid., 455). Powell seems to agree when he gives 3 August (*Ferryman*, 93). Gilbert implies the night of 1 August (*Churchill*, 725). For West it was 'a few minutes after midnight, on Sunday, August 3, 1942 ...' (*The Man*, 102).

17 Churchill, *Hinge of Fate*, 456. See also West, *The Man*, 102–14.

18 Churchill, *Hinge of Fate*, 458–9 and 463–4; Gilbert, *Churchill*, 726

19 Churchill, *Hinge of Fate*, 524. See also ibid., 473 and 500; Gilbert, *Churchill*, 726; and West, *The Man*, 115–33.

20 Quoted in Gilbert, *Churchill*, 730

21 See, for example, the unidentified clippings, dated 29 and 31 August

1942, apparently from *The Gazette* and *The Star*, Montreal newspapers, in Lillian Hanson Wheeler's scrapbook, copy at DHist.

22 West, *The Man*, 156–78

23 Powell, *Ferryman*, 93 and 125; Wheeler scrapbook, DHist

24 Fred Hatch, '"COMMANDO": The Rebirth and Demise of a Famous Aircraft,' *CAHS Journal* 15, 3 (fall 1977), 94; Powell, *Ferryman*, 94; West, *The Man*, 195

25 F/O Hodgins, 'O.T.U.'s under the B.C.A.T.P.; No. 32 O.T.U.,' unpublished narrative [1945], DHist 74/13

26 Ibid.; F.J. Hatch, *The Aerodrome of Democracy: Canada and the British Commonwealth Air Training Plan, 1939–1945* (Ottawa 1983), 78–9 and 188; W.A.B. Douglas, *The Creation of a National Air Force*, Official History of the Royal Canadian Air Force, vol. 2 (Toronto and Ottawa 1986), 288–9

27 No. 32 OTU, daily diary and operations record book (ORB), DHist

28 Hodgins, 'O.T.U.'s under the B.C.A.T.P.; No. 5 O.T.U.,' DHist 74/13

29 'Strength returns RCAF officers (and other ranks) on strength of No. 45 (AT) Group, RAF Station Dorval,' 'nominal roll RCAF officers on strength of no. 111 OTU, Nassau, Bahamas, 25 March 1945,' and 'nominal roll RCAF other ranks on strength of no. 111 OTU Nassau, Bahamas, 25 March 1945,' RCAF file S.21-6-7, DHist 181.005 (D863)

30 Jack Leslie Plant, 'The Royal Air Force in Nassau,' *Nassau: Magazine of International Life in the Bahamas* 12, 1 (Dec. 1945), 10. I am indebted to Mary Kelloway, who worked during the war at 113 Wing, for making copies of this magazine available to me.

31 RCAF Station North Bay, daily diary, DHist

32 *Atlantic Bridge*, 42–3

33 Reports for June 1944 to May 1945, PRO, AIR 25/648

34 Robert Byrne to his sister Frances, 12 and 15 Jan. 1943, copy in his biographical file, DHist. I am indebted to Gerald Forrette for sending me copies of the letters written by his uncle, Robert Byrne, describing his time with RAF Ferry Command. For details on this scheme to have USAAF personnel obtain training and experience with RAF Ferry Command, see LCol Francis J. Graling, acting military attaché, Legation of the USA, Ottawa, to G/C H.R. Stewart, director of air intelligence, Ottawa, 15 Oct. 1942 (copy, apparently sent to C.P. Edwards, deputy minister DOT), file 5250-7, NA, RG 12, vol. 599.

35 Byrne to his sister, 20 Jan. and 22 Feb. 1943, Robert Byrne biographical file, DHist. The account of Byrne's time with Ferry Command is based on this correspondence. Comments on the city and its women can be found in several of Byrne's letters from Montreal. For a similar view, see

interview transcripts, 328–9, in the Sheldon Luck papers, NA, Manuscript Group (MG) 31 A 11.

36 Gerald B. Forrette to author, 25 Sept. 1989, copy ibid.

37 Compilation of Ferry Command losses, DHist. The Ferry Command crew assignment cards record the loss of J.C. Ford, USATC (with no rank given), a radio operator in Catalina FP116 which crashed out of Bermuda on 13 March 1943. The other five known USAAF fatalities came when Liberator BZ935 disappeared over the North Atlantic on 1 March 1944. The USAAF supplied the entire crew: the pilot, 1st Lt C.M. Dorsett; the co-pilot, 2nd Lt O.E. Hess; the navigator, 1st Lt G.L. McBride; the radio operator, SSgt J.W. Wiant; and the flight engineer, Sgt R.F. Mennig. DHist 84/44/3. See also the diary of RCAF Station Gander, entry for 1 March, DHist.

38 The compilation of statistics showing the numbers of aircraft ferried across the North and South Atlantic, not to mention the Pacific, presents a difficult problem. The most complete statistical summary of aircraft delivered to the United Kingdom and other theatres by the Air Services Department of the CPR, ATFERO, Ferry Command, and 45 Group is to be found in PRO, AIR 38/23, which covers the period from October 1940 to 30 April 1945. For some reason this record fails to make any mention of the Lancasters ferried to the United Kingdom in 1943, 1944, and 1945, and does not give a monthly breakdown of Mosquitoes and Dakotas delivered in 1943 and 1944 as it does for other aircraft. Information on the Lancasters, Mosquitoes, and Dakotas, and of course other types as well, can be obtained from the monthly reports of Bowhill and Marix to the Air Ministry and Transport Command headquarters in PRO, AIR 24/506, AIR 25/647, and AIR 25/648. As these cover the period from September 1941 only, they do not provide a complete statistical picture, but do supplement AIR 38/23. The sources do not always agree, especially in the case of the Lancasters omitted in AIR 38/23. A particular problem in using AIR 24/506, AIR 25/647, and AIR 25/648 arises in connection with accidents, as it appears that the delivery totals have not been adjusted to take into consideration aircraft that were lost or wrecked en route. At best, available statistics must be regarded as approximations. Yet, imperfect as they are, they provide a measure of the dimensions of the transatlantic ferry service.

39 A/M Harris to CAS (chief of the air staff), weekly letter, week ending 9 Aug. 1941, app. 11, PRO, AIR 2/7526

40 Owen Thetford, *Aircraft of the Royal Air Force, 1918–1957* (London 1957), 346–7 and 190–1

41 No. 405 Squadron, flying with No. 8 (Pathfinder) Group, was equipped with British Lancasters. Three other Canadian squadrons used British-made Lancaster IIs for a short time, but converted to Halifaxes in 1944. Spencer Dunmore and William Carter, *Reap the Whirlwind: The Untold Story of 6 Group, Canada's Bomber Force of World War II* (Toronto 1991), passim; and William S. Carter, *Anglo-Canadian Relations, 1939–1945: RAF Bomber Command and No. 6 (Canadian) Group* (New York 1991), 53–65

42 Reports for Aug. 1943 to Sept. 1945 (PRO, AIR 25/647 and AIR 25/648) give a total of 390 Lancasters and 626 Mosquitoes delivered. K.M. Molson and H.A. Taylor, in *Canadian Aircraft since 1909* (Stittsville, Ont. 1982), 69, report that 422 Lancaster Xs were built in Canada and that all were ferried to Britain. The same source says that 1033 Mosquitoes were built in Canada (255), but does not indicate how many were delivered overseas.

43 C. Frank Turner, 'The Ruhr Express: Quick off the Line, Slow off the Mark,' *Airforce* 6, 3 (Sept. 1982), 5; Division of Aeronautical Engineering, 'Consolidated Progress Reports to 9 Aug. 1943,' DHist 181.003 (D3410); Molson and Taylor, *Canadian Aircraft*, 66

44 R.J. Lane biographical file, DHist; *The Aeroplane* 65 (July–Dec. 1943), 344

45 Quoted in Turner, 'The Ruhr Express,' 5 and 16

46 Powell, *Ferryman*, 79; Molson and Taylor, *Canadian Aircraft*, 67; Marix to AOC-in-C, 13 Sept. and 12 Oct. 1943, PRO, AIR 25/647

47 Powell, *Ferryman*, 79; Molson and Taylor, *Canadian Aircraft*, 69–70; Brereton Greenhous, Stephen J. Harris, William C. Johnston, and William G.P. Rawling, *The Crucible of War, 1939–1945*, Official History of the Royal Canadian Air Force, vol. 3 (Toronto and Ottawa 1994), 757–8

48 See the daily diaries and ORBs of the squadrons, DHist. The 6 Group aircraft inventory is summarized in a table in Greenhous et al., *Crucible of War*, 637 (see 863 for 'Tiger Force'). See also Carter, *Anglo-Canadian Wartime Relations*, 63; and Major John G. Armstrong, 'The Canadian Built Lancaster X; Complicated Answers to Simple Questions,' RCAF History, vol. 3 preliminary narrative (17 Nov. 1988), 26–8, DHist.

49 C. Martin Sharp and Michael J.F. Bowyer, *Mosquito* (London 1967), 102–5

50 Molson and Taylor, *Canadian Aircraft*, 254

51 Powell, *Ferryman*, 79 and 81–2

52 Don McVicar, *North Atlantic Cat* (Shrewsbury, Eng. 1983), 168 and generally 154–69

53 Ibid., 169. See also Powell, *Ferryman*, 81–2; and Harry Moyle, *The Hampden File* (Tonbridge, Eng. 1989), 175.

54 McVicar, *North Atlantic Cat*, 174. See also Powell, *Ferryman*, 81–2.

55 *Atlantic Bridge*, 46–50; Powell, *Ferryman*, 82; McVicar, *North Atlantic Cat*, 174; West, *The Man*, 140–55; Moyle, *The Hampden File*, 175

56 'Report on the Second Experimental Flight between Edmonton Alta. Canada and Prestwick, Scotland,' DHist. See also McVicar, *North Atlantic Cat*, 180–2.

57 The flying log attached to the report on the flight gives 23 hours 33 minutes ('Second Experimental Flight,' DHist); McVicar says 24 hours 15 minutes. (*North Atlantic Cat*, 183).

58 'Second Experimental Flight,' DHist

59 Powell, *Feeryman*, 106

60 Teulon to author, 16 Jan. 1993, and excerpts from his logbook, copies in A.P. Teulon biographical file, DHist, Teulon gives the number of flying boats in this allotment as twenty-five, rather than the forty-eight quoted by Powell in *Ferryman*.

61 Powell, *Ferryman*, 107. See also Teulon to author, 16 Jan. 1993, and logbook excerpts, Teulon biographical file, DHist. Teulon remembers the southern route deliveries with the Soviets as coming *after* the USSR had taken PBYs from California to Siberia.

62 Bowhill to undersecretary of state for air, 8 Feb. 1943, PRO, AIR 24/506; Marix to AOC-in-C Transport Command, 14 June and 16 July 1943, PRO, AIR 25/647; *The Aeroplane* 65, 1675 (2 July 1943), 30; Hitchins to Ralston, 27 Feb. 1948, DHist 181.009 (D5054); 'Address by W/C F.M. Gobeil to the annual convention of the Canadian Aviation Historical Society, Toronto, June 1973,' DHist 73/1449; photographs, DHist 73/328; various clippings, F.M. Gobeil biographical file, DHist; file 1008-1-186, NA, RG 24, vol. 4898

63 See the various reports and returns for Sept. 1941–Oct. 1945, in PRO, AIR 24/5493, AIR 25/647, and AIR 25/648.

64 Sully to RCAF liaison officer, 19 Dec. 1941, in 'Correspondence to RCAF Liaison Officer RAF Ferry Command, Dorval Quebec, Relating to Policy on Discipline for RCAF,' RCAF file S18/1, DHist 181.009 (D3442)

65 Crew assignment cards, DHist 84/44

66 The women co-pilots, apparently ATA, were Opal Anderson, from Chicago (Catalina JV935, 30 Oct. 1943); Ethel Ruth Ballard, Maidenhead, Eng. (Liberator AM861, 8–9 Oct. 1944); Dorothy Rita Bragg, from New Orleans (Mitchell FV967, 15–21 Sept. 1943); Suzanne H. Ford, from New York (Liberator EW613, 18–19 June 1944); Helen Marcelle Harrison, from Toronto (Mitchell FR185, 19–24 Sept. 1943); Mary Estelle Hooper, from Marquette, Michigan (Mitchell FV956, 10–13 Sept. 1943); Nancy Jane Miller, from Los Angeles (Liberator KH303, 26–29 Oct. 1944); Marion

Orr, from Toronto (Fortress HB815, 10–11 June 1944); Edith Foltz Stearns, from Portland, Oregon (Liberator BZ944, 30 Oct.–11 Nov. 1943); Grace Stevenson, from Holdenville, Oklahoma (Mitchell FV958, 11–15 Sept. 1943); and Ann Watson Wood, from Waldoboro, Maine (Mitchell FV959, 10–15 Sept. 1943). While these eleven women flew as supernumerary crew on deliveries, there is some evidence of three other women passing through Dorval: Roberta Sandoz Leveaux, from Chewelan, Washington (given as 'SNY,' supernumerary, with no aircraft or date); Virginia Parr, from New Jersey (mentioned in a newspaper clipping, as one of six 'ATA girls' in Montreal to fly as co-pilots); and Catharine Van Doozer, from Los Angeles (passenger, 7–9 Oct. 1943). Crew assignment cards, DHist 84/44; Wheeler scrapbook, DHist; and Gander Ferry Command diary, PRO, AIR 38/4. See also Shirley Render, *No Place for a Lady: The Story of Canadian Women Pilots, 1928–1992* (Winnipeg 1992), 85 and 89; Helen Harrison Bristol, 'Flying Back When,' *Airforce* 5, 2 (June 1982), 40–2; LCol Nancy B. Samuelson, 'Equality in the Cockpit: A Brief History of Women in Aviation,' *Air University Review* 35, 4 (May–June 1984), 35–46; Vi Lee Warren Doerr, 'Flying the WASP Way,' *Airforce* 10, 2 (July–Aug.–Sept. 1986), 8–9, also published in *CAHS Journal* 25, 1 (spring 1987), 20–2; and PRO, Foreign Office (FO) 371/26205.

67 Jacqueline Cochran and Maryann Bucknum Brinley, *Jackie Cochran: An Autobiography* (New York 1987), 167–79. See also Sholto Watt, *I'll Take the High Road: A History of the Beginning of the Atlantic Air Ferry in Wartime* (Fredericton NB 1960), 152–5. This story was confirmed in conversations with the author, without prompting, by Ferry Command veterans who were there at the time. In Cochran's version she and Carlisle, along with a radio operator who had volunteered to join them, had almost to sneak away from St Hubert in their delivery aircraft.

68 PRO, FO 371/26205

69 Powell, *Ferryman*, 54–5

70 McVicar, *North Atlantic Cat*, 167–8

71 Reports and returns, PRO, AIR 24/5493, AIR 25/647, and AIR 25/648

72 Ferry Command Association, 'Canadian Civilian Aircrew, Ferry Command,' attached to Wheeler to Douglas, 14 Aug. 1975, DHist

73 BAC (British Air Commission) to MAP (Ministry of Aircraft Production), 28 July 1941, PRO, AIR 2/705

74 Newfoundland Airport Watch Log, 11 July 1941, copy, DHist 79/1 LG; *The Gazette* (Montreal), 8 Feb. 1971; Fred Hatch interview with Al Lilly, A.J. Lilly biographical file, DHist; interview transcripts, 320, Sheldon

Luck Papers, NA, MG 31 A 11; Bowhill to undersecretary of state for air, 9 April 1943, PRO, AIR 24/506

75 Griffith Powell, *'Per Ardua Ad Astra': A Story of the Atlantic Air Ferry* (Montreal [1945]), np. Military members also received recognition for contributions to the ferry service, with at least a dozen members of the RCAF receiving Air Force Crosses for services to Ferry Command. F/L George Gordon Wright made seventy Atlantic and six Pacific crossings with the British ferry service and 168 Squadron of the RCAF. I am indebted to Hugh Halliday for making this information available.

76 'Statistics of the "Silent Keys,"' *The Transat: Bulletin of the Trans-Oceanic Radio Officers Association* 2, 2 (Oct. 1945), 8, copy at DHist

CHAPTER 10 Mosquito Deliveries

1 C. Martin Sharp, *D.H.: A History of de Havilland*, rev. ed. (Shrewsbury, Eng. 1982), 183. See also C. Martin Sharp and Michael J. Bowyer, *Mosquito* (London 1967), for the definitive book on the aircraft and its development; and Joe Holliday, *Mosquito: The Wooden Wonder Aircraft of World War II* (Markham, Ont. 1980), 30–3.

2 Sharp, *D.H.*, 178–86; Graham M. Simons, *Mosquito: The Original Multi-Role Aircraft* (London 1990), 25–32; Michael J.F. Bowyer and Bryan Philpott, *Mosquito* (Cambridge, Eng. 1980), 11–15; M.J. Hardy, *The de Havilland Mosquito* (New York 1977), 63–5; Sharp and Bowyer, *Mosquito*, 23–5; and Holliday, *Mosquito*, 241–2 and passim

3 Sharp, *D.H.*, 177–8 and 181; K.M. Molson and H.A. Taylor, *Canadian Aircraft since 1909* (Stittsville, Ont. 1982), 254; Simons, *Mosquito*, 35; and Holliday, *Mosquito*, 36 and 94–5

4 Sharp and Bowyer, *Mosquito*, app. 8, 409–10, and app. 5, 401–3; Simons, *Mosquito*, 25 and passim; and Hardy, *The de Havilland Mosquito*, 121

5 W.J. McDonough, 'Canada's Aircraft Industry: Text of Address by W.J. McDonough, President of Central Aircraft Mfg. Co. Ltd. before the Canadian Section, Society of Automotive Engineers, Royal York Hotel, Toronto, Ontario, Wednesday, November 15, 1944,' 8, copy of transcript in A.G. Sims Papers, National Archives of Canada (NA), Manuscript Group (MG) 30 A 76. The production figures vary slightly depending on the source. Sharp (in *D.H.*, 188–9) says that 5570 Mosquitoes were manufactured in Britain, 1134 in Canada, and 108 in Australia, for a total of 6812. In *Mosquito*, he and Bowyer give a wartime production total of 6710, including 1032 in Canada (81). They list forty-nine variants (app. 4,

393–400). Molson and Taylor (*Canadian Aircraft*, 225) list the total Canadian production at 1034. Fred Hotson (in *DH Canada Story* [Toronto 1978], 26) cites de Havilland Canada documents for a total of 1133. He admits: 'A photograph of that era plainly advertises "Mossie" 1,134 as our "LAST" and only adds to the confusion.' Simons (*Mosquito*, 134) claims: 'Production eventually reached a worldwide total of approaching 8,000.' He undoubtedly includes postwar construction. He sets the Canadian total at 1034 (40). Hardy notes (*The de Havilland Mosquito*, 115): 'On 15 November 1950, the 7,781st and last Mosquito to be built ... was completed.'

6 Holliday, *Mosquito*, 130–1. Taffy Powell, inexplicably, claims 'zero losses' for the Mosquito deliveries. See Griffith Powell, *Ferryman: From Ferry Command to Silver City* (Shrewsbury, Eng.), 116.

7 Simons, *Mosquito*, 39; Hardy, *The de Havilland Mosquito*, 90; Molson and Taylor, *Canadian Aircraft*, 258; Sharp and Bowyer, *Mosquito*, 102; and Holliday, *Mosquito*, 128–9. Later, Holliday says that the first Canadian Mosquito was flown by F/O T. Murray Mitchell of Toronto with F/O B. Stovel of Winnipeg as his radio navigator (191).

8 [John Pudney], *Atlantic Bridge: The Official Account of R.A.F. Transport Command's Ocean Ferry* (London 1945), 53. A newspaper report of 29 April 1943 credits May with a takeoff-to-landing time of 7 hours 40 minutes. Pudney, however, would surely have seen official documents. See 'Strong Tail Wind Helped May Make Record Flight,' *Ottawa Evening Journal*, clipping in file 5250-7 NA, Record Group (RG) 12, vol. 599.

9 Holliday, *Mosquito*, 192–4, 146–7, and 243–4; and Hardy, *The de Havilland Mosquito*, 90. See also Simons, *Mosquito*, 40; Molson and Taylor, *Canadian Aircraft*, 257–8; and Sharp and Bowyer, *Mosquito*, 104. Gill's radio-navigator for his November 1944 record-setting crossing was J.P. Lagadec. See 'New Air Record Is Set for Atlantic Crossing,' *Montreal Gazette*, 30 Nov. 1944, clipping in file 5250-7, NA, RG 12, vol. 599

10 Don McVicar, *A Change of Wings* (Shrewsbury, Eng. 1984), 63–70; crew assignment cards, Directorate of History, Department of National Defence (DHist) 84/44

11 McVicar, *Change of Wings*, 23–4, 66, and 71–4

12 Don McVicar, *North Atlantic Cat* (Shrewsbury, Eng. 1983), 127

13 Ibid., 129

14 Ibid., 130

15 Ibid., 131–2

16 Ibid., 132–3

17 Ibid., 133

18 Ibid.

19 McVicar, *Change of Wings*, 1–2

20 Ibid., 2–3. McVicar refers to the Greenland strip as BW-8, but he seems to mean BW-1, an interpretation supported by the crew assignment cards for him and Eby in DHist 84/44. It is unclear what type of surfacing one could find on the Greenland runways at this time. McVicar mentions concrete; some other sources say steel mat.

21 McVicar, *Change of Wings*, 4

22 No. 45 Group to Air Ministry, no. 06892, 8 May [1944], HQ 235-5-3 pt 1, NA, RG 24, acc. no. 83-84/049, box 199; and crew assignment cards DHist 84/44

23 Holiday, *Mosquito*, 132; G/C Best, chief engineer officer, 45 Group, 'Delivery of Mosquito Aircraft, November 1944–March 1945,' 7 April 1945, paragraph 1, copy in file generously provided by Fred Hotson (copy now at DHist as acc. no. 93/91)

24 'Notes of an interview with Mr. A.G. Sims concerning his operations with Ferry Command and No. 45 Transport Group, by F.J. Hatch, 28 October 1975,' A.G. Sims biographical file, DHist

25 Crew assignment cards, DHist 84/44; 'Statistics of the "Silent Keys,"' *The Transat: Bulletin of the Trans-Oceanic Radio Officers Association* 2, 2 (Oct. 1945), 8; and unidentified clipping, Lillian Hanson Wheeler scrapbook, copy at DHist

26 RCAF Station Goose Bay, daily diary, entry for 26 or 27 Aug. 1944 (it is impossible to discern which marginal date applies), DHist. See also crew assignment card, DHist 84/44/3; and unidentified clipping, dated 30 Aug. 1944, Wheeler scrapbook, DHist.

27 Best, 'Delivery of Mosquito Aircraft,' especially app. A, DHist 93/91

28 Ibid., paragraph 2

29 Ibid., paragraph 3

30 Crew assignment cards, DHist 84/44; RCAF Station Gander, daily diary, DHist; 45 Group, monthly accident reports, DHist 181.003 (D4286); Tom McGrath, diary, DHist 74/635; RCAF casualties, DHist 90/19; 'Statistics,' *Transat* (Oct. 1945), 8. G/C Best records the second of these two losses as KB536. 'Delivery of Mosquito Aircraft,' paragraph 3, DHist 93/91

31 Best, 'Delivery of Mosquito Aircraft,' especially app. A, DHist 93/91. According to McVicar, it was Huss's first Mosquito delivery. *Change of Wings*, 66. His crew assignment card has him piloting one other Mosquito to the United Kingdom, in October. Crew assignment card, DHist 84/44

32 Crew assignment cards, DHist 84/44; 45 Group, monthly accident reports, DHist 181.003 (D4286); RCAF casualties, DHist 90/19; John

Butler Wood, '"Over Seas" with the Royal Air Force Transport Command,' unpublished memoir, 127, copy, DHist

33 Best, 'Delivery of Mosquito Aircraft,' paragraphs 4, 5, and 6, and app. P, George Blakely's report, 'AN/Gyro Horizon in Mosquito at De Havilland,' 2, DHist 93/91

34 Best, 'Delivery of Mosquito Aircraft,' paragraph 6, DHist 93/91; crew assignment cards, DHist; 45 Group, monthly accident reports, DHist 181.003 (D4286); 'Statistics,' *Transat* (Oct. 1945), 8. There is also an obscure reference to the loss of 'Mos KB 563' with two civilians, A. Copp and J.E. Rogers, sometime in December 1944. RCAF casualties, DHist 90/19

35 Best, 'Delivery of Mosquito Aircraft,' paragraph 6, DHist 93/91

36 Ibid., paragraph 7

37 Ibid., app. B

38 Ibid., paragraph 10

39 Ibid., app. C, HQ No. 45 Group to HQ Transport Command, Harrow, Harvey from Powell, SASO-5380, 20 Dec. 1945

40 Ibid., paragraph 11, and app. D, W/C J.R. Bradford, 'Mosquito Preparation and Despatching Unit, Crumlin Airport, London, Ontario' (Organization Memorandum 21), 21 Jan. 1945

41 Ibid., paragraph 14

42 See the technical details in the memoranda and reports collected as ibid., app. I and app. J.

43 Ibid., Best, 'Delivery of Mosquito Aircraft,' paragraph 15

44 Ibid., paragraph 16

45 Testimony of 19th witness, Mathias Hinton, 'Proceedings of Investigation into the Loss of Mosquito KB 370,' HQ 235-5-3 pt 1, NA, RG 24, acc. 83-84/049, box 199. On this date, Capt John Frederick Bradley (from Calgary) and John Donald McIntyre (from Toronto) died when 'pilot shot up Amherst [NS] airfield at low altitude and high speed. Pulled up in climbing turn and wings failed near L.R. tanks, crashed and burned. Two crew killed.' 45 Group, monthly accident reports, DHist 181.003 (D4286). The names can be found in the crew assignment cards, DHist 84/44. See also 'Statistics,' *Transat* (Oct. 1945), 8; and unidentified clipping, dated 5 Feb. 1945, Wheeler scrapbook, DHist.

46 Testimony of 14th witness, F/L William H. McDonald, acting station navigating officer, 45 Group, Dorval, 'Investigation ... KB 370,' 11, HQ 235-5-3 pt 1, NA, RG 24, acc. 83-84/049, box 199

47 Testimony of 15th witness, Richard W. Haigh, ibid., 12

48 Testimony of 16th witness, F/L Dennis Walker Fenton, acting chief flying instructor, Training Wing, ibid., 12

49 S/L Ed Coristine's testimony, ibid., 12–13

50 Ibid.; testimony of 12th witness, F/L Cyril George Minchinton, operations control officer, 84 Staging Post, Goose Bay, ibid., 10; testimony of 11th witness, S/L John Beard, signals officer, 84 Staging Post, Goose Bay, ibid., 9

51 Minchinton testimony, ibid., 10

52 Testimony of 10th witness, James McRobb, a civilian engineer employed by RAF Transport Command as foreman in charge of maintenance of all RAF, BOAC, and TCA aircraft passing through Goose Bay, ibid., 8

53 Testimony of 2nd witness, Alfred Aaron Elkin, ibid., 2

54 Testimony of 18th witness, F/O Alan Dixon, ibid., 13–14

55 Testimony of 3rd witness, George C. Krewson, 2nd Lt, USAAF, ibid., 3–4

56 Testimony of 1st witness, F/O William H. Edwards, ibid., 1

57 Elkin testimony, ibid., 1

58 Testimony of 7th witness, Capt John J. Sullivan, USAAF, operations officer at the 67th AACS Group stationed at BW-1, ibid., 7

59 Testimony of 5th witness, S/Sgt Robert L. Kress, ibid, 5–6, and log exhibits K and M

60 Ibid.

61 RAF form 412, 'Proceedings of Investigation,' section 10, 'Conclusions,' paragraph (a), 3–4, ibid. See also the summary on the crash card at DHist.

62 W/C Jones comments, RAF form 412, section 10, 'Conclusions,' paragraph (a), 4, HQ 235-5-3 pt 1, NA, RG 24, acc. 83-84/049, box 199

63 Fletcher's comments, ibid.

64 Best, 'Delivery of Mosquito Aircraft,' paragraph 17, DHist 93/91

65 G.E. Ferguson, 'Report on Snags and Trouble on Aircraft via the Southern and Northern route,' 27 Feb. 1945, and covering letter to Best, same date, ibid., app. L

66 See the memoranda, minutes, and reports collected as app. L, M, and N to Best's report, ibid.

67 Crew assignment cards, DHist 84/44; 45 Group, monthly accident reports, DHist 181.003 (D4286)

68 Best, 'Delivery of Mosquito Aircraft,' paragraph 21, DHist 93/91. The crew names are taken from the crew assignment cards, DHist 84/44. See also 45 Group, monthly accident reports, DHist 181.003 (D4286); and 'Statistics,' *Transat* (Oct. 1945), 8.

69 Best, 'Delivery of Mosquito Aircraft,' paragraph 18, DHist 93/91

70 Ibid., 'Summary.' For more on Mosquito modifications, see 'Notes of an Interview on 27 and 28 October, 1975 with Captain A.J. Lilly … concerning his service with the Air Service Department of the C.P.R., ATFERO, Ferry Command and No. 45 Transport Group during the Second World War; by F.J. Hatch, Directorate of History, D.N.D. Ottawa,' A.J. Lilly biographical file, DHist. There was considerable pressure at this time to get Mosquitoes, and spare parts for them, to the United Kingdom. See the correspondence between the manufacturers and the government officials responsible for moving air cargo (up to and including C.D. Howe) in file 5252-4 pt 1, NA, RG 12, vol. 599, about the problem of moving Mosquito spare parts to Britain.

71 Sharp and Bowyer, *Mosquito*, 104–5, and photograph following 112. See also interview transcript, A.G. Sims biographical file, DHist.

72 Interview, 11–12, A.J. Lilly biographical file, DHist

73 No. 45 Group, monthly accident reports, DHist 181.003 (D4286); RCAF Station Goose Bay, daily diary, DHist. The pilots and radio navigators lost were: in KA968, F/O W. Wielondek and F/O M. Zajac; in KA153, F/O F.W. Clarke and F/L K.W. Grist; and in KA237, Capt H.S. Wright and J.R. Woodyard. Crew assignment cards, DHist 84/44; RCAF casualties, DHist 90/19. On 10 May the experienced RAF operational crew of F/L John Maurice Winnington Briggs and F/O J.C. Baker perished when Mosquito LR503 flew into the control tower during a demonstration flight at Calgary.

74 Testimony of 12th witness, Frances Archibald Innes, meteorological assistant, Department of Transport, stationed at the Mosquito Preparation and Development Unit, Crumlin Airport, London, transcript of the investigation report of the court of inquiry into the crash of Mosquito KB370, 6, HQ 235-5-3 pt 1, NA, RG 24, acc. 83-84/049, box 199. See also testimony of 13th witness, F/O Stanley Frederick Harvey Thompson, ibid., 7.

75 Testimony of 14th witness, Capt Thomas Givens Smith, chief flying instructor, 45 Group, Dorval, 'Proceedings of Investigation,' carbon copy, 7, ibid.

76 Testimony of 15th witness, ibid.

77 Testimony of 16th witness, ibid., 8

78 Testimony of 10th witness, Joseph LeRoy Dunn, ibid., 4. For these and other details, see also the summation by the investigating officers, F/Ls John H. Battison and D.R. Thoday, ibid., section 10, 3.

79 Testimony of 5th witness, F/O Bruce Montgomery Smith, RCAF, ibid., 2. See also the testimony of the 4th witness, Sgt Vincent Pelletier, flying control, 6 REMU, Mont Joli, ibid., and also the testimony of the 1st

witness, Douglas William James Stewart, RAFTC liaison officer, Mont
Joli, ibid., 1.

80 Testimony of 6th witness, Wilfred Ross, ibid., 3
81 Testimony of 3rd, 7th, 8th and 9th witnesses, F/O John Watson Moore,
Noel Belanger, George Thomas, and Dr Adrien Lepage, ibid., 2–4
82 Moore testimony, ibid., 2
83 Stewart testimony, ibid., 1
84 Testimony of 11th witness, S/L Henry Cobb, inspector of accidents,
AFHQ, ibid., 4–5
85 'Proceedings of Court of Inquiry,' section 10, 3, ibid.
86 Ibid., 4
87 Ibid.
88 Crew assignment cards and aircraft log record sheets, DHist 84/44;
RCAF casualties, DHist 90/19
89 Molson and Taylor, *Canadian Aircraft*, 257–8
90 McVicar, *Change of Wings*, 124
91 *The Transat: Bulletin of Trans-Oceanic Radio Officers Association* 2, 1 (Jan.
1945), 13

CHAPTER 11 No Piece of Cake

1 'Statistics of the "Silent Keys,"' *The Transat: Bulletin of Trans-Oceanic Radio
Officers Association* 2, 2 (Oct. 1945), 8. Three men may have been killed in
this crash, but no records could be located.
2 Newfoundland Airport Watch Log, 26 May 1941, copy, Directorate of
History, National Defence Headquarters (DHist) 79/1 LG. See also crew
assignment cards, DHist 84/44
3 No Christian names or initials could be found for Turner or Laing. A
radio officer named George Laing is recorded in the crew assignment
cards, but the first entry for him is dated 26 June 1941 with the delivery
of Hudson AM722. DHist 84/44
4 T.M. McGrath, diary, entry for 15 Sept. 1941, copy, DHist 74/635
5 RSC PS to CAS, 11 June 1941, Public Record Office (PRO), AIR 8/474
6 Watch log, 14 June 1941, DHist 79/1 LG; crew assignment cards, DHist
84/44
7 Crew assignment cards, DHist 84/44; 'Statistics,' *Transat* (Oct. 1945), 8
8 RCAF Station Gander, daily diary, 5 Aug. 1941, DHist; RCAF casualties,
DHist 90/19; crew assignment cards, DHist 84/44; 'Statistics,' *Transat*
(Oct. 1945), 8. Unfortunately, no file has come to light that provides
definitive details on the losses of personnel or aircraft by Ferry

Command. Consequently, it is often necessary to cite several sources for a loss, with each document providing a small piece of the puzzle.

9 George Lothian, *Flight Deck: Memoirs of an Airline Pilot* (Toronto 1979), 83–4 and 86–8

10 Edgar J. Wynn, *Bombers Across* (New York 1944), 52 and, generally, 51–3. Capt Wynn was killed in a plane crash in Florida in 1946 ('Casualties,' *Transat* 3, 1 [Feb 1948], 5). See also Henry Flory's unpublished memoirs, 120–1, copy, DHist.

11 Ralph Barker writes, in *Survival in the Sky* (London 1976), 93–101, that White and Cripps switched flights. Had they not, he says, White would have flown Liberator 915, with Lord Beaverbrook on board, into Goat Fell. It is a good story and it may be true. However, no archival substantiation has been found to support it.

12 '22 Killed in Air Crash: Scots Victim,' unidentified clipping [13 Aug. 1941], E.L. Thompson Papers, DHist. See also the Ferry Command account of the crash, apparently for staff more than for public consumption, ibid.

13 Letter, E.G. Palmer (Ex-AB), *Navy News* (Jan. 1976), 6

14 The pilots were Josiah James Anderson (of Charlottetown), Francis Delaforce Bradbrooke (who had a modest reputation as an aviation writer in Britain), Daniel J. Duggan (from Boston), George Thomas Harris (Lawrence, Kansas), Hoyt Ralph Judy (Dallas), Watt Miller King (Little Rock, Arkansas), John Evan Price (from Australia), John James Roulstone (Los Angeles), Harold Clifford Wesley Smith (Montreal), Ernest Robert Bristow White (Prestwick), and Jack Wixen (Los Angeles); the radio operators, Ralph Bruce Brammer (Toronto), John Beatty Drake (New Westminister, British Columbia), Henry Samuel Green (Whitechurch, England), Wilfred Graves Kennedy (Ottawa), George Laing (Halifax), Hugh Cameron McIntosh (Scarborough, Ontario), William Kenneth Marks (Stratford, Ontario), Albert Alexander Oliver (Swindon, England), George Herbert Powell (Derby, England), and Herbert David Rees (Llanelly, Wales); and the flight engineer, Ernest George Reeves (Somerville, New Jersey). See crew assignment cards, DHist 84/44; E.L. Thompson Papers, DHist; PRO, AIR 38/2; and 'Statistics,' *Transat* (Oct. 1945), 8. The crash is mentioned in the RCAF Station Gander daily diary, DHist; and BOAC Return Ferry Service (RFS), 'Operations Movements Book, No. 1' (hereafter log), DHist.

15 Wynn, *Bombers Across*, 54–5

16 Watch Log, DHist 79/1 LG

17 Wynn, *Bombers Across*, 57

18 Ibid.
19 Ibid.; Flory memoirs, 120, DHist
20 Wynn, *Bombers Across*, 58. See also Stafford's crew assignment card, DHist 84/44/3. He had 4500 hours as a pilot when he joined ATFERO in the fall of 1940.
21 Flory memoirs, 120, DHist
22 Ibid., 121
23 Ibid.
24 Ibid., 121–2
25 Ibid., 122
26 Ibid.
27 In addition to Stafford, the pilots in the second crash were Elbert Beard Anding (from Merrick, New York), Murray Benjamin Dilley (Kansas City), Alton Chester Earl (Huntington, West Virginia), Edward Hamel (Mount Vernon, New York), Gerald Hull (Royal Oak, Michigan), John Joseph Kerwin (Oakland, California), Philip Francis Lee Jr (Frederick, Maryland), James John Moffat (Toronto), Walter L. Trimble (Fort Worth, Texas), Earl Wellington Watson (Torrance, California), and Martin Joseph Wetzel (Jamesburg, New Jersey); the radio operators, Richard Coates (Dartmouth, Nova Scotia), Joseph Patrick Culbert (Liverpool, England), Robert Arnold Duncan (Fort William, Ontario), Wesley Francis James Goddard (Toronto), Donald Norman Hannant (Victoria), John Joseph MacDonald (Sydney, Nova Scotia), Glenwood McKay (Toronto), and Albert Tamblin (Port Arthur, Ontario); and the flight engineer Roland Fulford Davis (Seattle, Washington). Davis's crew assignment card calls him a USN Reserve pilot, but he was working as the flight engineer on this trip (DHist 84/44). See also 'Statistics,' *Transat* (Oct. 1945), 8. An early press report confused McKay with Joe Mackey and erroneously named the latter as one of the victims. See unidentified clipping in uncatalogued air force scrapbook, DHist. For more on the 14 August crash, see PRO, AIR 38/2.
28 RAF Ferry Command, 'Funeral Service at Lamlash Cemetery, Isle of Aaran [sic],' nd, and 'Hillside Grave for Plane Crash Victims,' *Daily Record and Mail*, 16 Aug. 1941, E.L. Thompson Papers, DHist; Wynn, *Bombers Across*, 59
29 RAF Ferry Command, 'Extract from "The Gazette," Montreal P.Q., August 15th, 1941,' E.L. Thompson Papers, DHist
30 RAF Ferry Command, 'Extract from "The Gazette," Tuesday, August 19th, 1941,' ibid.
31 Flory memoirs, 121, DHist

32 Crew assignment cards, DHist 84/44; Flory memoirs, 122, DHist; and
McGrath diary, DHist 74/635. The passengers were E. Taylor, Dr
Benjamin, Professor Mowat, Col Wrongham, Capt Pickering, and Count
de Bailler-Letour. The Watch Log (DHist 79/1 LG) is the only source that
mentions them.

33 On 21 September 1941, F/L R.F. Leavitt, RAF (pilot, from Regina,
Saskatchewan), Sgt Elwood Wallace McFall, RCAF (navigator, Ottawa)
and Robert Desmond Anderson (radio operator, Newcastle, New Bruns-
wick) disappeared in Hudson AE545. On 27 September F/O Harold
Wilson Oldham, RCAF (pilot, Dartmouth, Nova Scotia), Sgt William
Ronald Lance, RCAF (navigator, Hamilton, Ontario), and Cyril Harvey
Small (radio operator, St John's, Newfoundland) were 'lost at sea' in
Hudson AM940. On the same night Hudson AE577 crashed at Dundalk,
killing F/L Louis Romeo Dubuc, RCAF (pilot, Fort Saskatchewan,
Alberta), Sgt Frederick James Goodwin, RAF (navigator, Staffordshire,
England), and Samuel Raymond Kenny (radio operator, Louisburg, Nova
Scotia). On 11 October 1941 Hudson AM951 was 'lost at sea' with an all-
civilian crew: William James Guy (captain-navigator, Cardiff, Wales),
William Allen Herron (1st officer, Philadelphia, Pennsylvania), and
Clinton Lloyd Larder (radio operator, Consort, Alberta). This information
was put together from the crew assignment cards, DHist 84/44; the
Newfoundland Airport Watch Log, DHist 79/1 LG; the RCAF Station
Gander daily diary, DHist; McGrath diary, DHist 74/635; lists of RCAF
casualties, DHist 90/19; and 'Statistics,' *Transat* (Oct. 1945), 8. McGrath
records that 'AE 577 landed Baldonnell (Dublin) departed for Aldergrove
crashed and all killed.'

34 See the chronological card file on losses (citing sources for each name)
built up during the research for this book, now deposited at DHist. The
tabular summary shows the pattern at a glance.

35 No definitive file on the losses of ferry service aircraft has been located
at the PRO in London, the National Archives of Canada (NA), or DHist
in Ottawa. The figures quoted here are from the record of losses
compiled by the author from a number of sources at all three
repositories. A copy of the file thus created has been deposited for
public consultation at DHist. The key sources used to put this file
together were the crew assignment cards and the few aircraft log sheets
in DHist 84/44; PRO, AIR 38 (especially AIR 38/3 and AIR 38/4), AIR
2/4575, AIR 8/474, AIR 8/479; the daily diaries of RCAF Stations
Gander, Goose Bay, Mont Joli, and St Hubert at DHist (others were
checked but were no help); Headquarters No. 45 Group, 'Monthly

Accident Investigation Reports,' Sept. 1944–Oct. 1945, DHist 181.003
(D4286); RCAF casualties, DHist 90/19; McGrath diary, DHist 74/635;
Lillian Hanson Wheeler scrapbook, copy, DHist; BOAC RFS log, DHist;
crash cards for RCAF accidents in Canada (occasionally including Ferry
Command and 45 Group losses, apparently in error), DHist; 'Statistics of
the "Silent Keys,"' *Transat* (Oct. 1945), 8; and accident investigation
report files at the National Archives of Canada in Record Group (RG) 24,
especially file HQ 235-5-3, 'Flying Accidents: Non-Service Aircraft; RAF
Ferry Command Aircraft,' RG 24, acc. 83-84/049, box 199. Many RCAF
fatalities can be verified in the microfilm of the old Canadian Forces
Records Centre Index, held at DHist as 76/10 mfm. Ultimate verification
would necessitate checking individual personnel files at the Personnel
Records Centre of the National Archives of Canada. Research identified
at least 144 lost or disappeared aircraft involving ferry personnel
(excluding three RFS Liberators and two USATC losses that took 45
Group lives). A table, 'Disposition of Delivery Aircraft Received but Not
Delivered to the U.K. as of April 30th, 1945,' in PRO, AIR 38/23 gives
'186' as the total 'Lost or Struck Off.' It seems safe to assume that the
figures quoted in this book for losses are all on the low side.

36 Don McVicar, *North Atlantic Cat* (Shrewsbury, Eng. 1983), 113, and
generally 104–13. See also PRO, AIR 38/3; McGrath diary, 74/635; BOAC
RFS, 'Operations Movements Book, No. 3,' DHist. The signal from G/C
F.S. Wilkins, the RCAF's chief inspector of accidents, to the minister, 15
Feb. 1943, claims that the plane made two passes over the field before it
'struck a hill in the vicinity of the airport.' HQ 235-5-3 pt 1, NA, RG 24,
acc. 83-84/049, box 199

37 Entry for 9 Feb. 1943, PRO, AIR 38/3

38 McVicar, *North Atlantic Cat*, 11–12

39 Entry for 10 Feb. 1943, PRO, AIR 38/3

40 Ibid., 11 Feb. 1943

41 The Ferry Command fatalities were Frederick Joseph Brown (radio
operator, from Carnforth, Lancashire), Fortune Anthony Dugan (pilot,
New Orleans, Louisiana), Sgt James Robert Eding, RAF (pilot, Botley,
Oxford), G.P.M. 'Pat' Eves (pilot, Warlingham, Surrey), T.R. Harmes
(pilot, Crawley, Sussex), John David Jones (radio operator, Southampton,
England), Sgt Wilton Henry Kyle, RCAF (navigator, Winnipeg, Mani-
toba), Sgt Howell Leonard Benjamin Lewis, RAF (pilot, Devon, England),
Robert Marvin Lloyd (pilot, Hollywood, California), Ernest Graham
Longley (flight engineer, Winnipeg), J.B. Merriman (flight engineer,
Devon), Sgt David Jervis Owen, RAF (pilot, Cornwall, England), Sgt

Graham Pritchard Pollard, RAF (pilot, Wales), P/O Robert Irving Scott, RCAF (navigator, Govan, Saskatchewan), Frederick Scrafton (radio operator, Toronto), Jack Stagner (pilot, Dallas), Reginald Wadsworth (radio operator, Blackpool, England), and Ivan Wilmot Wilson (flight engineer, Vancouver). Crew assignment cards, DHist 84/44; unidentified clippings, Wheeler scrapbook, DHist

42 '19 Die in Newfoundland Ferry Command Bomber Crash,' 'Probe Opens into Air Crash,' and 'Dorval Plane Crashes, 16 Die,' unidentified clippings [file on 26 Oct. 1942 Ventura crash], Wheeler scrapbook, DHist; crash card, Liberator 3701, 10 Oct. 1943, DHist

43 Including the ATC crew, the transport carried twenty-six people. The RAFFC personnel lost were F/O Geoffrey A. Clegg, RAF (pilot), Sgt John Lowery Bell, RAF (navigator, from Durham, England), and FSgt Norman Patrick Drury, RCAF (radio operator), who had just delivered Baltimore FA175 to West Africa; Paul Blecker Makepeace (pilot, Houston, Texas), F/O Peter Charles Zoephel, RCAF (navigator, Christchurch, Kent), and Clinton Blackwell Berry (radio operator, Cobden, Ontario) – Baltimore FA300; William Richard Nixon (pilot, Ottawa), P/O William Thomas Wright Smithson, RAAF (navigator, New South Wales), and Otway Cecil McCombie (radio operator, New Westminster, British Columbia) – Baltimore FA157; and F/L Herbert James Martin, RCAF (pilot, Cannington, Ontario), Sgt John Henry Warman, RCAF (navigator, Bass River Point, New Brunswick), and Sgt Harold Victor Lamb, RAAF (radio operator, Victoria, Australia) – Baltimore FA176. Crew assignment cards, DHist 84/44; unidentified clippings, Wheeler scrapbook, DHist; RCAF casualties, DHist 90/19; and 'Statistics,' *Transat* (Oct. 1945), 8

44 Crew assignment cards, DHist 84/44; RCAF casualties, DHist 90/19; McGrath diary, DHist 74/635; unidentified clippings, Wheeler scrapbook, DHist; 'Statistics,' *Transat* (Oct. 1945), 8. Besides Samuel Howard McCawley, the crew members of the Catalina were Andrew Eugene Bleau (pilot, from Groton, Connecticut), P/O Edward Dennis Markham, RAF (navigator, Bedford, England), Sgt Thomas Clarence Judiesch, RCAF (radio operator, Victoria, British Columbia), Stephen Francis Whitmore (radio operator, Birmingham, England), and Sgt Cecil Stanley Rumble, RAF (flight engineer, London, England). Sgt Antony Manderson Harris, RAF (pilot, Orpington, Kent) and FSgt Ronald Charles Brooks, RCAF (radio operator, Westboro, Ontario) were killed when Hudson FH235 crashed at Whiteface Mountain, New York.

45 The American captain was John Kilby Cummings (from St Louis, Missouri), the RAF pilot, FSgt David Gale (Cheshire, England). The RCAF pilots were P/O William Alexander Gardner (Gilbert Plains, Manitoba) and P/O Eric Ogilvy Smith (born in Vancouver, but giving Seattle, Washington, as his permanent address); the RCAF navigators were Sgt John Samuel Cram (Morden, Manitoba), Sgt Samuel Jacob Donen (Winnipeg), and F/O John Scott MacLean (Toronto); and the RCAF radio operators were Sgt Ronald Cyrus Lounsbury (Windsor, Ontario), Sgt John MacRae (Winnipeg), and FSgt Erle Donald Rennick (Vancouver). Crew assignment cards, DHist 84/44; RCAF casualties, DHist 90/19. On 12 April 1989 the former Canadian minister of veterans affairs, the Honourable George Hees, in his capacity as ambassador-at-large, laid a wreath at the cross of sacrifice in Christiansborg war cemetery, Accra, in tribute to these men who gave their lives delivering military aircraft during the Second World War. See a text of the press release in Department of National Defence (DND) file 1325-500/00 (DHist).

46 PRO, AIR 38/3; Wheeler scrapbook, DHist; crew assignment cards, DHist 84/44; RCAF casualties, DHist 90/19. In addition to Carl Frederick Kaiser and Arthur Harold Down, the fatalities were the civilians Charles Herbert Cole (of R.H. Steen & Co., Toronto – entered as both Coke and Cole in DHist 90/19), H.S. Millan (of the Department of Transport in Montreal), and John T. Barry and Morris S. Myles (of the Canadian Ice Machine Company, Toronto), and the RCAF airmen, LAC D.A. Abbott, LAC K.D. Campbell, LAC J.F. Carr, Cpl C.T. Christopherson, LAC W.B. Danielson, Cpl M.J. Kasey, LAC B.E. Malone, LAC V.F. Peebles, AC1 L.V. Sparkes, and LAC P.J. Tennant.

47 On 8 October, Sgt Derrick Wallsh, RAF (pilot, from London, England), Sgt Thomas Geoffrey Knowles, RAF (pilot, Sunderland, England), Sgt Dennis Frederick John Jupp, RAF (navigator, Banstead, Surrey), and Sgt John Robert Weldon Grant, RCAF (radio operator, Dominion, Nova Scotia) took off from Gander in Ventura AJ450 and were never seen again. On 14 October Thomas Leonard Livermore (pilot, Sarasota, Florida), William Campbell Chitty (pilot, New York), George Frederic Johnston (navigator, Beaumont, Texas), Clarence Victor Atkinson (radio operator, Sydney, Nova Scotia), and Charles Frederick McDougall (flight engineer, Granum, Alberta) died in a Liberator crash on the southern route. On 15 October, Mitchell FR369 went missing out of Gander with its crew, F/L Russell Laurence Moss, RAF (pilot, Lancashire, England), P/O Francis John Pook, RAF (pilot, Plymouth, England), Sgt Michael

John Gardner, RAF (navigator, Epsom, Surrey), and Leonard R.J. Vine (radio operator, Wembley, England). Finally, on the same day that Kaiser crashed, 26 October, QM Nils Bjorn Rasmussen, RNAF pilot, drowned when Boston BZ200 crash-landed in an Irish bog and flipped over. Crew assignment cards, DHist 84/44; RCAF casualties, DHist 90/19; RCAF Station Gander, daily diary, DHist; Henry Flory memoirs, DHist; PRO, AIR 38/3; 'Statistics,' *Transat* (Oct. 1945), 8; HQ 235-5-3 pt 1, NA, RG 24, acc. 83-84/049, box 199

48 Flory memoirs, 132, DHist

49 Several clippings from Montreal newspapers, Wheeler scrapbook, DHist; crew assignment cards, DHist 84/44; RCAF casualties, DHist 90/19; and a brief mention in HQ 235-5-3 pt 1, NA, RG 24, acc. 83-84/049, box 199. One newspaper report claimed that the pilot survived.

50 This author has seen nothing in official archival sources about General Sikorski's misadventures in Ferry Command aircraft. The whole story has been chronicled by David Irving in *Accident: The Death of General Sikorski* (London 1967). For the Dorval incident, see 158–63 and 221–2. Sikorski flew to Washington in an American Liberator the next day. Irving claims that the pilot of the Hudson at Dorval was S/L R.E. Marrow. He then charges Ferry Command with denying this information and with downplaying the seriousness of the incident. Irving was unable to find any record of Marrow in RAF sources. Perhaps this was because he, or the Poles, confused Marrow with S/L R.E.E. Morrow, RCAF, who was with Ferry Command for a short period at this time. Morrow had commanded 402 Squadron in Britain prior to a brief sojourn in Canada in the fall of 1942. Like many other pilots needing to get overseas, he volunteered to fly an aircraft over for Ferry Command. The plane he was delivering, Boston BZ277, crashed at Conche Harbour, Newfoundland, on 30 November 1942, with no fatalities. Morrow, however, did not make it back to the United Kingdom. He subsequently served in the Aleutians, as commanding officer of the RCAF's 'X' Wing, and at various stations in Canada. *RCAF List*; crew assignment cards, DHist 84/44/3; RCAF Station Gander, daily diary, DHist; W.A.B. Douglas, *The Creation of a National Air Force*, Official History of the Royal Canadian Air Force, vol. 2 (Toronto and Ottawa 1986), 419

51 'Report of 9 April 1945 crash of a Liberator at St. Hyacinthe, PQ,' HQ 235-5-3 pt 1, NA, RG 24, acc. 83-84/049, box 199. There is little documentary evidence of the 13 March crash. The RCAF casualty list in DHist 90/19 links F/L Jarvis to Liberator EW626 of 45 Group on that date. For more on the crash-landing of Liberator AM929 on 9 April, see

45 Group Headquarters, 'Monthly Accident Reports,' DHist 181.003 (D4286), and unidentified clippings, Wheeler scrapbook, DHist.

52 Addendum to Aug. 1945 report, 45 Group Headquarters, 'Monthly Accident Reports,' DHist 181.003 (D4286). Besides Evans, the crew members were John W. Ross (co-pilot, from Portland, Oregon), Cyril P.J. 'Red' Meagher (radio operator, Halifax, Nova Scotia), F/O Roy Holden Marshall Patterson, RCAF (navigator, born in Chile, but giving Montreal as his home address), Gayle B. Swaney (flight engineer, Dayton, Ohio), and Sgt William T. Keates, RAF (flight clerk, London, England). The passengers were Sir William Malkin, Miss M.J.C. Scupham, Miss J. M. Cole-Hamilton, Miss A.M. Collard, and Miss D. Smith (all of the Foreign Office); R.T. Peel and Miss B. Hibberd (India Office); Col D.C. Capel-Dunn (Ministry of Defence); and Miss P.S. Spurway (Cabinet Office). Crash card, DHist; Wheeler scrapbook, DHist; RCAF casualties, DHist 90/19; 'Statistics,' *Transat* (Oct. 1945), 8

53 Report for Aug. 1945, 45 Group Headquarters, 'Monthly Accident Reports,' DHist 181.003 (D4286). Thirteen men allegedly died in this crash, but only eleven could be identified by the author. They were: pilots, F/O K.H.L. Houghton, F/O Stanley Albert Bennett, RAF (from Torquay, England), and F/L J.A. Sprigge; navigator, Sgt E.F. Rogers, RAF; wireless operators, Sgt R.R. Gibson, Sgt M.A. Hammond; air gunners, Sgt Dennis Gordon Longhurst, RAF (Brookham, Surrey), Sgt Robert Reade Milligan, RAF (Glasgow), Sgt Terence Phillip Pipe, RAF (St Albans, England), and Sgt W.F. Reeks; and flight engineer, Sgt Ralph Meanley, RAF (Darleston, Staffordshire). DHist 84/44/5 and DHist 84/44/6

54 'Local Man Burned One Dead in Crash,' unidentified clipping, and 'Plane Mishap; Landing Made in Storm,' *Herald* (Montreal), 21 Feb. 1946, Wheeler scrapbook, DHist

55 Unidentified clipping in ibid. Nothing could be found on this incident in Ferry Command records. If it was the Marion Bowers Darling listed on the microfilm of RCAF personnel at DHist (76/10), she was overseas for only a few months and was discharged in July 1943.

56 Barker, *Survival in the Sky*, 59–65; unidentified clippings, Wheeler scrapbook, DHist

57 See, for example, Air Ministry, Air Historical Branch, *The Second World War, 1939–1945, Royal Air Force: Air/Sea Rescue*, Air Publication 3232 (London 1952).

58 For the loss of Dakota KN271, see 45 Group Headquarters, 'Monthly Accident Reports,' DHist 181.003 (D4286); crew assignment cards and aircraft log sheet, DHist 84/44; RCAF casualties, DHist 90/19; and F/O

Alexander's memorandum, HQ 235-5-3 pt 1, NA, RG 24, acc. 83-84/049, box 199. The missing crew was made up of S/L Zozislaw Waclaw Hirsz, RAF (pilot, from Poland), P/O Denis Washer, RAF (pilot, Beckenham, Kent), FSgt William Roy Gregory, RAF (navigator, London, England), and F/L Herbert Bond Clarke, RAF (radio operator, St John's, Newfoundland).

59 F/O R.R. Alexander, 112 Wing ASRO to Group ASRO, 14 March 1945, 3, attached to report on loss of Mosquito KB370 on 11 Feb. 1945, HQ 235-5-3 pt 1, NA, RG 24, acc. 83-84/049, box 199

60 No. 112 Wing ASRO to Group ASRO, 14 March 1945, 1–2, ibid.

61 Ibid., 2

62 Ibid.

63 Canadian Forces, Air Command, *ATG Airlift Operations – Search and Rescue* (CFACM 60-2605; Ottawa 1990), 8-2-1. In fact, for a creeping-line-ahead search pattern (such as that used by 1st Arctic out of BW-1 in February 1945), this current operational guide gives the search visibility as one mile.

64 No. 112 Wing ASRO to Group ASRO, 14 March 1945, 3, HQ 235-5-3 pt 1, NA, RG 24, acc. 83-84/049, box 199

65 The captain was F/O J.W. Newman, RCAF, and the radio operator WO2 Patrick Lavin, RAF (of Bannockburn, Scotland). Less information was found on the two other members of the crew, F/L H.R. Hannaford (who appears to have been a pilot) and FSgt A.D.C. Jamieson, RAF. Crew assignment cards and aircraft log sheets, DHist 84/44; RCAF casualties, DHist 90/19

66 No. 45 Group Headquarters, 'Monthly Accident Reports,' DHist 181.003 (D4286); aircraft log sheet, DHist 84/44/5. The crew was F/O W. Wielondek, captain, and F/O M. Zajac, radio-navigator.

67 RCAF Station Goose Bay, daily diary, 10 June 1945, DHist. The captain of KA237 was the civilian, Howard Stanley Wright, and the radio operator, James Douglas Woodyard. Aircraft log sheet DHist 84/44/5; RCAF casualties, DHist 90/19; 'Statistics,' *Transat* (Oct. 1945), 8. There is some evidence that SAR procedures may have been a little better at some other stations. See, for example, RCAF file, 'Eastern Air Command – Searches for Missing Aircraft – 20 Dec. 1943 to 10 May 1944,' DHist 181.003 (D3439).

68 RCAF Station Gander, daily diary, 9 May 1942, DHist

69 RAFFC Gander, diary, 10–26 Nov. 1942, PRO, AIR 38/3. See also HQ 235-5-3 pt 1, NA, RG 24, acc. 83-84/049, box 199.

70 C.B. Wall, 'Arctic Ordeal,' *Maclean's* (15 May 1943), 8. An abridged version from Reader's Digest is available under the title, 'Fourteen Days

of Hell on an Icecap,' in *Secrets and Stories of the War* (Montreal 1963), vol. 2, 405–11. The article was partially reprinted again by Reader's Digest in *The Canadians at War 1939/45* ([Montreal] 1969), 1: 117–21. Newspapers carried the story in late January and early February. See Wheeler scrapbook, DHist.

71 Wall, 'Arctic Ordeal,' *Maclean's* (15 May 1943), 9 and 56

72 Ibid., 56–7

73 Ibid., 57

74 Canadian Press, 'Robbed of Furlough Pay,' unidentified clipping (dateline Toronto, 14 Jan. 1943), Wheeler scrapbook, DHist

75 RAFFC Gander, diary, 8–11 Dec. 1942, PRO, AIR 38/3. See also RCAF Station Gander, daily diary, DHist (which indicates another Boston 'crash landed on edge of runway'); and HQ 235-5-3 pt 1, NA, RG 24, acc. 83-84/049, box 199

76 Entries for 12, 19, 21, and 23 Dec. 1942, PRO, AIR 38/3. See also crew assignment cards, DHist 84/44.

77 RCAF Station Gander, daily diary, 20 June 1943, DHist. Given that these documents were frequently written long after the events they record, this date is probably in error. The usually accepted date of 25 June for the discovery of Hogan and Butt is undoubtedly correct, and consistent with the oft-quoted figure of forty-nine to fifty days in the wilderness. The Gander Ferry Command diary recorded the rescue on 26 June (PRO, AIR 38/4). For more on this incident, see also earlier entries in this diary in PRO, AIR 38/3; Tom McGrath's diary, DHist 74/635; and Ted Beaudoin's interview with Sheldon Luck, transcript, 84–7, NA, Manuscript Group (MG) 31 A 11. For the establishment and responsibilities of the Newfoundland Ranger Force, see Peter Neary, *Newfoundland in the North Atlantic World, 1929–1949* (Kingston and Montreal 1988), 51. See also Judy McGrath, ed., *'On the Goose': The Story of Goose Bay* (special edition of *Them Days Magazine*, Happy Valley, Goose Bay, Labrador, vol. 12, 4, June 1987), 109.

78 Glenn Gilbert, 'Battle with the Wilderness,' *Standard Magazine* (Montreal), 31 July 1943

79 Ted Beaudoin, in his biography of Sheldon Luck, *Walking on Air* (Vernon, BC 1986), 208–9, claims that two of the jumpers left the plane without parachutes and that one 'had his body severed by the horizontal section of the twin rudder tail boom. Neither body was ever found.' Luck, in an interview with Beaudoin, said that one passenger jumped without a parachute and was 'cut in 2 by the horizontal stabilizer.' Luck interview, 86, NA, MG 31 A 11

80 Unidentified clippings (some apparently from Nashville), Wheeler scrapbook, DHist. See also HQ 235-5-3 pt 1, NA, RG 24, acc. 83-84/049, box 199; and crew assignment cards, DHist 84/44.
81 Peter Bailey, 'Forty years ago "luckiest flier" hung from a plane – and lived,' *Toronto Star*, 19 Dec. 1982
82 Ibid.
83 Ibid.
84 Wheeler scrapbook, DHist. For more on this incident, see Barker, *Survival in the Sky*, 26–32; and Griffith Powell, *Ferryman: From Ferry Command to Silver City* (Shrewsbury, Eng. 1982), 65–6.
85 'Divers Searching for Bodies of "Pat" Christie, 2 Others,' unidentified clipping, Wheeler scrapbook, DHist. The scrapbook contains a couple of other informative clippings on the subject. See also crew assignment cards, DHist 84/44; and RCAF casualties, DHist 90/19.
86 Flory memoirs, 132, DHist
87 Henry Flory to author, 30 Nov. 1991, copy, Henry Flory biographical file, DHist. The account of the accident by A. Mowatt Christie in his unpublished biography of his brother, George Patterson Christie, says simply that 'no satisfactory explanation of the accident was presented following the Court of Inquiry' (unpublished manuscript, 118, excerpt at DHist). The author is not related to Pat Christie.
88 For a run of *Tee Emm*, see DHist 77/509.
89 HQ 235-5-3 pt 1, NA, RG 24, acc. 83-84/049, box 199
90 Ibid. See also crew assignment cards, DHist 84/44; and RCAF casualties, DHist 90/19.
91 HQ 235-5-3 pt 1, NA, RG 24, acc. 83-84/049, box 199
92 Ibid. The crew, listed in the file as F/O J.I. St John, RCAF (pilot); F/L A.R. Macdonald, RCAF (navigator); and E.W. McIlrey (undoubtedly Earl McIlroy, civilian radio operator), were uninjured. There is no indication of how the question of the claim was ultimately resolved. Earl McIlroy kindly provided a personal documentary of his Ferry Command recollections, including this incident, on a VHS cassette sent to the author, 20 May 1990. See also crew assignment cards, DHist 84/44.
93 RAFFC Gander, diary, PRO, AIR 38/3 and AIR 38/4; RCAF Station Gander, daily diary, DHist
94 See entry for 19 April 1943, PRO, AIR 38/3.
95 Ibid.
96 Ibid.
97 Ibid.
98 Ibid., 1, 3, 8, and 10 May 1943

99 McVicar, *North Atlantic Cat*, 176–82; crew assignment card, DHist 84/44
100 There is no authoritative file on losses. This rough conservative estimate is
   based on the numerous sources consulted by the author in the course of
   building his own record of aircraft and personnel losses, now deposited at
   DHist. In fact, several hundred (perhaps about 800) aircraft were received
   from the manufacturers but not delivered overseas. See the incomplete
   statistical breakdown of receipts and deliveries, PRO, AIR 38/23, printed
   in Paul Bridle, ed., *Documents on Relations between Canada and Newfoundland*, vol. 2: *1935–1945; Defence, Civil Aviation and Economic Affairs* (Ottawa
   1974), 1407–8. Not all of these were writeoffs. Some undoubtedly went to
   OTUs in Canada and Nassau, while others were used for training and
   general purposes within Ferry Command and 45 Group.

CHAPTER 12 Lasting Legacy

  1 Sinclair to Moore-Brabazon, 15 Aug. 1941, Public Record Office (PRO),
    AIR 2/5340
  2 Extract from Bowhill's report of 28 June 1941, ibid.
  3 Bowhill to Street, 8 Aug. 1941, ibid.
  4 Street to Bowhill, 9 Aug. 1941, ibid. This file contains additional
    correspondence between various officials which reflects Ferry Command
    and Air Ministry thinking on this issue.
  5 Sinclair to Moore-Brabazon, 15 Aug. 1941, ibid.
  6 Sinclair to Beaverbrook, 2 Sept. 1941, ibid. and Beaverbrook Papers,
    copies in Directorate of History, National Defence Headquarters (DHist)
    74/527, folder E, 7
  7 Undersecretary of state to secretary of state, 30 Aug. 1941, PRO, AIR
    2/5340
  8 Beaverbrook to Sinclair, 29 Aug. 1941, Beaverbrook Papers, DHist
    74/527, folder E, 6
  9 Sinclair to Beaverbrook, 2 Sept. 1941, ibid., folder E, 7, and PRO, AIR
    2/5340. See also Balfour minute, 30 Aug. 1941, ibid.
 10 'Direction to the British Overseas Airways Corporation under section 12
    of the British Overseas Airways Corporation Act, 1939,' 11 Sept. 1941,
    PRO, AIR 2/5340
 11 *Globe and Mail* (Toronto), 21 Aug. 1941
 12 George Lothian, *Flight Deck: Memoirs of an Airline Pilot* (Toronto 1979),
    83–4
 13 Vincent Massey, *What's Past Is Prologue: The Memoirs of the Right
    Honourable Vincent Massey* (Toronto 1963), 403. Harold Balfour

experienced the 'primitive comfort' of a transatlantic Liberator on more than one occasion. Harold Balfour, *Wings over Westminster* (London 1973), 161 and 208

14 'RCAF liaison officer, Dorval, Quebec, No. 45 (Atlantic Transport) Group, RAF, traffic notices,' 22 Sept. 1945, traffic notice 5, DHist 181.009 (D3482). See also the booklet given to people flying on Transport Command aircraft, *Passengers Your Crew*, in file 14 of the J.E. Briggs Papers, National Archives of Canada (NA), Manuscript Group (MG) 30 E 453.

15 William Lyon Mackenzie King, diary, NA, MG 26 J 13

16 H.J. Cooper, passenger service assistant, Traffic Department, 45 Group, Dorval, to AOC (air officer commanding), 31 Jan. 1944, file 5250-7, NA, Record Group (RG) 12, vol. 599

17 'Scheduled Air Services, R.A.F. Transport Command – Passenger Service,' 25 Jan. 1944, Department of Transport (DOT) file 5250-7, NA, RG 12, vol. 599. See also 'Notes on the BOAC–Pan American Route, London– Ottawa,' by an unidentified RCAF officer, nd, enclosed in L.B. Pearson to undersecretary of state for external affairs, 4 March 1943, HQC 15-24-19 pt 2, NA, RG 24, vol. 5200.

18 Warren F. Kimball, ed., *Churchill and Roosevelt: The Complete Correspondence*, 2: *Alliance Forged, November 1942–February 1944* (Princeton, NJ 1984), 291, 297, and 171–2. See also Gabriel Taschereau, *Du Salpêtre dans le Gruau: Souvenirs de l'escradrille (1939–1945)* (Sillery, Que. 1993), 308–10.

19 Bowhill to Street, 8 Aug. 1941, PRO, AIR 2/5340

20 King diary; Robert Spaight, *Vanier* (Toronto 1970), 230–1

21 Massey, *Memoirs*, 316–17

22 King diary

23 [John Pudney], *Atlantic Bridge: The Official Account of R.A.F. Transport Command's Ocean Ferry* (London 1945), 52. See also 'Strong Tail Wind Helped May Make Record Flight,' *Ottawa Evening Journal*, 29 April 1943, clipping on file 5250-7, NA, RG 12, vol. 599.

24 Beaverbrook to Sinclair, 10 Oct. 1941, PRO, AIR 2/5362

25 Sinclair to Beaverbrook, 17 Oct. 1941, ibid.

26 Massey to the secretary of state for external affairs, 6 Dec. 1941, 'Commercial Trans-Atlantic Flights,' HQC 15-24-19 pt 1, NA, RG 24, vol. 5200. Massey's proposal prompted the Departments of National Defence, Transport, and External Affairs to initiate discussions on this subject.

27 Paul Bridle, ed., *Documents on Relations between Canada and Newfoundland*, 1: *1935–1949; Defence, Civil Aviation and Economic Affairs* (Ottawa 1974),

1070–1180, 1117–39, 1144–64; Leonard Bridgman, comp., *Jane's All the World's Aircraft, 1934–44* (New York 1945), Part B, 'A Review of the World's Civil Aviation, 1943,' 48b–49b

28 Early in 1942 the production of DC-4s was commandeered by the USAAF and the aircraft was given the designation C-54 Skymaster. It saw worldwide service with USAAF Air Transport Command, and twenty-five were supplied to the RAF. Canada was unable to acquire any. F.G. Swanborough, *United States Military Aircraft since 1907* (London 1963), 242–6; Owen Thetford, *Aircraft of the Royal Air Force, 1918–1957* (London 1957), 490

29 Balfour to Street, 27 May 1942, PRO, AIR 2/5362; W/C H.H.C. Rutledge, DD plans, to D plans, 1 June 1942, HQC 15-24-19 pt 1, NA, RG 24, vol. 5200

30 Symington to Runciman, 16 June 1942, Runciman to Hildred, 23 June 1942, PRO, AIR 2/5362

31 Balfour to MacDonald, 25 June 1942, ibid.

32 Larson to Symington, 16 Oct. 1942, NA, RG 70, vol. 6

33 Howe to Symington, 11 Sept. 1942, ibid.

34 Bowhill to Street, 28 Sept. 1942, PRO, AIR 2/5362. One of the TCA captains was George Lothian. See *Flight Deck*, 89–104 and appendix [197].

35 Bowhill to Street, 2 Sept. 1942, PRO, AIR 2/5362

36 DOCA to DGCA, 24 March 1943, ibid.

37 Street to secretary of state, 6 Oct. 1942, ibid.

38 Minutes of Cabinet War Comittee meeting, 21 Oct. 1942, Bridle, *Documents*, 1080

39 Bruce Robertson, comp., *Lancaster: The Story of a Famous Bomber* (Letchworth, Eng. 1964), 106, 148; K.M. Molson and H.A. Taylor, *Canadian Aircraft since 1909* (Stittsville, Ont. 1982), 74

40 'TCA-100,' *Canadian Aviation* (Aug. 1944), 80; RCAF Station Goose Bay, daily diary, 27 Sept. 1942, DHist; Molson and Taylor, *Canadian Aircraft*, 74–5

41 Canada, Parliament, House of Commons, *Debates*, 1943, vol. 4, 3696–7. See also DOT file 5250-7, 'Air Traffic, General, Royal Air Force Transport Command, Trans-Atlantic,' NA, RG 12, vol. 599. Howe's announcement came earlier than planned because the Montreal *Gazette* of that date reportedly disclosed the plans to establish the Canadian government transatlantic air service. Secretary of state for external affairs to high commissioner for Canada in Ireland, 16 June 1943, HQC 15-24-19 pt 3, NA, RG 24, vol. 5200

42 Bowhill to Hildred, 15 March 1943, PRO, AIR 2/5362

43 C.P. Edwards, DM (deputy minister), DOT to S.L. de Carteret, DM, DND (Department of National Defence) for Air, 22 June 1943, HQ 1008-1-173, NA, RG 24, vol. 4897

44 J.R.K. Main, *Voyageurs of the Air: A History of Civil Aviation in Canada, 1858–1967* (Ottawa 1967), 154. A DOT civil servant, Main was responsible for allocating priorities to air cargo requests during the war. See, for example, file 5252-4 in NA, RG 12, vol. 599. The way in which the system worked, at least as it affected companies shipping through the Department of Munitions and Supply, is explained in B.S. Liberty, assistant deputy transport controller, DOT, to W/C D.W. McDonagh, RAF Delegation, Toronto, 13 Dec. 1944, file 5252-10 pt 1, ibid.

45 Molson and Taylor, *Canadian Aircraft*, 75–6. Another source says TCA acquired three Lancasters in 1945. See Ewart Young, 'Trans-Atlantic Service,' *Canadian Aviation* (Feb. 1945), 59.

46 See, for example, the files in NA, RG 12, vol. 599.

47 Canada, Parliament, House of Commons, *Debates*, 1943, vol. 2, 1776–7

48 No. 12 (Communications) Squadron, daily diary, 17 July 1940, DHist

49 McDougall to Pope, 30 Sept. 1942, DHist 181.009 (D4907); Secret Organization Order No. 108, 3 Feb. 1943, 'Formation of 164 Transport Squadron,' in 164 Squadron, daily diary, DHist

50 'Transport Organization, 1939–1945,' in folder k, 5 Feb. 1943 to 31 May 1949, RCAF Air Transport Command, daily diary, DHist; 165 and 168 Squadron, daily diaries, DHist. For more on the bomber mail squadron's activities, see C.R. Vincent, *Consolidated Liberator and Boeing Fortress*, Canada's Wings, vol. 2 (Stittsville, Ont. 1975), 118–47; and Carl Christie and Fred Hatch, 'The Directorate of Air Transport Command and the Growth of RCAF Transport Operations during the Second World War,' *Canadian Defence Quarterly* 16, 1 (summer 1986), 50–7. See also Z.L. Leigh's memoirs, *And I Shall Fly* (Toronto 1985), especially chapter 23, 'Foundations of a Command,' 145ff. The unedited manuscript can be consulted in NA, MG 31 G 11, and DHist 77/13.

51 'Summary of Operations Performed by No. 168 (H.T.) Squadron,' app. C, remarks quoted in Curtis to AOC No. 9 Transport Group, 13 July 1945, Air Transport Command, daily diary, DHist

52 Canada, Parliament, House of Commons, *Debates*, 1943, vol. 2, 1777. For a good, brief description of Canadian civil aviation policy as the war came to a close, see David MacKenzie, *Inside the Atlantic Triangle: Canada and the Entrance of Newfoundland into Confederation, 1939–1949* (Toronto 1986), 121.

53 C.P. Stacey, *Arms, Men and Governments: The War Policies of Canada, 1939–1945* (Ottawa 1970), 379–82. For more on the Northwest Staging

Route, see the chapter by Carl Christie in *For King and Country: Alberta in the Second World War* (Edmonton, Alta 1995); Stanley W. Dziuban, *Military Relations between the United States and Canada, 1939–1945* (Washington 1959), 216; Deane R. Brandon, 'ALSIB: The Northwest Ferrying Route through Alaska, 1942–45,' *Journal American Aviation Historical Society* (summer 1975); John Stewart, 'Canada and the Air Corridor to Alaska, 1935–42' (undergraduate thesis, Mount Allison University, Sackville, NB 1981), copy, DHist 81/332; K.C. Eyre, 'Custos Borealis: The Military in the Canadian North' (PhD thesis, University of London 1981), 82–95; and Wesley Frank Craven and James Lea Cate, *The Army Air Forces in World War II, 7: Services Around the World* (Chicago 1958; reprinted 1983), 152–72. There are a large number of underutilized files on the Northwest Staging Route at the NA, in the DOT, as well as in DND holdings, RG 12 and RG 24, and also in some private collections, such as the A.G.L. McNaughton papers, MG 30 E 133, and those of S/L Joachim Jaworski, MG 30 E 214. In addition, DHist still holds several extremely useful files on the subject.

54 Massey, *Memoirs*, 371
55 Canada, Parliament, House of Commons, *Debates*, 1943, vol. 1, 21
56 Dziuban, *Military Relations*, app. A, 358–9; RCAF file S.262-5, 'Curtailment of US activities over the North West Staging Route,' DHist 181.009 (D3293); and Canada, Parliament, House of Commons, *Debates*, 1944, vol. 3, 2227
57 'Report of the Advisory Committee on Post-War Hostilities Problems, "Post-War Canadian Defence Relationship with the United States: General Considerations," 23 January 1945,' paragraph 3, in James Eayrs, *In Defence of Canada: Peacemaking and Deterrence* (Toronto 1972), 376. Some of the best sources on the handover of facilities from US to Canadian control can be found in DOT files, such as 6800-18 pt 1, 'Stations, Radio, Government Owned, Northeast Staging Route, General,' Sept. 1942–Dec. 1947, NA, RG 12, vol. 1222; and 5150 pts 5 and 6, 'Airports & Airharbours, Northwest Staging Route, General Correspondence,' Aug. 1945–July 1949, ibid., vol. 1406.
58 Massey, *Memoirs*, 396–7
59 Minute, Hull to AOC (air officer commanding), 9 Aug. 1942, Western Air Command (WAC) file S.204-2-1, 'Operational Procedure & Control, vol. 1, Supporting Data,' DHist 181.002 (D164); 'Secret Organization Order No. 93,' 12 Aug. 1942, No. 1 School of Flying Control, daily diary, DHist
60 Dziuban, *Military Relations*, 356
61 'Western Air Command,' unpublished narrative, nd, section 8, 1–4,

DHist 74/3; WAC Headquarters (HQ), daily diary, Dec. 1941 to Feb. 1942, DHist

62 'Joint Agreement between the Commander, Northwest Sea Frontier, US Navy and the AOC, Western Air Command, RCAF,' 10 Nov. 1942, WAC HQ, daily diary, DHist

63 'Joint Agreement between CNWSF, WAC, WDC and ATC, 17 Feb. 1943,' and 'Minutes of Meeting of the JAN-CAN Committee at Western Defence Command on June 23rd, 1943,' DHist 181.002 (D164)

64 W.G. Goddard, 'North West Air Command,' unpublished narrative, nd, chapter 2, section 21, DHist 74/6; and Stevenson to air member for air services, 26 July 1943, DHist 181.002 (D164). In fact, DOT officials were not impressed with the abilities of the first RCAF graduates of DOT's Montreal-based air traffic control school who were posted to Northwest Staging Route stations. See DOT file 11-4-39 pt 1, 'Defence Measures and Regulations, Aviation, Traffic Control Officers – Northwest Staging Route,' July 1942–July 1943, NA, RG 12, vol. 615. See also DHist 181.009 (D5286).

65 Costello to AOC WAC, 4 Aug. 1943, DHist 181.002 (D164)

66 'Minutes of meeting at RCAF Headquarters, Lisgar Building, Ottawa, 19 Aug. 1943,' ibid.; Stacey, Arms, Men and Governments, 346–7

67 'Air Traffic Control: Sub-Committee Minutes,' 20–30 Aug. 1943, DHist 181.002 (D164)

68 Ibid.; Goddard, 'North West Air Command,' chapter 2, C, section 33, DHist 74/6

69 Dziuban, Military Relations, 305–6

70 R.C.A.F. Regulations for Control of Aircraft Movements (CAP 365, 2nd ed., May 1944), DHist 89/331

71 Canada, Parliament, House of Commons, Debates, 1944, vol. 2, 1578

72 Main, Voyageurs, 193–4. Although Main says the choice of Montreal as the headquarters of the Provisional International Civil Aviation Organization was unanimous, 'the final vote on the actual site was 27 for Montreal, 9 for Paris, 4 for Geneva, and 1 for China. After the vote had been taken the French graciously acknowledged the appropriateness of Montreal.' Report of the Delegation to the First Meeting of the Interim Assembly of PICAO, 1946, Donald M. Page, ed., Documents on Canadian External Relations (DCER), 12: 1946 (Ottawa 1977), 523. See also the memo by the first secretary, 'Mr. Symington's Visit to Washington,' 10 April 1946, John Hilliker, ed., DCER, 11: 1944–1945 Part II (Ottawa 1990), 559; and Canada, Parliament, House of Commons, Debates, 1946, 585–6.

73 Griffith Powell, Ferryman: From Ferry Command to Silver City (Shrewsbury, Eng. 1982), 123

74 Don McVicar, A Change of Wings (Shrewsbury, Eng. 1984), 119–20

75 Ibid., 74–120; Powell, *Ferryman*, 120 and 126–7; *Confidential Air Force List,*
    March 1946; Air Force List, April 1946
76 Jimmy Jubb to author, 18 March 1993, copy in J.N. Jubb biographical file,
    DHist
77 Ibid.
78 Ann Bond, 'RAFTC Is Gone, Its Work Done; Busses Disappear, Skies
    Quiet,' unidentified clipping, Lillian Hanson Wheeler scrapbook, copy,
    DHist. See also 'RAF Ensign Is Lowered at Dorval Ceremony
    "Demobilizes" Airport,' 'RAFTC Sets Moving date,' and 'Noble Task
    Accomplished,' ibid. In fact, Montreal has two bronze plaques to
    commemorate Ferry Command. One is in the main foyer of the com-
    munity centre of the City of Dorval; the newer, bilingual plaque, is in
    the main terminal building at Dorval airport.
79 T.M. McGrath, *History of Canadian Airports* (Ottawa 1992), 149
80 At a conservative estimate, the collection of Ferry Command personnel re-
    cords transferred by the British Air Ministry to DHist in 1984 contains a
    little over 10,000 employment record cards for civilian personnel who
    worked with the CPR Air Services Department, ATFERO, Ferry Com-
    mand, and No. 45 Group in a variety of roles, from basic labourer to
    executive. The collection also includes more than 6000 aircrew assignment
    cards for air force and civilian aircrew who passed through the Ferry
    Command organization during the war. Those trained but not accepted for
    a delivery flight assignment are included and thus swell the apparent
    aircrew total. Similarly, the appearance of civilian aircrew in both card
    files means that one cannot simply say that 16,000 people worked for or
    passed through the ferry service. See DHist 84/44. On the other hand,
    neither card file includes the large numbers of service personnel (mostly
    Canadian, but also from other belligerent nations, particularly Britain)
    stationed as groundcrew and administrative support staff not only at
    Dorval but at every staging post virtually around the world. The total
    number of people who worked in some capacity for the British ferry ser-
    vice at some time during its brief history may well be 15,000 or even more.

APPENDIX B Losses

1 For the sources used in the compilation of this list, see chapter 11, note
   35, 390–1.

Note on Sources

The activities of Royal Air Force Ferry Command, its precursors and its successors during the Second World War, are mentioned in a large number of unpublished and published sources, but few concentrate on the subject. There are undoubtedly many reasons for this relative neglect. Beyond the policy of wartime secrecy, however, there are primarily two explanations. In the first place, the ferry scheme began and grew in an informal ad hoc fashion, and no one nation or service has claimed responsibility for the contributions made by the mixture of military and civilian personnel from various Allied nations. Second, these contributions were not as obvious or as exciting and dangerous as operational flying against enemy targets that could shoot a plane down. Nonetheless, the understandable concentration on the exploits of fighting airmen should not diminish the key role played by the unsung heroes who pioneered air routes throughout the world by delivering aircraft to operational theatres of war.

Not surprisingly, the Ferry Command archival record is dispersed. Official British government documents are housed in the Public Record Office at Kew in southwest London. There, among the vast holdings from the Air Ministry and the Royal Air Force, the inquirer into the Ferry Command story will find the following classes particularly useful: AIR 2, registered correspondence; AIR 4, aircrews' flying logbooks; AIR 8, chief of the air staff, office records; AIR 19, private office papers of the secretary of state for air; AIR 20, unregistered papers from Air Ministry branches; AIR 24, command operations record books; AIR 25, group operations record books; AIR 38, Ferry and Transport Command records; and AIR 45, RAF Delegation, Washington.

In the Government Archives Division of the National Archives of Canada (NA) in Ottawa, Record Group (RG) 12, Department of Transport (DOT), particularly volumes 599, 615, 643, 645, 1222, 1405-6, 2358, and accession no. 84-

85/073, box 29, contains wartime files that reveal a number of contacts between DOT officials and Ferry Command. RG 24, Department of National Defence (DND) records, also includes files with relevance to Ferry Command – but not as many as one might expect. This was probably due to the informal nature of the ferry service's relationship with the Canadian government. The most useful volumes are 2791, 4888–98, 5200–2, 5372, 5420, 10995, and acc. no. 83-84/049, box 199. Contacts with Ferry Command, and/or discussions about its activities can also be found in the records of Trans-Canada Air Lines (RG 70, especially volume 6) and the National Research Council (RG 77, primarily volume 237).

The Manuscript Division of the National Archives holds private papers of interest to anyone looking into the Ferry Command story. At the highest level, the papers of Prime Minister William Lyon Mackenzie King (Manuscript Group [MG] 26 J) include a handful of references to the subjects in this book, as do those of A.G.L. McNaughton (MG 30 E 133) and J.A. Wilson (MG 30 E 243). MG 31 G 11, the papers of Z.L. Leigh, provides little that is not available in his published autobiography. A number of airmen have deposited useful personal papers which touch on Ferry Command. Those that were helpful were MG 30 A 76, A.G. Simms; MG 30 A 81, George Lothian; MG 30 E 177, Leeroy Brown; MG 30 E 214, Joachim Jaworski; MG 30 E 453, J.E. Briggs; and MG 31 A 11, Sheldon Luck.

The National Archives also holds a large and valuable collection of photographic negatives that proved extremely useful for this study. In addition to private collections, the archives has acquired negatives from *The Star* and *The Gazette*, Montreal newspapers that reported on a number of Ferry Command activities. These complement the vast array of DND photographic negatives now housed at the National Archives. To use these priceless collections properly takes an interminable length of time, but the results can be worth it – both for the particular images identified for use in a publication and also for the general enhancement of understanding from looking at so many pictures of the era.

The Directorate of History of the Department of National Defence (DHist) has become the key repository for Ferry Command research. This is primarily because of the thousands of Ferry Command employment record and aircrew assignment cards transferred there from the British Air Ministry more than a decade ago (accessioned as 84/44). DHist already held the original RCAF unit diaries and operations record books (ORBs) for formations and units from the command level to individual stations and squadrons (also available at the PRO and on microfilm at the National Archives). Many of these organizations had dealings with Ferry Command; a careful reading can thus reveal useful information.

In addition to the official records, DHist archivists have also built up some extremely useful informal reference and biographical files on formations, units, aircraft, and individuals. The miscellaneous press releases, clippings, booklets, and photographs in these files are often joined by notes and transcripts of interviews. DHist's Kardex Collection includes a number of RCAF files (mostly from the commands, and sometimes incomplete) not yet transferred to the National Archives. The Document Collection, which has replaced Kardex as the home for new material, is a growing series containing a variety of documents and files acquired by DHist since the Kardex Collection was closed in 1971. It also includes copies of all the PRO items cited in this book.

The reference notes reveal the specific DHist permanent reference files, biographical files, Kardex and Document Collection files, as well as RCAF diaries and ORBs that proved most valuable in the Ferry Command research.

Other archival institutions hold useful documentation. The Newfoundland Provincial Archives includes the transcript of the 'Enquiry into Death of Sir Frederick Banting, Wireless Operator William Snailham and Navigator William Bird.' The Harriet Irving Library of the University of New Brunswick holds, as part of the Bryan Priestman papers (RG 210), some Ferry Command navigation maps. Finally, the James Richardson Papers at the Provincial Archives of Manitoba include information peripheral to the early part of this story.

As the notes reveal, published government lists, reports, and collections of documents are virtually indispensable for a work of this kind. The Air Ministry's *Confidential Air Force List* (CD 200; London 1940–6) records the growth of the RAF's various far-flung commands and groups, including Ferry Command and 45 Group. *The Air Force List* (London 1940–6) and the *RCAF List* (Ottawa 1940–6) allow one to trace or verify an individual officer's promotions during the war. For policy, particularly from the Canadian perspective, the series of volumes, *Documents on Canadian External Relations*, vols 7–12: *1939–1946* (Ottawa 1973–90), is essential, as is the related *Documents on Relations between Canada and Newfoundland, 1: 1935–1949; Defence, Civil Aviation and Economic Affairs* (Ottawa 1974).

While official histories are useful for context, neither the British nor the Canadian say much about Ferry Command. W.A.B. Douglas's *The Creation of a National Air Force*, Official History of the Royal Canadian Air Force, vol. 2 (Toronto and Ottawa 1986) devotes a short appendix to the subject; volume 3 of the same series, *The Crucible of War, 1939–1945* (Toronto and Ottawa 1994), by Brereton Greenhous, Stephen J. Harris, William C. Johnston, and William G.P. Rawling, contains only two brief mentions of Ferry Command. Fred Hatch's *Aerodrome of Democracy: Canada and the British Commonwealth Air Training Plan, 1939–1945* (Ottawa 1983) is important for the BCATP, the Clayton Knight Committee, and related matters (as indeed is the second volume of the RCAF history). The earlier volumes, *The RCAF Overseas*, 3 vols (Toronto 1944–9), provide a little detail on some individuals. C.P. Stacey, *Arms, Men and Governments; the War Policies of Canada, 1939–1945* (Ottawa 1970), is essential reading.

Except for Denis Richards and Hilary St George Saunders, *Royal Air Force, 1939–1945*, 3 vols (London 1953–4), the British official histories tend to be organized by function rather than service. Still, Ferry Command rates nary a mention, although H. Duncan Hall, *North American Supply* (London 1955), and *Studies of Overseas Supply* (London 1956) by Hall and C.C. Wrigley, offer important background and context, and the *Statistical Digest of the War: Prepared in the Central Statistical Office* (London 1956) is helpful. The Air Ministry's Air Historical Branch series of special studies gives useful information. See particularly *The Second World War, 1939–1945: Meteorology* (CD 1134; London 1954); and the similar titles on *Maintenance* (CD 1131; London 1954), *Air/Sea Rescue* (Air Publication 3232; London 1952), *Works* (Air Publication 3236; London 1956), and also the Air Member for Training's *Notes on the History of RAF Training, 1939–44* ([London] 1945). Other British government-sponsored publications released near the end of the war are useful, particularly the Ministry of Information's brief *Atlantic Bridge: The Official Account of R.A.F. Transport Command's Ocean Ferry* [apparently by John Pudney] (London 1945), and *Merchant Airmen: The Air Ministry Account of British Civil Aviation, 1939–1944* (London 1946). Background on policy comes from Llewellyn Woodward, *British Foreign Policy in the Second World War* (London 1962). John Terraine's *The Right of the Line: The Royal Air Force in the European War, 1939–1945* (London 1985) has the look and heft of an official history, but in fact is not. It does, however, at least refer to Ferry Command on a couple of occasions.

The US official histories offer much useful information germane to the RAF Ferry Command story. Wesley Frank Craven and James Lea Cate's *The Army Air Forces in World War II*, 7 vols (Chicago 1948–58; reprinted 1983) is a remarkable achievement when one considers it was published so soon after the war. Volume 1, *Plans and Early Operations, January 1939 to August 1942*, and volume 7, *Services around the World*, proved especially useful. So too did Stanley W. Dziuban, *Military Relations between the United States and Canada, 1939–1945* (Washington 1959), and, to a lesser extent, Setson Conn and Byron Fairchild, *The Western Hemisphere: The Framework of Hemisphere Defense*, United States Army in World War II (Washington 1960), and Samuel Eliot Morison, *History of the United States Naval Operations in World War II*, 1: *The Battle of the Atlantic, September 1939–May 1943* (Boston 1947).

A number of personal memoirs were used and can be identified in the notes. However, a few bear special mention. D.C.T. Bennett's *Pathfinder: A War Auto-*

biography (London 1958; reprinted 1983) and Griffith 'Taffy' Powell's *Ferryman: From Ferry Command to Silver City* (Shrewsbury, Eng. 1982) tell the Ferry Command story from the perspective of two of the key leaders of the operation. Don McVicar, in *Ferry Command, North Atlantic Cat*, and *Change of Wings* (Shrewsbury, Eng. 1981–3), offers the reader a colourful personal memoir of what one might expect the typical swashbuckling ferry pilot to have been. George Lothian's *Flight Deck: Memoirs of an Airline Pilot* (Toronto 1979) is a more sober account from a TCA veteran who spent some time with Ferry Command. Bernt Balchen's *Come North with Me: An Autobiography* (New York 1958) chronicles an amazing career in aviation. Edgar Wynn's *Bombers Across* (New York 1944) is essential reading.

When it comes to leaders, it is impossible to ignore Winston S. Churchill, *The Second World War*, 6 vols (Boston 1948–53), now wonderfully supported by the British prime minister's correspondence with the US president in Warren F. Kimball, ed., *Churchill and Roosevelt: The Complete Correspondence*, 3 vols (Princeton, NJ 1984). It is amazing to see how far down Roosevelt's interest reached and how much influence he had on British policy on ferrying. In a somewhat similar manner, Vincent Massey watched from afar. See his *What's Past is Prologue: The Memoirs of the Right Honourable Vincent Massey* (Toronto 1963). Harold Balfour was more intimately involved, making his *Wings over Westminster* (London 1973) a valuable little book. The memoirs of two British air marshals with no direct involvement in the Ferry Command story also make some interesting mentions of ferrying. Sir John Slessor's *The Central Blue: Recollections and Reflections* (London 1956) and Lord Tedder's *With Prejudice: The War Memoirs of Marshal of the Royal Air Force Lord Tedder G.C.B.* (London 1966) are worth reading.

Biographies can be helpful, although there are few available with much on Ferry Command. Alan Bramson's *Master Airman: A Biography of Air Vice-Marshal Donald Bennett, CB, CBE, DSO* (Shrewsbury, Eng. 1985) and A.S. Jackson's *Pathfinder Bennett – Airman Extraordinary; Air Vice Marshal D.C.T. Bennett CB CBE DSO* (Lavenham, Eng. 1991) are disappointing on the subject. Even those on Lord Beaverbrook tell us little about his role in starting the delivery scheme: Tom Driberg, *Beaverbrook: A Study in Power and Frustration* (London 1956); A.J.P. Taylor, *Beaverbrook* (London 1972); and Anne Chisholm and Michael Davie, *Beaverbrook: A Life* (London 1992). Robert Daley, in *An American Saga: Juan Trippe and His Pan Am Empire* (New York 1980), and Marilyn Bender and Selig Altschul, in *The Chosen Instrument – Pan Am, Juan Trippe: The Rise and Fall of an American Entrepreneur* (New York 1982), give us more about Juan Trippe's support of wartime ferrying. D.H. Miller-Barstow's *Beatty of the C.P.R.* (Toronto 1951) and David Cruise and Alison Griffiths's *Lords of the Line* (Markham, Ont.

1988) flesh out Sir Edward Beatty, a key figure at the start of the ferry scheme. John Swettenham in *McNaughton*, 3 vols (Toronto 1968–9) does likewise for an important figure in early Canadian aviation policy. Robert Bothwell and William Kilbourn's *C.D. Howe: A Biography* (Toronto 1979) says nothing about Ferry Command. Michael Bliss, in *Banting: A Biography* (Toronto 1984), and Lloyd Stevenson, in *Sir Frederick Banting* (Toronto 1946), helped me understand their subject's motivation in the winter of 1940–1. Bruce West's *The Man Who Flew Churchill* (Toronto 1975) is the only known biography of a pilot who spent the war with Ferry Command. Ted Beaudoin's *Walking on Air* (Vernon, BC 1986) presents a colourful picture of Sheldon Luck's time ferrying out of Montreal.

Ferry Command receives little mention in conventional histories, although Sholto Watt made a beginning with *I'll Take the High Road: A History of the Beginning of the Atlantic Air Ferry in Wartime* (Fredericton, NB 1960), and Griffith 'Taffy' Powell produced a slim souvenir volume, *'Per Ardua Ad Astra': A Story of the Atlantic Air Ferry* (Montreal [1945]). For the early period of British civil aviation, Robin Higham, *Britain's Imperial Air Routes, 1918 to 1939: The Story of Britain's Overseas Airlines* (Hamden, Conn. 1961), is the standard work. Too bad there is not an adequate continuation. John Stroud, *Annals of British and Commonwealth Air Transport, 1919–1960* (London 1962), offers some help filling the gaps in the later period. Peter Neary's impressive *Newfoundland in the North Atlantic World, 1929–1949* (Kingston and Montreal 1988) is good on Gander and Goose Bay, as is David MacKenzie on civil aviation matters in *Inside the Atlantic Triangle: Canada and the Entrance of Newfoundland into Confederation, 1939–1949* (Toronto 1986). J.R.K. Main, in *Voyageurs of the Air: A History of Civil Aviation in Canada, 1858–1967* (Ottawa 1967), makes a start at a subject crucial to Canada's development that cries out for more work. Ferry Command does get some treatment in three anecdotal works, *Sixty Years: The RCAF and CF Air Command, 1924–1984*, edited by Larry Milberry (Toronto 1984), and the Reader's Digest's *The Canadians at War, 1939/45*, 2 vols (np 1969) and *Secrets and Stories of the War* (Montreal 1963). Bernt Balchen, Corey Ford, and Oliver La Farge tell the story of the war in Greenland in *War below Zero* (Boston 1944).

If little has been written about Ferry Command, much has been published on the aircraft industry as well as on many of the aeroplanes featured in this book. Some of the genre found helpful include Michael J.F. Bowyer and Bryan Philpott's *Mosquito* (Cambridge, Eng. 1980); G.R. Duval, *British Flying-Boats and Amphibians, 1909–1952* (London 1966); M.J. Hardy, *The de Havilland Mosquito* (New York 1977); Andrew Hendrie, *Seek and Strike: The Lockheed Hudson in World War II* (London 1983); Joe Holliday, *Mosquito: The Wooden Wonder Aircraft of World War II* (Markham, Ont. 1980); Fred Hotson, *DeHavilland Canada Story* (Toronto 1983); Geoffrey P. Jones, *Attacker: The Hudson and Its Flyers* (London

1980); Harry Moyle, *The Hampden File* (Tonbridge, Eng. 1989); Bruce Robertson, comp., *Lancaster: The Story of A Famous Bomber* (Letchworth, Eng. 1964); C. Martin Sharp and Michael J.F. Bowyer, *Mosquito* (London 1967); C. Martin Sharp, *D.H.: A History of de Havilland* (Shrewsbury, Eng. 1982); Graham M. Simons, *Mosquito: The Original Multi-Role Aircraft* (London 1990); and C.R. Vincent, *Consolidated Liberator and Boeing Fortress* (Stittsville, Ont. 1975). For more general reference on aircraft, *Jane's All the World's Aircraft*, edited and compiled by C.H. Grey and Leonard Bridgman (London 1927–46), was almost indispensable. Also useful were F.G. Swanborough, *United States Military Aircraft since 1907* (London 1963); K.M. Molson and H.A. Taylor, *Canadian Aircraft since 1909* (Stittsville, Ont. 1982); and Owen Thetford, *Aircraft of the Royal Air Force, 1918–1957* (London 1957). Tom McGrath, *History of Canadian Airports* (Ottawa 1992), is a useful encyclopedic guide.

No systematic check was made of contemporary newspapers and popular periodical literature. However, the research inevitably led to a number of articles, as revealed in the reference notes. Some of them can be found in the *Hamilton Spectator* Collection, now held by DHist. In addition, two scrapbook collections were used: the uncatalogued series of air force scrapbooks at DHist and the thick personal scrapbook kept by Lillian Hanson Wheeler, secretary to Jimmy Jubb at Ferry Command Headquarters in Montreal. She maintained close contact with many of the aircrew during and after the war and married Lloyd Wheeler, one of Jubb's civilian radio operators.

Most recent articles bearing on Ferry Command tend to have appeared in popular periodicals or in those specializing in aviation history; occasionally they are published in military history or professional military journals. Where appropriate, they have been cited in the reference notes.

Index